Al-Muwatta

Al-Muwatta

of Imām Mālik

Translated by

Aisha Abdurrahman Bewley

DIWAN PRESS

Classical and Contemporary Books on Islam and Sufism

First edition: Diwan Press 1982
Second edition: Madinah Press 1989
Third edition: Diwan Press 2014

Al-Muwatta

Published by: Diwan Press Ltd.
6 Terrace Walk,
Norwich
NR1 3JD
UK
Website: www.diwanpress.com
E-mail: info@diwanpress.com

Author: Imam Malik ibn Anas
Translation: Aisha Bewley
Typeset by: Abdassamad Clarke
Cover design by: Abdassamad Clarke
A catalogue record of this book is available from the British Library.

ISBN-13: 978-1-908892-36-2 (hardback)
978-1-908892-35-5 (paperback)

Printed and bound by: Lightning Source

Contents

Translation of Al-Muwatta

Al-Muwatta does not need an introduction as its author, the Faqih of Madina, Malik bin Anas, may Allah be pleased with him, is the founder of the school of hadith and Islamic fiqh. The maliki madhab is the madhab followed by the majority of the muslims in north and west Africa and in some parts of the Arabian peninsula. It is almost certain that most of the followers of the madhab are from non arabic speaking peoples and that the majority of these are from areas where the english language is in use. Therefore the translation of Al-Muwatta into this language is an essential work in that it makes the text accessible to the large numbers of english speakers in the Islamic world and the west.

This translation features two important advantages: firstly it is a translation that is not only accurate and honest but also a translation that the english reader can understand as it is not a 'literal' translation in which the meaning is lost nor is it a 'free' translation that deviates from what is intended, rather it has gathered eloquence of expression (as the translators are english muslims) and a true rendering of the original meaning (as it has been checked and corrected by an arabic scholar). Secondly it contains a complete glossary of all the terms of fiqh that are used in the text which facilitates the reader's use of the book and makes it a reference book for the student of law in both the Islamic and western schools, and in universities.

The translation of this book into the english language deserves every encouragement and support as it is a great weapon for the da^c^wa to the deen of Allah. It also clarifies the superior qualities of the noble shari^c^a in the language which is normally used to mislead and distract the reader from the truth.

May Allah give us success to work in the Way of His deen and guide us on the straight path.

Dr Muhammad Abu'l Khayr Zaki Badawi
Director, Islamic Cultural Centre & Central Mosque
London England.

بسم الله الرحمن الرحيم

THE ISLAMIC CULTURAL CENTRE

146 PARK ROAD (OFF BAKER STREET) LONDON NW8 7RG TEL (01)724 3363-7

DIRECTOR: Dr M A ZAKI BADAWI

ترجمة كتاب الموطأ

ان كتاب الموطأ ليس بحاجة الى تعريف فمؤلفه فقيه المدينة مالك بن أنس رضي الله عنه وهو رأس مدرسة الحديث في الفقه الاسلامي ، ومذهب مالك هو المذهب الذي يتبعه المسلمون في شمال وغرب افريقيا وفي بعض مناطق الجزيرة العربية ويكاد يجزم ان معظم أتباع المذهب من غير الناطقين باللغة العربية وان أكثريتهم من المناطق التي تستعمل اللغة الانجليزية ، فترجمة الكتاب الى هذه اللغة ضروري ليرجع اليه هذا العدد الكبير من المتحدثين بها في العالم الاسلامي وفي الغرب ، وأهم ما يميز هذه الترجمة أمران، أولا : انها ترجمة لاتتسم بالدقة والأمانة فحسب بل هي كذلك ترجمة يستطيع القارئ الانجليزي ان يفهمها فهي ليست ترجمة "حرفية" يضيع فيها المعنى وليست ترجمة "حرة" تنحرف عن المقصود وانما جمعت بين سلامة التعبير (فالمترجمون انجليز مسلمون) وصدق المعنى (فالمراجع عالم عربي) وثانيا : انها تحتوي على ملحق شامل للمصطلحات الفقهية المستعملة في الكتاب وهذا مما يسهل على القارئ استعمال الكتاب كما يجعله مرجعا لدارس القانون في المدارس والجامعات الاسلامية والعربية .

ان هذا العمل جدير بكل تشجيع وعون فهو سلاح عظيم من اسلحة الدعوة لدين الله وابراز لمحاسن الشريعة الغراء في لغة حفلت بكل مايضلل القارئ ويصرفه عن الحق.

وفقنا الله للعمل في سبيل دينه وهدانا الى الصراط المستقيم .

د . محمد أبو الخير زكي بدوي

مدير المركز الثقافي الاسلامي

لندن

ISLAMIC CULTURAL CENTRE and LONDON CENTRAL MOSQUE ★ LONDON

Introduction

Praise be to Allah, who sent our Prophet Muḥammad as a mercy to the whole universe. He sent down the Noble Qur'ān through him as a light and guidance for those who are godfearing. He commanded him to clarify what had been revealed to people so that they might reflect. His words and actions made clear to them everything they needed to know. He instructed those who were present with him to convey his teaching to those who were not there.

Blessings and peace be upon him and upon his family and his good and pure Companions who expended their property and their lives to spread the *dīn* of Islam. By means of them Allah preserved His *Sharī'a* enabling it to survive through the passage of time down to the present time. Their hearts were the vessels which contained and preserved the *ayats* of the Clear Book and the *Sunna* of the Seal of the Prophets and the Imām of the Messengers. Then those who followed them, and those who followed them in turn, undertook this task. The people who wrote down and recorded this knowledge appeared in the time of the third generation. The greatest of them was the Imām of the Abode of the *Hijra*, the Imām of the Imāms, Abū 'Abdullāh Mālik ibn Anas al-Aṣbaḥī al-Madanī. He took it upon himself to serve the *Sharī'a* and to preserve the Prophetic *Sunna*. He did this by relaying it from those notable *Tābi'ūn* with whose knowledge he was satisfied and whose words he thought worthy of conveying and by his work he opened the way for all later writers and cleared a path for the compilation of Islamic law. He selected those transmitters who were reliable and rejected those who were weak. His book, *al-Muwaṭṭa'*, was the greatest book written at that time. It was the most precise in layout and the best of them in its choice of chapters. The other books written at the same time as his book have vanished but Allah had decreed that his book would remain until this time and indeed until the first of the two worlds comes to an end, when Allah will inherit the earth and all those on it. This has come about by the permission of the One Who created the two worlds and the jinn and mankind.

I have been asked by some of our brothers, who desire to disseminate knowledge and to renew the call of Islam, to write an introduction to this edition of the *Muwaṭṭa'*, which is the first translation of the *Muwaṭṭa'* in the English language. I have complied with their request hoping for an abundant reward from Allah since we are well aware of the importance of this book, its blessings, the abundant knowledge to be found in it and its fame, both past and present, among the books written on the science of *ḥadīth* by the Imāms who are worthy of emulation.

We have divided this introduction into the following topics:

The lineage of Imām Mālik, his family, birth and autobiography

His full name is Mālik ibn Anas ibn Mālik ibn Abī 'Āmir al-Aṣbaḥī and he was related to Dhū Aṣbaḥ, a sub-tribe of Ḥimyar, one of the Qahtani tribes who held sway over an immense kingdom during the period of the *Jāhiliyya*. Their kingdom was known as the Tabābi'a (pl. of Tubba'). Tubba' is mentioned in two places in the Noble Qur'ān.

His father's grandfather, Abū 'Āmir, is considered by some to have been one of the Companions and it is mentioned that he went on all the raids with the Messenger of Allah ﷺ except Badr. However, Ibn Ḥajar mentioned in the *Iṣāba* from adh-Dhahabī that he did not find anyone who mentioned him as being one of the Companions, although he was certainly alive in the time of the Prophet ﷺ. As for Mālik ibn Abī 'Āmir, the grandfather of the Imām, he was one of the great scholars of the *Tābi'ūn*. He was one of those who assisted in the writing out of the noble *Muṣḥaf* at the time of the *Amīr al-Mu'minīn*, 'Uthmān ibn 'Affān ﵁.

He had four children: Anas, the father of the Imām, Abū Suhayl whose name was Nāfi', ar-Rabī', and Uways the grandfather of Ismā'īl ibn Abī

Uways and his brother, 'Abd al-Ḥamīd. These two (Ismā'īl and 'Abd al-Ḥamīd) were among the students of Mālik and among the transmitters of the *Ṣaḥīḥ*. The four brothers (i.e. Anas, Mālik's father, and his brothers) transmitted from their father, Mālik ibn Abī 'Āmir, and others, in turn, transmitted from them. The most famous of them in knowledge and transmission was Abū Suhayl. Imām Mālik related from him as did the compilers of the *Ṣaḥīḥ* collections. Al-Bukhārī, Muslim, and others transmitted a lot from Mālik ibn Abī 'Āmir and from his son, Abū Suhayl.

From this it is evident that the Imām was a branch from a good tree whose men were famous for transmitting and serving knowledge. Part of the excellence of this family lies in the fact that it gave birth to Imām Mālik. It is said that this took place in 90 A.H. although there are other opinions. He died when he was 87 according to the soundest report although it is also said that he was 90. Mālik, may Allah have mercy on him, was tall and slightly corpulent. He was bald, with a large head and well-shaped eyes, a fine nose and a full beard. Muṣ'ab az-Zubayrī said, "Mālik was one of the most handsome people in his face and the sweetest of them in eye, the purest of them in whiteness and the most perfect of them in height and the most excellent in body." Another said, "Mālik was of medium height." The first is better known.

His quest for knowledge

At the time when Mālik grew up, and during the time immediately preceding him, *Madīna al-Munawarra* was flourishing with the great scholars who were the direct inheritors of the knowledge of the Companions, may Allah be pleased with them. They included "the seven *fuqahā*'" of Madīna (or the ten) and their companions who took from them. Mālik himself was always eager for knowledge and devoted himself to the assemblies of eminent men of knowledge. He drank and drank again from the sweet, quenching springs of knowledge.

He was instructed in the learning and recitation of the Noble Qur'ān by Imām Nāfi' ibn 'Abd ar-Raḥmān ibn Abī Nu'aym, the Imām of the reciters of Madīna and one of the "seven reciters". Abū 'Amr ad-Dānī, who included the biography of Imām Mālik in his book *Ṭabaqāt al-*

Qurrā', considered him to be to be one of the reciters. He mentioned that Imām al-Awzā'ī related the Qur'ān from Mālik, he being concerned with the meaning of its commentary. In the *Muwaṭṭa'*, you will find some of his commentaries on certain *ayat*s.

He occupied himself with those who knew *ḥadīths*, both in transmission and knowledge, and was a master in *fiqh*, knowing how to derive judgements and join statements together and how to weigh one proof against another. Part of his good fortune was that two of his shaykhs, Muḥammad ibn Shihāb az-Zuhrī and 'Abdullāh ibn Abī Bakr ibn Muḥammad ibn 'Amr ibn Ḥazm al-Anṣārī, were instrumental in the beginning of the process of recording the *ḥadīths*.

Imām Mālik met an extraordinary number of men of knowledge who related from the Companions or from the great *Tābi'ūn*. He did not attend the circle of everyone who sat teaching in the mosque of the Prophet ﷺ or leaned against one of its pillars relating *ḥadīth* to the people from the Messenger of Allah ﷺ but used to take only from those men that he saw possessed *taqwā*, scrupulousness, good memory, knowledge and understanding, and who clearly knew that they would be accountable for what they said on the Day of Rising. Shu'ba ibn al-Ḥajjāj, who was one of the great scholars of *ḥadīth*, said that Mālik was most discriminating, saying about him that: "He did not write down from everyone."

Knowing, as we do, that Imām Mālik came from a family of learning and grew up in *Madīna al-Munawarra* which was the capital of knowledge at that time, especially the knowledge of *ḥadīths*, and also knowing the strength of Mālik's predisposition for retention, understanding and *taqwā* and his perseverance and steadfastness in the face of all the obstacles he met in the path of knowledge, it is hardly surprising to discover that he graduated at a very young age. Reliable transmitters relate that he sat to give *fatwā* when he was seventeen years old. This was not from the impetuosity of youth or because of love of appearance but only after seventy Imāms had testified that he was worthy to give *fatwā* and teach. Such people would only testify when it was absolutely correct to do so. Indeed, the testimony of any two of them would have been sufficient.

People's praise of him and their testimony that he was the greatest of the Imāms in knowledge

The notable scholars at the time of Mālik and those who came after him all agree about his pre-eminent worth and consider him to be a pillar of knowledge and one of its firm bulwarks, celebrated for his *taqwā*, his retentive memory, his reliability in transmission, and his ability in giving *fatwās*. He was well known for his turning towards true knowledge and away from what did not concern him, and for cutting himself off from the caliphs and amirs who would liberally bestow money on those men of knowledge who attached themselves to them. He had overwhelming respect for the *ḥadīths* of the Messenger of Allah ﷺ, and this was considered enough by the notable men of *ḥadīth* and *fuqahā'* who related from him and used his transmission as a proof, putting it ahead of the transmission of many of his peers. They followed him in declaring different transmitters reliable or unreliable.

There is no disagreement on the fact that al-Layth, al-Awzā'ī, the two Sufyāns, Ibn al-Mubārak, Shu'ba ibn al-Ḥajjāj, 'Abd ar-Razzāq and other great scholars like them transmitted from Mālik. Imām ash-Shāfi'ī was one of his most prominent pupils as was Imām Muḥammad ibn al-Ḥasan, the companion of Abū Ḥanīfa. Qāḍī Abū Yūsuf, who met and spoke with him, also related from him via an intermediary. It is also true that Abū Ḥanīfa related from him as did a group of his shaykhs, including Muḥammad ibn Shihāb az-Zuhrī, Rabi'a ibn Abī 'Abd ar-Raḥmān, Abū al-Aswad Muḥammad ibn 'Abd ar-Raḥmān known as the 'orphan of 'Urwa', Yaḥyā ibn Sa'īd al-Anṣārī, Ayyūb as-Sakhtiyānī and others. There were none in their time greater than these men. Some of them were *fuqahā'* and others were *ḥadīth* relaters. Most of them were both.

Those who came after them all related from Mālik except for those who were prevented from doing so by circumstances. Why indeed should they not relate from him? Was not the Imām someone who combined justice, precision, examination, and criticism in his evaluation of men and avoided transmission from the weak? There is only one man he related from who is considered weak. He was 'Abd al-Karīm ibn Abī al-Makhāriq al-Baṣrī, and this only happened because he was not one of the people of Mālik's own land and Mālik was deceived by his scrupulousness and the way he performed *hajj*.

If you have any doubts about what we have said, then look in any of the books of *ḥadīths* and you will find the name of Mālik constantly repeated by the tongues and pens of the transmitters. Enough for us is the frequent repetition of his name in the *Ṣaḥīḥ* volumes of al-Bukhārī and Muslim. The *Kitāb al-Umm* of Imām ash-Shāfi'ī and his *Kitāb ar-Risāla* both begin with the words, "Mālik reported to us." When the *Musnad* of ash-Shāfi'ī was compiled, it also began with the same words.

We find that Ḥāfiẓ Abū Bakr al-Bayhaqī began his great *Sunan* with the *ḥadīth* "Its water is pure" which is from the transmission of ash-Shāfi'ī from Mālik and from the transmission of Abū Dāwūd from Mālik. He mentioned that ash-Shāfi'ī said, "There is someone in the *isnād* whom I do not know." Then al-Bayhaqī said at the end of it, "However, that which establishes the soundness of its *isnād* was the reliability Mālik gave it in the *Muwaṭṭa'*." These words indicate the position of Mālik and that the people of his time and those after them, who were not partisan, acknowledged his pre-eminence in the preservation of *ḥadīth*, in his ability to distinguish the sound from the weak, and in his knowledge of the science of men and their states, whether they were reliable or unreliable.

Those early Imāms were not content to remain silent about him, but spoke out using their tongues and their pens, clearly stating his eminence and the extent of his fame. In *Iṣ'āf al-mubaṭṭa bi-rijāl al-Muwaṭṭa'*, Jalāl ad-Dīn as-Suyūṭī said that Bishr ibn 'Umar az-Zahrānī said that he asked Mālik about a man and he said, "Do you see him in my books?" He replied, "No." Mālik said, "If he had been reliable, you would have seen him in my books." Ibn al-Madīnī said, "I never knew Mālik to reject a man unless there was something wrong about his *ḥadīths*." Ibn al-Madīnī also said, "When Mālik brings you a *ḥadīth* from someone from Sa'īd ibn al-Musayyib, I prefer that to Sufyān from someone from Ibrāhīm. Mālik only relates from people who are reliable." Yaḥyā ibn Ma'īn said, "All of those from whom Mālik ibn Anas relates are reliable except for 'Abd al-Karīm al-Baṣrī Abū Umayya."

Aḥmad ibn Ṣāliḥ said, "I do not know of anyone who was more careful in his selection of men and scholars than Mālik. I do not know of anyone who has related anything wrong about anyone among those he chose. He related from people none of whom are rejected." An-Nasā'ī said, "The trustees of Allah over the knowledge of the Messenger of Allah ﷺ were Shu'ba ibn al-Ḥajjāj, Mālik ibn Anas and Yaḥyā ibn Sa'īd al-Qaṭṭān." He said, "Ath-Thawrī was an Imām, but he related from weak men. It was the same with Ibn al-Mubārak." Then he indicated the pre-eminence of Mālik over Shu'ba and Yaḥyā ibn Sa'īd al-Qaṭṭān. He said, "There are none among the *Tābi'ūn* trusted in *ḥadīths* more than these three, and none who had fewer weak transmissions."

Ismā'īl ibn Abī Uways said, "I heard my uncle, Mālik, say, 'This knowledge is a *dīn*, so look to those from whom you take your *dīn*. I met seventy men who said, "The Messenger of Allah ﷺ said by these pillars..." and I did not take anything from them. Yet if any one of them were to be trusted with the treasury, he would have been trustworthy. This is because they were not men of this business. But when Ibn Shihāb came to us, we crowded around his door. Yaḥyā ibn Ma'īn said from Sufyān ibn 'Uyayna, "Who are we in comparison to Mālik? We merely follow in the tracks of Mālik. We looked to see if Mālik took from a shaykh. If not we left him."

Ashhab said that Mālik was asked, "Should one take from someone who does not memorise, but is reliable and accurate in writing? Can *ḥadīths* be taken from such a man?" Mālik replied, "I fear that he might add to his books at night." Al-Athrim said, "I asked Aḥmad ibn Ḥanbal about 'Amr ibn Abī 'Amr, the client of al-Muṭṭalib, and he said, 'His transmission is excellent in my opinion. Mālik related from him.'" Abū Sa'īd ibn al-A'rābī said, "If Mālik related from a man, Yaḥyā ibn Ma'īn declared him reliable. More than one person was asked and said, 'He is reliable. Mālik related from him.'"

Qarād Abū Nūḥ said, "Mālik mentioned something and was asked, 'Who related it to you?' He said. 'We did not use to sit with fools.'" 'Abdullāh ibn Aḥmad ibn Ḥanbal said, "I heard my father mentioning this and he said, 'There is no statement in the world more noble than this regarding the virtues of scholars - Mālik ibn Anas mentioned that he did not sit with fools. This statement is not valid from anyone else except Mālik.'

In *Tadhkira al-Ḥuffāẓ*, adh-Dhahabī mentioned some of people's praise of him, including the famous statement of ash-Shāfi'ī, "When the *'ulamā'* are mentioned, Mālik is the star." Aḥmad ibn al-Khalīl said that he heard Isḥāq ibn Ibrāhīm (i.e. Ibn Rahwayh) say, "When ath-Thawrī, Mālik and al-Awzā'ī agree on a matter, it is *sunna*, even if there is no text on it."

After mentioning much of the praise of the people of knowledge for him, adh-Dhahabī said, "I put Mālik's biography on its own in a section in my *Tārīkh al-Kabīr.* It is agreed that Mālik had virtues which are not known to have been combined in anyone else. The first of them was the length of his life and extent of his transmission. The second was his piercing mind. The third was the agreement of the Imāms that he is a proof, sound in transmission. The fourth is that they agree on his *dīn*, justice and following of the *sunna*. The fifth is his pre-eminence in *fiqh*, *fatwā* and the soundness of his foundations."

In *Taqrīb at-Tahdhīb*, Ibn Ḥajar says, "Mālik ibn Anas ibn Mālik ibn Abī 'Āmir al-Aṣbaḥī, Abū 'Abdullāh, al-Madanī, the *faqīh*, the Imām of the Abode of the *Hijra*, the chief of those who have *taqwā* and the greatest of those who are confirmed, of whom al-Bukhārī said, 'The soundest *isnād*s of all are those of Mālik from Nāfi' from Ibn 'Umar.'"

This is just a brief collection of a few of the things that have been said about him by scholars who do not follow the school of Mālik. Their words in no way disagree with anything that has been written by the Mālikī scholars who follow him. The reader will be able to find a lot of what they have said in the books of Abū 'Umar ibn 'Abd al-Barr, the *Tartīb al-Madārik* of Qāḍī Abū al-Faḍl 'Iyāḍ, and *ad-Dībāj al-Mudhahhab* by Burhān ad-Dīn ibn Farḥūn, and other books of earlier and later writers.

Among the Mālikīs and others Imām Mālik is known as the Imām of the Imāms. It is easy to see why this is so. We know that those Imāms whose schools, *fatwās* and transmissions are followed were his students, either directly or via an intermediary. Imām ash-Shāfi'ī was one of Imām Mālik's most famous students and Imām Aḥmad was one of the most famous students of ash-Shāfi'ī. Muḥammad ibn al-Ḥasan was one of the transmitters of the *Muwaṭṭa'*. Abū Yūsuf also related it from Mālik via an intermediary. One scholar confirmed that Imām Abū Ḥanīfa also related from him, and no objection was made to him for stating that. Some shaykhs like Ibn Shihāb and ar-Rabī'a related from Mālik as we have already mentioned. We also mentioned that al-Layth, al-Awzā'ī, the two Sufyāns and Ibn al-Mubārak related from him, and there is no disagreement about that. Scholars of *ḥadīths* who are famous for writing in that field, or from whom others have transmitted, transmitted from him. We say that today there is no scholar of the Islamic *Sharī'a* who is not a student of Mālik. That is because, first of all, it is not valid to count someone as a scholar of the *Sharī'a* if he is ignorant of the *Muwaṭṭa'*, the Six Books, the *Musnad* of Aḥmad and the rest of the books which are consulted in *ḥadīths*. All of those who relate these books or some of them must relate from Mālik. Therefore they must respect this Imām from whom they relate and acknowledge his position and ask for mercy on him.

One of the extraordinary things about the people who came to Mālik for transmission is that there was not a single small region subject to the rule of Islam in his time but that a group of their noble sons set out to visit him. The number of those whose name was Muḥammad who related from him is more than a hundred. The number of those called 'Abdullāh is about sixty, of those called Yaḥyā about forty, and of those called Sa'īd more than twenty. If you were to imagine his circle of study, you would find Andalusians, Khorasanis, Syrians, Moroccans, Egyptians, Iraqis, Yemenis, and others all sitting in a circle around him with their different languages, colours, and clothing. It must have been an amazing sight. We do not believe that such a group has ever been gathered together at the feet of a scholar before or after him, in Madīna or elsewhere.

The shaykhs from whom he transmitted

It is known that Imām Mālik grew up in *Madīna al-Munawwara* and that those who sought knowledge travelled there from all the regions of Islam because Madīna had an unrivalled number of scholars compared with the rest of the Muslim world. In Madīna Mālik met all the great men who had a major part in the transmission of *ḥadīths* and the sayings of the Companions and the great *Tābi'ūn*. He found such a wealth of knowledge there that he did not need to travel anywhere else. He related from nine hundred shaykhs or more and with his own hand wrote down a hundred thousand *ḥadīths*. His book, the *Muwaṭṭa'*, which we are discussing, contains eighty-four men of the *Tābi'ūn*, all of whom were people of Madīna except for six. These six were Abū az-Zubayr from Makka, Ḥamīd aṭ-Ṭawīl and Ayyūb as-Sakhtiyānī from Basra, 'Aṭā' ibn Abī Muslim from Khorasan, 'Abd al-Karīm al-Jazarī from Jazira (Mesopotamia) in northern Iraq, and Ibrāhīm ibn Abī 'Abla from Syria. Mālik is famous for the fact that he did not transmit from a number of scholars whom he met, even though they were people of *dīn* and correct action, because he thought that they did not transmit properly.

Al-Ghāfiqī said that the number of his shaykhs whom he named (i.e. in the *Muwaṭṭa'*) was ninety-five.

The transmitters who transmitted from him

In the introduction to *Tanwīr al-Ḥawālik*, as-Suyūṭī says that so many people related from him that no other Imām is known to have had a transmission like his. He says that Abū Bakr al-Khaṭīb al-Baghdadī devoted a book to those who transmitted from Mālik and it included 993 men. Qāḍī 'Iyāḍ mentioned that he wrote a book on those who transmitted from Mālik in which he enumerated over 1300 men. As-Suyūṭī said that he had enumerated the names of all of them in his *Great Commentary*. The transmitters of *al-Muwaṭṭa'* alone are of a number which it is difficult to count.

Qāḍī 'Iyāḍ mentioned that the number of transmissions which he read or came across in the transmissions of his shaykhs reached twenty, and some of them mention thirty. Another thing that indicates the great number of the transmitters of the *Muwaṭṭa'* is that Aḥmad ibn Ḥanbal said, "I heard the *Muwaṭṭa'* from about ten of the companions of Mālik who had mentioned it but I revised it with ash-Shāfi'ī because I found him to be the most correct of them." Shaykh Muḥammad Ḥabīb-Allāh ibn Māyābā ash-Shinqīṭī said in *Iḍā'a al-Ḥālik* that Ibn Nāṣir ad-Dīn ad-Dimashqī wrote a book about the transmitters of the *Muwaṭṭa'* and he mentioned that there were seventy-nine. Among those who transmitted the *Muwaṭṭa'* from Mālik were his son, Yaḥyā, and his daughter, Fāṭima.

The position of the *Muwaṭṭa'* and people's concern for it

In the introduction to *Tanwīr al-Ḥawālik*, as-Suyūṭī said that ash-Shāfi'ī said, "After the Book of Allah, there is no book on the face of the earth sounder than the book of Mālik." In another statement he said, "No book has been placed on the earth closer to the Qur'ān than the book of Mālik." In a third he said, "After the Book of Allah, there is no book more useful than the *Muwaṭṭa'*." 'Alā' ad-Dīn Maghlaṭāy al-Ḥanafī said, "The first person to compile the *ṣaḥīḥ* was Mālik."

Ibn Ḥajar said, "The book of Mālik is sound by all the criteria that are demanded as proofs in the *mursal, munqaṭi'* and other types of transmission." Then as-Suyūṭī followed what Ibn Ḥajar said here and said, "The *mursal ḥadīths* in it are a proof with him (ash-Shāfi'ī) as well because the *mursal* is a proof with us when it is properly supported. Every *mursal* report in the *Muwaṭṭa'* has one or more supports as will be made clear in this commentary (i.e. *Tanwīr al-Ḥawālik*). It is absolutely correct to say that the *Muwaṭṭa'* is sound (*ṣaḥīḥ*) without exception."

Ibn 'Abd al-Barr collected together all the *mursal, munqaṭi'* and *mu'ḍal ḥadīths* in the *Muwaṭṭa'* and said that the total number of *ḥadīths* in the *Muwaṭṭa'* which do not have an *isnād* are sixty-one. He stated that he found the *isnāds* of all of them in other sources with the exception of four *ḥadīths*. The erudite scholar of *ḥadīth*, Shaykh Muḥammad Ḥabīb-Allāh ibn Māyābā ash-Shinqīṭī says in *Iḍā'a al-Ḥālik* that he had found witnesses for these four *ḥadīths* and he then mentioned these witnesses. He said, "Some of the people of knowledge made these *isnāds* complete." He mentioned from Ibn 'Abd al-Barr that there are no *munkar ḥadīths* in the *Muwaṭṭa'* nor anything fundamentally refuted. In *Dalīl as-Sālik* in the margin of *Iḍā'a al-Ḥālik* he mentioned that Ibn Ḥajar retracted what he had previously said which was what had been followed by as-Suyūṭī. From this it is clear that everything in the *Muwaṭṭa'* has an *isnād*. The people of knowledge rely on the *ḥadīths* in it and transmit and record them in their books, including al-Bukhārī and Muslim who transmitted most of its *ḥadīths* and included them in their *Ṣaḥīḥ* collections. The rest of the authors of the six books did the same as did the Imām of the *ḥadīth* scholars, Aḥmad ibn Ḥanbal, and others.

It should be pointed out that the *ḥadīths* of Mālik are not confined to those he included in the *Muwaṭṭa'*. This is clearly shown by the *ḥadīths* we find transmitted from Mālik in the two *Ṣaḥīḥ* volumes which are not found in the *Muwaṭṭa'*. There is a *ḥadīth* which al-Bukhārī relates in the chapter on the description of the Garden: "The people there look at the people of the chambers from above them." There is a second *ḥadīth* related by Mālik commenting on *Surat al-Muṭaffafīn* (83) where the Prophet ﷺ said, " 'The Day when people stand before the Lord of the Worlds' until one of them disappears immersed in his sweat up to his ears." There is a third *ḥadīth* related by Muslim in the chapter forbidding *ṣadaqa* to the family of the Prophet ﷺ which he related from 'Abdullāh ibn Muḥammad ibn Asmā' aḍ-Ḍaba'ī from his uncle, Juwayriya ibn Asmā', from Mālik.

There are two areas which particularly interest people regarding the *Muwaṭṭa'*. One of them is its transmission and the other is its commentary and the discussion about its transmitters and the different expressions they use and so forth. As for interest in its transmitters, we have already shown how the seekers of knowledge in Mālik's time came from East, West, South and North out of the desire to sit in his circle and take from him. Many of this group related the *Muwaṭṭa'* from him and preserved it in their hearts or in writing. The men of the generation after their generation were also concerned with it.

We have enough evidence for what we say in the fact that Imām Aḥmad ibn Ḥanbal related it first from ten men and then finally from Imām ash-Shāfi'ī. Similarly ash-Shāfi'ī first learned it in Makka and then went to Madīna to Mālik and took it directly from him. That is also what Yaḥyā ibn Yaḥyā al-Andalusī did – he first learned it in his own country from Ziyād ibn 'Abd ar-Raḥmān Shabṭūn and then travelled from Andalusia to Madīna and read it directly with Mālik in the year in which Imām Mālik died, may Allah have mercy on him.

As for interest in its commentary, discussion about its transmitters and whether the different versions are shorter or longer, and commentary on what is *gharib* in it and that sort of thing, people evince more interest in writing about these matters in the case of the *Muwaṭṭa'* than they do for any other book of *ḥadīth*. A great number of people have written about these things and some of them have composed several books. For instance, Ibn 'Abd al-Barr wrote three books: *at-Tamhīd*, *al-Istidhkār* and *at-Tajrīd* which is also *called "at-Taqaṣṣī"*. Qāḍī Abū al-Walīd al-Bājī wrote three commentaries called *al-Istīfā'*, *al-Muntaqā*, and *al-Īmā'*. He wrote a fourth book on the different versions of the *Muwaṭṭa'*. Jalāl ad-Dīn as-Suyūṭī wrote two commentaries on it. One of them, called *Kashf al-Mughaṭṭā*, is voluminous, and the other is a summary called *Tanwīr al-Ḥawālik*. He wrote a third book called *Iṣ'āf al-Mubaṭṭa' bi-rijāl al-Muwaṭṭa'*.

The most famous transmission of the *Muwaṭṭa'* is that of Yaḥyā ibn Yaḥyā al-Laythī al-Andalusī so that when the name the *Muwaṭṭa'* is used, it is this transmission that is referred to. There are about a hundred commentaries on it. This is what Shaykh Muḥammad Ḥabīb-Allāh ibn Māyābā ash-Shinqīṭī was indicating in the *Dalīl as-Sālik* when he said:

> The most famous *Muwaṭṭa'*
> If the truth be known
> Is that of Imām Yaḥyā al-Laythī.
> Who else's can be compared with his?

He also said:

> It is the one on which the critics comment and in
> whose lustre the slaves find benefit.
> There are about a hundred commentaries on it,
> all of them about what it contains.

Another version of the *Muwaṭṭa'* worthy of mention is that of Imām Muḥammad ibn al-Ḥasan ash-Shaybānī which has great distinction. It includes the transmission of many traditions intended to support his *madhhab* and the *madhhab* of his Imām, Abū Ḥanīfa. Sometimes he mentions that Abū Ḥanīfa agrees with Mālik regarding the matter under discussion.

It appears that the Andalusians had a great deal of interest in the *Muwaṭṭa'* as anyone will know who has studied the names of the scholars who made commentaries on it or spoke about the people in it and its different versions or wrote on its *gharīb ḥadīths.*

It should also be noted that those who were interested in the *Muwaṭṭa'* were not only Mālikīs or people from one particular region. They were from different groups and schools and from all parts of the Muslim world.

Clarification of the meaning of "*Muwaṭṭa'*", its excellent layout and fine style

"*Muwaṭṭa'*" is a passive participle from the verb "*tawṭi'a*". One says that the thing is smoothed (*waṭṭa'a*) and "I prepared the thing for you" and "The bed is laid out" and "The seat is made comfortable for you". Ibn Manẓūr said in *al-Lisān*, "In the *ḥadīth*: 'Shall I tell you of the one among you I love the most and who will sit closest to me on the Day of Rising? – Those who are easy-going (*muwaṭṭa' al-aknāf*) who are friendly and bring people together.'" Ibn al-Athīr said, "This comes from *tawṭi'a* which means to smooth and make lower. Thus *Muwaṭṭa'* means the clear book which smooths the way and is not difficult for the seeker of knowledge to grasp. It is also related that Mālik gave his book this title because he read it to a group of the people of knowledge and they agreed with him about it (*wāṭa'a*). In this case the name would be derived from *muwāṭa'a* which means agreement. However, the first meaning is more likely because it is supported by the rules of derivation although both of them apply since the way is prepared and smoothed by it and people agree about it and admire it.

If you look at the *Muwaṭṭa'* in an unbiased way, you will find that it prepares and smooths the way and is easy to grasp, even though it is one of the oldest books now in our possession. No earlier book from the people of knowledge is known. Its author made it an example to be imitated, particularly in the way in which it is arranged.

We find that Mālik begins with the chapters on the acts of worship, which are the pillars of Islam. He put the prayer first, it being the greatest of the pillars. Since the prayer only becomes obligatory when its time comes, he began by talking about the times of prayer. Then he spoke about purity in all its forms because purification is obligatory after the time for prayer has come. Then he spoke about what it is obligatory to do in the prayer and what is not obligatory and things that can happen to people in the prayer. Then he spoke about *zakāt* and so on until he had covered all the acts of worship. Then he spoke about the rest of the matters of *fiqh* and divided each chapter into small sections so as to make it easier to grasp. He finished the book with a chapter called "General Matters" which contains various things which did not fit under the other headings, and since it was not possible to devote a whole chapter to each of them and he did not want to go on at length, he combined them and called it "General Matters". As Ibn al-'Arabī says, other authors found in this arrangement a new way of organising their material.

What he did in the book as a whole he also did in certain chapters. For instance at the end of the chapter on prayer, he has a section entitled "Prayer in General". He also has a section on "Funerals in General," "Fasting in General," "General chapter on what is not permitted of marriage," and "General chapter on sales," etc. This shows the excellence of the way he arranged the book and the precision of the system he used. This is so much the case that if one of us today, in this age of systems, wanted to organise it, it would be very difficult to come up with a better arrangement than the one it already has.

If the reader looks at the *Muwaṭṭa'* with respect to its language, he will find that its language shows that the author was a pure Arab. His language has both force and simplicity. Its terms are neither odd nor hackneyed. His style is free of oversimplification, unnecessary complexity or triteness. Despite its length, the book does not contain any linguistic or grammatical errors nor any of the faults which the scholars of rhetoric warn against.

Consequently we do not find that any of those who have made commentaries on it or spoken about it, despite their great number and their different times, places and backgrounds, directed any criticism at it on these grounds, neither in respect of what the Imām himself wrote nor in respect of the transmissions of Prophetic *ḥadīths* and other traditions ascribed to the Companions and the *Tābi'ūn*. By that we mean that there is no criticism at all that cannot easily be answered. It is always possible for criticism to be made by people whose understanding is inadequate and who lack sufficient knowledge. "How many there are who find fault with a sound statement while their trouble is faulty understanding."

The noble reader should also be aware of the fact that Imām Mālik has other works than the *Muwaṭṭa'* even though they are not as famous.

These works are:

1. A letter on *Qadar* and refutation of the Qadariyya. He wrote it to 'Abdullāh ibn Wahb, one of his eminent students.

2. A book on the stars and reckoning the passage of time and the stages of the moon.

3. A letter on judgements which he wrote to some judges.

4. A letter on *fatwā* which was addressed to Abū Ghassān Muḥammad ibn Muṭarrif al-Laythī, one of his great students.

5. A letter on the *ijmā'* of the people of Madīna which he sent to Imām al-Layth ibn Sa'd.

6. A book on the *tafsīr* of rare words in the Qur'ān.

7. A letter on manners and admonitions which he sent to Hārūn ar-Rashīd which is not acknowledged by a group of notable Mālikīs.

8. A book called *Kitāb as-Sirr*.

This introduction is only a drop in the ocean. It has not covered everything by any means but I hope it has mentioned a few salient points.

Allah is the One we ask for help and on Whom we rely. May Allah bless our master Muḥammad and his family and Companions and grant them peace abundantly.

The late Shaykh Aḥmad ibn 'Abd al-'Azīz Al Mubārak

Head of the Sharī'a Court

United Arab Emirates

1. The Times of Prayer

1.1 The times of prayer

1 He said, "Yaḥyā ibn Yaḥyā al-Laythī related to me from Mālik ibn Anas from Ibn Shihāb that one day 'Umar ibn 'Abd al-'Azīz delayed the prayer. 'Urwa ibn az-Zubayr went to him and told him that al-Mughīra ibn Shu'ba had delayed the prayer one day while he was in Kūfa and Abū Mas'ūd al-Anṣārī had gone to him and asked, 'What is this, Mughīra? Do you not know that the angel Jibrīl came down and prayed and the Messenger of Allah ﷺ prayed. Then he prayed again, and the Messenger of Allah ﷺ prayed. Then he prayed again, and the Messenger of Allah ﷺ prayed. Then he prayed again, and the Messenger of Allah ﷺ prayed. Then he prayed again, and the Messenger of Allah ﷺ prayed. Then he said, "This is what I was ordered to do."'"

'Umar ibn 'Abd al-'Azīz said, "Be sure of what you relate, 'Urwa. Was it definitely Jibrīl who established the times of the prayers for the Messenger of Allah?"

'Urwa replied, "That is how it was related to Bashīr ibn Abī Mas'ūd al-Anṣārī by his father."

2 'Urwa said, "'Ā'isha, the wife of the Prophet ﷺ related to me that the Messenger of Allah ﷺ used to pray *'Aṣr* while the sunlight was pouring into her room, before the sun itself had become visible (i.e. because it was still high in the sky)."

3 Yaḥyā related to me from Mālik from Zayd ibn Aslam that 'Aṭā' ibn

Yasār said, "A man came to the Messenger of Allah ﷺ and asked him about the time of the *Ṣubḥ* prayer. The Messenger of Allah ﷺ did not answer him, but in the morning he prayed *Ṣubḥ* at first light. The following morning he prayed *Ṣubḥ* when it was much lighter, and then asked, 'Where is the man who was asking about the time of the prayer?' The man replied, 'Here I am, Messenger of Allah.' He said, 'The time is between these two.'"

4 Yaḥyā related to me from Mālik from Yaḥyā ibn Sa'īd from 'Amra bint 'Abd ar-Raḥmān that 'Ā'isha, the wife of the Prophet ﷺ said, "The Messenger of Allah ﷺ used to pray *Ṣubḥ* and then the women would leave wrapped in their garments while they could not yet be recognised in the darkness."

5 Yaḥyā related to me from Mālik from Zayd ibn Aslam from 'Aṭā' ibn Yasār and from Busr ibn Sa'īd and from al-A'raj – all of whom related it to him from Abū Hurayra – that the Messenger of Allah ﷺ said, "Whoever manages to perform a *rak'a* of *Ṣubḥ* before the sun has risen has done *Ṣubḥ* within the time, and whoever manages to perform a *rak'a* of *'Aṣr* before the sun has set has done *'Aṣr* within the time."

6 Yaḥyā related to me from Mālik from Nāfi', the *mawlā* of 'Abdullāh ibn 'Umar, that 'Umar ibn al-Khaṭṭāb wrote to his governors, saying, "The most important of your affairs in my view is the prayer. Whoever protects it and observes it carefully is protecting his *dīn,* while whoever is negligent about it will be even more negligent about other things."

Then he added, "Pray *Ẓuhr* any time from when the afternoon shade is the length of your forearm until the length of your shadow matches your height. Pray *'Aṣr* when the sun is still pure white, so that a rider can travel two or three farsakhs before the sun sets. Pray *Maghrib* when the sun has set. Pray *'Ishā'* any time after the redness in the western sky has disappeared up until a third of the night has passed – and a person who sleeps, may he have no rest; a person who sleeps, may he have no rest; a person who sleeps, may he have no rest. Pray *Ṣubḥ* when all the stars are visible and mixed together in the sky."

7 Yaḥyā related to me from Mālik from his uncle Abū Suhayl from his father that 'Umar ibn al-Khattāb wrote to Abū Mūsā saying that he should pray *Ẓuhr* when the sun had started to decline, *'Aṣr* when the sun was still pure white before it was tinged with any yellowness, *Maghrib* when the sun had set, and to delay *'Ishā'* as long as he did not sleep, and to pray *Ṣubḥ* when the stars were all visible and mixed together in the sky, reciting in it two long *sūras* from the *Mufaṣṣal.*

8 Yaḥyā related to me from Mālik from Hishām ibn 'Urwa from his father that 'Umar ibn al-Khaṭṭāb wrote to Abū Mūsā al-Ash'arī that he should pray *'Aṣr* when the sun was still pure white so that a man could ride three farsakhs (before *Maghrib*) and that he should pray *'Ishā'* during the first third of the night, or, if he delayed it, then up until the middle of the night, and he warned him not to be forgetful.

9 Yaḥyā related to me from Mālik from Yazīd ibn Ziyād that 'Abdullāh ibn Rāfi', the *mawlā* of Umm Salama, the wife of the Prophet ﷺ, asked Abū Hurayra about the times of the prayers. Abū Hurayra said, "I will tell you. Pray *Ẓuhr* when the length of your shadow matches your height, *'Aṣr* when your shadow is twice your height, *Maghrib* when the sun has set, *'Ishā'* in the first third of the night, and *Ṣubḥ* in the very first light of dawn," i.e. when the dawn has definitely come.

10 Yaḥyā related to me from Mālik from Ishāq ibn 'Abdullāh ibn Abī Ṭalḥa that Anas ibn Mālik said, "We used to pray the *'Aṣr* prayer, and then if one of us went out to the Banū 'Amr ibn 'Awf, we would find them praying *'Aṣr.*"

11 Yaḥyā related to me from Mālik from Ibn Shihāb that Anas ibn Mālik said, "We used to pray *'Aṣr* and then it was still possible for one of us to go to Qubā' and arrive there while the sun was still high."

12 Yaḥyā related to me from Mālik from Rabi'a ibn Abī 'Abd ar-Raḥmān that al-Qāsim ibn Muḥammad said, "None of the Companions that I met prayed *Ẓuhr* until well after noon," (i.e. until when the sun had lost it fierceness).

1.2 The time of the *jumu'a* prayer

13 Yaḥyā related to me from Mālik from his uncle Abū Suhayl ibn Mālik that his father said, "I used to see a carpet belonging to 'Āqil ibn Abī Ṭālib spread out on the day of *jumu'a* up to the west wall of the mosque. When the shadow of the wall covered the whole carpet, 'Umar ibn al-Khaṭṭāb would come out and pray the *jumu'a* prayer." Mālik, Abū Suhayl's father, added, "We would then return after the *jumu'a* prayer and take our midday sleep".

14 Yaḥyā related to me from Mālik from 'Amr ibn Yaḥyā ibn Yaḥyā al-Māzinī from Ibn Abī Salīt that 'Uthmān ibn 'Affān prayed *jumu'a* in Madīna and *'Aṣr* at Malal. Mālik commented, "That was due to praying *jumu'a* just past midday and then travelling fast."

1.3 Whoever catches a *rak'a* of the *ṣalāh*

15 Yaḥyā related to me from Mālik from Ibn Shihāb from Abū Salama ibn 'Abd ar-Raḥmān from Abū Hurayra that the Messenger of Allah ﷺ said, "Whoever catches a *rak'a* of the prayer has caught the prayer."

16 Yaḥyā related to me from Mālik from Nāfi' that 'Abdullāh ibn 'Umar ibn al-Khaṭṭāb used to say, "If you have missed *rukū'*, you have missed the *sajda*."

17 Yaḥyā related to me from Mālik that he had heard that 'Abdullāh ibn 'Umar and Zayd ibn Thābit used to say, "Whoever catches the *rukū'* has caught the *sajda*."

18 Yaḥyā related to me from Mālik that he had heard that Abū Hurayra used to say, "Whoever catches the *rukū'* has caught the *sajda* and whoever misses the recitation of the *Umm al-Qur'ān* has missed much good."

1.4 *Dulūk ash-shams* and *ghasaq al-layl*

19 Yaḥyā related to me from Mālik from Nāfi' that 'Abdullāh ibn 'Umar used to say, "*Dulūk ash-Shams* begins from when the sun passes the meridian."

20 Yaḥyā related to me from Mālik that Dā'ūd ibn al-Ḥusayn said that someone had told him that 'Abdullāh ibn 'Abbās used to say, "*Dulūk ash-Shams* begins from when the sun passes the meridian. *Ghasaq al-layl* is the gathering of the night and its darkness."

1.5 The times of prayer in general

21 Yaḥyā related to me from Mālik from Nāfi' from 'Abdullāh ibn 'Umar that the Messenger of Allah ﷺ said, "If someone misses the *'Aṣr* prayer it is as if he has been deprived of his family and all his wealth."

22 Yaḥyā related to me from Mālik from Yaḥyā ibn Sa'īd that once 'Umar ibn al-Khattāb left after performing the *'Aṣr* prayer and met a man who had not been present for *'Aṣr*. 'Umar asked him what had kept him from the *'Aṣr* prayer, and even though the man gave a good reason, 'Umar said, "You have given yourself short measure."

Yaḥyā added that Mālik commented, "It is said that everything has a short measure and a full measure."

23 Yaḥyā related to me from Mālik that Yaḥyā ibn Sa'īd used to say, "Even if someone manages to pray before the time of the prayer has passed, the time that has passed him by is more important – or better – than his family and wealth."

Yaḥyā said that Mālik said, "If the time for a prayer comes and a traveller delays the prayer through neglect or forgetfulness until he reaches his family, he should do that prayer in full if he arrives within the time. But if he arrives after the time has passed, he should do the travelling prayer – that way he only repays what he owes."

Mālik said, "This is what I have found the people and men of knowledge in our land doing."

Mālik explained that *shafaq* is the redness in the sky after the sun has set and said, "When the redness has gone then the *'Ishā'* prayer is due and you have left the time of *Maghrib*."

24 Yaḥyā related to me from Mālik from Nāfi' that once 'Abdullāh ibn 'Umar fainted and lost consciousness and he did not make up the prayer.

Mālik commented, "We consider that that was because, and Allah knows best, the time had passed. Someone who recovers within the time still has to pray."

1.6 Sleeping through the prayer

25 Yaḥyā related to me from Mālik from Ibn Shihāb from Sa'īd ibn al-Musayyab that the Messenger of Allah ﷺ travelled by night on the way back from Khaybar. Towards the end of the night he stopped for a rest and told Bilāl, "Keep watch for the *Ṣubḥ* prayer." The Messenger of Allah ﷺ and his companions slept. Bilāl stayed on watch for as long as was decreed for him and then he leant against his riding camel facing the direction of the dawn and sleep overcame him and neither he nor the Messenger of Allah ﷺ nor any of the party woke up until the sun's rays struck them. The Messenger of Allah ﷺ was alarmed. Bilāl said, "Messenger of Allah! The One who took your soul was the One who took my soul." The Messenger of Allah ﷺ said, "Move on." So they roused their mounts and rode on a short distance. The Messenger of Allah ﷺ ordered Bilāl to give the *iqāma* for the prayer and then led them in the *Ṣubḥ* prayer. When he finished the prayer he said, "A person who forgets a prayer should pray it when he remembers. Allah the Blessed and Exalted says in His book, 'Establish the prayer to remember Me.' (20:14)"

26 Yaḥyā related to me from Mālik that Zayd ibn Aslam said, "The Messenger of Allah ﷺ stopped for a rest one night on the road to Makka and appointed Bilāl to wake them up for the prayer. Bilāl slept and everyone else slept and none of them woke up until the sun had risen.

When they did wake up they were all alarmed. The Messenger of Allah ﷺ ordered them to ride out of the valley, saying that there was a *shayṭān* in it. So they rode out of the valley and the Messenger of Allah ﷺ ordered them to dismount and do *wuḍū'* and he told Bilāl either to call the prayer or to give the *iqāma*. The Messenger of Allah ﷺ then led them in prayer. Noticing their uneasiness, he went to them and said, 'O people! Allah seized our spirits (*arwāḥ*) and if He had wished He would have returned them to us at a time other than this. So if you sleep through the time for a prayer or forget it and then are anxious about it, pray it as if you were praying it in its time.' The Messenger of Allah ﷺ turned to Abū Bakr and said, 'Shayṭān came to Bilāl when he was standing in prayer and made him lie down and lulled him to sleep like a small boy.' The Messenger of Allah ﷺ then called Bilāl and told him the same as he had told Abū Bakr. Abū Bakr declared. 'I bear witness that you are the Messenger of Allah.'"

1.7 Not doing the prayer at the hottest hour of the day

27 Yaḥyā related to me from Mālik from Zayd ibn Aslam from 'Aṭā' ibn Yasār that the Messenger of Allah ﷺ said, "Scorching heat comes from the blast of Jahannam. So when the heat is fierce, delay the prayer until it gets cooler." He added in explanation, "The Fire complained to its Lord and said, 'My Lord, part of me has eaten another part,' so He allowed it two breaths in every year, a breath in winter and a breath in summer."

28 Mālik related to us from 'Abdullāh ibn Yazīd, the *mawlā* of al-Aswad ibn Sufyān, from Abū Salama ibn 'Abd ar-Raḥmān from Muḥammad ibn 'Abd ar-Raḥmān ibn Thawbān from Abū Hurayra that the Messenger of Allah ﷺ said, "When the heat is fierce, delay the prayer until it gets cooler, for scorching heat comes from the blast of Jahannam."

He added, "The Fire complained to its Lord, so He allowed it two breaths in each year, a breath in the winter and a breath in summer."

29 Yaḥyā related to me from Mālik from Abū az-Zinād from al-A'raj from Abū Hurayra that the Messenger of Allah ﷺ said, "When the heat is fierce, wait until it gets cooler before you do the prayer, for scorching heat comes from the blast of Jahannam."

1.8 Not entering the mosque smelling of garlic and not covering the mouth in prayer

30 Yaḥyā related to me from Mālik from Ibn Shihāb from Sa'īd ibn al-Musayyab that the Messenger of Allah ﷺ said, "Anyone who eats this plant should not come near our mosques. The smell of the garlic will offend us."

31 Yaḥyā related to me from Mālik from 'Abd ar-Raḥmān ibn al-Mujabbar that he used to see Sālim ibn 'Abdullāh pull the cloth away fiercely from the mouth of any man he saw covering his mouth while praying.

2. Book of Purity

2.1 How to perform *wuḍū'*

1 Yaḥyā related to me from Mālik from 'Amr ibn Yaḥyā al-Māzinī that his father once asked 'Abdullāh ibn Zayd ibn 'Āṣim, the grandfather of 'Amr ibn Yaḥyā al-Māzinī and one of the companions of the Messenger of Allah ﷺ, "Can you show me how the Messenger of Allah ﷺ used to perform *wuḍū'*?" 'Abdullāh ibn Zayd ibn 'Āṣim replied, "Yes," and asked for water to do *wuḍū'*. He poured some water on to his hand and washed his hands twice and then rinsed his mouth and snuffed water up his nose and blew it out twice. Then he washed his face three times and both of his arms up to the elbows twice. He then wiped his head with both hands, taking his hands from his forehead to the nape of his neck and then bringing them back to where he had begun. Then he washed his feet.

2 Yaḥyā related to me from Mālik from Abū'z-Zinād from al-A'raj from Abū Hurayra that the Messenger of Allah ﷺ said, "When you do *wuḍū'*, snuff water into your nose and blow it out, and if you use stones to clean your private parts use an odd number."

3 Yaḥyā related to me from Ibn Shihāb from Abū Idrīs al-Khawlānī from Abū Hurayra that the Messenger of Allah ﷺ said, "The person doing *wuḍū'* should snuff water up his nose and blow it out again, and if you use stones to clean your private parts use an odd number."

4 Yaḥyā said that he heard Mālik say that there was no harm in washing the mouth and cleaning the nose using only one handful of water.

5 Yaḥyā related to me from Mālik that he had heard that 'Abd ar-Raḥmān ibn Abī Bakr was visiting 'Ā'isha, the wife of the Prophet ﷺ, on the day that Sa'd ibn Abī Waqqāṣ died, and he asked for some water to do *wuḍū'*. 'A'isha said to him, "'Abd ar-Raḥmān! Perform your *wuḍū'* fully, for I heard the Messenger of Allah ﷺ say, 'Woe to the heels in the fire!'"

6 Yaḥyā related to me from Mālik from Yaḥyā ibn Muḥammad ibn Ṭalḥa from 'Uthmān ibn 'Abd ar-Raḥmān that his father related to him that he had heard that 'Umar ibn al-Khaṭṭāb used to wash what was beneath his waist-wrapper with water.

7 Yaḥyā said that Mālik was asked what a man should do if, when he did *wuḍū'*, he forgot and washed his face before he had rinsed his mouth, or washed his forearms before he had washed his face. He said, "If someone washes his face before rinsing his mouth, he should rinse his mouth and not wash his face again. If someone washes his forearms before his face, however, he should wash his forearms again so that he has washed them after his face. This is if he is still near the place (of *wuḍū'*)."

8 Yaḥyā said that Mālik was asked about what a man should do if he does not remember that he has not rinsed his mouth and nose until after he has prayed. He said, "He does not have to repeat the prayer, but he should rinse his mouth and nose if he wishes to do any more prayers after that."

2.2 *Wuḍū'* for praying after sleep

9 Yaḥyā related to me from Mālik from Abū'z-Zinād from al-A'raj from Abū Hurayra that the Messenger of Allah ﷺ said, "When one of you wakes up from sleep, he should wash his hands before putting them in the *wuḍū'* water for none of you knows where his hands were during the night."

10 Yaḥyā related to me from Mālik from Zayd ibn Aslam that 'Umar ibn al-Khaṭṭāb said, "If you fall asleep lying down you must do *wuḍū'* (before you pray)."

Yaḥyā related to me from Mālik from Zayd ibn Aslam that the *āyat "You who believe, when you get up to pray, wash your faces and your arms to the elbows, and wipe over your heads, and [wash] your feet up to the ankles,"* (5:6) refers to rising from one's bed, meaning sleep.

11 Yaḥyā said that Mālik said, "The position with us is that you do not have to perform *wuḍū'* on account of a nosebleed, or for blood, or on account of pus issuing from the body. You only have to perform *wuḍū'* on account of impurities which issue from the genitals or the anus, or for sleep."

Yaḥyā related to me from Mālik from Nāfi' that Ibn 'Umar used to sleep while sitting and then would pray without performing *wuḍū'*.

2.3 What is pure for *wuḍū'*

12 Yaḥyā related to me from Mālik from Ṣafwān ibn Sulaym from Sa'īd ibn Salama of the Banū Azraq from al-Mughīra ibn Abī Burda of the tribe of Banu 'Abd ad-Dār that he heard Abū Hurayra speak about a man who came to the Messenger of Allah ﷺ and said, "Messenger of Allah! We travel by sea and we do not carry much fresh water with us so if we do *wuḍū'* with it we go thirsty. Can we do *wuḍū'* with sea-water?" The Messenger of Allah ﷺ replied, "Its water is pure, and its dead creatures are *ḥalāl*."

13 Yaḥyā related to me from Mālik from Isḥāq ibn 'Abdullāh ibn Abī Ṭalha from Ḥumayda bint Abī 'Ubayda ibn Farwa that her maternal aunt, Kabsha bint Ka'b ibn Mālik, who was the wife of the son of Abū Qatāda al-Anṣārī, told her that once Abū Qatāda was visiting her and she poured out some water for him to do *wuḍū'* with. Just then a cat came to drink from it, so he tilted the vessel toward it to let it drink. Kabsha continued, "He saw me looking at him and said, 'Are you surprised, daughter of my brother?' I said, 'Yes.' He replied that the Messenger of Allah ﷺ said, 'Cats are not impure. They intermingle with you.'"

Yaḥyā said that Mālik said, "There is no harm in that unless one sees impurities on the cat's mouth."

14 Yaḥyā related to me from Mālik from Yaḥyā ibn Sa'īd from Muḥammad ibn Ibrāhīm ibn al-Ḥārith at-Taymī from Yaḥyā ibn 'Abd ar-Raḥmān ibn Ḥāṭib that 'Umar ibn al-Khaṭṭāb set out on one occasion with a party of riders, one of whom was 'Amr ibn al-'Āṣ. They came to a watering place and 'Amr ibn al-'Āṣ asked the man who owned it whether wild beasts drank from it. 'Umar ibn al-Khaṭṭāb told the owner of the watering place not to answer, since the people drank after the wild beasts and the wild beasts drank after them.

15 Yaḥyā related to me from Mālik from Nāfi' that 'Abdullāh ibn 'Umar used to say that men and women used to do *wuḍū'* together in the time of the Messenger of Allah ﷺ.

2.4 Things which do not break *wuḍū'*

16 Yaḥyā related to me from Mālik from Muḥammad ibn 'Umara from Muḥammad ibn Ibrāhīm that the mother of the son of Ibrāhīm ibn 'Abd ar-Rahmān ibn 'Awf questioned Umm Salama, the wife of the Prophet ﷺ and said, "I am a woman who wears a long skirt and (sometimes) I walk in dirty places." Umm Salama replied, "The Messenger of Allah ﷺ said, 'What follows it (i.e. clean places) purifies it.'"

17 Yaḥyā related to me from Mālik that he saw Rabi'a ibn 'Abd ar-Raḥmān regurgitate several times when he was in the mosque and he did not leave nor did he do *wuḍū'* before he prayed.

Yaḥyā said that Mālik was asked whether a man who regurgitated food had to do *wuḍū'* and he said, "He does not have to do *wuḍū'*, but he should rinse the inside of his mouth and wash his mouth out."

18 Yaḥyā related to me from Mālik from Nāfi' that 'Abdullāh ibn 'Umar prepared the body of one of Sa'īd ibn Zayd's sons for burial and carried it and then entered the mosque and prayed without doing *wuḍū'*.

Yaḥyā said that Mālik was asked whether it was necessary to do *wuḍū'* because of regurgitating undigested food and he said, "No, *wuḍū'* is not necessary, but the mouth should be rinsed."

2.5 Not doing *wuḍū'* on account of eating cooked food

19 Yaḥyā related to me from Mālik from Zayd ibn Aslam from 'Aṭā' ibn Yasār from 'Abdullāh ibn 'Abbās that the Messenger of Allah ﷺ ate a shoulder of lamb and then prayed without doing *wuḍū'*.

20 Yaḥyā related to me from Mālik from Yaḥyā ibn Sa'īd from Bushayr ibn Yasār, the *mawlā* of the Banu Ḥāritha, that Suwayd ibn an-Nu'mān told him that he went with the Messenger of Allah ﷺ on the expedition to Khaybar. When they reached aṣ-Ṣahbā', which was near Khaybar, the Messenger of Allah ﷺ stopped and prayed *'Aṣr*. He asked for food but only parched barley (*sawīq*) was brought, so he asked for it to be moistened. The Messenger of Allah ﷺ ate and we ate with him. Then he got up to pray *Maghrib* and rinsed his mouth and we rinsed ours. Then he prayed without doing *wuḍū'* again."

21 Yaḥyā related to me from Mālik that both Muḥammad ibn al-Munkadir and Ṣafwān ibn Sulaym transmitted to him from Muḥammad ibn Ibrāhīm ibn al-Ḥārith at-Taymī from Rabī'a ibn 'Abdullāh ibn al-Hudayr that he had eaten an evening meal with 'Umar ibn al-Khaṭṭāb who then prayed without doing *wuḍū'*.

22 Yaḥyā related to me from Mālik from Ḍamra ibn Sa'īd al-Māzinī from Abān ibn 'Uthmān that 'Uthmān ibn 'Affān ate bread and meat, rinsed his mouth out, washed his hands and wiped his face with them, and then prayed without doing *wuḍū'*.

23 Yaḥyā related to me from Mālik that he had heard that 'Alī ibn Abī Ṭālib and 'Abdullāh ibn 'Abbās did not do *wuḍū'* after eating cooked food.

24 Yaḥyā related to me from Mālik from Yaḥyā ibn Sa'īd that he asked 'Abdullāh ibn 'Āmir ibn Rabi'a whether a man who did *wuḍū'* for prayer and then ate cooked food had to perform *wuḍū'* again. He said, "I saw my father do that without doing *wuḍū'* again."

25 Yaḥyā related to me from Mālik from Abū Nu'aym Wahb ibn Kaysān that he heard Jābir ibn 'Abdullāh al-Anṣārī saying, "I saw Abū Bakr aṣ-Ṣiddīq eat meat and then pray without doing *wuḍū'*."

26 Yaḥyā related to me from Mālik from Muḥammad ibn al-Munkadir that the Messenger of Allah ﷺ was invited to eat, and some bread and meat was brought to him. He ate some of it, and then did *wuḍū'* and prayed. Then more of the same food was brought and he ate some more and then prayed without doing *wuḍū'*.

27 It was related to me from Mālik from Mūsā ibn 'Uqba from 'Abd ar-Raḥmān ibn Yazīd al-Anṣārī that when Anas ibn Mālik came back from Iraq, Abū Ṭalḥa and Ubayy ibn Ka'b visited him. He brought them some cooked food and they ate, and then Anas got up and did *wuḍū'*. Abū Ṭalha and Ubayy ibn Ka'b asked, "What is this, Anas? Is this an Iraqi custom?" Anas said, "I wish I had not done it (i.e. *wuḍū'*)." Abū Talḥa and Ubayy ibn Ka'b both got up and prayed without doing *wuḍū'*.

2.6 *Wuḍū'* in general

28 Yaḥyā related to me from Mālik from Hishām ibn 'Urwa from his father that the Messenger of Allah ﷺ was asked about cleaning oneself after excretion. He replied, "Are any of you unable to find three stones?"

29 Yaḥyā related to me from Mālik from al-'Alā' ibn 'Abd ar-Raḥmān from his father from Abū Hurayra that the Messenger of Allah ﷺ went to the burial grounds and said, "Peace be upon you, home of a people who believe! We shall join you, Allah willing. I wish that I had seen our brothers!" The people with him said, "Messenger of Allah! Are we not your brothers?" "No," he said, "You are my companions. Our brothers are those who have not yet come. And I will precede them to the *Ḥawḍ*." They asked him, "Messenger of Allah! How will you recognise those of your community who come after you?" He replied, "Does not a man who has horses with white legs and white blazes on their foreheads among totally black horses recognise which ones are his own?" They answered, "Of course, Messenger of Allah." He went on, "Even so will they come on the day of rising with white marks on their foreheads, hands and feet from *wuḍū'*, and I will precede them to the *Ḥawḍ*. Some men will be driven away from the *Ḥawḍ* as if they were straying camels and I shall call out to them, 'Will you not come? Will you not come? Will you not come?' and someone will say, 'They

changed things after you,' so I shall say, 'Then away with them, away with them, away with them!'"

30 Yaḥyā related to me from Mālik from Hishām ibn 'Urwa from his father from Ḥumrān, the *mawlā* of 'Uthmān ibn 'Affān, that 'Uthmān ibn 'Affān was once sitting on the *Maqā'id* (the benches surrounding the mosque in Madīna, or else a stone near 'Uthmān ibn 'Affān's house where he sat to discuss with people), when the *mu'adhdhin* came and told him that it was time for the *'Aṣr* prayer. He called for water and performed *wuḍū'*. Then he said, "By Allah, I shall tell you something which I would not tell you if it were not in the Book of Allah. I heard the Messenger of Allah ﷺ say, 'If anyone does *wuḍū'*, and does it well, and then performs the prayer, he will be forgiven everything that he does between then and the time when he prays the next prayer.'"

Yaḥyā said that Mālik said, "I believe he meant this *āyat*: 'Establish the prayer at each end of the night and in the first part of the night. Good actions eradicate bad actions. This is a reminder for people who pay heed.' (11:114)."

31 Yaḥyā related to me from Mālik from Zayd ibn Aslam from 'Aṭā' ibn Yasār from 'Abdullāh aṣ-Ṣanābiḥī that the Messenger of Allah ﷺ said, "When a believer does *wuḍū'*, as he rinses his mouth the wrong actions leave it. As he cleans his nose the wrong actions leave it. As he washes his face, the wrong actions leave it, even from underneath his eyelashes. As he washes his hands the wrong actions leave them, even from underneath his fingernails. As he wipes his head the wrong actions leave it, even from his ears. And as he washes his feet the wrong actions leave them, even from underneath the toenails of both his feet." He added, "Then his walking to the mosque and his prayer are an extra reward for him."

32 Yaḥyā related to me from Mālik from Suhayl ibn Abī Ṣāliḥ from his father from Abū Hurayra that the Messenger of Allah ﷺ said, "The Muslim (or the believer) does *wuḍū'* and, as he washes his face, every wrong action he has seen with his eyes leaves with the water (or the last drop of water). As he washes his hands every wrong action he has done with his hands leaves with the water (or the last drop of water). And as

he washes his feet every wrong action his feet have walked to leaves with the water (or the last drop of water), so that he comes away purified of wrong actions."

33 Yaḥyā related to me from Mālik from Isḥāq ibn 'Abdullāh ibn Abī Ṭalḥa that Anas ibn Mālik said, "I saw the Messenger of Allah ﷺ when it was near the time of *'Aṣr*. People were looking for water for *wuḍū'* but could not find any. Then the Messenger of Allah ﷺ was brought some water in a vessel. He put his hand into that vessel and told them all to do *wuḍū'* from it." Anas added, "I saw water gushing up from under his fingers. Then all of them to the last man did *wuḍū'*."

34 Yaḥyā related to me from Mālik from Nu'aym ibn 'Abdullāh al-Madanī al-Mujmir that he heard Abū Hurayra say, "If someone does *wuḍū'* and does it correctly and then goes off intending to do the prayer, he is in prayer as long as he intends to do the prayer. A good action is written for every alternate step he makes and a wrong action is erased for the other. When you hear the *iqāma* do not lengthen your stride, and the one who has the greatest reward is the one whose house is furthest away." They said, "Why, Abū Hurayra?" He replied, "Because of the greater number of steps."

35 Yaḥyā related to me from Mālik from Yaḥyā ibn Sa'īd that he heard someone ask Sa'īd ibn al-Musayyab about washing off excreta with water. Sa'īd said, "That is the way women wash."

36 Yaḥyā related to me from Mālik from Abū az-Zinād from al-A'raj from Abū Hurayra that the Messenger of Allah ﷺ said, "If a dog drinks from a vessel belonging to one of you, he should wash it seven times."

37 Yaḥyā related to me from Mālik that he heard that the Messenger of Allah ﷺ said, "Try to go straight, although you will not be able to do so. Act, and the best of your actions is the prayer. And only a believer is constant in his *wuḍū'*."

2.7 Wiping the head and ears

38 Yaḥyā related to me from Mālik from Nāfiʿ that ʿAbdullāh ibn ʿUmar used two fingers to bring up water to his ears.

39 Yaḥyā related to me from Mālik that he had heard that Jābir ibn ʿAbdullāh al-Anṣārī was asked about wiping over the turban. He said, "Not unless you have wiped over your hair with water."

40 Yaḥyā related to me from Mālik from Hishām ibn ʿUrwa that Abū ʿUrwa ibn az-Zubayr used to take off his turban and wipe his head with water.

41 Yaḥyā related to me from Mālik from Nāfiʿ that he saw Ṣafiyya bint Abī ʿUbayd, the wife of ʿAbdullah ibn ʿUmar, remove her head-covering and wipe her head with water. Nāfiʿ was a child at the time.

Mālik was asked about wiping over the turban and the head-covering. He said, "Neither the man nor the woman should wipe over the turban or the head-covering. They should wipe over the head itself."

Mālik was asked about someone who did *wuḍū'* but forgot to wipe his head until the water had dried. He said, "I think that he should wipe his head and then repeat the prayer if he has already performed it."

2.8 Wiping over leather socks

42 Yaḥyā related to me from Mālik from Ibn Shihāb from ʿAbbād ibn Ziyād, a descendant of al-Mughīra ibn Shuʿba, from his father from al-Mughīra ibn Shuʿba that the Messenger of Allah ﷺ went to relieve himself during the expedition of Tabūk. Mughīra said, "I went with him, taking water. Then the Messenger of Allah ﷺ came back and I poured out the water for him. He washed his hands and then went to bring his arms out of the sleeves of his garment, but could not do so because of their narrowness. So he brought his arms out from underneath his garment. Then he washed his arms, wiped his head and wiped over his leather socks. When the Messenger of Allah ﷺ returned ʿAbd ar-Raḥmān

ibn 'Awf was leading the people in prayer, and he had already finished one *rak'a* with them. The Messenger of Allah ﷺ prayed the remaining *rak'a* with them to everyone's concern. When the Messenger of Allah ﷺ finished he said, 'You have acted correctly.'"

43 Yaḥyā related to me from Mālik that Nāfi' and 'Abdullāh ibn Dīnār told him that 'Abdullāh ibn 'Umar arrived at Kufa and went to Sa'd ibn Abī Waqqāṣ, who was the governor of Kufa at that time. 'Abdullāh ibn 'Umar saw him wiping over his leather socks and disapproved of it. So Sa'd told to him, "Ask your father when you get back." 'Abdullāh returned but forgot to ask 'Umar about the matter until Sa'd arrived and said, "Have you asked your father?" and he answered, "No." 'Abdullāh then asked 'Umar and 'Umar replied, "If your feet are ritually pure when you put them in the leather socks then you can wipe over the socks." 'Abdullāh said, "What about if we have just come from relieving ourselves?" 'Umar said, "Yes, even if you have just come from relieving yourself."

44 Yaḥyā related to me from Mālik from Nāfi' that 'Abdullāh ibn 'Umar urinated in the market place and then did *wuḍū'*, washing his face and hands and wiping his head. Then as soon as he had come into the mosque, he was called to pray over a dead person, so he wiped over his leather socks and prayed over him.

45 Yaḥyā related to me from Mālik that Sa'īd ibn 'Abd ar-Raḥmān ibn Ruqaysh said, "I saw Anas ibn Mālik come, squat and urinate. Then water was brought and he did *wuḍū'*. He washed his face, then his arms to the elbows, and then he wiped his head and wiped over his leather socks. Then he came to the mosque and prayed."

Yaḥyā said: Mālik was asked whether someone who did *wuḍū'* for prayer and then put on his leather socks, and then urinated and took them off and put them back on again, should begin *wuḍū'* afresh. Mālik replied, "He should take off his socks and wash his feet. Only someone who puts on leather socks when his feet are (already) ritually purified by *wuḍū'* can wipe over them. Someone who puts on leather socks when his feet are not ritually purified by *wuḍū'* should not wipe over them."

He said: Mālik was asked about someone who did *wuḍū'* with his leather socks on and forgot to wipe over them until the water was dry and he had prayed, and he said, "He should wipe over his socks and repeat the prayer but not repeat *wuḍū'*."

Mālik was asked about someone who washed his feet and put on his leather socks and then started doing *wuḍū'*, and he said, "He should take off his socks and do *wuḍū'* and wash his feet."

2.9 How to wipe over leather socks

46 Yaḥyā related to me from Mālik from Hishām ibn 'Urwa that he saw his father wiping over his leather socks. He said, "When he wiped over his socks he would never do more than wipe the tops and he would not wipe the bottoms."

47 Yaḥyā related to me from Mālik asked Ibn Shihāb how to wipe over leather socks. Ibn Shihāb put one hand under the sock and his other hand above the sock and then passed them over it.

Yaḥyā said that Mālik said, "Of all that I have heard about the matter I prefer the verdict of Ibn Shihāb."

2.10 Nosebleeds in the prayer

48 Yaḥyā related to me from Mālik from Nāfi' that 'Abdullāh ibn 'Umar would leave and do *wuḍū'* if he had a nosebleed and then return and complete his prayer without speaking.

49 Yaḥyā related to me from Mālik from Nāfi' that 'Abdullāh ibn 'Abbās used to have nosebleeds and would leave to wash off the blood. He would then return and complete his prayer.

50 Yaḥyā related to me from Mālik from Yazīd ibn 'Abdullāh Qusayṭ al-Laythī that he saw Sa'īd ibn al-Musayyab having a nosebleed while praying. He went off to the room of Umm Salama, the wife of the Prophet

ﷺ and water was brought to him and he did *wuḍū'*." He then returned and completed his prayer.

2.11 Nosebleeds in general

51 Yaḥyā related to me that 'Abd ar-Raḥmān ibn Harmala al-Aslamī said, "I saw Sa'īd ibn al-Musayyab with his nose bleeding and the blood was pouring out of it so that his fingers were all red from the blood coming out of his nose, and prayed without doing *wuḍū'*.

52 Yaḥyā related to me from Mālik from 'Abd ar-Raḥmān ibn al-Mujabbar that he saw Sālim ibn 'Abdullāh with blood running from his nose so that his fingers were all coloured red. Then he rubbed his nose and he prayed without doing *wuḍū'*."

2.12 Bleeding from a wound or a nosebleed

53 Yaḥyā related to me from Hishām ibn 'Urwa from his father that al-Miswar ibn Makhrama told him that he had visited 'Umar ibn al-Khaṭṭāb on the night he was stabbed and had woken him up for *Ṣubḥ* and 'Umar had said, "Yes. Whoever stops doing the prayer will get nothing from Islam," and he did the prayer with blood pouring from his wound.

54 Yaḥyā related to me from Mālik from Yaḥyā ibn Sa'īd that Sa'īd ibn al-Musayyab was asked, "What do you say about someone who is afflicted by a nosebleed which does not stop?" Mālik stated that Yaḥyā ibn Sa'īd said that Sa'īd ibn al-Musayyab said, "I say that he should gesture with his head." (i.e. instead of doing *sajda* or *rukū'*.)

Yaḥyā said that Mālik said, "That is what I like most out of what I have heard about the matter."

2.13 *Wuḍū'* on account of prostatic fluid

55 Yaḥyā related to me from Mālik from Abū an-Naḍr, the *mawlā* of

ʿAbdullāh ibn ʿUbaydullāh, from Sulaymān ibn Yasār from al-Miqdād ibn al-Aswad that ʿAlī ibn Abī Ṭālib told him to ask the Messenger of Allah ﷺ what a man should do, who, when close to his wife, had a flow of prostatic fluid. ʿAlī explained that the daughter of the Messenger of Allah ﷺ was living with him then and he was too shy to ask for himself. Al-Miqdād said, "I asked the Messenger of Allah ﷺ about it, and he said, 'When that happens, wash your genitals with water and do *wuḍū'* as for prayer.'"

56 Yaḥyā related to me from Zayd ibn Aslam from his father that ʿUmar ibn al-Khaṭṭāb said, "I find it dropping from me like small beads. When that happens, wash your penis and do *wuḍū'* as for prayer."

57 Yaḥyā related to me from Mālik from Zayd ibn Aslam from his father that Jundub, the *mawlā* of ʿAbdullāh ibn ʿAyyāsh, said, "I asked ʿAbdullāh ibn ʿUmar about prostatic fluid and he said, 'When you find it, wash your genitals and do *wuḍū'* as for prayer.'"

2.14 Indulgence about not having to do *wuḍū'* on account of prostatic fluid

58 Yaḥyā related to me from Mālik from Yaḥyā ibn Saʿīd that he was listening to Saʿīd ibn al-Musayyab and a man questioned him saying, "I discover a discharge when I am praying. Should I leave?" Saʿīd ibn al-Musayyab said to him, "Even if it were to flow on my leg I would not leave until I had finished the prayer."

59 Yaḥyā related to me from Mālik that aṣ-Ṣalt ibn Zubayd said, "I asked Sulaymān ibn Yasār about a discharge I discovered. He said, 'Wash what is under your garments with water and forget about it.'"

2.15 *Wuḍū'* on account of touching the genitals

60 Yaḥyā related to me from Mālik that ʿAbdullāh ibn Abī Bakr ibn Muḥammad ibn ʿAmr ibn Ḥazm heard ʿUrwa ibn az-Zubayr saying, "I went to see Marwān ibn al-Ḥakam and we were talking about what you

had to do *wuḍū'* for, and Marwān mentioned that you had to do *wuḍū'* if you touched your penis." 'Urwa said, "I did not know that." Marwān ibn al-Ḥakam said that Busra bint Ṣafwān had told him that she heard the Messenger of Allah ﷺ say, "If any of you touches his penis he should do *wuḍū'*."

61 Yaḥyā related to me from Mālik from Ismā'īl ibn Muḥammad ibn Sa'd ibn Abī Waqqāṣ that Muṣ'ab ibn Sa'd ibn Abī Waqqāṣ said, "I was holding the Qur'ān for Sa'd ibn Abī Waqqāṣ and I rubbed myself. Sa'd enquired whether I had touched my penis. I replied that I had and he told me to get up and do *wuḍū'*. So I got up and did *wuḍū'* and then returned."

62 Yaḥyā related to me from Mālik from Nāfi' that 'Abdullāh ibn 'Umar used to say, "If you touch your penis you have to do *wuḍū'*."

63 Yaḥyā related to me from Mālik from Hishām ibn 'Urwa that his father used to say, "If any of you touches his penis he has to do *wuḍū'*."

64 Yaḥyā related from Mālik from Ibn Shihāb that Sālim ibn 'Abdullāh said, "I saw my father, 'Yaḥyā ibn 'Umar, do *ghusl* and then do *wuḍū'*. I asked him, 'Father, is *ghusl* not enough for you?' He said, 'Of course, but sometimes I touch my penis, so I do *wuḍū'*.'"

65 Yaḥyā related to me from Mālik from Nāfi' that Sālim ibn 'Abdullāh said, "I was with 'Abdullāh ibn 'Umar on a journey and after the sun had risen I saw him do *wuḍū'* and then pray, so I remarked to him, 'This is not a prayer that you normally do.' He said, 'After I had done *wuḍū'* for *Ṣubḥ*, I touched my genitals. Then I forgot to do *wuḍū'*. So I did *wuḍū'* again and repeated my prayer.'"

2.16 *Wuḍū'* on account of a man kissing his wife

66 Yaḥyā related to me from Mālik from ibn Shihāb from Sālim ibn 'Abdullāh that his father 'Abdullāh ibn 'Umar used to say, "A man's kissing his wife and fondling her with his hands are part of intercourse. Someone who kisses his wife or fondles her with his hand must perform *wuḍū'*."

67 Yaḥyā related to me from Mālik that he had heard that ʿAbdullāh ibn Masʿūd used to say, "*Wuḍū'* is necessary if a man kisses his wife."

68 Yaḥyā related to me from Mālik that Ibn Shihāb used to say, "*Wuḍū'* is necessary if a man kisses his wife."

Nāfiʿ said that Mālik said, "That is what I like most out of what I have heard."

2.17 How to perform *ghusl* on account of major ritual impurity

69 Yaḥyā related to me from Mālik from Hishām ibn 'Urwa from his father from 'Ā'isha, *Umm al-Mūminīn*, that whenever the Messenger of Allah ﷺ did *ghusl* for major ritual impurity, he would begin by washing his hands, and then do *wuḍū'* as for prayer. He would then put his fingers in the water and rub the roots of his hair with them. Then he would pour as much water as two hands can hold on to his head three times, and pour it over the entire surface of his skin.

70 Yaḥyā related to me from Mālik from ibn Shihāb from 'Urwa ibn az-Zubayr from 'Ā'isha, the *Umm al-Mūminīn*, that the Messenger of Allah ﷺ used to do *ghusl* for major ritual impurity from a vessel called a *faraq*.

71 Yaḥyā related to me from Mālik from Nāfiʿ that when ʿAbdullāh ibn 'Umar used to do *ghusl* for major ritual impurity he would begin by pouring water on his right hand and washing it. Then, in order, he would wash his genitals, rinse his mouth, snuff water in and out of his nose, wash his face and splash his eyes with water. Then he would wash his right arm and then his left, and after that he would wash his head. He would finish by having a complete wash and pouring water all over himself.

72 Yaḥyā related to me from Mālik that he heard that 'Ā'isha was asked about how a woman should perform *ghusl* for major ritual impurity. She said, "She should scoop water over her head with both hands three times and rub the roots of her hair with her hands."

2.18 *Ghusl* from the two "circumcised parts" meeting

73 Yaḥyā related to me from Mālik from ibn Shihāb from Sa'īd ibn al-Musayyab that 'Umar ibn al-Khaṭṭāb, 'Uthmān ibn 'Affān and 'Ā'isha, the wife of the Prophet ﷺ used to say, "When the circumcised part touches the circumcised part, then *ghusl* is obligatory."

74 Yaḥyā related to me from Mālik from Abū an-Naḍr, the *mawlā* of 'Umar ibn 'Abdullāh that Abū Salama ibn 'Abd ar-Raḥmān ibn 'Awf related that he had asked 'Ā'isha, the wife of the Prophet ﷺ, what made *ghusl* obligatory. She said, "Do you know what you are like, Abū Salama? You are like a chick when it hears the cocks crowing and so crows with them. When the circumcised part passes the circumcised part, *ghusl* becomes obligatory."

75 Yaḥyā related to me from Mālik from Yaḥyā ibn Sa'īd from Sa'īd ibn al-Musayyab that Abū Mūsā al-Ash'arī came to 'Ā'isha, the wife of the Prophet ﷺ and said to her, "The disagreement of the Companions about a matter which I hate to bring before you has distressed me." She asked, "What is that? You did not ask your mother about it, so ask me." He said, "A man penetrates his wife, but becomes listless and does not ejaculate." She answered, "When the circumcised part passes the circumcised part *ghusl* is obligatory." Abū Mūsā added, "I shall never ask anyone about this after you."

76 Yaḥyā related to me from Mālik from Yaḥyā ibn Sa'īd from 'Abdullāh ibn Ka'b, the *mawlā* of 'Uthmān ibn 'Affān, that Maḥmūd ibn Labīd al-Anṣārī asked Zayd ibn Thābit about a man who penetrated his wife but became listless and did not ejaculate. Zayd ibn Thābit said, "He does *ghusl*." Maḥmūd said to him, "Ubayy ibn Ka'b used not to think that *ghusl* was necessary" but Zayd ibn Thābit said, "Ubayy ibn Ka'b retracted that position before he died."

77 Yaḥyā related to me from Mālik from Nāfi' that 'Abdullāh ibn 'Umar used to say, "*Ghusl* becomes obligatory when the circumcised part touches the circumcised part."

2.19 *Wuḍū'* of a person in a state of major ritual impurity (*janāba*) when he wants to go to sleep or eat before having a *ghusl*

78 Yaḥyā related to me from Mālik from 'Abdullāh ibn Dīnār that 'Abdullah ibn 'Umar related that 'Umar ibn al-Khaṭṭāb mentioned to the Messenger of Allah ﷺ that he would sometimes become *junub* in the night. The Messenger of Allah ﷺ said to him, "Do *wuḍū'* and wash your penis, and then go to sleep."

79 Yaḥyā related to me from Mālik from Hishām ibn 'Urwa from his father that 'Ā'isha, the wife of the Prophet ﷺ used to say, "If you have intercourse with your wife and then wish to go to sleep before doing *ghusl*, do not sleep until you have done *wuḍū'* as you do it for prayer."

80 Yaḥyā related to me from Mālik from Nāfi' that 'Abdullāh ibn 'Umar, if he wished to sleep or eat while *junub*, would wash his face and his arms to the elbows and wipe his head. Then he would eat or sleep.

2.20 The repetition of the prayer by a person in a state of major ritual impurity, his doing *ghusl* when he has prayed without remembering it, and his washing his garments

81 Yaḥyā related to me from Mālik from Ismā'īl ibn Abī Ḥakīm that 'Aṭā' ibn Yasār told him that the Messenger of Allah ﷺ said the *takbīr* in one of the prayers and then indicated to them with his hand to stay in place. He left and then returned with traces of water on his skin.

82 Yaḥyā related to me from Mālik from Hishām ibn 'Urwa that Zubayd ibn aṣ-Ṣalṭ said, "I went with 'Umar ibn al-Khaṭṭāb to Juruf and he looked down and noticed that he had had a wet dream and had prayed without doing *ghusl*. He exclaimed, 'By Allah, I realise that I have had a wet dream and did not know it and I have not done *ghusl*!' So he did *ghusl* and washed off whatever he saw on his garment, and sprinkled with water whatever he did not see. Then he gave the *adhān* or the *iqāma* and prayed in the mid-morning."

83 Yaḥyā related to me from Mālik from Ismā'īl ibn Abī Ḥakim from

Sulaymān ibn Yasār that 'Umar ibn al-Khaṭṭāb went out early in the morning to his land in Juruf and found semen on his garment. He said, "I have been tried with wet dreams since I was entrusted with governing the people." He did *ghusl,* washed any semen that he saw from his garment, and then prayed after the sun had risen.

84 Yaḥyā related to me from Mālik from Yaḥyā ibn Sa'īd from Sulaymān ibn Yasār that 'Umar ibn al-Khattāb led the people in the Ṣubh prayer and then went out to his land in Juruf and found semen on his clothes. He said, "Since we have been eating rich meat our veins have become fulsome." He did *ghusl,* washed the semen from his clothing, and did his prayer again.

85 Yaḥyā related to me from Mālik from Hishām ibn 'Urwa from his father from Yaḥyā ibn 'Abd ar-Raḥmān ibn Ḥāṭib that he had set off for *'umra* with 'Umar ibn al-Khaṭṭāb in a party of riders among whom was 'Amr ibn al-'As. 'Umar ibn al-Khaṭṭāb dismounted for a rest late at night on a certain road near a certain oasis. 'Umar had a wet dream when it was almost dawn and there was no water among the riding party. He rode until he came to some water and then he began to wash off what he saw of the semen until it had gone. 'Amr ibn al-'Āṣ said to him, "It is morning and there are clothes with us, so allow your garment to be washed." 'Umar ibn al-Khaṭṭāb said to him, "I am surprised at you, 'Amr ibn al-'Āṣ! Even if you can find clothes, is everybody be able to find them? By Allah, if I were to do that, it would become a *sunna.* No, I wash what I see, and I sprinkle with water what I do not see."

Mālik spoke about a man who found traces of a wet dream on his clothes and did not know when it had occurred and did not remember anything he had seen in his sleep. He said, "Let the intention of his *ghusl* be from the time when he last slept, and if he has prayed since that last sleep he should repeat it. This is because sometimes a man has a wet dream and sees nothing, and sometimes he sees something but does not have an emission. So if he finds liquid on his garment he must do *ghusl.* This is because 'Umar repeated what he had prayed after the time he had last slept and not what was before it."

2.21 *Ghusl* of a woman when she experiences the same as a man in her sleep

86 Yaḥyā related to me from Mālik from Ibn Shihāb from 'Urwa ibn az-Zubayr that Umm Sulaym asked the Messenger of Allah ﷺ, "Should a woman do *ghusl* when she experiences the same as a man in her sleep?" The Messenger of Allah ﷺ said to her, "Yes, she should have a *ghusl*. 'Ā'isha said to her, "Shame on you! Does a woman see that?" (i.e. a liquid.) The Messenger of Allah ﷺ said to her, "May your right hand be full of dust. From where does family resemblance come?"

87 Yaḥyā related to me from Mālik from Hishām ibn 'Urwa from his father from Zaynab bint Abī Salama that Umm Salama, the wife of the Prophet ﷺ, said, "Umm Sulaym, the wife of Abū Ṭalḥa al-Anṣārī, came to the Messenger of Allah ﷺ and said, "Messenger of Allah! Allah is not shy about the truth – does a woman have to do *ghusl* if she has had an erotic dream?" He said, 'Yes, if she has a visible discharge.'"

2.22 *Ghusl* for major ritual impurity

88 Yaḥyā related to me from Mālik from Nāfi' that 'Abdullāh ibn 'Umar used to say, "There is no harm in doing *ghusl* with water that has been used by one's wife as long as she is not menstruating or in a state of major ritual impurity (*janāba*)."

89 Yaḥyā related to me from Mālik from Nāfi' that 'Abdullāh ibn 'Umar used to sweat in a garment while he was in *janāba* and then pray wearing it.

90 Yaḥyā related to me from Mālik from Nāfi' that the slave-girls of 'Abdullāh ibn 'Umar used to wash his feet and bring him a mat of palm-leaves while they were menstruating.

Mālik was asked whether a man who had wives and slave-girls could have intercourse with all of them before he did *ghusl*. He said, "There is no harm in a man having intercourse with two of his slave-girls before he does *ghusl*. It is disapproved of, however, to go to a free woman on another's day. There is no harm having intercourse first with one slave girl and then with another when one is *junub*."

Mālik was asked about a man who was *junub* and water was put down for him to do *ghusl* with. Then he forgot and put his finger into it to find out whether it was hot or cold. Mālik said, "If no impurity has soiled his fingers, I do not consider that that makes the water impure."

2.23 *Tayammum*

91 Yaḥyā related to me from Mālik from 'Abd ar-Raḥmān ibn al-Qāsim from his father that 'Ā'isha, *Umm al-Mūminīn*, said, "We went out on a journey with the Messenger of Allah ﷺ and, when we came to Baydā' or Dhāt al-Jaysh, a necklace of mine broke. The Messenger of Allah ﷺ stopped to look for it and the people stopped with him. There was no water nearby and the people were not carrying any with them, so they went to Abū Bakr aṣ-Ṣiddīq and said, 'Do you not see what 'Ā'isha has done? She has made the Messenger of Allah ﷺ and the people stop when there is no water nearby and they are not carrying any with them.'"

'Ā'isha continued, "Abū Bakr came and the Messenger of Allah ﷺ had fallen asleep with his head on my thigh. Abū Bakr said, 'You have made the Messenger of Allah ﷺ and the people stop when there is no water nearby and they are not carrying any with them.'"

She continued, "Abū Bakr remonstrated with me and said whatever Allah willed him to say, and began to poke me in the waist. The only thing that stopped me from moving was that the Messenger of Allah ﷺ had his head on my thigh. The Messenger of Allah ﷺ slept until morning found him with no water. Allah, the Blessed and Exalted, sent down the *āyat* of *tayammum* and so they did *tayammum*. Usayd ibn Huḍayr said, 'This is not the first blessing from you, O family of Abū Bakr.'"

'Ā'isha added, "We roused the camel I had been on and found the necklace under it."

Mālik was asked whether someone who did *tayammum* for one prayer should do *tayammum* when the time of the next prayer came or whether the first *tayammum* was enough. He said, "No, he does *tayammum* for every prayer, because he has to look for water for every prayer. If he looks for it and does not find it then he does *tayammum*."

Mālik was asked whether a man who did *tayammum* could lead others in prayer if they were in *wuḍū'*. He said, "I prefer that someone else should lead them. However, I see no harm in it if he does lead them in prayer."

Yaḥyā said that Mālik said that if a man did *tayammum* because he could not find any water, and then stood and said the *takbīr* and entered into the prayer, and then someone came with some water, he does not stop his prayer but completes it with *tayammum* and then does *wuḍū'* for future prayers.

Yaḥyā said that Mālik said, "Whoever gets up to pray and does not find water and so does what Allah has ordered him to do of *tayammum* has obeyed Allah. Someone who does find water is neither purer than him nor more perfect in prayer, because both have been commanded and each does as Allah has commanded. What Allah has commanded as far as *wuḍū'* is concerned is for the one who finds water, and *tayammum* is for the one who does not find water before he enters into the prayer."

Mālik said that a man who was in a state of major ritual impurity could do *tayammum* and read his portion of Qur'ān and do voluntary prayers as long as he did not find any water. This applied only to circumstances in which it was allowable to pray with *tayammum*.

2.24 How to do *tayammum*

92 Yaḥyā related to me from Mālik from Nāfi' that 'Abdullāh ibn 'Umar and he were approaching Juruf. When they got to Mirbad, 'Abdullāh got down and did *tayammum* with some good earth. He wiped his face, and his arms to the elbows, and then prayed.

93 Yaḥyā related to me from Mālik from Nāfi' that 'Abdullāh ibn 'Umar used to do *tayammum* up to his elbows.

Mālik was asked about how *tayammum* was done and what parts were covered and he said, "Strike the ground once for the face and once for the arms and wipe them to the elbows."

2.25 *Tayammum* of someone in a state of major ritual impurity

94 Yaḥyā related to me from Mālik from 'Abd ar-Raḥmān ibn Ḥarmala that a man asked Sa'īd ibn al-Musayyab about what a man who was *junub* and had done *tayammum* should do when he found water. Sa'īd said, "When he finds water he must do *ghusl* for what comes after."

Mālik said about someone who had a wet dream while he was on a journey and there was only enough water for *wuḍū'* and he was not thirsty so he did not need to use it for drinking. "Let him wash his genitals, and whatever the semen has fallen on, with the water and then he does *tayammum* with good earth as Allah has ordered him."

Mālik was asked whether a man who was *junub* and wished to do *tayammum* but could only find salty earth could do *tayammum* with that earth, and whether it was disapproved of to pray on salty earth. He said, "There is no harm in praying on salty earth or in using it to do *tayammum* because Allah the Blessed and Exalted has said, '...and do *tayammum* with good earth.' One is purified by *tayammum* with everything that is earth, whether it is salty or otherwise."

2.26 What is permitted to a man from his wife when she is menstruating

95 Yaḥyā related to me from Mālik from Zayd ibn Aslam that a man questioned the Messenger of Allah ﷺ, saying, "What is permitted to me from my wife when she is menstruating?" The Messenger of Allah ﷺ said, "Let her wrap her waist-wrapper round herself tightly, and then what is above that is your concern."

96 Yaḥyā related to me from Mālik from Rabi'a ibn Abī 'Abd ar-Raḥmān that on one occasion 'Ā'isha, the wife of the Prophet ﷺ was sleeping with the Messenger of Allah ﷺ, in one garment, when suddenly she jumped up sharply. The Messenger of Allah ﷺ said to her, "What's the matter with you? Are you losing blood?" meaning menstruating. She said, "Yes." He said, "Wrap your waist-wrapper tightly about you, and return to your sleeping-place."

97 Yaḥyā related to me from Mālik from Nāfi' that 'Ubaydullāh ibn 'Abdullāh ibn 'Umar sent a question to 'Ā'isha asking her, "May a man fondle his wife when she is menstruating?" She replied, "Let her wrap her waist-wrapper around her lower part and then he may fondle her if he wishes."

98 Yaḥyā related to me from Mālik that he had heard that Sālim ibn 'Abdullāh and Sulaymān ibn Yasār were asked whether the husband of a menstruating woman could have sexual intercourse with her when she saw that she was pure but before she had had a *ghusl*. They said, "No, not until she has had a *ghusl*."

2.27 The purity of a woman after menstruation

99 Yaḥyā related to me from Mālik from 'Alqama ibn Abī 'Alqama that his mother, the *mawlā* of 'Ā'isha, *Umm al-Mūminīn*, said, "Women used to send little boxes to 'Ā'isha, *Umm al-Mūminīn*, with a piece of cotton cloth in each one on which was yellowness from menstrual blood, asking her about the prayer. She said to them, "Do not be hasty until you see a white discharge." By that she meant purity from menses.

100 Yaḥyā related to me from Mālik from 'Abdullāh ibn Abī Bakr from his paternal aunt from the daughter of Zayd ibn Thābit that she had heard that women used to ask for lamps in the middle of the night to check their purity. She would criticise them for this saying, "Women never used to do this," i.e. in the time of the Companions.

101 Mālik was asked whether a woman whose period had finished could do *tayammum* to purify herself if she could not find water and he said,

"Yes, because she is like some one in a state of major ritual impurity, who, if he cannot find water, does *tayammum*."

2.28 Menstruation in general

102 Yaḥyā related to me from Mālik that he had heard that 'Ā'isha, the wife of the Prophet ﷺ, said that a pregnant woman who noticed bleeding left off from prayer.

103 Yaḥyā related to me from Mālik that he asked Ibn Shihāb about a pregnant woman who noticed bleeding. Ibn Shihāb replied, "She refrains from prayer."

Yaḥyā said that Mālik said, "That is what is done in our community."

104 Yaḥyā related to me from Mālik from Hishām ibn 'Urwa from his father that 'Ā'isha, the wife of the Prophet ﷺ, said, "I used to comb the head of the Messenger of Allah ﷺ while I was menstruating."

105 Yaḥyā related to me from Mālik from Hishām ibn 'Urwa from his father from Fāṭima bint al-Mundhir ibn az-Zubayr that Asmā' bint Abī Bakr aṣ-Ṣiddīq said, "A woman asked the Messenger of Allah ﷺ saying, 'What do you think a woman should do if menstrual blood gets on her clothes?' The Messenger of Allah ﷺ said, "If menstrual blood gets onto the clothes of any of you, she should gather up the place in her fingers, rub it, and wash it with water and then she can pray in it.'"

2.29 Bleeding as if menstruating

106 Yaḥyā related to me from Mālik from Hishām ibn 'Urwa from his father that 'Ā'isha, the wife of the Prophet ﷺ, said, "Fāṭima bint Abī Ḥubaysh said, 'Messenger of Allah, I never become pure. Should I abandon the prayer?' The Messenger of Allah ﷺ said, 'That is due to a vein, not menstruation. So when your period comes, leave off from the prayer, and when its normal length ends, wash the blood from yourself and pray.'"

107 Yaḥyā related to me from Mālik from Nāfi' from Sulaymān ibn Yasār from Umm Salama, the wife of the Prophet ﷺ, that a certain woman in the time of the Messenger of Allah ﷺ used to bleed profusely, so Umm Salama consulted the Messenger of Allah ﷺ for her, and he said, "She should calculate the number of nights and days a month that she used to menstruate before it started happening, and she should leave off from prayer for that much of the month. When she has completed that she should do *ghusl*, bind her private parts with a cloth, and then pray."

108 Yaḥyā related to me from Mālik from Hishām ibn 'Urwa from his father from Zaynab, the daughter of Umm Salama, that she saw Zaynab bint Jaḥsh, the wife of 'Abd ar-Raḥmān ibn 'Awf, and she used to bleed as if menstruating. She would have a *ghusl* and pray.

109 Yaḥyā related to me from Mālik from Sumayy, the *mawlā* of Abū Bakr ibn 'Abd ar-Raḥmān that al-Qa'qā' ibn Ḥakīm and Zayd ibn Aslam sent him to Sa'īd ibn al-Musayyab to ask how a woman, who was bleeding as if menstruating, should have a *ghusl*. Sa'īd said, "She does a *ghusl* to cover from the end of one period to the end of the next, and does *wuḍū'* for every prayer, and if bleeding overtakes her she should bind her private parts."

110 Yaḥyā related to me from Mālik from Hishām ibn 'Urwa that his father said, "A woman who bleeds as if menstruating only has to do one *ghusl*, and then after that she does *wuḍū'* for each prayer."

Yaḥyā said that Mālik said, "The position with us is that when a woman who bleeds as if menstruating starts to do the prayer again, her husband can have sexual intercourse with her. Similarly, if a woman who has given birth sees blood after she has reached the fullest extent that bleeding normally restrains women, her husband can have sexual intercourse with her and she is in the same position as a woman who bleeds as if menstruating."

Yaḥyā said that Mālik said, "The position with us concerning a woman who bleeds as if menstruating is founded on the *ḥadīth* of Hishām ibn 'Urwa from his father, and it is what I prefer the most of what I have heard about the matter."

2.30 The urine of an infant boy

111 Yaḥyā related to me from Mālik from Hishām ibn 'Urwa from his father that 'Ā'isha, the wife of the Prophet ﷺ, said, "An infant boy was brought to the Messenger of Allah ﷺ and it urinated on him. The Messenger of Allah ﷺ called for some water and rubbed over the urine with it."

112 Yaḥyā related to me from Mālik from Ibn Shihāb from 'Ubaydullāh ibn 'Abdullāh ibn 'Utba ibn Mas'ūd from Umm Qays ibn Miḥṣan that she brought a baby boy of hers who was not yet eating food to the Messenger of Allah ﷺ and he sat him in his lap and and the boy urinated on his clothes, so the Messenger of Allah ﷺ called for some water and sprinkled over it but did not wash it.

2.31 Urinating standing and otherwise

113 Yaḥyā related to me from Mālik that Yaḥyā ibn Sa'īd said, "A Bedouin came into the mosque and uncovered his private parts to urinate. The people called out to him and began to raise their voices but the Messenger of Allah ﷺ said, 'Let him be.' So they let him be and he urinated. Then the Messenger of Allah ﷺ ordered a bucketful of water to be brought and it was poured on the place."

114 Yaḥyā related to me from Mālik that 'Abdullāh ibn Dīnār said, "I saw 'Abdullāh ibn 'Umar urinating while standing."

Yaḥyā said that Mālik was asked if any *ḥadīth* had come down about washing the private parts from urine and faeces and he said, "I have heard that some of those who have passed away used to wash themselves after defecating. I like to wash my private parts from urine."

2.32 The tooth-stick (*siwāk*)

115 Yaḥyā related to me from Mālik from Ibn Shihāb from Ibn as-Sabbāq that the Messenger of Allah ﷺ said in a *jumu'a*, "Muslims! Allah has made

this day a festival day so do *ghusl*, and it will do no harm if whoever has perfume to applies some of it, and use a tooth-stick."

116 Yaḥyā related to me from Mālik from Abū'z-Zinād from al-A'raj from Abū Hurayra that the Messenger of Allah ﷺ said, "Were it not that I would be overburdening my community I would have ordered them to use the tooth-stick."

117 Yaḥyā related to me from Mālik from Ibn Shihāb from Ḥumayd ibn 'Abd ar-Raḥmān ibn 'Awf that Abū Hurayra said, "Were it not that he would have been overburdening his community he (the Messenger of Allah ﷺ) would have ordered them to use the tooth-stick with each *wuḍū'*."

3. Prayer

3.1 The call to prayer

1 Yaḥyā related to me from Mālik that Yaḥyā ibn Sa'īd said, "The Messenger of Allah ﷺ had wanted to take two pieces of wood to strike them together to gather people for the prayer, and 'Abdullāh ibn Zayd al-Anṣārī, of the tribe of Ḥārith ibn al-Khazraj, was shown two pieces of wood in his sleep. He said, 'These are close to what the Messenger of Allah ﷺ wants.' Then it was said, 'Do you not call to the prayer?' When he woke up he went to the Messenger of Allah ﷺ and mentioned the dream to him. The Messenger of Allah ﷺ ordered the *adhān*."

2 Yaḥyā related to me from Mālik from Ibn Shihāb from 'Aṭā' ibn Yazīd al-Laythī from Abū Sa'īd al-Khudrī that the Messenger of Allah ﷺ said, "When you hear the *adhān*, repeat what the *mu'adhdhin* says."

3 Yaḥyā related to me from Mālik from Sumayy, the *mawlā* of Abū Bakr ibn 'Abd ar-Raḥmān, from Abū Hurayra that the Messenger of Allah ﷺ stated, "If people only knew what was in the call to prayer and the first row, and could find no other way to get it than drawing lots for it, they would draw lots for it. If they only knew what was in going early to the prayer, they would race each other to get there. And if they only knew what was in the prayers of *'Ishā'* and *Ṣubḥ*, they would come to them even if they had to crawl."

4 Yaḥyā related to me from Mālik from al-'Alā' ibn 'Abd ar-Raḥmān ibn Ya'qūb from his father and Isḥāq ibn 'Abdullāh that they informed him that they heard Abū Hurayra say, "The Messenger of Allah ﷺ said, 'When

the *iqāma* is called for prayer, do not come to it running, but come with calmness. Pray what you catch and complete what you miss. You are in prayer as long as your aim is the prayer.'"

5 Yaḥyā related to me from Mālik from 'Abd ar-Raḥmān ibn 'Abdullāh ibn 'Abd ar-Raḥmān ibn Abī Ṣa'ṣa'a al-Anṣārī, later al-Māzinī, that his father told him that Abū Sa'īd al-Khudrī had said to him, "I see that you love sheep and the desert. When you are among your sheep or in the desert, call the prayer and raise your voice in the *adhān* because I heard the Messenger of Allah ﷺ say, 'No jinn or man or anything within range hears the voice of the *mu'adhdhin* without bearing witness for him on the Day of Rising.'"

6 Yaḥyā related to me from Mālik from Abū az-Zinād from Al-A'raj from Abū Hurayra that the Messenger of Allah ﷺ said, "When the call to prayer is made Shayṭān retreats, passing wind, so that he will not hear it. When the *adhān* is completed he comes back, until, when the *iqāma* is said, he retreats again. When the *iqāma* is completed, he comes back, until he comes between a man and his self and says, 'Think of such and such, think of such and such,' which he was not thinking about before, until the man does not know how much he has prayed."

7 Yaḥyā related to me from Mālik from Abū Ḥāzim ibn Dīnār that Sahl ibn Sa'd as-Sā'idī said, "There are two times when the gates of heaven are opened, and few who make supplication have it returned to them unanswered. They are at the time of the *adhān*, and when in a rank of people fighting in the way of Allah."

Mālik was asked whether the *adhān* on the day of *jumu'a* was called before the time had come for the prayer and he said, "It is not called until after the sun has passed the meridian."

Mālik was asked about doubling the *adhān* and the *iqāma*, and at what point people had to stand when the *iqāma* for the prayer was called. He said, "I have heard nothing about the *adhān* and *iqāma* except what I have seen people do. As for the *iqāma*, it is not doubled. That is what the people of knowledge in our region continue to do. As for people standing up when the *iqāma* for the prayer is called, I have not heard of any definite point at which it is begun, and I consider it rather to be according to people's (individual) capacity, for some people are heavy and some are light, and they are not able to act as one person."

Mālik was asked about a gathering of people who wished to perform the prescribed prayer calling the *iqāma* but not the *adhān*, and he said, "It is enough for them. The *adhān* is only obligatory in mosques where the prayer is performed in congregation."

Mālik was asked about the *mu'adhdhin* saying "Peace be upon you" to the imām and calling him to the prayer, and he was asked who was the first person to whom such a greeting was made. He replied, "I have not heard that this greeting occurred in the first community."

Yaḥyā said that Mālik was asked whether a *mu'adhdhin* who called the people to prayer and then waited to see if anyone would come and no one did, so he said the *iqāma* and did the prayer by himself and then people came after he had finished, should repeat the prayer with them. Mālik said, "He does not repeat the prayer, and whoever comes after he has finished should do the prayer by himself."

Yaḥyā said that Mālik was asked about a *mu'adhdhin* who called the *adhān* for a group of people, did voluntary prayers, and then the group of people wanted to do the prayer with some one else saying the *iqāma*. He said, "There is no harm in that. His *iqāma* or somebody else's are the same."

Yaḥyā said that Mālik said, "The *Ṣubḥ* prayer is still called before dawn. As for the other prayers, we believe that they should only be called after the time has started."

8 Yaḥyā related to me from Mālik that he had heard that the *mu'adhdhin* came to 'Umar ibn al-Khaṭṭāb to call him to the *Ṣubḥ* prayer and found him asleep, so he said, "Prayer is better than sleep," and 'Umar ordered him to put that in the *adhān* for *Ṣubḥ*.

9 Yaḥyā related to me from Mālik from his paternal uncle Abū Suhayl ibn Mālik that his uncle's father said, "I recognise nothing nowadays of

what I saw the people (i.e. the Companions of the Messenger ﷺ) doing except the call to prayer."

10 Yaḥyā related to me from Mālik that 'Abdullāh ibn 'Umar heard the *iqāma* while he was in Baqī', so he quickened his pace in walking to the mosque.

3.2 The *adhān* on a journey and without *wuḍū'*

11 Yaḥyā related to me from Mālik from Nāfi' that 'Abdullāh ibn 'Umar called the *adhān* on a cold and windy night and included the phrase, "Pray in your houses." Then he said, "The Messenger of Allah ﷺ used to order the *mu'adhdhin* to say, 'Pray in your houses' when it was a cold, rainy night."

12 Yaḥyā related to me from Mālik from Nāfi' that when he was on a journey 'Abdullāh ibn 'Umar did no more than call the *iqāma*, except in the case of *Ṣubḥ*, when he called both the *adhān* and the *iqāma*. 'Abdullāh ibn 'Umar used to say, "The *adhān* is for an imām whom people join [for the prayer]."

13 Yaḥyā related to me from Mālik from Hishām ibn 'Urwa that his father told him, "When you are on a journey you can, if you wish, call both the *adhān* and the *iqāma*, or, if you wish, the *iqāma* and not the *adhān*."

Yaḥyā said that he heard Mālik say, "There is no harm in a man calling the *adhān* while riding."

14 Yaḥyā related to me from Mālik from Yaḥyā ibn Sa'īd that Sa'īd ibn al-Musayyab used to say, "If someone prays in waterless, desolate land, an angel prays on his right and an angel prays on his left. When he calls both the *adhān* and the *iqāma* for the prayer, or calls out the *iqāma*, mountains of angels pray behind him."

3.3 The meal before dawn (*saḥūr*) in relation to the *adhān*

15 Yaḥyā related to me from Mālik from 'Abdullāh ibn Dīnār from 'Abdullāh ibn 'Umar that the Messenger of Allah ﷺ said, "Bilāl calls the *adhān* whilst it is still night so eat and drink until Ibn Umm Maktūm calls the *adhān*."

16 Yaḥyā related to me from Mālik from Ibn Shihāb from Sālim ibn 'Abdullāh that the Messenger of Allah ﷺ said, "Bilāl calls the *adhān* in the night, so eat and drink until Ibn Umm Maktūm calls the *adhān*." Ibn Umm Maktūm was a blind man who did not call the *adhān* until someone said to him, "The morning has come. The morning has come."

3.4 The opening of the prayer

17 Yaḥyā related to me from Mālik from Ibn Shihāb from Sālim ibn 'Abdullāh from 'Abdullāh ibn 'Umar that the Messenger of Allah ﷺ used to raise his hands level with his shoulders when he began the prayer, and when he raised his head from *rukū'* he raised them in the same way, saying, "Allah hears whoever praises him, our Lord and praise belongs to You." He did not do that in the *sujūd*.

Sami'a'llāhu liman ḥamidah. Rabbanā wa laka'l-ḥamd.

18 Yaḥyā related to me from Mālik from Ibn Shihāb that 'Alī ibn Ḥusayn ibn 'Alī ibn Abī Ṭālib said, "The Messenger of Allah ﷺ used to say, 'Allah is greater' whenever he lowered himself and raised himself, and he continued to pray like that until he met Allah."

19 Yaḥyā related to me from Mālik from Yaḥyā ibn Sa'īd from Sulaymān ibn Yasār that the Messenger of Allah ﷺ used to raise his hands in the prayer.

20 Yaḥyā related to me from Mālik from Ibn Shihāb from Abū Salama ibn 'Abd ar-Raḥmān ibn 'Awf that Abū Hurayra used to lead them in prayer and would say "Allah is greater" whenever he lowered himself and raised himself. When he had finished he would say, "By Allah, I am

the person whose prayer most resembles the prayer of the Messenger of Allah ﷺ."

21 Yaḥyā related to me from Mālik from Ibn Shihāb from Sālim ibn 'Abdullāh that 'Abdullah ibn 'Umar used to say "Allah is greater" in the prayer whenever he lowered himself and raised himself.

Yaḥyā related to me from Mālik from Nāfi' that 'Abdullāh ibn 'Umar used to raise his hands to the level of his shoulders when he began the prayer and when he came up from *rukū'* he would raise them less than that.

22 Yaḥyā related to me from Mālik from Abū Nu'aym Wahb ibn Kaysān that Jābir ibn 'Abdullāh used to teach them the *takbīr* in the prayer. Abū Nu'aym said, "He used to tell us to say 'Allah is greater' whenever we lowered or raised ourselves."

23 Yaḥyā related to me from Mālik that Ibn Shihāb used to say, "When a man catches the *rak'a* he says, 'Allah is greater' once, and that *takbīr* is enough for him."

Mālik added, "That is if he intended to begin the prayer by that *takbīr*."

Mālik was asked about a man who began the prayer with the imām but forgot the opening *takbīr* and the *takbīr* of the *rukū'* until he had done one *rak'a*. Then he remembered that he had not said the *takbīr* at the opening nor in the *rukū'*, so he said the *takbīr* in the second *rak'a*. He said, "I prefer that he start his prayer again, but if he forgets the opening *takbīr* with the imām and says the *takbīr* in the first *rukū'*, I consider that enough for him if he intends by it the opening *takbīr*."

Mālik said about someone who prayed by himself and forgot the opening *takbīr*, "He should begin his prayer afresh."

Mālik said about an imām who forgot the opening *takbīr* until he had finished his prayer, "I think that he should do the prayer again, and those behind him, even if they have said the *takbīr*."

3.5 The recitation of Qur'ān in the *Maghrib* and *'Ishā'* prayers

24 Yaḥyā related to me from Mālik from Ibn Shihāb from Muḥammad ibn Jubayr ibn Muṭ'im that his father said, "I heard the Messenger of Allah ﷺ recite *aṭ-Ṭūr* (*sūra* 52) in the *Maghrib* prayer."

25 Yaḥyā related to me from Mālik from Ibn Shihāb from 'Ubaydullāh ibn 'Abdullāh ibn 'Utba ibn Mas'ūd from 'Abdullāh ibn 'Abbās that Umm al-Faḍl bint al-Ḥārith heard him reciting *al-Mursalāt* (*sūra* 77) and she said to him, "My son, you have reminded me by reciting this *sūra* that it was what I last heard the Messenger of Allah ﷺ recite in the *Maghrib* prayer."

26 Yaḥyā related to me from Mālik from Abū 'Ubayd, the *mawlā* of Sulaymān ibn 'Abd al-Mālik, from 'Ubāda ibn Nusayy from Qays ibn al-Ḥārith that Abū 'Abdullāh aṣ-Ṣunābiḥī said, "I arrived in Madīna during the khalifate of Abū Bakr aṣ-Ṣiddīq, and I prayed *Maghrib* behind him. He recited the *Umm al-Qur'ān* and two *sūras* from the shorter ones of the *Mufaṣṣal* in the first two *rak'as*. Then he stood up in the third and I drew so near to him that my clothes were almost touching his clothes. I heard him reciting the *Umm al-Qur'ān* and this *āyat*, 'Our Lord, do not make our hearts deviate after You have guided us. And give us mercy from You. You are the Ever-Giving.'" (3:8).

27 Yaḥyā related to me from Mālik from Nāfi' that 'Abdullāh ibn 'Umar used to recite in all four *rak'as* when he prayed alone – in every *rak'a* the *Umm al-Qur'ān* and another *sūra* from the Qur'ān. Sometimes he would recite two or three *sūras* in one *rak'a* in the obligatory prayer. Similarly, he recited the *Umm al-Qur'ān* and two *sūras* in the first two *rak'as* of *Maghrib*.

28 Yaḥyā related to me from Mālik from Yaḥyā ibn Sa'īd from 'Adī ibn Thābit al-Anṣārī that al-Barā' ibn 'Āzib said, "I prayed *'Ishā'* with the Messenger of Allah ﷺ and he recited *at-Tīn* (*sūra* 95) in it."

3.6 Behaviour in the recitation

29 Yaḥyā related to me from Mālik from Nāfi' from Ibrāhīm ibn 'Abdullah ibn Ḥunayn from his father from 'Alī ibn Abī Ṭālib that the Messenger of Allah ﷺ forbade wearing the *qassī* (an Egyptian garment, striped with silk), wearing gold rings, and reciting the Qur'ān in *rukū'*.

30 Yaḥyā related to me from Mālik from Yaḥyā ibn Sa'īd from Muḥammad ibn Ibrāhīm ibn al-Ḥārith at-Taymī from Abū Ḥāzim at-Tammār from al-Bayāḍī that the Messenger of Allah ﷺ came out to the people while they were praying and their voices were raised in the recitation. He said, "When you pray you are talking confidentially to your Lord. So look to what you confide to Him, and do not say the Qur'ān out loud so that others hear it."

31 Yaḥyā related to me from Mālik from Ḥumayd aṭ-Ṭawīl that Anas ibn Mālik said, "I stood behind Abū Bakr and 'Umar and 'Uthmān and none of them used to recite 'In the Name of Allah, the All-Merciful, the Most Merciful' when they began the prayer."

32 Yaḥyā related to me from Mālik from his paternal uncle Abū Suhayl ibn Mālik that his father said, "We heard the recitation of 'Umar ibn al-Khaṭṭāb when we were at the home of Abū Jahm in al-Balāṭ."

33 Yaḥyā related to me from Mālik from Nāfi' that when 'Abdullāh ibn 'Umar missed anything of a prayer in which the imām had recited out loud, he would stand up when the imām had said the *taslīm* and recite what he owed out loud by himself.

34 Yaḥyā related to me from Mālik that Yazīd ibn Rumān said, "I used to pray next to Nāfi' ibn Jubayr ibn Mut'im and he would nudge me to prompt him while we were praying."

3.7 The recitation in the *Ṣubḥ* prayer

35 Yaḥyā related to me from Mālik from Hishām ibn 'Urwa from his father that Abū Bakr aṣ-Ṣiddīq prayed *Ṣubḥ* and recited *Sūrat al-Baqara* in the two *rak'as*.

36 Yaḥyā related to me from Mālik from Hishām ibn 'Urwa that his father heard 'Abdullāh ibn 'Āmir ibn Rabi'a say, "We prayed *Ṣubḥ* behind 'Umar ibn al-Khaṭṭāb and he recited *Sūra Yūsuf* (*sūra* 12) and *Sūrat al-Ḥajj* (*sūra* 22) slowly."

"I (Hishām's father) said, 'By Allah, then it must have been his habit to get up at the crack of dawn.' He said, 'Of course.'"

37 Yaḥyā related to me from Mālik from Yaḥyā ibn Sa'īd and Rabi'a ibn Abī 'Abd ar-Rahmān from al-Qāsim ibn Muḥammad that al-Furāfiṣa ibn 'Umayr al-Ḥanafī said, "I only learnt *Sūra Yūsuf* (*sūra* 12) from the recitation of it by 'Uthmān ibn 'Affān in the *Ṣubḥ* prayer because of the great number of times he repeated it to us."

38 Yaḥyā related to me from Mālik from Nāfi' that 'Abdullāh ibn 'Umar used to recite the first ten *sūras* of the *Mufaṣṣal* in the *Ṣubḥ* prayer, and on a journey he would recite the *Umm al-Qur'ān* and a *sūra* in every *rak'a*.

3.8 The *Umm al-Qur'ān*

39 Yaḥyā related to me from Mālik from al-'Alā' ibn 'Abd ar-Raḥmān ibn Ya'qūb that Abū Sa'īd, the *mawlā* of 'Āmir ibn Kurayz, told him that the Messenger of Allah ﷺ called to 'Ubayy ibn Ka'b while he was praying. When 'Ubayy had finished his prayer he joined the Messenger of Allah ﷺ and the Messenger of Allah put his hand upon his hand, and he was intending to leave by the door of the mosque, so the Messenger of Allah ﷺ said, "I hope that you will not leave the mosque until you know a *sūra* whose like Allah has not sent down in the Torah nor in the Gospel nor in the Qur'ān." 'Ubayy said, "I began to slow down my pace in the hope of that. Then I said, 'Messenger of Allah, the *sūra* you promised me!' He said, 'What do you recite when you begin the prayer?' I recited the *Fātiḥa* (*sūra* 1) until I came to the end of it, and the Messenger of Allah ﷺ said, 'It is this *sūra*, and it is the "Seven Oft-Repeated" and the " Magnificent Qur'ān" which I was given.'"

40 Yaḥyā related to me from Mālik from Abū Nu'aym Wahb ibn Kaysān that he heard Jābir ibn 'Abdullāh say, "Someone who prays a *rak'a*

without reciting the *Umm al-Qur'ān* in it has not performed the prayer, unless he is praying behind an imām."

3.9 Reciting to oneself behind the imām when he does not recite aloud

41 Yaḥyā related to me from Mālik from al-'Alā' ibn 'Abd ar-Raḥmān ibn Ya'qūb that he heard Abū as-Sā'ib, the *mawlā* of Hishām ibn Zuhra, say he had heard Abū Hurayra say, "I heard the Messenger of Allah ﷺ say, 'If someone prays a prayer without reciting the *Umm al-Qur'ān* in it, his prayer is aborted, it is aborted. It is aborted, incomplete.' So I said, 'Abū Hurayra, sometimes I am behind the imām.' He pulled my forearm and said, 'Recite it to yourself, O Persian, for I heard the Messenger of Allah ﷺ say that Allah the Blessed, the Exalted, said, "I have divided the prayer into two halves between me and my slave. One half of it is for Me and one half of it is for My slave, and My slave has what he asks for."' The Messenger of Allah ﷺ said, "Recite." The slave says, '*Praise be to Allah, the Lord of the Worlds.*' Allah the Blessed, the Exalted, says, 'My slave has praised Me.' The slave says, '*The All-Merciful, the Most Merciful.*' Allah says, 'My slave has spoken well of Me.' The slave says, '*King of the Day of the Dīn.*' Allah says, 'My slave has glorified Me.' The slave says, '*You alone we worship and You alone we ask for help.*' Allah says, 'This *āyat* is between Me and My slave, and for My slave is what he asks for.' The slave says, '*Guide us on the straight Path, the Path of those whom You have blessed, not of those with whom You are angry, nor those who are in error.*' Allah says, 'These are for My slaves, and for My slave is what he asks for.'"

42 Yaḥyā related to me from Mālik from Hishām ibn 'Urwa that his father used to recite behind the imām when the imām did not recite aloud.

43 Yaḥyā related to me from Mālik from Yaḥyā ibn Sa'īd and from Rabī'a ibn Abī 'Abd ar-Raḥmān that al-Qāsim ibn Muḥammad used to recite behind the imām when the imām did not recite aloud.

44 Yaḥyā related to me from Mālik from Yazīd ibn Rūmān that Nāfi' ibn Jubayr ibn Muṭ'im used to recite behind the imām when he did not recite aloud.

Mālik said, "That is what I prefer of what I have heard about the matter."

3.10 Not reciting behind the imām when he recites aloud

45 Yaḥyā related to me from Mālik from Nāfi' that 'Abdullāh ibn 'Umar, when asked if anyone should recite behind an imām, said, "When you pray behind an imām then the recitation of the imām is enough for you, and when you pray on your own you must recite."

Nāfi' added, "'Abdullāh ibn 'Umar used not to recite behind the imām."

Yaḥyā said that he heard Mālik say, "The position with us is that a man recites behind the imām when the imām does not recite aloud and he refrains from reciting when the imām recites aloud."

46 Yaḥyā related to me from Mālik from Ibn Shihāb from Ibn Ukayma al-Laythī from Abū Hurayra that the Messenger of Allah ﷺ finished a prayer in which he had recited aloud and asked, "Did any of you recite with me just now?" One man said, "Yes, I did, Messenger of Allah." The Messenger of Allah ﷺ said, "I was saying to myself, 'Why am I distracted from the Qur'ān?'" When the people heard the Messenger of Allah ﷺ say that, they refrained from reciting with the Messenger of Allah ﷺ when he recited aloud.

3.11 Saying '*amīn*' behind the imām

47 Yaḥyā related to me from Mālik from Ibn Shihāb that Sa'īd ibn al-Musayyab and Abū Salama ibn 'Abd ar-Raḥmān told him from Abū Hurayra that the Messenger of Allah ﷺ said, "When the imām says '*Amīn*', say '*Amīn*'. If someone's '*Amīn*' coincides with that of the angels, he will be forgiven his past wrong actions."

Ibn Shihāb said, "The Messenger of Allah ﷺ used to say '*Āmīn*' (extending it)."

48 Yaḥyā related to me from Mālik from Sumayy, the *mawlā* of Abū Bakr, from Abū Ṣāliḥ as-Sammān, from Abū Hurayra that the Messenger of

Allah ﷺ said, "When the imām has said, '*not of those with anger on them nor of those who are in error*,' say '*Amīn*', for the past wrong actions of all those whose utterance coincides with that of the angels are forgiven them."

49 Yaḥyā related to me from Mālik from Abū az-Zinād from al-A'raj from Abū Hurayra that the Messenger of Allah ﷺ said, "When any of you say '*Amīn*' and the angels in the heavens also say '*Amīn*' so that the one coincides with the other, his past wrong actions are forgiven him."

50 Yaḥyā related to me from Mālik from Sumayy, the *mawlā* of Abū Bakr, from Abū Ṣāliḥ as-Sammān from Abū Hurayra that the Messenger of Allah ﷺ said, "When the imām says, 'Allah hears whoever praises Him,' say, 'O Allah, our Lord, praise belongs to You.' Anyone whose words coincide with those of the angels will be forgiven his past wrong actions.'"

3.12 Behaviour in the sitting in the prayer

51 Yaḥyā related to me from Mālik from Muslim ibn Abī Maryam that 'Alī ibn 'Abd ar-Raḥmān al-Mu'āwī said, "'Abdullāh ibn 'Umar saw me playing with some small pebbles in the prayer. When I finished he forbade me [to do that], saying, 'Do as the Messenger of Allah ﷺ did.' I asked, 'What did the Messenger of Allah ﷺ do?' He replied, 'When he sat in the prayer, he placed his right hand on his right thigh and he closed his fist and pointed his index finger, and he placed his left hand on his left thigh. That is what he used to do.'"

52 Yaḥyā related to me from Mālik from 'Abdullāh ibn Dīnār that he had seen 'Abdullāh ibn 'Umar praying with a man beside him. When the man sat in the fourth *rak'a*, he put both feet to one side and crossed them. When 'Abdullāh finished, he disapproved of that to him, and the man protested, "But you do the same." 'Abdullāh ibn 'Umar said, "I am ill."

53 Yaḥyā related to me from Mālik from Ṣadaqa ibn Yasār that al-Mughīra ibn Ḥakīm saw 'Abdullāh ibn 'Umar sit back from the two

sajdas of the prayer onto the top of his feet. When he had finished, al-Mughīra mentioned it to him, and ʿAbdullāh ibn ʿUmar explained, "It is not a *sunna* of the prayer. I do it because I am ill."

54 Yaḥyā related to me from Mālik from ʿAbd ar-Raḥmān ibn al-Qāsim that ʿAbdullāh ibn ʿUmar told him that he used to see ʿAbdullāh ibn ʿUmar cross his legs in the sitting position of the prayer. He said, "So I did the same, and I was young at the time. ʿAbdullah ibn ʿUmar forbade me to do it, saying, 'The *sunna* of the prayer is that you keep your right foot vertical and lay your left foot down.' I told him, 'But you were doing that.' He answered, 'My feet do not support me.'"

55 Yaḥyā related to me from Mālik from Yaḥyā ibn Saʿīd that al-Qāsim ibn Muḥammad showed them how to sit in the *tashahhud*, and he kept his right foot vertical and laid his left foot down, and sat on his left haunch not on his foot. Then he said, "ʿAbdullāh ibn ʿAbdullāh ibn ʿUmar saw me doing this and related to me that his father used to do the same thing."

3.13 *Tashahhud* in the prayer

56 Yaḥyā related to me from Mālik from Ibn Shihāb from ʿUrwa ibn az-Zubayr from ʿAbd ar-Raḥmān ibn ʿAbd al-Qārī that he heard ʿUmar ibn al-Khaṭṭāb say, while he was teaching people the *tashahhud* from the minbar, "Say, 'Greetings belong to Allah. Pure actions belong to Allah. Good words and prayers belong to Allah. Peace on you, Prophet, and the mercy of Allah and His blessings. Peace be upon us and on the slaves of Allah who are right-acting. I testify that there is no god except Allah. And I testify that Muḥammad is His slave and His Messenger.'"

At-tāḥiyyatu lillāh, az-zākiyātu lillāh, aṭ-ṭayyibātu wa'ṣ-ṣalawātu lillāh. As-salāmu ʿalayka ayyuhā'n-nabiyyu wa raḥmatu'llāhi wa barakātuhu. As-salāmu ʿalaynā wa ʿalā ʿibādi'llāhi'ṣ-ṣāliḥīn. Ash-hadu an lā ilaha illā'llāh wa ash-hadu anna Muḥammadan ʿabduhu wa rasulūh.

57 Yaḥyā related to me from Mālik from Nāfiʿ that ʿAbdullāh ibn ʿUmar used to say the *tashahhud* saying, "In the Name of Allah. Greetings belong to Allah. Prayers belong to Allah. Pure actions belong to Allah. Peace be

on the Prophet and the mercy of Allah and His blessings. Peace be on us and on the slaves of Allah who are right-acting. I testify that there is no god except Allah. I testify that Muḥammad is the Messenger of Allah."

Bismillāh, at-tāḥiyyatu lillāh, aṣ-ṣalawātu lillāh, az-zākiyātu lillāh. As-salāmu 'alā'n-nabiyyi wa raḥmatu'llāhi wa barakātuhu. As-salāmu 'alaynā wa 'alā 'ibādi'llāhi'ṣ-ṣāliḥīn. Shahidtu an la ilaha illallāh. Shahidtu anna Muḥammadan rasūlu'llāh.

He used to say this after the first two *rak'as* and he would make supplication with whatever seemed fit to him when the *tashahhud* was completed. When he sat at the end of the prayer, he did the *tashahhud* in a similar manner, except that after the *tashahhud* he made supplication with whatever seemed fit to him. When he had completed the *tashahhud* and intended to say the *taslīm*, he said, "Peace be on the Prophet and His mercy and blessings. Peace be upon us and on the slaves of Allah who are right-acting."

"As-salāmu 'alā'n-nabiyyi wa raḥmatu'llāhi wa barakātuhu. As-salāmu 'alaynā wa 'alā 'ibādi'llāhi'ṣ-ṣāliḥīn."

He then said, "Peace be upon you" to his right, and would return the greeting to the imām, and if anyone said "Peace be upon you" from his left he would return the greeting to him.

58 Yaḥyā related to me from Mālik from 'Abd ar-Raḥman ibn al-Qāsim from his father that 'Ā'isha, the wife of the Prophet ﷺ used to say in the *tashahhud*, "Greetings, good words, prayers, pure actions belong to Allah. I testify that there is no god except Allah, alone without partner, and that Muḥammad is His slave and His Messenger. Peace be on you, Prophet, and the mercy of Allah and His blessings. Peace be on us and on the slaves of Allah who are right-acting. Peace be upon you."

"At-tāḥiyyatu, aṭ-ṭayyibātu, aṣ-ṣalawātu, az-zākiyātu lillāh. Ashhadu an lā ilaha illā'llāh, waḥdahu lā sharīka lah, wa anna Muḥammadan 'abduhu wa rasuluhu. As-salāmu 'alayka ayyuhā'n-nabiyyu wa raḥmatu'llāhi wa barakātuhu. As-salāmu 'alaynā wa 'alā 'ibādi'llāhi'ṣ-ṣāliḥīn. As-salāmu 'alaykum."

59 Yaḥyā related to me from Mālik from Yaḥyā ibn Sa'īd al-Anṣārī that al-Qāsim ibn Muḥammad ibn Muḥammad told him that 'Ā'isha, the wife of the Prophet ﷺ, used to say in the *tashahhud*, "Greetings, good words, prayers, pure actions belong to Allah. I testify that there is no god except Allah, alone without partner, and I testify that Muḥammad is the slave of Allah and His Messenger. Peace be upon you, Prophet, and the mercy of Allah and His blessings. Peace be upon us and on the slaves of Allah who are right-acting. Peace be upon you."

"At-tāḥiyyatu, aṭ-ṭayyibātu, aṣ-ṣalawātu, az-zākiyātu lillāh. Ash-hadu an lā ilaha illā'llāh, waḥdahu lā sharīka lah wa ash-hadu anna Muḥammadan 'abduhu wa rasūluhu. As-salāmu 'alayka ayyuhā'n-nabiyyu wa raḥmatu'llāhi wa barakātuhu. As-salāmu 'alaynā wa 'alā 'ibādi'llāhi'ṣ-ṣāliḥīn. As-salāmu 'alaykum."

60 Yaḥyā related to me from Mālik that he asked Ibn Shihāb and Nāfi', the *mawlā* of Ibn 'Umar, whether a man who joined an imām who had already done a *rak'a* should say the *tashahhud* with the imām in the second and fourth *rak'as*, even though these were odd for him? They said, "He should say the *tashahhud* with him."

Mālik said, "That is the position with us."

3.14 What to do if one raises one's head before the imām

61 Yaḥyā related to me from Mālik from Muḥammad ibn 'Amr ibn 'Alqama from Mālik ibn 'Abdullāh as-Sa'dī that Abū Hurayra said, "The forelock of someone who raises his head and lowers it before the imām is in the hand of a *shayṭān*."

Mālik said concerning some one who forgot and raised his head before the imām in *rukū'* or *sujūd*, "The *sunna* of that is to return to bowing or prostrating and not to wait for the imām to come up. What he has done is a mistake, because the Messenger of Allah ﷺ said, 'The imām is appointed to be followed, so do not differ with him.' Abū Hurayra said, 'The forelock of someone who raises his head and lowers it before the imām is in the hand of a *shayṭān*.'"

3.15 What to do if through forgetfulness one says the *taslīm* after two *rak'as*

62 Yaḥyā related to me from Mālik from Ayyūb ibn Abī Tamīma as-Sakhtiyānī from Muḥammad ibn Sīrīn from Abū Hurayra that the Messenger of Allah ﷺ finished the prayer after two *rak'as* and Dhū al-Yadayn asked him, "Has the prayer been shortened or did you forget, Messenger of Allah?" The Messenger of Allah ﷺ said, "Has Dhū al-Yadayn spoken the truth?" The people said, "Yes," and the Messenger of Allah ﷺ stood and prayed another two *rak'as* and then said, "Peace be upon you." Then he said, "Allah is greater" and went into a *sajda* as long as his usual prostration or longer. Then he came up from *sajda* and said, "Allah is greater" and went into a *sajda* as long as his usual prostration or longer and then came up.

63 Yaḥyā related to me from Mālik from Dāwūd ibn al-Ḥuṣayn that Abū Sufyān, the *mawlā* of Ibn Abī Aḥmad, said that he heard Abū Hurayra say, "The Messenger of Allah ﷺ prayed *'Aṣr* and said the *taslīm* after two *rak'as*. Dhū al-Yadayn stood up and said, 'Has the prayer been shortened, Messenger of Allah, or did you forget?' The Messenger of Allah ﷺ stood up and completed what remained of the prayer, and then, remaining sitting after saying the *taslīm*, he made two prostrations."

64 Yaḥyā related to me from Mālik from Ibn Shihāb that Abū Bakr ibn Sulaymān ibn Abī Ḥathma said, "I have heard that the Messenger of Allah ﷺ prayed two *rak'as* of one of the two day-time prayers, *Ẓuhr* or *'Aṣr*, and said the *taslīm* after two *rak'as*. Dhū ash-Shamālayn asked him, 'Has the prayer been shortened, Messenger of Allah, or did you forget?' The Messenger of Allah ﷺ said, 'The prayer has not been shortened and I did not forget.' Dhū ash-Shamālayn said, 'It was certainly one of those, Messenger of Allah.' The Messenger of Allah ﷺ approached the people and said, 'Has Dhū ash-Shamālayn spoken the truth?' They replied, 'Yes, Messenger of Allah,' and the Messenger of Allah ﷺ completed what remained of the prayer, and then said, 'Peace be upon you.'"

65 Yaḥyā related the same as that to me from Mālik from Ibn Shihāb from Sa'īd ibn al-Musayyab, and from Abū Salama ibn 'Abd ar-Raḥmān.

Mālik said, "For every forgetfulness which decreases from the prayer, prostrations for it are done before the greeting, and for every forgetfulness which is an addition to the prayer, prostrations are done for it come after the greeting."

3.16 Completing what is recalled when uncertain how much has been prayed

66 Yaḥyā related to me from Mālik from Zayd ibn Aslam from 'Aṭā' ibn Yasār that the Messenger of Allah ﷺ said, "If you are uncertain in the prayer and do not know whether you have prayed three or four *rak'as*, then pray a *rak'a* and make two prostrations from the sitting position before the *taslīm*. If the *rak'a* that you prayed was the fifth, then you make it even by these two *sajdas*, and if it was the fourth, then the two prostrations spite Shayṭān."

67 Yaḥyā related to me from Mālik from 'Umar ibn Muḥammad ibn Zayd from Sālim ibn 'Abdullāh that 'Abdullāh ibn 'Umar used to say, "If you become uncertain in the prayer, estimate what you think you have forgotten of the prayer and repeat it, then do the two *sajdas* of forgetfulness from the sitting position."

68 Yaḥyā related to me from Mālik from 'Afīf ibn 'Amr as-Sahmī that 'Aṭā' ibn Yasār said, "I asked 'Abdullāh ibn 'Amr ibn al-'Āṣ and Ka'b al-Aḥbar about someone who was uncertain in his prayer and did not know whether he had prayed three or four *rak'as*. Both of them said, 'He should pray another *rak'a* and then do two *sajdas* from the sitting position.'"

69 Yaḥyā related to me from Mālik from Nāfi' that 'Abdullāh ibn 'Umar, when questioned about forgetfulness in the prayer, said, "If you think that you have forgotten part of the prayer, then you should pray it."

3.17 What to do if one stands after the completion of the prayer or after two *rak'as*

70 Yaḥyā related to me from Mālik from Ibn Shihāb from al-A'raj that 'Abdullāh ibn Buḥayna said, "The Messenger of Allah ﷺ prayed two *rak'as* with us then got up without sitting back and the people stood with him. When he had finished the prayer and we had seen him say the *taslīm*, he said 'Allah is greater' and did two *sajdas* from the sitting position and then said the *taslīm* again."

71 Yaḥyā related to me from Mālik from Yaḥyā ibn Sa'īd from 'Abd ar-Raḥmān ibn Hurmuz that 'Abdullāh ibn Buḥayna said, "The Messenger of Allah ﷺ prayed *Ẓuhr* with us and he stood straight up after two *rak'as* without sitting. When he had finished the prayer, he did two *sajdas* and then said the *taslīm* after that."

Mālik said, concerning someone who forgot in his prayer and stood up after he had completed four *rak'as* and recited and then went into *rukū'* and then, when he raised his head from *rukū'*, remembered that he had already completed (his prayer), "He returns to a sitting position and does not do any *sajda*. If he has already done one *sajda* I do not think he should do another. Then, when his prayer is finished, he does two *sajdas* from the sitting position after saying the *taslīm*."

3.18 Distraction in the prayer

72 Yaḥyā related to me from Mālik from 'Alqama ibn Abī 'Alqama from his mother that 'Ā'isha, the wife of the Prophet ﷺ, said, "Abū Jahm ibn Ḥudhayfa gave the Messenger of Allah ﷺ a fine striped garment from Syria and he performed the prayer in it. When he had finished he said, 'Give this garment back to Abū Jahm. I looked at the stripes in the prayer and they almost distracted me.'"

73 Mālik related to me from Hishām ibn 'Urwa from his father that the Messenger of Allah ﷺ wore a fine striped garment from Syria, and then gave it to Abū Jahm and took a plain, rough, garment in return. Abū Jahm asked, "Messenger of Allah! Why?" He said, "I looked at the stripes in the prayer."

74 Mālik related to me from ʿAbdullāh ibn Abī Bakr that Abū Ṭalḥa al-Anṣārī was praying in his garden when a wild pigeon flew in and began to fly to and fro trying to find a way out. The sight was pleasing to him and he let his eyes follow the bird for a time and then he went back to his prayer but could not remember how much he had prayed. He said, "A trial has befallen me in this property of mine." So he came to the Messenger of Allah ﷺ and mentioned the trial that had happened to him in his garden and said, "Messenger of Allah, it is a *ṣadaqa* for Allah, so dispose of it wherever you wish."

75 Yaḥyā related to me from Mālik from ʿAbdullāh ibn Abī Bakr that a man from the Anṣār was praying in a garden of his in Quff, one of the valleys of Madīna, during the date season and the branches of the palms were sagging with fruit on all sides. He stared at their fruitfulness in amazement. Then he went back to his prayer and he did not know how much he had prayed. He said, "A trial has befallen me in this property of mine." So he went to ʿUthmān ibn ʿAffān, who was the *khalīfa* at the time, and mentioned it to him and said, "It is *ṣadaqa*, so give it away in the paths of good." ʿUthmān ibn ʿAffān sold it for fifty thousand and so that property became known as the Fifty.

4. Forgetfulness in the Prayer

4.1 What to do if one forgets in prayer

1 Yaḥyā related to me from Mālik from Ibn Shihāb from Abū Salama ibn 'Abd ar-Raḥmān ibn 'Awf from Abū Hurayra that the Messenger of Allah ﷺ said, "When one of you stands in prayer, Shayṭān comes to him and confuses him until he does not know how much he has prayed. When one of you experiences that, he should do two *sajdas* from the sitting position."

2 Yaḥyā related to me from Mālik that he had heard that the Messenger of Allah ﷺ said, "I forget, or I am made to forget, in order that I may establish the *sunna*."

3 Yaḥyā related to me from Mālik that he had heard that a man questioned al-Qāsim ibn Muḥammad saying, "My imagination gets carried away in the prayer, and that happens to me a lot." Al-Qāsim ibn Muḥammad said, "Go on with your prayer, for it will not leave you alone until you go away saying, 'I have not completed my prayer.'"

5. *Jumu'a*

5.1 *Ghusl* on the day of *jumu'a*

1 Yaḥyā related to me from Mālik from Sumayy, the *mawlā* of Abū Bakr ibn 'Abd ar-Raḥmān, from Abū Ṣāliḥ as-Sammān from Abū Hurayra that the Messenger of Allah ﷺ said, "If someone does *ghusl* for major ritual impurity (*janāba*) on the day of *jumu'a* and then goes to the prayer in the first part of the time, it is as if he has offered up a camel. If he goes in the second part of the time, it is as if he has offered up a cow. If he goes in third part of the time, it is as if he has offered up a horned ram. If he goes in the fourth part of the time, it is as if he has offered up a hen. If he goes in the fifth part of the time, it is as if he has offered up an egg. And when the imām comes out, the angels settle down listening to the *dhikr* (remembrance of Allah)."

2 Yaḥyā related to me from Mālik from Sa'īd ibn Abī Sa'īd al-Maqburī that Abū Hurayra used to say, "Doing *ghusl* as prescribed for major ritual impurity (*janāba*) on the day of *jumu'a* is incumbent (*wājib*) on every male who has reached puberty."

3 Yaḥyā related to me from Mālik from Ibn Shihāb that Sālim ibn 'Abdullāh said, "One of the Companions of the Messenger of Allah ﷺ came into the mosque on the day of *jumu'a* while 'Umar ibn al-Khaṭṭāb was already giving the *khuṭba*. 'Umar asked, 'What (kind of) time is this (to arrive)?' He replied, '*Amīr al-Mu'minīn*, I returned from the market and heard the call to prayer, so I did no more than do *wuḍū'*.' 'Umar said, 'You only did *wuḍū'* as well? You know that the Messenger of Allah ﷺ used to instruct people to do *ghusl*.'"

4 Yaḥyā related to me from Mālik from Ṣafwān ibn Sulaym from 'Aṭā' ibn Yasār from Abū Sa'īd al-Khudrī that the Messenger of Allah ﷺ said, "*Ghusl* on the day of *jumu'a* is incumbent on every male who has reached puberty."

5 Yaḥyā related to me from Mālik from Nāfi' from Ibn 'Umar that the Messenger of Allah ﷺ said, "When one of you goes to *jumu'a*, perform *ghusl*."

Mālik said, "It is not enough for someone to have a *ghusl* on the day of *jumu'a* and intend by it the *ghusl* for *jumu'a* unless he does *ghusl* and then sets off. That is because the Messenger of Allah ﷺ said in the *ḥadīth* related by Ibn 'Umar, 'When one of you goes to *jumu'a*, perform *ghusl*.'"

Mālik said, "If someone does *ghusl* on the day of *jumu'a* and intends by it the *ghusl* of the day of *jumu'a* and then sets out, whether early or late, and does something which breaks his *wuḍū'*, he only has to perform *wuḍū'* and his *ghusl* remains valid for him."

5.2 Paying attention when the imām is giving the *khuṭba* on the day of *jumu'a*

6 Yaḥyā related to me from Mālik from Abū az-Zinād from al-A'raj from Abū Hurayra that the Messenger of Allah ﷺ said, "Even saying to your companion 'Listen' while the imām is giving the *khuṭba* on the day of *jumu'a* constitutes foolish chatter."

7 Yaḥyā related to me from Mālik from Ibn Shihāb that Tha'laba ibn Abī Mālik al-Quraẓī informed him that in the time of 'Umar ibn al-Khaṭṭāb they used to pray on the day of *jumu'a* until 'Umar came out, and when 'Umar came out and sat on the minbar and the *mu'adhdhin*s called the *adhān*, they would sit and talk, and then when the *mu'adhdhin*s were silent and 'Umar stood to give the *khuṭba*, they would pay attention and no one would speak.

Ibn Shihāb said, "The imām coming out stops prayer and his speaking stops conversation."

8 Yaḥyā related to me from Mālik from Abū an-Naḍr, the *mawlā* of 'Umar ibn 'Ubaydullāh, from Mālik ibn Abī 'Āmir that 'Uthmān ibn 'Affān used to say in *khuṭbas*, and he would seldom omit it if he was giving the *khuṭba*, "When the imām stands to deliver the *khuṭba* on the day of *jumu'a*, listen and pay attention, for there is the same portion for someone who pays attention but cannot hear as for someone who pays attention and hears. And when the *iqāma* of the prayer is called, straighten your rows and make your shoulders adjacent to each other, because the straightening of the rows is part of the completion of the prayer." Then he would not say the *takbīr* until some men who had been entrusted with straightening the rows came and told him that they were straight. Then he would say the *takbīr*.

9 Yaḥyā related to me from Mālik from Nāfi' that 'Abdullāh ibn 'Umar saw two men talking while the imām was giving the *khuṭba* on the day of *jumu'a* and he threw pebbles at them to alert them to be quiet.

10 Yaḥyā related to me from Mālik that he had heard that a man sneezed on the day of *jumu'a* while the imām was giving the *khuṭba*, and a man by his side asked Allah to bless him. Sa'īd ibn al-Musayyab was asked about that and disapproved of what the man had done and said, "Do not do it again."

11 Yaḥyā related to me from Mālik that when he asked Ibn Shihāb about talking in the *jumu'a* after the imām had come down from the minbar but before he had said the *takbīr* Ibn Shihāb said, "There is no harm in that."

5.3 Catching a *rak'a* of the *jumu'a* prayer

12 Yaḥyā related to me from Mālik that Ibn Shihāb used to say, "Someone who catches a *rak'a* of the *jumu'a* prayer should pray another *rak'a* with it." Ibn Shihāb said, "That is the *sunna*."

Mālik said, "I saw the people of knowledge in our city doing that. That is because the Messenger of Allah ﷺ said, 'Whoever catches a *rak'a* of the prayer has caught the prayer.'"

Mālik said concerning someone who was in a crowd on the day of *jumu'a* and did the *rukū'* but was not able to go into *sajda* until the imām had risen or finished his prayer, "If he is able to do the *sajda* and has already done the *rukū'* then he should do the *sajda* when the people stand up. If he is unable to do the *sajda* until after the imām has finished the prayer, then I prefer that he begins the prayer again and does the four *rak'as* of *Ẓuhr*."

5.4 Nose-bleeds on the day of *jumu'a*

13 Mālik said, "If someone has a nosebleed on the day of *jumu'a* while the imām is giving the *khuṭba* and leaves and does not come back until the imām has finished the prayer, he should pray four *rak'as*."

Mālik said that if someone prayed a *rak'a* with the imām on the day of *jumu'a* and then his nose started to bleed so he left and came back and found that the imām had prayed both *rak'as*, he should then complete the prayer with a second *rak'a* as long as he had not spoken.

Mālik said, "Someone who has a nosebleed or something else happen to him that forces him to leave does not have to ask permission of the imām if he wants to leave on the day of *jumu'a*."

5.5 Making haste on the day of *jumu'a*

14 Yaḥyā related to me from Mālik that he had asked Ibn Shihāb about the words of Allah, the Majestic, the Mighty, "*O you who believe! When the prayer is called on the Day of jumu'a, hasten to the remembrance of Allah*" (62:9). Ibn Shihāb said, "'Umar ibn al-Khaṭṭāb used to recite, 'When the call is made for the prayer on the day of *jumu'a*, go to the remembrance of Allah.'"

Mālik said, "Making haste in the Book of Allah is only deed and action. Allah the Blessed, the Exalted, says '*When he leaves you, he goes about the earth*' (2:205), and He, the Exalted, said, '*But as for him who comes to you eagerly showing fearfulness*' (80:8-9), and He said, '*Then he hastily backed away'* (79:22), and He said, '*There is a vast difference in your striving*'" (92:4).

Mālik said, "Thus the making haste which Allah mentions in His Book is not running on the feet or exertion. It only means deed and actions."

5.6 The Imām's stopping off in a town on the day of *jumu'a*

15 Mālik said, "If the Imām stops off on a journey in a settlement where *jumu'a* is obligatory and he gives a *khuṭba* and leads them in the *jumu'a* prayer, then the people of the town and any other people present perform the *jumu'a* prayer with him."

Mālik said, "If the Imām gathers people for prayer while he is travelling in a settlement where the *jumu'a* prayer is not obligatory, then there is no *jumu'a* for him, nor for the people of the town, nor for anyone else who joins them for the prayer in congregation, and the people of the settlement and anyone else who is not travelling should perform the full prayer."

Mālik added, "*jumu'a* is not obligatory for a traveller."

5.7 The special time in the day of *jumu'a*

16 Yaḥyā related to me from Mālik from Abū az-Zinād from al-A'raj from Abū Hurayra that the Messenger of Allah ﷺ mentioned the day of *jumu'a* and said, "There is a time in it when Allah gives to a Muslim standing in prayer whatever he asks for," and the Messenger of Allah ﷺ indicated with his hand how small it was.

17 Yaḥyā related to me from Mālik from Yazīd ibn 'Abdullāh ibn al-Hād from Muḥammad ibn Ibrāhīm ibn al-Hārith at-Taymī from Abū Salama ibn 'Abd ar-Raḥmān ibn 'Awf that Abū Hurayra said, "I went out to aṭ-Ṭūr (Mount Sinai) and met Ka'b al-Ahbar and sat with him. He related to me things from the Torah and I related to him things from the Messenger of Allah ﷺ. Among the things I related to him was that the Messenger

of Allah ﷺ said, 'The best of days on which the sun rises is the day of *jumu'a*. On it Adam was created, and on it he fell from the Garden. On it he was forgiven, and on it he died. On it the Final Hour will take place, and every moving thing listens from morning till the sun disappears in apprehension of the Final Hour except jinn and men. During it there is a time when Allah gives to a Muslim slave standing in prayer whatever he asks for.' Ka'b said, 'That is one day in every year.' I said, 'No, rather every *jumu'a*.' Then Ka'b recited the Torah and said, 'The Messenger of Allah ﷺ has spoken the truth.'"

Abū Hurayra continued, "I met Baṣra ibn Abī Baṣra al-Ghifārī and he asked, 'Where have you come from?' I replied, 'From aṭ-Ṭūr.' He said, 'If I had seen you before you left, you would not have gone. I heard the Messenger of Allah ﷺ say, "Only make a special journey to three mosques: the mosque of the *Ḥaram* (Makka), this mosque (Madīna), and the mosque of Ilyā' or the Bait al-Maqdis (two names of Jerusalem)."'" (He was not sure which expression was used.)

Abū Hurayra continued, "Then I met 'Abdullāh ibn Salām and I told him that I had sat with Ka'b al-Aḥbar, and I mentioned what I had related to him about the day of *jumu'a*, and told him that Ka'b had said, 'That is one day in every year.' 'Abdullāh ibn Salām said, 'Ka'b lied,' and I added, 'Ka'b then recited the Torah and said, "No, it is every *jumu'a*."' 'Abdullāh ibn Salām said, 'Ka'b spoke the truth.' Then 'Abdullāh ibn Salām said, 'I know what time that is.'"

Abū Hurayra continued, "I said to him, 'Let me know it – do not keep it from me.' 'Abdullāh ibn Salām said, 'It is the last period of time in the day of *jumu'a*.'"

Abū Hurayra continued, "I asked, 'How can it be the last period of time in the day of *jumu'a*, when the Messenger of Allah ﷺ said, "a Muslim standing in prayer", and that is a time when there is no prayer?' 'Abdullāh ibn Salām replied, 'Did not the Messenger of Allah ﷺ say, "Whoever sits waiting for the prayer is in prayer until he prays?"'"

Abū Hurayra added, "I said, 'Of course.' He said, 'Then it is that.'"

5.8 Good appearance and not stepping over people and facing the imām on the day of *jumu'a*

18 Yaḥyā related to me from Mālik from Yaḥyā ibn Sa'īd that he had heard that the Messenger of Allah ﷺ said, "There is nothing wrong in wearing two garments which are not work-clothes for *jumu'a*."

19 Yaḥyā related to me from Mālik from Nāfi' that 'Abdullāh ibn 'Umar would never go to *jumu'a* without wearing oil and perfume except when it was forbidden (i.e. when he was in *iḥrām*).

20 Yaḥyā related to me from Mālik from Nāfi' from 'Abdullāh ibn Abī Bakr ibn Ḥazm from whoever related it to him that Abū Hurayra used to say, "It is better for a man to pray on the surface of al-Ḥarra (a rocky area in Madīna) than for him to wait until the imām stands to give the *khuṭba* and then come and step over people's necks."

Mālik said, "The *sunna* with us is that the people face the imām on the day of *jumu'a* when he intends to give the *khuṭba*, whether they are near the *qibla* or elsewhere."

5.9 The recitation in the *jumu'a* prayer, the sitting, and missing the prayer without a reason

21 Yaḥyā related to me from Mālik from Ḍamra ibn Sa'īd al-Māzinī from 'Ubaydullāh ibn 'Abdullāh ibn 'Utba ibn Mas'ūd that aḍ-Ḍaḥḥāk ibn Qays asked an-Nu'mān ibn Bashīr, "What did the Messenger of Allah ﷺ used to recite on the day of *jumu'a* after *Sūrat al-jumu'a* (*sūra* 62)?" He said, "He used to recite *Sūrat al-Ghāshiya* (*sūra* 88)."

22 Yaḥyā related to me from Mālik that Ṣafwān ibn Sulaym said, "If anyone misses *jumu'a* three times without reason or illness, Allah will set a seal on his heart." Mālik said, "I do not know if it was from the Messenger of Allah ﷺ or not."

23 Yaḥyā related to me from Mālik from Ja'far ibn Muḥammad from his father that the Messenger of Allah ﷺ gave two *khuṭbas* on the day of *jumu'a* and sat down between them.

6. Prayer in Ramadan

6.1 Stimulation of the desire for prayer in Ramaḍān

1 Yaḥyā related to me from Mālik from Ibn Shihāb from 'Urwa ibn az-Zubayr from 'Ā'isha, the wife of the Prophet ﷺ, that the Messenger of Allah ﷺ prayed in the mosque one night and people prayed behind him. Then he prayed the next night and there were more people. Then they gathered on the third or fourth night and the Messenger of Allah ﷺ did not come out to them. In the morning, he said, "I saw what you were doing and the only thing that prevented me from coming out to you was that I feared that it would become obligatory (*farḍ*) for you." This happened in Ramaḍān.

2 Yaḥyā related to me from Mālik from Ibn Shihāb from Abū Salama ibn 'Abd ar-Raḥmān ibn 'Awf from Abū Hurayra that the Messenger of Allah ﷺ used to exhort people to spend the night in prayer in Ramaḍān but never gave a definite order to do it. He used to say, "Anyone who stands in prayer in the night during Ramaḍān with belief and expecting the reward will be forgiven all his previous wrong actions."

Ibn Shihāb said, "The Messenger of Allah ﷺ died while that was still the custom, and it continued to be the custom in the khalifate of Abū Bakr and at the beginning of the khalifate of 'Umar ibn al-Khaṭṭāb."

6.2 Praying at night during Ramaḍān

3 Mālik related to me from Ibn Shihāb from 'Urwa ibn az-Zubayr that

'Abd ar-Raḥmān ibn 'Abd al-Qārī said, "I went out with 'Umar ibn al-Khaṭṭāb in Ramaḍān to the mosque and found the people there were spread out in groups. Some men were praying by themselves, whilst others were praying in small groups. 'Umar said, 'By Allah, I think that it would be better for all these people to join together behind one reciter.' So he gathered them behind Ubayy ibn Ka'b. Then I went out with him another night and the people were praying behind their Qur'ān reciter. 'Umar said, 'This is an excellent innovation! But the one they sleep through is better than the one they are praying,' meaning the last part of the night, and people used to pray at the beginning of the night."

4 Yaḥyā related to me from Mālik from Muḥammad ibn Yūsuf that as-Sā'ib ibn Yazīd said, "'Umar ibn al-Khaṭṭāb ordered Ubayy ibn Ka'b and Tamīm ad-Dārī to lead the people in praying eleven rak'as. The reciter of the Qur'ān would recite the Mi'īn (a group of medium-sized *sūras*) until we would be leaning on our staffs on account of having stood so long in prayer. And we would not leave until the approach of dawn."

5 Yaḥyā related to me from Mālik that Yazīd ibn Rūmān said, "The people used to pray twenty-three *rak'as* at night during Ramaḍān in the time of 'Umar ibn al-Khaṭṭāb."

6 Yaḥyā related to me from Mālik from Dāwūd ibn al-Ḥusayn that he heard al-A'raj say, "I never saw the people in Ramaḍān but that they were cursing the disbelievers." He added, "The reciter of Qur'ān used to recite *Sūrat al-Baqara* in eight *rak'as* and if he did it in twelve *rak'as* the people would think that he had made it easy."

7 Yaḥyā related to me from Mālik that 'Abdullāh ibn Abī Bakr said, "I heard my father say, 'We finished praying in Ramaḍān and the servants hurried with the food, fearing the approach of dawn.'"

8 Yaḥyā related to me from Mālik from Hishām ibn 'Urwa from his father that Dhakwān Abū 'Amr (a slave belonging to 'Ā'isha, the wife of the Prophet ﷺ, who was freed by her after her death) used to stand in prayer and recite for her in Ramaḍān.

7. *Tahajjud*

7.1 Concerning prayer in the night

1 Yaḥyā related to me from Mālik from Muḥammad ibn al-Munkadir from Saʿīd ibn al-Jubayr that a man who has his approval (as a relater of *ḥadīth*), told him that 'A'isha, the wife of the Prophet ﷺ said, "If a man prays in the night and sleep overcomes him during it, Allah writes for him the reward of his prayer, and his sleep is *ṣadaqa* for him."

2 Yaḥyā related to me from Mālik from Abū an-Naḍr, the *mawlā* of 'Umar ibn 'Ubaydillāh, from Abū Salama ibn 'Abd ar-Raḥmān that 'Ā'isha, the wife of the Prophet ﷺ said, "I used to sleep directly in front of the Messenger of Allah ﷺ and my legs were in his *qibla*. When he prostrated, he would nudge me and I would pull up my legs. When he stood up, I stretched them out again." She added, "In those days there were no lamps in the houses."

3 Yaḥyā related to me from Mālik from Hishām ibn 'Urwa from his father from 'Ā'isha, the wife of the Prophet ﷺ that the Messenger of Allah ﷺ said, "When one of you nods off while he is praying, he should go and lie down until he is no longer sleepy. If someone prays when he is drowsy, he may not know whether he is asking for forgiveness or asking for something bad for himself."

4 Yaḥyā related to me from Mālik from Ismāʿīl from Ibn Abī Ḥakīm that he had heard that the Messenger of Allah ﷺ heard a woman praying at night. He asked, "Who is that?" and someone told him, "It is al-Ḥawlā' bint Tuwayt. She does not sleep in the night." The Messenger of Allah ﷺ

disapproved of that and his disapproval showed in his face. Then he said, "Allah, the Blessed and Exalted, does not become weary, but you become weary. Take on whatever is within your capability."

5 Yaḥyā related to me from Mālik from Zayd ibn Aslam from his father that 'Umar ibn al-Khaṭṭāb used to pray as much as Allah willed in the night until he would wake his family at the end of the night for the prayer. He used to say to them, "The prayer, the prayer." Then he would recite the *āyat*, *"Command your family to pray, and be constant in it. We do not ask you for provision. We provide for you. And the best end result is gained by taqwā."* (20:132)

6 Yaḥyā related to me from Mālik that he had heard that Sa'īd ibn al-Musayyab used to say, "Sleep is disapproved of before *'Ishā'* as is conversation after it."

7 Yaḥyā related to me from Mālik that he had heard that 'Abdullāh ibn 'Umar used to say, "(Voluntary) prayers, whether in the day or the night, are done two at a time with a *taslīm* after every pair of *rak'as*."

Mālik said, "That is the custom among us."

7.2 How the Prophet ﷺ prayed the *witr*

8 Yaḥyā related to me from Mālik from Ibn Shihāb from 'Urwa ibn az-Zubayr from 'Ā'isha, the wife of the Prophet ﷺ, that the Messenger of Allah ﷺ used to pray eleven *rak'as* in the night, making them odd with a single one, and when he had finished he lay down on his right side.

9 Yaḥyā related to me from Mālik from Sa'īd ibn Abī Sa'īd al-Maqburī from Abū Salama ibn 'Abd ar-Raḥmān ibn 'Awf that he asked 'Ā'isha, the wife of the Prophet ﷺ, what the prayer of the Messenger of Allah ﷺ was like during Ramadān. She said, "The Messenger of Allah ﷺ did not exceed eleven *rak'as* in Ramadan or at any other time. He prayed four – do not ask me about their beauty or length. Then he prayed another four – do not ask me about their beauty and length. Then he prayed three."

'Ā'isha continued, "I said, 'Messenger of Allah, do you sleep before you do the *witr*?' He said, "Ā'isha, my eyes sleep but my heart does not sleep.'"

10 Yaḥyā related to me from Mālik from Hishām ibn 'Urwa from his father that 'Ā'isha, *Umm al-Mūminīn* said, "The Messenger of Allah ﷺ used to pray thirteen *rak'as* in the night and then would pray two *rak'as* when he heard the *adhān* for the *Ṣubḥ* prayer."

11 Yaḥyā related to me from Mālik from Makhrama ibn Sulaymān from Kurayb, the *mawlā* of Ibn 'Abbās, that 'Abdullāh ibn 'Abbās told him that he had spent a night at the house of Maymūna, the wife of the Prophet ﷺ, who was also Ibn 'Abbās's mother's sister. Ibn 'Abbās said, "I lay down with my head on the breadth of the cushion, and the Messenger of Allah ﷺ and his wife lay down with their heads on its length. The Messenger of Allah ﷺ slept, until, halfway through the night or a little before or after it, he awoke and sat up and wiped the sleep away from his face with his hand. Then he recited the last ten *āyats* of *Sūra Āl 'Imrān* (*sūra* 3). Then he got up and went over to a water-skin which was hanging up and did *wuḍū'* from it, doing his *wuḍū'* thoroughly, and then he stood in prayer."

Ibn 'Abbās continued, "I stood up and did the same and then went and stood by his side. The Messenger of Allah ﷺ put his right hand on my head and took my right ear and tweaked it. He prayed two *rak'as*, then two *rak'as*, then two *rak'as*, then two *rak'as*, then two *rak'as*, then two *rak'as*, and then prayed an odd *rak'a*. Then he lay down until the *mu'adhdhin* came to him, and then prayed two quick *rak'as*, and went out and prayed *Ṣubḥ*."

12 Yaḥyā related to me from Mālik from 'Abdullāh ibn Abī Bakr from his father that 'Abdullāh ibn Qays ibn Makhrama told him that Zayd ibn Khālid al-Juhanī said one night that he had gone to observe the prayer of the Messenger of Allah ﷺ. He said, "I rested my head on his threshold. The Messenger of Allah ﷺ got up and prayed two long, long, long *rak'as*. Then he prayed two *rak'as* which were slightly less long than the two before them. Then he prayed two *rak'as* which were slightly less long than the two before them. Then he prayed two *rak'as* which were slightly less long than the two before them. Then he prayed two *rak'as* which were slightly less long than the two before them. Then he prayed

two *rak'as* which were slightly less long than the two before them. Then he prayed an odd *rak'a*, making thirteen *rak'as* in all."

7.3 The command to pray the *witr*

13 Yaḥyā related to me from Mālik from Nāfi' and 'Abdullāh ibn Dīnār from 'Abdullāh ibn 'Umar that a man asked the Messenger of Allah ﷺ about night prayers. The Messenger of Allah ﷺ said, "Night prayers are done two by two, and when you are afraid that dawn is approaching, then pray one *rak'at* as *witr* to make what you have prayed odd."

14 Yaḥyā related to me from Mālik from Yaḥyā ibn Sa'īd from Muḥammad ibn Yaḥyā ibn Ḥibbān from Ibn Muḥayriz that a man from the Kināna tribe called al-Mukhdajī heard a man in Syria known as Abū Muḥammad saying, "The *witr* is obligatory (*farḍ*)." Al-Mukhdajī said, "I went to 'Ubāda ibn aṣ-Ṣāmit and presented myself to him as he was going to the mosque, and told him what Abū Muḥammad had said. 'Ubāda said that Abū Muḥammad had lied and that he had heard the Messenger of Allah ﷺ say, 'Allah the Majestic and Mighty has written five prayers for mankind, and whoever does them and does not waste anything of them by making light of what is due to them, there is a pact for him with Allah that He will admit him into the Garden. Whoever does not do them, there is no pact for him with Allah. If He wishes, He punishes him, and if He wishes, He admits him into the Garden.'"

15 Yaḥyā related to me from Mālik from Abū Bakr ibn 'Umar that Sa'īd ibn Yasār said, "I was travelling with 'Abdullāh ibn 'Umar on the road to Makka, and fearing that it was nearly dawn I dismounted, prayed the *witr* and then caught up with him. 'Abdullāh said, 'Do you not have a good enough example in the Messenger of Allah ﷺ?' I said, 'Of course, by Allah!' He said, 'The Messenger of Allah ﷺ used to pray the *witr* on his camel.'"

16 Yaḥyā related to me from Mālik from Yaḥyā ibn Sa'īd that Sa'īd ibn al-Musayyab said, "Abū Bakr aṣ-Ṣiddīq used to pray the *witr* when he wished to go to bed, and 'Umar ibn al-Khaṭṭāb used to pray the *witr* at the end of the night. As for me, I pray the *witr* when I go to bed."

17 Yaḥyā related to me from Mālik that he had heard that a man asked 'Abdullāh ibn 'Umar whether the *witr* was obligatory and 'Abdullāh ibn 'Umar replied, "The Messenger of Allah ﷺ prayed the *witr*, and the Muslims prayed the *witr*." The man began repeating his question, and 'Abdullāh ibn 'Umar kept saying, "The Messenger of Allah ﷺ prayed the *witr*, and the Muslims prayed the *witr*."

18 Yaḥyā related to me from Mālik that he had heard that 'Ā'isha, the wife of the Prophet ﷺ, used to say, "If someone fears that he will sleep through till the morning, let him pray the *witr* before he goes to sleep, and if someone hopes to wake for the last part of the night, let him delay his *witr*."

19 Yaḥyā related to me from Mālik that Nāfi' said, "I was with 'Abdullāh ibn 'Umar in Makka. The sky was clouded over and 'Abdullāh was worried that dawn was approaching so he prayed one *rak'a* for *witr*. Then the clouds cleared and he saw that it was still night, so he made his prayers even by praying one *rak'a*. Then he continued to pray two *rak'as* at a time until, fearing that dawn was approaching, he prayed one *rak'a* for *witr*."

20 Yaḥyā related to me from Mālik from Nāfi' that 'Abdullāh ibn 'Umar used to say the *taslīm* between the two *rak'as* and the one *rak'a* of *witr* so that he could ask for something he needed.

21 Yaḥyā related to me from Mālik from Ibn Shihāb that Sa'd ibn Abī Waqqāṣ used to pray *witr* after *'Ishā'* with one *rak'a*.

Mālik said, "This is not the practice with us. Rather three is the minimum for *witr*."

22 Yaḥyā related to me from Mālik from 'Abdullāh ibn Dīnār that 'Abdullāh ibn 'Umar used to say, "The *Maghrib* prayer is the *witr* of the daytime prayers."

Mālik said, "If someone prays the *witr* at the beginning of the night and goes to sleep and then wakes up and it seems good to him to pray, let him pray two *rak'as* at a time. That is what I like most of what I have heard."

7.4 Praying the *witr* after the break of dawn

23 Yaḥyā related to me from Mālik from 'Abd al-Karīm ibn Abī al-Mukhāriq al-Baṣrī from Sa'īd ibn Jubayr that 'Abdullāh ibn 'Abbas went to sleep, and when he woke up, he said to his servant, "Go and see what the people have done," (by that time his sight had gone.) The servant went out and returned saying, "The people have left from *Ṣubḥ*," so 'Abdullāh ibn 'Abbās got up and prayed the *witr* and then prayed *Ṣubḥ*.

24 Yaḥyā related to me from Mālik that he had heard that 'Abdullāh ibn 'Abbās and 'Ubāda ibn aṣ-Ṣāmit and al-Qāsim ibn Muḥammad and 'Ābdullāh ibn 'Āmir ibn Rabi'a had all prayed the *witr* after the break of dawn.

25 Yaḥyā related to me from Mālik from Hishām ibn 'Urwa from his father that 'Abdullāh ibn Mas'ūd said, "I do not mind if the *iqāma* for the *Ṣubḥ* prayer is called while I am still praying the *witr*."

26 Yaḥyā related to me from Mālik that Yaḥyā ibn Sa'īd said, "'Ubāda ibn aṣ-Ṣāmit used to lead the people in prayer. One day he came out for *Ṣubḥ* and the *mu'adhdhin* began to give the *iqāma* for the *Ṣubḥ* prayer. 'Ubāda silenced him, prayed the *witr* and then led them in *Ṣubḥ*."

27 Yaḥyā related to me from Mālik that 'Abd ar-Raḥmān ibn al-Qāsim said, "I heard 'Abdullāh ibn 'Āmir ibn Rabi'a say, 'I sometimes pray the *witr* while hearing the *iqāma* or after the break of dawn.'" 'Abd ar-Raḥmān was not certain which he said.

28 Mālik related to me that 'Abd ar-Raḥmān ibn al-Qāsim heard his father al-Qāsim ibn Muḥammad say, "I have prayed the *witr* after dawn."

Mālik said, "Only a person who oversleeps so that he has not done the *witr* prays it after dawn. No one should intentionally do his *witr* after dawn."

7.5 The two *rak'as* of *Fajr*

29 Yaḥyā related to me from Mālik from Nāfi' from 'Abdullāh ibn 'Umar that Hafṣa, the wife of the Prophet ﷺ told him that the Messenger of Allah ﷺ used to pray two quick *rak'as* after the *mu'adhdhin* had finished the *adhān* for the *Ṣubḥ* prayer before the *iqāma* was said for the prayer.

30 Mālik related to me from Yaḥyā ibn Sa'īd that 'Ā'isha, the wife of the Prophet ﷺ, said, "The Messenger of Allah ﷺ used to pray the two *rak'as* of the dawn (fajr) so quickly that I would ask myself whether he had recited the *Umm al-Qur'ān* or not.'"

31 Yaḥyā related to me from Mālik from Sharīk ibn 'Abdullāh ibn Abī Namir that Abū Salama ibn 'Abd ar-Raḥmān said, "Some people heard the *iqāma* and started to pray. The Messenger of Allah ﷺ came out and said, 'Are you doing two prayers at the same time? Are you doing two prayers at the same time?' That was about the *Ṣubḥ* prayer and the two *rak'as* before *Ṣubḥ*."

"Are you doing two prayers at the same time?" Al-Bājī said that this is an objection and rebuke.

32 Yaḥyā related to me from Mālik that he had heard that 'Abdullāh ibn 'Umar missed the two *rak'as* of dawn and then prayed them after the sun had risen.

33 Yaḥyā related to me from Mālik from 'Abd ar-Raḥman ibn al-Qāsim that al-Qāsim ibn Muḥammad had done the same as Ibn 'Umar.

8. Prayer in Congregation

8.1 The superiority of prayer in congregation over prayer alone

1 Yaḥyā related to me from Mālik from Nāfi‘ from ‘Abdullāh ibn ‘Umar that the Messenger of Allah ﷺ said, "Prayer in a group is twenty-seven times better than the prayer of a man by himself."

2 Yaḥyā related to me from Mālik from Ibn Shihāb from Sa‘īd ibn al-Musayyab from Abū Hurayra that the Messenger of Allah ﷺ said, "Prayer in a group is twenty-five degrees times better than the prayer of one of you on his own."

3 Yaḥyā related to me from Mālik from Abū az-Zinād from al-A‘raj from Abū Hurayra that the Messenger of Allah ﷺ said, "By Him in Whose hand my soul is, I seriously considered ordering someone to collect firewood, ordering the prayer be called, appointing a man to lead the prayer and then coming up behind certain men and burning their houses down about them! By Him in whose hand my soul is, if any of them had known they would find a meaty bone or two good hooves, they would have attended *‘Ishā’*."

4 Yaḥyā related to me from Mālik from Abū an-Naḍr, the *mawlā* of ‘Umar ibn ‘Ubaydullāh, from Busr ibn Sa‘īd that Zayd ibn Thābit said, "The most excellent prayer is your prayer in your house, except for the prescribed prayers."

8.2 The *'Ishā'* and *Ṣubḥ* prayers

5 Yaḥyā related to me from Mālik from 'Abd ar-Raḥmān ibn Ḥarmala al-Aslamī from Sa'īd ibn al-Musayyab that the Messenger of Allah ﷺ said, "What separates us from the hypocrites is being present at *'Ishā'* and *Ṣubḥ*. They cannot do it," or words to that effect.

6 Yaḥyā related to me from Mālik from Sumayy, the *mawlā* of Abū Bakr ibn 'Abd ar-Raḥmān from Abū Ṣāliḥ from Abū Hurayra that the Messenger of Allah ﷺ said, "If a man who is walking along a road finds a branch of thorns on the road and removes it, Allah thanks him for doing that and forgives him."

He also said, "There are five categories who are considered martyrs: someone killed by a plague, someone killed by a disease of the belly, someone who drowns, someone killed by a collapsing building and the one who is martyred in the Path of Allah."

He also said, "If people knew what there was in the call to prayer and the first row, and they could find no other way except to draw lots for it, they would draw lots for it. And if they knew what there was in performing *Ẓuhr* at its time, they would race each other to it. And if they knew what there was in the prayers of *'Ishā'* and *Ṣubḥ*, they would come to them even if they had to crawl."

7 Yaḥyā related to me from Mālik from Ibn Shihāb from Abū Bakr ibn Sulaymān ibn Abī Ḥathma that 'Umar ibn al-Khaṭṭāb missed Sulaymān ibn Abī Ḥathma in the *Ṣubḥ* prayer. In the morning he went to the market, and Sulaymān's house was between the market and the Prophet's mosque. He passed ash-Shifā', Sulaymān's mother, and said to her, "I did not see Sulaymān at *Ṣubḥ*." She replied, "He spent the night in prayer and sleep overcame him." 'Umar said, "I would rather be present at *Ṣubḥ* than stand the whole night in prayer."

8 Yaḥyā related to me from Mālik from Yaḥyā ibn Sa'īd from Muḥammad ibn Ibrāhīm that 'Abd ar-Raḥmān ibn Abī 'Amra al-Anṣārī said that 'Uthmān ibn 'Affān came to the *'Ishā'* prayer and, seeing only a few people in the mosque, he lay down at the back of the mosque to wait for the

number of people to increase. Ibn Abī 'Amra went and sat down beside him and 'Uthmān asked him who he was, so he told him. 'Uthmān said, "What have you memorised of the Qur'ān?" and he told him. 'Uthmān said, "If someone is present at *'Ishā'*, it is as if he had stood in prayer for half a night, and if someone is present at *Ṣubḥ*, it is as if he had stood in prayer for a whole night."

8.3 Repeating the prayer with the imām

9 Yaḥyā related to me from Mālik from Zayd ibn Aslam from a man of the Banū ad-Dīl called Busr ibn Miḥjan from his father, Miḥjan, that he was in a gathering with the Messenger of Allah ﷺ when the call to prayer was made. The Messenger of Allah ﷺ rose and prayed and then returned. Miḥjan remained sitting and did not pray with him. The Messenger of Allah ﷺ asked, "What prevented you from praying with the people? Are you not a Muslim?" He replied, "Of course, Messenger of Allah, but I have already prayed with my family." The Messenger of Allah ﷺ said, "When you come, pray with the people even if you have prayed already."

10 Yaḥyā related to me from Mālik from Nāfi' that a man asked 'Abdullāh ibn 'Umar, "Sometimes I pray in my house and then catch the prayer with the imām, should I pray with him?" 'Abdullāh ibn 'Umar said to him, "Yes," and the man said, "Which of them do I make my prayer?" 'Abdullāh ibn 'Umar said, "Is that up to you? It is up to Allah. He will decide on whichever of them He wishes."

11 Yaḥyā related to me from Mālik from Yaḥyā ibn Sa'īd that a man asked Sa'īd ibn al-Musayyab, "I pray in my house and then I come to the mosque and find the imām praying, should I pray with him?" Sa'īd answered, "Yes", and the man said, "Which of them is my prayer?" Sa'īd replied, "Are you the one to decide that? That is up to Allah."

12 Yaḥyā related to me from Mālik from 'Afīf as-Sahmī that a man from the tribe of Banū Asad asked Abū Ayyūb al-Anṣārī, "Sometimes I pray in my house and then come to the mosque and find the imām praying, should I pray with him?" Abū Ayyūb said, "Yes, pray with him,

for someone who does so has the reward of the group or the equivalent of the reward of the group."

13 Yaḥyā related to me from Mālik from Nāfi' that 'Abdullāh ibn 'Umar used to say, "Someone who prays *Maghrib* or *Ṣubḥ* and then catches them with the imām should not repeat them."

Mālik said, "I do not see any harm in someone who has already prayed in his house praying with the imām, except for *Maghrib*, because if he repeats it, he makes it even."

8.4 Praying in a group of people

14 Yaḥyā related to me from Mālik from Abū az-Zinād from al-A'raj from Abū Hurayra that the Messenger of Allah ﷺ said, "When you lead people in the prayer, make it short, because there are among them some people who are weak, ill and old. But when you pray on your own, make it as long as you wish."

15 Yaḥyā related to me from Mālik that Nāfi' said, "I stood behind 'Abdullāh ibn 'Umar in one of the prayers when there was no one else with him, and he reached behind with his hand and placed me beside him."

16 Yaḥyā related to me from Mālik from Yaḥyā ibn Sa'īd that a man used to lead the people in prayer in al-'Aqīq (a place near Madīna), and 'Umar ibn 'Abd al-'Azīz sent a message to him forbidding him to do so.

Mālik said, "He only forbade him because his father was not known."

8.5 Prayer behind an imām when he prays sitting

17 Yaḥyā related to me from Mālik from Ibn Shihāb from Anas ibn Mālik that the Messenger of Allah ﷺ fell off his horse when riding, and his right side was grazed, so he did one of the prayers sitting, and we prayed behind him sitting. When he left he said, "The imām is appointed to be

followed. If he prays standing, then pray standing, and when he goes into *rukū'*, go into *rukū'*, and when he rises, rise, and when he says, 'Allah hears whoever praises him,' say, 'Our Lord, praise belongs to You', and if he prays sitting, then all of you pray sitting."

18 Yaḥyā related to me from Mālik from Hishām ibn 'Urwa from his father that 'Ā'isha, the wife of the Prophet ﷺ said, "When the Messenger of Allah ﷺ prayed while he was ill, he prayed sitting; some people prayed behind him standing, and he indicated to them to sit down. When he finished, he said, 'The imām is only appointed to be followed. When he goes into *rukū'*, go into *rukū'* and when he rises, rise and if he prays sitting, pray sitting.'"

19 Yaḥyā related to me from Mālik from Hishām ibn 'Urwa from his father that the Messenger of Allah ﷺ came out during his illness and found Abū Bakr standing, leading the people in prayer. Abū Bakr began to move back, but the Messenger of Allah ﷺ indicated to him to stay where he was. The Messenger of Allah ﷺ sat by the side of Abū Bakr, and Abū Bakr prayed following the prayer of the Messenger of Allah ﷺ who was sitting, and the people prayed following the prayer of Abū Bakr.

8.6 The excellence of prayer standing over prayer sitting

20 Yaḥyā related to me from Mālik from Ismā'īl ibn Muḥammad ibn Sa'īd ibn Abī Waqqās from a *mawlā* of 'Amr ibn al-'Āṣ or of 'Abdullāh ibn 'Amr ibn al-'Ās that the Messenger of Allah ﷺ said, "The prayer of one of you sitting down is only equal to half the prayer of one of you when he is standing."

21 Yaḥyā related to me from Mālik from Ibn Shihāb that 'Abdullāh ibn 'Amr ibn al-'Āṣ said, "When we arrived at Madīna we were struck down by a severe epidemic which debilitated us greatly. The Messenger of Allah ﷺ came out to the people while they were praying *nawāfil* prayers sitting down. The Messenger of Allah ﷺ said, 'The prayer of the one sitting is equal to only half the prayer of the one standing.'"

8.7 Praying voluntary prayers (*nawāfil*)

22 Yaḥyā related to me from Mālik from Ibn Shihāb from as-Sā'ib ibn Yazīd from al-Muṭṭalib ibn Abī Wadā'a as-Sahmī that Ḥafṣa, the wife of the Prophet ﷺ, said, "I never saw the Messenger of Allah ﷺ praying *nawāfil* prayers sitting until a year before his death, when he began to pray them sitting. He would recite the *sūra* with a measured slowness so that it would seem to be longer than other *sūras* which were actually longer than it."

23 Yaḥyā related to me from Mālik from Hishām ibn 'Urwa from his father that 'Ā'isha, the wife of the Prophet ﷺ, told him that she had never seen the Messenger of Allah ﷺ doing night prayers sitting down until he was getting on in years. He would recite sitting down until when he wanted to go into *rukū'*, he would stand up and recite about thirty or forty *āyats* and then go into *rukū'*.

24 Yaḥyā related to me from Mālik from 'Abdullāh ibn Yazīd al-Madanī and from Abū an-Naḍr from Abū Salama ibn 'Abd ar-Raḥmān from 'Ā'isha, the wife of the Prophet ﷺ, that the Messenger of Allah ﷺ used to pray sitting. He would recite sitting, and then, when about thirty or forty *āyats* of what he was reciting remained, he would stand up and recite standing and then go into *rukū'* and *sajda*. He would do the same in the second *rak'a*.

25 Yaḥyā related to me from Mālik that he had heard that 'Urwa ibn az-Zubayr and Sa'īd ibn al-Musayyab used to pray voluntary prayers sitting.

8.8 The middle prayer

26 Yaḥyā related to me from Mālik from Zayd ibn Aslam from al-Qa'qā' ibn Ḥakīm that Abū Yūnus, the *mawlā* of 'Ā'isha, *Umm al-Mūminīn*, said, "'Ā'isha ordered me to write out a Qur'ān for her. She said, 'When you reach this *āyat*, let me know: "Safeguard the prayer – especially the middle prayer. Stand in obedience to Allah."' When I reached it I told her, and she dictated to me, '*Safeguard the prayer – especially the middle prayer and the 'Aṣr prayer. Stand in obedience to Allah.*' 'Ā'isha said, 'I heard it from the Messenger of Allah ﷺ.'"

27 Yaḥyā related to me from Mālik from Zayd ibn Aslam that 'Amr ibn Rāfi' said, "I was writing out a Qur'ān for Ḥafṣa, *Umm al-Mūminīn*, and she said, 'When you reach this *āyat*, let me know, "*Safeguard the prayer – especially the middle prayer. Stand in obedience to Allah.*" (2:238)' When I reached it I told her and she dictated to me, 'Safeguard the prayer – especially the middle prayer and the *'Aṣr* prayer. Stand in obedience to Allah.'"

28 Yaḥyā related to me from Mālik from Dāwūd ibn al-Ḥuṣayn that Ibn Yarbū' al-Makhzūmī said, "I heard Zayd ibn Thābit say, 'The middle prayer is the *Ẓuhr* prayer.'"

29 Yaḥyā related to me from Mālik that he had heard that 'Alī ibn Abī Ṭālib and 'Abdullāh ibn 'Abbās used to say, "The middle prayer is the *Ṣubḥ* prayer."

Mālik said, "Out of all that I have heard about the matter, I prefer what 'Alī ibn Abī Ṭālib and 'Abdullāh ibn 'Abbās said."

8.9 Permission to pray in one garment

30 Yaḥyā related to me from Mālik from Hishām ibn 'Urwa from his father that 'Umar ibn Abī Salama saw the Messenger of Allah ﷺ praying in one garment in the house of Umm Salama. He was completely covered by it, and had put both ends crossed over his shoulders.

31 Yaḥyā related to me from Mālik from Ibn Shihāb from Sa'īd ibn al-Musayyab from Abū Hurayra that someone asked the Messenger of Allah ﷺ about praying in one garment and the Messenger of Allah ﷺ said, "Do you all have two garments?"

32 Yaḥyā related to me from Mālik from Ibn Shihāb that Sa'īd ibn al-Musayyab said that Abū Hurayra was asked, "May a man pray in one garment?" "Yes," he replied. The man then asked him, "Do you do that?" and he answered, "Yes, I pray in one garment while my clothes are on the clothes-rack."

33 Yaḥyā related to me from Mālik that he had heard that Jābir ibn 'Abdullāh used to pray in one garment.

34 Yaḥyā related to me from Mālik from Rabi'a ibn Abī 'Abd ar-Raḥmān that Muḥammad ibn 'Amr ibn Ḥazm used to pray in a single long shirt.

35 Yaḥyā related to me from Mālik that he had heard from Jābir ibn 'Abdullāh that the Messenger of Allah ﷺ said, "Let anyone who cannot find two garments pray in one garment and wrap himself in it, and if the garment is short, let him wrap it around his waist."

Mālik said, "In my view it is preferable for someone who prays in a single shirt to put a garment or a turban over his shoulders."

8.10 Permission for a woman to pray in a shift and head-covering

36 Yaḥyā related to me from Mālik that he had heard that 'Ā'isha, the wife of the Prophet ﷺ used to pray in a shift and head-covering.

37 Yaḥyā related to me from Mālik from Muḥammad ibn Zayd ibn Qunfudh that his mother asked Umm Salama, the wife of the Prophet ﷺ, what clothes a woman could wear in the prayer. She answered, "She can pray in a shift that reaches down and covers the top of her feet."

38 Yaḥyā related to me from Mālik from a reliable source from Bukayr ibn 'Abdullāh ibn al-Ashajj from Busr ibn Sa'īd that when 'Ubaydullāh ibn al-Aswad al-Khawlānī was in the room of Maymūna, the wife of the Prophet ﷺ, she used to pray in a shift and head-covering, without a waist-wrapper.

39 Yaḥyā related to me from Mālik from Hishām ibn 'Urwa from his father that a woman asked him for a decision, saying, "Waist-wrappers are painful to me. Can I pray in a shift and head-covering?" He replied, "Yes, if the shift is long."

9. Shortening the Prayer

9.1 Joining two prayers when settled and when travelling

1 Yaḥyā related to me from Mālik from Dāwūd ibn al-Huṣayn from al-A'raj from Abū Hurayra that the Messenger of Allah ﷺ joined the *Ẓuhr* and *'Aṣr* prayers on his journey to Tabūk.

2 Yaḥyā related to me from Mālik from Abū az-Zubayr al-Makkī from Abū aṭ-Ṭufayl 'Āmir ibn Wāthila that Mu'ādh ibn Jabal told him that they went out with the Messenger of Allah ﷺ in the year of Tabūk, and the Messenger of Allah ﷺ joined *Ẓuhr* with *'Aṣr* and *Maghrib* with *'Ishā'*. Mu'ādh said, "One day he delayed the prayer and then came out and prayed *Ẓuhr* and *'Aṣr* together. Then he said, 'Tomorrow, Allah willing, you will reach the spring of Tabūk. But you will not get there until well into the morning. No one who arrives should touch any of its water until I arrive.' We reached it and found that two men had got to it before us and the spring was dripping with only a little water. The Messenger of Allah ﷺ asked them, 'Have you touched any of its water?' They said, 'Yes.' The Messenger of Allah ﷺ upbraided them and said what Allah wished him to say. Then they took water with their hands from the spring little by little until it had been collected in something. Then the Messenger of Allah ﷺ washed his face and hands in it. Then he put it back into the spring and the spring flowed with an abundance of water and the people drew water from it. The Messenger of Allah ﷺ said, 'If you live long enough, Mu'ādh, you will see this place filled with gardens.'"

3 Yaḥyā related to me from Mālik from Nāfi' that 'Abdullāh ibn 'Umar

said, "The Messenger of Allah ﷺ used to join *Maghrib* and *'Ishā'* together when he was in a hurry to travel."

4 Yaḥyā related to me from Mālik from Abū az-Zubayr al-Makkī from Sa'īd ibn Jubayr that 'Abdullāh ibn 'Abbās said, "The Messenger of Allah ﷺ prayed *Ẓuhr* and *'Aṣr* together and *Maghrib* and *'Ishā'* together, and not out of fear nor because of travelling."

Mālik said, "I believe that was during rain."

5 Yaḥyā related to me from Mālik from Nāfi' that 'Abdullāh ibn 'Umar used to join the prayer behind the governors if they joined *Maghrib* and *'Ishā'* in the rain.

6 Yaḥyā related to me from Mālik from Ibn Shihāb that he had asked Sālim ibn 'Abdullāh, "Can you join *Ẓuhr* and *'Aṣr* when travelling?" He answered, "Yes, there is no harm in doing that. Have you not seen the people praying at 'Arafa?"

7 Yaḥyā related to me from Mālik that he had heard that 'Alī ibn Ḥusayn used to say, "The Messenger of Allah ﷺ would join *Ẓuhr* and *'Aṣr* if he wished to travel the same day, and he would join *Maghrib* and *'Ishā'* if he wished to travel the same night."

9.2 Shortening the prayer in travel

8 Yaḥyā related to me from Mālik from Ibn Shihāb from a man of the family of Khālid ibn Asīd who said to 'Abdullāh ibn 'Umar, "Abū 'Abd ar-Raḥmān, we find the Fear Prayer and the prayer when resident mentioned in the Qur'ān, but we do not find any mention of the travelling prayer in it." Ibn 'Umar said, "Son of my brother! Allah the Mighty and Majestic sent us Muḥammad ﷺ and we knew nothing. We only do as we saw him doing."

9 Yaḥyā related to me from Mālik from Ṣāliḥ ibn Kaysān from 'Urwa ibn az-Zubayr that 'Ā'isha, the wife of the Prophet ﷺ said, "The prayer was prescribed as two *rak'as*, whether resident or travelling. Then the

travelling prayer was kept the same but the residential prayer was increased."

10 Yaḥyā related to me from Mālik from Yaḥyā ibn Sa'īd that he asked Sālim ibn 'Abdullāh what was the latest he had seen his father delay *Maghrib* while on a journey and Sālim replied, "One time the sun set when we were at Dhāt al-Jaysh and he prayed *Maghrib* at al-'Aqīq."[1]

9.3 Circumstances in which the prayer has to be shortened

11 Yaḥyā related to me from Mālik from Nāfi' that 'Abdullāh ibn 'Umar began to shorten the prayer at Dhū al-Ḥulayfa when he left for *ḥajj* or *'umra*.

12 Yaḥyā related to me from Mālik from Ibn Shihāb from Sālim ibn 'Abdullāh that his father rode for some distance and shortened the prayer on the journey.

Mālik said, "That was about four mail-stages." (approximately forty-eight miles)

13 Yaḥyā related to me from Mālik from Nāfi' from Sālim ibn 'Abdullāh that 'Abdullāh ibn 'Umar rode to Dhāt an-Nuṣub and shortened the prayer on the journey.

Mālik said, "There are four mail-stages between Dhāt an-Nuṣub and Madīna."

14 Yaḥyā related to me from Mālik from Nāfi' from Ibn 'Umar that he used to travel to Khaybar and would shorten the prayer.

15 Yaḥyā related to me from Mālik from Ibn Shihāb from Sālim ibn 'Abdullāh that 'Abdullāh ibn 'Umar used to shorten the prayer when he travelled for a whole day.

1 There are 12 miles between them.

16 Yaḥyā related to me from Mālik from Nāfi' that he used to travel one mail-stage with Ibn 'Umar and he would not shorten the prayer.

17 Yaḥyā related to me from Mālik that he had heard that 'Abdullāh ibn 'Abbās used to shorten the prayer when he travelled a distance equivalent to that between Makka and Ṭā'if, and that between Makka and 'Usfān, and that between Makka and Jidda.

Mālik said, "That is four mail-stages, and to me that is the most preferable distance for shortening the prayer."

Mālik said, "Someone who intends to travel does not shorten the prayer until he has left the houses of the settlement, and he does not perform it in full until he reaches the first houses of his place of destination, or is close to it."

9.4 The prayer of a traveller when undecided whether to remain in a place or not

18 Yaḥyā related to me from Mālik from Ibn Shihāb from Sālim ibn 'Abdullāh that 'Abdullāh ibn 'Umar used to say, "I pray the prayer of a traveller as long as I am undecided whether to remain somewhere or not, even if I am detained for twelve nights."

19 Yaḥyā related to me from Mālik from Nāfi' that Ibn 'Umar stayed in Makka for ten nights, shortening the prayer, except when he prayed it behind an imām, in which case he followed the imām's prayer.

9.5 Doing the full prayer when one decides to remain in a place

20 Yaḥyā related to me from Mālik from 'Aṭā' al-Khurasāni that he heard Sa'īd ibn al-Musayyab say, "A traveller who has decided to remain somewhere for four nights does the prayer in full."

Mālik said, "That is what I prefer most out of what I have heard."

When Mālik was asked about the prayer of a prisoner, he said, "It is the same as the prayer of a person who remains in one place unless he is travelling."

9.6 The prayer of a traveller when acting as imām, or when praying behind an imām

21 Yaḥyā related to me from Mālik from Ibn Shihāb from Sālim ibn 'Abdullāh from his father that when 'Umar ibn al-Khaṭṭāb went to Makka, he used to lead them in prayer and do two *rak'as* and then say, "People of Makka, complete the prayer, we are a group who are travelling."

22 Yaḥyā related to me from Mālik from Nāfi' that 'Abdullāh ibn 'Umar used to pray four *rak'as* behind the imām at Mina, but when he prayed by himself he would pray two *rak'as*.

23 Yaḥyā related to me from Mālik from Ibn Shihāb that Ṣafwān said, "'Abdullāh ibn 'Umar used to come and visit 'Abdullāh ibn Ṣafwān and he would lead us in the prayer for two *rak'as*, and when he finished we would stand and complete the prayer."

9.7 Voluntary prayers while travelling, by day and at night, and praying on a riding beast

24 Yaḥyā related to me from Mālik from Nāfi' that 'Abdullāh ibn 'Umar never used to pray any prayer besides the *farḍ* prayer, either before it or after it, while travelling, except in the depths of the night. He would pray on the ground or on his mount, whichever direction it was facing.

25 Yaḥyā related to me from Mālik that he had heard that al-Qāsim ibn Muḥammad and 'Urwa ibn az-Zubayr and Abū Bakr ibn 'Abd ar-Raḥmān used to pray *nāfila* prayers when travelling.

26 Yaḥyā related to me that Mālik said. "I have heard from Nāfi' that 'Abdullāh ibn 'Umar used to see his son, 'Ubaydullāh ibn 'Abdullāh, doing voluntary prayers on a journey and he did not disapprove of it."

27 Yaḥyā related to me from Mālik from 'Amr ibn Yaḥyā al-Māzinī from Abū al-Ḥubāb Sa'īd ibn Yasār that 'Abdullāh ibn 'Umar said, "I saw the Messenger of Allah ﷺ praying on a donkey while heading towards Khaybar."

28 Yaḥyā related to me from Mālik from 'Abdullāh ibn Dīnār from 'Abdullāh ibn 'Umar that the Messenger of Allah ﷺ used to pray on his mount while travelling, whichever way it was facing.

29 Yaḥyā related to me from Mālik that Yaḥyā ibn Sa'īd said, "I saw Anas ibn Mālik on a journey praying on a donkey facing away from the *qibla*. He did *rukū'* and prostration by motioning with his head without putting his face on anything."

9.8 The *Ḍuḥā* prayer

30 Yaḥyā related to me from Mālik from Mūsā ibn Maysara from Abū Murra, the *mawlā* of 'Aqīl ibn Abī Ṭālib, that Umm Hāni' bint Abī Ṭālib told him that in the Year of the Conquest the Messenger of Allah ﷺ prayed eight *rak'as*, wrapping himself in a single garment.

31 Yaḥyā related to me from Mālik from Abū an-Naḍr, the *mawlā* of 'Umar ibn 'Ubaydullāh, that Abū Murra, the *mawlā* of 'Aqīl ibn Abī Ṭālib, told him that he heard Umm Hāni' bint Abī Ṭālib say, "I went to the Messenger of Allah ﷺ in the Year of the Conquest and found him doing *ghusl* while his daughter, Fāṭima, was screening him with a garment. I said to him, 'Peace be upon you,' and he asked, 'Who is that?' I replied, 'Umm Hāni' bint Abī Tālib,' and he said, 'Welcome, Umm Hāni'!' When he had finished his *ghusl*, he stood and prayed eight *rak'as*, covering himself with one garment, and then came away. I said, 'Messenger of Allah, the son of my mother, 'Alī, says that he is determined to kill so-and-so, son of Hubayra, a man I have placed under my protection.' The Messenger of Allah ﷺ said, 'We give protection to whoever you have given protection to, Umm Hāni'.'"

Umm Hāni' related that this incident happened in the morning.

32 Yaḥyā related to me from Mālik from Ibn Shihāb from 'Urwa ibn az-Zubayr that 'Ā'isha, the wife of the Prophet ﷺ said, "I never once saw the Messenger of Allah ﷺ doing the voluntary prayer of *Ḍuḥā*, but I myself would perform it. Sometimes the Messenger of Allah ﷺ would refrain from a practice that he loved to do, fearing that people would do the same and it would become obligatory (*farḍ*) for them."

33 Yaḥyā related to me from Mālik from Zayd ibn Aslam that 'Ā'isha used to pray *Ḍuḥā* with eight *rak'as*, and she would say, "I would never stop doing them even if my parents were to be brought back to life."

9.9 General remarks about the voluntary prayer of *Ḍuḥā*

34 Yaḥyā related to me from Mālik from Isḥāq ibn 'Abdullāh ibn Abī Ṭalḥa from Anas ibn Mālik that his grandmother, Mulayka, invited the Messenger of Allah ﷺ for some food and he ate some of it. Then the Messenger of Allah ﷺ said, "Get up and I will lead you in prayer."

Anas said, "I stood up and took a woven mat belonging to us that had become black through long use and sprinkled it with water, and the Messenger of Allah ﷺ stood on it. The orphan and I formed a row behind him, and the old woman stood behind us. He prayed two *rak'as* with us and then left."

35 Yaḥyā related to me from Mālik from Ibn Shihāb that 'Ubaydullāh ibn 'Abdullāh ibn 'Utba said, "I visited 'Umar ibn al-Khaṭṭāb just before noon and found him praying a voluntary prayer, so I stood behind him, but he pulled me nearer and put me next to him on his right hand side, and then Yarfā came and I moved back and we formed a row behind him."

9.10 Strong warning against passing in front of a person praying

36 Yaḥyā related to me from Mālik from Zayd ibn Aslam from 'Abd ar-Raḥmān ibn Abī Sa'īd al-Khudrī from his father that the Messenger of Allah ﷺ said, "Do not let anyone pass in front of you when you are

praying. Repel him as much as you can, and, if he refuses, fight him, for he is only a *shayṭān*."

37 Yaḥyā related to me from Mālik from Abū an-Naḍr, the *mawlā* of 'Umar ibn 'Ubaydullāh, from Busr ibn Sa'īd that Zayd ibn Khālid al-Juhanī sent him to Abū Juhaym to ask him what he had heard from the Messenger of Allah ﷺ about passing in front of someone praying. Abū Juhaym said, "The Messenger of Allah ﷺ said, 'If the person passing in front of a man praying knew what he was incurring, he would find it preferable to wait forty rather than pass in front of him.'"

Abū an-Naḍr said, "I do not know whether he said forty days or months or years."

38 Yaḥyā related to me from Mālik from Zayd ibn Aslam from 'Aṭā' ibn Yasār that Ka'b al-Aḥbar said, "If the person who passed in front of a man praying knew what he was bringing on himself, it would seem better to him to sink into the ground than to pass in front of him."

39 Yaḥyā related to me from Mālik that he had heard that 'Abdullāh ibn 'Umar used to disapprove of passing in front of women while they were praying.

40 Yaḥyā related to me from Mālik from Nāfi' that 'Abdullāh ibn 'Umar would neither pass in front of anyone nor let anyone pass in front of him.

9.11 Permission to pass in front of someone praying

41 Yaḥyā related to me from Mālik from Ibn Shihāb from 'Ubaydullāh ibn 'Abdullāh ibn 'Utba ibn Mas'ūd that 'Abdullāh ibn 'Abbās said, "I came riding up on a donkey while the Messenger of Allah ﷺ was leading the people in prayer at Mina, and I was at that time nearing puberty. I passed in front of part of the row, dismounted, sent the donkey off to graze, and then joined the row, and no one rebuked me for doing so."

42 Yaḥyā related to me from Mālik that he had heard that Sa'īd ibn Abī

Waqqāṣ used to pass in front of some of the rows while the prayer was in progress.

Mālik said, "I consider that it is permissible to do that if the *iqāma* for the prayer has been said and the imām has said the initial *takbīr* and a man cannot find any way into the mosque except by going between the rows."

43 Yaḥyā related to me from Mālik that he had heard that 'Alī ibn Abī Ṭālib said, "Something passing in front of a man praying does not break his prayer."

Yaḥyā related to me from Mālik from Ibn Shihāb from Sālim ibn 'Abdullāh that 'Abdullāh ibn 'Umar used to say, "Something passing in front of a man praying does not break his prayer."

9.12 The *sutra* of a traveller praying

44 Yaḥyā related to me from Mālik that he had heard that 'Abdullāh ibn 'Umar would use the animal he was riding as a *sutra* when he prayed.

Yaḥyā related to me from Mālik from Hishām ibn 'Urwa that his father used to pray in the desert without a *sutra*.

9.13 Brushing away small stones in the prayer

45 Yaḥyā related to me from Mālik that Abū Ja'far al-Qārī said, "I saw 'Abdullāh ibn 'Umar quickly brush away the small stones from the place where he was going to put his forehead as he was going down into *sajda*."

46 Yaḥyā related to me from Mālik from Yaḥyā ibn Sa'īd that he had heard that Abū Dharr used to say, "Brush away the small stones with one sweep, but leaving them is better than obtaining a red camel."

9.14 Straightening the rows

47 Yaḥyā related to me from Mālik from Nāfi' that 'Umar ibn al-Khaṭṭāb used to order the rows to be straightened, and when they had come to him and told him that the rows were straight, then he would say the *takbīr*.

48 Yaḥyā related to me from Mālik from his paternal uncle, Abū Suhayl ibn Mālik, that his father said, "I was with 'Uthmān ibn 'Affān when the *iqāma* was said for the prayer and I was talking to him about being assigned a definite allowance by him. I continued talking to him while he was levelling some small stones with his sandals, and then some men that he had entrusted to straighten the rows came and told him that the rows were straight. He said, to me, 'Line up in the row,' and then he said the *takbīr*."

9.15 Placing one hand on the other in the prayer

49 Yaḥyā related to me from Mālik that 'Abd al-Karīm ibn Abī al-Mukhāriq al-Baṣrī said, "Among things the Prophet ﷺ said and did are: 'As long as you do not feel ashamed, do whatever you wish', the placing of one hand on the other in prayer (one places the right hand on the left), being quick to break the fast, and delaying the meal before dawn."

50 Yaḥyā related to me from Mālik from Abū Ḥāzim ibn Dīnār that Sahl ibn Sa'd said, "People used to be ordered to place their right hands on their left forearms in the prayer."

Abū Ḥāzim added, "I know for sure that Sahl traces that back to the Prophet ﷺ."

9.16 *Qunūt* in the *Ṣubḥ* prayer

51 Yaḥyā related to me from Mālik from Nāfi' that 'Abdullāh ibn 'Umar did not say the *qunūt* in any of the prayers.

9.17 Prohibition against a man praying when wishing to relieve himself

52 Yaḥyā related to me from Mālik from Hishām ibn 'Urwa from his father that 'Abdullāh ibn al-Arqam used to lead his companions in prayer. The time for prayer came one day and he went to relieve himself. When he returned, he said, "I heard the Messenger of Allah ﷺ say, 'If you wish to defecate, you should do so before the prayer.'"

53 Yaḥyā related to me from Mālik from Zayd ibn Aslam that 'Umar ibn al-Khaṭṭāb said, "You should not pray while you are holding your bowels."

9.18 Waiting for the prayer and walking to it

54 Yaḥyā related to me from Mālik from Abū az-Zinād from al-A'raj from Abū Hurayra that the Messenger of Allah ﷺ said, "The angels ask for blessings on each one of you as long as he is in the place where he has prayed and has not broken *wuḍū'*, saying, 'Allah, forgive him. Allah have mercy on him.'"

Mālik said, "I do not consider that his words refer to anything other than the discharges that break *wuḍū'*."

55 Yaḥyā related to me from Mālik from Abū az-Zinād from al-A'raj from Abū Hurayra that the Messenger of Allah ﷺ said, "You are in prayer as long as the prayer detains you and there is nothing that prevents you from returning to your family except the prayer."

56 Yaḥyā related to me from Mālik from Sumayy, the *mawlā* of Abū Bakr, that Abū Bakr ibn 'Abd ar-Raḥmān used to say, "Someone who goes to the mosque in the morning or the afternoon with no intention of going anywhere else, either to learn good or teach it, is like someone who does *jihād* in the way of Allah and returns with booty."

57 Yaḥyā related to me from Mālik from Nu'aym ibn 'Abdullāh al-Mujmir that he heard Abū Hurayra say, "If any one of you prays and then sits

down in the spot where he has prayed, the angels ask blessings on him saying, 'Allah, forgive him. Allah, have mercy on him.' And if he moves from the spot where he has prayed and sits elsewhere in the mosque waiting for the prayer, he remains in prayer until he prays."

58 Yaḥyā related to me from Mālik from al-'Alā' ibn 'Abd ar-Raḥmān ibn Ya'qūb from his father from Abū Hurayra that the Messenger of Allah ﷺ said, "Shall I tell you the things by which Allah erases wrong actions and by which He raises ranks: the complete and correct performance of *wuḍū'* in adverse conditions, a great number of steps towards the mosque, and waiting after one prayer for the next prayer. That is the firm handhold, that is the firm handhold, that is the firm handhold."

59 Yaḥyā related to me from Mālik that he had heard that Sa'īd ibn al-Musayyab said, "It is said that no one except a hypocrite leaves the mosque after the call to prayer, except for someone who intends to return."

60 Yaḥyā related to me from Mālik from 'Āmir ibn 'Abdullāh ibn az-Zubayr from 'Amr ibn Sulaym az-Zuraqī from Abū Qatāda al-Ansārī that the Messenger of Allah ﷺ said, "When you enter the mosque, you should pray two *rak'as* before you sit down."

61 Yaḥyā related to me from Mālik from Abū an-Naḍr, the *mawlā* of 'Umar ibn 'Ubaydullāh, that Abū Salama ibn 'Abd ar-Raḥmān asked him, "Did I not see your master sit down before praying after he had entered the mosque?"

Abū an-Naḍr said, "By that he meant 'Umar ibn 'Ubaydullāh, and he was finding fault with him for sitting down before praying after he had come into the mosque."

Yaḥyā said that Mālik said, "It is good to do that but not obligatory."

9.19 Placing the hands flat on the surface by the face in prostration

62 Yaḥyā related to me from Mālik from Nāfi' that 'Abdullāh ibn 'Umar

used to place his palms flat on the surface where he put his forehead. Nāfi' said, "I have seen him take his hands out from under his burnous on a very cold day and place them on the ground."

63 Yaḥyā related to me from Mālik from Nāfi' that 'Abdullāh ibn 'Umar used to say, "When any of you puts his forehead on the ground he should put his palms on the surface on which he puts his forehead. Then, when he rises, he should raise them, for the hands prostrate just as the face prostrates."

9.20 Turning around and clapping when necessary during the prayer

64 Yaḥyā related to me from Mālik from Abū Ḥāzim Salama ibn Dīnār from Sahl ibn Sa'īd as-Sā'idī that the Messenger of Allah ﷺ went to the tribe of Banū 'Amr ibn 'Awf to settle their disputes. The time for the prayer came and the *mu'adhdhin* came to Abū Bakr aṣ-Ṣiddīq and asked, "Could you lead the people in prayer and I will say the *iqāma*?" He said, "Yes", and Abū Bakr started to pray. The Messenger of Allah ﷺ arrived while the people were doing the prayer and went through until he was standing in the row. People clapped, but Abū Bakr did not turn round from his prayer. When the people increased their clapping, he turned and saw the Messenger of Allah ﷺ and the Messenger of Allah ﷺ indicated to him to stay in his place. Abū Bakr raised his hands and praised Allah that the Messenger of Allah ﷺ had told him to do that. Then he drew back until he was in the row, and the Messenger of Allah ﷺ stepped forward and led the prayer. When he had finished he said, "Abū Bakr, what stopped you from staying put like I told you?" Abū Bakr replied, "It is not for Ibn Abī Quḥāfa to pray in front of the Messenger of Allah ﷺ."

The Messenger of Allah ﷺ said, "Why did I see you all clapping so much? If something happens while you are in the prayer you should say '*Subḥānallāh*' (Glory be to Allah), and when you say '*Subḥānallāh*', attention will be paid to it. Clapping is for women."

65 Yaḥyā related to me from Mālik from Nāfi' that Ibn 'Umar would never turn around when praying.

66 Yaḥyā related to me from Mālik that Abū Ja'far al-Qārī said, "I was praying, and 'Abdullāh ibn 'Umar was behind me and I was not aware of it. Then I turned round and he prodded me (in disapproval)."

9.21 Joining the prayer while the imām is in *rukū'*

67 Yaḥyā related to me from Mālik from Ibn Shihāb that Abū Umāma ibn Sahl ibn Ḥunayf said, "Zayd ibn Thābit entered the mosque and found the people in *rukū'*, so he went into *rukū'* and then moved slowly forward until he reached the row."

68 Yaḥyā related to me from Mālik that he had heard that 'Abdullāh ibn Mas'ūd used to move forward while in *rukū'*.

9.22 The prayer on the Prophet ﷺ

69 Yaḥyā related to me from Mālik from 'Abdullāh ibn Abī Bakr ibn Ḥāzim from his father that 'Amr ibn Sulaym az-Zuraqī said, "Abū Humayd as-Sā'idī told me that they asked the Messenger of Allah ﷺ how they were to ask for blessings upon him and he replied that they should say, 'O Allah, bless Muḥammad and his wives and his descendants as You blessed the family of Ibrāhīm, and grant blessing to Muḥammad and his wives and his descendants as You granted blessing to the family of Ibrāhīm. You are worthy of Praise and Glorious.'"

"Allāhumma ṣalli 'alā Muḥammad wa azwājihi wa dhuriyyatihi kamā ṣallayta 'alā āli Ibrāhīm, wa bārik 'alā Muḥammad wa azwājihi wa dhuriyyatihi kamā bārakta 'alā āli Ibrāhīm, innaka ḥamīdun majīd."

70 Yaḥyā related to me from Mālik from Nu'aym ibn 'Abdullāh al-Mujmir that Muḥammad ibn 'Abdullāh ibn Zayd told him that Abū Mas'ūd al-Anṣārī said, "The Messenger of Allah ﷺ came to us at the gathering of Sa'd ibn 'Ubāda. Bashīr ibn Sa'd said to him, 'Allah has ordered us to ask for blessings on you, Messenger of Allah. How should we do it?' The Messenger of Allah ﷺ remained silent until we wished we had not asked him. Then he told us to say, "O Allah, bless Muḥammad and the family of

Muḥammad as You blessed Ibrāhīm, and grant blessing to Muḥammad and the family of Muḥammad as You granted blessing to the family of Ibrāhīm in all the worlds. You are worthy of Praise and Glorious,' and then give the *taslīm* as you have learnt."

"Allāhumma ṣalli 'alā Muḥammad wa āli Muḥammad kama ṣallayta 'alā Ibrāhīm, wa bārik 'alā Muḥammad wa āli Muḥammad kama bārakta 'alā āli Ibrāhīm fī'l 'alamīn. Innaka ḥamīdun majīd."

71 Yaḥyā related to me from Mālik that 'Abdullāh ibn Dīnār said, "I saw 'Abdullāh ibn 'Umar stop by the grave of the Prophet ﷺ and ask for blessings on the Prophet ﷺ and on Abū Bakr and 'Umar."

9.23 How to perform the prayer in general

72 Yaḥyā related to me from Mālik from Nāfi' from Ibn 'Umar that the Messenger of Allah ﷺ used to pray two *rak'as* before *Ẓuhr* and two *rak'as* after it, two *rak'as* after *Maghrib*, in his house, and two *rak'as* after *'Ishā'*. He did not pray after *jumu'a* until he had left the mosque, and then he prayed two *rak'as*.

73 Yaḥyā related to me from Mālik from Abū az-Zinād from al-A'raj from Abū Hurayra that the Messenger of Allah ﷺ said, "Do you see the direction I am facing here? By Allah, neither your humbleness nor your *rukū'* is hidden from me. I can see you behind my back."

74 Yaḥyā related to me from Mālik from Nāfi' from 'Abdullāh ibn 'Umar that when the Messenger of Allah ﷺ used to go to Qubā' (to pray), he would walk as well as ride.

75 Yaḥyā related to me from Mālik from Yaḥyā ibn Sa'īd from an-Nu'mān ibn Murra that the Messenger of Allah ﷺ said, "What do you think about drunkenness, stealing and adultery?" That was before anything had been revealed about them. They answered, "Allah and His Messenger know best." He said, "They are detestable acts and there is a punishment for them. But the worst thief is the one who steals his prayer." They asked, "How can someone steal his prayer,

Messenger of Allah?" He replied, "By not performing *rukū'* or *sajda* properly."

76 Yaḥyā related to me from Mālik from Hisham ibn 'Urwa from his father that the Messenger of Allah ﷺ said, "Perform some of the prayers in your houses."

77 Yaḥyā related to me from Mālik from Nāfi' that 'Abdullāh ibn 'Umar used to say, "When a sick man is unable to prostrate he should motion with his head and not raise anything to his forehead."

78 Yaḥyā related to me from Mālik from Rabi'a ibn Abī 'Abd ar-Raḥmān that if 'Abdullāh ibn 'Umar arrived at the mosque when the people had already prayed, he would begin with the obligatory prayer and not pray anything before it.

79 Yaḥyā related to me from Mālik from Nāfi' that 'Abdullāh ibn 'Umar passed by a man who was praying and said, "Peace be upon you," and the man replied to him. 'Abdullāh ibn 'Umar returned to him and said, "When someone says, 'Peace be upon you' to you while you are praying do not reply, but give a signal with your hand."

80 Yaḥyā related to me from Mālik from Nāfi' that 'Abdullāh ibn 'Umar used to say, "Someone who only remembers that he has forgotten a prayer when he is praying the next prayer behind an imām should pray the prayer he has forgotten after the imām has said the *taslīm* and then pray the other one again."

81 Yaḥyā related to me from Mālik from Yaḥyā ibn Sa'īd from Muḥammad ibn Yaḥyā ibn Ḥabbān that his paternal uncle, Wāsi' ibn Ḥabbān, said, "I was praying, and 'Abdullāh ibn 'Umar was resting his back against the wall of the *qibla*. When I had finished the prayer I turned towards him on my left-hand side. 'Abdullāh ibn 'Umar said, 'What stopped you from turning away to your right?' I replied, 'I saw you and turned towards you.' 'Abdullāh said, 'You are correct. People say that you should turn away to your right, but when you pray you can turn whichever way you wish. If you like, to your right, and if you like, to your left."

82 Yaḥyā related to me from Mālik from Hishām ibn 'Urwa from his father that one of the Muhājirūn, in whom he saw no harm, asked 'Abdullāh ibn 'Amr ibn al-'Āṣ, "Can I pray in a place where camels are watered?" 'Abdullāh replied, "No, but you can pray in a sheep-pen."

83 Yaḥyā related to me from Mālik from Ibn Shihāb that Sa'īd ibn al-Musayyab asked, "In which prayer do you sit in every *rak'a*?" Sa'īd replied, "It is *Maghrib* when you have missed one *rak'a*, and that is the *sunna* in all the prayers."

9.24 Prayer in general

84 Yaḥyā related to me from Mālik from 'Āmir ibn 'Abdullāh ibn az-Zubayr from 'Amr ibn Sulaym az-Zuraqi from Abū Qatāda al-Anṣārī that the Messenger of Allah ﷺ used to pray carrying Umāma, the daughter of Zaynab, the daughter of the Messenger of Allah ﷺ, and Abū al-'Āṣ ibn Rabi'a ibn 'Abd Shams. When he prostrated, he put her down. When he stood up, he lifted her up again.

85 Yaḥyā related to me from Abū az-Zinād from al-A'raj from Abū Hurayra that the Messenger of Allah ﷺ said, "There are angels which take turns in being with you in the night which are followed by other angels in the day, and they meet together at the *'Aṣr* and *Fajr* prayers. Then the ones who were with you during the night ascend and Allah asks them – although He knows better than they do – 'How were My slaves when you left them?' They reply, 'When we left them they were praying and when we came to them, they were praying.'"

86 Yaḥyā related to me from Mālik from Hishām ibn 'Urwa from his father from 'Ā'isha, the wife of the Prophet ﷺ, that the Messenger of Allah ﷺ said, "Tell Abū Bakr to lead the people in prayer." 'Ā'isha said, "Messenger of Allah, when Abū Bakr stands in your place his voice does not reach the ears of the people because of his weeping, so tell 'Umar to lead the people in prayer." He said, "Tell Abū Bakr to lead the people in prayer."

'Ā'isha continued, "I told Ḥafṣa to tell him that when Abū Bakr stood in his place his voice did not reach the ears of the people because of his weeping, and that he should tell 'Umar to lead the people in prayer. Ḥafṣa did so, and the Messenger of Allah ﷺ said, 'You are the companions of Yūsuf!' (referring to the women who cut their hands when they saw the beauty of Yūsuf thereby displaying their hidden opposition). Tell Abū Bakr to lead the people in prayer!'"

'Ā'isha added that Ḥafṣa said to her, "I have never had anything good from you!"

87 Yaḥyā related to me from Mālik from Ibn Shihāb from 'Aṭā' ibn Yazīd al-Laythī that 'Ubaydullāh ibn 'Adī ibn al-Khiyār said, "Once when the Messenger of Allah ﷺ sitting with some people, a man came to him and spoke secretly to him. Nobody knew what he had said until the Messenger of Allah ﷺ disclosed that he had asked for permission to kill one of the hypocrites. When he disclosed this, the Messenger of Allah ﷺ said, 'Does he not testify that there is no god but Allah and that Muḥammad is the Messenger of Allah?' The man replied, 'Of course, but it is not a true testimony.' He asked, 'Does he not do the prayer?' and the man replied, 'Of course, but it is not a true prayer.' The Prophet ﷺ said, 'Those are the ones whom Allah has forbidden me (to kill).'"

88 Yaḥyā related to me from Mālik from Zayd ibn Aslam from 'Aṭā' ibn Yasār that the Messenger of Allah ﷺ said, "O Allah! Do not make my grave an idol that is worshipped. The anger of Allah on those who took the graves of their Prophets as places of worship was terrible."

89 Yaḥyā related to me from Mālik from ibn Shihāb from Maḥmūd ibn Rabī' al-Anṣārī that 'Itbān ibn Mālik, who was a blind man, used to lead his people in prayer, and he said to the Messenger of Allah ﷺ, "Sometimes it is dark and rainy and there is a lot of water around outside, and I am a man who has lost his sight. Messenger of Allah, pray in a certain place in my house so that I can take it as a place to pray." The Messenger of Allah ﷺ came to him and asked, "Where would you like me to pray?" He indicated a place to him and the Messenger of Allah ﷺ prayed there.

90 Yaḥyā related to me from Mālik from Ibn Shihāb from 'Abbād ibn Tamīm from his paternal uncle that he saw the Messenger of Allah ﷺ lying down in the mosque with one foot on top of the other.

Yaḥyā related to me from Mālik from Ibn Shihāb from Sa'īd ibn al-Musayyab that 'Umar ibn al-Khaṭṭāb and 'Uthmān ibn 'Affān ﷺ used to do the same.

91 Yaḥyā related to me from Mālik from Yaḥyā ibn Sa'īd that 'Abdullāh ibn Mas'ūd said to a certain man, "You are living in a time when men of understanding (*fuqahā'*) are many and Qur'ān reciters are few, when the *ḥudūd* defined in the Qur'ān are guarded and its letters are neglected, when few people ask and many give, when they make the prayer long and the *khuṭba* short, and put their good actions before their desires. A time will come upon people when their *fuqahā'* are few but their Qur'ān reciters are many, when the letters of the Qur'ān are guarded carefully but its *ḥudūd* are neglected, when many ask but few give, when they make the *khuṭba* long but the prayer short, and put their desires before their actions."

92 Yaḥyā related to me from Mālik that Yaḥyā ibn Sa'īd said, "I have heard that the first of the actions of a slave to be considered on the Day of Rising will be the prayer. If it is accepted from him the rest of his actions will be considered, and if it is not accepted from him, then none of his actions will be considered."

93 Yaḥyā related to me from Mālik from Hishām ibn 'Urwa from his father that 'Ā'isha, the wife of the Prophet ﷺ said, "The actions which the Messenger of Allah ﷺ loved most were those which were done most constantly."

94 Yaḥyā related to me from Mālik that he had heard from 'Āmir ibn Sa'd ibn Abī Waqqāṣ that his father said, "There were two brothers, one of whom died forty nights before the other. The merit of the first was being mentioned in the presence of the Messenger of Allah ﷺ and he said, 'Was the other one not a Muslim?' They answered, 'Of course, Messenger of Allah, and there was no harm in him.' The Messenger of Allah ﷺ said, 'What will make you realise what his prayer has brought him? The prayer is like a deep river of sweet water running by your door into which you plunge five times a day. How much of your dirtiness do you think that will leave? You do not realise what his prayer has brought him?'"

95 Yaḥyā related to me from Mālik that he had heard that if anyone passed by 'Aṭā' ibn Yasār in the mosque with something to trade, he would call him and ask, "What is the matter with you? What do you want?" If the man said that he wished to trade with him, he would say, "You need the market of this world. This is the market of the Next World."

96 Yaḥyā related to me from Mālik that he had heard that 'Umar ibn al-Khaṭṭāb set aside an area near the mosque called al-Buṭayḥā' and said, "Whoever wishes to talk nonsense or recite poetry or raise his voice should go to this area."

9.25 Stimulation of the desire for prayer in general

97 Yaḥyā related to me from Mālik from his paternal uncle Abū Suhayl ibn Mālik that his father heard Ṭalḥa ibn 'Ubaydullāh say, "Once one of the people of Najd came to the Messenger of Allah ﷺ. He had dishevelled hair and although his voice could be heard we could not make out what he was saying until he drew nearer and then we found he was asking about Islam. The Messenger of Allah ﷺ said to him, 'There are five prayers during the day and the night.' He asked, 'Do I have to do anything else besides that?' He answered, 'No, except what you do of your own accord.' The Messenger of Allah ﷺ then added, 'And fasting the month of Ramaḍān.' He said, 'Is there anything else I have to do?' He said, 'No, except what you do of your own accord.' The Messenger of Allah ﷺ then mentioned *zakāt*. The man said, 'Is there anything else that I have to do?' He replied, 'No, except what you do of your own accord.'

He continued, "The man went away saying, 'By Allah, I will not do any more than this nor will I do any less.' The Messenger of Allah ﷺ said, 'That man will be successful if he is telling the truth.'"

98 Yaḥyā related to me from Mālik from Abū az-Zinād from al-A'raj from Abū Hurayra that the Messenger of Allah ﷺ said, "Shayṭān ties three knots at the back of your head when you sleep, and he seals the place of each knot with 'You have a long night ahead, so sleep.' If you wake up and remember Allah, a knot is untied. When you do *wuḍū'*, a

knot is untied. When you pray, a knot is untied, and morning finds you lively and in good spirits, and if not, morning finds you in bad spirits and lazy."

10. The Two *'Īds*

10.1 *Ghusl* for the two *'Īd*s, the call to prayer for them, and the *iqāma*

1 Yaḥyā related to me from Mālik that he had heard more than one of their men of knowledge say, "There has been no *adhān* or *iqāma* for the *'Īd al-Fiṭr* or the *'Īd al-Aḍḥā* since the time of the Messenger of Allah ﷺ."

Mālik said, "That is the *sunna* and there is no disagreement about it among us."

2 Yaḥyā related to me from Mālik from Nāfi' that 'Abdullāh ibn 'Umar used to have a *ghusl* on the day of *'Īd al-Fiṭr* before going to the place of prayer.

10.2 The order to pray before the *khuṭba* on the two *'Īd*s

3 Yaḥyā related to me from Mālik from Ibn Shihāb that the Messenger of Allah ﷺ used to pray before the *khuṭba* on the days of *'Īd al-Fiṭr* and the day of *'Īd al-Aḍḥā.*

4 Yaḥyā related to me from Mālik that he had heard that Abū Bakr and 'Umar used to do that.

5 Yaḥyā related to me from Mālik from Ibn Shihāb that Abū 'Ubayd, the *mawlā* of Ibn Azhar said, "I was present at one of the *'Īd*s with 'Umar ibn al-Khaṭṭāb. He prayed, and then after he had prayed he gave a *khuṭba* to the people and said, 'The Messenger of Allah ﷺ forbade fasting on these

two days – the day you break your fast (after Ramaḍān), and the day you eat from your sacrifice (after the *Ḥajj*).'"

Abū 'Ubayd continued, "Then I was present at one of the *'Īd*s with 'Uthmān ibn 'Affān. He came and prayed, and when he had finished he gave a *khuṭba* and said, 'Two *'īds* have been joined together for you on this day of yours. If any of the people of al-'Āliyya (the hills outlying Madīna) want to wait for the *jumu'a* they can do so, and if any of them want to return, I have given them permission.'"

Abū 'Ubayd continued, "Then I was present at an *'Īd* with 'Alī ibn Abī Ṭālib (at the time when 'Uthmān was under siege). He came and prayed, and then after he had prayed he gave a *khuṭba*."

10.3 The order to eat before going out on the morning of the *'Īd*

6 Yaḥyā related to me from Mālik from Hishām ibn 'Urwa from his father that he used to eat on the day of the *'Īd al-Fiṭr* before going out.

7 Yaḥyā related to me from Mālik from Ibn Shihāb that Sa'īd al-Musayyab told him that people used to be told to eat on the day of *Fiṭr* before setting out.

Mālik said that he did not consider that people had to do that on the *'Īd al-Aḍḥā*.

10.4 The *takbīrs* and the recitation in the prayer of the two *'Īd*s

8 Yaḥyā related to me from Mālik from Ḍamra ibn Sa'īd al-Māzinī from 'Ubaydullāh ibn 'Abdullāh ibn 'Utba ibn Mas'ūd that 'Umar ibn al-Khaṭṭāb asked Abū Wāqid al-Laythī what the Messenger of Allah ﷺ used to recite in the prayers of *Aḍḥā* and *Fiṭr*. He said, "He used to recite *Sūra Qāf* (50) and *Sūrat al-Inshiqāq* (84)."

9 Yaḥyā to me from Mālik that Nāfi', the *mawlā* of 'Abdullāh ibn 'Umar said, "I attended *Aḍḥā* and *Fiṭr* with Abū Hurayra and he said 'Allah is

greater' seven times in the first *rak'a*, before the recitation, and five times in the second, before the recitation."

Mālik said, "That is the position with us."

Regarding a man who finds that people have finished the *'Īd* prayer, Mālik said that he did not think that he had to pray either in the place where the prayer was performed nor in his house. If he does perform the prayer in the place or in his house, he did not see any harm in doing that. He says the *takbīr* seven times in the first *rak'a* before the recitation and five times in the second before the recitation.

10.5 Refraining from praying before and after the two *'Īd* prayers

10 Yaḥyā related to me from Mālik from Nāfi' that 'Abdullāh ibn 'Umar did not pray either before the prayer or after it on the day of *Fiṭr*.

11 Yaḥyā related to me from Mālik that he had heard that Sa'īd ibn al-Musayyab used to go to the place of prayer after praying *Ṣubḥ*, and before the sun rose.

10.6 Permission to pray before and after the two *'Īd* prayers

12 Yaḥyā related to me from Mālik from 'Abd ar-Raḥmān ibn al-Qāsim that his father used to pray four *rak'as* before he went to the place of prayer.

13 Yaḥyā related to me from Hishām ibn 'Urwa that his father used to pray in the mosque on the day of *Fiṭr* before the prayer.

10.7 The coming of the imām on the Day of the *'Īd* and waiting for the *khuṭba*

14 Yaḥyā related to me that Mālik said, "The *sunna* concerning the time of prayer on the *'Īds* of *Fiṭr* and *Aḍḥā* – and there is no disagreement

amongst us about it – is that the imām leaves his house and as soon as he has reached the place of prayer the prayer falls due."

Yaḥyā said that Mālik was asked whether a man who prayed with the imām could leave before the *khuṭba*, and he said, "He should not leave until the imām leaves."

11. The Fear Prayer

11.1 The Fear Prayer

1 Yaḥyā related to me from Mālik from Yazīd ibn Rūmān from Ṣāliḥ ibn Khawwāt from someone who had prayed (the fear prayer) with the Messenger of Allah ﷺ on the day of Dhāt ar-Riqā' that one group had formed a row with him and one group had formed a row opposite the enemy. He then prayed one *rak'a* with the group he was with, and then remained standing while they finished by themselves. They then left and formed a row opposite the enemy, and then the other group came and he prayed the remaining *rak'a* of his prayer with them, and then remained sitting while they finished by themselves. Then he said the *taslīm* with them.

2 Yaḥyā related to me from Mālik from Yaḥyā ibn Sa'īd from al-Qāsim ibn Muḥammad from Ṣāliḥ ibn Khawwāt that Sahl ibn Abī Ḥathma related to him that the form of the fear prayer was that the imām stood with a group of his companions, while another group faced the enemy. The imām prayed one *rak'a* with them, including the prostration, and then stood. He remained standing while they completed the remaining *rak'a* by themselves. They then said the *taslīm*, left, and formed up opposite the enemy while the imām remained standing. Then the others who had not prayed came forward and said the *takbīr* behind the imām and he prayed one *rak'a* with them, including the prostration. He then said the *taslīm*, while they stood up and prayed the remaining *rak'a* by themselves. Then they said the *taslīm*.

3 Yaḥyā related to me from Mālik from Nāfi' that 'Abdullāh ibn 'Umar,

when asked about the fear prayer said, "The imām and a group of people go forward and the imām prays a *rak'a* with them, while another group, who have not yet prayed, position themselves between him and the enemy. When those who are with him have prayed a *rak'a* they draw back to where those who have not prayed are, and do not say the *taslīm*. Then those who have not prayed come forward and pray a *rak'a* with him. Then the imām leaves, as he has now prayed two *rak'as*. Everyone else in both groups stands and prays a *rak'a* by himself after the imām has left. In this way each of the two groups will have prayed two *rak'as*. If the fear is greater than that, then the men pray standing on their feet or mounted, either facing the *qibla* or otherwise."

Mālik said that Nāfi' said, "I do not believe that 'Abdullāh ibn 'Umar related it from anyone other than the Messenger of Allah ﷺ."

4 Yaḥyā related to me from Mālik from Yaḥyā ibn Sa'īd that Sa'īd ibn al-Musayyab said, "The Messenger of Allah ﷺ did not pray *Ẓuhr* and *'Aṣr* on the Day of the Trench until after the sun had set."

Mālik said, "The *ḥadīth* of al-Qāsim ibn Muḥammad from Ṣāliḥ ibn Khawwāt is the one I like most out of what I have heard about the Fear Prayer."

12. The Eclipse Prayer

12.1 How to pray the Eclipse Prayer

1 Yaḥyā related to me from Mālik from Hishām ibn 'Urwa from his father that 'A'isha, the wife of the Prophet ﷺ said, "There was an eclipse of the sun in the time of the Messenger of Allah ﷺ and the Messenger of Allah ﷺ led the people in prayer. He stood, and did so for a long time. Then he went into *rukū'*, and made the *rukū'* long. Then he stood again, and did so for a long time, though not as long as the first time. Then he went into *rukū'*, and made the *rukū'* long, though not as long as the first time. Then he rose, and went down into *sajda*. He then did the same in the second *rak'a*, and by the time he had finished the sun had appeared. He then gave a *khuṭba* to the people, in which he praised Allah and then said, 'The sun and the moon are two of Allah's signs. They are not eclipsed for anyone's death nor for anyone's life. When you see an eclipse, call on Allah and say, "Allah is greater" and give *ṣadaqa*.' Then he said, 'O community of Muḥammad! By Allah, there is no one more jealous than Allah of a male or female slave of his who commits adultery. O community of Muḥammad! By Allah, if you knew what I knew, you would laugh little and weep much.'"

2 Yaḥyā related to me from Mālik from Zayd ibn Aslam from 'Aṭā' ibn Yasār that 'Abdullāh ibn 'Abbās said, "There was an eclipse of the sun and the Messenger of Allah ﷺ prayed, and the people prayed with him. He stood for a long time, nearly as long as (it takes to recite) *Sūrat al-Baqara* (2), and then went into *rukū'* for a long time. Then he rose and stood for a long time, though less than the first time. Then he went into *rukū'* for a long time, though less than the first time. Then he went down

into *sajda*. Then he stood for a long time, though less than the first time. Then he went into *rukūʿ* for a long time, though less than the first time. Then he rose and stood for a long time, though less than the first time. Then he went into *rukūʿ* for a long time, though less than the first time. Then he went down into *sajda*, and by the time he had finished the sun had appeared. Then he said, 'The sun and the moon are two of Allah's signs. They do not eclipse for anyone's death nor for anyone's life. When you see an eclipse, remember Allah.' They said, 'Messenger of Allah, we saw you reach out for something while you were standing here and then we saw you withdraw.' He said, 'I saw the Garden and I reached out for a bunch of grapes from it, and if I had taken it you would have been able to eat from it for as long as this world lasted. Then I saw the Fire – and I have never seen anything more hideous than what I saw today – and I saw that most of its people were women.' They said, 'Why, Messenger of Allah?' He said, 'Because of their ungratefulness (*kufr*).' Someone asked, 'Are they ungrateful to Allah?' He said, 'And they are ungrateful to their husbands and they are ungrateful for good behaviour (towards them). Even if you were to behave well towards one of them for a whole lifetime and then she were to see you do something (that she did not like) she would say that she had never seen anything good from you.'"

3 Yaḥyā related to me from Mālik from Yaḥyā ibn Saʿīd from 'Amra bint 'Abd ar-Raḥmān from 'Ā'isha, the wife of the Prophet ﷺ that a Jewish woman came to beg from her and said, "May Allah give you refuge from the punishment of the grave." So 'Ā'isha asked the Messenger of Allah ﷺ, "Are people punished in their graves?" and the Messenger of Allah ﷺ took refuge in Allah from that. Then one morning the Messenger of Allah ﷺ out on a journey and there was an eclipse of the sun, and he returned in the late morning and passed through his apartments. Then he stood and prayed, and the people stood behind him. He stood for a long time, and then went into *rukūʿ* for a long time. Then he rose and stood for a long time, though less than the first time, and then went into *rukūʿ* for a long time, though less than the first time. Then he rose, and went down into *sajda*. Then he stood for a long time, though less than the time before, and then went into *rukūʿ* for a long time, though less than the time before. Then he rose and stood for a long time, though less than the time before, and then went into *rukūʿ* for a long time though less than the time before. Then he rose, and went down into *sajda*. When he

had finished he said what Allah willed him to say, and then he told them to seek protection for themselves from the punishment of the grave."

12.2 About the Eclipse Prayer

4 Yaḥyā related to me from Mālik from Hishām ibn 'Urwa from Fāṭima bint al-Mundhir that Asmā' bint Abī Bakr aṣ-Ṣiddīq said, "I went to 'Ā'isha, the wife of the Prophet ﷺ during an eclipse of the sun, and everybody was standing in prayer, and she too was standing praying. I asked, 'What is everybody doing?' She pointed towards the sky with her hand and said, 'Glory be to Allah.' I said, 'A sign?' She indicated 'Yes' with her head."

She continued, "I stood until I had almost fainted, and I began to pour water over my head. The Messenger of Allah ﷺ praised Allah and spoke well of Him, and then said, 'There is nothing which I had previously not seen beforehand that I have not now seen while standing – even the Garden and the Fire. It has been revealed to me that you will be tried in your graves with a trial, like, or near to, the trial of the Dajjāl (I do not know which one Asmā' said). Everyone of you will have someone who comes to him and asks him, 'What do you know about this man?' A believer (*mu'min*), or one who has certainty (*mūqin*) (I do not know which one Asmā' said), will say, 'He is Muḥammad, the Messenger of Allah ﷺ, who came to us with clear proofs and guidance, and we answered and believed and followed.' He will then be told, 'Sleep in a good state. We know now that you were a believer.' A hypocrite, however, or one who has doubts (I do not know which one Asmā' said), will say, 'I do not know, I heard everybody saying something and I said it.'"

13. Praying for Rain

13.1 How to pray for rain

1 Yaḥyā related to me from Mālik from 'Abdullāh ibn Abī Bakr ibn 'Amr ibn Ḥazm that he had heard 'Abbād ibn Tamīm say that he had heard 'Abdullāh ibn Zayd al-Māzinī say, "The Messenger of Allah ﷺ came out to the place of prayer and asked for rain, and when he faced the *qibla* he turned his cloak inside out."

Mālik was asked how many *rak'as* there were in the prayer of asking for rain and he said, "Two *rak'as*, and the imām does the prayer before he gives the *khuṭba*. He prays two *rak'as*, and then he gives a *khuṭba* and makes supplication, facing the *qibla* and turning his cloak inside out. He recites out loud in both *rak'as*, and when he turns his cloak inside out he puts what is on his right on his left and what is on his left on his right, and all the people turn their cloaks inside out when the imām does so and face the *qibla*, sitting."

13.2 What is reported about praying for rain

2 Yaḥyā related to me from Mālik from Yaḥyā ibn Sa'īd from 'Amr ibn Shu'ayb that the Messenger of Allah ﷺ said, when he asked for rain, "O Allah, give water to Your slaves and Your animals, and spread Your mercy, and give life to Your dead land."

3 Yaḥyā related to me from Mālik from Sharīk ibn 'Abdullāh ibn Abī Namir that Anas ibn Mālik said, "A man came to the Messenger of Allah

ﷺ and said, 'Messenger of Allah, our animals are dying and our camels are too weak to travel, so make supplication to Allah.' The Messenger of Allah ﷺ, made supplication, and then it rained on us from one *jumu'a* to the next."

Anas continued, "Then a man came to the Messenger of Allah ﷺ and said, 'Messenger of Allah, our houses have fallen down, the paths are blocked, and our flocks are dying.' The Messenger of Allah ﷺ said, 'O Allah, (only) the mountain and hill-tops, the valley bottoms, and the places where trees grow.'"

Anas added, "It cleared away from Madīna like a garment being removed."

Mālik said, about a man who missed the prayer of asking for rain but caught the *khuṭba* and wished to pray in the mosque, or in his house when he returned, "He is free to do so, or not, as he wishes."

13.3 About asking the stars for rain

4 Yaḥyā related to me from Mālik from Ṣāliḥ ibn Kaysān from 'Ubaydullāh ibn 'Abdullāh ibn 'Utba ibn Mas'ūd that Zayd ibn Khālid al-Juhanī said, "The Messenger of Allah ﷺ led us in the *Ṣubḥ* prayer at Ḥudaybiya after it had rained in the night. When he had finished he went up to the people and asked, 'Do you know what your Lord has said?' They replied, 'Allah and His Messenger know best.' He said, 'Some of My slaves have begun the morning believing in Me, and others have begun it rejecting Me. As for those who say, "We had rain through the overflowing favour of Allah and His mercy," they believe in Me and reject the stars. But as for those who say, "We had rain through such and such a star, they reject Me and believe in the stars."'"

5 Yaḥyā related to me from Mālik that he had heard that the Messenger of Allah ﷺ used to say, "When a cloud appears from the direction of the sea and then goes towards Syria, it will be an abundant source of rain."

6 Yaḥyā related to me from Mālik that he had heard that Abū Hurayra used to say, when morning came after it had rained on the people, "We

have been rained upon by the rain of Allah's opening," and would then recite the *āyat*, "*Whatever mercy Allah opens up to people no one can withhold, and whatever He withholds no one can afterwards release.*" (35:2)

14. The *Qibla*

14.1 The prohibition against relieving oneself facing the *qibla*

1 Yaḥyā related to me from Mālik from Isḥāq ibn 'Abdullāh ibn Abī Ṭalḥa that Rāfi' ibn Isḥāq, a *mawlā* of the family of ash-Shifā' who was known as the *mawlā* of Abū Ṭalḥa, heard Abū Ayyūb al-Anṣārī, one of the Companions of the Messenger of Allah ﷺ say while he was in Egypt, "By Allah! I do not know how to deal with these lavatories since the Messenger of Allah ﷺ said, 'When you go to defecate or urinate, do not expose your genitals towards the *qibla*, and do not put your back to it.'"

2 Yaḥyā related to me from Mālik from Nāfi' from one of the Anṣār that the Messenger of Allah ﷺ forbade defecating or urinating while facing the *qibla*.

14.2 Permission to face the *qibla* when urinating or defecating

3 Yaḥyā related to me from Mālik from Yaḥyā ibn Sa'īd from Muḥammad ibn Yaḥyā ibn Ḥabbān from his paternal uncle, Wāsi' ibn Ḥabbān, that 'Abdullah ibn 'Umar said, "People used to say, 'When you sit to relieve yourself, do not face the *qibla* or Jerusalem.'"

'Abdullāh continued, "I went up on top of a house of ours and saw the Messenger of Allah ﷺ (squatting) on two unfired bricks facing Jerusalem, relieving himself."

Ibn 'Umar added, "Perhaps you are one of those who pray folded on their haunches."[2]

Wāsi' replied, "I do not know, by Allah!"

Mālik said that he meant those who pray without lifting themselves from the ground properly, who cleave close to the ground in prostration.

14.3 The prohibition of spitting towards the *Qibla*

4 Yaḥyā related to me from Mālik from Nāfi' from 'Abdullāh ibn 'Umar that the Messenger of Allah ﷺ saw spittle on the wall of the *qibla* and scraped it off. Then he went up to the people and said, "Do not spit in front of you when you are praying, because Allah, the Blessed and Exalted, is in front of you when you pray."

5 Yaḥyā related to me from Mālik from Hishām ibn 'Urwa from his father from 'Ā'isha, the wife of the Prophet ﷺ, that the Prophet ﷺ saw spittle, or mucus or phlegm, on the wall of the *qibla* and scraped it off.

14.4 About the *qibla*

6 Yaḥyā related to me from Mālik from 'Abdullāh ibn Dīnar that 'Abdullāh ibn 'Umar said, "On one occasion when the people were praying *Ṣubḥ* at Qubā a man came to them and said, 'A piece of Qur'ān was sent down to the Messenger of Allah ﷺ last night, and he was ordered to face the Ka'ba, so face it.' They had been facing Syria, so they turned round and faced the Ka'ba."

7 Yaḥyā related to me from Mālik from Yaḥyā ibn Sa'īd that Sa'īd ibn al-Musayyab said, "The Messenger of Allah ﷺ prayed towards Jerusalem for sixteen months after arriving in Madīna. Then the *qibla* was changed two months before the battle of Badr."

2 By saying this, he was making reference to his ignorance of the proper way of doing things.

8 Yaḥyā related to me from Mālik from Nāfi' that 'Umar ibn al-Khaṭṭāb said, "Any direction that is between East and West can be taken as a *qibla* if the person praying is face-on to the House."

14.5 The Mosque of the Prophet

9 Yaḥyā related to me from Mālik from Zayd ibn Rabāḥ and 'Ubaydullāh ibn Abī 'Abdullāh Salmān al-Agharr from Abū Hurayra that the Messenger of Allah ﷺ said, "A prayer in this mosque of mine is better than a thousand prayers in any other mosque, except the *Masjid al-Ḥarām* (in Makka)."

10 Yaḥyā related to me from Mālik from Khubayb ibn 'Abd ar-Raḥmān from Ḥafṣ ibn 'Āṣim from Abū Hurayra or from Abū Sa'īd al-Khudrī that the Messenger of Allah ﷺ said, "What is between my house and my minbar is one of the meadows of the Garden, and my minbar is on my watering-place (*al-Ḥawḍ*)."

11 Yaḥyā related to me from Mālik from 'Abdullāh ibn Abī Bakr from 'Abbād ibn Tamīm from 'Abdullāh ibn Zayd al-Māzinī that the Messenger of Allah ﷺ said, "What is between my house and my minbar is one of the meadows of the Garden"

14.6 Women going out to the mosque

12 Yaḥyā related to me from Mālik that he had heard that 'Abdullāh ibn 'Umar said, "The Messenger of Allah ﷺ said, 'Do not forbid the female slaves of Allah from (going to) the mosques of Allah.'"

13 Yaḥyā related to me from Mālik that he had heard from Busr ibn Sa'īd that the Messenger of Allah ﷺ said, "None of you women should use perfume when you attend at the *'Ishā'* prayer."

14 Yaḥyā related to me from Mālik from Yaḥyā ibn Sa'īd that 'Atika bint Zayd ibn 'Amr ibn Nufayl, the wife of 'Umar al-Khaṭṭāb, used to ask 'Umar ibn al-Khaṭṭāb for permission to go to the mosque. He would keep

silent, so she would say, "By Allah, I will go out, unless you forbid me," and he did not forbid her.

15 Yaḥyā related to me from Mālik from Yaḥyā ibn Sa'īd from 'Amra bint 'Abd ar-Raḥmān that 'A'isha, the wife of the Prophet ﷺ, said, "If the Messenger of Allah ﷺ had seen what women do now, he would have forbidden them to go into the mosques, just as the women of the tribe of Israel were forbidden."

Yaḥyā ibn Sa'īd said that he asked 'Amra, "Were the women of the tribe of Israel forbidden to go into mosques?" and she replied, "Yes."

15. The Qur'ān

15.1 The command to be in *wuḍū'* (when touching the Qur'ān)

1 Yaḥyā related to me from Mālik from 'Abdullāh ibn Abī Bakr ibn Ḥazm that it said in a letter sent by the Messenger of Allah ﷺ to 'Amr ibn Ḥazm that no one should touch the Qur'ān unless he was pure.

Mālik said, "No one should carry the Qur'ān by its strap, or on a cushion, unless he is pure. If it were permissible to do so, it would also have been permissible to carry it in its cover. This is not because of there being something on the hands of the one who carries it by which the Qur'ān will be soiled, but because it is disapproved of for someone to carry the Qur'ān without being pure out of respect for the Qur'ān, and in order to honour it."

Mālik said, "The best thing that I have heard about this is the *āyat* '*No one may touch it except the purified.*' (56:79) It ranks with the *āyats* in *Sūrat 'Abasa* where Allah, the Blessed and Exalted, says, '*Truly it is a reminder, and whoever wills pays heed to it. Inscribed on honoured pages, exalted, purified, by the hands of scribes, noble, virtuous.*' (80:11-16)"

15.2 Allowance to recite the Qur'ān while not in *wuḍū'*

2 Yaḥyā related to me from Mālik from Ayyūb ibn Abī Tamīma as-Sakhtayānī from Muḥammad ibn Sīrīn that 'Umar ibn al-Khaṭṭāb was with some people who were reciting Qur'ān. He went to relieve himself and then came back and recited Qur'ān. One of the men said to him,

"*Amīr al-Mūminīn*, are you reciting the Qur'ān without being in *wuḍū'*?" Umar replied, "Who gave you a verdict on this? Was it Musaylima?"

15.3 The division of the Qur'ān into sections (*ḥizb*s)

3 Yaḥyā related to me from Mālik from Dāwūd ibn al-Ḥuṣayn from al-A'raj from 'Abd ar-Raḥmān ibn 'Abd al-Qāri' that 'Umar ibn al-Khaṭṭāb said, "If someone misses reading his *ḥizb* at night and reads it between the time when the sun has passed the meridian and the *Ẓuhr* prayer, he has not missed it, or it is as if he has caught it."

4 Yaḥyā related to me from Mālik that Yaḥyā ibn Sa'īd said, "Once while Muḥammad ibn Yaḥyā ibn Ḥabbān and I were sitting down, Muḥammad called a man over to him and said to him, 'Tell me what you have heard from your father.' The man replied that his father had told him that he went to Zayd ibn Thābit and asked him, 'What do you think of reciting the entire Qur'ān in seven days?' Zayd said, 'That is good, but I prefer to recite it over two weeks or ten days. Ask me why that is.' He said, 'I ask you why then.' Zayd said, 'So that I can reflect on it and pause in it.'"

15.4 About the Qur'ān

5 Yaḥyā related to me from Mālik from Ibn Shihāb from 'Urwa ibn az-Zubayr that 'Abd ar-Raḥmān ibn 'Abd al-Qāri' said that he had heard 'Umar ibn al-Khaṭṭāb say, "I heard Hishām ibn Ḥakīm ibn Ḥizām reciting *Sūrat al-Furqān* (25) differently from me, and it was the Messenger of Allah ﷺ who had recited it to me. I was about to rush up to him but I granted him a respite until he had finished his prayer. Then I grabbed him by his cloak and took him to the Messenger of Allah ﷺ and said, 'Messenger of Allah, I heard this man reciting *Sūrat al-Furqān* differently from the way you recited it to me.' The Messenger of Allah ﷺ said, 'Let him go.' Then he said, 'Recite, Hishām,' and Hishām recited as I had heard him recite. The Messenger of Allah ﷺ said, 'It was sent down like that.' Then he said to me, 'Recite,' and I recited the *sūra*, and he said, 'It was sent down like that. This Qur'ān was sent down in seven (different) modes, so recite from it whatever is easy for you.'"

6 Yaḥyā related to me from Mālik from Nāfi' from 'Abdullāh ibn 'Umar that the Messenger of Allah ﷺ said, "A man who knows the Qur'ān well is like a man who has a hobbled camel. If he takes care of it, he keeps it, and if he lets it go, it gets away."

7 Yaḥyā related to me from Mālik from Hishām ibn 'Urwa from his father from 'Ā'isha, the wife of the Prophet ﷺ that al-Ḥārith ibn Hishām asked the Messenger of Allah ﷺ, "How does revelation come to you?" and the Messenger of Allah ﷺ replied, "Sometimes it comes to me like the ringing of a bell, and that is the hardest for me, and when it leaves me I remember what has been said. And sometimes the angel appears to me in the likeness of a man and talks to me and I remember what he says."

'Ā'isha added, "I saw it coming down on him on an intensely cold day, and when it had left him his forehead was dripping with sweat."

8 Yaḥyā related to me from Mālik from Hishām ibn 'Urwa that his father said that *Sūrat 'Abasa* (80) was revealed about 'Abdullāh ibn Umm Maktūm. He came to the Prophet ﷺ and began to say, "O Muḥammad, show me a place near you (where I can sit)," whilst one of the leading men of the idol-worshippers was in audience with the Prophet ﷺ. The Prophet ﷺ began to turn away from him and give his attention to the other man, and he said to him, "Father of so-and-so, do you see any harm in what I am saying?" And he said, "No, by the blood (of our sacrifices) I see no harm in what you are saying." And then *'Abasa – "He frowned and turned away when the blind man came"* – was sent down.

9 Yaḥyā related to me from Mālik from Zayd ibn Aslam from his father that the Messenger of Allah ﷺ was on one of his journeys and one night 'Umar ibn al-Khaṭṭāb, who was travelling with him, asked him about something, but he did not answer him. He asked him again, but he did not answer him. Then he asked him again, and again he did not answer him. 'Umar said, "May your mother be bereaved of you, 'Umar. Three times you have importuned the Messenger of Allah ﷺ with a question and he has not answered you at all."

'Umar continued, "I got my camel moving until, when I was out ahead of the people, I feared that a piece of Qur'ān was being sent down about me. It was not long before I heard a crier calling for me, and I said that I feared that a piece of Qur'ān had been sent down about me."

He continued, "I came to the Messenger of Allah ﷺ and said, 'Peace be upon you' to him, and he said, 'A *sūra* has been sent down to me this night that is more beloved to me than anything on which the sun rises.'" Then he recited *Sūrat al-Fatḥ* (48).

10 Yaḥyā related to me from Mālik from Yaḥyā ibn Sa'īd from Muḥammad ibn Ibrāhīm ibn al-Ḥārith at-Taymī from Abū Salama ibn 'Abd ar-Raḥmān that Abū Sa'īd said that he had heard the Messenger of Allah ﷺ say, "A group of people will appear among you whose prayer, fasting and deeds will make you think little of your own prayer, fasting and deeds. They will recite the Qur'ān but it will not get past their throats, and they will pass through the *dīn* like an arrow passes through game. You look at the arrowhead and you see nothing, and you look at the shaft and you see nothing, and you look at the flights and you see nothing, and you are in doubt about the notch."

11 Yaḥyā related to me from Mālik that he had heard that it took 'Abdullāh ibn 'Umar eight years to learn *Sūrat al-Baqara*.

15.5 The prostration of the Qur'ān

12 Yaḥyā related to me from Mālik from 'Abdullāh ibn Yazīd, the *mawlā* of al-Aswad ibn Sufyān, from Abū Salama ibn 'Abd ar-Raḥmān that Abū Hurayra recited *Sūrat al-Inshiqāq* (*sūra* 84) to them and prostrated in it. When he had finished he told them that the Messenger of Allah ﷺ had prostrated in it.

13 Yaḥyā related to me from Mālik from Nāfi', the *mawlā* of Ibn 'Umar, that a man from Egypt told him that 'Umar ibn al-Khaṭṭāb recited *Sūrat al-Ḥajj* (*sūra* 22) and prostrated twice in it, and then said, "This *sūra* has been given special preference by having two prostrations in it."

14 Yaḥyā related to me from Mālik that 'Abdullāh ibn Dīnār said, "I saw 'Abdullāh ibn 'Umar prostrate twice in *Sūrat al-Ḥajj* (22)."

15 Yaḥyā related to me from Mālik from Ibn Shihāb from al-A'raj that 'Umar ibn al-Khaṭṭāb recited *Sūrat an-Najm* (53) and prostrated in it, and then got up and recited another *sūra.*

16 Yaḥyā related to me from Mālik from Hishām ibn 'Urwa from his father that 'Umar ibn al-Khaṭṭāb once recited a piece of Qur'ān requiring a prostration while he was on the minbar on the day of *jumu'a*, and he came down and prostrated, and everyone prostrated with him. Then he recited it again the next *jumu'a* and everybody prepared to prostrate but he said, "At your ease. Allah has not prescribed it for us unless we wish." He did not prostrate and he stopped them from prostrating.

Mālik said, "The imām does not come down and prostrate when he recites a piece of Qur'ān requiring a prostration while he is on the minbar."

Mālik said, "The position with us is that there are eleven prescribed prostrations in the Qur'ān, none of which are in the *Mufaṣṣal.*"

Mālik said, "No one should recite any of the pieces of Qur'ān that require a prostration after the prayers of *Ṣubḥ* and *'Aṣr.* This is because the Messenger of Allah ﷺ forbade prayer after *Ṣubḥ* until after the sun had risen, and after *'Aṣr* until the sun had set, and prostration is part of the prayer. So no one should recite any piece of Qur'ān requiring a prostration during these two periods of time."

Mālik was asked whether a menstruating woman could prostrate if she heard someone reciting a passage of Qur'ān requiring a prostration, and he said, "Neither a man nor a woman should prostrate unless they are ritually pure."

Mālik was asked whether a man in the company of a woman who was reciting a passage of Qur'ān requiring a prostration should prostrate with her, and he said, "He does not have to prostrate with her. The prostration is only obligatory for people who are with a man who is leading them. He recites the piece and they prostrate with him. Someone who hears a piece of Qur'ān that requires a prostration being recited by a man who is not leading him in prayer does not have to do the prostration."

15.6 About reciting *Sūrat al-Ikhlāṣ* and *Sūrat al-Mulk*

17 Yaḥyā related to me from Mālik from 'Abd ar-Rahmān ibn 'Abdullāh ibn Ṣa'ṣa'a from his father that Abū Sa'īd al-Khudrī heard a man reciting *Sūrat al-Ikhlāṣ* (112), repeating it over and over again. In the morning he went to the Messenger of Allah ﷺ and mentioned it to him as if he thought little of it. The Messenger of Allah ﷺ said, "By the One in whose hand my self is, it is equal to one third of the Qur'ān."

18 Yaḥyā related to me from Mālik from 'Ubaydullāh ibn 'Abd ar-Raḥmān that 'Ubayd ibn Ḥunayn, the *mawlā* of the family of Zayd ibn al-Khaṭṭāb, mentioned that he had heard Abū Hurayra say, "I was going along with the Messenger of Allah ﷺ when he heard a man reciting *Sūrat al-Ikhlāṣ* (112). The Messenger of Allah ﷺ said, 'It is obligatory,' and I asked him, 'What is, Messenger of Allah?' and he said, 'The Garden.' I wanted to tell the man the good news but I was afraid that I would miss the midday meal with the Messenger of Allah ﷺ and I preferred to eat with the Messenger of Allah ﷺ. When I went to the man afterwards I found him gone."

19 Yaḥyā related to me from Mālik from Ibn Shihāb that Ḥumayd ibn 'Abd ar-Raḥmān ibn 'Awf had told him that *Sūrat al-Ikhlāṣ* (112) was equal to a third of the Qur'ān and that *Sūrat al-Mulk* (67) pleaded for its owner.

15.7 *Dhikr* (Remembrance) of Allah, the Blessed and Exalted

20 Yaḥyā related to me from Mālik from Sumayy, the *mawlā* of Abū Bakr, from Abū Ṣāliḥ as-Sammān from Abū Hurayra that the Messenger of Allah ﷺ said, "Whoever says 'There is no god but Allah, alone, without any partner. The Kingdom and praise belong to Him and He has power over everything' (*Lā ilaha illā'llāh, waḥdahu lā sharīka lah, lahu'l-mulku wa lahu'l-ḥamd, wa huwa 'alā kulli shay'in qadīr*) one hundred times a day, it is the same for him as freeing ten slaves. One hundred good actions are written for him and one hundred wrong actions are erased for him, and it is a protection from Shayṭān for that day until the night. No one does anything more excellent than what he does except someone who does more than that."

21 Yaḥyā related to me from Mālik from Sumayy, the *mawlā* of Abū Bakr, from Abū Ṣāliḥ as-Sammān from Abū Hurayra that the Messenger of Allah ﷺ said, "Whoever says, 'Glory be to Allah and with His praise' (*Subḥāna'llāh wa bi-ḥamdihi*) one hundred times in a day will have his wrong actions taken away from him, even if they are as abundant as the foam on the sea."

22 Yaḥyā related to me from Mālik from Abū 'Ubayd, the *mawlā* of Sulaymān ibn 'Abd al-Mālik, from 'Aṭā' ibn Yazīd al-Laythī that Abū Hurayra said, "Whoever says 'Glory be to Allah' (*subḥāna'llāh*) thirty-three times and 'Allah is Greater' (*Allāhu akbar*) thirty-three times and 'Praise be to Allah' (*al-ḥamdu lillāh*) thirty-three times, and seals the hundred with 'There is no god but Allah, alone without any partner. The Kingdom and praise belong to Him and He has power over everything' (*Lā ilaha illā'llāh, waḥdahu la sharīka lah, lahu'l-mulku wa lahu'l-ḥamd, wa huwa 'alā kulli shay'in qadīr*) after every prayer will have his wrong actions forgiven him even if they are abundant as the foam on the sea."

23 Yaḥyā related to me from Mālik that 'Umāra ibn Ṣayyād heard Sa'īd ibn al-Musayyab say about 'abiding good deeds' that they were a slave's saying 'Allah is greater' (*Allāhu akbar*) and 'Glory be to Allah' (*subḥāna'llāh*) and 'Praise be to Allah' (*al-ḥamdu lillāh*) and 'There is no god but Allah and there is no power and no strength except by Allah.' (*Lā ilaha illā'llāh wa lā ḥawla wa lā quwwata illā bi'llāh.*)

24 Yaḥyā related to me from Mālik that Ziyād ibn Abī Ziyād mentioned that Abū ad-Dardā' said, "Shall I not tell you the best of your deeds, and those that give you the highest rank, and those that are the purest with your King, and are better for you than giving gold and silver, and better for you than meeting your enemy and striking their necks?" They answered, "Of course." He said, "Remembrance (*dhikr*) of Allah *ta'ālā*."

Ziyād ibn Abī Ziyād said that Mu'ādh ibn Jabal said, "There is no action which is more likely to save one from Allah's punishment than remembrance (*dhikr*) of Allah."

25 Mālik related to me from Nu'aym ibn 'Abdullāh ibn al-Mujmir from 'Alī ibn Yaḥyā az-Zuraqī from his father that Rifā'a ibn Rāfi' said, "One day

we were praying behind the Messenger of Allah ﷺ when the Messenger of Allah ﷺ raised his head from *rukū'* and said, 'Allah hears the one who praises Him' (*Sami' Allāhu liman ḥamidah*). A man behind him said, 'Our Lord, praise belongs to You – blessed, pure and abundant praise' (*Rabbanā wa laka'l-ḥamd kathīran ṭayyiban mubārakan fīhi*). When the Messenger of Allah ﷺ had finished, he said, 'Who was it who spoke just now?' The man said, 'I did, Messenger of Allah,' and the Messenger of Allah ﷺ said, 'I saw more than thirty angels rushing to see which one of them would record it first.'"

15.8 *Du'ā'* (supplication)

26 Yaḥyā related to me from Mālik from Abū az-Zinād from al-A'raj from Abū Hurayra that the Messenger of Allah ﷺ said, "Every Prophet is given a supplication (*du'ā'*), and I wish to preserve my supplication as intercession for my community in the next world."

27 Yaḥyā related to me from Mālik from Yaḥyā ibn Sa'īd that he had heard that the Messenger of Allah ﷺ used to say the following supplication: "O Allah, it is You who makes the dawn break and makes the night a time for rest and appoints the sun and moon to reckon by. Relieve me of debt and enrich me from poverty and let me enjoy my hearing, my sight and my strength in Your way."

Allāhumma fāliqa'l-iṣbāḥ, wa jā'ila'l-layli sakana, wa'sh-shamsi wa'l-qamari ḥusbāna. Iqḍa 'anniy ad-dayna, wa'ghnaniy mina'l-faqr. Amti'ni bi sam'ī wa basarī wa quwwatī fi sabīlik.

28 Yaḥyā related to me from Mālik from Abū az-Zinād from al-A'raj from Abū Hurayra that the Messenger of Allah ﷺ said, "When you are making supplication do not say, 'O Allah, forgive me if You wish. O Allah, forgive me if You wish.' You should be firm in your asking, for there is no compelling Him."

29 Yaḥyā related to me from Mālik from Ibn Shihāb from Abū 'Ubayd, the *mawlā* of Ibn Azhar, from Abū Hurayra that the Messenger of Allah

ﷺ said, "You will be answered as long as you are not impatient and say, 'I have made a supplication and it has not been answered for me.'"

30 Yaḥyā related to me from Mālik from Ibn Shihāb from Abū 'Abdullāh al-Agharr and from Abū Salama from Abū Hurayra that the Messenger of Allah ﷺ said, "Our Lord, the Blessed and Exalted, descends every night to the heaven of this world when the last third of the night is still to come and says, 'Who will call on Me so that I may answer him? Who will ask Me so that I may give him? Who will ask forgiveness of Me so that I may forgive him?'"

31 Yaḥyā related to me from Mālik from Yaḥyā ibn Sa'īd from Muḥammad ibn Ibrāhīm ibn al-Ḥārith at-Taymī that 'Ā'isha, *Umm al-Mu'minīn*, said, "I was sleeping by the side of the Messenger of Allah ﷺ I missed him in the night, so I felt for him with my hand and I put my hand on his feet and he was in *sajda* saying, 'I seek refuge in Your pleasure from Your wrath, and in Your pardon from Your punishment, and in You from You. I cannot enumerate Your praises as You praise Yourself.'"

A'ūdhu bi riḍāka min sakhaṭika, wa bi mu'āfātika min 'uqūbatika wa bika minka, la uḥṣiy thanā'an 'alayka, anta kamā athnayta 'alā nafsika.

32 Yaḥyā related to me from Mālik from Ziyād ibn Abī Ziyād from Ṭalḥa ibn 'Ubaydullāh ibn Kurayz that the Messenger of Allah ﷺ said, "The best supplication is supplication on the day of 'Arafat, and the best thing that I or the Prophets before me have said is 'There is no god but Allah, alone, without any partner' (*Lā ilaha illā'llāh, waḥdahu lā sharīka lah.*)"

33 Yaḥyā related to me from Mālik from Abū az-Zubayr al-Makkī from Ṭāwus al-Yamānī from 'Abdullāh ibn 'Abbās that the Messenger of Allah ﷺ used to teach this supplication in the same way that he would teach them a *sūra* of the Qur'ān, "O Allah, I seek refuge in You from the torment of Hellfire, and I seek refuge in You from the trial of the Dajjāl, and I seek refuge in You from the trial of life and death."

Allāhumma inniy a'ūdhu bika min 'adhābi jahannama, wa a'ūdhu bika min 'adhābi'l-qabri, wa a'ūdhu bika min fitnati'l-maḥyā wa mamāti.

34 Yaḥyā related to me from Mālik from Abū az-Zubayr al-Makkī from Tāwus al-Yamāni from 'Abdullāh ibn 'Abbās that the Messenger of Allah ﷺ used to say when he rose for prayer in the middle of the night, "O Allah, praise belongs to You. You are the light of the heavens and the earth and praise belongs to You. You are the Sustainer of the heavens and the earth and praise belongs to You. You are the Lord of the heavens and the earth and whoever is in them. You are the Truth and Your words are true. Your promise is true and the meeting with You is true. The Garden is true, the Fire is true and the Hour is true. O Allah, I submit to You and I accept You and I trust in You and I turn to You and I argue by You and I look to You for judgement. Forgive me what I have sent before me and what I have left behind, what I have kept secret and what I have proclaimed, You are my god – there is no god but You."

Allāhumma laka'l-ḥamdu anta nuru's-samawāti wa'l-ardi, wa laka'l-ḥamdu anta qayāmu's-samawāti wa'l-arḍi, wa laka'l-ḥamdu anta rabbu's-samawāti wa'l-arḍi, wa man fīhinna. Anta'l-ḥaqqu, wa qawluka'l-ḥaqqu, wa wa'duka'l-ḥaqqu, wa liqā'uka ḥaqqun, wa'l-jannatu ḥaqqun, wa'n-nāru ḥaqqun, wa's-sā'atu ḥaqqun. Allāhumma laka aslamtu, wa bika amantu, wa 'alayka tawakkaltu, wa ilayka anabtu, wa bika khāṣamtu, wa ilayka ḥakamtu, fa'ghfirliy ma qadamtu wa akhartu wa asrartu wa a'lantu. Anta ilahiy, lā ilaha illā ant.

35 Yaḥyā related to me from Mālik that 'Abdullāh ibn 'Abdullāh ibn Jābir ibn 'Atīk said that 'Abdullāh ibn 'Umar had come to them in Banū Mu'āwiya, one of the villages of the Anṣār, and said, "Do you know where the Messenger of Allah ﷺ prayed in this mosque of yours?" I told him, "Yes," and I pointed out a place near where he was. He asked, "Do you know the three things for which he made supplication here?" I answered, "Yes." He said, "Tell me them then." I said, "He asked that Allah would not make an enemy from among the non-believers triumph over the believers and that He would not destroy the believers by bad harvests, and he was given both these things. And he asked that He would not make the believers fight among themselves, and that was refused." Ibn 'Umar said, "You have told the truth," and he added, " Turmoil will not cease until the Day of Rising."

36 Yaḥyā related to me from Mālik that Zayd ibn Aslam used to say, "No

one makes a supplication without one of three things happening: either it is answered, or it is stored up for him, or wrong actions are expiated by it."

15.9 Making supplication (*du'ā'*)

37 Yaḥyā related to me from Mālik that 'Abdullāh ibn Dīnār said, "'Abdullāh ibn 'Umar saw me when I was making supplication and I was pointing with two fingers, one from each hand, and he forbade me to do that."

38 Yaḥyā related to me from Mālik from Yaḥyā ibn Sa'īd that Sa'īd ibn al-Musayyab used to say, "A man is raised in degrees by the supplication of his son after his death." He spoke with his hands turned upwards, and then lifted them up.

39 Yaḥyā related to me from Mālik from Hishām ibn 'Urwa that his father said, "The following *āyat* was revealed about supplication: '*Do not be too loud in your prayer or too quiet in it, but try and find a way between the two.*'" (17:110)

Yaḥyā said that Mālik was asked about making supplication in obligatory prayers and he said, "There is no harm in making supplication in them."

40 Yaḥyā related to me from Mālik that he had heard that the Messenger of Allah ﷺ used to make supplication saying, "O Allah, I ask You for good actions and for leaving what is disapproved of and for love of the poor. And if You wish to try people, then bring me to You without being tried.'"

Allāhumma innī asa'luka fi'la'l-khayrāti, wa tarka'l-munkarāti, wa ḥubba'l-masākīn, wa idhā aradta fi'n-nāsi fitnatan fa'qbiḍnī ilayka ghayra maftūn.

41 Yaḥyā related to me from Mālik that he had heard that the Messenger of Allah ﷺ said, "No one calls to guidance without having the same reward as those who follow him, without diminishing their rewards at all. And no one calls to error without having the same burdens as they do, without diminishing their burdens at all."

42 Yaḥyā related to me from Mālik that he had heard that 'Abdullāh ibn 'Umar said, "O Allah, make me one of the leaders of the people of *taqwā*!"

Allāhumma ja'lnī min a'immati'l-muttaqīn.

43 Yaḥyā related to me from Mālik that he had heard that Abū ad-Dardā' used to rise in the middle of the night and say, "Eyes have slept, and stars have set, and You are the Living and Self-Subsistent."

Nāmati'l-'uyūnu wa ghāriti'n-nujūm wa anta'l-Ḥayyu-l-Qayyūm.

"Stars have set," i.e. disappeared under the horizon.

15.10 Prayer forbidden after *Ṣubḥ* and after *'Aṣr*

44 Yaḥyā related to me from Mālik from Zayd ibn Aslam from 'Aṭā' ibn Yasār from 'Abdullāh aṣ-Ṣunābiḥī that the Messenger of Allah ﷺ said, "The sun rises and with it is the horn of Shayṭān and when the sun gets higher the horn leaves it. Then when the sun reaches the meridian the horn joins it and when the sun declines the horn leaves it, and when the sun has nearly set it joins it again." The Messenger of Allah ﷺ forbade prayer at these times.

45 Yaḥyā related to me from Mālik from Hishām ibn 'Urwa that his father said that the Messenger of Allah ﷺ used to say, "Delay the prayer when the edge of the sun appears until it is completely in view, and delay the prayer when the edge of the sun is disappearing until it has completely disappeared."

46 Yaḥyā related to me from Mālik that al-'Alā' ibn 'Abd ar-Rahmān said, "We visited Anas ibn Mālik after *Ẓuhr* and he stood up and prayed *'Aṣr*. When he had finished his prayer, we mentioned doing prayers early in their time, or he mentioned it, and he said that he had heard the Messenger of Allah ﷺ say, 'The prayer of the hypocrites, the prayer of the hypocrites, the prayer of the hypocrites is that one of them sits until the sun becomes yellow and is between the horns of Shayṭān, or on

the horn of Shayṭān, and then gets up and rattles off four *rak'as*, hardly remembering Allah in them at all.'"

47 Yaḥyā related to me from Mālik from Nāfi' from 'Abdullāh ibn 'Umar that the Messenger of Allah ﷺ said, "None of you should seek to pray as the sun is rising or as it is setting."

48 Yaḥyā related to me from Mālik from Muḥammad ibn Yaḥyā ibn Ḥabbān from al-A'raj from Abū Hurayra that the Messenger of Allah ﷺ forbade prayer after *'Aṣr* until the sun had set, and prayer after *Ṣubḥ* until the sun had risen.

49 Yaḥyā related to me from Mālik from 'Abdullāh ibn Dīnār from 'Abdullāh ibn 'Umar that 'Umar ibn al-Khaṭṭāb used to say, "Do not seek to do your prayer at either sunrise or sunset, for the horns of Shaytān rise with the rising of the sun and set with its setting."

'Umar used to beat people for that kind of prayer.

50 Yaḥyā related to me from Mālik from Ibn Shihāb from as-Sā'ib ibn Yazīd that he saw 'Umar ibn al-Khaṭṭāb beating al-Munkadir for praying after *'Aṣr*.

16. Burials

16.1 Washing the dead

1 Yaḥyā related to me from Mālik from Ja'far ibn Muḥammad from his father that the Messenger of Allah ﷺ was washed while wearing a long shirt.

2 Yaḥyā related to me from Mālik from Ayyūb ibn Abī Tamīma as-Sakhtiyāni from Muḥammad ibn Sīrīn that Umm 'Aṭiyya al-Anṣāriyya said, "The Messenger of Allah ﷺ came to us when his daughter died and said, 'Wash her three times, or five, or more than that if you think it necessary, with water and lotus leaves, and at the end put on some camphor, or a little camphor, and when you have finished let me know.' When we finished we told him, and he gave us his waist-wrapper and said, 'Shroud her with this.'"

3 Yaḥyā related to me from Mālik from 'Abdullāh ibn Abī Bakr that Asmā' bint 'Umays washed Abū Bakr aṣ-Ṣiddīq when he died. Then she went out and asked some of the Muhājirūn who were there, "I am fasting and this is an extremely cold day. Do I have to do *ghusl*?" They answered, "No."

4 Yaḥyā related to me from Mālik that he had heard people of knowledge say, "When a woman dies and there are no women with her to wash her and no man who has the right by blood ties to take charge of that for her and no husband to take charge of it for her, she should be purified by means of *tayammum*, that is, by wiping her face and hands with earth."

Mālik said, "When a man dies and there are only women with him, they also should purify him with earth."

Mālik said, "There is no particular way with us for washing the dead nor any recognised way to do it. They are just washed and purified."

16.2 Shrouding the dead

5 Yaḥyā related to me from Mālik from Hishām ibn 'Urwa from his father from 'Ā'isha, the wife of the Prophet ﷺ, that the Messenger of Allah ﷺ was shrouded in three *Saḥūlī* white cotton garments, none of which was a long shirt or turban.

6 Yaḥyā related to me from Mālik that Yaḥyā ibn Sa'īd said that he had heard that when Abū Bakr aṣ-Ṣiddīq was ill he asked 'Ā'isha, "How many shrouds did the Messenger of Allah ﷺ have?" and she replied, "Three *Saḥūlī* white cotton garments." Abū Bakr said, "Take this garment (a garment he was wearing on which red clay or saffron had fallen) and wash it. Then shroud me in it with two other garments." 'Ā'isha said, "Why is that?" and Abū Bakr replied, "The living have greater need of the new than the dead. This is only for the body fluids that come out as the body decays."

7 Yaḥyā related to me from Mālik from Ibn Shihāb from Ḥumayd ibn 'Abd ar-Raḥmān ibn 'Awf that 'Abdullāh ibn 'Amr ibn al-'Āṣ said, "A dead man is clothed in a shirt and a waist-wrapper and then wrapped in a third, and if he only has one garment he is shrouded in that."

16.3 Preceeding the bier

8 Yaḥyā related to me from Mālik from Ibn Shihāb that the Messenger of Allah ﷺ, and Abū Bakr and 'Umar as well as the *khalīfas* up until this time and 'Abdullāh ibn 'Umar would walk in front of the bier.

9 Yaḥyā related to me from Muḥammad ibn al-Munkadir that Rabi'a

ibn ʿAbdullāh ibn al-Hadīr told him that he had seen ʿUmar ibn al-Khaṭṭāb leading people in front of the bier at the funeral of Zaynab bint Jaḥsh.

10 Yaḥyā related to me from Mālik that Hishām ibn ʿUrwa said, "I only ever saw my father in front of a funeral procession." He added, "Then he would come to al-Baqīʿ and sit down until the procession passed him."

11 Yaḥyā related to me from Mālik that Ibn Shihāb said, "Walking behind the bier is contrary to the *sunna*."

16.4 The prohibition against following the bier with a burning torch

12 Yaḥyā related to me from Mālik from Hishām ibn ʿUrwa that Asmāʾ bint Abī Bakr said to her family, "Perfume my clothes with incense when I die and then embalm me. Do not put any of the embalming substance on my shroud, and do not follow me with a burning torch."

13 Yaḥyā related to me from Mālik from Saʿīd ibn Abī Saʿīd al-Maqburī that Abū Hurayra forbade anyone to follow him with a burning torch after his death. Yaḥyā said, "I heard Mālik disapprove of that."

16.5 The *takbīrs* in funerals

14 Yaḥyā related to me from Mālik from Ibn Shihāb from Saʿīd ibn al-Musayyab from Abū Hurayra that the Messenger of Allah ﷺ announced the death of the Negus to the people on the day that he died, and went out with them to the place of prayer, and then formed them into rows and said "Allah is greater" four times.

15 Yaḥyā related to me from Mālik from Ibn Shihāb that Abū Umāma ibn Sahl ibn Ḥunayf told him that once a poor woman fell ill and the Messenger of Allah ﷺ was told of her illness, and the Messenger of Allah ﷺ used to visit poor people frequently and ask after them. The Messenger of Allah ﷺ said, "Let me know if she dies." Her bier was brought out at night-time and they did not want to wake up the Messenger of Allah ﷺ.

In the morning the Messenger of Allah ﷺ was told what had happened to her and he said, "Did I tell not you to let me know if she died?" They replied, "Messenger of Allah, we did not want to wake you up and make you come out in the night." Then the Messenger of Allah ﷺ went out and formed everyone into rows by her grave and said "Allah is greater" four times.

16 Yaḥyā related to me that Mālik asked Ibn Shihāb about a man who caught some of the *takbīrs* said over the corpse and missed the rest, and Ibn Shihāb said, "He completes what he has missed."

16.6 What to say in the prayer for the dead

17 Yaḥyā related to me from Mālik from Sa'īd ibn Abī Sa'īd al-Maqburī from his father that he had asked Abū Hurayra, "How do you pray over the dead?" and Abū Hurayra replied, "By the Life of Allah, I will tell you! I follow with the family and when the corpse is put down I say, 'Allah is greater' and praise Allah and ask for blessings on His Prophet. Then I say, 'O Allah, he is Your slave and the son of Your male slave and Your female slave. He used to testify that there is no god but You and that Muḥammad is Your slave and Your Messenger, and You know that best. O Allah! If he acted well, then increase for him his good action, and if he acted wrongly, then overlook his wrong actions. O Allah! Do not deprive us of his reward, and do not try us after him.'"

Allāhumma innahu 'abduka wa'bnu 'abdika wa'bnu amatika. Kāna yashhadu an lā ilaha illā anta wa anna Muḥammadan 'abduka wa rasūluka, wa anta 'alamu bihi. Allāhumma in kana muḥsinan zid fi iḥsānihi, wa in kāna musiyan fa tajāwaz 'an sayyiātihi. Allāhumma la taḥrimnā ajrahu wa lā taftinnā ba'dahu.

18 Yaḥyā related to me from Mālik that Yaḥyā ibn Sa'īd said that he heard Sa'īd ibn al-Musayyab say, "I once prayed behind Abū Hurayra over a child who had never done a wrong action and I heard him say, 'O Allah, give him protection from the torment of the grave.'"

"Allāhumma a'idh hu min 'adhāb al-qabr."

19 Yaḥyā related to me from Mālik from Nāfiʻ that 'Abdullāh ibn 'Umar used not to recite Qur'ān when praying over a dead person.

16.7 Permission to pray over the dead after *Ṣubḥ* until the dawn is clear and after *'Aṣr* until the sun turns yellow

20 Yaḥyā related to me from Mālik from Muḥammad ibn Abī Ḥarmala, the *mawlā* of 'Abd ar-Raḥmān ibn Abī Sufyān ibn Ḥuwaytib, that Zaynab bint Abī Salama died during the time that Ṭāriq was governor of Madīna and her bier was brought out after *Ṣubḥ* and put in al-Baqīʻ. He said that Ṭāriq used to pray *Ṣubḥ* right at the beginning of its time. He added, "I heard 'Abdullāh ibn 'Umar say to the family, 'You can either pray over your dead now or you can wait until the sun comes up.'"

21 Yaḥyā related to me from Mālik from Nāfiʻ that 'Abdullāh ibn 'Umar said, "The prayer for a dead person can be done after *'Aṣr* and *Ṣubḥ* if these have been prayed at their times."

16.8 Doing the prayer for the dead in mosques

22 Yaḥyā related to me from Mālik from Abū an-Naḍr, the *mawlā* of 'Umar ibn 'Ubaydullāh that 'Ā'isha, the wife of the Prophet ﷺ, ordered that the body of Sa'd ibn Abī Waqqāṣ be brought past her in the mosque so that she could make supplication for him. Some people disapproved of her doing that, and she said, "How hasty people are! The Messenger of Allah ﷺ only prayed over Suhayl ibn Bayḍā' in the mosque."

23 Yaḥyā related to me from Mālik from Nāfiʻ that 'Abdullāh ibn 'Umar said, "The prayer over 'Umar ibn al-Khaṭṭāb was done in the mosque."

16.9 The prayer over the dead in general

24 Yaḥyā related to me from Mālik that he had heard that 'Uthmān ibn 'Affān, 'Abdullāh ibn 'Umar and Abū Hurayra used to pray over the dead,

both men and women, in Madīna. They would put the men nearer to the imām and the women nearer to the *qibla*.

25 Yaḥyā related to me from Mālik from Nāfi' that 'Abdullāh ibn 'Umar, when he prayed over the dead, would say, "Peace be upon you" loud enough for whoever was near to him to hear.

26 Yaḥyā related to me from Mālik from Nāfi' that 'Abdullāh ibn 'Umar used to say, "No one should pray over a dead person unless he is in *wuḍū'*."

Yaḥyā said that he heard Mālik say, "I have not seen any person of knowledge disapproving of praying over either a child born of adultery or its mother."

16.10 Burying the dead

27 Yaḥyā related to me from Mālik that he had heard that the Messenger of Allah ﷺ died on Monday and was buried on Tuesday and people prayed over him individually with no one leading them. Some people said that he would be buried near the minbar, and others said that he would be buried in al-Baqī'. Abū Bakr aṣ-Ṣiddīq came and said, "I heard the Messenger of Allah ﷺ say, 'No Prophet was ever buried except in the place where he died.'" So a grave was dug for him there. When he was about to be washed they wished to take off his shirt but they heard a voice saying "Do not remove his shirt," so they did not take off his shirt and he ﷺ was washed with it on.

28 Yaḥyā related to me from Mālik from Hishām ibn 'Urwa that his father said, "There were two men in Madīna, one of whom dug graves with a niche in the side wall for the body, and the other who did not, and they said, 'Whichever one comes first can do the job,' and the one who dug graves with a niche came first and dug the grave of the Messenger of Allah ﷺ."

29 Yaḥyā related to me from Mālik that he had heard that Umm Salama, the wife of the Prophet ﷺ used to say, "I did not believe that the Messenger of Allah ﷺ had died until I heard the pickaxes fall."

30 Yaḥyā related to me from Mālik from Yaḥyā ibn Sa'īd that 'Ā'isha, the wife of the Prophet ﷺ said, "I dreamt that three moons fell into my room, and I related my vision to Abū Bakr aṣ-Ṣiddīq. Then, when the Messenger of Allah ﷺ died and was buried in my house, Abū Bakr said to me, 'This is one of your moons, and he is the best of them.'"

31 Yaḥyā related to me from Mālik from more than one reliable source that Sa'd ibn Abī Waqqāṣ and Sa'īd ibn Zayd ibn 'Amr ibn Nufayl died at al-'Aqīq and were carried to Madīna and buried there.

32 Yaḥyā related to me from Mālik from Hishām ibn 'Urwa that his father said, "I would not want to be buried in al-Baqī'. I would prefer to be buried elsewhere. The one who is buried in al-Baqī' is one of two people: either he is unjust (*ẓālim*), and I would not like to be buried with him, or he is righteous (*ṣāliḥ*), and I would not like his bones to be disturbed for me."

16.11 Stopping for funerals and sitting in graveyards

33 Yaḥyā related to me from Mālik from Yaḥyā ibn Sa'īd from Wāqid ibn 'Amr ibn Sa'd ibn Mu'ādh from Nāfi' ibn Jubayr ibn Muṭ'im from Mas'ūd ibn al-Ḥakam from 'Alī ibn Abī Ṭālib that the Messenger of Allah ﷺ used to stand up when a funeral procession passed by, and then sit down again afterwards.

34 Yaḥyā related to me from Mālik that he had heard that 'Alī ibn Abī Tālib used to rest his head on graves and lie on them.

Mālik said, "We think that it is only forbidden to sit on graves to relieve oneself."

35 Yaḥyā related to me from Mālik from Abū Bakr ibn 'Uthmān ibn Sahl ibn Ḥunayf that he had heard Abū Umāma ibn Sahl ibn Ḥunayf say, "We used to attend funeral processions, and the last of the people would not sit until they had been given permission."

16.12 The prohibition of weeping over the dead

36 Yaḥyā related to me from Mālik from ʿAbdullāh ibn ʿAbdullāh ibn Jābir ibn ʿAtīk that ʿAtīk ibn al-Ḥārith, the grandfather of ʿAbdullāh ibn ʿAbdullāh ibn Jābir on his mother's side, told him that Jābir ibn ʿAtīk had told him that the Messenger of Allah ﷺ came to visit ʿAbdullāh ibn Thābit and found him in his death-throes. He called to him but he did not reply. The Messenger of Allah ﷺ said, "We belong to Allah, and to Him we are returning," and added, "You are being taken from us, Abū ar-Rabīʿ." The women cried out and wept and Jābir began to silence them. The Messenger of Allah ﷺ said, "Leave them, and it is necessary, none of the women should cry." They said, "Messenger of Allah, what do you mean by 'necessary'?" and he replied, "When he dies." The dying man's daughter said, "By Allah, I hope that you will be a martyr, for you have completed your preparations for battle," and the Messenger of Allah ﷺ said, "Allah has made his reward fall according to his intention. What do you consider martyrdom to be?" They said, "Death in the way of Allah." The Messenger of Allah ﷺ said, "There are seven kinds of martyr other than those killed in the way of Allah. Someone who is killed by the plague is a martyr, someone who drowns is a martyr, someone who dies of pleurisy is a martyr, someone who dies of a disease of the belly is a martyr, someone who dies by fire is a martyr, someone who dies under a falling building is a martyr and a woman who dies in childbirth is a martyr."

37 Yaḥyā related to me from Mālik from ʿAbdullāh ibn Abī Bakr from his father that ʿAmra bint ʿAbd ar-Raḥmān told him that she had heard ʿĀʾisha, the *Umm al-Muʾminīn*, say (when it was mentioned to her that ʿAbdullāh ibn ʿUmar used to say, "The dead are tormented by the weeping of the living"), "May Allah forgive Abū ʿAbd ar-Raḥmān. Of course he has not lied, but he has forgotten or made a mistake. The Messenger of Allah ﷺ passed by a Jewish woman whose family were crying over her and he said, 'You are crying over her, and she is being tormented in her grave.'"

16.13 Fortitude in the face of misfortune

38 Yaḥyā related to me from Mālik from Ibn Shihāb from Saʿīd ibn al-Musayyab from Abū Hurayra that the Messenger of Allah ﷺ said, "No

Muslim who has three children die will be touched by the Fire except to fulfil Allah's oath."

39 Yaḥyā related to me from Mālik from Muḥammad ibn Abī Bakr ibn 'Amr ibn Ḥazm from his father from Ibn an-Naḍr as-Salamī that the Messenger of Allah ﷺ said, "If three of a Muslim's children die, and he remains content with that, they will be a protection for him from the Fire." A woman who was with the Messenger of Allah ﷺ said, "Or two, Messenger of Allah?" and he said, "Or two."

40 Yaḥyā related to me from Mālik that he had heard from Abū al-Ḥubāb Sa'īd ibn Yasār from Abū Hurayra that the Messenger of Allah ﷺ said, "The believer continues to be struck by misfortune in his children and close friends until he meets Allah with no wrong actions."

16.14 Fortitude in the face of misfortune generally

41 Yaḥyā related to me from Mālik from 'Abd ar-Raḥmān ibn al-Qāsim ibn Muḥammad ibn Abī Bakr that the Messenger of Allah ﷺ said, "Let the misfortune that befalls me be a comfort to the Muslims in their misfortunes."

42 Yaḥyā related to me from Mālik from Rabi'a ibn Abī 'Abd ar-Raḥmān from Umm Salama, the wife of the Prophet ﷺ, that the Messenger of Allah ﷺ said, "If a misfortune befalls someone and he says, as Allah has ordered, 'We belong to Allah and to Him we are returning. O Allah, reward me in my misfortune and give me better than it afterwards,' Allah will do that for him." (*Innā lillāhi wa innā ilayhi rāji'ūn. Allāhumma ijurnī fī muṣībatī, wa 'aqibnī khayran minhā.*) Umm Salama said, "When Abū Salama died I said that, and then I said, 'Who is better than Abū Salama?'" And then Allah left her the Messenger of Allah ﷺ and he married her.

43 Yaḥyā related to me from Mālik from Yaḥyā ibn Sa'īd that al-Qāsim ibn Muḥammad said, "One of my wives died and Muḥammad ibn Ka'b al-Quraẓī came to console me about her. He told me of a certain man from the tribe of Israel who was a diligent, worshipping, knowledgeable and understanding man who had a wife that he admired and loved, and she

died. He grieved over her intensely and lamented to such an extent that he withdrew into a room and locked himself in, hidden from everyone, and no one visited him. A woman heard about him and went to him, saying, 'I need for him to give me a legal opinion. Nothing will satisfy me except what he says about it.' Everyone went away but she stayed at his door and said, 'I must speak to him.' Someone said to him, 'There is a woman who wishes to ask your opinion about something.' She said, 'I will only speak to him.' When everyone had gone away and she still had not left his door, he said, 'Let her in.' So she went in and saw him and said, 'I have come to ask your opinion about something.' 'What is it?' he asked. She said, 'I borrowed a piece of jewellery from a neighbour of mine, and I have worn it and used it for a long time. Then they sent to me for it. Should I let them have it back?' He said, 'Yes, by Allah.' She said, 'I have had it for a long time.' He said, 'It is more correct for you to return it to them since they have lent it to you for such a long time.' She said, 'Yes. May Allah have mercy on you. Do you then grieve over what Allah has lent you and then taken from you, when He has a greater right to it than you?' Then he saw the situation he was in, and Allah helped him by her words."

16.15 Exhumation

44 Yaḥyā related to me from Mālik that Abū ar-Rijāl Muḥammad ibn 'Abd ar-Raḥmān heard his mother 'Amra bint 'Abd ar-Raḥmān say, "The Messenger of Allah ﷺ cursed both men and women who dug up," meaning those who dug up graves.

45 Yaḥyā related to me from Mālik that he had heard that 'Ā'isha, the wife of the Prophet ﷺ used to say, "Breaking the bone of a Muslim when he is dead is like breaking it when he is alive." She meant if done in wrong action.

16.16 Burial in general

46 Yaḥyā related to me from Mālik from Hishām ibn 'Urwa from 'Abbād ibn 'Abdullāh ibn az-Zubayr that 'Ā'isha, the wife of the Prophet ﷺ, told him that she had heard the Messenger of Allah ﷺ say before he died,

while he was leaning on her breast and she was listening to him, "O Allah, forgive me and have mercy on me and join me with the Highest Company."

47 Yaḥyā related to me from Mālik that he heard that 'Ā'isha said, "The Messenger of Allah ﷺ, said, 'No prophet dies until he is given the choice.' She continued, "I heard him say, 'O Allah, the Highest Company,' and I knew that he was going."

48 Yaḥyā related to me from Mālik from Nāfi' that 'Abdullāh ibn 'Umar said that the Messenger of Allah ﷺ said, "When you die, your place will be shown to you in the morning and the evening. If you are one of the people of the Garden, then you will be with the people of the Garden, and if you are one of the people of the Fire, then you will be with the people of the Fire. You will be told, 'This is your place of waiting until Allah raises you on the day of rising.'"

49 Yaḥyā related to me from Mālik from Abū az-Zinād from al-A'raj from Abū Hurayra that the Messenger of Allah ﷺ said, "The earth consumes all of the son of Ādam except the coccyx. He was created from it, and from it he will be reconstituted."

50 Yaḥyā related to me from Mālik from Ibn Shihāb that 'Abd ar-Raḥmān ibn Ka'b ibn Mālik al-Anṣārī told him that his father, Ka'b ibn Mālik, used to relate that the Messenger of Allah ﷺ said, "The soul of the believer is a bird that sits in the trees of the Garden until Allah returns it to his body on the day He raises him."

51 Yaḥyā related to me from Mālik from Ibn Shihāb that 'Abd ar-Raḥmān ibn Ka'b ibn Mālik al-Anṣārī told him that his father, Ka'b ibn Mālik, used to relate that the Messenger of Allah ﷺ said, "The soul of the believer is a bird that sits in the trees of the Garden until Allah returns it to his body on the day He raises him."

52 Yaḥyā related to me from Mālik from Abū az-Zinād from al-A'raj from Abū Hurayra that the Messenger of Allah ﷺ said, "A man said to his family that he had never done a good action, and that when he died they were to burn him and then scatter half of him on the land and half

of him on the sea, for by Allah, if Allah destined it for him, He would punish him with a punishment which He had not punished anyone else with in all the worlds. When the man died, they did as he had told them. Then Allah told the land to collect everything that was in it, and told the sea to collect everything that was in it, and then He said to the man, 'Why did you do this?' and he said, 'From fear of You, Lord, and You know best.'"

Abū Hurayra added, "And He forgave him."

53 Yaḥyā related to me from Mālik from Abū az-Zinad from al-A'raj from Abū Hurayra that the Messenger of Allah ﷺ said, "Every child is born in the *fiṭra* (natural form) and it is his parents who make him a Jew or a Christian. It is just as a camel is born whole – do you perceive any defect?" They asked, "Messenger of Allah, what happens to people who die when they are (very) young?" He replied, "Allah knows best what they used to do."

54 Yaḥyā related to me from Mālik from Abū az-Zinād from al-A'raj from Abū Hurayra that the Messenger of Allah ﷺ said, "The Final Hour will not come until a man passes by the grave of another and says, 'If only I were in his place.'"

55 Yaḥyā related to me from Mālik from Muḥammad ibn 'Amr ibn Ḥalḥala ad-Dīlī from Ma'bad ibn Ka'b ibn Mālik that Abū Qatāda ibn Rib'ī used to relate that a funeral procession passed by the Messenger of Allah ﷺ and he said, "One is relieved and another others are relieved from." They said, "Who is the one relieved and the one from whom others are relieved?" He said, "A slave who is a believer is the one who is relieved from the exhaustion and suffering of this world to the mercy of Allah, and a wrong-acting slave is the one from whom people, towns, trees and animals are relieved."

56 Yaḥyā related to me from Mālik that Abū an-Naḍr, the *mawlā* of 'Umar ibn 'Ubaydullāh, said that the Messenger of Allah ﷺ said when 'Uthmān ibn Maẓ'ūn's funeral procession passed by him, "You have gone and you were not involved in any of it."

57 Mālik related to me from 'Alqama ibn Abī 'Alqama that his mother said that she had heard 'Ā'isha, the wife of the Prophet ﷺ, say, "The Messenger of Allah ﷺ rose one night and put on his clothes and then went out. I ordered my slave-girl, Barīra, to follow him, and she followed him until he got to al-Baqī'. He stood near it as long as Allah willed and then he left. Barīra arrived back before him and told me and I did not say anything to him until morning, and then I mentioned it to him and he explained, 'I was sent out to the people of al-Baqī' to pray for them.'"

58 Yaḥyā related to me from Mālik from Nāfi' that Abū Hurayra said, "Make your funerals speedy, for it is only good that you are advancing him towards, or evil that you are taking off your necks."

17. Zakāt

17.1 Things subject to *zakāt*

1 Yaḥyā related to me from Mālik from 'Amr ibn Yaḥyā al-Māzinī that his father said that he had heard Abū Sa'īd al-Khudrī say that the Messenger of Allah ﷺ said, "There is no *zakāt* due on less than five camels, there is no *zakāt* due on less than five *awāq* (two hundred dirhams of pure silver) and there is no *zakāt* due on less than five *awsāq* (three hundred *ṣā's*)."

2 Yaḥyā related to me from Mālik from Muḥammad ibn 'Abdullāh ibn 'Abd ar-Rahmān ibn Abī Ṣa'ṣa'a al-Anṣārī from al-Māzinī from his father from Abū Sa'īd al-Khudrī that the Messenger of Allah ﷺ said, "There is no *zakāt* due on less than five *awsāq* of dates, there is no *zakāt* due on less than five *awāq* of silver and there is no *zakāt* due on less than five camels."

3 Yaḥyā related to me from Mālik that he had heard that 'Umar ibn 'Abd al-'Azīz wrote to his governor in Damascus about *zakāt* saying, "*Zakāt* is paid on the produce of cultivated land, on gold and silver, and on livestock."

Mālik said, "*Zakāt* is only paid on three things: the produce of cultivated land, gold and silver, and livestock."

17.2 The *zakāt* on gold and silver coins

4 Yaḥyā related to me from Mālik that Muḥammad ibn 'Uqba, the *mawlā* of az-Zubayr, asked al-Qāsim ibn Muḥammad whether he had to pay any *zakāt* on a large sum given to him by his slave to buy his freedom. Al-Qāsim said, "Abū Bakr aṣ-Ṣiddīq did not take *zakāt* from anyone's property until it had been in his possession for a year."

Al-Qāsim ibn Muḥammad continued, "When Abū Bakr gave men their stipends he would ask them, 'Do you have any property on which *zakāt* is due?' If they said, 'Yes,' he would take the *zakāt* on that property out of their stipends. If they said, 'No,' he would hand over their stipends to them without deducting anything from them."

5 Yaḥyā related to me from Mālik from 'Urwa ibn Husayn from 'Ā'isha bint Qudāma that her father said, "When I used to come to 'Uthmān ibn 'Affān to collect my stipend he would ask me, 'Do you have any property on which *zakāt* is due?' If I answered, 'Yes,' he would deduct the *zakāt* on that property from my stipend, and if I said, 'No,' he would pay me my stipend (in full)."

6 Yaḥyā related to me from Mālik from Nāfi' that 'Abdullāh ibn 'Umar used to say, "*Zakāt* is not due on property until it has been in one's possession for a year."

7 Yaḥyā related to me from Mālik that Ibn Shihāb said, "The first person to deduct *zakāt* from stipends was Mu'āwiya ibn Abī Sufyān." (i.e. the deduction being made automatically).

Mālik said, "The agreed *sunna* with us is that *zakāt* has to be paid on twenty dinars (of gold coin) in the same way as it has to be paid on two hundred dirhams (of silver)."

Mālik said, "There is no *zakāt* to pay on (gold) that is clearly less than twenty dinars (in weight) but if it increases so that by the increase the amount reaches a full twenty dinars in weight then *zakāt* has to be paid. Similarly there is no *zakāt* to pay on (silver) that is clearly less than two hundred dirhams (in weight), but if it increases so that by the increase the amount reaches a full two hundred dirhams in weight then *zakāt* has to be paid. If it passes the full weight, then I think there is *zakāt* to pay whether it be dinars or dirhams." (i.e. the *zakāt* is assessed by the weight and not the number of the coins.)

Mālik said that a man who had one hundred and sixty dirhams by weight when the exchange rate in his town was eight dirhams to a dinar did not have to pay any *zakāt*. *Zakāt* had only to be paid on twenty dinars of gold or two hundred dirhams.

Mālik said about the case of a man who acquired five dinars from a transaction, or in some other way, which he then invested in trade, that, as soon as it increased to a zakatable amount and a year had elapsed since the original transaction, he had to pay *zakāt* on it, even if the zakatable amount was reached one day before or one day after the passing of a year. There was then no *zakāt* to pay on it from the day the *zakāt* was taken until a year had elapsed over it.

Mālik said about the similar case of a man who had in his possession ten dinars which he invested in trade, and which reached twenty dinars by the time one year had elapsed over them, that he paid *zakāt* on them right then and did not wait until a year had elapsed over them, (counting) from the day when they actually reached the zakatable amount. This was because a year had elapsed over the original dinars and there were now twenty of them in his possession. There was then no *zakāt* to pay on it until a year after the day it reached the zakatable amount.

Mālik said, "What we are agreed upon (here in Madīna) regarding income from hiring out slaves, rent from property, and the instalments received when a slave buys his freedom, is that no *zakāt* is due on any of it, whether great or small, from the day the owner takes possession of it until a year has elapsed over it from the day when the owner takes possession of it."

Mālik said, in the case of gold and silver which was shared between two co-owners, that *zakāt* was due from anyone whose share reached twenty dinars of gold or two hundred dirhams of silver, and that no *zakāt* was due from anyone whose share fell short of this zakatable amount. If all the shares reached the zakatable amount and the shares were not equally divided, *zakāt* was taken from each man according to the measure of his share. This applied only when the share of each man among them reached the zakatable amount, because the Messenger of Allah ﷺ said, "There is no *zakāt* on less than five *awāq* of silver."

Mālik commented, "This is what I prefer most out of what I have heard about the matter."

Mālik said, "When a man has gold and silver dispersed among various people he must add it all up together and then take out the *zakāt* due on the total sum."

Mālik said, "No *zakāt* is due from someone who acquires gold or silver until a year has elapsed since the day he acquired it."

17.3 *Zakāt* on mines

8 Yaḥyā related to me from Mālik from Rabi'a ibn Abī 'Abd ar-Raḥmān from more than one source that the Messenger of Allah ﷺ assigned the mines of al-Qabaliyya, which lie in the direction of al-Fur', to Bilāl ibn Ḥārith al-Māzinī, and nothing except *zakāt* has been taken from them up to this day.

Mālik said, "In my opinion, and Allah knows best, nothing is taken from what comes out of mines until what comes out of them reaches a value of twenty gold dinars or two hundred silver dirhams. When it reaches that amount there is *zakāt* to pay on it where it is on the spot. *Zakāt* is levied on anything over that according to how much of it there is, as long as there continues to be a supply from the mine. If the vein runs out and then, after a while, more becomes obtainable, the new supply is dealt with in the same way as the first, and payment of *zakāt* on it is begun as it was begun on the original supply."

Mālik said, "Mines are dealt with like crops, and the same procedure is applied to both. *Zakāt* is deducted from what comes out of a mine on the day it comes out without waiting for a year, just as a tenth is taken from a crop at the time it is harvested without waiting for a year to elapse over it."

17.4 *Zakāt* on buried treasure (*rikāz*)

9 Yaḥyā related to me from Mālik from Ibn Shihāb from Sa'īd ibn al-Musayyab and from Abū Salama ibn 'Abd ar-Raḥmān from Abū Hurayra that the Messenger of Allah ﷺ said, "There is a tax of a fifth due on buried treasure."

Mālik said, "The position which we are agreed upon, and which I have heard the people of knowledge mentioning, is that *rikāz* refers to treasure which has been found which was buried during the *Jāhiliyya*, as long as neither capital is required, nor is expense, great labour or inconvenience incurred in recovering it. If capital is required or great labour is incurred, or on one occasion the mark is hit and on another it is missed, then it is not *rikāz*."

17.5 Non-zakatable items of jewelry, bits of gold and silver, and amber

10 Yaḥyā related to me from Mālik from 'Abd ar-Rahmān ibn al-Qāsim from his father that 'Ā'isha, the wife of the Prophet ﷺ, used to look after the orphaned daughters of her brother in her house. They had jewellery (which they wore) and she did not pay *zakāt* on this jewelry of theirs.

11 Yaḥyā related to me from Mālik from Nāfi' that 'Abdullāh ibn 'Umar used to adorn his daughters and slave-girls with gold jewellery and he did not take any *zakāt* on their jewellery.

Mālik said, "Anyone who has unminted gold or silver, or gold and silver jewellery which is not used for wearing, must pay *zakāt* on it every year. It is weighed and one-fortieth is taken unless it falls short of twenty dinars of gold or two hundred dirhams of silver, in which case there is no *zakāt* to pay. *Zakāt* is paid only when jewellery is kept for purposes other than wearing. Bits of gold and silver or broken jewellery which the owner intends to mend to wear are in the same position as goods which are worn by their owner – no *zakāt* has to be paid on them by the owner."

Mālik said, "There is no *zakāt* (to pay) on pearls, musk or amber."

17.6 *Zakāt* on the property of orphans and trading for orphans

12 Yaḥyā related to me from Mālik that he had heard that 'Umar ibn al-Khaṭṭāb said, "Trade with the property of orphans and then it will not be eaten away by *zakāt*."

13 Yaḥyā related to me from Mālik from 'Abd ar-Raḥmān ibn al-Qāsim that his father said, "'Ā'isha used to look after me and one of my brothers – we were orphans – in her house, and she would take the *zakāt* from our property."

14 Yaḥyā related to me from Mālik that he had heard that 'Ā'isha, the wife of the Prophet ﷺ, used to give the property of the orphans that were in her house to whoever would use it to trade with on their behalf.

15 Yaḥyā related to me from Mālik that Yaḥyā ibn Sa'īd bought some property on behalf of his brother's sons who were orphans in his house, and that the property was sold afterwards for a great deal of profit.

Mālik said, "There is no harm in using the property of orphans to trade with on their behalf if the one in charge of them has permission to do so. Furthermore, I do not think that he is subject to any liability."

17.7 *Zakāt* on inheritance

16 Yaḥyā related to me that Mālik said, "I consider that if a man dies and he has not paid *zakāt* on his property, then *zakāt* is taken from the third of his property (from which he can make bequests), and the third is not exceeded and the *zakāt* is given priority over bequests. In my opinion it is the same as if he had a debt, which is why I think it should be given priority over bequests."

Mālik continued, "This applies if the deceased has asked for the *zakāt* to be deducted. If the deceased has not asked for it to be deducted, but his family do so, then that is good, but it is not binding upon them if they do not do it."

Mālik continued, "The *sunna* which we are all agreed upon is that *zakāt* is not due from someone who inherits a debt (i.e. wealth that was owed to the deceased), or goods, or a house, or a male or female slave, until a year has elapsed over the price realised from whatever he sells (i.e. slaves or a house which are not zakatable) or over the wealth he inherits, from the day he sold the things or took possession of them."

Mālik said, "The *sunna* with us is that *zakāt* does not have to be paid on wealth that is inherited until a year has elapsed over it."

17.8 *Zakāt* on debts

17 Yaḥyā related to me from Mālik from Ibn Shihāb from as-Sā'ib ibn Yazīd that 'Uthmān ibn 'Affān used to say, "This is the month in which you pay your *zakāt*. If you have any debts then pay them off so that you can sort out your wealth and take the *zakāt* from it."

18 Yaḥyā related to me from Mālik from Ayyūb ibn Abī Tamīma as-Sakhtayānī that 'Umar ibn 'Abd al-'Azīz wrote an order that some property, which one of his governors had collected unjustly, be returned to its owner and that *zakāt* be taken from it for the years that had passed. Then shortly afterwards he revised his order with a message that *zakāt* should only taken from it once since it was a bad debt.

19 Yaḥyā related to me from Mālik from Yazīd ibn Khuṣayfa that he had asked Sulaymān ibn Yasār whether *zakāt* was due from a man who had wealth in hand but also owed a debt for the same amount, and he replied, "No."

Mālik said, "Our position, about which we have no disagreement, concerning a debt is that the lender of it does not pay *zakāt* on it until he gets it back. Even if it stays with the borrower for a number of years before the lender collects it, the lender only has to pay *zakāt* on it once. If he collects an amount of the debt which is not zakatable, and has other wealth which is zakatable, then what he has collected of the debt is added to the rest of his wealth and he pays *zakāt* on the total sum."

Mālik continued, "If he has no ready money other than that which he has collected from his debt, and that does not reach a zakatable amount, then he does not have to pay any *zakāt*. He must, however, keep a record of the amount that he has collected and if, later, he collects another amount which, when added to what he has already collected, brings *zakāt* into effect, then he has to pay *zakāt* on it."

Mālik continued, "*Zakāt* is due on this first amount, together with what he has further collected of the debt owed to him, regardless of whether or not he has used up what he first collected. If what he takes back reaches twenty dinars of gold or two hundred dirhams of silver, he pays *zakāt* on it. He pays *zakāt* on anything else he takes back after that, whether it be a large or small amount, according to the amount."

Mālik said, "What shows that *zakāt* is only taken once from a debt, which is out of hand for some years before it is recovered, is that if goods remain with a man for trading purposes for some years before he sells them, he only has to pay *zakāt* on their prices once. This is because the one who is owed the debt or owns the goods should not have to take the *zakāt* on the debt or the goods from anything else, since the *zakāt* on anything is only taken from the thing itself and not from anything else."

Mālik said, "Our position regarding someone who owes a debt and has goods which are worth enough to pay off the debt, and who also has an amount of ready money which is zakatable, is that he pays *zakāt* on the ready money which he has to hand. If, however, he only has enough goods and ready money to pay off the debt, then he does not have to pay any *zakāt*. But if the ready money that he has reaches a zakatable amount over and above the amount of the debt that he owes, then he must pay *zakāt* on it."

17.9 *Zakāt* on merchandise

20 Yaḥyā related to me from Mālik from Yaḥyā ibn Sa'īd that Zurayq ibn Ḥayyān, who was in charge of admission to Egypt in the time of al-Walīd, Sulaymān, and 'Umar ibn 'Abd al-'Azīz, mentioned that 'Umar ibn 'Abd al-'Azīz had written to him saying, "Assess the Muslims that pass you and take from their apparent wealth and whatever merchandise is in their charge, one dinar for every forty dinars, and the same proportion from what is less than that down to twenty dinars, and if the amount falls short of that by one third of a dinar then leave it and do not take anything from it. As for the People of the Book that pass you, take from the merchandise in their charge one dinar for every twenty dinars and the same proportion from what is less than that down to ten dinars, and if the amount falls short by one third of a dinar, leave it and do not take anything from it. Give them a receipt for what you have taken from them until the same time next year."

Mālik said, "The position among us (in Madīna) concerning goods with a constant turnover is that if a man pays *zakāt* on his wealth and then buys goods with it, whether cloth, slaves or something similar, and then sells them before a year has elapsed over them, he does not pay *zakāt* on that wealth until a year elapses over it from the day he paid *zakāt* on it. He does not have to pay *zakāt* on any of the goods if he does not sell them for some years, and even if he keeps them for a very long time he still only has to pay *zakāt* on them once when he sells them."

Mālik said, "The position among us concerning a man who uses gold or silver to buy wheat, dates, or whatever, for trading purposes and keeps that until a year has elapsed over it and then sells it, is that he only has to pay *zakāt* on it at the time when he sells it, if the price reaches a zakatable amount. This is therefore not the same as the harvest crops that a man reaps from his land, or the dates that he harvests from his palms."

Mālik said, "A man who has wealth which he invests in trade, but which does not realise a zakatable profit for him, fixes a month in the year when he takes stock of what goods he has for trading, and counts the gold and silver that he has in ready money, and if all of it comes to a zakatable amount he then pays *zakāt* on it."

Mālik said, "The position is the same for Muslims who trade and Muslims who do not. They only have to pay *zakāt* once in any one year, whether they trade in that year or not."

17.10 Wealth which has been hidden away (*kanz*)

21 Yaḥyā related to me from Mālik that 'Abdullāh ibn Dīnār said, "I heard 'Abdullāh ibn 'Umar being asked what *kanz* was and he said, 'It is wealth on which *zakāt* has not been paid.'"

22 Yaḥyā related to me from Mālik from 'Abdullāh ibn Dīnār from Abū aṣ-Ṣāliḥ as-Sammān that Abū Hurayra used to say, "Anyone who has wealth on which he has not paid *zakāt* will, on the Day of Rising, find that his wealth will take the form of a white-headed serpent with two black spots over its eyes which will seek him out until it has him in its power, saying, 'I am the wealth that you had hidden away.'"

17.11 *Zakāt* on livestock

23 Yaḥyā related to me from Mālik that he had read what 'Umar ibn al-Khaṭṭāb had written about *zakāt*, and in it he found:

"In the name of Allah, the Merciful, the Compassionate

The Book of *Zakāt*

On twenty-four camels or less *zakāt* is paid in sheep, one ewe for every five camels.

On anything above that, up to thirty-five camels, a she-camel in its second year, and, if there is no she-camel in its second year, a male camel in its third year.

On anything above that, up to forty-five camels, a she-camel in its third year.

On anything above that, up to sixty camels, a she-camel in its fourth year that is ready to be sired.

On anything above that, up to seventy-five camels, a she-camel in its fifth year.

On anything above that, up to ninety camels, two she-camels in their third year.

On anything above that, up to one hundred and twenty camels, two she-camels in their fourth year that are ready to be sired.

On any number of camels above that, for every forty camels, a she-camel in its third year, and for every fifty, a she-camel in its fourth year.

On grazing sheep and goats, if they come to forty or more, up to one hundred and twenty head, one ewe.

On anything above that, up to two hundred head, two ewes.

On anything above that, up to three hundred, three ewes.

On anything above that, for every hundred, one ewe.

A ram should not be taken for *zakāt*, nor an old or injured ewe, except as the *zakāt* -collector thinks fit. Those separated should not be gathered together, nor should those gathered together be separated, in order to avoid paying *zakāt*. Whatever belongs to two associates is settled between them proportionately.

On silver, if it reaches five *awāq*, one fortieth is paid."

17.12 *Zakāt* on cattle

24 Yaḥyā related to me from Mālik from Ḥumayd ibn Qays al-Makkī from Ṭāwus al-Yamānī that from thirty cows, Mu'ādh ibn Jabal took one cow in its second year, and from forty cows, one cow in its third

or fourth year, and when less than that (i.e. thirty cows) was brought to him he refused to take anything from it. He said, "I have not heard anything about it from the Messenger of Allah ﷺ. When I meet him, I will ask him." But the Messenger of Allah ﷺ died before Mu'ādh ibn Jabal returned.

Yaḥyā said that Mālik said, "The best that I have heard about someone who has sheep or goats with two or more shepherds in different places is that they are added together and the owner then pays the *zakāt* on them. This is the same situation as a man who has gold and silver scattered in the hands of various people. He must add it all up and pay whatever *zakāt* there is to pay on the sum total."

Yaḥyā said that Mālik spoke about a man who had both sheep and goats, saying that they were added up together for the *zakāt* to be assessed, and if, between them, they came to a number on which *zakāt* was due, he paid *zakāt* on them. Mālik added, "They are all considered as a single category as 'sheep', and in 'Umar al-Khaṭṭāb's letter it says, 'On grazing sheep and goats, if they come to forty or more, one ewe is owed.'"

Mālik said, "If there are more sheep than goats and their owner only has to pay one ewe, the *zakāt* collector takes the ewe from the sheep. If there are more goats than sheep, he takes it from the goats. If there is an equal number of sheep and goats, he takes the ewe from whichever kind he wishes."

Yaḥyā said that Mālik said, "Similarly, Dromedary and Bactrian camels are added up together in order to assess the *zakāt* that the owner has to pay. They are all considered as camels. If there are more Dromedaries than Bactrians and the owner only has to pay one camel, the *zakāt* collector takes it from the Dromedaries. If, however, there are more Bactrian camels he takes it from those. If there is an equal number of both, he takes the camel from whichever kind he wishes."

Mālik said, "Similarly, cows and water buffalo are added up together and are all considered as cattle. If there are more cows than water buffalo and the owner only has to pay one cow, the *zakāt* collector takes it from the cows. If there are more water buffalo, he takes it from them. If there is an equal number of both, he takes the cow from whichever kind he wishes. So if *zakāt* is necessary, it is assessed taking both kinds as one group."

Yaḥyā said that Mālik said, "No *zakāt* is due from anyone who comes into possession of livestock, whether camels or cattle or sheep and goats, until a year has elapsed over them from the day he acquired them, unless he already has in his possession a zakatable number of livestock (i.e. five camels, or thirty cattle, or forty sheep and goats). If he already has five camels, or thirty cattle, or forty sheep and goats, and he then acquires additional camels, or cattle, or sheep and goats, either by trade, or gift, or inheritance, he must pay *zakāt* on them when he pays *zakāt* on the livestock he already has, even if a year has not elapsed over the acquisition. And even if the additional livestock that he acquires has had *zakāt* taken from it the day before he bought it or the day before he inherited it, he must still pay *zakāt* on it when he pays *zakāt* on the livestock he already has."

Yaḥyā said that Mālik said, "This is the same situation as someone who has some silver on which he pays *zakāt* and then uses to buy some goods with from somebody else. He then has to pay *zakāt* on those goods when he sells them. It could be that one man will have to pay *zakāt* on them one day, and by the following day the other man will also have to pay."

Mālik said about the case of a man who had sheep and goats which did not reach the zakatable amount and who then bought or inherited an additional number of sheep and goats well above the zakatable amount, that he did not have to pay *zakāt* on all his sheep and goats until a year had elapsed over them from the day he acquired the new animals, whether he bought them or inherited them. This was because none of the livestock that a man had, whether it be camels, or cattle, or sheep and goats, was counted as a zakatable amount (*niṣāb*) until there was enough of any one kind for him to have to pay *zakāt* on it. This was the *niṣāb* which was used for assessing the *zakāt* on what the owner had additionally acquired, whether it were a large or small amount of livestock.

Mālik said, "If a man has enough camels, or cattle, or sheep and goats, for him to have to pay *zakāt* on each kind, and then he acquires another camel, or cow, or sheep, or goat, it must be included with the rest of his animals when he pays *zakāt* on them."

Yaḥyā said that Mālik said, "This is what I like most out of what I heard about the matter."

Mālik said about the case of a man who does not have the animal required of him for the *zakāt*, "If it is a two-year-old she-camel that he does not have, a three-year-old male camel is taken instead. If it is a three or four or five-year-old she-camel that he does not have, then he must buy the required animal so that he gives the collector what is due. I do not like it if the owner gives the collector the equivalent value."

Mālik said about camels used for carrying water and cattle used for working water-wheels or ploughing, "I think that *zakāt* is paid on all such animals when *zakāt* is due on them."

17.13 *Zakāt* of associates

25 Yaḥyā said that Mālik said concerning two associates, "If they share the same herdsman, one male animal, the same pasture and the same watering-place, then the two men are associates as long as each one of them can distinguish his own property from that of his companion. If someone cannot tell his property apart from that of his fellow, he is not an associate but a co-owner."

Mālik said, "It is not obligatory for both associates to pay *zakāt* unless both of them have a zakatable amount (of livestock). If, for instance, one of the associates has forty or more sheep and goats and the other has less than forty sheep and goats, then the one who has forty has to pay *zakāt* and the one who has less does not. If both of them have a zakatable amount (of livestock) then both of them are assessed together (i.e. the flock is assessed as one) and both of them have to pay *zakāt*. If one of them has a thousand sheep, or less, that he has to pay *zakāt* on, and the other has forty, or more, then they are associates, and each one pays his contribution according to the number of animals he has – so much from the one with a thousand, and so much from the one with forty."

Mālik said, "Two associates in camels are the same as two associates in sheep and goats, and, for the purposes of *zakāt*, they are assessed together if each one of them has a zakatable amount (of camels). That is because the Messenger of Allah ﷺ said, 'There is no *zakāt* on less than five head of camels,' and 'Umar ibn al-Khaṭṭāb said, 'On grazing sheep and goats, if they come to forty or more – one ewe.'"

Yaḥyā said that Mālik said, "This is what I like most out of what I have heard about the matter."

Mālik said that when 'Umar ibn al-Khaṭṭāb said, "Animals which are separated should not be gathered together nor should those gathered together be separated in order to avoid paying *zakāt*," what he meant was the owners of livestock.

Mālik said, "What he meant when he said, 'Animals which are separated should not be gathered together' is, for instance, that there is a group of three men, each of whom has forty sheep and goats, and each of whom thus has to pay *zakāt*. Then, when the *zakāt* collector is on his way, they gather their flocks together so that they only owe one ewe between them. They are forbidden to do that.

"What he meant when he said, 'nor should those gathered together be separated,' is, for instance, that there are two associates, each one of whom has a hundred and one sheep and goats, and each of whom must therefore pay three ewes. Then, when the *zakāt* collector is on his way, they split up their flocks so that they only have to pay one ewe each. They are forbidden to do that. And thus it is said, 'Animals which are separated should not be gathered together nor should those gathered together be separated in order to avoid paying *zakāt*.'"

Mālik said, "This is what I have heard about the matter."

17.14 Counting lambs and kids when assessing *zakāt*

26 Yaḥyā related to me from Mālik from Thawr ibn Zayd ad-Dīlī from a son of 'Abdullāh ibn Sufyān ath-Thaqafī from his grandfather Sufyān

ibn ʻAbdullāh that ʻUmar ibn al-Khaṭṭāb once sent him to collect *zakāt*. He used to include *sakhlas* (when assessing *zakāt*), and they said, "Do you include *sakhlas* even though you do not take them (as payment)?" He returned to ʻUmar ibn al-Khaṭṭāb and mentioned that to him and ʻUmar said, "Yes, you include a *sakhla* which the shepherd is carrying, but you do not take it. Neither do you take an *akūla*, or a *rubbā*, or a *mākhiḍ*, or rams. You take goats in their second and third years, and this is a just compromise between the young of sheep and goats and the best of them."

Mālik said, "A *sakhla* is a new-born lamb or kid. A *rubbā* is a mother that is looking after her offspring, a *mākhiḍ* is a pregnant ewe or goat, and an *akūla* is a sheep or goat that is being fattened for meat."

Mālik said about a man who had sheep and goats on which he did not have to pay any *zakāt*, but which increased by birth to a zakatable amount on the day before the *zakāt* collector came to them, "If the number of sheep and goats along with their (new-born) offspring reaches a zakatable amount then the man has to pay *zakāt* on them. That is because the offspring of the sheep are part of the flock itself. It is not the same situation as when someone acquires sheep by buying them, or is given them, or inherits them. Rather, it is like when merchandise whose value does not come to a zakatable amount is sold, and with the profit that accrues it then comes to a zakatable amount. The owner must then pay *zakāt* on both his profit and his original capital, taken together. If his profit had been a chance acquisition or an inheritance he would not have had to pay *zakāt* on it until one year had elapsed over it from the day he had acquired it or inherited it."

Mālik said, "The young of sheep and goats are part of the flock in the same way that profit from wealth is part of that wealth. There is, however, one difference, in that when a man has a zakatable amount of gold and silver and then acquires an additional amount of wealth, he leaves aside the wealth he has acquired and does not pay *zakāt* on it when he pays the *zakāt* on his original wealth but waits until a year has elapsed over what he has acquired from the day he acquired it. Whereas a man who has a zakatable amount of sheep and goats, or cattle, or camels, and then acquires another camel, cow, sheep or goat, pays *zakāt* on it at the same time that he pays the *zakāt* on the others of its kind, if he already has a zakatable amount of livestock of that particular kind."

Mālik said, "This is the best of what I have heard about this."

17.15 *Zakāt* when two years are assessed together

27 Yaḥyā said that Mālik said, "The position with us concerning a man who has *zakāt* to pay on one hundred camels but then the *zakāt* collector does not come to him until *zakāt* is due for a second time and by that time all his camels have died except five, is that the *zakāt* collector assesses the two amounts of *zakāt* that are due from the owner of the animals from the five camels, which in this case is only two sheep, one for each year. This is because the only *zakāt* which an owner of livestock has to pay is what is due from him on the day that the *zakāt* is (actually) assessed. His livestock may have died or it may have increased, and the *zakāt* collector only assesses the *zakāt* on what he (actually) finds in his possession, and if his livestock has died, or several payments of *zakāt* are due from him and nothing is taken until all his livestock has died, or has been reduced to an amount below that on which he has to pay *zakāt*, then he does not have to pay any *zakāt*, and there is no liability (on him) for what has died or for the years that have passed.

17.16 The prohibition of making things difficult for people in taking *zakāt*

28 Yaḥyā related to me from Mālik from Yaḥyā ibn Sa'īd from Muḥammad ibn Yaḥyā ibn Ḥabbān from al-Qāsim ibn Muḥammad that 'Ā'isha, the wife of the Prophet ﷺ, said, "Sheep from the *zakāt* were brought past 'Umar ibn al-Khaṭṭāb and he saw amongst them a sheep with a large udder, ready to give milk, and he asked, 'What is this sheep doing here?' and they replied, 'It is one of the sheep from the *zakāt*.' 'Umar said, 'The owners did not give this sheep willingly. Do not subject people to trials. Do not take from the Muslims those of their animals which are the best food-producers.'"

29 Yaḥyā related to me from Mālik from Yaḥyā ibn Sa'īd that Muḥammad

ibn Yaḥyā ibn Ḥabbān said, "Two men from the Ashja' tribe told me that Muḥammad ibn Maslama al-Anṣārī used to come to them to collect their *zakāt*, and he would say to anyone who owned livestock, 'Select (the animal for) the *zakāt* due on your livestock and bring it to me,' and he would accept any sheep that was brought to him provided it met the requirements of what the man owed."

Mālik said, "The *sunna* with us, and what I have seen the people of knowledge doing in our city, is that things are not made difficult for the Muslims in their paying *zakāt*, and whatever they offer of their livestock is accepted from them."

17.17 Receiving *zakāt*, and who is permitted to receive it

30 Yaḥyā related to me from Zayd ibn Aslam from 'Aṭā' ibn Yasār that the Messenger of Allah ﷺ said, "*Zakāt* is not permissible for someone who is not in need except in five cases: someone fighting in the way of Allah, someone who collects *zakāt*, someone in debt, someone who buys it with his own money, and someone who has a poor neighbour who receives some *zakāt* and gives some as a present to the one who is not in need."

Mālik said, "The position with us concerning the dividing up of *zakāt* is that it is up to the individual judgement of the man in charge (*wālī*). Whichever categories of people are in most need and are most numerous are given preference, according to how the man in charge sees fit. It is possible that it may change after one year, or two, or more, but it is always those who are in need and are most numerous that are given preference, whatever category they may belong to. This is what I have seen done by people of knowledge with whom I am satisfied."

Mālik said, "There is no fixed share for the collector of the *zakāt*, except according to what the ruler sees fit."

17.18 Collecting *zakāt* and being firm in doing so

31 Yaḥyā related to me from Mālik that he had heard that Abū Bakr aṣ-Ṣiddīq said, "If they withhold even a hobbling cord I will fight them over it."

32 Yaḥyā related to me from Mālik that Zayd ibn Aslam said, "'Umar ibn al-Khaṭṭāb drank some milk which he liked (very much) and he asked the man who had given it to him, 'Where did this milk come from?' The man told him that he had come to a watering-place, which he named, and had found grazing livestock from the *zakāt* watering there. He was given some of their milk, which he then put into his water-skin, and that was the milk in question. 'Umar ibn al-Khaṭṭāb then put his hand into his mouth to make himself vomit."

Mālik said, "The position with us is that if anyone refuses to honour one of the obligatory demands of Allah, and the Muslims are unable to get it, then they have the right to fight him until they get it from him."

33 Yaḥyā related to me from Mālik that he had heard that one of the administrators of 'Umar ibn 'Abd al-'Azīz wrote to him mentioning that a man had refused to pay *zakāt* on his property. 'Umar wrote to the administrator and told him to leave the man alone and not to take any *zakāt* from him when he took it from the other Muslims. The man heard about this and the situation became unbearable for him, and after that he paid the *zakāt* on his property. The administrator wrote to 'Umar and mentioned that to him, and 'Umar wrote back telling him to take the *zakāt* from him.

17.19 *Zakāt* on estimated yields of date-palms and vines

34 Yaḥyā related to me from Mālik from a reliable source from Sulaymān ibn Yasār and from Busr ibn Sa'īd that the Messenger of Allah ﷺ said, "There is a tenth (*'ushr*) due on land that is watered by rain or springs or any natural means. There is half of an *'ushr* (a twentieth) on irrigated land."

35 Yaḥyā related to me from Mālik from Ziyād ibn Sa'd that Ibn Shihāb said, "Neither *ju'rūr*, nor *muṣrān al-fāra*, nor *'adhq ibn ḥubayq* should be taken as *zakāt* from dates. They should be included in the assessment but not taken as *zakāt*."

Mālik said, "This is the same as with sheep and goats, whose young are included in the assessment but are not (actually) taken as *zakāt*. There are also certain kinds of fruit which are not taken as *zakāt*, such as *burdī* dates (one of the finest kinds of dates), and similar varieties.

"Neither the lowest quality (of any property) nor the highest should be taken. Rather, *zakāt* should be taken from average quality property."

Mālik said, "The position that we are agreed upon concerning fruit is that only dates and grapes are estimated while still on the trees. They are estimated when their usability is clear and they are lawful to sell. This is because the fruit of date-palms and vines is eaten straightaway in the form of fresh dates and grapes, and so the assessment is done by estimation to make things easier for people and to avoid causing them trouble. Their produce is estimated and then they are given a free hand in using their produce as they wish, and later they pay the *zakāt* on it according to the estimation that was made."

Mālik said, "Crops which are not eaten fresh, such as grains and seeds, which are only eaten after they have been harvested, are not estimated. The owner, after he has harvested, threshed and sifted the crop, so that it is then in the form of grain or seed, has to fulfil his trust himself and deduct the *zakāt* he owes if the amount is large enough for him to have to pay *zakāt*. This is the position about which there is no disagreement here (in Madīna)."

Mālik said, "The position that we are all agreed upon here (in Madīna) is that the produce of date-palms is estimated while it is still on the trees, after it has ripened and become lawful to sell, and the *zakāt* on it is deducted in the form of dried dates at the time of harvest. If the fruit is damaged after it has been estimated, and the damage affects all the fruit, then no *zakāt* has to be paid. If some of the fruit remains unaffected, and this fruit amounts to five *awsāq* or more using the *ṣā'* of the Prophet ﷺ, then *zakāt* is deducted from it. *Zakāt* does not have to be paid, however, on the fruit that was damaged. Grape-vines are dealt with in the same way.

"If a man owns various pieces of property in various places, or is a co-owner of various pieces of property in various places, none of which individually comes to a zakatable amount, but which, when added together, do come to a zakatable amount, then he adds them together and pays the *zakāt* that is due on them."

17.20 *Zakāt* on seeds and olives

36 Yaḥyā related to me from Mālik that he asked Ibn Shihāb about olives and he said, "There is a tenth due on them."

Mālik said, "The tenth that is taken from olives is taken after they have been pressed, and the olives must reach a minimum amount of five *awsāq*. If there are less than five *awsāq* of olives, no *zakāt* has to be paid. Olive trees are like date-palms in so far as there is a tenth on whatever is watered by rain or springs or any natural means, and a twentieth on whatever is irrigated. Olives, however, are not estimated while still on the trees.

"The *sunna* with us concerning grain and seeds which people store and eat is that a tenth is taken from whatever has been watered by rain or springs or any natural means, and a twentieth from whatever has been irrigated, that is, as long as the amount comes to five *awsāq* or more using the aforementioned *ṣāʿ*, that is, the *ṣāʿ* of the Prophet ﷺ. *Zakāt* must be paid on anything above five *awsāq* according to the amount involved."

Mālik said, "The categories of grain and seeds which are subject to *zakāt* are: wheat, barley, *sult* (a kind of barley), sorghum, pearl millet, rice, lentils, peas, beans, sesame seeds and other such grains and seeds which are used for food. *Zakāt* is taken from them after they have been harvested and are in the form of grain or seed."

He said, "People are entrusted with the assessment and whatever they hand over is accepted."

Mālik was asked whether the tenth or the twentieth was taken out of olives before they were sold or after and he said, "The sale is not taken into consideration. It is the people who produce the olives that are asked about the olives, just as it is the people who produce foodstuffs that are asked about it, and *zakāt* is taken from them on the basis of what they say. Someone who gets five *awsāq* or more of olives from his olive trees has a tenth taken from the oil after pressing. Whereas someone who does not get five *awsāq* from his trees does not have to pay any *zakāt* on the oil."

Mālik said, "Someone who sells his crops when they are ripe and are ready in the husk has to pay *zakāt* on them but the one who buys them does not. The sale of crops is not valid until they are ready in the husk and no longer need water."

Mālik said, concerning the words of Allah the Exalted, *"pay their due on the day of their harvest,"* (6:141), that it referred to *zakāt*, and that he had heard people saying that.

Mālik said, "If someone sells his garden or his land, on which are crops or fruit which have not yet ripened, then it is the buyer who has to pay the *zakāt*. If, however, they have ripened, it is the seller who has to pay the *zakāt*, unless paying the *zakāt* is one of the conditions of the sale."

17.21 Non-zakatable fruits

37 Mālik said, "If a man has four *awsāq* of dates he has harvested, four *awsāq* of grapes he has picked, or four *awsāq* of wheat he has reaped or four *awsāq* of pulses he has harvested, the different categories are not added together, and he does not have to pay *zakāt* on any of the categories – the dates, the grapes, the wheat or the pulses – until any one of them comes to five *awsāq* using the *ṣā'* of the Prophet ﷺ as the Messenger of Allah ﷺ said, 'There is no *zakāt* (to pay) on anything less than five *awsāq* of dates.'

"If any of the categories comes to five *awsāq*, then *zakāt* must be paid. If none of the categories comes to five *awsāq*, then there is no *zakāt* to pay. The explanation of this is that when a man harvests five *awsāq* of dates (from his palms), he adds them all together and deducts the *zakāt* from them even if they are all of different kinds and varieties. It is the same with different kinds of cereal, such as brown wheat, white wheat, barley and *sult*, which are all considered as one category. If a man reaps five *awsāq* of any of these, he adds it all together and pays *zakāt* on it. If it does not come to that amount he does not have to pay any *zakāt*. It is the same (also) with grapes, whether they be black or red. If a man picks five *awsāq* of them he has to pay *zakāt* on them, but if they do not come to that amount he does not have to pay any *zakāt*. Pulses also are considered as one category in the same way as cereals, dates and grapes, even if they are of different varieties and are called by different names. Pulses include chick-peas, lentils, beans, peas, and anything which is agreed by everybody to be a pulse. If a man harvests five *awsāq* of pulses, measuring by the aforementioned *ṣā'*, the *ṣā'* of the Prophet ﷺ, he collects them all together and must pay *zakāt* on them, even if they are from all kinds of pulse and not just one kind."

Mālik said, "'Umar ibn al-Khaṭṭāb drew a distinction between pulses and wheat in what he took from the Nabatean Christians. He considered all pulses to be one category and took a tenth from them, and from cereals and raisins he took a twentieth."

Mālik said, "If someone asks, 'How can pulses be added up all together when assessing the *zakāt* so that there is just one payment, when a man can barter two of one kind for one of another, while cereals cannot be bartered at a rate of two to one?', then tell him, 'Gold and silver are collected together when assessing the *zakāt*, even though an amount of gold dinars can be exchanged hand to hand for many times that amount of silver dirhams.'"

Mālik said regarding date-palms which are shared equally between two men, and from which eight *awsāq* of dates are harvested, "They do not have to pay any *zakāt* on them. If one man owns five *awsāq* of what is harvested from the one piece of land, and the other owns four *awsāq* or less, the one who owns the five *awsāq* has to pay *zakāt*, and the other one, who harvested four *awsāq* or less, does not have to pay *zakāt*. This is how things are done whenever there are associates in any crop, whether the crop is grain or seeds that are reaped, or dates that are harvested, or grapes that are picked. Any one of them that harvests five *awsāq* of dates, or picks five *awsāq* of grapes, or reaps five *awsāq* of wheat, has to pay *zakāt*, and whoever's portion is less than five *awsāq* does not have to pay *zakāt*. *Zakāt* only has to be paid by someone whose harvesting or picking or reaping comes to five *awsāq*."

Mālik said, "The *sunna* with us regarding anything from any of these categories, i.e. wheat, dates, grapes and any kind of grain or seed, which has had the *zakāt* deducted from it and is then stored by its owner for a number of years after he has paid the *zakāt* on it until he sells it, is that he does not have to pay any *zakāt* on the price he sells it for until a year has elapsed over it from the day he made the sale, as long as he got it through (chance) acquisition or some other means and it was not intended for trading. Cereals, seeds and trade-goods are the same, in that if a man acquires some and keeps them for a number of years and then sells them for gold or silver, he does not have to pay *zakāt* on their price until a year has elapsed over it from the day of sale. If, however, the goods were intended for trade then the owner must pay *zakāt* on them when he sells them, as long as he has had them for a year from the day when he paid *zakāt* on the property with which he bought them."

17.22 Non-zakatable fruits, animal fodder and vegetables

Mālik said, "The *sunna* that we are all agreed upon here (in Madīna) and which I have heard from the people of knowledge, is that there is no *zakāt* on any kind of fresh (soft) fruit, whether it be pomegranates, peaches, figs or anything that is like them or not like them as long as it is fruit."

He continued, "No *zakāt* has to be paid on animal fodder or herbs and vegetables of any kind, and there is no *zakāt* to pay on the price realised on their sale until a year has elapsed over it from the day of sale when the seller receives the sum, as long as it reaches the *niṣāb*."

17.23 *Zakāt* on slaves, horses and honey

38 Yaḥyā related to me from Mālik from 'Abdullāh ibn Dīnār from Sulaymān ibn Yasār from 'Irāk ibn Mālik from Abū Hurayra that the Messenger of Allah ﷺ said, "A Muslim does not have to pay any *zakāt* on his slaves or his horses."

39 Yaḥyā related to me from Mālik from Ibn Shihāb from Sulaymān ibn Yasār that the people of Syria said to Abū 'Ubayda ibn al-Jarrāḥ, "Take *zakāt* from our horses and slaves," and he refused. Then he wrote to 'Umar ibn al-Khaṭṭāb and he (also) refused. Again they talked to him and again he wrote to 'Umar, and 'Umar wrote back to him saying, "If they want, take it from them and (then) give it back to them and give their slaves provision."

Mālik said, "What he means, may Allah have mercy upon him, by the words 'and give it back to them' is 'to their poor'."

40 Yaḥyā related to me from Mālik that 'Abdullāh ibn Abī Bakr ibn 'Amr ibn Ḥazm said, "A message came from 'Umar ibn 'Abd al-'Azīz to my father when he was in Minā telling him not to take *zakāt* from either honey or horses."

41 Yaḥyā related to me from Mālik that 'Abdullāh ibn Dīnār said, "I asked Sa'īd ibn al-Musayyab about *zakāt* on work-horses, and he said, 'Is there any *zakāt* due on horses?'"

17.24 *Jizya* imposed on the People of the Book and Magians

42 Yaḥyā related to me from Mālik that Ibn Shihāb said, "I have heard that the Messenger of Allah ﷺ took *jizya* from the Magians of Bahrain, that 'Umar ibn al-Khaṭṭāb took it from the Magians of Persia and that 'Uthmān ibn 'Affān took it from the Berbers."

43 Yaḥyā related to me from Mālik from Ja'far ibn Muḥammad ibn 'Alī from his father that 'Umar ibn al-Khaṭṭāb mentioned the Magians and said, "I do not know what to do about them." 'Abd ar-Raḥmān ibn 'Awf

said, "I bear witness that I heard the Messenger of Allah ﷺ say, 'Follow the same *sunna* with them as you follow with the People of the Book.'"

44 Yaḥyā related to me from Mālik from Nāfi' from Aslam, the *mawlā* of 'Umar ibn al-Khattāb, that 'Umar ibn al-Khattāb imposed a *jizya* tax of four dinars on those living where gold was the currency, and forty dirhams on those living where silver was the currency. In addition, they had to provide for the Muslims and receive them as guests for three days.

45 Yaḥyā related to me from Mālik from Zayd ibn Aslam from his father that he said to 'Umar ibn al-Khattāb, "There is a blind she-camel behind the house," so 'Umar said, "Hand it over to a household so that they can make (some) use of it." He said, "But she is blind." 'Umar replied, "Then put it in a line with other camels." He said, "How will it be able to eat from the ground?" 'Umar asked, "Is it from the livestock of the *jizya* or the *zakāt*?" and Aslam replied, "From the livestock of the *jizya*." 'Umar said, "By Allah, you wish to eat it." Aslam said, "It has the brand of the *jizya* on it." So 'Umar ordered it to be slaughtered. He had nine platters, and on each of the platters he put some of every fruit and delicacy that was available and then sent them to the wives of the Prophet ﷺ and the one he sent to his daughter Ḥafṣa was the last of them all, and if there was any deficiency in any of them it was in Ḥafṣa's portion.

"He put meat from the slaughtered animal on the platters and sent them to the wives of the Prophet ﷺ and he ordered what was left of the meat of the slaughtered animal to be prepared. Then he invited the Muhājirūn and the Anṣār to eat it."

Mālik said, "I do not think that livestock should be taken from people who pay the *jizya* other than what is included in their *jizya*."

46 Yaḥyā related to me from Mālik that he had heard that 'Umar ibn 'Abd al-'Azīz wrote to his governors telling them to relieve any people who paid the *jizya* from paying the *jizya* if they became Muslims.

Mālik said, "The past *sunna* is that there is no *jizya* due from women or children of People of the Book, and that *jizya* is only taken from men who have reached puberty. The people of *dhimma* and the Magians do not have to pay any *zakāt* on their palms or their vines or their crops or their livestock. This is because *zakāt* is imposed on the Muslims to purify them and to be given back to their poor, whereas *jizya* is imposed on the People of the Book to humble them. As long as they are in the country they have agreed to live in, they do not have to pay anything on their property except the *jizya*. If, however, they trade in Muslim countries, coming and going in them, a tenth is taken from what they invest in such trade. This is because *jizya* is only imposed on them according to conditions which they have agreed on, namely that they will remain in their own countries, and that war will be waged for them on any enemy of theirs, and that if they then leave that land to go anywhere else to do business they will have to pay a tenth. Whoever among them does business with the people of Egypt, and then goes to Syria to do business with the people of Syria and then goes to Iraq to do business with them and then goes on to Madīna, or Yemen, or other similar places, has to pay a tenth.

"People of the Book and Magians do not have to pay any *zakāt* on any of their property, livestock, produce or crops. That is still the *sunna*. They remain in the *dīn* they were in, and they continue to do what they used to do. If in any one year they frequently come and go in Muslim countries then they have to pay a tenth every time they do so, since that is outside what they have agreed upon and not one of the conditions stipulated for them. This is what I have seen the people of knowledge of our city doing."

17.25 The *'ushr* for the People of *Dhimma*

47 Yaḥyā related to me from Ibn Shihāb from Sālim ibn 'Abdullāh from his father that 'Umar ibn al-Khaṭṭāb used to take a twentieth from the cereals and olive oil of the Nabatean Christians, intending by that to increase the supply to Madīna. He would take a tenth from pulses.

48 Yaḥyā related to me from Mālik from Ibn Shihāb that as-Sā'ib ibn Yazīd said, "As a young man I used to work with 'Abdullāh ibn 'Utba ibn Mas'ūd in the market of Madīna in the time of 'Umar ibn al-Khaṭṭāb and we used to take a tenth from the Nabateans."

49 Yaḥyā related to me from Mālik that he had asked Ibn Shihāb why 'Umar ibn al-Khaṭṭāb used to take a tenth from the Nabateans, and Ibn Shihāb replied, "It used to be taken from them in the *Jāhiliyya*, and 'Umar imposed it on them."

17.26 Selling *ṣadaqa* and taking it back

50 Yaḥyā related to me from Zayd ibn Aslam that his father said that he had heard 'Umar ibn al-Khaṭṭāb say, "I once gave someone a noble horse to carry him in the way of Allah, and the man neglected it. I wished to buy it back from him and I thought that he would sell it cheaply. I asked the Messenger of Allah ﷺ about it and he said, 'Do not buy it, even if he gives it to you for one dirham, for someone who takes back his *ṣadaqa* is like a dog swallowing its own vomit.'"

51 Yaḥyā related to me from Mālik from Nāfi' from 'Abdullāh ibn 'Umar that 'Umar ibn al-Khaṭṭāb gave a horse to carry someone in the way of Allah, and then he wished to buy it back. So he asked the Messenger of Allah ﷺ about it, and he said, "Do not buy or take back your *ṣadaqa*."

Yaḥyā said that Mālik was asked about whether a man who gave some *ṣadaqa*, and then found it being offered back to him for sale by someone other than the man to whom he had given it, could buy it or not, and he said, "I would prefer that he leave it."

17.27 Who pays the *Zakāt al-Fiṭr*

52 Yaḥyā related to me from Mālik from Nāfi' that 'Abdullāh ibn 'Umar used to pay the *Zakāt al-Fiṭr* for those slaves of his that were at Wādī al-Qurā and Khaybar.

Yaḥyā related to me that Mālik said, "The best that I have heard about the *Zakāt al-Fiṭr* is that a man has to pay for every person that he is responsible for supporting and whom he must support. He has to pay for all his *mukātab* slaves, his *mudabbar* slaves, and his ordinary slaves, whether they are present or absent, as long as they are Muslim, and whether or not they are for trade. However, he does not have to pay *zakāt* on any of them that are not Muslim."

Mālik said, concerning a runaway slave, "I think that his master should pay the *zakāt* for him, whether or not he knows where he is, if it has not been long since the slave ran away and his master hopes that he is still alive and will return. If it has been a long time since he ran away and his master has despaired of him returning, then I do not think that he should pay *zakāt* for him."

Mālik said, "*Zakāt al-Fiṭr* has to be paid by people living in the desert (i.e. nomadic people) just as it has to be paid by people living in villages (i.e. settled people), because the Messenger of Allah ﷺ made the *Zakāt al-Fiṭr* at the end of Ramaḍān obligatory on every Muslim, whether freeman or slave, male or female."

17.28 Measuring the *Zakāt al-Fiṭr*

53 Yaḥyā related to me from Mālik from Nāfi' from 'Abdullāh ibn 'Umar that the Messenger of Allah ﷺ made the *zakāt* of breaking the fast at the end of Ramaḍān obligatory on every Muslim, whether freeman or slave, male or female, and stipulated it as a *ṣā'* of dates or a *ṣā'* of barley.

54 Yaḥyā related to me from Mālik from Zayd ibn Aslam from 'Iyāḍ ibn 'Abdullāh ibn Sa'd ibn Abī Sarḥ al-'Āmirī that he had heard Abū Sa'īd al-Khudrī say, "We used to pay the *Zakāt al-Fiṭr* with a *ṣā'* of wheat, or a *ṣā'* of barley, or a *ṣā'* of dates, or a *ṣā'* of dried sour milk, or a *ṣā'* of raisins, using the *ṣā'* of the Prophet ﷺ."

55 Yaḥyā related to me from Mālik from Nāfi' that 'Abdullāh ibn 'Umar would always pay the *Zakāt al-Fiṭr* in dates, except once, when he paid it in barley.

Mālik said, "Payment of all types of *kaffāra* (expiation), of *Zakāt al-Fiṭr* and of the *zakāt* on grains for which a tenth or a twentieth is due, is made using the smaller *mudd*, which is the *mudd* of the Prophet ﷺ except in the case of *ẓihār* divorce, when the *kaffāra* is paid using the *mudd* of Hishām, which is the larger *mudd*."

17.29 When to send the *Zakāt al-Fiṭr*

56 Yaḥyā related to me from Mālik from Nāfi' that 'Abdullāh ibn 'Umar used to send the *Zakāt al-Fiṭr* to the one with whom it was collected together two or three days before the day of breaking the fast.

57 Yaḥyā related to me that Mālik had seen that the people of knowledge used to like to pay the *Zakāt al-Fiṭr* after dawn had broken on the day of the *Fiṭr* before they went to the place of prayer.

Mālik said, "There is leeway in this, if Allah wills, in that it can be paid either before setting out (for the prayer) on the day of *Fiṭr* or afterwards."

17.30 People who are not obliged to pay the *Zakāt al-Fiṭr*

58 Yaḥyā related to me that Mālik said, "A man does not have to pay *zakāt* for the slaves of his slaves, or for someone employed by him, or for his wife's slaves, except for anyone who serves him and whose services are indispensable to him, in which case he must pay *zakāt*. He does not have to pay *zakāt* for any of his slaves that are unbelievers and have not become Muslim, whether they be for trade or otherwise."

18. Fasting

18.1 Sighting the new moon for beginning and ending the fast of Ramaḍān

1 Yaḥyā related to me from Mālik from Nāfi' from 'Abdullāh ibn 'Umar that the Messenger of Allah ﷺ once mentioned Ramaḍān and said, "Do not begin the fast until you see the new moon, and do not break the fast (at the end of Ramaḍān) until you see it. If the new moon is obscured from you, then calculate (when it should be)."

2 Yaḥyā related to me from Mālik from 'Abdullāh ibn Dīnār from 'Abdullāh ibn 'Umar that the Messenger of Allah ﷺ said, "The month has twenty-nine days in it. Do not start the fast or break it until you see the new moon. If the new moon is obscured from you, then calculate (when it should be)."

3 Yaḥyā related to me from Mālik from Thawr ibn Zayd ad-Dīlī from 'Abdullāh ibn 'Abbās that the Messenger of Allah ﷺ once mentioned Ramaḍān and said, "Do not start the fast or break it until you see the new moon. If the new moon is obscured from you, then complete a full thirty days."

4 Yaḥyā related to me from Mālik that he had heard that once in the time of 'Uthmān ibn 'Affān the new moon was seen in the afternoon but 'Uthmān did not break his fast until evening had come and the sun had set.

Yaḥyā said that he had heard Mālik say that someone who sees the new moon of Ramaḍān when he is on his own should start the fast and not break it if he knows that that day is part of Ramaḍān.

He added, "Someone who sees the new moon of Shawwāl when he is on his own does not break the fast, because people suspect the trustworthiness of someone among them who breaks the fast. Such people should say when they sight the new moon, 'We have seen the new moon.' Whoever sees the new moon of Shawwāl during the day should not break his fast but should continue fasting for the rest of that day. This is because it is really the new moon of the night that is coming."

Yaḥyā said that he heard Mālik say, "If people are fasting on the Day of *Fiṭr* thinking that it is still Ramaḍān and then definite evidence comes to them that the new moon of Ramaḍān had been seen one day before they began to fast and that they are now into the thirty-first day, then they should break the fast on that day at whatever time the news comes to them. However, they do not pray the *'Īd* prayer if they hear the news after the sun has begun to decline."

18.2 Making the intention to fast before dawn

5 Yaḥyā related to me from Mālik from Nāfi' that 'Abdullāh ibn 'Umar used to say, "Only someone who makes the intention to fast before dawn (actually) fasts."

Yaḥyā related to me from Mālik from Ibn Shihāb that 'Ā'isha and Ḥafṣa, the wives of the Prophet ﷺ also said that.

18.3 Being quick to break the fast

6 Yaḥyā related to me from Mālik from Abū Ḥazm ibn Dīnār from Sahl ibn Sa'd as-Sā'idī that the Messenger of Allah ﷺ said, "People will continue to be all right as long as they hurry to break the fast."

7 Yaḥyā related to me from Mālik from 'Abd ar-Raḥmān ibn Ḥarmala al-

Aslamī from Sa'īd ibn al-Musayyab that the Messenger of Allah ﷺ said, "People will continue to be all right as long as they hurry to break the fast."

8 Yaḥyā related to me from Mālik from Ibn Shihāb from Ḥumayd ibn 'Abd ar-Rahmān that 'Umar ibn al-Khaṭṭāb and 'Uthmān ibn 'Affān would pray *Maghrib* when they saw the night darkening, before they broke their fast, and then they would break their fast. That was during Ramaḍān.

18.4 Fasting when someone finds himself in *janāba* in the morning during Ramaḍān

9 Yaḥyā related to me from Mālik from 'Abdullāh ibn 'Abd ar-Raḥmān ibn Ma'mar al-Anṣārī from Abū Yūnus, the *mawlā* of 'Ā'isha, from 'Ā'isha that she overheard a man standing at the door saying to the Messenger of Allah ﷺ, "Messenger of Allah, I get up in the morning in *janāba* (in a state of major ritual impurity) and want to fast," and the Messenger of Allah ﷺ said, "I too get up in the morning in *janāba* and want to fast, so I do *ghusl* and fast." The man said to him, "You are not the same as us. Allah has forgiven you all your wrong actions that have gone before and those that have come after." The Messenger of Allah ﷺ got angry and said, "By Allah, I hope that I am the most fearful of you with respect to Allah and the most knowledgeable of you in how to fear Allah."

10 Yaḥyā related to me from Mālik from 'Abd Rabbihi ibn Sa'īd from Abū Bakr ibn 'Abd ar-Raḥmān ibn al-Ḥārith ibn Hishām from 'Ā'isha and Umm Salama, the wives of the Prophet ﷺ, that the Prophet ﷺ used to get up in the morning in *janāba* as a result of intercourse, not a dream, in Ramaḍān, and then he would fast."

11 Yaḥyā related to me from Mālik from Sumayy, the *mawlā* of Abū Bakr ibn 'Abd ar-Raḥmān ibn al-Ḥārith ibn Hishām that he heard Abū Bakr ibn 'Abd ar-Raḥmān ibn al-Ḥārith ibn Hishām say, "My father and I were with Marwān ibn al-Ḥakam at the time when he was governor of Madīna, and someone mentioned to him that Abū Hurayra used to say, 'If someone begins the morning in *janāba*, he has broken the fast for that

day.' Marwān said, 'I swear to you, 'Abd ar-Raḥmān, you must go to the two *Umm al-Mu'minīn*, 'Ā'isha and Umm Salama, and ask them about it.'

"'Abd ar-Raḥmān went to visit 'Ā'isha and I accompanied him. He greeted her and then said, '*Umm al-Mu'minīn*, we were with Marwān ibn al-Ḥakam and someone mentioned to him that Abū Hurayra used to say that if someone had begun the morning in *janāba*, he had broken the fast for that day.' 'Ā'isha said, 'It is not as Abū Hurayra says, 'Abd ar-Raḥmān. Do you dislike what the Messenger of Allah ﷺ used to do?' and 'Abd ar-Raḥmān said, 'No, by Allah.' 'Ā'isha said, 'I bear witness that the Messenger of Allah ﷺ used to get up in the morning in *janāba* from intercourse, not a because of a dream, and would then fast for that day.'"

He continued, "Then we went and visited Umm Salama, and 'Abd ar-Raḥmān asked her about the same matter and she said the same as 'Ā'isha had said. Then we went off until we came to Marwān ibn al-Ḥakam. 'Abd ar-Raḥmān told him what they had both said and Marwān said, 'I swear to you, Abū Muḥammad, you must use the mount which is at the door, and go to Abū Hurayra, who is on his land at al-'Aqīq, and tell him this.' So 'Abd ar-Raḥmān rode off, and I went with him, until we came to Abū Hurayra. 'Abd ar-Raḥmān talked with him for a while, and then mentioned the matter to him, and Abū Hurayra said, 'I don't know anything about it. I was just told that by someone.'"

12 Yaḥyā related to me from Mālik from Sumayy, the *mawlā* of Abū Bakr, from Abū Bakr ibn 'Abd ar-Raḥmān that 'Ā'isha and Umm Salama, the wives of the Prophet ﷺ, said, "The Messenger of Allah ﷺ used to get up in the morning in *janāba* from intercourse, not on account of a dream, and would then fast."

18.5 Permission for a fasting man to kiss

13 Yaḥyā related to me from Mālik from Zayd ibn Aslam from 'Aṭā' ibn Yasār that a certain man kissed his wife while he was fasting in Ramaḍān. This made him very anxious, and so he sent his wife to the Prophet ﷺ to ask him about that for him. She went in and saw Umm Salama, the wife of the Prophet ﷺ, and mentioned the matter to her,

and Umm Salama told her that the Messenger of Allah ﷺ used to kiss while he was fasting. So she went back and told her husband that, but it only made him find fault all the more and he said, "We are not like the Messenger of Allah ﷺ. Allah makes permissible for the Messenger of Allah ﷺ whatever He wishes."

His wife then went back to Umm Salama and found the Messenger of Allah ﷺ with her. The Messenger of Allah ﷺ said, "What is the matter with this woman?" and Umm Salama told him. The Messenger of Allah ﷺ said, "Did you not tell her that I do that myself?" and she said, "I told her, and she went to her husband and told him, but it only made him find fault all the more and say, 'We are not like the Messenger of Allah ﷺ. Allah makes permissible for His Messenger ﷺ whatever He wishes.'" The Messenger of Allah ﷺ got angry and said, "By Allah, I am the one with the most *taqwā* of Allah of you all, and of you all the one who best knows His limits."

14 Yaḥyā related to me from Mālik from Hishām ibn 'Urwa from his father that 'Ā'isha, *Umm al-Mu'minīn* ؓ said, "The Messenger of Allah ﷺ used to kiss certain of his wives when fasting," and then she laughed.

15 Yaḥyā related to me from Mālik from Yaḥyā ibn Sa'īd that 'Ātika bint Zayd ibn 'Amr ibn Nufayl, the wife of 'Umar ibn al-Khaṭṭāb, used to kiss 'Umar ibn al-Khaṭṭāb's head while he was fasting, and he did not forbid her.

16 Yaḥyā related to me from Mālik from Abū an-Naḍr, the *mawlā* of 'Umar ibn 'Ubaydullāh that 'Ā'isha bint Ṭalḥa told him that she was once with 'Ā'isha, the wife of the Prophet ﷺ, and her husband, who was fasting, came and visited her there. (He was 'Abdullāh ibn 'Abd ar-Raḥmān ibn Abī Bakr aṣ-Ṣiddīq). 'Ā'isha said to him, "What's stopping you from coming close to your wife and kissing her and joking with her?" He asked, "Can I kiss her when I am fasting?" She answered, "Yes."

17 Yaḥyā related to me from Mālik from Zayd ibn Aslam that Abū Hurayra and Sa'd ibn Abī Waqqāṣ used to say that someone who was fasting was allowed to kiss.

18.6 Being strict about kissing when fasting

18 Yaḥyā related to me from Mālik that he had heard that 'Ā'isha, the wife of the Prophet ﷺ, would say, when she mentioned that the Messenger of Allah ﷺ used to kiss while fasting, "And who among you is more able to control himself than the Messenger of Allah ﷺ?"

Yaḥyā said that Mālik said that Hishām ibn 'Urwa ibn az-Zubayr had said, "I do not think that kissing invites people who are fasting to good."

19 Yaḥyā related to me from Mālik from Zayd ibn Aslam from 'Aṭā' ibn Yasār that 'Abdullāh ibn 'Abbās was asked about people kissing while fasting and he said that he allowed it for old men but disapproved of it for young men.

20 Yaḥyā related to me from Mālik from Nāfi' that 'Abdullāh ibn 'Umar used to forbid kissing and fondling for people who were fasting.

18.7 Fasting while travelling

21 Yaḥyā related to me from Mālik from Ibn Shihāb from 'Ubaydullāh ibn 'Abdullāh ibn 'Utba ibn Mas'ūd from 'Abdullāh ibn 'Abbās that the Messenger of Allah ﷺ left for Makka in Ramaḍān during the Year of the Conquest [of Makka], and fasted until he reached al-Kadīd. He then broke the fast, and so everyone else did so as well. What people used to do was act according to whatever the Messenger of Allah ﷺ had done most recently.

22 Yaḥyā related to me from Mālik from Sumayy, the *mawlā* of Abū Bakr ibn 'Abd ar-Raḥmān, from Abū Bakr ibn 'Abd ar-Raḥmān from one of the Companions of the Messenger of Allah ﷺ, that the Messenger of Allah ﷺ ordered everyone to break the fast on the journey he made in the Year of the Conquest saying, "Be strong for your enemy," while the Messenger of Allah ﷺ kept on fasting. Abū Bakr said that the one who related this to him said, "I saw the Messenger of Allah ﷺ pouring water over his head at al-'Arj, either from thirst or from the heat. Then someone said to the Messenger of Allah ﷺ, 'Messenger of Allah, a group of people kept on fasting when

you did.' Then when the Messenger of Allah was at al-Kadīd, he asked for a drinking-bowl and drank, and everyone broke the fast."

23 Yaḥyā related to me from Mālik from Ḥumayd aṭ-Ṭawīl that Anas ibn Mālik said, "We once travelled with the Messenger of Allah ﷺ in Ramaḍān, and those who were fasting did not find fault with those who were not, and those who were not fasting did not find fault with those who were."

24 Yaḥyā related to me from Mālik from Hishām ibn 'Urwa from his father that Ḥamza ibn 'Amr al-Aslamī once said to the Messenger of Allah ﷺ, "Messenger of Allah, I am a man who fasts. Can I fast when travelling?" The Messenger of Allah ﷺ replied, "If you want you can fast, and if you want you can break the fast."

25 Yaḥyā related to me from Mālik from Nāfi' that 'Abdullāh ibn 'Umar used not to fast while travelling.

26 Yaḥyā related to me from Mālik that Hishām ibn 'Urwa said, "My father, 'Urwa, used to travel in Ramaḍān and we would travel with him, and he used to fast while we would break the fast and he would not tell us to fast."

18.8 Returning from a journey in Ramaḍān and intention to travel in Ramaḍān

27 Yaḥyā related to me from Mālik that he had heard that 'Umar ibn al-Khaṭṭāb, if he was travelling in Ramaḍān and knew that he would reach Madīna at the beginning of the day, would do so fasting.

Yaḥyā said that Mālik said, "If someone is travelling and knows that he will be reaching his people in the first part of the day, and then dawn breaks before he gets there, he should be fasting when he gets there."

Mālik said, "If someone intends to go away (on a journey) in Ramaḍān, and then dawn breaks while he is still on his land before he has left, he should fast that day."

Mālik said that a man who returns from a journey in Ramaḍān and is not fasting may have sexual intercourse with his wife if he wishes, if she is not fasting and she has just become pure after her menses.

18.9 *Kaffāra* (making amends) for breaking the fast in Ramaḍān

28 Yaḥyā related to me from Mālik from Ibn Shihāb from Ḥumayd ibn 'Abd ar-Raḥmān ibn 'Awf from Abū Hurayra that a man broke the fast in Ramaḍān and the Messenger of Allah ﷺ ordered him to make *kaffāra* by freeing a slave, or fasting two consecutive months, or feeding sixty poor people, and he said, "I cannot do it." Someone brought a large basket of dates to the Messenger of Allah ﷺ and he said, "Take this and give it away as *ṣadaqa*." He said, "Messenger of Allah, there is no one more needy than I am." The Messenger of Allah ﷺ smiled until his molars showed and then said, "Eat them."

29 Yaḥyā related to me from Mālik from 'Aṭā' ibn 'Abdullāh al-Khurasānī that Sa'īd ibn al-Musayyab said, "A bedouin came to the Messenger of Allah ﷺ beating his breast and tearing out his hair and saying, 'I am destroyed!' The Messenger of Allah ﷺ said, 'Why is that?', and he said, 'I had intercourse with my wife while fasting in Ramaḍān.' The Messenger of Allah ﷺ asked him, 'Are you able to free a slave?' and the man said, 'No.' Then he asked him, 'Are you able to give away a camel?' and the man replied, 'No.' He said, 'Sit down.' Someone brought a large basket of dates to the Messenger of Allah ﷺ and he said to the man, 'Take this and give it away as *ṣadaqa*.' The man said, 'There is no one more needy than me,' and (the Messenger of Allah ﷺ said, 'Eat them, and fast one day for the day when you had intercourse.'"

Mālik said that 'Aṭā' said that he had asked Sa'īd ibn al-Musayyab how many dates there were in that basket, and he said, "Between fifteen and twenty *ṣā's*."

Mālik said, "I have heard people of knowledge saying that the *kaffāra* specified by the Messenger of Allah ﷺ for a man who has intercourse with his wife during the day in Ramaḍān is not due from someone who, on a day when he is making up the fast of Ramaḍān, breaks his fast by having intercourse with his wife, or whatever. He only has to make up for that day."

Mālik said, "This is what I like most out of what I have heard about the matter."

18.10 Cupping a man who is fasting

30 Yaḥyā related to me from Mālik from Nāfi' that 'Abdullāh ibn 'Umar used to be cupped while he was fasting. Nāfi' said, "He later stopped doing that, and would not be cupped when he was fasting until he had broken the fast."

31 Yaḥyā related to me from Mālik from Ibn Shihāb that Sa'd ibn Abī Waqqāṣ and 'Abdullāh ibn 'Umar used to be cupped while they were fasting.

32 Yaḥyā related to me from Mālik from Hishām ibn 'Urwa that his father used to be cupped while he was fasting and he would not then break his fast. Hishām added, "I only ever saw him being cupped when he was fasting."

Mālik said, "Cupping is only disapproved of for someone who is fasting out of fear that he will become weak and if it were not for that it would not be disapproved of. I do not think that a man who is cupped in Ramaḍān and does not break his fast owes anything, and I do not say that he has to make up for the day on which he was cupped, because cupping is only disapproved of for someone fasting if his fast is endangered. I do not think that someone who is cupped, and is then well enough to keep the fast until evening, owes anything, nor does he have to make up for that day."

18.11 Fasting the Day of *'Āshūrā'* (the 10th of Muḥarram)

33 Yaḥyā related to me from Mālik from Hishām ibn 'Urwa from his father that 'Ā'isha, the wife of the Prophet ﷺ said, "The Day of *'Āshūrā'* was a day the Quraysh used to fast in the *Jāhiliyya*, and the Messenger of Allah

ﷺ, used also to fast it during the *Jāhiliyya*. Then when the Messenger of Allah ﷺ came to Madīna he fasted it and ordered that it be fasted. Then Ramaḍān was made obligatory, and that became the obligation instead of *'Āshūrā'*, but whoever wanted to, fasted it, and whoever did not want to, did not fast it."

34 Yaḥyā related to me from Mālik from Ibn Shihāb that Ḥumayd ibn 'Abd ar-Raḥmān ibn 'Awf heard Mu'āwiya ibn Abī Sufyān say from the minbar on the Day of *'Āshūrā'* in the year in which he went on *ḥajj*, "People of Madīna, where are your learned men? I heard the Messenger of Allah ﷺ say about this day, 'This is the Day of *'Āshūrā'*, and fasting it has not been prescribed for you. I am fasting it, and whoever of you wants to fast it can do so, and whoever does not want to does not have to.'"

35 Yaḥyā related to me from Mālik that he had heard that 'Umar ibn al-Khaṭṭāb had sent (the following message) to al-Ḥārith ibn Hishām, "Tomorrow is the Day of *'Āshūrā'*, so fast (it) and tell your family to fast (also)."

18.12 Fasting the Days of *Fiṭr* and *Aḍḥā* and fasting continuously

36 Yaḥyā related to me from Mālik from Muḥammad ibn Yaḥyā ibn Ḥabbān from al-A'raj from Abū Hurayra that the Messenger of Allah ﷺ forbade fasting on two days, the Day of *Fiṭr* and the Day of *Aḍḥā*.

37 Yaḥyā related to me from Mālik that he used to hear the people of knowledge say, "There is no harm in fasting continuously as long as one breaks the fast on the days on which the Messenger of Allah, ﷺ forbade fasting, namely, the days of Minā, the Day of *Aḍḥā* and the Day of *Fiṭr*, according to what we have heard."

Mālik said, "This is what I like most out of what I have heard about the matter."

18.13 The prohibition against fasting for two days or more without breaking the fast in between (*wiṣāl*)

38 Yaḥyā related to me from Mālik from Nāfi' from 'Abdullah ibn 'Umar that the Messenger of Allah ﷺ forbade fasting for two days or more without breaking the fast in between. They said, "But Messenger of Allah, you practice *wiṣāl*." He replied, "I am not the same as you. I am fed and given to drink."

39 Yaḥyā related to me from Mālik from Abū az-Zinād from al-A'raj from Abū Hurayra that the Messenger of Allah ﷺ said, "Beware of *wiṣāl*. Beware of *wiṣāl*." They said, "But you practise *wiṣāl*, Messenger of Allah." He replied, "I am not the same as you. My Lord feeds me and gives me to drink."

18.14 Fasting on account of manslaughter or for pronouncing the *ẓihār* form of divorce

40 Yaḥyā related to me, and I (myself) heard Mālik say, "The best that I have heard about someone who has to fast for two consecutive months because of having killed someone by mistake, or having pronounced the *ẓihār* form of divorce, becoming very ill and having to break his fast is that, if he recovers from his illness and is strong enough to fast, he must not delay doing so. He continues his fast from where he left off.

"Similarly, a woman who has to fast because of having killed someone by mistake should not delay resuming her fast when she has become pure after her period. She continues her fast from where she left off.

"No one who, by the Book of Allah, has to fast for two consecutive months may break his fast except for reason of illness or menstruation. He must not travel and break his fast."

Mālik said, "This is the best that I have heard about the matter."

18.15 Illness and the fast

41 Yaḥyā said that he heard Mālik say, "What I have heard from the people of knowledge is that, if a man succumbs to an illness which makes fasting very difficult for him and exhausts him and wears him out, he can break his fast. This is the same as the case of a sick man in the prayer who finds standing to be too difficult and exhausting (and Allah knows better than the slave that it is an excuse for him) and other matters which are not described. If someone is in such a condition he prays sitting, and the *dīn* of Allah is ease.

"Allah has permitted a traveller to break the fast when travelling, and he has more strength for fasting than a sick man. Allah, the Exalted, says in His says in His Book, *'But any of you who are ill or on a journey should fast a number of other days,'* (2:185) and Allah has thus permitted a traveller to break his fast when on a journey, and he is more capable of fasting than a sick man."

"This is what I most prefer of what I had heard, and it is the practice on which there is consensus among us."

18.16 The vow to fast, and fasting on behalf of a dead person

42 Yaḥyā related to me from Mālik that he had heard that Sa'īd ibn al-Musayyab was asked whether a man who had vowed to fast a month could fast voluntarily, and Sa'īd said, "He should fulfil his vow before he does any voluntary fasting."

Mālik said, "I have heard the same thing from Sulaymān ibn Yasār."

Mālik said, "If someone dies with an unfulfilled vow to free a slave or to fast or to give *ṣadaqa* or to give away a camel, and makes a bequest that his vow should be fulfilled from his estate, then the *ṣadaqa* or the gift of the camel is taken from one third of his estate. Preference is given to it over other bequests, except things of a similar nature, because by his vow it has become incumbent on him, and this is not the case with something he donates voluntarily. They (vows and voluntary donations) are settled from one-third of his estate, and not from the whole of it, since if the dying man were free to dispose of all of his estate, he might delay settling what had become incumbent on him (i.e. his vows), so that when death came and the estate passed into the hands of his heirs, he would have bequeathed such things (i.e. his vows) that were not claimed by anyone (like debts). If that (i.e. to dispose freely of his property) were allowed him, he would delay these things (i.e. his vows) until when he was near death, he would designate them and they might take up all of his estate. He must not do that."

43 Yaḥyā related to me from Mālik that he had heard that 'Abdullāh ibn 'Umar used to be asked, "Can someone fast for someone else, or do the prayer for someone else?" and he would reply, "No one can fast or do the prayer for anyone else."

18.17 Making up days missed in Ramaḍān, and the *kaffāra*

44 Yaḥyā related to me from Mālik from Zayd ibn Aslam from his brother Khālid ibn Aslam that 'Umar ibn al-Khaṭṭāb once broke the fast on a cloudy day thinking that evening had come and the sun had set. Then a man came to him and said, "*Amīr al-Mu'minīn*, the sun has come out," and 'Umar said, "That is an easy matter. It was our deduction (*ijtihād*)."

Mālik commented, "According to what we think, Allah knows best, what he was referring to when he said, 'That is an easy matter' was making up the fast, and how slight the effort involved was and how easy it was. He was saying (in effect), 'We will fast another day in its place.'"

45 Yaḥyā related to me from Mālik from Nāfi' that 'Abdullāh ibn 'Umar used to say, "Someone who breaks the fast in Ramaḍān because he is ill or travelling should make up the days he has missed consecutively."

46 Yaḥyā related to me from Mālik from Ibn Shihāb that 'Abdullah ibn 'Abbās and Abū Hurayra differed about making up days missed in Ramaḍān. One of them said that they were done separately and the other said that they were done consecutively. He did not know which one of them it was who said that they were done separately.

47 Yaḥyā related to me from Mālik from Nāfi' that 'Abdullāh ibn 'Umar used to say, "If someone makes himself vomit while he is fasting he has to make up a day, but if he cannot help vomiting he does not have to make up anything."

48 Yaḥyā related to me from Mālik from Yaḥyā ibn Sa'īd that he heard Sa'īd ibn al-Musayyab being asked about making up days missed in Ramaḍān, and Sa'īd said, "What I like best is for days missed in Ramaḍān to be made up consecutively and not separately."

Yaḥyā said that he had heard Mālik say, about someone who made up the days he had missed in Ramaḍān separately that he did not have to repeat them. (What he had done) was enough for him. It was, however, preferable to do them consecutively.

Mālik said, "Whoever eats or drinks thoughtlessly or forgetfully in Ramaḍān, or during any other obligatory fast that he must do, has to fast another day in its place."

49 Yaḥyā related to me from Mālik that Ḥumayd ibn Qays al-Makkī told him, "I was with Mujāhid while he was performing *ṭawāf* around the Ka'ba, and a man came to him and asked whether the days (of fasting) for *kaffāra* (making amends) had to be fasted consecutively, or whether they could be split up. I said to him, 'Yes, they can be split up, if the person so wishes.' Mujāhid said, 'He should not split them up, because in Ubayy ibn Ka'b's recitation they are referred to as three consecutive days."

Mālik said, "What I like most is what Allah has specified in the Qur'ān, that is that they are fasted consecutively."

Mālik was asked about a woman who began the day fasting in Ramaḍān and, though it was outside of the time of her period, fresh blood (i.e. not menstrual blood) flowed from her. She then waited until evening to see the same, but did not see anything. Then, on the next day in the morning she had another flow, though less than the first. Then, some days before her period, the flow stopped completely. Mālik was asked what she should do about her fasting and prayer, and he said, "This blood is like menstrual blood. When she sees it she should break her fast, and then make up the days she has missed. Then, when the blood has completely stopped, she should have a *ghusl* and fast."

Mālik was asked whether someone who became Muslim on the last day of Ramaḍān had to make up all of Ramaḍān or whether he just had to make up the day when he became Muslim, and he said, "He does not have to make up any of the days that have passed. He begins fasting from that day onwards. What I like most is that he makes up the day on which he became Muslim."

18.18 Making up voluntary fasts

50 Yaḥyā related to me from Mālik from Ibn Shihāb that 'Ā'isha and Ḥafṣa, the wives of the Prophet ﷺ began fasting voluntarily one morning and then food was given to them and they broke their fast with it. Then the Messenger of Allah ﷺ came in. 'Ā'isha said, "Ḥafṣa asked, anticipating me in speech – she took after her father 'Umar – 'Messenger of Allah, 'Ā'isha and I began the morning fasting voluntarily and then food was given us and we broke the fast with it.' The Messenger of Allah ﷺ said, 'Fast another day in its place.'"

Yaḥyā said that he heard Mālik say, "Someone who eats or drinks out of absent-mindedness or forgetfulness during a voluntary fast does not have to repeat his fast, but he should continue fasting for the rest of any day, in which he eats or drinks while fasting voluntarily, and not stop fasting. Someone to whom something unexpected happens, which causes him to break his fast while he is fasting voluntarily, does not have to repeat his fast if he has broken it for a reason and not simply because he decided to break his fast, just as I do not think that someone has to repeat a voluntary prayer if he has had to stop it because of some discharge which he could not prevent and which meant that he had to repeat his *wuḍū'*."

Mālik said, "Once a man has begun doing any of the right actions such as the prayer, the fast and the *ḥajj*, or similar right actions of a voluntary nature, he should not stop until he has completed it, according to what the *sunna* for that action is. If he says the *takbīr* he should not stop until he has prayed two *rak'as*. If he is fasting he should not break his fast until he has completed that day's fast. If he goes into *iḥrām* he should not return until he has completed his *ḥajj*, and if he begins doing *ṭawāf* he should not stop doing so until he has gone around the Ka'ba seven times. He should not stop doing any of these actions once he has started them until he has completed them, except if something happens such as illness or some other matter by which a man is excused. This is because Allah, the Blessed and Exalted, says in His Book, *'Eat and drink until you can clearly discern the white thread from the black thread of the dawn. Then complete the fast until the night appears'* (2:187), and so he must complete his fast as Allah has said. Allah, the Exalted, (also) says, *'Perform the ḥajj and 'umra for Allah,'* (2:196) and so if a man were to go into *iḥrām* for a voluntary *ḥajj*, having performed his one obligatory *ḥajj* (on a previous occasion), he could not then stop doing his *ḥajj* having once begun it and come out of *iḥrām* while in the middle of his *ḥajj*. Anyone that begins a voluntary act must complete it once he has begun doing it, just as an obligatory act must be completed. This is the best of what I have heard."

18.19 The *fidya* (compensation) for breaking the fast in Ramaḍān for a reason

51 Yaḥyā related to me from Mālik that he had heard that Anas ibn Mālik used to pay *fidya* when he had grown old and was no longer able to fast.

Mālik said, "I do not consider that to do so is obligatory, but what I like most is that a man does the fast when he is strong enough. Whoever pays compensation gives one *mudd* of food in place of every day, using the *mudd* of the Prophet ﷺ."

52 Yaḥyā related to me from Mālik that he had heard that 'Abdullāh ibn 'Umar was asked about what a pregnant woman should do if the fast became difficult for her and she feared for her child, and he said, "She should break the fast and feed a poor man one *mudd* of wheat in place of every day missed, using the *mudd* of the Prophet ﷺ."

Mālik said, "The people of knowledge consider that she has to make up for each day of the fast that she misses as Allah, the Exalted and Glorified, says, '*But any of you who are ill or on a journey should fast a number of other days,*' (2:185) and they consider this pregnancy as a sickness, in addition to her fear for her child."

53 Yaḥyā related to me from Mālik from 'Abd ar-Raḥmān ibn al-Qāsim that his father used to say, "If someone has to make up for days not fasted in Ramaḍān and does not do them before the next Ramaḍān comes although he is strong enough to do so, he should feed a poor man with a *mudd* of wheat for every day that he has missed, and he has to fast the days he owes as well."

Yaḥyā related to me from Mālik that he had heard the same thing from Sa'īd ibn Jubayr.

18.20 Making up days of Ramaḍān in general

54 Yaḥyā related to me from Mālik from Yaḥyā ibn Sa'īd from Abū Salama ibn 'Abd ar-Raḥmān that he heard 'Ā'isha, the wife of the Prophet ﷺ, say, "I used to have to make up days from Ramaḍān and not be able to do them until Sha'bān came."

18.21 Fasting the "Day of Doubt"

55 Yaḥyā related to me from Mālik that he had heard the people of knowledge telling people not to fast on the day in Sha'bān when there was doubt (about whether it was Sha'bān or Ramaḍān), if they intended by it the fast of Ramaḍān. They considered that whoever fasted on that day without having seen (the new moon) had to make up that day if it later became clear that it really was part of Ramaḍān. They did not see any harm in voluntary fasting on that day.

Mālik said, "This is what we do, and what I have seen the people of knowledge in our city doing."

18.22 The Fast in General

56 Yaḥyā related to me from Mālik from Abū an-Naḍr, the *mawlā* of ʿUmar ibn ʿUbaydullāh, from Abū Salama ibn ʿAbd ar-Rahmān that ʿĀʾisha, the wife of the Prophet ﷺ, said, "The Messenger of Allah ﷺ used to fast for so long that we thought he would never stop fasting, and he would go without fasting for so long that we thought he would never fast again. I never saw the Messenger of Allah ﷺ fast for a complete month except for Ramaḍān, and I never saw him fast more in any one month than he did in Shaʿbān."

57 Yaḥyā related to me from Mālik from Abū az-Zinād from al-Aʿraj from Abū Hurayra that the Messenger of Allah ﷺ said, "Fasting is a protection for you, so when you are fasting, do not behave obscenely or foolishly, and if anyone argues with you or abuses you, say, 'I am fasting, I am fasting.'"

58 Yaḥyā related to me from Mālik from Abū az-Zinād from al-Aʿraj from Abū Hurayra that the Messenger of Allah ﷺ said, "By the One in Whose hand my self is, the smell of the breath of a man fasting is better with Allah than the scent of musk. Allah says, 'He leaves his desires and his food and drink for My sake. Fasting is for Me and I reward it. Every good action is rewarded by ten times its kind, up to seven hundred times, except fasting, which is for Me, and I reward it.'"

59 Yaḥyā related to me from Mālik from his paternal uncle Abū Suhayl ibn Mālik from his father that Abū Hurayra said, "When Ramaḍān comes the gates of the Garden are opened and the gates of the Fire are locked, and the *shayṭāns* are chained."

60 Yaḥyā related to me from Mālik that he had heard that the people of knowledge did not disapprove of fasting people using tooth-sticks at any hour of the day in Ramaḍān, whether at the beginning or the end, nor had he heard any of the people of knowledge disapproving of or forbidding the practice.

Yaḥyā said that he heard Mālik say, about fasting for six days after breaking the fast at the end of Ramaḍān, that he had never seen any of the people of knowledge and fiqh fasting them. He said, "I have not heard that any of our predecessors used to do that, and the people of knowledge disapprove of it and they are afraid that it might become an innovation and that common and ignorant people might join to Ramaḍān what does not belong to it, if they were to think that the people of knowledge had given permission for that to be done and were seen doing it."

Yaḥyā said that he heard Mālik say, "I have never heard any of the people of knowledge and fiqh and those whom people take as an example forbidding fasting on the day of *jumu'a* (Friday). Fasting on it is good, and I have seen one of the people of knowledge fasting it, and it seemed to me that he was keen to do so."

19. *I'tikāf* in Ramaḍān

19.1 Concerning *i'tikāf* (retreat)

1 Yaḥyā related to me from Mālik from Ibn Shihāb from 'Urwa ibn az-Zubayr from 'Amra bint 'Abd ar-Raḥmān that 'Ā'isha, the wife of the Prophet ﷺ, said, "When the Messenger of Allah ﷺ did *i'tikāf* he would bring his head near to me and I would comb it. He would only go into the house to relieve himself."

2 Yaḥyā related to me from Mālik from Ibn Shihāb from 'Amra bint 'Abd ar-Raḥmān that when 'Ā'isha was doing *i'tikāf* she would only ask after sick people if she was walking but not if she was standing still.

Mālik said, "A person doing *i'tikāf* should not carry out his worldly obligations nor leave the mosque for them, nor should he help anyone. He should only leave the mosque to relieve himself. If he were able to go out to do things for people, then visiting the sick, praying over the dead and following funeral processions would be the things with the most claim on his going out."

Mālik said, "A person doing *i'tikāf* is not doing *i'tikāf* until he avoids what someone doing *i'tikāf* should avoid, namely, visiting the sick, praying over the dead, and going into houses, except to relieve himself."

3 Yaḥyā related to me from Mālik that he had asked Ibn Shihāb whether someone doing *i'tikāf* could go into a house to relieve himself, and he said, "Yes, there is no harm in that."

Mālik said, "The situation that we are all agreed upon here (in Madīna) is that there is no disapproval of anyone doing *i'tikāf* in a mosque where *jumu'a* is held. The only reason I see for disapproving of doing *i'tikāf* in a mosque where *jumu'a* is not held is that the man doing *i'tikāf* would have to leave the mosque where he was doing *i'tikāf* in order to go to *jumu'a*, or else not go to it at all. If, however, he is doing *i'tikāf* in a mosque where *jumu'a* is not held, and he does not have to go to *jumu'a* in any other mosque, then I see no harm in him doing *i'tikāf* there, because Allah, the Blessed and Exalted, says, '*While you are doing i'tikāf in mosques*,' (2:187) and refers to all mosques in general, without specifying any particular kind."

Mālik continued, "Accordingly, it is permissible for a man to do *i'tikāf* in a mosque where *jumu'a* is not held if he does not have to leave it to go to a mosque where *jumu'a* is held."

Mālik said, "A person doing *i'tikāf* should not spend the night anywhere except in the mosque where he is doing *i'tikāf*, unless his tent is in one of the courtyards of the mosque. I have never heard that someone doing *i'tikāf* can put up a shelter anywhere except in the mosque itself or in one of the courtyards of the mosque.

"Part of what shows that the person doing *i'tikāf* must spend the night in the mosque is 'Ā'isha saying that when the Messenger of Allah ﷺ, was doing *i'tikāf*, he would only go into the house to relieve himself. Nor should someone do *i'tikāf* on the roof of the mosque or in the minaret."

Mālik said, "The person who is going to do *i'tikāf* should enter the place where he wishes to do *i'tikāf* before the sun sets on the night when he wishes to begin his *i'tikāf*, so that he is ready to begin the *i'tikāf* at the beginning of the night when he is going to start his *i'tikāf*. A person doing *i'tikāf* should be occupied with his *i'tikāf*, and not turn his attention to other things which might occupy him, such as trading or whatever. There is no harm, however, if someone doing *i'tikāf* tells someone to do something for him regarding his estate, or the affairs of his family, or tells someone to sell some property of his, or something else that does not occupy him directly. There is no harm in him arranging for someone else to do that for him if it is a simple matter."

Mālik said, "I have never heard any of the people of knowledge mentioning any modification as far as how to do *i'tikāf* is concerned. *I'tikāf* is an act of worship like the prayer, fasting, the *Ḥajj*, and similar acts, whether they are obligatory or voluntary. Anyone who begins doing any of these acts should do them according to what has come down in the *Sunna*. He should not start doing anything in them that the Muslims have not done, whether it is a modification that he imposes on others, or one that he begins doing himself. The Messenger of Allah ﷺ practised *i'tikāf*, and the Muslims know what the *sunna* of *i'tikāf* is."

Mālik said, "*I'tikāf* and *jiwār* mean the same, and *i'tikāf* is the same for the village-dweller as it is for the nomad."

19.2 Essentials of *i'tikāf*

4 Yaḥyā related to me from Mālik that he had heard that al-Qāsim ibn Muḥammad and Nāfi', the *mawlā* of 'Abdullāh ibn 'Umar said, "You cannot do *i'tikāf* unless you are fasting, because of what Allah, the Blessed and Exalted, says in His Book, '*And eat and drink until the white thread becomes clear to you from the black thread of dawn, then complete the fast until night-time, but do not have intercourse with them while you are doing i'tikāf in mosques.*' (2:187) Allah only mentions *i'tikāf* together with fasting."

Mālik said, "That is the practice with us in Madīna. *I'tikāf* must be done while fasting."

19.3 Leaving *i'tikāf* for the *'Īd*

5 Yaḥyā related to me that Ziyād ibn 'Abd ar-Raḥmān said, "Mālik related to us from Sumayy, the *mawlā* of Abū Bakr ibn 'Abd ar-Raḥmān, that Abū Bakr ibn 'Abd ar-Raḥmān was once doing *i'tikāf* and he would go out to relieve himself in a closed room under a roofed passage in Khālid ibn Walīd's house. Otherwise he did not leave his place of *i'tikāf* until he went to pray the *'Īd* with the Muslims."

6 Yaḥyā related to me from Ziyād from Mālik that he saw some of the people of knowledge who, when they did *i'tikāf* in the last ten days of Ramaḍān, would not go back to their families until they had attended the *'Īd al-Fiṭr* with the people.

Ziyād said that Mālik said, "I heard this from the people of excellence who have passed away, and it is what I like most out of what I have heard about the matter."

19.4 Making up for the *i'tikāf* (not done)

7 Ziyād related to me from Mālik from Ibn Shihāb from 'Amra bint 'Abd ar-Raḥmān from 'Ā'isha that the Messenger of Allah ﷺ wanted to do *i'tikāf*, and, when he went off to the place where he wanted to do *i'tikāf*, he found some tents there, which were 'Ā'isha's tent, Ḥafsa's tent, and Zaynab's tent. When he saw them he asked about them and someone told him that they were the tents of 'Ā'isha, Ḥafsa and Zaynab. The Messenger of Allah ﷺ said, "Do you say they intended piety by them?" Then he left, and did not do *i'tikāf* until Shawwāl, when he then did it for ten days.

Mālik was asked whether someone who went into a mosque to do *i'tikāf* for the last ten days of Ramaḍān and stayed there for a day or two but then became ill and left the mosque had to do *i'tikāf* for the number of days that were left from the ten or not, and if he did have to do so, then what month should he do it in, and he replied, "He should make up whatever he has to do of the *i'tikāf* when he recovers, whether in Ramaḍān or otherwise. I have heard that the Messenger of Allah ﷺ once wanted to do *i'tikāf* in Ramaḍān, but then came back without having done so, and then when Ramaḍān had gone, he did *i'tikāf* for ten days in Shawwāl.

"Someone who does *i'tikāf* voluntarily in Ramaḍān and someone who has to do *i'tikāf* are in the same position regarding what is lawful for them and what is unlawful. I have not heard that the Messenger of Allah ﷺ ever did *i'tikāf* other than voluntarily."

Mālik said that if a woman went into *i'tikāf* and then menstruated during her *i'tikāf*, she should return to her house and, when she was pure again, then she should return to the mosque at whatever time it was that she became pure. She should then continue her *i'tikāf* from where she left off. This ruling is the same for a woman who had to fast two consecutive months, who then menstruates and then becomes pure: she too continues the fast from where she had to stop and does not delay doing so.

8 Ziyād related to me from Mālik from Ibn Shihāb that the Messenger of Allah ﷺ used to go to relieve himself in houses.

Mālik said, "Someone doing *i'tikāf* should not leave for his parents' funeral or for anything else."

19.5 Marriage in *i'tikāf*

Mālik said, "There is no harm in someone who is in *i'tikāf* entering into a marriage contract as long as there is no physical relationship. A woman in *i'tikāf* may also be betrothed as long as there is no physical relationship. What is forbidden for someone in *i'tikāf*, in relation to his womenfolk during the day, is also forbidden for him during the night."

Yaḥyā said that Ziyād said that Mālik said, "It is not lawful for a man to have intercourse with his wife while he is in *i'tikāf*, nor for him to take pleasure in her by kissing her, or whatever. However, I have not heard anyone disapproving of a man or woman in *i'tikāf* getting married as long as there is no physical relationship. Marriage is not disapproved of for someone fasting. There is, however, a distinction between the marriage of someone in *i'tikāf* and that of someone who is *muḥrim*, in that someone who is in *iḥrām* can eat, drink, visit the sick and attend funerals, but cannot put on perfume, whilst a man or woman in *i'tikāf* can put on oil and perfume and groom their hair, but cannot attend funerals or pray over the dead or visit the sick. Thus their situations with regard to marriage are different. This is the *sunna* as it has come down to us regarding marriage for those who are in *iḥrām*, doing *i'tikāf*, or fasting."

19.6 *Laylat al-Qadr* (The Night of Power)

9 Yaḥyā related to me from Mālik from Yazīd ibn 'Abdullāh ibn al-Hādi from Muḥammad ibn Ibrāhīm al-Hārith at-Taymi from Abū Salama ibn 'Abd ar-Raḥmān that Abū Sa'īd al-Khudrī said, "The Messenger of Allah ﷺ used to do *i'tikāf* in the middle ten days of Ramaḍān. One year he was doing *i'tikāf* and then, when it came to the night of the twenty-first, which was the night before the morning when he would normally have finished his *i'tikāf*, he said, 'Those who have done *i'tikāf* with me should continue doing *i'tikāf* for the last ten days. I was shown this night in a dream and then I was made to forget it. I saw myself prostrating the following morning in water and mud. Look for it during the last ten days, and look for it on the odd nights."

Abū Sa'īd continued, "The sky poured with rain that night and the mosque, which had a roof (made of palm-fronds), was soaked. With my own eyes I saw the Messenger of Allah ﷺ leave with traces of water and mud on his forehead and nose, in the morning after the night of the twenty-first."

10 Ziyād related to me from Mālik from Hishām ibn 'Urwa from his father that the Messenger of Allah ﷺ said, "Search for *Laylat al-Qadr* in the last ten days of Ramaḍān."

11 Ziyād related to me from Mālik from 'Abdullāh ibn Dīnar from 'Abdullāh ibn 'Umar that the Messenger of Allah ﷺ said, "Search for *Laylat al-Qadr* in the last seven days."

12 Ziyād related to me from Mālik from Abū an-Naḍr, the *mawlā* of 'Umar ibn 'Ubaydullāh, that 'Abdullāh ibn Unays al-Juhanī said to the Messenger of Allah ﷺ, "Messenger of Allah, I am a man whose house is a long way off. Tell me one night so that I can stop my journey for it." The Messenger of Allah ﷺ said, "Stop on the twenty-third night of Ramaḍān."

13 Ziyād related to me from Mālik from Ḥumayd aṭ-Ṭawīl that Anas ibn Mālik said, "The Messenger of Allah ﷺ came out to us in Ramaḍān and said, 'I was shown a certain night in Ramaḍān and then two men quarrelled and it was taken away. Look for it on the twenty-seventh, twenty-ninth and twenty-fifth.'"

14 Ziyād related to me from Mālik from Nāfi' from Ibn 'Umar that some of the Companions of the Messenger of Allah ﷺ were shown in a dream that the *Laylat al-Qadr* is during the last seven days. The Messenger of Allah ﷺ said, "I think that your dreams agree about the last seven nights. Those who want to look for it, should look for it in the last seven nights."

15 Ziyād related to me from Mālik that he had heard a man he trusted of the people of knowledge say, "The Messenger of Allah ﷺ was shown the life-spans of the people (who had gone) before him, or what Allah willed of that, and it was as if the lives of the people of his community had become too short for them to be able to do as many good actions as others before them had been able to do with their long lives, so Allah gave him *Laylat al-Qadr*, which is better than a thousand months."

16 Ziyād related to me from Mālik that he had heard that Sa'īd ibn al-Musayyab used to say, "Whoever is present at *'Ishā'* on *Laylat al-Qadr* has taken his portion from it."

20. Ḥajj

20.1 The *ghusl* of *iḥrām*

1 Yaḥyā related to me from Mālik from 'Abd ar-Raḥmān ibn al-Qāsim from his father from Asmā' bint 'Umays that she gave birth to Muḥammad ibn Abī Bakr at al-Bayḍā'. Abū Bakr mentioned this to the Messenger of Allah ﷺ and he said, "Tell her to do *ghusl* and then enter *iḥrām*."

2 Yaḥyā related to me from Mālik from Yaḥyā ibn Sa'īd from Sa'īd ibn al-Musayyab that Asmā' bint 'Umays gave birth to Muḥammad ibn Abī Bakr at Dhū al-Ḥulayfa and Abū Bakr told her to do *ghusl* and then enter *iḥrām*.

3 Yaḥyā related to me from Mālik from Nāfi' that 'Abdullāh ibn 'Umar used to do *ghusl* for *iḥrām* before he entered *iḥrām*, and for entering Makka, and for standing on the afternoon of 'Arafa.

20.2 *Ghusl* in *iḥrām*

4 Yaḥyā related to me from Mālik from Zayd ibn Aslam from Ibrāhīm ibn 'Abdullāh ibn Ḥunayn from his father 'Abdullāh ibn Ḥunayn that 'Abdullāh ibn 'Abbās and al-Miswar ibn Makhrama once had a disagreement at al-Abwā'. 'Abdullah said that someone in *iḥrām* could wash his head, and al-Miswar ibn Makhrama maintained that someone in *iḥrām* could not wash his head.

'Abdullāh ibn Ḥunayn continued, "'Abdullāh ibn 'Abbās sent me to Abū

Ayyūb al-Anṣārī, and I found him doing *ghusl* between the posts of a well, screened by a garment. I greeted him and he said, 'Who is that?' I replied, 'I am 'Abdullāh ibn Ḥunayn. 'Abdullāh ibn 'Abbās sent me to you to ask how the Messenger of Allah ﷺ, used to wash his head when he was in *iḥrām*.'"

He continued, "Abū Ayyūb put his hand on the garment and pulled it down until I could see his head. He said to the man who was pouring out the water for him, 'Pour,' and he poured some over his head. Then he passed his hands over his head from the front to the back and then to the front again, and then said, 'I saw the Messenger of Allah ﷺ doing it like this.'"

5 Mālik related to me from Ḥumayd ibn Qays from 'Aṭā' ibn Abī Rabāḥ that 'Umar ibn al-Khaṭṭāb once asked Ya'lā ibn Munya, who was pouring out water for him while he was having a *ghusl*, to pour some on his head. Ya'lā said, "Are you trying to make me responsible? I will only pour it out if you tell me to do so." 'Umar ibn al-Khaṭṭāb said, "Pour: it will only make (my head) more unkempt."

6 Mālik related to me from Nāfi' that 'Abdullāh ibn 'Umar would spend the night between the two trails in the valley of Dhū Ṭuwā when he was approaching Makka. Then he would pray *Ṣubḥ*, and after that he would enter Makka by the trail which is at the highest part of Makka. He would never enter Makka if he was coming for *ḥajj* or *'umra* without doing *ghusl* beforehand when he was near Makka at Dhū Ṭuwā, and he would tell whoever was with him to do likewise.

7 Yaḥyā related to me from Mālik from Nāfi' that 'Abdullāh ibn 'Umar would never wash his head while he was in *iḥrām* unless if he had to do *ghusl* because of a wet dream.

Mālik said, "I have heard the people of knowledge say that there is no harm in someone who is in *iḥrām* rubbing his head with certain kinds of plants after he has stoned the *Jamrat al-'Aqaba* but before he has shaved his head, because once he has finished stoning the *Jamrat al-'Aqaba* it is *ḥalāl* for him to kill lice, to shave his head, to clean himself of body hair, and to wear normal clothes."

20.3 Clothes forbidden in *iḥrām*

8 Yaḥyā related to me from Mālik from Nāfi' from 'Abdullāh ibn 'Umar that a man once asked the Messenger of Allah ﷺ what clothes someone in *iḥrām* could wear, and the Messenger of Allah ﷺ said, "Do not wear shirts, turbans, trousers, burnouses, or leather socks except if you cannot find sandals. In that case you can wear leather socks, but cut them off below the ankles. Do not wear any clothes that have been touched by saffron or yellow dye (*wars*)."

Yaḥyā said that Mālik was asked about the *ḥadīth* attributed to the Prophet ﷺ, "Whoever cannot find a waist-wrapper should wear trousers," and he said, "I have never heard this, and I do not think that someone who is in *iḥrām* can wear trousers, because among the things which the Prophet ﷺ forbade someone in *iḥrām* to wear were trousers, and he did not make any exception for them although he did make an exception for leather socks."

20.4 Clothes worn in *iḥrām*

9 Yaḥyā related to me from Mālik from 'Abdullāh ibn Dīnār that 'Abdullāh ibn 'Umar said, "The Messenger of Allah ﷺ forbade anyone in *iḥrām* to wear a garment which had been dyed with saffron or yellow dye (*wars*), and said, 'Anyone that cannot find sandals can wear leather socks, but he should cut them off below the ankles.'"

10 Yaḥyā related to me from Mālik from Nāfi' that he had heard Aslam, the *mawlā* of 'Umar ibn al-Khaṭṭāb, telling 'Abdullāh ibn 'Umar that 'Umar ibn al-Khaṭṭāb once saw a dyed garment on Ṭalḥa ibn 'Ubaydullāh while he was in *iḥrām* and 'Umar said, "What is this dyed garment, Talḥa?" and Ṭalha said, "*Amīr al-Mu'minīn*, it is only mud." 'Umar said, "You and your like are taken by people as imāms, and if an ignorant man were to see this garment he would say that Ṭalha ibn 'Ubaydullāh used to wear a dyed robe while he was in *iḥrām*. So do not wear any form of dyed clothes."

11 Yaḥyā related to me from Mālik from Hishām ibn 'Urwa from his

father that Asmā' bint Abī Bakr had worn clothes that were completely dyed with safflower while she was in *iḥrām* – there was not any saffron on them, though.

Yaḥyā said that Mālik was asked if a garment which had been perfumed could be used for *iḥrām* if the smell of the perfume had gone, and he said, "Yes, as long as there is no saffron or yellow dye (*wars*) on it."

20.5 Wearing a belt in *iḥrām*

12 Yaḥyā related to me from Mālik from Nāfi' that 'Abdullāh ibn 'Umar used to disapprove of anybody wearing a belt or girdle while in *iḥrām*.

13.1 Yaḥyā related to me from Mālik from Yaḥyā ibn Sa'īd that he heard Sa'īd ibn al-Musayyab say, about the girdle worn by some one in *iḥrām* under his clothes, "There is no harm in it if he ties the ends together as a belt."

Mālik said, "This is what I like most out of what I have heard about the matter."

20.6 Veiling the face in *iḥrām*

13.2[3] Yaḥyā related to me from Mālik from Yaḥyā ibn Sa'īd that al-Qāsim ibn Muḥammad said that al-Furāfiṣa ibn 'Umayr al-Ḥanafī saw 'Uthmān ibn 'Affān at al-'Arj, and he was covering his face while in *iḥrām*.

13.3[3] Yaḥyā related to me from Mālik from Nāfi' that 'Abdullāh ibn 'Umar used to say that a man in *iḥrām* should not veil anything above his chin.

14 Yaḥyā related to me from Mālik from Nāfi' that 'Abdullāh ibn 'Umar shrouded his son Wāqid ibn 'Abdullāh, who had died at al-Juḥfa while in *iḥrām*, and he veiled his head and face and said, "If we had not been in *iḥrām* we ourselves would have perfumed him."

3 The Arabic Edition repeats the numbering on these *ḥadīths*.

Mālik commented, "A man can only do things while he is alive. When he is dead, his actions stop."

15 Yaḥyā related to me from Mālik from Nāfiʿ that 'Abdullāh ibn 'Umar used to say that a woman in *iḥrām* should wear neither a veil nor gloves.

16 Yaḥyā related to me from Mālik from Hishām ibn 'Urwa that Fāṭima bint al-Mundhir said, "We used to veil our faces when we were in *iḥrām* in the company of Asmā' bint Abī Bakr aṣ-Ṣiddiq."

20.7 Wearing perfume during *ḥajj*

17 Yaḥyā related to me from Mālik from 'Abd ar-Raḥmān ibn al-Qāsim from his father that 'Ā'isha, the wife of the Prophet ﷺ, said, "I perfumed the Messenger of Allah ﷺ for his *iḥrām* before he entered *iḥrām*, and when he came out of *iḥrām* before he did *ṭawāf* of the House."

18 Yaḥyā related to me from Mālik from Ḥumayd ibn Qays from 'Aṭā' ibn Rabāḥ that a bedouin came to the Messenger of Allah ﷺ when he was at Ḥunayn, and he was wearing a shirt with traces of yellow on it. He said, "Messenger of Allah, I have entered *iḥrām* for *'umra*. What should I do?" The Messenger of Allah ﷺ told him, "Take off your shirt and wash off this yellowness and do in *'umra* as you would do on *ḥajj*."

19 Yaḥyā related to me from Mālik from Nāfiʿ from Aslam, the *mawlā* of 'Umar ibn al-Khaṭṭāb, that 'Umar ibn al-Khaṭṭāb noticed the smell of perfume while he was at ash-Shajara and asked, "Who is this smell of perfume coming from?" Mu'āwiya ibn Abī Sufyān answered, "From me, *Amīr al-Mu'minīn*." 'Umar said, "From you? By the life of Allah!" Mu'āwiya explained, "Umm Habība perfumed me, *Amīr al-Mu'minīn*." 'Umar then said, "You must go back and wash it off."

20 Yaḥyā related to me from Mālik from aṣ-Ṣalt ibn Zubayd from more than one of his family that 'Umar ibn al-Khaṭṭāb noticed the smell of perfume while he was at ash-Shajara. Kathīr ibn aṣ-Ṣalt was at his side, and 'Umar asked, "Who is this smell of perfume coming from?" and Kathīr answered, "From me, *Amīr al-Mu'minīn*. I matted my hair with

perfume and I intended not to shave it." 'Umar said, "Go to a *sharaba* and rub your head until it is clean," and Kathīr did so.

Mālik explained, "A *sharaba* is the ditch at the base of a date-palm."

21 Yaḥyā related to me from Mālik from Yaḥyā ibn Sa'īd and 'Abdullāh ibn Abī Bakr and Rabī'a ibn Abī 'Abd ar-Raḥmān that al-Walīd ibn 'Abd al-Mālik asked Sālim ibn 'Abdullāh and Khārija ibn Zayd ibn Thābit if he could use perfume after he had stoned the *jamra* and shaved his head but before he had left for the *Ṭawāf al-Ifāḍa*. Sālim forbade him to do so, but Khārija ibn Zayd ibn Thābit said that he could.

Mālik said, "There is no harm in a man oiling himself with an oil which does not have any perfume in it, either before he enters *iḥrām*, or before he leaves Mina for the *Ṭawāf al-Ifāḍa*, if he has stoned the *jamra*."

Yaḥyā said that Mālik was asked whether someone in *iḥrām* could eat food with saffron in it, and he said, "There is no harm in someone in *iḥrām* eating it if it has been cooked. If, however, it has not been cooked he should not eat it."

20.8 Points of entry for *iḥrām* (*mawāqīt*)

22 Yaḥyā related to me from Mālik from Nāfi' from 'Abdullāh ibn 'Umar that the Messenger of Allah ﷺ said, "The people of Madīna should enter *iḥrām* at Dhū al-Ḥulayfa, the people of Syria should do so at al-Juḥfa, and the people of Najd should do so at Qarn."

'Abdullāh ibn 'Umar added, "I have heard that the Messenger of Allah ﷺ said, 'The people of Yemen should enter *iḥrām* at Yalamlam.'"

23 Yaḥyā related to me from Mālik from 'Abdullāh ibn Dīnār that 'Abdullāh ibn 'Umar said, "The Messenger of Allah ﷺ told the people of Madīna to enter *iḥrām* at Dhū al-Ḥulayfa, the people of Syria to do so at al-Juḥfa, and the people of Najd to do so at Qarn."

24 'Abdullāh ibn 'Umar said, "I heard these three from the Messenger of

Allah ﷺ. I was also told that the Messenger of Allah ﷺ said, 'The people of Yemen should enter *iḥrām* at Yalamlam.'"

25 Yaḥyā related to me from Mālik from Nāfi' that 'Abdullāh ibn 'Umar once entered *iḥrām* at al-Fur'.

26 Yaḥyā related to me from Mālik from a reliable source that 'Abdullāh ibn 'Umar once entered *iḥrām* at Ilyā' (Jerusalem).

27 Yaḥyā related to me from Mālik that he had heard that the Messenger of Allah ﷺ once entered *iḥrām* at al-Ji'irrāna (near Makka) for an *'umra.*

20.9 The method of entering *iḥrām*

28 Yaḥyā related to me from Mālik from 'Abdullāh ibn 'Umar that the *talbiya* of the Messenger of Allah ﷺ was, "I am at Your service, O Allah, I am at Your service. I am at Your service, You have no partner. I am at Your service. Praise and blessing belong to You, and the Kingdom. You have no partner."

Labbayk Allāhumma labbayk. Labbayka lā sharīka laka labbayk. Inna'l-ḥamda wa'n-ni'mata laka wa'l-mulk. Lā sharīka lak.

Mālik said that 'Abdullāh ibn 'Umar used to add, "I am at Your service, I am at Your service. I am at Your service and at Your call. Good is in Your hands, and I am at Your service. Our desire is for You, and our action."

Labbayka labbayka labbayka wa sa'dayk. Wa'l-khayru bi yadayka labbayk. Wa'r-raghbā'u ilayka wa'l-'amal.

29 Yaḥyā related to me from Mālik from Hishām ibn 'Urwa from his father that the Messenger of Allah ﷺ used to pray two *rak'as* in the mosque at Dhū al-Ḥulayfa, and then, when he had got on to his camel and it had stood up, he would begin doing *talbiya.*

30 Yaḥyā related to me from Mālik from Musā ibn 'Uqba that Sālim ibn 'Abdullāh heard his father say, "Your claim that the Messenger of Allah

ﷺ began doing *talbiya* from this desert of yours is not true, because he only began doing *talbiya* from the mosque, i.e. the mosque of Dhū al-Ḥulayfa."

"Your claim that the Messenger of Allah ﷺ began doing *talbiya* from this desert of yours is not true." i.e. you say that he assumed *iḥrām* from there when he did not, in fact, do so.

31 Yaḥyā related to me from Mālik from Sa'īd ibn Abī Sa'īd al-Maqburī that 'Ubayd ibn Jurayj once said to 'Abdullāh ibn 'Umar, "Abū 'Abd ar-Raḥmān, I have seen you doing four things which I have never seen any of your companions doing." He said, "What are they, Ibn Jurayj?" and he replied, "I have seen you touching only the two Yamānī corners, I have seen you wearing hairless sandals, I have seen you using yellow dye, and, when you were at Makka and everybody had started doing *talbiya* after seeing the new moon, I saw that you did not do so until the eighth of Dhū al-Ḥijja."

'Abdullāh ibn 'Umar replied, "As for the corners, I only ever saw the Messenger of Allah ﷺ touching the two Yamānī corners. As for the sandals, I saw the Messenger of Allah ﷺ wearing hairless sandals and doing *wuḍū'* in them, and I like wearing them. As for using yellow dye, I saw the Messenger of Allah ﷺ using it, and I also like to use it for dyeing things with. As for doing *talbiya*, I never saw the Messenger of Allah ﷺ begin doing so until he had set out on the animal he was riding on (i.e. for Minā and 'Arafa)."

32 Yaḥyā related to me from Mālik from Nāfi' that 'Abdullah ibn 'Umar used to pray in the mosque of Dhū al-Ḥulayfa, and then go outside and get on his camel and when his camel had stood up he would begin to do *talbiya*.

33 Yaḥyā related to me from Mālik that he had heard that 'Abd al-Mālik ibn Marwān had started to do *talbiya* at the mosque of Dhū al-Ḥulayfa, after the animal he was riding on had stood up, and that Abān ibn 'Uthmān had told him to do this.

20.10 Raising the voice in *talbiya*

34 Yaḥyā related to me from Mālik from 'Abdullāh ibn Abī Bakr ibn Muḥammad ibn 'Amr ibn Ḥazm from 'Abd al-Mālik ibn Abī Bakr ibn al-Ḥārith ibn Hishām from Khallād ibn as-Sā'ib al-Anṣārī from his father that the Messenger of Allah ﷺ said, "Jibrīl came to me and told me to tell my Companions, or whoever was with me, to raise their voices when doing *talbiya*."

35 Yaḥyā related to me from Mālik that he had heard the people of knowledge say, "Women do not have to raise their voices when they are doing *talbiya*, and a woman should only speak loudly enough to hear herself."

Mālik said, "Someone who is in *iḥrām* should not raise his voice when doing *talbiya* if he is in a mosque where there are groups of people. He should only speak loudly enough for himself and those who are near him to be able to hear, except in the *Masjid al-Ḥarām* and the mosque at Minā where he should raise his voice."

Mālik said, "I have heard some of the people of knowledge recommending (people to do) *talbiya* at the end of every prayer and at every rise on the route."

20.11 *Ḥajj al-ifrād*

36 Yaḥyā related to me from Mālik from Abū al-Aswad Muḥammad ibn 'Abd ar-Raḥmān, from 'Urwa ibn az-Zubayr, that 'Ā'isha, the wife of the Prophet ﷺ, said, "We set out with the Messenger of Allah ﷺ in the year of the Farewell *Ḥajj*, and some of us went into *iḥrām* to perform *'umra*, some of us went into *iḥrām* to perform *ḥajj* and *'umra*, and some of us went into *iḥrām* to perform *ḥajj* on its own. The Messenger of Allah ﷺ went into *iḥrām* to perform *ḥajj* on its own. Those who had gone into *iḥrām* perform do *'umra* came out of *iḥrām* (after doing *'umra*). Those who had gone into *iḥrām* to perform hajj on its own (*Ḥajj al-ifrād*), or to perform both *ḥajj* and *'umra* (*Ḥajj al-qirān*), did not come out of *iḥrām* until the Day of the Sacrifice."

37 Yaḥyā related to me from Mālik, from 'Abd ar-Raḥmān ibn al-Qāsim, from his father, from 'Ā'isha, *Umm al-Mu'minīn*, that the Messenger of Allah ﷺ performed *Ḥajj al-Ifrād.*

38 Yaḥyā related to me from Mālik, from Abū al-Aswad Muḥammad ibn 'Abd ar-Raḥmān, from 'Urwa ibn az-Zubayr, from 'Ā'isha, *Umm al-Mu'minīn*, that the Messenger of Allah ﷺ performed *Ḥajj* al-Ifrād.

39 Yaḥyā related to me from Mālik that he had heard the people of knowledge say, "If someone goes into *iḥrām* to perform *Ḥajj al-ifrād*, he cannot then go into *iḥrām* to perform *'umra.*"

Mālik said, "This is what I have found the people of knowledge in our city doing."

20.12 Performing *ḥajj* and *'umra* together (*Ḥajj al-Qirān*)

40 Yaḥyā related to me from Mālik, from Ja'far ibn Muḥammad, from his father, that al-Miqdād ibn al-Aswad once went to see 'Alī ibn Abī Ṭālib at as-Suqyā, where he was feeding some young camels of his with a mash of meal and leaves, and he said to him, "This man 'Uthmān ibn 'Affān is telling people that they cannot perform *Ḥajj al-qirān.*"

Al-Miqdād said, "'Alī ibn Abī Ṭālib went off with bits of meal and leaves on his forearms – and I shall never forget the sight of the meal and the leaves on his arms – and went to see 'Uthmān ibn 'Affān and asked him, 'Are you saying then that people cannot perform *Ḥajj al-Qirān?*' 'Uthmān replied, 'That is my opinion.' Whereupon 'Alī got angry and went out saying, 'I am at your service, O Allah, I am at your service for *Ḥajj al-Qirān.*'"

Mālik said, "Our position (here in Madīna) is that someone who does *Ḥajj al-qirān* should not remove any of his hair, nor should he come out of *iḥrām* in any way until he has sacrificed an animal, if he has one. He should come out of *iḥrām* at Minā, on the Day of Sacrifice."

41 Yaḥyā related to me from Mālik from Muḥammad ibn 'Abd ar-

Raḥmān, from Sulaymān ibn Yasār, that when the Messenger of Allah ﷺ, set out for *ḥajj* in the year of the Farewell *Ḥajj*, some of his companions went into *iḥrām* to perform *ḥajj* on its own, some of them combined *ḥajj* and *'umra*, and some went into *iḥrām* to perform *'umra* on its own. Those who had gone into *iḥrām* to perform *ḥajj*, or *ḥajj* and *'umra* together, did not come out of *iḥrām*, whilst those who had gone into *iḥrām* to perform *'umra* (on its own) came out of *iḥrām*.

42 Yaḥyā related to me from Mālik that he had heard some of the people of knowledge say, "If someone goes into *iḥrām* to perform *'umra* and then wants to go into *iḥrām* to do *ḥajj* as well, he can do so, as long as he has not done *ṭawāf* of the House and *sa'y* between Safā and Marwa. This is what 'Abdullāh ibn 'Umar did when he said, 'If I am blocked from the House we shall do what we did when we were with the Messenger of Allah ﷺ.' He then turned to his companions and said, 'It is the same either way. I call you to witness that I have decided in favour of *ḥajj* and *'umra* together.'"

Mālik said, "The Companions of the Messenger of Allah ﷺ went into *iḥrām* to perform *'umra* in the year of the Farewell *Ḥajj*, and the Messenger of Allah ﷺ, said to them, 'Anyone that has a sacrificial animal with him should go into *iḥrām* to perform *ḥajj* and *'umra* together, and he should not come out of *iḥrām* until he has finished both.'"

20.13 When to stop the *talbiya*

43 Yaḥyā related to me from Mālik that Muḥammad ibn Abī Bakr ath-Thaqafī once asked Anas ibn Mālik, while the two of them were going from Minā to 'Arafa, "What did you use to do on this day when you were with the Messenger of Allah ﷺ?" He said, "Those of us who were saying the *talbiya* would continue doing so, and no one disapproved of it, and those of us who were saying *'Allāhu akbar'* would continue doing so, and no one disapproved of that either."

44 Yaḥyā related to me from Mālik, from Ja'far ibn Muḥammad, from his father, that 'Alī ibn Abī Ṭālib used to say the *talbiya* while on *ḥajj* until after noon on the Day of 'Arafa, when he would stop doing so.

Yaḥyā said that Mālik said, "This is what the people of knowledge in our city are still doing."

45 Yaḥyā related to me from Mālik, from 'Abd ar-Raḥmān ibn al-Qāsim, from his father, that 'Ā'isha, the wife of the Prophet ﷺ, would stop saying the *talbiya* when she arrived at the place of standing (i.e. 'Arafa).

46 Yaḥyā related to me from Mālik, from Nāfi', that when 'Abdullāh ibn 'Umar was doing *ḥajj* he would keep saying the *talbiya* until he reached the *Ḥaram* and did *ṭawāf* of the House and *sa'y* between Safā and Marwa. He would then say the *talbiya* until he left Minā to go to 'Arafa, at which point he would stop doing so. If he was doing *'umra* he would stop saying the *talbiya* on entering the *Ḥaram*.

47 Yaḥyā related to me from Mālik that Ibn Shihāb used to say, "'Abdullāh ibn 'Umar would never say the *talbiya* while he was doing *ṭawāf* of the House."

48 Yaḥyā related to me from Mālik from 'Alqama ibn Abī 'Alqama from his mother that 'Ā'isha, *Umm al-Mu'minīn*, used to camp on the plain of 'Arafa at a place called Namira, and then later she changed to another place called al-Arak. She said, "'Ā'isha, and those who were with her, would say the *talbiya* while she was at the place where they were camping, and then, when she had mounted and set out towards the place of standing, she would stop doing so."

She continued, "'Ā'isha used to perform *'umra* when she was in Makka after the *Ḥajj* was over, in the month of Dhū al-Ḥijja. Then she stopped doing that, and instead would set out before the new moon of Muḥarram for al-Juḥfa, where she would stay until she saw the new moon, and then, when she had seen the new moon, she would go into *iḥrām* to perform *'umra*."

49 Yaḥyā related to me from Mālik from Yaḥyā ibn Sa'īd that 'Umar ibn 'Abd al-'Azīz was once going from Minā (to 'Arafa) on the Day of 'Arafa and heard the *takbīr* being said loudly, so he sent the guard to shout out to the people, "O people, you should be saying the *talbiya*."

20.14 How the people of Makka, and those besides them living there, go into *iḥrām*

50 Yaḥyā related to me from Mālik from 'Abd ar-Rahmān ibn al-Qāsim from his father that 'Umar ibn al-Khaṭṭāb said, "People of Makka, why is it that people arrive dishevelled while you still have oil on your hair? Go into *iḥrām* when you see the new moon."

51 Yaḥyā related to me from Mālik from Hishām ibn 'Urwa that 'Abdullāh ibn az-Zubayr stayed in Makka for nine years. He would go into *iḥrām* for *ḥajj* at the beginning of Dhū al-Ḥijja, and 'Urwa ibn az-Zubayr, who was with him, would do likewise.

Yaḥyā said that Mālik said, "The people of Makka and whoever else is living there besides them should go into *iḥrām* for *ḥajj* if they are in Makka, and anyone that is living in the centre of Makka and is not one of the people of Makka should not leave the *Ḥaram*."

Yaḥyā said that Mālik said, "Someone who goes into *iḥrām* for *ḥajj* in Makka should delay *ṭawāf* of the House and the *sa'y* between Safā and Marwa until he has come back from Minā, which is what 'Abdullāh ibn 'Umar used to do."

Mālik was asked what the people of Madīna, or anybody else, should do about *ṭawāf* if they went into *iḥrām* in Makka at the beginning of Dhū al-Ḥijja, and he said, "They should delay the obligatory *ṭawāf*, which is the one they combine with the *sa'y* between Ṣafā and Marwa, but they can do whatever other *ṭawāf* they want to, and they should pray two *rak'as* every time they complete seven circuits, which is what the Companions of the Messenger of Allah ﷺ, did when they had gone into *iḥrām* to do *ḥajj*. They delayed the *ṭawāf* of the House and the *sa'y* between Ṣafā and Marwa until they had come back from Mina. 'Abdullāh ibn 'Umar also did this, going into *iḥrām* for *ḥajj* in Makka at the beginning of Dhū al-Ḥijja, and then delaying *ṭawāf* of the House and the *sa'y* between Safā and Marwa until he had come back from Minā."

Mālik was asked whether one of the people of Makka could go into *iḥrām* to do *'umra* in the centre of Makka, and he said, "No. He should go outside the *Ḥaram* and go into *iḥrām* there."

20.15 Situations when *iḥrām* is not obligatory for garlanding sacrificial animals

52 Yaḥyā related to me from Mālik from 'Abdullāh ibn Abī Bakr ibn Muḥammad that 'Amra bint 'Abd ar-Raḥmān told him that Ziyād ibn Abī Sufyān once wrote to 'Ā'isha, the wife of the Prophet ﷺ, saying "'Abdullāh ibn 'Abbās said that whatever was unlawful for someone performing *ḥajj* was also unlawful for someone who sent a sacrificial animal until the animal was sacrificed. I have sent one, so write and tell me what you say about this, or tell the man in charge of the animal what to do."

'Amra said that 'Ā'isha said, "It is not as Ibn 'Abbās has said. I once plaited the garlands for the sacrificial animal of the Messenger of Allah ﷺ, with my own two hands. Then after that the Messenger of Allah ﷺ put the garlands on the animal and then sent it with my father. And there was nothing that Allah had made lawful for the Messenger of Allah ﷺ that was unlawful for him until such time as the animal had been sacrificed."

53 Yaḥyā related to me from Mālik that Yaḥyā ibn Sa'īd said, "I asked 'Amra bint 'Abd ar-Raḥmān if there was anything that was unlawful for someone who sent a sacrificial animal (to Makka) but did not go there himself, and she told me that she had heard 'Ā'isha say, 'It is only someone who goes into *iḥrām* for *ḥajj* and begins saying the *talbiya* for whom things are unlawful.'"

54 Yaḥyā related to me from Mālik from Yaḥyā ibn Sa'īd from Muḥammad ibn Ibrāhīm ibn al-Hārith at-Taymī that Rabi'a ibn 'Abdullāh ibn al-Ḥudayr once saw a man in a state of *iḥrām* in Iraq. So he asked people about him and they said, "He has given directions for his sacrificial animal to be garlanded, and it is for that reason that he has put on *iḥrām*." Rabi'a said, "I then met 'Abdullāh ibn az-Zubayr and so I mentioned this to him and he said, 'By the Lord of the Ka'ba, an innovation!'"

Mālik was asked about someone who set out with his own sacrificial animal and marked it and garlanded it at Dhū al-Ḥulayfa, but did not go into *iḥrām* until he had reached al-Juḥfa, and he said, "I do not like that, and whoever does so has not acted properly. He should only garland his sacrificial animal or mark it when he goes into *iḥrām* unless it is someone who does not intend to do *ḥajj*, in which case he sends it off and stays with his family."

Mālik was asked if someone who was not in *iḥrām* could set out with a sacrificial animal, and he said, "Yes. There is no harm in that."

He was also asked to comment on the different views people had about what became unlawful for someone who garlanded a sacrificial animal but did not intend to perform either *ḥajj* or *'umra*, and he said, "What we go by as far as this is concerned is what 'Ā'isha, *Umm al-Mu'minīn*, said: 'The Messenger of Allah ﷺ sent his sacrificial animal off and did not go there himself, and there was nothing that Allah had made lawful for him that was unlawful for him until the animal had been sacrificed.'"

20.16 Menstruating women on *ḥajj*

55 Yaḥyā related to me from Mālik from Nāfi' that 'Abdullāh ibn 'Umar used to say, "A menstruating woman who wants to go into *iḥrām* to perform either *ḥajj* or *'umra* can do so if she so wishes, but she cannot do *ṭawāf* of the House nor the *sa'y* between Ṣafā and Marwa. She can participate in all the rituals along with everybody else, except that she cannot do *ṭawāf* of the House, nor the *sa'y* between Ṣafā and Marwa, nor can she come near the mosque until she is pure."

20.17 *'Umra* in the months of *ḥajj*

56 Yaḥyā related to me from Mālik that he had heard that the Messenger of Allah ﷺ performed *'umra* three times: in the year of Ḥudaybiya, in the year of *al-Qaḍiyya* (the Fulfilled *'Umra*), and in the year of al-Ji'irrāna.

57 Yaḥyā related to me from Mālik from Hishām ibn 'Urwa from his

father, that the Messenger of Allah ﷺ only performed three *'umras*, one of them in Shawwāl, and two in Dhū al-Qa'da.

58 Yaḥyā related to me from Mālik from 'Abd ar-Rahmān ibn Ḥarmala al-Aslamī that somebody asked Sa'īd ibn al-Musayyab, "Can I perform *'umra* before I perform *ḥajj*?" and Sa'īd said, "Yes, the Messenger of Allah ﷺ performed *'umra* before performing *ḥajj*."

59 Yaḥyā related to me from Mālik, from Ibn Shihāb from Sa'īd ibn al-Musayyab that 'Umar ibn Abī Salama once asked 'Umar ibn al-Khaṭṭāb for permission to perform *'umra* in Shawwāl. He gave him permission, so he perform *'umra* and then went back to his family, and he did not perform *ḥajj*.

20.18 When to stop saying the *talbiya* for *'umra*

60 Yaḥyā related to me from Mālik from Hishām ibn 'Urwa that this father would stop saying the *talbiya* when he entered the *Ḥaram* if he was performing *'umra*.

Mālik said that someone who went into *iḥrām* at at-Tan'īm should stop saying the *talbiya* when he saw the House.

Yaḥyā said that Mālik was asked where a man from the people of Madīna, or elsewhere, who had begun doing *'umra* at one of the *mīqāts*, should stop saying the *talbiya*, and he said, "Someone who goes into *iḥrām* at one of the *mīqāts* should stop saying the *talbiya* when he arrives at the *Ḥaram*."

Mālik added, "I have heard that 'Abdullāh ibn 'Umar used to do that."

20.19 *Ḥajj at-Tamattu'*

61 Yaḥyā related to me from Mālik from Ibn Shihāb that Muḥammad ibn 'Abdullāh ibn al-Ḥārith ibn Nawfal ibn 'Abd al-Muṭṭalib told him that in the year when Mu'āwiya ibn Abī Sufyān went on *ḥajj* he had heard

Sa'd ibn Abī Waqqāṣ and aḍ-Ḍaḥḥāk ibn Qays discussing *tamattu'* and combining *'umra* and *ḥajj*. Aḍ-Ḍaḥḥāk ibn Qays said, "Only someone who is ignorant of what Allah, the Exalted and Glorified, says would do that." Whereupon Sa'd said, "How wrong is what you have just said, son of my brother!" Aḍ-Ḍaḥḥāk said, "'Umar ibn al-Khattāb forbade that," and Sa'd retorted, "The Messenger of Allah ﷺ did it and we did it with him."

62 Yaḥyā related to me from Mālik from Ṣadaqa ibn Yasār that 'Abdullāh ibn 'Umar said, "By Allah, I would rather perform *'umra* before *ḥajj* and sacrifice an animal than perform *'umra* after *ḥajj* in the month of Dhū al-Ḥijja."

63 Yaḥyā related to me from Mālik from 'Abdullāh ibn Dīnār that 'Abdullāh ibn 'Umar used to say, "Anyone who performs *'umra* in the months of *ḥajj*, that is, in Shawwāl, Dhū al-Qa'da, or Dhū al-Ḥijja before the *ḥajj*, and then stays in Makka until the time for *ḥajj*, is performing *tamattu'* if he then performs *ḥajj*. He must sacrifice whatever animal it is easy for him to obtain, and if he cannot find one then he must fast three days during *ḥajj* and seven days when he returns."

Mālik said, "This is only the case if he stays until the *ḥajj* and performs *ḥajj* in that same year."

Mālik said that if someone who was from Makka, but had stopped living there and gone to live elsewhere, came back to perform *'umra* in the months of the *ḥajj* and then stayed in Makka to begin *ḥajj* there, he was performing *tamattu'* and had to offer up a sacrificial animal, or fast if he could not find one. He was not the same as the people of Makka.

Mālik was asked whether someone, who was not from Makka and entered Makka to perform *'umra* in the months of *ḥajj* with the intention of staying on to begin his *ḥajj* there, was performing *tamattu'* or not, and he said, "Yes, he is performing *tamattu'*, and he is not the same as the people of Makka, even if he has the intention of staying there. This is because he has entered Makka, but is not one of its people, and making a sacrifice or fasting is incumbent on anyone who is not from Makka, and, although he intends to stay, he does not know what possibilities might arise later. He is not one of the people of Makka."

64 Yaḥyā related to me from Mālik that Yaḥyā ibn Sa'īd used to hear Sa'īd ibn al-Musayyab say, "Anyone who performs *'umra* in Shawwāl, Dhū al-Qa'da or Dhū al-Ḥijja and then stays in Makka until it is time for the *ḥajj* is performing *tamattu'* if he then does *ḥajj*. He must sacrifice whatever animal it is easy for him to obtain, and if he cannot find one then he must fast three days during *ḥajj* and seven days when he returns."

20.20 Circumstances in which *tamattu'* is not obligatory

65 Mālik said, "Someone who performs *'umra* in Shawwāl, Dhū al-Qa'da or Dhū al-Ḥijja and then goes back to his people, and then returns and performs *ḥajj* in that same year does not have to sacrifice an animal. Sacrificing an animal is only incumbent on someone who performs *'umra* in the months of *ḥajj*, and then stays in Makka and then performs *ḥajj*. A person not from Makka who moves to Makka and establishes his home there and performs *'umra* in the months of the *ḥajj* and then begins his *ḥajj* there is not performing *tamattu'*. He does not have to sacrifice an animal nor does he have to fast. He is in the same position as the people of Makka if he is one of those who are living there."

Mālik was asked whether a man from Makka who had gone to live in another town or had been on a journey and then returned to Makka with the intention of staying there, regardless of whether he had a family there or not, and entered it to perform *'umra* in the months of the *ḥajj*, and then began his *ḥajj* there, beginning his *'umra* at the *mīqāt* of the Prophet ﷺ or at a place nearer than that, was doing *tamattu'* or not? Mālik answered, "He does not have to sacrifice an animal or fast as someone who is doing *tamattu'* has to do. This is because Allah, the Blessed and Exalted, says in His Book, 'That is for someone whose family are not present at the *Masjid al-Ḥarām*.'"

20.21 About *'umra* in general

66 Yaḥyā related to me from Mālik from Sumayy, the *mawlā* of Abū Bakr ibn 'Abd ar-Rahmān, from Abū Ṣāliḥ as-Sammān from Abū Hurayra that the Messenger of Allah ﷺ said, "*'Umra* is an expiation for what is

between it and the next *'umra*, and the only reward for an accepted *ḥajj* is the Garden."

67 Yaḥyā related to me from Mālik that Sumayy, the *mawlā* of Abū Bakr ibn 'Abd ar-Raḥmān, heard Abū Bakr ibn 'Abd ar-Raḥmān say, "A woman came to the Messenger of Allah ﷺ and said, 'I had arranged to perform *ḥajj*, but I was prevented,' and the Messenger of Allah ﷺ said, 'Perform *'umra* in Ramaḍān, for performing *'umra* in it is like performing *ḥajj*.'"

68 Yaḥyā related to me from Mālik from Nāfi' from 'Abdullāh ibn 'Umar that 'Umar ibn al-Khaṭṭāb said, "Keep your *ḥajj* separate from your *'umra*: that way your *ḥajj* will be more complete, and your *'umra* will be more complete if you perform it outside of the months of the *ḥajj*."

69 Yaḥyā related to me from Mālik that he had heard that 'Uthmān ibn 'Affān would sometimes never dismount from the animal he was riding on when he was doing *'umra* until he had returned.

Mālik said, "*'Umra* is a *sunna*, and we do not know of any Muslim who has ever said that it is permissible not to do it."

Mālik said, "I do not think that anyone can do more than one *'umra* in any one year."

Mālik said that someone doing *'umra* who had sexual intercourse with his wife had to sacrifice an animal and do a second *'umra*, which he had to begin when he had finished the one that he had spoiled and that he should go into *iḥrām* at the same place where he went into *iḥrām* for the *'umra* which he had spoiled, except if he had entered into *iḥrām* at a place further away than his *mīqāt*. This was because he only had to go into *iḥrām* from his *mīqāt*.

Mālik said, "Someone who enters Makka to perform *'umra*, and does *ṭawāf* of the House and *sa'y* between Ṣafā and Marwa while he is in *janāba*, or not in *wuḍū'*, and afterwards has intercourse with his wife and then remembers, should do *ghusl* or *wuḍū'*, and then go back and do *ṭawāf* around the House and *sa'y* between Ṣafā and Marwa and perform another *'umra* and sacrifice an animal. A woman should do the same if her husband has intercourse with her while she is in *iḥrām*."

Mālik said, "As for beginning *'umra* at at-Tan'īm, (it is not the only alternative). It is permissible if Allah wills for some one to leave the *Ḥaram* and go into *iḥrām* if he wishes, but the best way is for him to go into *iḥrām* at the *mīqāt* which the Messenger of Allah ﷺ used (i.e. at-Tan'īm) or one which is further away."

20.22 Marriage while in *iḥrām*

70 Yaḥyā related to me from Mālik from Rabī'a ibn Abī 'Abd ar-Raḥmān from Sulaymān ibn Yasār that the Messenger of Allah ﷺ sent Abū Rāfi' and a man of the Anṣār to arrange his marriage to Maymūna bint al-Ḥārith, and the Messenger of Allah ﷺ was in Madīna before he had left for *'umra*.

71 Yaḥyā related to me from Mālik from Nāfi', from Nubayh ibn Wahb, who was from the tribe of Banū 'Abd ad-Dār, that 'Umar ibn 'Ubaydullāh sent a message to Abān ibn 'Uthmān (who was amīr of the *ḥajj* at the time), while both of them were in *iḥrām*, saying "I want give the daughter of Shayba ibn Jubayr in marriage to Ṭalḥa ibn 'Umar and I want you to be present." Abān told him that he should not do that and said, "I heard 'Uthmān ibn 'Affān say that the Messenger of Allah ﷺ said, 'A man in *iḥrām* should not marry, or give in marriage, or get betrothed.'"

72 Yaḥyā related to me from Mālik from Dāwūd ibn al-Ḥusayn that Abū Ghaṭafān ibn Ṭarīf al-Murrī told him that his father Ṭarīf had married a woman while he was in *iḥrām*, and 'Umar ibn al-Khaṭṭāb had rescinded the marriage.

73 Yaḥyā related to me from Mālik from Nāfi' that 'Abdullāh ibn 'Umar used to say, "Someone in *iḥrām* may neither get married, nor arrange a marriage for himself or others."

74 Yaḥyā related to me from Mālik that he had heard that Sa'īd ibn al-Musayyab, Sālim ibn 'Abdullāh and Sulaymān ibn Yasār were asked about

whether someone in *iḥrām* could get married, and they said, "Someone in *iḥrām* may neither get married nor give someone in marriage."

Mālik said that a man who was in *iḥrām* could take his wife back, if he wanted to, if she was still in her *'idda* after she had been divorced from him.

20.23 Cupping while in *iḥrām*

75 Yaḥyā related to me from Mālik from Yaḥyā ibn Sa'īd from Sulaymān ibn Yasār that the Messenger of Allah ﷺ was once cupped on the top of his head while he was in *iḥrām* at Laḥya Jamal, which is a place on the road to Makka.

76 Yaḥyā related to me from Mālik from Nāfi' that 'Abdullāh ibn 'Umar used to say, "Someone in *iḥrām* should not be cupped except when there is no other alternative."

Mālik said, "Someone who is in *iḥrām* should not be cupped except when it is absolutely necessary."

20.24 Game that can be eaten by someone who is in *iḥrām*

77 Yaḥyā related to me from Mālik from Abū an-Naḍr, the *mawlā* of 'Umar ibn 'Ubaydullāh at-Taymī from Nāfi', the *mawlā* of Abū Qatāda al-Anṣārī, that Abū Qatāda was once with the Messenger of Allah ﷺ. When they got to one of the roads to Makka he fell behind with some Companions of his who were in *iḥrām*, while he was not. Then he saw a wild ass, so he got on his mount and asked his companions to give him his whip but they refused. Then he asked them for his spear and they refused to give it to him. So he took hold of it and attacked the ass and killed it. Some of the companions of the Messenger of Allah ﷺ ate from it, and others refused. When they had caught up with the Messenger of Allah ﷺ, they asked him about it and he said, "It is food that Allah has fed you with."

78 Yaḥyā related to me from Mālik from Hishām ibn 'Urwa from his father that az-Zubayr ibn al-'Awwām used to take dried gazelle meat (*ṣafīf aẓ-ẓibā'*) as provisions while he was in *iḥrām*.

Mālik explained, "*Ṣafīf* are dried strips of meat."

79 Yaḥyā related to me from Mālik from Zayd ibn Aslam that 'Atā' ibn Yasār had told him from Abū Qatāda the same *ḥadīth* about the wild ass as that of Abū an-Naḍr, except that in the *ḥadīth* of Zayd ibn Aslam the Messenger of Allah ﷺ asked, "Do you still have any of its meat?"

80 Yaḥyā related to me from Mālik that Yaḥyā ibn Sa'īd al-Anṣārī said that Muḥammad ibn Ibrāhīm ibn al-Ḥārith at-Taymī told him from 'Īsā ibn Ṭalha ibn 'Ubaydullāh, from 'Umayr ibn Salama aḍ-Ḍamri, from al-Bahzī, that the Messenger of Allah ﷺ set out once for Makka while in *iḥrām*. When they had reached ar-Rawḥā', they unexpectedly came upon a wounded wild ass. Someone mentioned it to the Messenger of Allah ﷺ and he said, "Leave it. The man to whom it belongs is about to come." Then al-Bahzī, the man himself, came to the Prophet ﷺ and said, 'Messenger of Allah, do whatever you want with this ass,' and the Messenger of Allah ﷺ told Abū Bakr to divide it up among the company. Then they went on until they came to the well of al-Uthāba, which was located between ar-Ruwaytha and al-'Arj (between Makka and Madīna), where they unexpectedly came upon a gazelle with an arrow in it, lying on its side in some shade. He claimed that the Messenger of Allah ﷺ told someone to stand by it to make sure no one disturbed it until everyone had passed by.

81 Yaḥyā related to me from Mālik from Yaḥyā ibn Sa'īd that he heard Sa'īd ibn al-Musayyab relating from Abū Hurayra that he was once coming back from Bahrain, and, when he reached ar-Rabadha, he found a caravan of people from Iraq in *iḥrām*, who asked him whether they could eat the meat of some game which they had found with the people of ar-Rabadha, and he told them they could eat it. He said, "Afterwards I had doubts about what I had told them to do, so when I got back to Madīna I mentioned the matter to 'Umar ibn al-Khaṭṭāb and he said, 'What did you tell them to do?' I said, 'I told them to eat it.' 'Umar ibn al-Khaṭṭāb said, threatening me, 'If you had told them to do anything else I would have done something to you.'"

82 Yaḥyā related to me from Mālik from Ibn Shihāb that Sālim ibn ʿAbdullāh heard Abū Hurayra relating to ʿAbdullāh ibn ʿUmar how a group of three people in *iḥrām* had passed him at ar-Rabadha and had asked him for a *fatwā* about eating game which people who were not in *iḥrām* were eating, and he told them that they could eat it. He said, "Then I went to ʿUmar ibn al-Khaṭṭāb in Madīna and asked him about it, and he said, 'What did you say to them?' and I said, 'I told them that they could eat it.' ʿUmar said, 'If you had told them anything else I would have done you an injury.'"

83 Yaḥyā related to me from Mālik from Zayd ibn Aslam from ʿAṭāʾ ibn Yasār that Kaʿb al-Aḥbar was once coming back from Syria with a group of riders, and at a certain point along the road they found some game-meat and Kaʿb said they could eat it. When they got back to Madīna they went to ʿUmar ibn al-Khaṭṭāb and told him about that, and he said, "Who told you that you could do that?" and they answered, "Kaʿb." He said, "He was indeed the one I put in charge of you until you should return."

Later, when they were on the road to Makka, a swarm of locusts passed them by and Kaʿb told them to catch them and eat them. When they got back to ʿUmar ibn al-Khaṭṭāb they told him about this, and he said (to Kaʿb), "What made you tell them they could do that?" Kaʿb said, "It is game of the sea." He said, "How do you know?" and Kaʿb said, "*Amīr al-Mu'minīn*, by the One in whose hand my self is, it is only the sneeze of a fish which it sneezes twice every year."

Mālik was asked whether someone in *iḥrām* could buy game that he had found on the way. He replied, "Game that is only hunted to be offered to people performing *ḥajj* I disapprove of and forbid, but there is no harm in game that a man has which he does not intend for those in *iḥrām*, but which a someone in *iḥrām* comes across and buys."

Mālik said, about someone who had some game with him that he had hunted or bought at the time when he had entered into *iḥrām*, that he did not have to get rid of it, and that there was no harm in him giving it to his family.

Mālik said that it was lawful for someone in *iḥrām* to fish in the sea or in rivers and lakes, etc.

20.25 Game that is not lawful to eat while in *iḥrām*

84 Yaḥyā related to me from Mālik from Ibn Shihāb from 'Ubaydullāh ibn 'Abdullāh ibn 'Utba ibn Mas'ūd from 'Abdullāh ibn 'Abbās that aṣ-Ṣa'b ibn Jaththāma al-Laythī once gave a wild ass to the Messenger of Allah ﷺ while he was at al-Abwā' or Waddān, and the Messenger of Allah ﷺ gave it back to him. However, when the Messenger of Allah ﷺ saw the expression on the man's face he said, "We only gave it back to you because we are in *iḥrām*."

85 Yaḥyā related to me from Mālik from 'Abdullāh ibn Abī Bakr that 'Abd ar-Raḥmān ibn 'Āmir ibn Rabi'a said, "I once saw 'Uthmān ibn 'Affān in *iḥrām* on a hot summer's day at al-'Arj, and he had covered his face with a red woollen cloth. Some game-meat was brought to him and he told his companions to eat. They asked, 'Will you not eat then?' and he replied, 'I am not in the same position as you. It was hunted for my sake.'"

86 Yaḥyā related to me from Mālik from Hishām ibn 'Urwa, from his father that 'Ā'isha, *Umm al-Mu'minīn*, said to him, "Son of my sister, it is only for ten nights, so if you get an urge for it, leave it," by which she meant eating game-meat.

Mālik said that if game was hunted for the sake of a man who was in *iḥrām* and it was prepared for him and he ate some of it knowing that it had been hunted for his sake, then he had to pay a forfeit for all of the game that had been hunted on his behalf.

Mālik was asked about whether someone who was forced to eat carrion while he was in *iḥrām* should hunt game and then eat that rather than the carrion, and he said, "It is better for him to eat the carrion, because Allah, the Blessed and Exalted, has not give permission for someone in *iḥrām* to either eat game or take it in any situation, but He has made allowances for eating carrion when absolutely necessary."

Mālik said, "It is not lawful for anyone, whether in *iḥrām* or not, to eat game which has been killed or sacrificed by someone in *iḥrām*, because, whether it was killed deliberately or by mistake, it was not done in a lawful manner, and so eating it is not lawful. I have heard this from more than one person. Somebody who kills game and then eats it only has to make a single *kaffāra*, which is the same as for somebody who kills game but does not eat any of it."

20.26 Hunting in the *Ḥaram*

87 Mālik said, "It is not lawful to eat any game that has been hunted in the *Ḥaram*, or has had a dog set after it in the *Ḥaram* and then been killed outside the *Ḥaram*. Anyone who does that has to pay a forfeit for what has been hunted. However, someone that sets his dog after game outside the *Ḥaram* and then follows it until it is hunted down in the *Ḥaram* does not have to pay any forfeit, unless he set the dog after the game near to the *Ḥaram*. The game, however, should not be eaten. If he set the dog loose near the *Ḥaram* then he has to pay a forfeit for the game."

20.27 Assessing the forfeit for hunting game animals

88 Mālik said, "Allah, the Blessed and Exalted, says, '*O you who believe, do not kill game while you are in iḥrām. If one of you kills any deliberately, the reprisal for it is a livestock animal equivalent to what he killed, as judged by two just men among you, a sacrifice to reach the Ka'ba, or expiation by feeding the poor, or fasting commensurate to that, so that he may taste the evil consequences of what he did.*'" (5:95).

Mālik said, "Someone who hunts game when he is not in *iḥrām* and then kills it while he is in *iḥrām* is in the same position as someone who buys game while he is in *iḥrām* and then kills it. Allah has forbidden killing it, and so a man who does so has to pay a forfeit for it. The position that we go by in this matter is that a forfeit is assessed for anyone who kills game while he is in *iḥrām*."

Yaḥyā said that Mālik said, "The best that I have heard about someone who kills game and is assessed for it is that the game which he has killed is assessed and its value in food is estimated and with that food he feeds each poor man a *mudd*, or fasts a day in place of each *mudd*. The number of poor men is considered, and if it is ten then he fasts ten days, and if it is twenty he fasts twenty days, according to how many people there are to be fed, even if there are more than sixty."

Mālik said, "I have heard that a forfeit is assessed for someone who kills game in the *Ḥaram* while he is not in *iḥrām* in the same way that it is assessed for someone who kills game in the *Ḥaram* while he is in *iḥrām*."

20.28 Animals that someone in *iḥrām* can kill

89 Yaḥyā related to me from Mālik from Nāfi' from 'Abdullāh ibn 'Umar that the Messenger of Allah ﷺ said, "There are five kinds of animal which it is not wrong for someone in *iḥrām* to kill: crows, kites, scorpions, rats and mice, and wild dogs."

90 Yaḥyā related to me from Mālik from 'Abdullah ibn Dinār from 'Abdullāh ibn 'Umar that the Messenger of Allah ﷺ said, "There are five (kinds of) animal which it is not wrong for someone in *iḥrām* to kill: scorpions, rats and mice, crows, kites and wild dogs."

91 Yaḥyā related to me from Mālik from Hishām ibn 'Urwa from his father that the Messenger of Allah ﷺ said, "There are five kinds of vicious animals that can be killed in the *Ḥaram*: rats and mice, scorpions, crows, kites and wild dogs."

92 Yaḥyā related to me from Mālik from Ibn Shihāb that 'Umar ibn al-Khaṭṭāb told people to kill snakes in the *Ḥaram*.

Mālik said, about the "wild dogs" which people were told to kill in the *Ḥaram*, that any animals that wounded, attacked or terrorised men, such as lions, leopards, cheetahs and wolves, were counted as "wild dogs." However, someone who was in *iḥrām* should not kill beasts of prey that did not attack (people), such as hyenas, foxes, cats and anything else like them, and if he did then he had to pay a forfeit for it. Similarly, someone in *iḥrām* should not kill any predatory birds except the kinds that the Prophet ﷺ specified, namely crows and kites. If someone in *iḥrām* killed any other kind of bird he had to pay a forfeit for it.

20.29 Things that someone in *iḥrām* is allowed to do

93 Yaḥyā related to me from Yaḥyā ibn Sa'īd from Muḥammad ibn Ibrāhīm ibn al-Ḥārith at-Taymī from Rabi'a ibn Abī 'Abdullāh ibn al-Hudayr that he saw 'Umar ibn al-Khaṭṭāb taking the ticks off a camel of his at as-Suqyā while he was in *iḥrām*.

Mālik said that he disapproved of that.

94 Yaḥyā related to me from Mālik from 'Alqama ibn Abī 'Alqama that his mother said, "I heard 'Ā'isha, the wife of the Prophet ﷺ being asked whether someone in *iḥrām* could scratch their body or not, and she said, 'Yes, he can scratch it and do so as hard as he pleases. I would scratch even if my hands were tied and I could only use my feet.'"

95 Yaḥyā related to me from Mālik from Ayyūb ibn Mūsā that 'Abdullāh ibn 'Umar once looked in the mirror for something that was irritating him while he was in *iḥrām*.

96 Yaḥyā related to me from Mālik from Nāfi' that 'Abdullāh ibn 'Umar did not like people who were in *iḥrām* removing mites or ticks from their camels.

Mālik said, "This is what I like most out of what I have heard about the matter."

97 Yaḥyā related to me from Mālik that Muḥammad ibn 'Abdullāh ibn Abī Maryam once asked Sa'īd ibn al-Musayyab about (what to do with) one of his nails that had broken while he was in *iḥrām* and Sa'īd said, "Cut it off."

Mālik was asked whether someone in *iḥrām* who had an ear-complaint could use medicinal oil which was not perfumed for dropping into his ears, and he said, "I do not see any harm in that, and even if he were to put it into his mouth I still would not see any harm in it."

Mālik said that there was no harm in someone in *iḥrām* lancing an abscess that he had, or a boil, or cutting a vein, if he needed to do so.

20.30 Performing the *ḥajj* for somebody else

98 Yaḥyā related to me from Mālik from Ibn Shihāb from Sulaymān ibn Yasār that 'Abdullāh ibn 'Abbās said, "Al-Faḍl ibn 'Abbās was riding behind the Messenger of Allah ﷺ when a woman from the Khath'ama tribe came to him to ask him for a *fatwā*. Al-Faḍl began to look at her, and she at him, and the Messenger of Allah ﷺ turned Faḍl's face away to the other side. The woman said, 'Messenger of Allah, Allah's making the *ḥajj* obligatory finds my father a very old man, unable to stay firm on his riding-beast. Can I do *ḥajj* on his behalf?' and he said, 'Yes.' This was during the Farewell *Ḥajj*."

20.31 Someone whose path (to the House) is blocked by an enemy

99 Yaḥyā related to me that Mālik said, "Someone whose passage to the House is blocked by an enemy is freed from every restriction of *iḥrām*, and should sacrifice his animal and shave his head wherever he has been detained, and there is nothing for him to make up afterwards."

Yaḥyā related to me from Mālik that he had heard that when the Messenger of Allah ﷺ and his Companions came out of *iḥrām* at al-Ḥudaybiya they sacrificed their sacrificial animals and shaved their heads, and were freed from all the restrictions of *iḥrām* without having done *ṭawāf* of the House and without their sacrificial animals *iḥrām* the Ka'ba.

There is nothing known about the Messenger of Allah ﷺ ever telling any of his companions or anybody else that was with him, to make up for anything they had missed or to go back to do anything they had not finished doing.

100 Yaḥyā related to me from Mālik from Nāfi' that when 'Abdullāh ibn 'Umar set out for Makka during the troubles (between al-Ḥajjāj ibn Yūsuf and Zubayr ibn al-'Awwām) he said, "If I am blocked from going to the House we shall do what we did when we were with the Messenger of Allah ﷺ," and he went into *iḥrām* for *'umra* because that was what the Messenger of Allah ﷺ did in the year of al-Ḥudaybiya. But afterwards he reconsidered his position and said, "It is the same either way." After that he turned to his companions and said, "It is the same either way. I call you to witness that I have decided in favour of *ḥajj* and *'umra* together." He then got through to the House (without being stopped) and did one *ṭawāf*, which he considered to be enough for himself, and sacrificed an animal.

Mālik said, "This is what we go by if someone is hindered by an enemy, as the Prophet ﷺ and his companions were. If someone is hindered by anything other than an enemy, he is only freed from *iḥrām* by *ṭawāf* of the House."

20.32 Someone who is prevented (from going to the House) by something other than an enemy

101 Yaḥyā related to me from Mālik from Ibn Shihāb from Sālim ibn 'Abdullāh that 'Abdullāh ibn 'Umar said, "Someone who is held back from going to the House by illness can only come out of *iḥrām* after he has done *ṭawāf* of the House and *sa'y* between Ṣafā and Marwa. If it is absolutely necessary for him to wear any ordinary clothes or undergo medical treatment, he should do that and pay compensation for it."

102 Yaḥyā related to me from Mālik from Yaḥyā ibn Sa'īd that he had heard that 'Ā'isha, the wife of the Prophet ﷺ, used to say, "Only the House frees a person in *iḥrām* from *iḥrām*."

103 Yaḥyā related to me from Mālik from Ayyūb ibn Abī Tamīma as-Sakhtiyānī that a very old man from Basra once said to him, "I set out for Makka but on the way there I broke my thigh, so I sent a message on to Makka. 'Abdullāh ibn 'Abbās and 'Abdullāh ibn 'Umar and the people were there, but no one allowed me to leave *iḥrām*, and I stayed there for seven months until I left *iḥrām* by doing an *'umra*."

104 Yaḥyā related to me from Mālik from Ibn Shihāb from Sālim ibn 'Abdullāh that 'Abdullāh ibn 'Umar said, "Someone who is detained by sickness before he has got to the House cannot leave *iḥrām* until he has done *ṭawāf* of the House and *sa'y* between Ṣafā and Marwa."

Yaḥyā related to me from Mālik from Yaḥyā ibn Sa'īd from Sulaymān ibn Yasār that Sa'īd ibn Ḥuzāba al-Makhzūmī was thrown off his mount while he was in *iḥrām* on the road to Makka. He asked after the person in charge of the relay station where he was injured and he found 'Abdullāh ibn 'Umar, 'Abdullāh ibn az-Zubayr and Marwān ibn al-Ḥakam there. He told them what had happened to him and all of them said that he should take whatever medicine he had to take and pay compensation for it. Then, when he got better again, he should perform *'umra* and come out of his *iḥrām*, after which he had to perform *ḥajj* the next year and to offer whatever sacrificial animal he was able to in the future.

Mālik said, "This is what we do here (in Madīna) if someone is detained by something other than an enemy. And when Abū Ayyūb al-Ansārī and Habbār ibn al-Aswad arrived on the Day of Sacrifice, having missed the *ḥajj*, 'Umar ibn al-Khaṭṭāb told them to come out of *iḥrām* by doing *'umra* and then to go home free of *iḥrām* and perform *ḥajj* sometime in the future and to sacrifice an animal, or, if they could not find one, to fast three days during the *ḥajj* and seven days after they had returned to their families."

Mālik said, "Anyone who is detained from performing *ḥajj* after he has gone into *iḥrām*, whether by illness or otherwise, or by an error in calculating the month or because the new moon is concealed from him, is in the same position as someone who is hindered from performing the *ḥajj* and must do the same as he does."

Yaḥyā said that Mālik was asked about the situation of someone from Makka who went into *iḥrām* for *ḥajj* and then broke a bone or had severe stomach pain, or of a woman who gives birth, and he said, "Someone to whom this happens is in the same situation as one who is hindered from performing *ḥajj*, and he must do the same as people from outlying regions do when they are hindered from performing *ḥajj*."

Mālik said about someone who arrived in the months of the *ḥajj* with the intention of performing *'umra*, and completed his *'umra* and went into *iḥrām* in Makka to perform *ḥajj*, and then broke a bone or something else happened to him which stopped him from being present at 'Arafa with everybody else: "I think that he should stay where he is until he is better and then go outside the area of the *Ḥaram*, and then return to Makka and do *ṭawāf* of the House and *sa'y* between Ṣafā and Marwa, and then leave *iḥrām*. He must then perform *ḥajj* again the next year and offer a sacrificial animal."

Mālik said about someone who left *iḥrām* in Makka, and then did *ṭawāf* of the House and *sa'y* between Ṣafā and Marwa, and then fell ill and was unable to be present with everybody at 'Arafa: "If someone miss the *ḥajj*, he should, if he can, go out of the area of the *Ḥaram* and then come back in again to perform *'umra* and do *ṭawāf* of the House and *sa'y* between Ṣafā and Marwa, because he had not intended his initial *ṭawāf* to be for an *'umra*, and so for this reason he does it again. He must perform the next *ḥajj* and offer a sacrificial animal.

"If he is not one of the people of Makka, and something happens to him which stops him from performing the *ḥajj*, but he does *ṭawāf* of the House and *sa'y* between Ṣafā and Marwa, he should come out of *iḥrām* by doing an *'umra* and then do *ṭawāf* of the House a second time, and *sa'y* between Ṣafā and Marwa, because his initial *ṭawāf* and *sa'y* were intended for the *ḥajj*. He must do the next *ḥajj* and offer a sacrificial animal.

20.33 Building the Ka'ba

105 Yaḥyā related to me from Mālik from Ibn Shihāb from Sālim ibn 'Abdullāh that 'Abdullāh ibn Muḥammad ibn Abī Bakr aṣ-Ṣiddīq told 'Abdullāh ibn 'Umar from 'Ā'isha, that the Prophet ﷺ said, "Do you not see that when your people built the Ka'ba they fell short of the foundations of Ibrāhīm?" 'Ā'isha said, "Messenger of Allah, will you not restore it to the foundations of Ibrāhīm?" and the Messenger of Allah ﷺ said, "If it were not that your people have only recently left disbelief, I would have done so."

Sālim ibn ʻAbdullāh added that ʻAbdullāh ibn ʻUmar said, "If ʻĀ'isha heard this from the Messenger of Allah ﷺ, then I consider that the Messenger of Allah ﷺ only refrained from greeting the two corners which are adjacent to the Ḥijr because the House had not been completed on the foundations of Ibrāhīm." (i.e. the corners he did not touch were not the original corners of the Kaʻba.)

106 Yaḥyā related to me from Mālik from Hishām ibn ʻUrwa from his father that ʻĀ'isha, *Umm al-Mu'minīn*, said, "I do not mind whether I pray in the Hijr or in the House." (i.e. praying in the Ḥijr is the same as praying in the House.)

107 Yaḥyā related to me from Mālik that he heard Ibn Shihāb say that he had heard one of the people of knowledge say that the Ḥijr was only enclosed so that people would go beyond it when they were making *ṭawāf*, and their *ṭawāf* would therefore encompass the original House.

20.34 Hastening (*raml*) in the *ṭawāf*

108 Yaḥyā related to me from Mālik from Jaʻfar ibn Muḥammad from his father that Jābir ibn ʻAbdullāh said, "I saw the Messenger of Allah ﷺ hastening from the Black Stone until he reached it again, three times."

Mālik said, "This is what is still done by the people of knowledge in our city (Madīna)."

109 Yaḥyā related to me from Mālik from Nāfiʻ that ʻAbdullāh ibn ʻUmar used to hasten from the Black Stone round to the Black Stone three times and then would walk four circuits normally.

110 Yaḥyā related to me from Mālik from Hishām ibn ʻUrwa that when his father did *ṭawāf* of the House he would hasten in the first three circuits and say in a low voice, "O Allah, there is no god but You, and You bring to life after You have made to die."

Allāhumma lā ilāha illā anta wa anta tuḥyī baʻda mā amatt.

111 Yaḥyā related to me from Mālik from Hishām ibn 'Urwa from his father that he saw 'Abdullāh ibn az-Zubayr go into *iḥrām* for *'umra* at at-Tan'īm. He said, "Then I saw him hasten around the House for three circuits."

112 Yaḥyā related to me from Mālik from Nāfi' that 'Abdullāh ibn 'Umar never used to do *ṭawāf* of the House or *sa'y* between Ṣafā and Marwa if he went into *iḥrām* in Makka until he had returned from Minā, nor would he hasten when doing *ṭawāf* of the House if he went into *iḥrām* in Makka.

20.35 Saluting the corners during *ṭawāf*

113 Yaḥyā related to me from Mālik that he had heard that when the Messenger of Allah ﷺ had finished his *ṭawāf* of the House and prayed two *rak'as*, and wanted to go to Ṣafā and Marwa, he would salute the corner of the Black Stone before he left.

114 Yaḥyā related to me from Mālik from Hishām ibn 'Urwa that his father said that the Messenger of Allah ﷺ once said to 'Abd ar-Raḥmān ibn 'Awf, "What do you do, Abū Muḥammad, when saluting the corner?" and 'Abd ar-Raḥmān said, "Sometimes I salute it, and sometimes I do not." The Messenger of Allah ﷺ said, "You are right."

115 Yaḥyā related to me from Mālik from Hishām ibn 'Urwa that his father used to salute all the corners when he did *ṭawāf* of the House and did not omit the Yamānī corner unless prevented.

20.36 Kissing the corner of the Black Stone when saluting the corners

116 Yaḥyā related to me from Mālik from Hishām ibn 'Urwa from his father that 'Umar ibn al-Khaṭṭāb said to the corner of the Black Stone while he was doing *ṭawāf* of the House, "You are only a stone, and if I had not seen the Messenger of Allah ﷺ kiss you, I would not do so." Then he kissed it.

Mālik said, "I have heard some of the people of knowledge recommending someone doing *ṭawāf* of the House to put his hand to his mouth when he takes it from the Yamānī corner."

20.37 The two *rak'as* of *ṭawāf*

117 Yaḥyā related to me from Mālik from Hishām ibn 'Urwa that his father would never do two sets of seven circuits together without praying between them. After every seven circuits he would pray two *rak'as*, sometimes at the *Maqām* of Ibrāhīm, and sometimes elsewhere.

Mālik was asked whether a man doing voluntary *ṭawāf* could, to make it easier on himself, join two or more sets of seven circuits and then pray whatever he owed for those sets of seven, and he said, "He should not do that. The *sunna* is that he does two *rak'as* after every seven circuits."

Mālik said about someone, who began doing *ṭawāf* and then forgot how many circuits he had done and did eight or nine, "He should stop when he knows that he has done more than the right number and then pray two *rak'as*, and he should not count the ones that he has done in excess. Neither should he build on the nine that he has done and then pray the *rak'as* for the two sets of seven circuits together, because the *sunna* is that you pray two *rak'as* after every seven circuits."

Mālik said, "Someone who was in doubt about his *ṭawāf* after he had prayed the two *rak'as* of *ṭawāf* should go back and complete his *ṭawāf* until he was certain of how much he had done. He should then repeat the two *rak'as*, because prayer when doing *ṭawāf* was only valid after completing seven circuits."

Mālik said, "If someone breaks his *wuḍū'* either while he is doing *ṭawāf*, or when he has finished *ṭawāf* but before he has prayed the two *rak'as* of *ṭawāf*, he should do *wuḍū'* and begin the *ṭawāf* and the two *rak'as* afresh."

Mālik said, "Breaking *wuḍū'* does not interrupt *sa'y* between Ṣafā and Marwa, but a person should not begin *sa'y* unless he is pure by being in *wuḍū'*.'"

20.38 Praying after *Ṣubḥ* and *'Aṣr* when doing *ṭawāf*

118 Yaḥyā related to me from Mālik from Ibn Shihāb from Ḥumayd ibn 'Abd ar-Raḥmān ibn 'Awf that 'Abd ar-Raḥmān ibn 'Abd al-Qārī mentioned to him that he once did *ṭawāf* of the House with 'Umar ibn al-Khaṭṭāb after *Ṣubḥ* and when 'Umar had finished his *ṭawāf* he looked and saw that the sun had not yet risen, so he rode on until he made his camel kneel at Dhū Ṭuwā, and he prayed two *rak'as*.

119 Yaḥyā related to me from Mālik that Abū az-Zubayr al-Makkī said, "I saw 'Abdullāh ibn 'Abbās doing *ṭawāf* after *'Aṣr*. Then he went into his room and I do not know what he did."

120 Yaḥyā related to me from Mālik that Abū az-Zubayr al-Makkī said, "I saw the House deserted both after *Ṣubḥ* and *'Aṣr*, with no one doing *ṭawāf*."

Mālik said, "If someone does some of his circuits and then *Ṣubḥ* and *'Aṣr* prayer is begun, he should pray with the imām and then complete the rest of his circuits but should not pray at all until the sun has either risen or set."

He added, "There is no harm in delaying the two *rak'as* until after he has prayed *Maghrib*."

Mālik said, "There is no harm in someone doing a single *ṭawāf* after *Ṣubḥ* or after *'Aṣr*, but not more than that, and even then only as long as he delays the two *rak'as* until after the sun has risen, as 'Umar ibn al-Khaṭṭāb did, or until after the sun has set if it is after *'Aṣr*. Then when the sun has set he can pray them if he wants, or, if he wants, he can delay them until after he has prayed *Maghrib*. There is no harm in that."

20.39 Taking leave of the House

121 Yaḥyā related to me from Mālik from Nāfi' from 'Abdullāh ibn 'Umar that 'Umar ibn al-Khaṭṭāb said, "No one should leave the *ḥajj* until he has done *ṭawāf* of the House, and *ṭawāf* of the House is the final rite."

Mālik said, commenting about 'Umar ibn al-Khaṭṭāb's saying '... *ṭawāf* of the House is the final rite', "In our opinion, and Allah knows best, that is because Allah, the Blessed and Exalted, says, '*As for those who honour Allah's sacred rites, that comes from the fear of Allah within their hearts*' (22:32), and He says, '*Then their place of sacrifice is by the Ancient House.*' (22:33) Therefore the place of all the rituals and their ending should be at the Ancient House."

122 Yaḥyā related to me from Mālik from Yaḥyā ibn Sa'īd that 'Umar ibn al-Khaṭṭāb refused to let one man who had not taken leave of the House pass aẓ-Ẓahrān, (a valley eighteen miles from Makka) until he had taken leave of it.

123 Yaḥyā related to me from Mālik from Hishām ibn 'Urwa that his father said, "Allah has completed the *ḥajj* of anyone who does the *Ṭawāf al-Ifāda*. It is fitting that *ṭawāf* of the House be the last of his affair, as long as nothing prevents him, and if something prevents him or an obstacle arises, then Allah has completed his *ḥajj*."

Mālik said, "I do not think that a man who does not come to know that the last of his affair is *ṭawāf* of the House until he has left owes anything unless he is nearby and can return, do *ṭawāf*, and then leave having done the *Ṭawāf al-Ifāda*."

20.40 *Tawāf* in general

124 Yaḥyā related to me from Mālik from Abū al-Aswad Muḥammad ibn 'Abd ar-Raḥmān ibn Nawfal from 'Urwa ibn az-Zubayr from Zaynab bint Abī Salama that Umm Salama, the wife of the Prophet ﷺ said, "I once complained to the Messenger of Allah ﷺ that I was ill and he said, 'Do *ṭawāf* riding behind the people.' So I performed *ṭawāf* riding my camel, while the Messenger of Allah ﷺ was praying by the side of the House, reciting *Sūrat at-Ṭūr* (52)."

125 Yaḥyā related to me from Mālik from Abū az-Zubayr al-Makkī that Abū Mā'iz al-Aslamī 'Abdullāh ibn Sufyān told him that once, when he was sitting with 'Abdullāh ibn 'Umar, a woman came to ask him for an

opinion. She said, "I set out intending to do *ṭawāf* of the House, but then, when I got to the gate of the Mosque, I started bleeding, so I went back until it had left me. Then I set out again, and then, when I got to the gate of the Mosque, I started bleeding, so I went back until it had left me. Then I set off again, and then, when I got to the gate of the Mosque, I started bleeding." 'Abdullāh ibn 'Umar said, "That is only an impulse from Shayṭān. Do *ghusl*, then bind your private parts with a cloth and do *ṭawāf*."

126 Yaḥyā related to me from Mālik that he had heard that if Sa'd ibn Abī Waqqāṣ entered Makka late, he would go to 'Arafa before doing *ṭawāf* of the House and *sa'y* between Ṣafā and Marwa, and then do *ṭawāf* when he got back.

Mālik said, "The leeway is broad, if Allah wills."

Mālik was asked whether somebody who was doing obligatory *ṭawāf* could stop and talk with another man, and he said, "I do not like him to do that."

Mālik said, "Only someone who is pure (by being in *wuḍū'*) should do *ṭawāf* of the House or *sa'y* between Ṣafā and Marwa."

20.41 Starting with Safā in the *sa'y*

127 Yaḥyā related to me from Mālik from Ja'far ibn Muḥammad ibn 'Alī from his father that Jābir ibn 'Abdullāh said, "I heard the Messenger of Allah ﷺ say as he left the Mosque, intending to go to Ṣafā, 'We begin with what Allah began,' and he began with Ṣafā."

128 Yaḥyā related to me from Mālik from Ja'far ibn Muḥammad ibn 'Alī from his father from Jābir ibn 'Abdullāh that the Messenger of Allah ﷺ used to say, "Allah is greater" three times when he stopped on Ṣafā, and "There is no god but Allah, alone, without any partner. To Him belong the Kingdom and praise, and He has power over everything" three times, and make supplication. He would then do the same on Marwa.

129 Yaḥyā related to me from Mālik from Nāfi' that he heard 'Abdullāh ibn 'Umar making supplication on Ṣafā saying, "O Allah, You have said, 'Call on Me – I will answer you' and You do not break Your promise. So I am asking You, in the same way that You have guided me to Islam, not to take it away from me, and that You make me die while I am Muslim."

20.42 *Sa'y* in general

130 Yaḥyā related to me from Mālik from Hishām ibn 'Urwa that his father said, "Once when I was young I said to 'Ā'isha, *Umm al-Mu'minīn*, "Have you heard the saying of Allah, the Blessed and Exalted, "*Ṣafā and Marwa are among the Sacred Landmarks of Allah, so anyone who goes on ḥajj to the House or does 'umra incurs no wrong in going back and forth between them*" (2:158)? So it follows that there should be no harm for someone who does not go between them. By Allah, so there is no harm in not going between Ṣafā and Marwa.' 'Ā'isha said, 'No, if it was as you say, it would have been, "There is no harm in him not doing going back and forth between them." However, this *āyat* was revealed about the Anṣār. They used to make pilgrimage to Manāt, and Manāt was an idol near Qudayd, and they used to avoid going between Ṣafā and Marwa, so when Islam came they asked the Messenger of Allah ﷺ about this and Allah, the Blessed and Exalted, revealed, "*Ṣafā and Marwa are among the Sacred Landmarks of Allah, so anyone who goes on ḥajj to the House or does 'umra incurs no wrong in going back and forth between them.*""

131 Yaḥyā related to me from Mālik from Hishām ibn 'Urwa that Sawda bint 'Abdullāh ibn 'Umar, who was in the household of 'Urwa ibn az-Zubayr, set off walking between Ṣafā and Marwa when doing either *ḥajj* or *'umra*. She was a heavy woman and she began when everybody was leaving after the *'Ishā'* prayer, and she still had not completed her circuits when the first call was given for *Ṣubḥ*, but finished them between the two calls to prayer. If 'Urwa saw people doing circuits on riding beasts he would tell them in very strong terms not to do so, and they would pretend to be ill, out of awe of him.

[Hishām added], "He used to say to us about them, 'These are the unsuccessful and have lost.'"

Mālik said, "Someone who forgets *sa'y* between Ṣafā and Marwa in an *'umra*, and does not remember until he is far from Makka, should return and do *sa'y*. If, in the meantime, he has had intercourse with a woman, he should return and do *sa'y* between Ṣafā and Marwa so as to complete what remains of that *'umra*, and then after that he has to perform another *'umra* and offer a sacrificial animal."

Mālik was asked about someone who met another man when doing *sa'y* between Ṣafā and Marwa and stopped to talk with him, and he said, "I do not like anyone to do that."

Mālik said, "If anyone forgets some of his *ṭawāf*, or is uncertain about it, and remembers only when he is doing *sa'y* between Ṣafā and Marwa, he should stop the *sa'y* and complete his *ṭawāf* of the House, apart from that about which he is certain. After that he prays the two *rak'as* of the *ṭawāf*, and then begins his *sa'y* between Ṣafā and Marwa."

132 Yaḥyā related to me from Mālik from Ja'far ibn Muḥammad from his father from Jābir ibn 'Abdullah that the Messenger of Allah ﷺ, walked when he came down from Ṣafā and Marwa and then, when he reached the middle of the valley, he broke into a light run until he had left it.

Mālik said, about a man who, out of ignorance, did the *sa'y* between Ṣafā and Marwa before he had done *ṭawāf* of the House, "He should go back and do *ṭawāf* of the House and then do *sa'y* between Ṣafā and Marwa. If he does not learn about this until he has left Makka and is far away, he should return to Makka and do *ṭawāf* of the House and *sa'y* between Ṣafā and Marwa. If in the meantime he has had intercourse with a woman, he should return and do *ṭawāf* of the House and *sa'y* between Ṣafā and Marwa so that he completes what he owes of that *'umra*. Then, after that, he has to perform another *'umra* and offer a sacrificial animal."

20.43 Fasting the Day of 'Arafa

133 Yaḥyā related to me from Mālik from Abū an-Naḍr, the *mawlā* of 'Umar ibn 'Ubaydullāh, from 'Umayr, the *mawlā* of 'Abdullāh ibn 'Abbās, from Umm al-Faḍl bint al-Ḥārith, that she was present when some

people were arguing on the Day of 'Arafa about whether the Messenger of Allah ﷺ was fasting or not. Some of them said he was fasting and some of them said he was not. So she sent a bowl of milk to him while his camel was standing still and he drank.

134 Yaḥyā related to me from Mālik from Yaḥyā ibn Sa'īd from al-Qāsim ibn Muḥammad that 'Ā'isha, *Umm al-Mu'minīn*, used to fast on the Day of 'Arafa.

Al-Qāsim said, "I saw her, when the imām began moving away (after sunset) on the afternoon of 'Arafa, stay where she was until the ground between her and the people became clear. Then she asked for something to drink and broke her fast."

20.44 Fasting on the Days of Minā

135 Yaḥyā related to me from Mālik from Abū an-Naḍr, the *mawlā* of 'Umar ibn 'Ubaydullāh, from Sulaymān ibn Yasār that the Messenger of Allah ﷺ forbade fasting on the Days of Minā.

136 Yaḥyā related to me from Mālik from Ibn Shihāb that the Messenger of Allah ﷺ sent 'Abdullāh ibn Ḥudhāfa out on the Days of Mina to circulate among the people to tell them those days were for eating and drinking and remembrance of Allah.

137 Yaḥyā related to me from Mālik from Muḥammad ibn Yaḥyā ibn Ḥabbān from al-A'raj from Abū Hurayra that the Messenger of Allah ﷺ forbade fasting on two days: the day of the *'Īd al-Fiṭr* and the day of the *'Īd al-Aḍḥā*.

138 Yaḥyā related to me from Mālik from Yazīd ibn 'Abdullāh ibn al-Hādi from Abū Murra, the *mawlā* of Umm Hāni', the sister of 'Aqīl ibn Abī Ṭālib, that 'Abdullāh ibn 'Amr ibn al-'Āṣ told him that he had visited his father 'Amr ibn al-'Āṣ and found him eating. His father had invited him to eat and, when he replied that he was fasting, his father said, "These are the days on which the Messenger of Allah ﷺ forbade us to fast, and told us to break the fast on them."

Mālik said, "These days are the Days of *Tashrīq*."

20.45 What are acceptable as sacrificial animals (*hadys*)

139 Yaḥyā related to me from Mālik from Nāfi' from 'Abdullāh ibn Abī Bakr ibn Muḥammad ibn 'Amr ibn Ḥazm that the Messenger of Allah ﷺ sacrificed a camel, which had belonged to Abū Jahl ibn Hishām, in either a *ḥajj* or an *'umra*.

140 Yaḥyā related to me from Mālik from Abū az-Zinād from al-A'raj from Abū Hurayra that the Messenger of Allah ﷺ saw a man driving forward a camel, which he was going to sacrifice, and he told him to ride it. The man said, "Messenger of Allah, it is an animal that I am going to sacrifice," and he replied, "Ride it, confound you!" either two or three times.

141 Yaḥyā related to me from Mālik from 'Abdullāh ibn Dīnār that he used to see 'Abdullāh ibn 'Umar sacrificing animals two at a time during *ḥajj* and one at a time during *'umra*. He said, "I saw him sacrifice an animal during an *'umra* outside the house of Khālid ibn Usayd, where he was staying. I saw him stick his spear in the throat of the animal he was going to sacrifice until the spear came out under its shoulder."

142 Yaḥyā related to me from Mālik from Yaḥyā ibn Sa'īd that 'Umar ibn 'Abd al-'Aziz once sacrificed a camel during a *ḥajj* or an *'umra*.

143 Yaḥyā related to me from Mālik from Abū Ja'far al-Qarī that 'Abdullāh ibn 'Ayyāsh ibn Abī Rabi'a al-Makhzūmī sacrificed two camels, one of them a Bactrian.

144 Yaḥyā related to me from Mālik from Nāfi' that 'Abdullāh ibn 'Umar used to say, "If a she-camel that is being driven as a sacrificial animal gives birth, the offspring should be carried along as well and they are sacrificed together with her, and if there is no place where they can be carried, they should be carried on the mother until they are all sacrificed."

145 Yaḥyā related to me from Mālik from Hishām ibn 'Urwa that his father said, "If necessary, ride on your sacrificial animal, without burdening it, and, if necessary, drink its milk after its young one has drunk its fill, and when you sacrifice it, sacrifice the young one with it."

20.46 Treatment of sacrificial animals while being driven to sacrifice

146 Yaḥyā related to me from Mālik from Nāfi' from 'Abdullāh ibn 'Umar that, when he brought an animal to be sacrificed from Madīna, he would garland it and brand it at Dhū al-Ḥulayfa, doing the garlanding before the branding, but doing both in the same place, while facing the *qibla*. He would garland the animal with two sandals and brand it on its left side. It would then be driven with him until he observed the standing along with everybody at 'Arafa. Then he would drive it on with him when everybody else moved on, and then when he arrived at Mina on the morning on the sacrifice, he would sacrifice the animal before he shaved his head. He would sacrifice the animals with his own hands, lining them up standing and facing the *qibla*. He would then eat some of the meat, and give some of it away.

147 Yaḥyā related to me from Mālik from Nāfi' that 'Abdullāh ibn 'Umar said, when nicking the hump of his sacrificial animal to brand it, "In the name of Allah, and Allah is greater."

148 Yaḥyā related to me from Mālik from Nāfi' that 'Abdullāh ibn 'Umar used to say, "A sacrificial animal is what has been garlanded, branded, and stood with on 'Arafa."

149 Yaḥyā related to me from Mālik from Nāfi' that 'Abdullāh ibn 'Umar used to drape his sacrificial animals in fine Egyptian linen, saddlecloths and sets of clothing, which he would afterwards send to the Ka'ba and have the Ka'ba draped with them.

150 Yaḥyā related to me from Mālik that he asked 'Abdullāh ibn Dīnār what 'Abdullāh ibn 'Umar used to do with the drapings of his animals when the Ka'ba began to be draped with the kiswa, and he said, "He gave them away as *ṣadaqa*."

151 Yaḥyā related to me from Mālik from Nāfi' that 'Abdullāh ibn 'Umar used to say, about sacrificial animals, "Six year-old camels, three-year old cows and sheep, or older than these."

152 Yaḥyā related to me from Mālik from Nāfi' that 'Abdullāh ibn 'Umar never used to tear the drapes of his sacrificial animals, and he would not drape them until he went from Minā to 'Arafa.

153 Yaḥyā related to me from Mālik from Hishām ibn 'Urwa that his father used to say to his sons, "My sons, let none of you sacrifice any animal which he would be ashamed to sacrifice for a noble woman, for surely Allah is the noblest of noble ones, and the most deserving of those for whom things are chosen."

20.47 Injury to sacrificial animals or their loss

154 Yaḥyā related to me from Mālik from Hishām ibn 'Urwa from his father that the man who was in charge of the sacrificial animal of the Messenger of Allah ﷺ said, "Messenger of Allah, what should I do with a sacrificial animal that gets injured?" The Messenger of Allah ﷺ said to him, "Slaughter any sacrificial animal that is injured. Then throw the garlands in its blood, and then give the people a free hand in eating it."

155 Yaḥyā related to me from Mālik from Ibn Shihāb that Sa'īd ibn al-Musayyab said, "If someone dedicates an animal voluntarily and then it is injured and he kills it and gives everyone a free hand in eating it, he owes nothing. If, however, he eats some of it himself, or tells certain other people to eat it, then he owes compensation."

156 Yaḥyā related the same as that to me from Mālik from Thawr ibn Zayd ad-Dīlī from 'Abdullāh ibn 'Abbās.

157 Yaḥyā related to me from Mālik that Ibn Shihāb said, "If someone dedicates an animal as compensation, or for a vow, or as the sacrifice for *Ḥajj* at-*tamattu'*, and misfortune befalls it on the road, he must provide a substitute."

158 Yaḥyā related to me from Mālik from Nāfi' that 'Abdullāh ibn 'Umar said, "If someone dedicates an animal and then it goes astray or dies, he should provide a substitute, if it was for a vow. If, however, it was voluntary, then he can either provide a substitute for it or not, as he wishes."

159 Yaḥyā related to me from Mālik that he had heard the people of knowledge say, "Someone who dedicates a sacrificial animal for compensation or as part of the *ḥajj* should not eat from it."

20.48 The animal to be sacrificed on account of intercourse in *iḥrām*

160 Yaḥyā related to me from Mālik that he had heard that 'Umar ibn al-Khaṭṭāb and 'Alī ibn Abī Ṭālib and Abū Hurayra were asked about a man who had intercourse with his wife while he was in *iḥrām* on *ḥajj*. They said, "The two of them should carry on and complete their *ḥajj*. Then they must perform *ḥajj* again the following year, and sacrifice an animal."

Mālik added that 'Alī ibn Abī Ṭālib said, "When they then go into *iḥrām* for *ḥajj* in the following year they should keep apart until they have completed their *ḥajj*."

161 Yaḥyā related to me from Mālik from Yaḥyā ibn Sa'īd that he heard Sa'īd ibn al-Musayyab asking a group of people, "What do you think about someone who has intercourse with his wife while he is in *iḥrām*?" and none of them answered him. Sa'īd said, "There is a man who has had intercourse with his wife while in *iḥrām* who has sent a message to Madīna asking about it." Some of them said, "They should be kept apart until the following year," and Sa'īd ibn al-Musayyab said, "They should carry on and complete the *ḥajj* which they have spoiled, and then return home when they have finished. When the following *ḥajj* comes, they must perform *ḥajj* and sacrifice an animal. They should go into *iḥrām* for the *ḥajj* that they have spoiled, and they should keep apart until they have finished their *ḥajj*."

Mālik said, "They should both sacrifice an animal."

Mālik said about a man who had intercourse with his wife during *ḥajj* after he had come back from 'Arafa but before he had stoned the *Jamra*, "He must sacrifice an animal and perform *ḥajj* again the following year. If, however, he had intercourse with his wife after he stoned the *Jamra*, he only has to do an *'umra* and sacrifice an animal and he does not have to perform another *ḥajj*."

Mālik explained, "What spoils a *ḥajj* or an *'umra,* and makes sacrificing an animal and repeating the *ḥajj* necessary, is the meeting of the two circumcised parts, even if there is no emission. It is also made necessary by an emission if it is the result of bodily contact. I do not think that a man who remembers something and has an emission owes anything."

Mālik said, "And if a man were to kiss his wife and no emission were to occur from that, he would only have to sacrifice an animal."

Mālik said, "A woman in *iḥrām* who has intercourse with her husband several times during *ḥajj* or *'umra* out of obedience to him only has to perform another *ḥajj* and sacrifice an animal. That is if her husband has intercourse with her while she is performing *ḥajj*. If he has intercourse with her while she is performing *'umra*, she must repeat the *'umra* she has spoiled and sacrifice an animal."

20.49 The animal to be sacrificed on account of missing the *ḥajj*

162 Yaḥyā related to me from Mālik that Yaḥyā ibn Sa'īd said that Sulaymān ibn Yasār told him that Abū Ayyūb al-Anṣārī once set off to perform *ḥajj* and then, when he reached an-Nāziya on the road to Makka, his riding beasts strayed. He reached 'Umar ibn al-Khaṭṭāb on the Day of Sacrifice and told him what had happened and 'Umar said, "Do what someone performing *'umra* would do, and then you can leave *iḥrām*, and then when the *ḥajj* next comes upon you, do it and sacrifice whatever animal is easy for you."

163 Mālik related to me from Nāfi' from Sulaymān ibn Yasār that Habbār ibn al-Aswad arrived on the Day of Sacrifice while 'Umar ibn al-Khaṭṭāb was sacrificing his animal and said, *"Amīr al-Mu'minīn,* we

made a mistake in our reckoning and we thought that today was the day of 'Arafa." 'Umar said, "Go to Makka, you and whoever else is with you, and do *ṭawāf* and sacrifice your animal if you have one with you, then shave or cut your hair and return home. Then, in another year, perform *ḥajj* and sacrifice an animal, and if you cannot find one, fast three days on *ḥajj* and seven when you return home."

Mālik said, "Someone who intends to perform *ḥajj* and *'umra* together (*Ḥajj al-Qirān*) and then misses the *ḥajj* must perform *ḥajj* again in another year, doing *Ḥajj al-Qirān* and offer two sacrificial animals, one for doing *Ḥajj al-Qirān*, and one for the hajj that he has missed."

20.50 Intercourse before the *Ṭawāf al-Ifāḍa*

164 Yaḥyā related to me from Mālik from Abū az-Zubayr al-Makkī from 'Aṭā' ibn Abī Rabāḥ that 'Abdullāh ibn 'Abbās was asked about a man who had had intercourse with his wife while at Minā before he had done the *Ṭawāf al-Ifāḍa*, and he told him to sacrifice an animal.

165 Yaḥyā related to me from Mālik from Thawr ibn Zayd ad-Dīlī that 'Ikrima, the *mawlā* of Ibn 'Abbās, said, (and Thawr believed it to be from 'Abdullāh ibn 'Abbās), "Someone who has intercourse with his wife before he has done the *Ṭawāf al-Ifāḍa* should perform an *'umra* and sacrifice an animal."

166 Yaḥyā related to me from Mālik that he had heard Rabi'a ibn Abī 'Abd ar-Raḥmān saying the same about that as what 'Ikrima related from Ibn 'Abbās.

Mālik said, "That is what I like most out of what I have heard about the matter."

Mālik was asked about a man who forgot the *Ṭawāf al-Ifāḍa* until he had left Makka and returned to his country and he said, "I think that he should go back and do the *Ṭawāf al-Ifāḍa* as long as he has not had sexual relations with women. If, however, he has had sexual relations with women, then he should not only return and do the *Ṭawāf al-Ifāḍa* but he should also perform an *'umra* and sacrifice an animal. He should not buy the animal in Makka and sacrifice it there, but if he has not brought one with him from wherever it was he set out to do *'umra*, he should buy one in Makka and then take it outside the limits of the *Ḥaram* and drive it from there to Makka and sacrifice it there."

20.51 The sacrificial animals considered least difficult

167 Yaḥyā related to me from Mālik from Ja'far ibn Muḥammad from his father that 'Alī ibn Abī Ṭālib used to say, "The least difficult thing acceptable as a sacrificial animal is a sheep."

168 Yaḥyā related to me from Mālik that he had heard that 'Abdullāh ibn 'Abbās used to say, "The least difficult thing acceptable as a sacrificial animal is a sheep."

Mālik said, "That is what I like most out of what I have heard about the matter, because Allah, the Blessed and Exalted, says in His Book, *'O you who believe, do not kill game while you are in iḥrām. If one of you kills any deliberately, the reprisal for it is a livestock animal equivalent to what he killed, as judged by two just men among you, a sacrifice to reach the Ka'ba, or expiation by feeding the poor, or fasting commensurate to that,'* (5:95) and a sheep is one of the animals which is judged to be acceptable as a sacrifice. Allah has called it a sacrificial animal, and there is no dispute among us about the matter. How, indeed, could anyone be in doubt about the matter? A sheep is the *kaffāra* for anything which does not reach the extent of something for which a camel or a cow would be the *kaffāra*, and the *kaffāra* for something which does not reach the extent of something for which a sheep would be the *kaffāra* is fasting, or feeding poor people."

169 Yaḥyā related to me from Mālik from Nāfi' that 'Abdullāh ibn 'Umar used to say, "The least thing that is acceptable as a sacrificial animal is a camel or a cow."

170 Yaḥyā related to me from Mālik from 'Abdullāh ibn Abī Bakr that a *mawlā* of 'Amra bint 'Abd ar-Raḥmān called Ruqayya told him that

she once set out with 'Amra bint 'Abd ar-Raḥman to go to Makka. She said, "'Amra entered Makka on the eighth of Dhū al-Ḥijja, and I was with her. She did *ṭawāf* of the House, and *sa'y* between Ṣafā and Marwa, and then entered the back of the mosque. She asked me, 'Do you have a pair of scissors with you?' and I answered, 'No.' She said, 'Then try and find some for me.' I went and looked for some and brought them back and she cut some hair from the tresses of her head. Then, on the Day of Sacrifice, she slaughtered a sheep."

20.52 Sacrificial animals in general

171 Yaḥyā related to me from Mālik from Ṣadaqa ibn Yasār al-Makkī that a man from the people of Yemen, who had his hair braided came to 'Abdullāh ibn 'Umar and said, "Abū 'Abd ar-Raḥmān, I have come to perform *'umra* on its own." 'Abdullāh ibn 'Umar said to him, "If I had been with you or you had asked me, I would have told you to perform *ḥajj* and *'umra* together." The Yemenī answered, "Then that is what I am doing," and 'Abdullāh ibn 'Umar said to him, "Cut off the locks that are hanging from your head and offer a sacrificial animal." A woman from Iraq asked, "What should his sacrificial animal be, Abū 'Abd ar-Raḥmān?" and he replied, "His sacrificial animal." She asked him again, "What should his sacrificial animal be?" 'Abdullāh ibn 'Umar replied, "If I could only find a sheep to sacrifice, I would prefer to do that than to fast."

172 Yaḥyā related to me from Mālik from Nāfi' that 'Abdullāh ibn 'Umar used to say, "A woman in *iḥrām* should not comb her hair when she leaves *iḥrām* until she has cut off some tresses from her hair, and if she has an animal for sacrifice with her she should not cut off any of her hair until the animal has been killed."

173 Yaḥyā related to me from Mālik that he had heard one of the people of knowledge say, "A man and wife should not share in one sacrificial animal. Each should sacrifice an animal separately."

Mālik was asked about whether someone who had been entrusted with an animal for him to sacrifice on *ḥajj*, who then went into *iḥrām* for *'umra*, should sacrifice it when he came out of *iḥrām* or postpone it so that he sacrificed it at the time of the *ḥajj,* having in the meantime come out of *iḥrām* from his *'umra.* He said, "He should postpone it so that he may sacrifice it at the time of the *ḥajj,* and meanwhile come out of *iḥrām* from his *'umra.*"

Mālik said, "If it is judged that someone must offer an animal for having killed game, or for any other reason, this animal can only be sacrificed at Makka, since Allah, the Blessed and Exalted, says, '*...a sacrifice to reach the Ka'ba.*' The fasting or *ṣadaqa* that is considered equivalent to offering a sacrifice can be done outside Makka, and the person who is doing it can do it wherever he likes."

174 Yaḥyā related to me from Mālik from Yaḥyā ibn Sa'īd from Ya'qūb ibn Khālid al-Makhzūmī that Abū Asmā', the *mawlā* of 'Abdullāh ibn Ja'far, told him that he was with 'Abdullāh ibn Ja'far when they set out once from Madīna. At as-Suqyā they passed by Husayn ibn 'Alī, who was ill at the time. 'Abdullāh ibn Ja'far stayed with him and then, when he feared that he was late (for the *ḥajj*), he left and sent for 'Alī ibn Abī Ṭālib and Asmā' bint 'Umays in Madīna, and they came to Ḥusayn. Then Ḥusayn pointed to his head, and 'Alī told someone to shave his head. Then he sacrificed an animal for him at as-Suqyā, killing a camel for him.

Yaḥyā ibn Sa'īd added, "Ḥusayn had set out with 'Uthmān ibn 'Affān on that particular journey to Makka."

20.53 The *wuqūf* (standing) at 'Arafa and Muzdalifa

175 Yaḥyā related to me from Mālik that he had heard that the Messenger of Allah ﷺ said, "The whole of 'Arafa is a standing-place, except the middle of 'Urana, and the whole of Muzdalifa is a standing-place, except for the middle of Muḥassir."

176 Yaḥyā related to me from Mālik from Hishām ibn 'Urwa that 'Abdullāh ibn az-Zubayr used to say, "Know that the whole of 'Arafa is a standing-place except for the middle of 'Urana, and that the whole of Muzdalifa is a standing-place except for the middle of Muḥassir."

Mālik said, "Allah, the Blessed and Exalted says, '*There is to be no rafath, no fusūq and no jidāl during the ḥajj.*'" (2:197).

He added, "*Rafath* is sexual relations with women, and Allah knows best. Allah, the Blessed and Exalted says, '*Rafath with your women is permitted to you on the night of the fast.*' (2:197). *Fusūq* are sacrifices made to idols, and Allah knows best. Allah, the Blessed and Exalted, says, '*Or a fisq offered up to other than Allah.*' (6:145) *Jidāl* (arguing) during the *ḥajj* refers to when the Quraysh used to stand near the *Mash'ar al-Harām* at Quzaḥ in Muzdalifa, while the Arabs and others would stand at 'Arafa, and they would argue about who was the more correct.

Allah, the Blessed and Exalted, says, "*We have appointed for every nation a rite that they observe. So let them not dispute with you about the matter. Call the people to your Lord. You are guided straight.*" (22:67) This is what *jidāl* refers to in our opinion, and Allah knows best. I have heard this from the people of knowledge."

20.54 *Wuqūf* while not in *wuḍū'*, and *wuqūf* on a riding beast

177 Mālik was asked about whether a man could stand at 'Arafa, or at Muzdalifa, or stone the *Jamras*, or do *sa'y* between Ṣafā and Marwa if he was not in *wuḍū'*, and he said, "Every practice in the *ḥajj* that a menstruating woman can take part in can be taken part in by a man who is not in *wuḍū'*, and there is nothing due from him for that. However, it is better for him to be in *wuḍū'* for all those things, and he should make a general practice of it."

Mālik was asked whether a man who was riding should get down to do the standing at 'Arafa, or if he could do the standing while mounted, and he said, "He can do the standing (*wuqūf*) while mounted, unless he or his riding beast has an illness, in which case Allah is the one who most often accepts an excuse."

20.55 The *wuqūf* at 'Arafa of someone who misses the *ḥajj*

178 Yaḥyā related to me from Mālik from Nāfi' that 'Abdullāh ibn 'Umar used to say, "Someone who does not stand at 'Arafa on the night of Muzdalifa before the dawn breaks has missed the *ḥajj*, and someone who stands at 'Arafa on the night of Muzdalifa before the dawn breaks has caught the *ḥajj*."

179 Yaḥyā related to me from Mālik from Hishām ibn 'Urwa that his father said, "Someone who does not stand at 'Arafa on the night of Muzdalifa before the dawn breaks has missed the *ḥajj*, and someone who stands at 'Arafa on the night of Muzdalifa before the dawn breaks has caught the *ḥajj*."

Mālik said about a slave freed during the *wuqūf* at 'Arafa, "His standing does not fulfil for him the *ḥajj* of Islam, except if he was not in *iḥrām* and then he went into *iḥrām* after he was freed and he stood at 'Arafa that same night before the dawn broke – in which case that is enough for him. If, however, he did not go into *iḥrām* until after the dawn had broken, he is in the same position as someone who misses the *ḥajj* by not catching the standing at 'Arafa before the breaking of the dawn on the night of Muzdalifa, and he will have to perform the *ḥajj* of Islam later."

20.56 Sending women and children ahead

180 Yaḥyā related to me from Mālik from Nāfi' from Sālim and 'Ubaydullāh, two sons of 'Abdullāh ibn 'Umar, that their father 'Abdullāh ibn 'Umar used to send his family and children from Muzdalifa to Minā ahead of him so that they could pray *Ṣubḥ* at Mina and throw the stones before everyone (else) arrived.

181 Yaḥyā related to me from Mālik from Yaḥyā ibn Sa'īd from 'Atā' ibn Abī Rabāḥ that a *mawlā* of Asmā' bint Abī Bakr told him, "We arrived at Minā with Asmā' bint Abī Bakr at the end of the night, and I said to her, 'We have arrived at Minā at the end of the night,' and she said, 'We used to do that with one who was better than you.'"

182 Yaḥyā related to me from Mālik that he had heard that Ṭalḥa ibn 'Ubaydullāh used to send his family and children from Muzdalifa to Minā ahead of him.

183 Yaḥyā related to me from Mālik that he had heard one of the people of knowledge disapproving of stoning the *jamra* until after dawn on the Day of Sacrifice, as it was lawful for whoever had thrown the stones to sacrifice.

184 Yaḥyā related to me from Mālik from Hishām ibn 'Urwa that Fāṭima bint al-Mundhir told him that she used to see Asmā' bint Abī Bakr at Muzdalifa telling whoever led the *Ṣubḥ* prayer for her and her companions to pray it as soon as the dawn broke, after which she would mount and go to Mina without stopping at all.

20.57 Going from 'Arafa to Muzdalifa

185 Yaḥyā related to me from Mālik from Hishām ibn 'Urwa that his father said, "I was sitting with Usāma ibn Zayd when someone asked him, 'How did the Messenger of Allah ﷺ travel when he went from 'Arafa to Muzdalifa during the Farewell *Ḥajj*?' and he replied, 'He went at a medium pace, but when he found a gap (in the crowds) he sped up.'"

186 Yaḥyā related to me from Mālik from Nāfi' that 'Abdullāh ibn 'Umar used to spur on his mount in the middle of Muḥassir over the distance of a stone's throw.

20.58 Sacrificing during the *ḥajj*

187 Yaḥyā related to me from Mālik that he had heard that the Messenger of Allah ﷺ once said at Minā, "This is the place of sacrifice, and the whole of Minā is a place of sacrifice", and he said on *'umra,* "This is the place of sacrifice," meaning Marwa, "and all the pathways of Makka and its roads are a place of sacrifice."

188 Yaḥyā related to me from Mālik that Yaḥyā ibn Sa'īd said that 'Amra

bint 'Abd ar-Raḥmān told him that she had heard 'Ā'isha, *Umm al-Mu'minīn*, saying, "We set out with the Messenger of Allah ﷺ when there were five nights left in Dhū al-Qa'da and we assumed that we must be setting out for *ḥajj*. When we got near to Makka, the Messenger of Allah ﷺ told everyone that did not have a sacrificial animal with them to leave *iḥrām* after they had done *ṭawāf* of the House and *sa'y* between Ṣafā and Marwa."

'Ā'isha added, "We were sent some beef on the Day of Sacrifice. I asked what it was and they said that the Messenger of Allah ﷺ had sacrificed for his wives."

Yaḥyā ibn Sa'īd said, "I mentioned this *ḥadīth* to Qāsim ibn Muḥammad and he said, 'She has given you the complete *ḥadīth*, by Allah.'"

189 Yaḥyā related to me from Mālik from Nāfi' from 'Abdullāh ibn 'Umar that Ḥafṣa, *Umm al-Mu'minīn*, once said to the Messnger of Allah ﷺ, "Why is it that everyone has left *iḥrām* and you still have not left *iḥrām* from your *'umra*?" and he replied, "I have gummed my hair and garlanded my sacrificial animal and will not leave *iḥrām* until I have sacrificed the animal."

20.59 How to make the sacrifice

190 Yaḥyā related to me from Mālik from Ja'far ibn Muḥammad from his father from 'Alī ibn Abī Ṭālib that the Messenger of Allah ﷺ killed some of his sacrificial animals himself, and someone else killed the rest.

191 Yaḥyā related to me from Mālik from Nāfi' that 'Abdullāh ibn 'Umar said, "Someone who vows to sacrifice a camel or a cow to Allah should garland it with two sandals about its neck, and brand it by causing blood to flow from its side. He should then sacrifice it either at the House or at Minā on the Day of Sacrifice. There are no other correct places apart from those. However, someone who vows to slaughter a camel or a cow simply as a sacrifice can sacrifice it wherever he wishes."

192 Yaḥyā related to me from Mālik from Hishām ibn 'Urwa that his father used to kill his sacrificial animals while they were standing.

Mālik said, "No one is permitted to shave his head until he has killed his sacrificial animal, and no one must sacrifice before dawn on the Day of Sacrifice. The things that should be done on the Day of Sacrifice are slaughtering, donning clothes, grooming the body generally (*at-tafath*) and shaving the head, and none of this may be done before the Day of Sacrifice."

20.60 Shaving the head

193 Yaḥyā related to me from Mālik from Nāfi' from 'Abdullāh ibn 'Umar that the Messenger of Allah ﷺ said, "O Allah, have mercy on those who shave their hair." They said, "And those who shorten (their hair), Messenger of Allah." He said, "O Allah, have mercy on those who shave." They said, "And those who shorten it, Messenger of Allah." He said, "And those who shorten it."

194 Yaḥyā related to me from Mālik from 'Abd ar-Raḥmān ibn al-Qāsim that his father used to go into Makka by night when he was doing *'umra* and do *ṭawāf* of the House and *sa'y* between Ṣafā and Marwa and delay the shaving until the morning, but he would not go back to the House and do *ṭawāf* again until he had shaved his head.

'Abd ar-Raḥmān added, "Sometimes he would enter the mosque and do the *witr* prayer there without actually going near the House."

Mālik said, "*At-tafath* is shaving the head, putting on normal clothes and things of that nature."

Yaḥyā said that Mālik was asked whether a man who forgot to shave (his head) at Minā during the *ḥajj* could shave in Makka, and he said, "That is permissible, but I prefer the shaving to be done at Mina."

Mālik said, "What we are all agreed upon here (in Madīna) is that no-one should shave his head or cut his hair until he has killed his sacrificial animal, if he has one, and things that are unlawful for him do not become lawful for him until he leaves *iḥrām* at Minā on the Day of Sacrifice. This is because Allah, the Blessed and Exalted, says, '*But do not shave your heads until the sacrificial animal has reached the place of sacrifice.'* (2:196)"

20.61 Cutting the Hair

195 Yaḥyā related to me from Mālik from Nāfi' that if 'Abdullāh ibn 'Umar had finished the fast of Ramaḍān and intended to do *ḥajj*, he would not cut his hair or beard at all until he had performed *ḥajj*.

Mālik said, "It is not necessary for people to do the same."

196 Yaḥyā related to me from Mālik from Nāfi' that 'Abdullah ibn 'Umar used to trim his beard and moustache when he shaved at the end of a *ḥajj* or *'umra*.

197 Yaḥyā related to me from Mālik from Rabī'a ibn Abī 'Abd ar-Raḥmān that a man came to Qāsim ibn Muḥammad and said, "I did the *Ṭawāf al-Ifāḍa* along with my wife, and then I went off onto a mountain path and approached my wife to make love to her, and she said, 'I have not cut my hair yet.' So I bit some of her hair off with my teeth and then had intercourse with her." Qāsim laughed and said, "Tell her to cut her hair with some scissors."

Mālik said, "To my liking, an animal should be sacrificed in an instance such as this, because 'Abdullāh ibn 'Abbās said, 'Whoever forgets any of his rites on *ḥajj* should sacrifice an animal.'"

198 Yaḥyā related to me from Mālik from Nāfi' that 'Abdullāh ibn 'Umar once met a relative of his called al-Mujabbar who had done the *Ṭawāf al-Ifāḍa* but, out of ignorance, had not shaved his head or cut his hair. 'Abdullah told him to go back and shave his head or cut his hair, and then go back and do the *Ṭawāf al-Ifāḍa*.

199 Yaḥyā related to me from Mālik that he had heard that when Sālim ibn 'Abdullāh intended to go into *iḥrām* he would call for some scissors and trim his moustache and beard before setting off and before going into *iḥrām*.

20.62 Gumming the hair

200 Yaḥyā related to me from Mālik from Nāfi' from 'Abdullāh ibn 'Umar that 'Umar ibn al-Khaṭṭāb said, "Someone who puts plaits in his hair should shave his head, and do not plait your hair in a such a way that it seems you have gummed it."

201 Yaḥyā related to me from Mālik from Yaḥyā ibn Sa'īd from Sa'īd ibn al-Musayyab that 'Umar ibn al-Khaṭṭāb said, "Anyone who has braided his hair, or plaited it, or gummed it must shave his head."

20.63 Performing the prayer in the House, shortening the prayer, and hastening the *khuṭba* at 'Arafa

202 Yaḥyā related to me from Mālik from Nāfi' from 'Abdullāh ibn 'Umar that the Messenger of Allah ﷺ entered the Ka'ba with Usāma ibn Zayd, Bilāl ibn Rabāḥ and 'Uthmān ibn Ṭalha al-Ḥajabī and locked it behind him and stayed there for some time.

'Abdullāh said that he asked Bilāl, when he came out, what the Messenger of Allah ﷺ had done there and he said, "He positioned himself with one support to his left, two supports to his right, and three behind him (the house had six supports at that time) and then he prayed."

203 Yaḥyā related to me from Mālik from Ibn Shihāb that Sālim ibn 'Abdullāh said, "'Abd al-Mālik ibn Marwān wrote to al-Ḥajjāj ibn Yūsuf telling him not to disagree with my father, 'Abdullāh ibn 'Umar, about anything to do with the *ḥajj*. Then, when the day of 'Arafa came, 'Abdullāh ibn 'Umar went to him just after noon, and I went with him. He called out to him outside his tent, 'Where is this man?' and al-Hajjāj came out to him, wearing a blanket dyed with safflower and said to him, 'What is it, Abū 'Abd ar-Raḥmān?' He replied, 'Hurry up if you want to follow the *sunna*.' Al-Ḥajjāj said, 'At this hour?' and he answered, 'Yes.' Al-Ḥajjāj said, 'Wait until I have poured some water over myself and then I will come out.' So 'Abdullāh dismounted and waited until al-Ḥajjāj came out. He passed between me and my father and I said to him, 'If you want to follow the *sunna* today, then make the *khuṭba* short, do not delay the

prayer and perform the prayer quickly.' Al-Ḥajjāj looked at my father, 'Abdullāh ibn 'Umar, to see if he would say the same thing, and when 'Abdullāh saw that, he said, 'What Sālim is saying is true.'"

20.64 Performing the prayer at Minā on the eighth day of Dhū al-Ḥijja, and the *jumu'a* at Minā and 'Arafa

204 Yaḥyā related to me from Mālik from Nāfi' that 'Abdullāh ibn 'Umar used to pray *Ẓuhr, 'Aṣr, Maghrib, 'Ishā'* and *Ṣubḥ* at Minā. Then in the morning, after the sun had risen, he would go to 'Arafa.

Mālik said, "What we are all agreed upon here (in Madīna) is that the imām does not recite the Qur'ān out loud in *Ẓuhr* on the Day of 'Arafa, and that he gives a *khuṭba* to the people on that day, and that the prayer on the day of 'Arafa is really a *Ẓuhr* prayer, and even if it coincides with a *jumu'a* it is still a *Ẓuhr* prayer, but one which has been shortened because of travelling."

Mālik said that the imām of the pilgrims should not pray the *jumu'a* prayer if the Day of 'Arafa, the Day of Sacrifice, or one of the three days after the Day of Sacrifice, was a Friday.

20.65 Performing the prayer at Muzdalifa

205 Yaḥyā related to me from Mālik from Ibn Shihāb from Sālim ibn 'Abdullāh from 'Abdullāh ibn 'Umar that the Messenger of Allah ﷺ prayed *Maghrib* and *'Ishā'* together at Muzdalifa.

206 Yaḥyā related to me from Mālik from Mūsā ibn 'Uqba that Kurayb, the *mawlā* of Ibn 'Abbās, heard Usāma ibn Zayd say, " The Messenger of Allah ﷺ left 'Arafa and then, when he reached ash-Shi'b, he dismounted and urinated and then did *wuḍū'*, though not thoroughly. I said to him, 'It is time for the prayer, Messenger of Allah,' and he answered, 'The prayer is ahead of you,' and then mounted. When we arrived at Muzdalifa he dismounted and did *wuḍū'* thoroughly. Then the *iqāma* was said for the prayer and he prayed *Maghrib*. After that everyone settled his camel in

its resting-place, and then the *iqāma* for *'Ishā'* was said and he prayed it, without having prayed anything between the two."

207 Yaḥyā related to me from Mālik from Yaḥyā ibn Sa'īd from 'Adī ibn Thābit al-Anṣārī that 'Abdullāh ibn Yazīd al-Khaṭmī told him that Abū Ayyūb al-Anṣārī told him that he prayed *Maghrib* and *'Ishā'* together at Muzdalifa during the Farewell *Ḥajj*, with the Messenger of Allah ﷺ.

208 Yaḥyā related to me from Mālik from Nāfi' that 'Abdullāh ibn 'Umar used to pray *Maghrib* and *'Ishā'* together at Muzdalifa.

20.66 Performing the prayer at Minā

209 Mālik said that the people of Makka who are performing the *ḥajj* should shorten the prayer to two *rak'as* when at Minā until they go back to Makka.

210 Yaḥyā related to me from Mālik from Hishām ibn 'Urwa from his father that the Messenger of Allah ﷺ prayed four *rak'a* prayers with only two *rak'as* when at Minā, and that Abū Bakr prayed them at Minā with only two *rak'as*, and that 'Umar ibn al-Khaṭṭāb prayed them at Minā with only two *rak'as*, and that 'Uthmān prayed them at Minā with only two *rak'as* for half of his caliphate, and then in the latter part completed them.

211 Yaḥyā related to me from Mālik from Ibn Shihāb from Sa'īd ibn al-Musayyab that 'Umar ibn al-Khaṭṭāb prayed two *rak'as* with everybody when he arrived in Makka. Then, when he had finished, he said, "People of Makka, complete your prayer, because we are a group of travellers." Later, 'Umar ibn al-Khaṭṭāb prayed two *rak'as* with them at Minā, but we have not heard that he said anything to them on that occasion.

212 Yaḥyā related to me from Mālik from Zayd ibn Aslam from his father that Umar ibn al-Khaṭṭāb prayed two *rak'as* with the people of Makka, and then, when he had finished, he said, "People of Makka, complete your prayer, because we are a group of travellers." Later, 'Umar prayed two *rak'as* with them at Mina, but we have not heard that he said anything to them on that occasion.

Mālik was asked whether the people of Makka should pray two *rak'as* at 'Arafa or four, and whether the amīr of the *ḥajj*, if he was a Makkan, should pray *Ẓuhr* and *'Aṣr* with four *rak'as* or two, and also how the people of Makka who were living (at Minā) should pray, and he said, "The people of Makka should pray only two *rak'as* at 'Arafa and Minā for as long as they stay there, and should shorten the prayer until they return to Makka. The amīr of the *ḥajj*, if he is a Makkan, should also shorten the prayer at 'Arafa and during the days of Minā. Anyone who is living at Mina as a resident should do the full prayer at Minā, and similarly anyone who lives at 'Arafa and is a resident there should do the full prayer at 'Arafa."

20.67 The prayer of a visitor to Makka or Minā

213 Yaḥyā related to me that Mālik said, "Someone who comes to Makka at or before the new moon of Dhū al-Ḥijja and goes into *iḥrām* for the *ḥajj* should do the full prayer until he leaves Makka for Minā, and then he should shorten the prayer. This is because he has decided to stay there for more than four nights."

20.68 Saying the *takbīr* during the Days of *Tashrīq*

214 Yaḥyā related to me from Mālik from Yaḥyā ibn Sa'īd that he had heard that on the day after the Day of Sacrifice 'Umar ibn al-Khaṭṭāb went out a little after the sun had risen and said the *takbīr*, and everyone repeated it after him. Then he went out a second time the same day when the sun was well up and said the *takbīr*, and everyone repeated it after him. Then he went out a third time after midday and said the *takbīr*, and everyone repeated it after him until it resounded from group to group until it reached the House and people knew that 'Umar had left to throw the stones.

Mālik said, "What we do here (in Madīna) is to say the *takbīr* during the Days of *Tashrīq* after each prayer. The first time is when the imām and everyone with him says the *takbīr* after the *Ẓuhr* prayer on the Day of Sacrifice, and the last is when the imām and everyone with him says the *takbīr* after *Ṣubḥ* on the last of the Days of *Tashrīq*, after which he stops saying the *takbīr*."

Mālik said, "The *takbīrs* during the Days of *Tashrīq* should be performed by both men and women, whether they are in a group or by themselves, at Minā or anywhere else, and all of the them are obligatory. In this everyone follows the imām of the *ḥajj* and the people at Minā, because when everyone returns (to Makka) and comes out of *iḥrām* they keep the same people as imāms while out of *iḥrām* (as they did when they were in *iḥrām*). Someone who is not performing *ḥajj* does not follow them except for the *takbīrs* during the Days of *Tashrīq*."

Mālik said, "The '*designated days*' (2:203) are the Days of *Tashrīq*."

20.69 Performing the prayer at al-Mu'arras and al-Muḥaṣṣab

215 Yaḥyā related to me from Mālik from Nāfi' from 'Abdullāh ibn 'Umar that the Messenger of Allah ﷺ made his camel kneel down at al-Baṭḥā', which is at Dhū al-Ḥulayfa, and prayed there.

Nāfi' said, "'Abdullāh ibn 'Umar used to do that."

Mālik said, "No one should go past al-Mu'arras, when he is returning from *ḥajj*, without praying there. If he passes it at a time when prayer is not permissible he should stay there until prayer is permissible and then pray whatever he feels is appropriate. (This is) because I have heard that the Messenger of Allah ﷺ stopped there to rest, and that 'Abdullāh ibn 'Umar stopped his camel there also."

216 Yaḥyā related to me from Mālik from Nāfi' that 'Abdullah ibn 'Umar used to pray *Ẓuhr*, *'Aṣr*, *Maghrib* and *'Ishā'* at al-Muḥaṣṣab, and then enter Makka at night and do *ṭawāf* of the House.

20.70 Staying overnight at Makka on the nights of Minā

217 Yaḥyā related to me from Mālik that Nāfi' said, "They say that 'Umar ibn al-Khaṭṭāb used to send men out to bring people in from beyond al-'Aqaba."

218 Yaḥyā related to me from Mālik from Nāfi' from 'Abdullah ibn 'Umar that 'Umar ibn al-Khaṭṭāb said, "No one performing *ḥajj* should spend the nights of Minā beyond al-'Aqaba."

219 Yaḥyā related to me from Mālik from Hishām ibn 'Urwa that his father said, talking about spending the nights of Minā at Makka: "No one should spend the night anywhere except Minā."

20.71 Stoning the *jamras*

220 Yaḥyā related to me from Mālik that he had heard that 'Umar ibn al-Khaṭṭāb used to stop at the first two *jamras* for such a long time that someone standing up would get tired.

221 Yaḥyā related to me from Mālik from Nāfi' that 'Abdullāh ibn 'Umar used to stop for a long time at the first two *jamras* saying, "Allah is greater", "Glory be to Allah", "Praise be to Allah", and making *du'ā*'s to Allah, but he did not stop at the *Jamrat al-'Aqaba*.

222 Yaḥyā related to me from Mālik from Nāfi' that 'Abdullāh ibn 'Umar used to say "Allah is greater" whenever he threw a pebble while stoning the *jamra*.

223 Yaḥyā related to me from Mālik that he had heard some of the people of knowledge saying, "The pebbles used for stoning the *jamras* should be like the stones used as slingshot."

Mālik said, "I like it better if they are a little larger than that."

Yaḥyā related to me from Mālik from Nāfi' that 'Abdullāh ibn 'Umar used to say, "Someone who is at Minā when the sun sets in the middle of the Days of *Tashrīq* must not leave until he has stoned the *jamras* on the following day."

224 Yaḥyā related to me from Mālik from 'Abd ar-Raḥmān ibn Qāsim from his father that when people went to stone the *jamras* they would walk both going there and coming back. The first one to ride was Mu'āwiya ibn Abī Sufyān.

225 Yaḥyā related to me from Mālik that he asked 'Abd ar-Raḥmān ibn Qāsim, "From where did Qasim stone the *Jamrat al-'Aqaba*?" and he replied, "From wherever it was possible."

Yaḥyā said that Mālik was asked whether someone else could throw the stones for a child or a sick man and he said, "Yes, and a sick man should inquire as to when the stones will be thrown for him and then say the *takbīr* while he is in the place where he is staying, and make a sacrifice. If a sick man regains his health during the Days of *Tashrīq*, he should stone whatever stoning has been done for him and he should sacrifice an animal."

Mālik said, "I do not consider that someone who stones the *jamras* or does *sa'y* between Ṣafā and Marwa without being in *wuḍū'* has to repeat anything, but he should not do so deliberately."

226 Yaḥyā related to me from Mālik from Nāfi' that 'Abdullāh ibn 'Umar used to say, "The *jamras* should not be stoned during the three days until after the sun has passed the meridian."

20.72 Indulgence with respect to stoning the jamras

227 Yaḥyā related to me from Mālik from 'Abdullāh ibn Abī Bakr ibn Ḥazm from his father that Abū al-Baddāḥ ibn 'Āṣim ibn 'Adī told him from his father that the Messenger of Allah ﷺ allowed the camel-herders to spend the night outside of Minā, and they threw the stones (once) on the Day of Sacrifice, and (once) for the following day and the day after that, and (once) on the day when they left Minā.

228 Yaḥyā related to me from Mālik that Yaḥyā ibn Sa'īd heard 'Aṭā' ibn Abī Rabāḥ mentioning that the camel-herders were allowed to throw the stones at night, and saying that this was in the early period (of Islam).

Mālik said, "The explanation of the *ḥadīth* in which the Messenger of Allah ﷺ allowed the camel-herders to delay the stoning of the *jamras* is, in our view, and Allah knows best, that they threw stones on the Day of Sacrifice, and then threw again two days later, which was the first possible day for leaving, and this throwing was for the day which had passed. They then threw again for the day itself, because it is only possible for someone to make up for something which is obligatory for him, and when something obligatory passes someone by (without him doing it) he must necessarily make it up afterwards (and not beforehand). So (in the case of the camel-herders), if it seemed appropriate for them to leave that day, they would have done all that they were supposed to do, and if they were to stay until the following day, they would throw stones with everybody else on the second and last day for leaving, and then leave."

229 Yaḥyā related to me from Mālik from Abū Bakr ibn Nāfi' from his father that the daughter of one of Ṣafiyya bint Abī 'Ubayd's brothers was bleeding after she had given birth to a child at Muzdalifa. She and Safiyya were delayed and did not arrive at Minā until after the sun had set on the Day of Sacrifice. 'Abdullāh ibn 'Umar told them both to stone the *jamra* at the time they arrived and he did not think that they owed anything.

Yaḥyā said that Mālik was asked about someone who forgot to stone one of the *jamras* on one of the days of Minā until it was evening and he said, "He should throw the stones at whatever time of day or night he remembers, just as he would pray the prayer if he forgot it and then remembered it at any time of day or night. If he remembers (that he has not done the stoning) after he has returned to Makka, or after he has left, he must sacrifice an animal."

20.73 The *Ṭawāf al-Ifāḍa*

230 Yaḥyā related to me from Mālik from Nāfi' and 'Abdullāh ibn Dīnār from 'Abdullāh ibn 'Umar that 'Umar ibn al-Khattāb gave a *khuṭba* to the people at 'Arafa and taught them the conduct of the *ḥajj*, and one of the things he said to them in his speech was, "When you get to Minā and have stoned the *jamra*, then whatever is unlawful for someone performing the *ḥajj* becomes lawful, except women and scent. No one should touch women or scent until he has done *ṭawāf* of the House."

231 Yaḥyā related to me from Mālik from Nāfi' and 'Abdullāh ibn Dīnār from 'Abdullāh ibn 'Umar that 'Umar ibn al-Khaṭṭāb said, "When someone has stoned the *jamra* and shaved his head or shortened some of his hair and sacrificed an animal, whatever was unlawful for him becomes lawful, except women and scent, (which remain lawful for him) until he has done *ṭawāf* of the House."

20.74 A menstruating woman's entering Makka

232 Yaḥyā related to me from 'Abd ar-Raḥmān ibn al-Qāsim, from his father that 'Ā'isha, *Umm al-Mu'minīn*, said, "We set out with the Messenger of Allah ﷺ, in the year of the Farewell *Ḥajj* and we went into *iḥrām* for *'umra*. Afterwards, the Messenger of Allah ﷺ said, 'Whoever has a sacrificial animal with him should go into *iḥrām* for *Ḥajj al-Qirān*, and he should not leave *iḥrām* without leaving *iḥrām* for both of them at the same time.'"

She continued, "I was menstruating when I got to Makka, so I did not do *ṭawāf* of the House or *sa'y* between Ṣafā and Marwa. I complained to the Messenger of Allah ﷺ and he said, 'Undo your hair and comb it and leave the *'umra* and go back into *iḥrām* for the *ḥajj*.'"

She said, "I did so, and when we had completed the *ḥajj*, the Messenger of Allah ﷺ sent me with 'Abd ar-Raḥmān ibn Abī Bakr as-Ṣiddīq to at-Tan'īm and I performed an *'umra* and he said, 'This is in place of your *'umra*.'"

"Those who had entered *iḥrām* for the *'umra* did *ṭawāf* of the House and *sa'y* between Ṣafā and Marwa, then left *iḥrām*. Then they did another *ṭawāf* after returning from Minā for their *ḥajj*, whereas those who entered *iḥrām* for the *ḥajj* or combined the *ḥajj* and the *'umra*, only did one *ṭawāf*."

Yaḥyā related the same as that to me from Mālik from Ibn Shihāb from 'Urwa ibn az-Zubayr from 'Ā'isha.

233 Yaḥyā related to me from Mālik from 'Abd ar-Raḥmān ibn al-Qāsim from his father that 'Ā'isha said, "I came to Makka at the time of my period so I did not do *ṭawāf* of the House or go between Ṣafā and Marwa. I complained to the Messenger of Allah ﷺ and he said, 'Do what the people performing *ḥajj* do except do not do *ṭawāf* of the House and go between Ṣafā and Marwa until you are pure.'"

Mālik said, concerning a woman who entered *iḥrām* for *'umra* at the time of *ḥajj*, and she arrived in Makka during her period and so could not do *ṭawāf* of the House, "When she fears that the time (for *ḥajj*) is getting close, she gets into *iḥrām* for the *ḥajj* and sacrifices an animal. She is like someone who combines the *ḥajj* and the *'umra*. One *ṭawāf* is enough for her. If a woman starts her period after she has already done *ṭawāf* of the House and prayed, she does *sa'y* between Safā and Marwa and stops at 'Arafa and Muzdalifa and stones the *jamras* but she does not do the *Ṭawāf al-Ifāḍa* until she is pure and has finished her menses."

20.75 The *Ṭawāf al-Ifāḍa* of a menstruating woman

234 Yaḥyā related to me from Mālik from 'Abd ar-Raḥmān ibn al-Qāsim from his father from 'Ā'isha, *Umm al-Mu'minīn*, that Ṣafiyya bint Ḥuyayy began menstruating and so she mentioned it to the Messenger of Allah ﷺ, and he asked, "Will she delay us?" and he was told, "She has already done the *Ṭawāf al-Ifāḍa*," and he said, "Then she will not delay us."

235 Yaḥyā related to me from Mālik from 'Abdullāh ibn Abī Bakr ibn Ḥazm from his father from 'Amra bint 'Abd ar-Raḥmān that 'Ā'isha, *Umm al-Mu'minīn*, said to the Messenger of Allah ﷺ, "Messenger of

Allah, Ṣafiyya bint Ḥuyayy has begun her period," and the Messenger of Allah ﷺ said, "Perhaps she will delay us. Has she done *ṭawāf* of the House with you?" They said, "Of course." He said, "So you are free to leave."

236 Yaḥyā related to me from Mālik from Abū ar-Rijāl Muḥammad ibn 'Abd ar-Raḥmān from 'Amra bint 'Abd ar-Raḥmān that when 'Ā'isha, *Umm al-Mu'minīn*, was performing *ḥajj* with women who were expecting their periods, she would hurry them to do the *Ṭawāf al-Ifāḍa* on the Day of Sacrifice. If they started to menstruate after the *Ṭawāf al-Ifāḍa* she did not stop for them but left with them while they were menstruating.

237 Yaḥyā related to me from Mālik from Hishām ibn 'Urwa from his father from 'Ā'isha, *Umm al-Mu'minīn*, that the Messenger of Allah ﷺ mentioned Ṣafiyya bint Ḥuyayy and he was told that she had started her period. The Messenger of Allah ﷺ said, "Perhaps she will delay us." They said, "Messenger of Allah, she has done *ṭawāf*," and the Messenger of Allah ﷺ said, "Then she will not delay us."

Mālik said that Hishām said that 'Urwa said that 'Ā'isha said, "We can remember, so why would people get their women to do the *ṭawāf* early if it wasn't of benefit to them? If it were as they say, more than six thousand menstruating women would still be in Minā in the morning, all of them having already done the *Ṭawāf al-Ifāḍa*.'"

238 Yaḥyā related to me from Mālik from 'Abdullāh ibn Abī Bakr from his father that Abū Salama ibn 'Abd ar-Raḥmān told him that Umm Sulaym bint Milḥān asked the Messenger of Allah ﷺ for advice one time when she had begun menstruating, or had given birth to a child, after she had done *Ṭawāf al-Ifāḍa* on the Day of Sacrifice. The Messenger of Allah ﷺ gave her permission to leave.

Mālik said, "A woman menstruating at Minā stays until she has done *ṭawāf* of the House. There is no escape from that for her. If she has already done the *Ṭawāf al-Ifāḍa* and she starts to menstruate afterwards, she may leave for her country, since permission for menstruating women to leave has been transmitted to us from the Messenger of Allah ﷺ."

He added, "If a woman starts her period at Minā before she does the

Ṭawāf al-Ifāḍa, and the period lasts longer than usual, she has to stay longer than the time that bleeding would usually detain women."

20.76 The compensation (*fidya*) for killing birds and wild animals while in *iḥrām*

239 Yaḥyā related to me from Mālik from Abū az-Zubayr that 'Umar ibn al-Khaṭṭāb gave the judgement of a ram for a hyena, a female goat for a gazelle, a she-goat less than one year old for a hare, and a four month old kid for a jerboa.

240 Yaḥyā related to me from Mālik from 'Abd al-Mālik ibn Qurayr from Muḥammad ibn Sīrīn that a man came to 'Umar ibn al-Khaṭṭāb and said, "I was racing a friend on horseback towards a narrow mountain trail and we killed a gazelle accidentally and we were in *iḥrām*. What is your opinion?" 'Umar said to a man by his side, "Come, so that you and I may make an assessment." They decided on a female goat for him, and the man turned away saying, "This *Amīr al-Mu'minīn* cannot even make an assessment in the case of a gazelle until he calls a man to decide with him." 'Umar overheard the man's words and called him and asked him, "Do you recite *Sūrat al-Mā'ida*?" and he answered, "No." He said, "Then do you recognize this man who has taken the decision with me?" and he answered, "No." He said, "If you had told me that you did recite *Sūrat al-Mā'ida*, I would have dealt you a blow." Then he said, "Allah the Blessed, the Exalted says in His Book, *'as judged by two just men among you, a sacrifice to reach the Ka'ba'* (5:95), and this is 'Abd ar-Raḥmān ibn 'Awf."

241 Yaḥyā related to me from Mālik from Hishām ibn 'Urwa that his father used to say, "For an oryx a cow is given and for the female of gazelles a sheep."

242 Yaḥyā related to me from Mālik from Yaḥyā ibn Sa'īd that Sa'īd ibn al-Musayyab used to say, "For a pigeon killed in Makka a sheep is due."

Mālik said, speaking about if a man of the people of Makka were to enter *iḥrām* for *ḥajj* or *'umra* and there were some Makkan nestlings in his house and they were shut in and died, "I think that he should pay for that with a sheep for each bird."

243 Mālik said, "I still hear that when a person in *iḥrām* kills an ostrich, a camel is due."

Mālik said, "I think that for an ostrich egg, one-tenth of the price of a camel is due in the same way that one pays the price of a slave, either male or female, for the unborn child of a free woman. The value of the slave is fifty dinars, and that is one-tenth of what the blood-money, (in compensation) for the mother would be.

Mālik said, "In the case of birds of prey, eagles or falcons or vultures count as game for which a price is paid just as a price is paid for any game which a person in *iḥrām* kills."

Mālik said, "For everything for which a penalty is paid, the assessment is the same, whether the animal is old or young. The analogy of that is that the blood-money for the young and the old freeman are considered to be the same."

20.77 The *fidya* for killing locusts in *iḥrām*

244 Yaḥyā related to me from Mālik from Zayd ibn Aslam that a man came to 'Umar ibn al-Khaṭṭāb and said, "*Amīr al-Mu'minīn*, I killed some locusts with my whip when I was in *iḥrām*," and 'Umar said to him, "Give a handful of food."

245 Yaḥyā related to me from Mālik from Yaḥyā ibn Sa'īd that a man came to 'Umar ibn al-Khaṭṭāb and asked him about some locusts he had killed while he was in *iḥrām*. 'Umar said to Ka'b, "Come, let us make an assessment." Ka'b said, "A dirham," and 'Umar said to Ka'b, "You can find dirhams. A date is better than a locust."

20.78 The *fidya* for shaving the head before sacrificing

246 Yaḥyā related to me from Mālik from 'Abd al-Karīm ibn Mālik al-Jazarī from 'Abd ar-Raḥmān ibn Abī Laylā from Ka'b ibn 'Ujra that one time he was with the Messenger of Allah ﷺ in *iḥrām*, and he was suffering from lice on his head. The Messenger of Allah ﷺ, told him to shave his head, saying, "Fast three days, or feed six poor people, two *mudds* for each person, or sacrifice a sheep. If you do any of those it will be enough for you."

247 Yaḥyā related to me from Mālik from Ḥumayd bin Qays from Mujāhid Abū al-Ḥajjāj from Ibn Abī Laylā from Ka'b ibn 'Ujra that the Messenger of Allah ﷺ said to him, "Perhaps your lice are troubling you?" He replied that indeed they were, and the Messenger of Allah ﷺ said, "Shave your head and fast three days or feed six poor men or sacrifice a sheep."

248 Yaḥyā related to me from Mālik that 'Aṭā' ibn 'Abdullāh al-Khurasānī said that an old man from Sūq al-Buram in Kufa had related to him that Ka'b ibn 'Ujra said, "The Messenger of Allah ﷺ came to me while I was blowing under a cooking pot belonging to my companions and my head and beard were full of lice. He took my forehead and said, 'Shave your hair and fast three days or feed six poor people.' The Messenger of Allah ﷺ was aware that I did not have anything with me to sacrifice.'"

Mālik said, concerning paying compensation (*fidya*) for the relief of physical discomfort, "The custom concerning it is that no one pays compensation until he has done something which makes it obligatory to pay compensation just as making amends (*kaffāra*) is only done when it has become obligatory for the one who owes it. The person can pay the compensation wherever he wishes, regardless of whether he has to sacrifice an animal or fast or give *ṣadaqa* – in Makka or in any other town."

Mālik said, "It is not correct for a person in *ihrām* to pluck out any of his hair or to shave it or cut it until he has left *ihrām*, unless he is suffering from an ailment of the head, in which case he owes the compensation Allah the Exalted has ordered. It is not correct for a person in *ihrām* to cut his nails, or to kill his lice, or to remove them from his head or from his skin or his garment to the ground. If a person in *ihrām* removes lice from his skin or his garment, he must give away the quantity of food that he can scoop up with both hands."

Mālik said, "Anyone who, while in *ihrām*, plucks out hairs from his nose or armpit or rubs his body with a depilatory agent or shaves the hair from around a head wound out of necessity or shaves his neck for the place of the cupping glasses, regardless of whether it is in forgetfulness or in ignorance, owes compensation in all these instances, and he must not shave the place of the cupping glasses. Someone, who, out of ignorance, shaves his head before he stones the *jamra*, must also pay compensation."

20.79 Forgetfulness in the rituals

249 Yaḥyā related to me from Mālik from Ayyūb ibn Abī Tamīma as-Sakhtayānī from Sa'īd ibn Jubayr that 'Abdullāh ibn 'Abbās said, "If someone forgets anything of the rituals or omits them intentionally, he must slaughter an animal."

Ayyūb added "I do not know if he said 'omits' or 'forgets'."

Mālik said, "If it is a sacrificial animal that has to be slaughtered, it may only be done in Makka, but if it is a sacrifice, it may be slaughtered wherever the one who owes the sacrifice prefers."

20.80 Compensation (*fidya*) in general

250 Mālik said concerning someone who wishes to wear clothes that a person in *iḥrām* must not wear, or cut his hair, or touch perfume without necessity, because he finds it easy to pay the compensation: "No one must do such things. They are only allowed in cases of necessity, and compensation is owed by whoever does them."

Mālik was asked whether the culprit could choose for himself the method of compensation he made, and he was asked what kind of animal was to be sacrificed, and how much food was to be given, and how many days were to be fasted, and whether the person could delay any of these, or if they had to be done immediately. He answered, "Whenever there are alternatives in the Book of Allah for the *kaffāra*, the culprit can choose to do whichever of the alternatives he prefers. The sacrifice is a sheep. Fasting is fasting for three days. Feeding consists of feeding six poor men: two *mudds* for every poor man, measured by the first *mudd*, the *mudd* of the Prophet ﷺ."

Mālik said, "I have heard one of the people of knowledge saying, 'When a person in *iḥrām* throws something and hits game unintentionally and kills it, he must pay compensation. In the same way, someone outside the *Ḥaram* who throws anything into the *Ḥaram* and hits game he did not intend to and kills it, has to pay compensation because the intentional and the accidental are in the same position in this matter.'"

Mālik said concerning people who kill game together while they are in *iḥrām* or in the *Ḥaram*, "I think that each one of them owes a full share. If a sacrificial animal is decided for them, each one of them owes one, and if fasting is decided for them, the full fasting is owed by each one of them. The analogy of that is a group of people who kill a man by mistake and the *kaffāra* for that is that each person among them must free a slave or fast two consecutive months."

Mālik said, "Anyone who throws something at game or hunts it after stoning the *jamra* and shaving his head but before he has performed the *Ṭawāf al-Ifāḍa* owes compensation for that game, because Allah the Blessed, the Exalted said, '*And when you leave iḥrām, then hunt*,' and restrictions still remain for someone who has not done the *Ṭawāf al-Ifāḍa* about touching perfume and women."

Mālik said, "Someone in *iḥrām* does not owe anything for plants he cuts down in the *Ḥaram* and it has not reached us that anyone has given a decision of anything for it, but what he has done is bad!"

Mālik said concerning someone who was ignorant of, or who forgot the fast of three days in the *ḥajj*, or who was ill during them and so did not fast them until he had returned to his community, "He must offer a sacrificial animal (*hady*) if he can find one and if not he must fast the three days among his people and the remaining seven after that."

20.81 The *ḥajj* in general

251 Yaḥyā related to me from Mālik from Ibn Shihāb from 'Īsā ibn Ṭalha that 'Abdullāh ibn 'Amr ibn al-'Āṣ said, "The Messenger of Allah ﷺ stopped for the people at Minā, and they questioned him. A man came and said to him, 'Messenger of Allah, I was unclear about what to do and I shaved before sacrificing,' and the Messenger of Allah ﷺ said, 'Sacrifice, and there is no harm.' Then another came to him and said, 'Messenger of Allah, I was unclear about what to do and I sacrificed before throwing the stones.' He advised, 'Throw, and there is no harm."

'Amr continued, saying that the Messenger of Allah ﷺ was not asked about anything that should be done before or after it without his saying, "Do it, and there is no harm."

252 Yaḥyā related to me from Mālik from Nāfi' from 'Abdullāh ibn 'Umar that when the Messenger of Allah ﷺ returned from a military expedition or a *ḥajj* or an *'umra*, he used to say three *takbīrs* on every elevated part of the land, and then he used to say, "There is no god but Allah, alone, without partner. To Him belongs the Kingdom and to Him belongs the praise and He has power over everything. Returning, repenting serving, prostrating, praising our Lord. Allah has promised truly and given His slave victory and defeated the tribes alone."

Lā ilāha illa'llāhu waḥdahu lā sharīka lah. Lahu'l-mulku wa lahu'l-ḥamd wa huwa 'alā kulli shay'in qadīr. Ā'ibūna tā'ibūna 'ābidūna sājidūna li rabbinā ḥāmidun. Ṣadaqa'llāhu wa'dahu wa naṣara 'abddahu wa hazama'al-aḥzāba waḥdah.

253 Yaḥyā related to me from Mālik from Ibrāhīm ibn 'Uqba from Kurayb the *mawlā* of 'Abdullāh ibn 'Abbās from Ibn 'Abbās that the Messenger of Allah ﷺ passed a woman in a litter and it was said to her, "This is the Messenger of Allah ﷺ," and she took the forearms of a young boy who

was with her and asked, "Does this one have a *ḥajj*, Messenger of Allah?" and he replied, "Yes, and you have a reward."

254 Yaḥyā related to me from Mālik from Ibrāhīm ibn Abī 'Abla from Ṭalḥa ibn 'Ubaydullāh ibn Kurayz that the Messenger of Allah ﷺ said, "Shaytān is not considered more abased or more cast out or more contemptible or more angry on any day than on the Day of 'Arafa. That is only because he sees the descent of the Mercy and the fact that Allah overlooks great wrong actions. That is except from what he was shown on the Day of Badr." Someone asked, "What was he shown on the Day of Badr, Messenger of Allah?" He replied, "Did he not see Jibrīl arranging the ranks of the angels?"

255 Yaḥyā related to me from Mālik from Ziyād ibn Abī Ziyād the *mawlā* of 'Abdullāh ibn 'Ayyāsh ibn Abī Rabi'a from Talha ibn 'Ubaydullāh ibn Kurayz that the Messenger of Allah ﷺ said, "The most excellent *du'ā'* is the *du'ā'* on the Day of 'Arafa, and the best of what I and the Prophets before me have said, is 'There is no god but Allah, alone, without partner.'"

Lā ilāha illa'llāhu waḥdahu lā sharīka lah.

256 Yaḥyā related to me from Mālik from Ibn Shihāb from Anas ibn Mālik that the Messenger of Allah ﷺ entered Makka in the Year of Victory wearing a helmet, and when he took it off a man came to him and said, "Messenger of Allah, Ibn Khaṭṭal is clinging to the covers of the Ka'ba", and the Messenger of Allah ﷺ said, "Kill him."

Mālik commented, "The Messenger of Allah ﷺ was not in *iḥrām* at the time, and Allah knows best."

257 Yaḥyā related to me from Mālik from Nāfi' that 'Abdullāh ibn 'Umar was coming from Makka and when he was at Qudayd, news came to him from Madīna and he returned and entered Makka without *iḥrām*.

Yaḥyā related the same as that to me from Mālik from Ibn Shihāb.

258 Yaḥyā related to me from Mālik from Muḥammad ibn 'Amr ibn Ḥalḥala ad-Dīlī from Muḥammad ibn 'Imrān al-Anṣārī that his father

said that ʿAbdullāh ibn ʿUmar came upon him while he was stopped for a rest under a tall tree on the road to Makka and he said, "What has made you stop under this tall tree?" He replied that he sought its shade. ʿAbdullāh ibn ʿUmar said, "Anything besides that?" and he said, "No, that was the only reason I have stopped for a rest," and ʿAbdullāh ibn ʿUmar said, "The Messenger of Allah ﷺ said, 'If you are between al-Akhshabayn (which are two mountains) near Minā, (indicating the east with his outspread hand) you will find a valley called as-Surar with a tree in it beneath which the umbilical cords of seventy Prophets have been cut.'"

259 Yaḥyā related to me from Mālik from ʿAbdullāh ibn Abī Bakr ibn Ḥazm from Ibn Abī Mulayka that ʿUmar ibn al-Khaṭṭāb passed a leprous woman doing *ṭawāf* of the House and he said to her, "Slave of Allah, do not make people uncomfortable. Better that you stay in your house," so she did so. A man passed by her after that and said to her, "The one who forbade you has died, so come out." She replied, "I am not going to obey him when he is alive and disobey him when he is dead."

260 Yaḥyā related to me from Mālik that he had heard that ʿAbdullāh ibn ʿAbbās used to say that the area between the corner of the Black Stone and the door of the Kaʿba was called *al-Multazam*.

261 Yaḥyā related to me from Mālik that Yaḥyā ibn Saʿīd heard Muḥammad ibn Yaḥyā ibn Ḥabbān mentioning that a certain man passed Abū Dharr at ar-Rabadha (which was about 30 miles from Madīna) and Abū Dharr asked him, "Where are you heading to?" and he replied, "I am intending to perform *ḥajj*." Abū Dharr asked, "Has anything else brought you out?" and on his saying, "No", Abū Dharr said, "Resume what you are doing whole-heartedly."

The man related, "I went on till I came to Makka and I stayed as long as Allah willed. Suddenly, one time, I was with a crowd of people thronging about a man and I pushed through the people to him and it was the old man that I had come across at ar-Rabadha. When he saw me, he recognized me and said, 'Ah, you have done what I told you.'"

262 Yaḥyā related to me from Mālik that he asked Ibn Shihāb about making a condition in the *ḥajj* that one could leave *iḥrām* at any place

where an obstacle befell one and he said, "Does anyone do that?" and disapproved of it.

Mālik was asked whether a man could cut plants from the *Ḥaram* for his mount, and he said, "No."

20.82 The *ḥajj* of a woman without a *maḥram*

263 Mālik said concerning a woman who had never been on *ḥajj*, "If she does not have a *maḥram* who can go with her, or if she has one but he cannot go with her, she does not abandon the obligation of the *ḥajj* which Allah has imposed on her. Let her go in a group of women."

20.83 Fasting in *Ḥajj at-Tamattu'*

264 Yaḥyā related to me from Mālik from Ibn Shihāb from 'Urwa ibn az-Zubayr that 'Ā'isha, *Umm al-Mu'minīn*, used to say, "Someone performing *Ḥajj at-Tamattu'* who does not have a sacrificial animal fasts (three days) from the time he enters *iḥrām* for the *ḥajj* till the Day of 'Arafa, and if he does not fast then, he fasts the days of Minā."

Yaḥyā related to me from Mālik from Ibn Shihāb from Sālim ibn 'Abdullāh that 'Abdullāh ibn 'Umar used to say the same concerning that as the words of 'Ā'isha ☙.

21. Jihād

21.1 Stimulation of desire for *jihād*

1 Yaḥyā related to me from Mālik from Abū az-Zinād from al-Aʿraj from Abū Hurayra that the Messenger of Allah ﷺ said, "Someone who does *jihād* in the way of Allah is like someone who fasts and prays constantly and does not slacken from his prayer and fasting until he returns."

2 Yaḥyā related to me from Mālik from Abū az-Zinād from al-Aʿraj from Abū Hurayra that the Messenger of Allah ﷺ said, "Allah guarantees either the Garden or a safe return to his home with whatever he has obtained of reward or booty for the one who does *jihād* in His way, if it is solely *jihād* and trust in His promise that brings him out of his house."

3 Yaḥyā related to me from Mālik from Zayd ibn Aslam from Abū Ṣāliḥ as-Sammān from Abū Hurayra that the Messenger of Allah ﷺ said, "Horses are a reward for one man, a protection for another, a burden for another. The one for whom they are a reward is the one who dedicates them for use in the Way of Allah, and tethers them in a meadow or grassland. Whatever the horse enjoys of the grassland or meadow in the length of its tether are good deeds for him. If it breaks its tether and goes over a hillock or two, its tracks and droppings are good deeds for him. If it crosses a river and drinks from it while he did not mean to allow it to drink it, that counts as good deeds for him, and the horse is a reward for him. Another man uses his horse to gain self reliance and to be able to refrain from asking for support from other people and does not forget Allah's right on their necks and backs. Horses are a protection for him. Another man uses them

out of pride to show them off and in hostility to the people of Islam. They are a burden for that man."

The Messenger of Allah ﷺ was asked about donkeys, and he said, "Nothing has been revealed to me about them except this single all-inclusive *āyat*, '*Whoever does an atom of good will see it, and whoever does an atom of evil will see it*' (99:7-8).

4 Yaḥyā related to me from 'Abdullāh ibn 'Abd ar-Raḥmān ibn Ma'mar al-Anṣārī that 'Aṭā' ibn Yasār said that the Messenger of Allah ﷺ, "Shall I tell you who has the best degree among people? A man who takes the rein of his horse to do *jihād* in the way of Allah. Shall I tell you who has the best degree among people after him? A man who lives alone with a few sheep, performs the prayer, pays the *zakāt*, and worships Allah without associating anything with Him."

5 Yaḥyā related to me from Mālik that Yaḥyā ibn Sa'īd said, "'Ubayda ibn al-Walīd ibn 'Ubāda ibn aṣ-Ṣāmit informed me from his father that his grandfather ('Ubāda) said, 'We made a contract with the Messenger of Allah ﷺ to hear and obey in ease and hardship, enthusiasm and reluctance, and not to dispute with people in authority and to speak or establish the truth wherever we were without worrying about criticism.'"

6 Yaḥyā related to me from Mālik that Zayd ibn Aslam had said that 'Ubayda ibn al-Jarrāḥ had written to 'Umar ibn al-Khaṭṭāb mentioning to him a great array of Byzantine troops and the anxiety they were causing him. 'Umar ibn al-Khaṭṭāb wrote in reply to him, "Whatever hardship befalls a believing slave, Allah will make an opening for him after it, and a hardship will not overcome two eases. Allah the Exalted says in His Book, '*O you who believe! Be steadfast; be supreme in steadfastness; be firm on the battlefield; and show fear of Allah – so that perhaps you will be successful*' (3:200)."

21.2 Prohibition against travelling with the Qur'ān in enemy territory

7 Yaḥyā related to me from Mālik from Nāfi' that 'Abdullāh ibn 'Umar said that the Messenger of Allah ﷺ forbade travelling with a Qur'ān in

the land of the enemy. Mālik commented, "That is out of fear that the enemy will get hold of it."

21.3 The prohibition against killing women and children in military expeditions

8 Yaḥyā related to me from Mālik from Ibn Shihāb that a son of Ka'b ibn Mālik (Mālik ibn Ka'b) said, "The Messenger of Allah ﷺ forbade those who fought Ibn Abī Ḥuqayq (a treacherous Jew from Madīna) to kill women and children. He said that one of the men fighting reported that the wife of Ibn Abī Ḥuqayq began screaming and he repeatedly raised his sword against her. Then he would remember the prohibition of the Messenger of Allah ﷺ so he would stop. Had it not been for that, we would have been rid of her."

9 Yaḥyā related to me from Mālik from Nāfi' from Ibn 'Umar that the Messenger of Allah ﷺ saw the corpse of a woman who had been slain in one of the expeditions and he disapproved of it and forbade the killing of women and children.

10 Yaḥyā related to me from Mālik from Yaḥyā ibn Sa'īd that Abū Bakr aṣ-Ṣiddīq was sending armies to Syria. He went for a walk with Yazīd ibn Abī Sufyān who was the commander of one of the battalions. It is claimed that Yazīd asked Abū Bakr, "Will you ride or shall I get down?" Abū Bakr replied, "I will not ride and you will not get down. I intend these steps of mine to be in the way of Allah." Then Abū Bakr advised Yazīd, "You will find a people who claim to have totally given themselves to Allah. Leave them to what they claim to have given themselves. You will find a people who have shaved the middle of their heads, strike what they have shaved with the sword.

"I give you ten orders. Do not kill women or children or an aged, infirm person. Do not cut down fruit-bearing trees. Do not destroy an inhabited place. Do not slaughter sheep or camels except for food. Do not burn bees and do not scatter them. Do not steal from the booty. And do not be cowardly."

11 Yaḥyā related to me from Mālik that he had heard that 'Umar ibn 'Abd al-'Azīz wrote to one of his governors, "It has been passed down to us that when the Messenger of Allah ﷺ sent out a raiding party, he would say to them, 'Make your raids in the name of Allah in the Way of Allah. Fight whoever denies Allah. Do not steal from the booty and do not act treacherously. Do not the mutilate and do not kill children.' Say the same to your armies and raiding parties, Allah willing. Peace be upon you."

21.4 Fulfilling safe conduct

12 Yaḥyā related to me from Mālik from a man of Kufa that 'Umar ibn al-Khaṭṭāb wrote to a commander of an army which he had sent out, "I have heard that it is the habit of some of your men to chase an unbeliever till he takes refuge in a high place. Then one man tells him in Persian not to be afraid, and when he comes up to him, he kills him. By Him in whose hand my self is, if I knew someone who had done that, I would strike off his head."

Yaḥyā said, I heard Mālik say, "This tradition is not unanimously agreed upon, so it is not acted upon."

Mālik, when asked whether safe conduct promised by a gesture had the same status as that promised by speech, said, 'Yes, I think that one can request an army not to kill someone by gesturing for safe conduct, because as far as I am concerned, gesture has the same status as speech. I have heard that 'Abdullāh ibn 'Abbās said, 'There is no people who betray a pledge, but that Allah gives their enemies power over them.'"

21.5 Giving in the Way of Allah

13 Yaḥyā related to me from Mālik from Nāfi' that when 'Abdullāh ibn 'Umar gave something in the Way of Allah, he would say to its owner, "When you reach Wādi al-Qurā (on the outskirts of Madīna) then it is your affair."

14 Yaḥyā related to me from Mālik from Yaḥyā ibn Saʿīd that Saʿīd ibn al-Musayyab used to say, "When a man is given something for a military expedition, and he brings it to the battlefield, it is his."

Mālik was asked about a man who pledged himself to go on a military campaign, equipped himself, and when he wanted to go out, one or both of his parents forbade him to go. He said, "He should not contradict them. Let him put it off for another year. As for the equipment, I think that he should store it until he needs it. If he fears that it will spoil, let him sell it and keep its price so that he can readily buy what is needed for a military expedition. If he is well-to-do, he will find the like of his equipment when he goes out, so let him do what he likes with his equipment."

21.6 Booty from war in general

15 Yaḥyā related to me from Mālik from Nāfiʿ from ʿAbdullāh ibn ʿUmar that the Messenger of Allah ﷺ sent a raiding party which included ʿAbdullāh ibn ʿUmar near Najd. They plundered many camels and their portions were twelve or eleven camels each. They divided it up camel by camel.

16 Yaḥyā related to me from Mālik from Yaḥyā ibn Saʿīd that he heard Saʿīd ibn al-Musayyab say, "When people in military expeditions divided the spoils, they made a camel equal to ten sheep."

Mālik said about the paid labourer in military expeditions, "If he is present at the battle and is with the people in the battle and he is a free man, he has his share. If he is not present, he has no share."

Mālik summed up, "I think that the booty is only divided among free men who have been present at the battle."

21.7 Things on which the tax of one-fifth (*khums*) is not obligatory

Mālik said about enemy soldiers who were found on the seashore of a

Muslim land and claimed that they were merchants and that the sea had driven them ashore, while the Muslims were not able to verify any of that nor that their ships had been damaged, or they were thirsty and had disembarked without the permission of the Muslims, "I think that it is up to the ruler to give his opinion about them, and I do not think that the tax of one-fifth is taken from them."

21.8 What it is permissible for the Muslims to eat before the spoils are divided

Mālik said, "I do not see that there is any harm in the Muslims eating whatever food they come across in enemy territory before the spoils are divided."

Mālik said, "I think that any camels, cattle and sheep (taken as booty) are considered as food which the Muslims can eat in enemy territory. If they could not be eaten until the people had gathered for the divisions and the spoils had been distributed among them, that would be harmful for the army. I do not see any objection to eating such things within acceptable limits. I do not think, however, that anyone should store up any of it to take back to his family."

Mālik was asked whether it was proper for a man who had obtained food in enemy territory and had eaten some of it and stocked up some of it as provision and some of it was left over – was it correct for him to keep it and then eat it with his family, or to sell before he had come to his country and make use of its price? He said, "If he sells it while he is on a military expedition, I think that he should put its price into the booty of the Muslims. If he takes it back to his country, I see no objection to his eating it and using it if it is a small amount."

21.9 Returning enemy plunder to the owner before the division of the spoils

17 Yaḥyā related to me from Mālik that it reached him that a slave of 'Abdullāh ibn 'Umar escaped and one of his horses wandered off, and

the idolaters seized them. Then the Muslims re-captured them, and they were returned to 'Abdullāh ibn 'Umar, before the division of the spoils took place.

I heard Mālik say about Muslim property that had been seized by the enemy, "If it is noticed before the distribution, then it is returned to its owner. Whatever has already been distributed is not returned to anyone."

Mālik, when asked about a man whose young male slave was taken by the idolaters and then the Muslims re-captured him, said, "The owner is more entitled to him without having to pay his price or value or having to incur any loss before the distribution takes place. If the distribution has already taken place, then I think that the slave belongs to his master for his price if the master wants him back."

Regarding an *umm walad* of a Muslim man who has been taken by the idol-worshippers and then re-captured by the Muslims and allotted in the distribution of spoils and then recognised by her master after the distribution. Mālik said, "She is not to be enslaved. I think that the ruler should pay a ransom for her for her master. If he does not do it, then her master must pay a ransom for her and not leave her. I do not think that she should be made a slave by whoever takes her nor is it lawful for him to have intercourse with her. She is in the position of a free woman because her master would be required to pay compensation if she injured somebody and so she is in the same position (as a wife). He should not leave an *umm walad* of his to be made a slave and intercourse with her to be made lawful."

Mālik was asked about a man who went to enemy territory to pay ransom or to trade, and he brought a free man or a slave, or they were given to him. He said, "As for the free man, the price he buys him for is a debt against the man and he is not made a slave. If the captive is given to him freely, he is free and owes nothing unless the man gave something in recompense for him. That is a debt against the free man, the same as if a ransom had been paid for him. As for a slave, his former master can choose to take him back and pay his price to the man who brought him or he can choose to leave him, as he wishes. If he was given to the man, the former master is more entitled to him, and he does nothing for him unless the man gave something for him in recompense. Whatever he gave for him is a loss against the master if he wants him back."

21.10 Stripping the slain of their personal effects in the booty

18 Yaḥyā related to me from Mālik from Yaḥyā ibn Sa'īd from 'Amr ibn Kathīr in Aflaḥ from Abū Muḥammad, the *mawlā* of Abū Qatāda, that Abū Qatāda ibn Rib'ī said, "We went out with the Messenger of Allah ﷺ in the year of Ḥunayn. When the armies met, the Muslims were put in disarray. I saw a man from the idolaters who had got the better of one of the Muslims, so I circled round and came up behind him and struck him with a sword on his shoulder-blade. He turned to me and grabbed me so hard that I felt the smell of death in it. Then death overcame him, and he let go of me."

He continued, "I met 'Umar ibn al-Khaṭṭāb and asked him, "What is going on with the people?' He replied, 'The Command of Allah.' Then the people returned from the battle and the Messenger of Allah ﷺ said, 'Whoever has killed one of the dead and can prove it, can strip him of his personal effects.' I stood up and said, 'Who will testify for me?' and then I sat down. The Messenger of Allah ﷺ repeated, 'Whoever has killed one of the dead and can prove it, can strip him of his personal effects.' I stood up and said, 'Who will testify for me?' then I sat down. Then he repeated his statement for a third time, so I stood up, and the Messenger of Allah ﷺ said, 'What is the matter with you, Abū Qatāda?' So I related my story to him. A man said, 'He has spoken the truth, Messenger of Allah. I have the effects of that slain person with me, so give him compensation for it, Messenger of Allah.'

Abū Bakr said, 'No, by Allah! He did not intend that one of the lions of Allah should fight for Allah and His Messenger and then give you his spoils.' The Messenger of Allah ﷺ said, 'He has spoken the truth, hand it over to him.' He gave it to me, and I sold the breast-plate and I bought a garden in the area of the Banū Salima with the money. It was the first property I had acquired since becoming Muslim."

19 Yaḥyā related to me from Mālik from Ibn Shihāb that al-Qāsim ibn Muḥammad said that he had heard a man asking Ibn 'Abbās about booty. Ibn 'Abbās said, "Horses are part of the booty and personal effects are as well."

Then the man repeated his question, and Ibn 'Abbās repeated his answer. Then the man asked, "What are the spoils which He, the Blessed, the Exalted, mentions in His Book?" He kept on asking until Ibn 'Abbās was on the verge of getting annoyed, then Ibn 'Abbās said, "Do you know who this man is like? He is like Ibn Ṣabīgh, who was beaten by 'Umar ibn al-Khaṭṭāb because he was notorious for asking foolish questions."

Yaḥyā said that Mālik was asked whether someone who killed one of the enemy could keep the man's effects without the permission of the ruler. He answered, "No one can do that without the permission of the ruler. Only the ruler can exercise his discretion. I have not heard that the Messenger of Allah ﷺ ever said, 'Whoever kills someone can have his effects' on any other day than the day of Ḥunayn."

21.11 Awarding extra portions from the fifth (*khums*)

20 Yaḥyā related to me from Mālik from Abū az-Zinād that Sa'īd ibn al-Musayyab said, "People used to be given extra portions from the *khums*."

Mālik said, "That is the best of what I have heard on the matter."

Mālik was asked about extra portions and whether they were taken from the first of the spoils, and he said, "That is only decided according to the discretion (*ijtihād*) of the ruler. We do not have a known reliable command about that other than it is up to the discretion of the ruler. I have not heard that the Messenger of Allah ﷺ gave extra portions in all his raids. I have only heard that he gave extra portions in one of them, namely the day of Ḥunayn. It depends on the discretion of the ruler whether they are taken from the first of the spoils or what is after it."

21.12 The share of the spoils allotted to cavalry in military expeditions

21 Yaḥyā related to me that Mālik said that he had heard that 'Umar ibn 'Abd al-'Azīz used to say, "A man on horse-back has two shares, and a man on foot has one."

Mālik added, "I continue to hear the same."

Mālik, when asked whether a man who was present with several horses took a share for all of them, said, "I have never heard that. I think that there is only a share for the horse on which he fought."

Mālik said, "I think that working horses and half-breeds are considered as horses because Allah, the Blessed, the Exalted, says in His Book, '*And horses, mules and donkeys both to ride and for adornment.*' (16:8) He said, the Mighty, the Majestic, '*Arm yourselves against them with all the firepower and cavalry you can muster, to terrify the enemies of Allah and your enemies.*' (8:60) I think that working breeds and half-breeds are considered as horses if the governor accepts them."

Sa'īd ibn al-Musayyab was asked about work-horses and whether there was *zakāt* on them. He said, "Is there any *zakāt* on horses?"

21.13 Stealing from the spoils

22 Yaḥyā related to me from Mālik from 'Abd ar-Raḥmān ibn Sa'īd from 'Amr ibn Shu'ayb that when the Messenger of Allah ﷺ came back from Ḥunayn heading for al-Ji'rāna, the people crowded around so much to question him that his she-camel backed into a tree, which became entangled in his cloak and pulled it off his back. The Messenger of Allah ﷺ said, "Return my cloak to me. Are you afraid that I will not distribute among you what Allah has given you as spoils? By Him in whose hand my self is! Had Allah given you as spoils as many camels as there are acacia trees in Tihāma, I would have distributed it among you. You will not find me to be miserly, cowardly, or a liar." Then the Messenger of Allah ﷺ got down and stood among the people, and said, "Hand over even the needle and

thread, for stealing from the spoils is disgrace, fire, ignominy on the Day of Rising for people who do it."

Then he took a bit of camel fluff or something from the ground and said, "By Him in whose hand my self is! What Allah has made spoils for you is not mine –- even the like of this! – except for the tax of one-fifth (*khums*), and the tax of one-fifth is returned to you."

23 Yaḥyā related to me from Mālik from Yaḥyā ibn Sa'īd from Muḥammad ibn Yaḥyā ibn Ḥabbān from Ibn Abī 'Amra that Zayd ibn Khālid al-Juhanī said, "A man died on the day of Hunayn, and they mentioned him to the Messenger of Allah ﷺ." Zayd claimed that the Messenger of Allah ﷺ said, "You pray over your companion." (i.e. he would not pray himself). The people's faces dropped at that. Zayd claimed that the Messenger of Allah ﷺ said, "Your companion stole from the spoils taken in the way of Allah." Zayd said, "So we opened up his baggage and found some Jews' beads worth about two dirhams."

24 Yaḥyā related to me from Mālik from Yaḥyā ibn Sa'īd from 'Abdullāh ibn al-Mughīra ibn Abī Burda al-Kinānī that he had heard that the Messenger of Allah ﷺ came to the people in their tribes and made supplication for them, but left out one of the tribes. 'Abdullāh related, "The tribe found an onyx necklace stolen from the booty in the saddle-bags of one of their men. The Messenger ﷺ, came to them, and then did the *takbīr* over them as one does the *takbīr* over the dead."

25 Yaḥyā related to me from Mālik from Thawr ibn Zayd ad-Dīlī from Abū al-Ghayth Sālim, the *mawlā* of Ibn Muṭī' that Abū Hurayra said, "We went out with the Messenger of Allah ﷺ in the year of Khaybar. We did not capture any gold or silver except for personal effects, clothes, and household goods. Rifā'a ibn Zayd gave a black slave-boy called Mid'am to the Messenger of Allah ﷺ. The Messenger of Allah ﷺ made for Wādi al-Qurā. After he arrived there, Mid'am was struck and killed by a stray arrow while unsaddling the camel of the Messenger of Allah ﷺ. The people said, 'Good luck to him! The Garden!'

The Messenger of Allah ﷺ said, 'No! By Him in whose hand my self is! The cloak which he took from the spoils on the Day of Khaybar before they were distributed will blaze with fire on him.' When the people heard that, a man brought a sandal-strap – or two sandal-straps – to the Messenger of Allah ﷺ. The Messenger of Allah ﷺ said, 'A sandal-strap – or two sandal-straps – of fire!'"

26 Yaḥyā related to me from Mālik from Yaḥyā ibn Sa'īd that he had heard that 'Abdullāh ibn 'Abbās said, "Stealing from the spoils does not appear in a people but that terror is cast into their hearts. Fornication does not spread in a people but that there is much death among them. A people do not lessen the measure and weight but that provision is cut off from them. A people do not judge without right but that blood spreads among them. A people do not betray the pledge but that Allah gives their enemies power over them."

21.14 Martyrs in the Way of Allah

27 Yaḥyā related to me from Mālik from Abū az-Zinād from al-A'raj from Abū Hurayra that the Messenger of Allah ﷺ said, "By Him in whose hand my self is! I would like to fight in the way of Allah and be killed, then brought to life again so I could be killed, and then brought to life again so I could be killed."

Abū Hurayra said three times, "I testify to it by Allah!"

28 Yaḥyā related to me from Mālik from Abū'z-Zinād from al-A'raj from Abū Hurayra that the Messenger of Allah ﷺ said, "Allah laughs over two men. One of them kills the other, but each of them will enter the Garden; one fights in the way of Allah and is killed, then Allah turns (in forgiveness) to the killer, so he fights (in the way of Allah) and also becomes a martyr."

29 Yaḥyā related to me from Mālik from Abū az-Zinād from al-A'raj from Abū Hurayra that the Messenger of Allah ﷺ said, "By Him in whose hand my self is! None of you is wounded in the way of Allah – and Allah knows best who is wounded in His way – but that when the Day of Rising comes, blood will gush forth from his wound. It will be the colour of blood, but its scent will be that of musk."

30 Yaḥyā related to me from Mālik from Zayd ibn Aslam that 'Umar ibn al-Khaṭṭāb used to say, "O Allah! Do not let me be slain by the hand of a man who has prayed a single prostration to You with which he will dispute with me before You on the Day of Rising!"

31 Yaḥyā related to me from Mālik from Yaḥyā ibn Sa'īd from Sa'īd al-Maqburī from 'Abdullāh ibn Abī Qatāda that his father said that a man came to the Messenger of Allah ﷺ and said, "O Messenger of Allah! If I am killed in the way of Allah, expecting the reward, sincere, advancing, and not retreating, will Allah pardon my faults?" The Messenger of Allah ﷺ answered, "Yes." When the man turned away, the Messenger of Allah ﷺ called him – or sent an order to him and he was called to him. The Messenger of Allah ﷺ said to him, "What did you say?" He repeated his words to him, and the Prophet ﷺ said to him, "Yes, except for debts. Jibrīl said that to me."

32 Yaḥyā related to me from Mālik from Abū an-Naḍr, the *mawlā* of 'Umar ibn 'Ubaydullāh, that he had heard that the Messenger of Allah ﷺ said over the martyrs of Uḥud, "I testify for them." Abū Bakr aṣ-Ṣiddīq said, "Messenger of Allah! Are we not their brothers? We entered Islam as they entered Islam and we did *jihād* as they did *jihād*." The Messenger of Allah ﷺ said, "Yes, but I do not know what you will do after me." Abū Bakr wept profusely and said, "Are we really going to outlive you!"

33 Yaḥyā related to me from Mālik that Yaḥyā ibn Sa'īd said, "The Messenger of Allah ﷺ was sitting by a grave which was being dug at Madīna. A man looked into the grave and said, 'An awful bed for the believer.' The Messenger of Allah ﷺ said, 'What you have said is awful.'

"The man said, 'I did not mean that, Messenger of Allah. I meant being killed in the way of Allah.' The Messenger of Allah ﷺ said, 'Being killed in the way of Allah has no like! There is no place on the earth where I would prefer my grave to be than here (meaning Madīna).' He repeated it three times."

21.15 Things in which martyrdom lies

34 Yaḥyā related to me from Mālik from Zayd ibn Aslam that ʿUmar ibn al-Khaṭṭāb used to say, "O Allah! I ask You for martyrdom in Your way and death in the city of Your Messenger!"

35 Yaḥyā related to me from Mālik from Yaḥyā ibn Saʿīd that ʿUmar ibn al-Khaṭṭāb said, "The nobility of the believer is his *taqwā*. His *dīn* is his noble descent. His manliness is his good character. Boldness and cowardice are but instincts which Allah places wherever He wills. The coward shrinks from defending even his father and mother, and the bold one fights for the sake of the combat not for the spoils. Being slain is but one way of meeting death, and the martyr is the one who gives himself, expectant of reward from Allah."

21.16 How to wash a martyr

36 Yaḥyā related to me from Mālik from Nāfiʿ from ʿAbdullāh ibn ʿUmar that ʿUmar ibn al-Khaṭṭāb was washed and shrouded and prayed over, yet he was a martyr, may Allah have mercy on him.

37 Yaḥyā related to me from Mālik that he had heard the people of knowledge say that martyrs in the way of Allah were not washed, nor were any of them prayed over. They were buried in the garments in which they were slain.

Mālik said, "This is the *sunna* for someone who is killed on the battlefield and is not reached until he is already dead. Someone who is carried off and lives for as long as Allah wills after it is washed and prayed over as was ʿUmar ibn al-Khaṭṭāb."

21.17 What is disliked to be done with something given in the Way of Allah

38 Yaḥyā related to me from Mālik from Yaḥyā ibn Saʿīd that ʿUmar ibn al-Khaṭṭāb in one year gave 40,000 camels as war-mounts. Sometimes he

would give one man a camel to himself. Sometimes he would give one camel between two men to take them to Iraq. A man from Iraq came to him and said, "Give me and Suḥaym a mount." 'Umar ibn al-Khaṭṭāb asked him, "I ask you by Allah, is *suḥaym* a water-skin?" He answered, "Yes."

21.18 Stimulation of desire for *jihād*

39 Yaḥyā related to me from Mālik from Isḥāq ibn 'Abdullāh ibn Abī Ṭalha that Anas ibn Mālik had said that when the Messenger of Allah ﷺ arrived at Qubā', he visited Umm Ḥarām bint Milḥan and she fed him. Umm Ḥarām was the wife of 'Ubāda ibn aṣ-Ṣāmit. One day the Messenger of Allah ﷺ had called on her and she had fed him, and sat down to delouse his hair. The Messenger of Allah ﷺ had dozed and woke up smiling. Umm Ḥarām said, "What is making you smile, Messenger of Allah?" He said, "Some of my community were presented to me, riding in the Way of Allah. They were riding in the middle of the sea, kings on thrones, or like kings on thrones." (Isḥāq was not sure). She said, "O Messenger of Allah! Ask Allah to put me among them!" So he made a supplication for her, and put his head down and slept. Then he had woken up smiling, and she said to him, "Messenger of Allah, why are you smiling?" He said, "Some of my community were presented to me, raiding in the way of Allah. They were kings on thrones or like kings on thrones," as he had said the first time. She said, "O Messenger of Allah! Ask Allah to let me be among them!" He said, "You are among the first."

Isḥāq added, "She travelled on the sea in the time of Mu'āwiya, and when she landed, she was thrown from her mount and killed."

40 Yaḥyā related to me from Mālik from Yaḥyā ibn Sa'īd from Abū Ṣāliḥ as-Sammān from Abā Hurayra that the Messenger of Allah ﷺ said, "Had I not been concerned for my community, I would have liked never to stay behind a raiding party going out in the way of Allah. However, I do not have the means to carry them to it, nor can they find for themselves anything on which to ride out and it is grievous for them to have to stay behind from me. I would like to fight in the way of Allah and then be killed, then brought back to life so that I could be killed and then brought back to life so that I could be killed."

41 Yaḥyā related to me from Mālik that Yaḥyā ibn Sa'īd said, "On the Day of Uḥud, the Messenger of Allah ﷺ said, 'Who will bring me news of Sa'īd ibn ar-Rabī' al-Anṣārī?' A man said, 'Me, Messenger of Allah!' So the man went around among the slain, and Sa'īd ibn ar-Rabī' said to him, 'What are you doing?' The man said to him, 'The Messenger of Allah ﷺ sent me to bring him news of you.' He said, 'Go to him, and give him my greetings, and tell him that I have been stabbed twelve times, and am mortally wounded. Tell your people that they will have no excuse with Allah if the Messenger of Allah ﷺ is slain while one of them is still alive.'"

42 Yaḥyā related to me from Mālik from Yaḥyā ibn Sa'īd that the Messenger of Allah ﷺ encouraged people to do *jihād* and mentioned the Garden. One of the Anṣār was eating some dates he had in his hand, and said, "Am I so desirous of this world that I should sit until I finish them?" He threw aside what was in his hand and took his sword and fought until he was slain.

43 Yaḥyā related to me from Mālik from Yaḥyā ibn Sa'īd that Mu'ādh ibn Jabal said, "There are two types of military expeditions. There is one military expedition in which valuables are spent, things are made easy for a fellow, authorities are obeyed, and corruption is avoided. That military expedition is all good. There is a military expedition in which valuables are not spent, things are not made easy, the authorities are not obeyed, and corruption is not avoided. The one who fights in that military expedition does not return with any reward."

21.19 Horses and racing them and financing in military expeditions

44 Yaḥyā related to me from Mālik from Nāfi' from 'Abdullāh ibn 'Umar that the Messenger of Allah ﷺ said, "Blessing is in the forelocks of horses until the Day of Rising."

45 Yaḥyā related to me from Mālik from Nāfi' from 'Abdullāh ibn 'Umar that the Messenger of Allah ﷺ held a race between horses which had been made lean by training, from al-Ḥafyā' to Thaniyyat al-Wadā'. He held a race between horses which had not been made lean from the

Thaniyya (a mountain pass near Madīna) to the mosque of the Banū Zurayq. 'Abdullāh ibn 'Umar was among those who raced them.

46 Yaḥyā related to me from Mālik that Yaḥyā ibn Sa'īd heard Sa'īd ibn al-Musayyab say, "There is no harm in placing stakes on horses if a third horse enters the race. The winner takes the stake, and the loser has no liability."

47 Yaḥyā related to me from Mālik from Yaḥyā ibn Sa'īd that the Messenger of Allah ﷺ was seen wiping the face of his horse with his cloak. He was questioned about it and said, "I was reproached in the night about horses," i.e. not taking proper care of them.

48 Yaḥyā related to me from Mālik from Ḥumayd aṭ-Ṭawīl from Anas ibn Mālik that when the Messenger of Allah ﷺ went out to Khaybar, he arrived there at night, and when he came upon a people by night, he did not attack until morning. In the morning, the Jews came out with their spades and baskets. When they saw him, they said, "Muḥammad! By Allah, Muḥammad and his army!" The Messenger of Allah ﷺ said, "Allah is greater! Khaybar is destroyed. When we come to a people, it is an evil morning for those who have been warned."

49 Yaḥyā related to me from Mālik from Ibn Shihāb from Ḥumayd ibn 'Abd ar-Raḥmān ibn 'Awf from Abū Hurayra that the Messenger of Allah ﷺ said, "Whoever hands over two of any type of property in the way of Allah is called to the Garden, with the words, 'O slave of Allah! This is good!' Whoever is among the people of prayer, is called from the gate of prayer. Whoever is among the people of *jihād* is called from the gate of *jihād*. Whoever is among the people of *ṣadaqa*, is called from the gate of *ṣadaqa*. Whoever is among the people of fasting, is called from the gate of the well-watered (*Bāb ar-Rayyān*)."

Abū Bakr aṣ-Ṣiddīq said, "Messenger of Allah! Is it absolutely necessary that one be called from one of these gates? Can someone be called from all of these gates?" He answered, "Yes, and I hope you are among them."

21.20 Acquisition of the land of *dhimmīs* who surrender

Mālik was asked whether he thought that when an imām had accepted *jizya* from a people and they gave it, the land of any of those who surrendered belonged to the Muslims. Mālik said, "That varies. As for the people who make a treaty – those of them who surrendered are entitled to their land and property. As for the people of force who are taken by force – if one of them surrenders, his land and property belong to the Muslims because the people of force have been overcome in their towns, and so this becomes booty for the Muslims. As for the people with a treaty, their property and lives are protected by the treaty they made. Only the terms of the treaty are demanded of them."

21.21 Burial in one grave by necessity and Abū Bakr's carrying out the promise of the Messenger of Allah ﷺ after the death of the Messenger ﷺ

50 Yaḥyā related to me from Mālik from 'Abd ar-Raḥmān ibn Abī Ṣa'ṣa'a that he had heard that 'Amr ibn al-Jamūḥ al-Anṣārī and 'Abdullāh ibn 'Umar al-Anṣārī, both of the tribe of Banū Salama, had their grave uncovered by a flood. Their grave was part of what was left after the flood. They were in the same grave, having been among those martyred at Uḥud. They were dug up so that they might be moved. They were found unchanged. It was as if they had only died the day before. One of them had been wounded, and he had put his hand over his wound and had been buried like that. His hand was pulled away from his wound and released, and it returned to where it had been. It was forty-six years between Uḥud and the day they were dug up.

Mālik said, "There is no harm in burying two or three men in the same grave due to necessity. The oldest one is put nearest to the *qibla*."

51 Yaḥyā related to me from Mālik from Rabi'a ibn Abī 'Abd ar-Raḥmān said, "Property was sent to Abū Bakr aṣ-Ṣiddīq from Bahrain. He said, 'If someone had a promise or a pledge with the Messenger of Allah ﷺ, let him come to me.' So Jābir ibn 'Abdullāh came to him, and he gave him three cupped handfuls."

22. Vows and Oaths

22.1 Fulfilling vows to walk

1 Yaḥyā related to me from Mālik from Ibn Shihāb from 'Ubaydullāh ibn 'Abdullāh ibn 'Utba ibn Mas'ūd from 'Abdullāh ibn 'Abbās that Sa'd ibn 'Ubāda asked the Messenger of Allah ﷺ for an opinion and said, "My mother died while she still had a vow which she had not fulfilled." The Messenger of Allah ﷺ said, "Fulfil it for her."

2 Yaḥyā related to me from Mālik from 'Abdullāh ibn Abī Bakr that his paternal aunt related that her grandmother made a vow to walk to the Qubā' mosque. She died and did not fulfil it, so 'Abdullāh ibn 'Abbās asked her daughter to walk on her behalf.

Yaḥyā said that he had heard Mālik say, "No one can walk for anyone else."

3 Yaḥyā related to me from Mālik that 'Abdullāh ibn Abī Ḥabība said, "I said to a man when I was young, 'A man who only says that he must walk to the House of Allah and does not say that he has vowed to walk, does not have to walk.'

"A man said, 'Shall I give you this small cucumber?' and he had a small cucumber in his hand, 'if you will say, "I must walk to the House of Allah?"' I answered, 'Yes,' and I said it since at that time I was still immature. Then, when I came of age, someone told me that I had to fulfil my vow. I went and asked Sa'īd ibn al-Musayyab about it, and he said to me, 'You must walk.' So I walked."

Mālik said, "That is the custom among us."

22.2 Making vows to walk to the House and not succeeding

4 Yaḥyā related to me from Mālik that 'Urwa ibn 'Udhayna al-Laythī said, "I went out with my grandmother who had vowed to walk to the House of Allah. When we had gone part of the way, she could not go on. I sent one of her *mawlās* to question 'Abdullāh ibn 'Umar and went with him. He asked 'Abdullāh ibn 'Umar, and 'Abdullāh ibn 'Umar said to him, 'Take her and let her ride, and when she has the strength let her ride back, and start to walk from the place from where she was unable to go on.'"

Yaḥyā said that he had heard Mālik say, "I think that she must sacrifice an animal."

Yaḥyā related to me from Mālik that he had heard that Sa'īd ibn al-Musayyab and Abū Salama ibn 'Abd ar-Raḥmān both said the same as 'Abdullāh ibn 'Umar.

5 Yaḥyā related to me from Mālik that Yaḥyā ibn Sa'īd said, "I vowed to walk, but I was struck by a pain in the kidney, so I rode until I came to Makka. I questioned 'Aṭā' ibn Abī Rabāḥ and others, and they said, 'You must sacrifice an animal.' When I came to Madīna I questioned the scholars there, and they told me to walk again from the place from which I was unable to go on. So I walked."

Yaḥyā said that he had heard Mālik say, "What is done among us regarding someone who makes a vow to walk to the House of Allah, and then cannot do it and so rides, is that he must return and walk from the place from which he was unable to go on. If he cannot walk, he should walk what he can and then ride, and he must sacrifice a camel, a cow, or a sheep if that is all that he can manage."

Mālik, when asked about a man who said to another, "I will carry you to the House of Allah", answered, "If he intended to carry him on his shoulders, by which he means hardship and exhaustion to himself, and does not have to do that, let him walk by foot after a sacrifice. If he did not intend anything, let him ride to *ḥajj*, and take the man with him. That is because he said, 'I will carry you to the House of Allah.' If the man refuses to perform *ḥajj* with him, then there is nothing against him, and what is demanded of him is revoked."

Yaḥyā said that Mālik was asked whether it is enough for a man who has made a vow that he will walk to the House of Allah a certain (large) number of times, or who has forbidden himself from talking to his father and brother, if he does not fulfil a certain vow, and he had taken upon himself, by the oath, something which he is incapable of fulfilling in his lifetime, even though he were to try every year, to fulfil only one or a (smaller) number of vows by Allah. Mālik said, "The only satisfaction I know for that is fulfilling what he has obliged himself to do. Let him walk for as long as he is able and draw near Allah the Exalted by what he can of good."

22.3 How to fulfil the oath of walking to the Ka'ba

Yaḥyā related to me from Mālik that what he preferred of what he had heard from the people of knowledge about a man or woman who vowed to walk to the House of Allah, was that they fulfilled the oath when performing *'umra*, by walking until they had done *sa'y* between Ṣafā and Marwa. When they had done *sa'y* it was finished. If they vowed to perform the *ḥajj* on foot, they walked until they came to Makka, then they walked until they had finished all the rites.

Mālik said, "Walking is only for *ḥajj* or *'umra*."

22.4 Vows not permitted in disobedience to Allah

6 Yaḥyā related to me from Mālik from that Ḥumayd ibn Qays and Thawr ibn Zayd ad-Dīlī both informed him that the Messenger of Allah ﷺ (and one of them gave more detail than the other), saw a man standing in the sun. The Messenger asked, "What is wrong with him?" The people said, "He has vowed not to speak or to seek shade from the sun or to sit, and

to fast." The Messenger of Allah ﷺ said, "Go and tell him to speak, seek shade, and sit, but let him complete his fast."

Mālik said, "I have not heard that the Messenger of Allah ﷺ ordered the man in question to do any *kaffāra*. The Messenger of Allah ﷺ only ordered him to complete that in which there was obedience to Allah and to abandon that in which there was disobedience to Allah."

7 Yaḥyā related to me from Mālik from Yaḥyā ibn Sa'īd that he heard al-Qāsim ibn Muḥammad say, "A woman came to 'Abdullāh ibn 'Abbās and said, 'I have vowed to sacrifice my son.' Ibn 'Abbas said, 'Do not sacrifice your son. Do *kaffāra* for your oath.' An old man with Ibn 'Abbās said, 'What *kaffāra* is there for this?' Ibn 'Abbās said, 'Allah the Exalted says, "*Those of you who say, regarding their wives. 'Be as my mother's back*'" (58:2) and then He went on to oblige the *kaffāra* for it as you have seen.'"

8 Yaḥyā related to me from Mālik from Ṭalḥa ibn Abī al-Mālik al-Aylī from al-Qāsim ibn Muḥammad ibn aṣ-Ṣiddīq from 'Ā'isha that the Messenger of Allah ﷺ said, "If someone vows to obey Allah, let him obey Him. If someone vows to disobey Allah, let him not disobey Him."

Yaḥyā said that he had heard Mālik say, "The meaning of the statement of the Prophet ﷺ, 'If someone vows to disobey Allah, let him not disobey Him' is that, for instance, a man who vows that, if he speaks to such-and-such a person, he will walk to Syria, Egypt, ar-Rabadha, or any other such things which are not considered as *'ibāda*, is not under any obligation by any of that, even if he were to speak to the man or to break whatever it was he swore, because Allah does not demand obedience in such things. He should only fulfil those things in which there is obedience to Allah."

22.5 Inadvertence in oaths

9 Yaḥyā related to me from Mālik from Hishām ibn 'Urwa from his father that "Ā'isha, *Umm al-Mu'minīn*, said, "Inadvertence in oaths is that a man says, 'By Allah! No, by Allah!'" i.e. out of habit.

Mālik said, "The best of what I have heard on the matter is that an inadvertent oath is when a man takes an oath on something which he feels certain is like he said, only to find that it is other than what he said. This is inadvertance."

Mālik said, "A binding oath is, for example, that a man says that he will not sell his garment for ten dinars, and then he sells it for that, or that he will beat his young slave and then does not beat him, and so on. One owes *kaffāra* for making such an oath, but there is no *kaffāra* for inadvertence."

Mālik said, "If someone makes an oath about something, knowing that he is acting wrongly, and he swears to a lie, when he knows it to be a lie, in order to please someone with it or to excuse himself to someone by it or to gain money by it, no *kaffāra* that he does for it can cover it."

22.6 Oaths for which *kaffāra* is not obligatory

10 Yaḥyā related to me from Mālik from Nāfi' that 'Abdullāh ibn 'Umar said, "If someone swears by Allah and then says, 'Allah willing' and then does not do what he has sworn to, he has not broken his oath."

Mālik said, "The best I have heard on this reservation is that it belongs to the statement made if the speaker does not break the normal flow of speech before he is silent. If he is silent and breaks the flow of speech, he has no such reservation."

Yaḥyā said, "Mālik said that a man who said that he had disbelieved or associated something with Allah and then broke his oath, owed no *kaffāra*, and he was not a disbeliever or one who associated something with Allah unless his heart concealed something of either of those. He should ask forgiveness of Allah and not do that again – but what he did was evil."

22.7 Oaths for which *kaffāra* is obligatory

11 Yaḥyā related to me from Mālik from Suhayl ibn Abī Ṣāliḥ from his father from Abū Hurayra that the Messenger of Allah ﷺ said, "Whoever

makes an oath and then sees that something else would be better than it, should do *kaffāra* for his oath and do what is better."

Yaḥyā said that he heard Mālik say, "Anyone who makes the form of a vow and then does not mention anything specific is still obliged to make the *kaffāra* for an oath (if he breaks it)."

Mālik says, "Emphasis is when a man swears one thing several times, repeating the oath in his speech time after time. For instance, the statement, 'By Allah, I will not decrease it from such-and-such,' sworn three times or more. The *kaffāra* of that is like the *kaffāra* of one oath. If a man swears, 'I will not eat this food or wear these clothes or enter this house,' that is all in one oath, and he is only obliged to do one *kaffāra*. It is the same for a man who says to his wife, 'You are divorced if I let you wear this garment or let you go to the mosque,' and it is one entire statement in the normal pattern of speech. If he breaks any of that oath, divorce is obliged, and there is no breaking of oath after that in whatever he does. There is only one oath to be broken in that."

Mālik said, "What we do about a woman who makes a vow without her husband's permission is that she is allowed to do so and she must fulfil it if it only concerns her own person and will not harm her husband. If, however, it will harm her husband, he may forbid her to fulfil it, but it remains an obligation against her until she has the opportunity to complete it."

22.8 What is done regarding the *kaffāra* of a broken oath

12 Yaḥyā related to me from Mālik from Nāfi' that 'Abdullāh ibn 'Umar said, "If someone breaks an oath which he has stressed, he has to free a slave, or clothe ten poor people. If someone breaks an oath, but has not stressed it, he only has to feed ten poor people and each poor person is fed a *mudd* of wheat. Someone who does not have the means for that should fast for three days."

13 Yaḥyā related to me from Mālik from Nāfi' that 'Abdullāh ibn 'Umar used to do *kaffāra* for a broken oath by feeding ten poor people. Each

person got a *mudd* of wheat. He sometimes freed a slave if he had repeated the oath.

Yaḥyā related to me from Mālik from Yaḥyā ibn Sa'īd that Sulaymān ibn Yasār said, "I understood from people that when they made the *kaffāra* for a broken oath, they gave a *mudd* of wheat according to the smaller *mudd*. They thought that such would compensate for them."

Mālik said, "The best of what I have heard about the one who does *kaffāra* for breaking his oath by clothing people is that, if he clothes men, he clothes them each in one garment. If he clothes women, he clothes them each in two garments, a long shift and a long scarf, because that is what is satisfactory for each of them in the prayer."

22.9 Oaths in general

14 Yaḥyā related to me from Mālik from Nāfi' from 'Abdullāh ibn 'Umar that one time the Messenger of Allah ﷺ was speaking to 'Umar ibn al-Khaṭṭāb while he was travelling in an expedition and 'Umar swore by his father. He (the Messenger) said, "Allah forbids you to swear by your fathers. If anyone swears, let him swear by Allah or keep silent."

15 Yaḥyā related to me from Mālik that he had heard that the Messenger of Allah ﷺ used to say, "No, by the Overturner of hearts."

16 Yaḥyā related to me from Mālik from 'Uthmān ibn Ḥafṣ ibn 'Umar ibn Khalda that Ibn Shihāb had heard that Abū Lubāba ibn 'Abd al-Mundhir, when Allah turned to him, said, "Messenger of Allah, should I leave my people's house in which I committed wrong action and keep your company, and give away all my property as *ṣadaqa* for Allah and His Messenger?" The Messenger of Allah ﷺ said, "Giving away a third of it is enough for you."

17 Yaḥyā related to me from Mālik from Ayyūb ibn Mūsā from Manṣūr ibn 'Abd ar-Rahmān al-Ḥajabī from, his mother that 'Ā'isha, *Umm al-Mu'minīn* ؓ was asked about a man who devoted his property to the door of the Ka'ba. She said, "Let him do *kaffāra* for it with the *kaffāra* of the oath."

Mālik said that someone who devoted all his property in the way of Allah, and then broke his oath, should put a third of his property in the Way of Allah, as that was what the Messenger of Allah ﷺ did in the case of Abū Lubāba.

23. Sacrificial Animals

23.1 Animals avoided as sacrifices

1 Yaḥyā related to me from Mālik from 'Amr ibn al-Ḥārith from 'Ubayd ibn Fayrūz from al-Barā' ibn 'Āzib that the Messenger of Allah ﷺ was asked what animals should be avoided as sacrifices. He indicated with his hand and said, "Four:" – Al-Barā' indicated with his hand and said, "My hand is shorter than the hand of the Messenger of Allah ﷺ." – "A lame animal whose lameness is evident, a one-eyed animal which is clearly one-eyed, an animal which is clearly ill, and an emaciated animal with no fat on it."

2 Yaḥyā related to me from Mālik from Nāfi' that 'Abdullāh ibn 'Umar would guard against animals and camels which were young or had physical defects as sacrifices.

Mālik said, "That is what I like best of what I have heard."

23.2 Animals desirable as sacrifices

3 Yaḥyā related to me from Mālik from Nāfi' that one time 'Abdullāh ibn 'Umar wanted to sacrifice an animal at Madīna. Nāfi' said, "He told me to buy him an excellent horned ram, then to sacrifice it on the Day of Sacrifice in the people's place of prayer." Nāfi' said, "So I did it, then it was carried to 'Abdullāh ibn 'Umar who shaved his head when the ram had been sacrificed. He was ill, and did not attend the *'Īd* with the people."

Nāfi' added, "'Abdullāh ibn 'Umar used to say, 'Shaving the head is not obligatory for someone who sacrifices an animal.' Ibn 'Umar would do so, however."

23.3 Prohibition against sacrificing an animal before the imām finishes

4 Yaḥyā related to me from Mālik from Yaḥyā ibn Sa'īd from Bushayr ibn Yasār that Abū Burda ibn Niyār sacrificed an animal before the Messenger of Allah ﷺ sacrificed on the Day of Sacrifice. He asserted that the Messenger of Allah ﷺ ordered him to sacrifice another animal, and he, Abū Burda, said, "What if I can only find an animal less than one year old, Messenger of Allah?" He had said, "If you can only find a young animal, then sacrifice it."

5 Yaḥyā related to me from Mālik from Yaḥyā ibn Sa'īd from 'Abbād ibn Tamīm that one time 'Uwaymir ibn Ashqar sacrificed his animal before the prayer on the morning of the Day of Sacrifice, and he mentioned that the Messenger of Allah ﷺ had ordered him to sacrifice another animal.

23.4 Storing meat from sacrificial animals

6 Yaḥyā related to me from Mālik from Abū az-Zubayr al-Makkī from Jābir ibn 'Abdullāh that the Messenger of Allah ﷺ forbade that the meat from sacrificial animals be eaten after three days. Then later he said, "Eat, give *ṣadaqa*, provide for yourselves and store up."

7 Yaḥyā related to me from Mālik from 'Abdullāh ibn Abī Bakr that 'Abdullāh ibn Wāqid said, "The Messenger of Allah ﷺ forbade eating the meat from sacrificial animals after three days."

'Abdullāh ibn Abī Bakr continued, "I mentioned that to 'Amra bint 'Abd ar-Raḥmān, and she affirmed that he had spoken the truth as she had heard 'Ā'isha, the wife of the Prophet ﷺ say, 'Some people from the desert came at the time of the sacrifice in the time of the Messenger of Allah ﷺ,

so the Messenger of Allah ﷺ said, "Store up for three days, and give what is left over as *ṣadaqa*.""

She said that afterwards someone said to the Messenger of Allah ﷺ that people had been accustomed to make use of their sacrificial animals, melting the fat and curing the skins. The Messenger of Allah ﷺ said, "What about it?" They said, "You have forbidden the meat of sacrificial animals after three days." The Messenger of Allah ﷺ said, "I only forbade you for the sake of the people who were coming to you. Eat, give *ṣadaqa*, and store up."

By these people, he meant the poor people who were coming to Madīna.

8 Yaḥyā related to me from Mālik from Rabi'a ibn Abī 'Abd ar-Raḥmān that Abū Sa'īd al-Khudrī returned from a journey and his family gave him some meat. He asked whether it was meat from the sacrifice. They replied that it was. Abū Sa'īd said, "Did not the Messenger of Allah ﷺ forbid that?" They said, "There has been a new command from the Messenger of Allah ﷺ since you went away." Abū Sa'īd went out and made enquiries about it and was told that the Messenger of Allah ﷺ had said, "I forbade you before to eat meat of the sacrifice after three days, but now eat, give *ṣadaqa*, and store up. I forbade you before to make *nabīdh* (by soaking raisins or dates in water), but now make *nabīdh*, but remember every intoxicant is forbidden. I forbade you to visit graves, but now visit them, and do not use bad language."

23.5 Sharing sacrificial animals

9 Yaḥyā related to me from Mālik from Abū az-Zubayr al-Makkī that Jābir ibn 'Abdullāh said, "We sacrificed with the Messenger of Allah ﷺ in the year of Ḥudaybiya, a camel shared between seven people, and a cow between seven people."

10 Yaḥyā related to me from Mālik from 'Umara ibn Yasār that 'Aṭā' ibn Yasār told him that Abū Ayyūb al-Anṣārī had told him, "We used to sacrifice one sheep, and a man sacrificed for himself and his family. Then later on people began to compete with each other and it became boasting."

Mālik said, "The best that I have heard about a single camel, cow, or sheep is that a man should sacrifice a camel for himself and his family. He should sacrifice a cow or a sheep which he owns for the family, and share with them in it. It is disapproved for a group of people to buy a camel, cow or sheep to share for the ritual and sacrifice, each giving a share of its price and taking a share of its meat. We have heard the tradition that people do not share in the ritual. However, it may be that the people of one household can share."

11 Yaḥyā related to me from Mālik that Ibn Shihāb said, "The Messenger of Allah ﷺ only sacrificed one camel or one cow for himself and his family."

Mālik said, "I do not know which of them Ibn Shihāb mentioned."

23.6 The sacrificial animal for the child in the womb and mention of the Days of Sacrifice

12 Yaḥyā related to me from Mālik from Nāfi' that 'Abdullāh ibn 'Umar said, "The sacrifice can be done up to two days after the Day of Sacrifice."

Yaḥyā related to me from Mālik that the same had reached him from 'Alī ibn Abī Ṭālib.

13 Yaḥyā related to me from Mālik from Nāfi' that 'Abdullāh ibn 'Umar did not sacrifice for the child still in the womb.

Mālik said, "The sacrifice is *sunna*, but it is not obligatory. I prefer that anyone who has the price of the animal should not abandon it."

24. Slaughtering Animals

24.1 Saying the Name of Allah over the slaughtered animal

1 Yaḥyā related to me from Mālik from Hishām ibn 'Urwa that his father said, "The Messenger of Allah ﷺ, was asked, 'Messenger of Allah! Some people from the desert bring us meat, and we do not know whether the name of Allah has been mentioned over it or not.' The Messenger of Allah ﷺ said, 'Mention the name of Allah over it and eat.'"

Mālik said, "That was at the beginning of Islam."

2 Yaḥyā related to me from Mālik from Yaḥyā ibn Sa'īd that 'Abdullāh ibn 'Ayyāsh ibn Abī Rabī'a al-Makhzūmī told one of his slaves to slaughter an animal. When he wanted to slaughter it, he said to him, "Mention Allah's name." The slave said to him, "I have mentioned the name!" He said to him, "Mention the name of Allah, bother you!" He said to him, "I have mentioned the name of Allah." 'Abdullāh ibn 'Ayyāsh said, "By Allah, I shall never eat it!"

24.2 Methods of slaughter permitted in necessity

3 Yaḥyā related to me from Mālik from Zayd ibn Aslam from 'Aṭā' ibn Yasār that a man of the Anṣār from the tribe of Banū Ḥāritha was herding a pregnant she-camel at Uḥud. It was about to die, so he slaughtered it with a sharp stake. The Messenger of Allah ﷺ was asked about that, and he said, "There is no harm in it, eat it."

4 Yaḥyā related to me from Mālik from Nāfi' from a one of the Anṣār from Mu'ādh ibn Sa'd or Sa'd ibn Mu'ādh that a slave-girl of Ka'b ibn Mālik was herding some sheep at Sal' (a mountain near Madīna). One of the sheep was about to die, so she went over to it and slaughtered it with a stone. The Messenger of Allah ﷺ was asked about that, and he said, "There is no harm in it, so eat it."

5 Yaḥyā related to me from Mālik from Thawr ibn Zayd ad-Dīlī that 'Abdullāh ibn 'Abbās was asked about animals slaughtered by the Christian Arabs. He said, "There is no harm in them," but he recited this *āyat, "Any of you who takes them as friends is one of them."* (5:54)

6 Yaḥyā related to me from Mālik that 'Abdullāh ibn 'Abbās used to say, "You can eat anything that has had its jugular vein cut."

Yaḥyā related to me from Mālik from Yaḥyā ibn Sa'īd that Sa'īd ibn al-Musayyab said, "There is no harm in whatever you slaughter with a cutting edge, as long as you are forced to do it by necessity."

24.3 What is disapproved of in slaughtering animals

7 Yaḥyā related to me from Mālik from Yaḥyā ibn Sa'īd that Abū Murra, the *mawlā* of 'Aqīl ibn Abī Ṭālib, asked Abū Hurayra about a sheep which was slaughtered and then part of it moved. He ordered him to eat it. Then he asked Zayd ibn Thābit about it, and he said, "Does a corpse move?" and he forbade eating its meat.

Mālik was asked about a sheep which fell down and injured itself badly and then its master reached it and slaughtered it. Blood flowed from it but it did not move. Mālik said, "If he kills it and blood flows from it and its eyes blink, he may eat."

24.4 Slaughtering what is in the womb of a slaughtered animal

8 Yaḥyā related to me from Mālik from Nāfi' that 'Abdullāh ibn 'Umar said, "When a she-camel is slaughtered, what is in its womb is included

in the slaughter if it is perfectly formed and its hair has begun to grow. If it comes out of its mother's womb, it is slaughtered so that blood flows from its heart."

9 Yaḥyā related to me from Mālik from Yazīd ibn 'Abdullāh ibn Qusayṭ al-Laythī that Sa'īd ibn al-Musayyab said, "The slaughter of what is in the womb is included in the slaughter of the mother if it is perfectly formed and its hair has begun to grow."

25. Game

25.1 Eating game killed with throwing sticks and by stones

1 Yaḥyā related to me from Mālik from Nāfi' who said, "I was at al-Juruf (near Madīna) and threw a stone at two birds, and hit them. One of them died, and 'Abdullāh ibn 'Umar threw it away, and then went to slaughter the other one with an adze. It died before he could slaughter it, so 'Abdullāh threw that one away as well."

2 Yaḥyā related to me from Mālik that he had heard that al-Qāsim ibn Muḥammad disapproved of eating game that had been killed with throwing sticks and by clay pellets.

3 Yaḥyā related to me from Mālik that he had heard that Sa'īd ibn al-Musayyab disapproved of killing domestic animals by any means that game was slain such as arrows and the like.

Mālik said, "I do not see any harm in eating game which is pierced by a throwing stick in a vital organ. Allah, the Blessed, the Exalted! said, '*O you who believe, Allah will test you with game animals which come within the reach of your hands and spears.*'" (5:97)

Mālik said, "So any game that a man obtains by his hand or by his spear or by any weapon which pierces it and reaches a vital organ, is acceptable as Allah, the Exalted, has indicated."

4 Yaḥyā related to me from Mālik that he had heard the people of knowledge say that when a man hit game and something else might

have contributed to death, like water or an untrained dog, such game was not to be eaten unless it was beyond doubt that it was the arrow of the hunter that had killed it by piercing a vital organ, so that it did not have any life after that.

Yaḥyā said that he heard Mālik say that there was no harm in eating game when you did not see it die if you found the mark of your dog on it or your arrow in it as long as it had not remained overnight. If it had remained overnight, then it was disapproved of to eat it.

25.2 Game caught by trained dogs

5 Yaḥyā related to me from Mālik from Nāfiʿ that ʿAbdullāh ibn ʿUmar said about a trained dog, "Eat whatever it catches for you whether it kills it or not."

6 Yaḥyā related to me from Mālik that he heard Nāfiʿ say that ʿAbdullāh ibn ʿUmar said, "Whether it eats from it or not."

7 Yaḥyā related to me from Mālik that he had heard that Saʿīd ibn Abī Waqqāṣ had said, when asked about a trained dog killing game, "Eat, even if only one piece of it remains."

8 Yaḥyā related to me from Mālik that he had heard some of the people of knowledge say that when falcons, eagles, and hawks and their like, understand as trained dogs understand, there is no harm in eating what they kill in the course of hunting, if the name of Allah is mentioned when they were sent out.

Mālik said, "The best of what I have heard about retrieving game from the falcon's talons or from the mouth of a dog and then waiting until it dies, is that it is not *ḥalāl* to eat it."

Mālik said, "The same applies to anything which could have been slaughtered by the hunter when it was in the talons of the falcon or the mouth of a dog. If the hunter leaves it until the falcon or dog has killed it, it is not lawful to eat it either."

He continued, "The same thing applies to any game hit by a hunter and caught while still alive, which he neglects to slaughter before it dies."

Mālik said, "It is generally agreed among us that it is lawful to eat the game that a hunting-dog belonging to a Magian hunts or kills if it is sent out by a Muslim and the animal is trained. There is no harm in it even if the Muslim does not actually slaughter it. That is like a Muslim using a Magian's knife to slaughter with or using his bow and arrows to shoot and kill with. The game he shoots and the animal he slaughters are *ḥalāl*. There is no harm in eating them. If a Magian sends out a Muslim's hunting dog for game, and it catches it, the game is not to be eaten unless it is slaughtered by a Muslim. That is like a Magian using a Muslim's bow and arrow to hunt game with, or like his using a Muslim's knife to slaughter with. It is not lawful to eat anything killed like that."

25.3 Catching sea animals

9 Yaḥyā related to me from Mālik from Nāfi' that 'Abd ar-Raḥmān ibn Abī Hurayra asked 'Abdullāh ibn 'Umar about eating what was cast up by the sea and he forbade him to eat it. Then 'Abdullāh turned and asked for a Qur'ān, and read, "*The game of the sea and its flesh are lawful for you.*" (5:96)

Nāfi' added, "'Abdullāh ibn 'Umar sent me to 'Abd ar-Raḥmān ibn Abī Hurayra to say that there was no harm in eating it."

10 Yaḥyā related to me from Mālik from Zayd ibn Aslam that Sa'īd al-Jārī, the *mawlā* of 'Umar ibn al-Khaṭṭāb, asked 'Abdullāh ibn 'Umar about fish which had killed each other or which had died from severe cold. He said, "There is no harm in eating them." Sa'd said, "I then asked 'Abdullāh ibn 'Amr ibn al-'Āṣ and he said the same."

11 Yaḥyā related to me from Mālik from Abū az-Zinād from Abū Salama ibn 'Abd ar-Raḥmān from Abū Hurayra and Zayd ibn Thābit that they saw no harm in eating what was cast up by the sea.

12 Yaḥyā related to me from Mālik from Abū az-Zinād from Abū Salama

ibn 'Abd ar-Raḥmān that some people from al-Jār came to Marwān ibn al-Ḥakam and asked him about eating what was cast up by the sea. He said, "There is no harm in eating it." Marwān said, "Go to Zayd ibn Thābit and Abū Hurayra and ask them about it, then come to me and tell me what they say." They went to them and asked them, and they both said, "There is no harm in eating it." They returned to Marwān and told him. Marwān said, "I told you."

Mālik added that there was no harm in eating fish caught by Magians, because the Messenger of Allah ﷺ said, "The water of the sea is pure, and its dead creatures are *ḥalāl*."

Mālik said, "Since that is eaten dead, it does not matter who has caught it."

25.4 Prohibition against eating animals with fangs

13 Yaḥyā related to me from Mālik from Ibn Shihāb from Abū Idrīs al-Khawlānī from Abū Tha'laba al-Khushanī that the Messenger of Allah ﷺ said, "It is unlawful to eat animals with fangs."

14 Yaḥyā related to me from Mālik from Ismā'īl ibn Abī Ḥakīm from 'Abīda ibn Sufyān al-Ḥaḍrami from Abū Hurayra that the Messenger of Allah ﷺ said, "Eating animals with fangs is *ḥarām*."

Mālik said, "This is the custom among us."

25.5 What is disapproved of regarding eating riding animals

15 Yaḥyā related to me from Mālik that the best of what he had heard about horses, mules and donkeys was that they were not eaten because Allah, the Blessed, the Exalted, says, "*And horses, mules and donkeys both to ride and for adornment.*" (16:8) He also says, may He be Blessed and Exalted, about livestock, "*Some for you to ride and some to eat.*" (40:79) He also says, the Blessed, the Exalted, "*So that they may mention the name of Allah over the livestock He has given them ... eat of them and feed both*

those who ask and (al-qāni') and those who are too shy to ask (al-mu'tarr)." (22:34-36)

Mālik commented, "Allah mentions horses, mules and donkeys for riding and adornment, and He mentions cattle for riding and eating."

Mālik said, "*Al-qāni'* also means the poor."

25.6 Using the skin of animals found dead

16 Yaḥyā related to me from Mālik from Ibn Shihāb from 'Ubaydullāh ibn 'Abdullāh ibn 'Utba ibn Mas'ūd that 'Abdullāh ibn 'Abbās said, "The Messenger of Allah ﷺ passed by a dead sheep which had been given to a *mawlā* of his wife, Maymūna. He asked, 'Are you not going to use its skin?' They answered, 'Messenger of Allah, but it is carrion.' The Messenger of Allah ﷺ said. 'Only eating it is *ḥarām*.'"

17 Mālik related to me from Zayd ibn Aslam from Ibn Wa'la al-Miṣrī from 'Abdullāh ibn 'Abbās that the Messenger of Allah ﷺ said, "A skin is pure when it has been tanned."

18 Yaḥyā related to me from Mālik from Yazīd ibn 'Abdullāh ibn Qusayṭ from Muḥammad ibn 'Abd ar-Raḥmān ibn Thawbān from his mother that 'Ā'isha, the wife of the Prophet ﷺ, said that the Messenger of Allah ﷺ ordered that the skins of carrion be used after they had been tanned."

25.7 Eating carrion when forced to, out of necessity

19 Yaḥyā related to me from Mālik that the best of what he had heard about a man who was forced by necessity to eat carrion was that he ate it until he was full and then took provision from it. If he found something which would enable him to dispense with it, he threw it away.

Mālik, when asked whether or not a man who had been forced by necessity to eat carrion, should eat it when he also found the fruit, crops or sheep of a people in that place, answered, "If he thinks that the owners of the fruit, crops or sheep will accept that it was a necessity so that he will not be deemed a thief and have his hand cut off, then I think that he should eat from what he finds whatever will remove his hunger but he should not carry any of it away. I prefer that he do that rather than eat carrion. If he fears that he will not be believed, and will be deemed a thief for what he has taken, then I think that it is better for him to eat the carrion, and he has leeway to eat carrion in this respect. Even so, I fear that someone who is not forced by necessity to eat carrion might exceed the limits out of a desire to consume other people's property, crops or fruit."

Mālik said, "That is the best of what I have heard."

26. The *'Aqīqa*

26.1 About the *'aqīqa*

1 Yaḥyā related to me from Mālik from Zayd ibn Aslam from a man of the Banū Ḍamra that his father said, "The Messenger of Allah ﷺ was asked about the *'aqīqa*. He said, 'I do not like disobedience (*'uqūq*),' as if he disliked the name. He said, 'If anyone has a child born to him, and wants to sacrifice for his child, then let him do it.'"

2 Yaḥyā related to me from Mālik from Ja'far ibn Muḥammad that his father said, "Fāṭima, the daughter of the Messenger of Allah ﷺ weighed the hair of Ḥasan, Ḥusayn, Zaynab and Umm Kulthum, and gave away in *ṣadaqa* an equivalent weight of silver."

3 Yaḥyā related to me from Mālik from Rabi'a ibn Abī 'Abd ar-Raḥman that Muḥammad ibn 'Alī ibn al-Ḥusayn said, " Fāṭima, the daughter of the Messenger of Allah ﷺ, weighed the hair of Ḥasan and Ḥusayn, and gave away in *ṣadaqa* the equivalent weight in silver."

26.2 Behaviour in the *'aqīqa*

4 Yaḥyā related to me from Mālik from Nāfi' that if any of 'Abdullāh ibn 'Umar's family asked him for an *'aqīqa*, he would give it to them. He gave a sheep as *'aqīqa* for both his male and female children.

5 Yaḥyā related to me from Mālik from Rabi'a ibn Abī 'Abd ar-Raḥmān that Muḥammad ibn al-Ḥārith at-Taymī said, "I heard my father say that the *'aqīqa* was desirable, even if it was only a sparrow."

6 Yaḥyā related to me from Mālik that he heard that there had been an *'aqīqa* for Ḥasan and Ḥusayn, the sons of 'Alī ibn Abī Ṭālib.

7 Yaḥyā related to me from Mālik from Hishām ibn 'Urwa that his father, 'Urwa ibn az-Zubayr made an *'aqīqa* for his male and female children of a sheep each.

Mālik said, "What we do about the *'aqīqa* is that if someone makes an *'aqīqa* for his children, he gives a sheep for both male and female. The *'aqīqa* is not obligatory but it is desirable to do it, and it is something which people continue to do here (i.e. Madīna). If someone makes an *'aqīqa* for his children, the same rules apply as with all sacrificial animals: one-eyed, emaciated, injured, or sick animals must not be used, and neither the meat or the skin is to be sold. The bones are broken and the family eat the meat and give some of it away as *ṣadaqa*. The child is not smeared with any of the blood."

27. Fixed Shares of Inheritance

27.1 Inheritance of direct descendants

Yaḥyā related to me from Mālik, "The generally agreed upon way of doing things among us and what I have seen the people of knowledge doing in our city about the fixed shares of inheritance (*farā'iḍ*) of children from the mother or father when one or other of them dies is that if they leave male and female children, the male takes the portion of two females. If there are only females, and there are more than two, they get two thirds of what is left between them. If there is only one, she gets a half. If people with fixed shares share with the children and there are males among them, the reckoner begins with the ones with fixed shares. What remains after that is divided among the children according to their inheritance.

"When there are no children, grandchildren through sons have the same position as children, so that grandsons are like sons and grand-daughters are like daughters. They inherit as they inherit and they preclude as the children preclude. If there are both children and grandchildren through sons, and there is a male among the children, then the grandchildren through sons do not share in the inheritance with him.

"If there are no surviving males among the children, and there are two or more daughters, grand-daughters through a son do not share in the inheritance with them unless there is a male who is in the same position as them in relation to the deceased, or further than them. His presence gives access to whatever is left over, if any, to whoever is in his position and whoever is above him of the grand-daughters through sons.

If something is left over, they divide it among them, and the male takes the portion of two females. If nothing is left over, they have nothing.

"If the only descendant is a daughter, she takes half, and if there are one or more grand-daughters through a son, who are in the same position to the deceased, they share a sixth. If there is a male in the same position as the grand-daughters through a son in relation to the deceased, they have no share and no sixth.

"If there is a surplus after the allotting of shares to the people with fixed shares, the surplus goes to the male and whoever is in his position and whoever is above him of the female descendants through sons. The male receives the share of two females. The one who is more distant in relationship than grandchildren through sons has nothing. If there is no surplus, they receive nothing. That is because Allah, the Blessed, the Exalted, says in is Book, *'Allah instructs you regarding your children: A male gets the same as the share of two females. If there are more than two daughters they get two-thirds of what you leave. If she is one on her own she gets a half.'*" (4:11)

27.2 Inheritance of husbands from wives and wives from husbands

Mālik said, "The inheritance of a husband from a wife, when she leaves no children or grandchildren through sons, is a half. If she leaves children or grandchildren through sons, male or female, by her present or any previous husband, the husband has a quarter after bequests or debts. The inheritance of a wife from a husband who does not leave children or grandchildren through sons is a quarter. If he leaves children or grandchildren through sons, male or female, the wife has an eighth after bequests and debts. That is because Allah, the Blessed, the Exalted! says in His Book, *'You get half of what your wives leave if they are childless. If they have children you get a quarter of what they leave after any bequest they make or any debts. They get a quarter of what you leave if you are childless. If you have children they get an eighth of what you leave after any bequest you make or any debts.'*" (4:12)

27.3 Inheritance of fathers and mothers from children

Mālik said, "The generally agreed-on way of doing things among us, about which there is no dispute and what I have seen the people of knowledge in our city doing, is that when a father inherits from a son or a daughter and the deceased leaves children or grandchildren through a son, the father has a fixed share of one sixth. If the deceased does leave any children or male grandchildren through a son, the apportioning begins with those with whom the father shares in the fixed shares. They are given their fixed shares. If a sixth or more is left over, the sixth and what is above it is given to the father, and if there is less than a sixth left, the father is given his sixth as a fixed share (i.e. the other shares are adjusted)."

"The inheritance of a mother from her child, if her son or daughter dies and leaves children, male or female, or grandchildren through a son, or leaves two or more full or half siblings, is a sixth. If the deceased does not leave any children or grandchildren through a son, or two or more siblings, the mother has a whole third except in two cases. One of them is if a man dies and leaves a wife and both his parents. The wife has a fourth, the mother a third of what remains (which is a fourth of the capital). The other is if a wife dies and leaves a husband and both her parents. The husband gets half, and the mother a third of what remains, (which is a sixth of the capital). That is because Allah, the Blessed, the Exalted, says in His Book, '*Each of your parents get a sixth of what you leave if you have children. If you are childless and your heirs are your parents your mother gets a third. If you have brothers or sisters your mother gets a sixth.*' (4:11) The *sunna* is that the siblings referred to be two or more."

27.4 Inheritance of maternal half-siblings

Mālik said, "The generally agreed-upon way of doing things among us is that maternal half-siblings do not inherit anything when there are children or grandchildren through sons, male or female. They do not inherit anything when there is a father or the father's father. They inherit in what is outside of that. If there is only one male or female, they are given a sixth. If there are two, each of them has a sixth. If there are more than that, they share in a third which is divided among them. The male does not have the portion of two females. That is because Allah, the Blessed, the Exalted, says in His Book, '*If a man or woman has no direct heirs but has a brother or sister, each of them gets a sixth. If there are more than that they share in a third.*'" (4:12) So males and females are alike in regard to this.

27.5 Inheritance of full-siblings

Mālik said, "The generally agreed-on way of doing things among us is that full-siblings do not inherit anything with sons nor anything with grandsons through a son, nor anything with the father. They do inherit with the daughters and the grand-daughters through a son when the deceased does not leave a paternal grandfather. They are considered in any property that is left over as paternal relations. One begins with the people who are allotted fixed shares. They are given their shares. If there is anything left over after that, it belongs to the full-siblings. They divide it between themselves according to the Book of Allah, whether they are male or female. The male has a portion of two females. If there is nothing left over, they receive nothing.

"If the deceased does not leave a father or a paternal grandfather or children or male or female grandchildren through a son, a single full sister gets a half. If there are two or more full sisters, they get two-thirds. If there is a brother with them, sisters, whether one or more, do not have a fixed share. One begins with whoever shares in the fixed shares. They are given their shares. Whatever remains after that goes to the full-siblings. The male has the portion of two females except in one case, in which the full-siblings have nothing. They share in this case the third of the half-siblings by the mother. That case is when a woman dies and leaves a husband, a mother, half-siblings by her mother, and full-siblings. The husband has a half. The mother has one sixth. The half-siblings by the mother have a third. Nothing is left after that, so the full-siblings share in this case with the half-siblings by the mother in their third. The males have the portion of two females inasmuch as all of them are siblings of the deceased by the mother. They inherit by the mother. That is because Allah, the Blessed, the Exalted, says in His Book, '*If a man or a woman has no direct heir and he has a brother or sister, each one of the two gets a sixth. If there are more than that, they share equally in the third.'* (4:12) They therefore share in this case because they all are siblings of the deceased by the mother."

27.6 Inheritance of paternal half-siblings

Mālik said, "The generally agreed-on way of doing things among us is that when there are no full-siblings with them, half-siblings by the father take the position of full-siblings. Their males are like the males of the full-siblings, and their females are like their females except in the case where the half-siblings by the mother and the full-siblings share, because they are not offspring of the mother who joins these."

Mālik said, "If there are both full-siblings and half-siblings by the father and there is a male among the full-siblings, none of the half-siblings by the father have any inheritance. If there is one or more females in the full-siblings and there is no male with them, the one full-sister gets a half, and the half-sister by the father gets a sixth, completing the two-thirds. If there is a male with the half-sisters by the father, they have no share. The people of fixed shares are given their shares and, if there is something left after that, it is divided between the half-siblings by the father. The male gets the portion of two females. If there is nothing left over, they get nothing. Half-siblings by the mother, full-siblings, and half-siblings by the father, each have a sixth (when they are only one). Two and more share a third. The male has the same portion as the female. They are in the same position in this case."

27.7 Inheritance of grandfathers

1 Yaḥyā related to me from Mālik from Yaḥyā ibn Sa'īd that he had heard that Mu'āwiya ibn Abī Sufyān wrote to Zayd ibn Thābit asking him about the grandfather. Zayd ibn Thābit wrote to him. "You have written to me asking me about the grandfather. Allah knows best. This belongs to those matters left to the determination of the commanders, i.e. the caliphs. I was present with two caliphs before you who gave the

grandfather a half with one sibling, and a third with two. If there were more siblings, they did not decrease his third."

2 Yaḥyā related to me from Mālik from Ibn Shihāb from Qabīṣa ibn Dhū'ayb that 'Umar ibn al-Khaṭṭāb gave the grandfather "what people him give today."

3 Yaḥyā related to me from Mālik that he had heard that Sulaymān ibn Yasār said, "'Umar ibn al-Khaṭṭāb, 'Uthmān ibn 'Affān, and Zayd ibn Thābit gave the grandfather a third with full-siblings."

Mālik said, "The generally agreed-on way of doing things among us and what I have seen the people of knowledge in our city doing is that the paternal grandfather does not inherit anything at all with the father. He is given a sixth as a fixed share with the son and the grandson through a son. Other than that, when the deceased does not leave a mother or a paternal aunt, one begins with whoever has a fixed share, and they are given their shares. If there is a sixth of the property left over, the grandfather is given a sixth as a fixed share."

Mālik said, "When someone shares with the grandfather and the full siblings in a specified share, one begins with whoever shares with them of the people of fixed shares. They are given their shares. What is left over after that belongs to the grandfather and the full-siblings. Then one sees which is the more favourable of two alternatives for the portion of the grandfather. Either a third is allotted to him and the siblings to divide between them, and he gets a share as if he were one of the siblings, or else he takes a sixth from all the capital. Whichever is the best portion for the grandfather is given to him. What is left after that goes to the full-siblings. The male gets the portion of two females except in one particular case. The division in this case is different from the preceding one. This case is when a woman dies and leaves a husband, mother, full sister and grandfather. The husband gets a half, the mother gets a third, the grandfather gets a sixth, and the full sister gets a half. The sixth of the grandfather and the half of the sister are joined and divided into thirds. The male gets the share of two females. Therefore, the grandfather has two thirds of it, and the sister has one third of it"

Mālik said, "The inheritance of the half-siblings by the father with the grandfather, when there are no full-siblings with them, is like the inheritance of the full-siblings (in the same situation). The males are the same as their males and the females are the same as their females. When there are both full-siblings and half-siblings by the father, the full-siblings include in their number the half-siblings by the father in order to limit the inheritance of the grandfather, i.e. if there was only one full-sibling with the grandfather, they would share, after the allotting of the fixed shares, the remainder of the inheritance between them equally. If there were also two half-siblings by the father, their number is added to the division of the sum, which would then be divided four ways. A quarter going to the grandfather and three-quarters going to the full-siblings who annex the shares technically allotted to the half-siblings by the father. They do not include the number of half-siblings by the mother because if there were only half-siblings by the father they would not inherit anything after the portion of the grandfather.

"It belongs to the full-siblings more than the half-siblings by the father, and the half-siblings by the father do not get anything with them unless the full-siblings consist of one sister. If there is one full sister, she includes the grandfather with the half-siblings by her father in the division, however many. Whatever remains for her and these half-siblings by the father goes to her rather than them until she has had her complete share, which is half of the total capital. If there is surplus beyond half of all the capital in what she and the half-siblings by the father acquire, it goes to them. The male receives the portion of two females. If there is nothing left over, they get nothing."

27.8 Inheritance of grandmothers

4 Yaḥyā related to me from Mālik from Ibn Shihāb from 'Uthmān ibn Isḥāq ibn Kharasha that Qabīṣa ibn Dhū'ayb said, "A grandmother came to Abū Bakr as-Ṣiddīq and asked him for her inheritance. Abū Bakr said to her, 'You have nothing in the Book of Allah, and I do not know that you have anything in the *sunna* of the Messenger of Allah ﷺ. Go away therefore, until I have questioned the people (i.e. the Companions).' He questioned the people, and al-Mughīra ibn Shu'ba said, 'I was present

with the Messenger of Allah ﷺ when he gave the grandmother a sixth.' Abū Bakr asked, 'Was there anybody else with you?' Muḥammad ibn Maslama al-Ansārī stood up and said the like of what al-Mughīra had said. Abū Bakr aṣ-Siddiq gave it to her. Then the other grandmother came to 'Umar ibn al-Khaṭṭāb and asked him for her inheritance. He said to her, 'You have nothing in the Book of Allah, and what has been decided is only for other than you, and I am not one to add to the fixed shares, other than that sixth. If there are two of you together, it is between you. If either of you is left alone with it, it is hers.'"

5 Yaḥyā related to me from Mālik from Yaḥyā ibn Sa'īd that al-Qāsim ibn Muḥammad said, "Two grandmothers came to Abū Bakr aṣ-Ṣiddīq, and he wanted to give the sixth to the one who was from the mother's side, and a man of the Ansār said, 'What? Are you omitting the one from whom he would inherit if she died while he was still alive?' Abū Bakr divided the sixth between them."

6 Yaḥyā related to me from Mālik from 'Abdu Rabbih ibn Sa'īd that Abū Bakr ibn 'Abd ar-Raḥmān ibn al-Ḥārith ibn Hishām only gave a fixed share to two grandmothers (together).

Mālik said, "The generally agreed-on way of doing things among us in which there is no dispute, and which I saw the people of knowledge in our city doing, is that the maternal grandmother does not inherit anything at all with the mother. Outside of that, she is given a sixth as a fixed share. The paternal grandmother does not inherit anything along with the mother of the father. Outside of that she is given a sixth as a fixed share."

If both the paternal grandmother and maternal grandmother are alive, and the deceased does not have a father or a mother other than them, Mālik said, "I have heard that if the maternal grandmother is the nearest of the two of them, then she has a sixth instead of the paternal grandmother. If the paternal grandmother is nearer, or they are in the same position in relation to the deceased, the sixth is divided equally between them."

Mālik said, "None of the female grandrelations except for these two has any inheritance because I have heard that the Messenger of Allah

ﷺ gave the grandmother inheritance, and then Abū Bakr asked about that until someone reliable related from the Messenger of Allah ﷺ that he had made the grandmother an heir and given a share to her. Another grandmother came to 'Umar ibn al-Khaṭṭāb, and he said, 'I am not one to add to the fixed shares. If there are two of you together, it is between you. If either of you is left alone with it, it is hers.'"

Mālik said, "We do not know of anyone who made other than the two grandmothers heirs from the beginning of Islam to this day."

27.9 Inheritance of persons without parents or offspring

7 Yaḥyā related to me from Mālik from Zayd ibn Aslam that 'Umar ibn al-Khaṭṭāb asked the Messenger of Allah ﷺ about someone who died without parents or offspring (i.e. he asked about "*kalāla*") and the Messenger of Allah ﷺ said to him, "The *āyat* which was sent down in the summer at the end of the Sūrat an-Nisā' (4) is enough for you."

Mālik said, "The generally agreed-on way of doing things among us, in which there is no dispute, and which I saw the people of knowledge in our city doing, is that the person who leaves neither parent or offspring can be of two types. As for the kind described in the *āyat* which was sent down at the beginning of Sūrat an-Nisā' in which Allah, the Blessed, the Exalted, says, '*If a man or a woman has no direct heir and he has a brother or sister, each one of the two gets a sixth. If there are more than that, they share equally in the third.*' (4:12) This heirless one does not have heirs among his mother's siblings since there are no children or parents. As for the other kind described in the *āyat* which comes at the end of the Sūrat an-Nisā', Allah, the Blessed, the Exalted, says in it, '*They will ask you for a definitive ruling. Say: "Allah gives you a definitive ruling about people who die without direct heirs: If a man dies childless but has a sister she gets half of what he leaves. And he is her heir if she dies childless. If there are two sisters they get two-thirds of what he leaves. If there are brothers and sisters the males get the share of two females. Allah makes things clear to you so you will not go astray. Allah has knowledge of all things.*"' (4:176)

Mālik said, "If this person without direct heirs (parents) or children has siblings by the father, they inherit with the grandfather from this person without direct heirs. The grandfather inherits with the siblings because he is more entitled to the inheritance than them. That is because he inherits a sixth with the male children of the deceased when the siblings do not inherit anything with the male children of the deceased. How can he not be like one of them when he takes a sixth with the children of the deceased? How can he not take a third with the siblings while the brother's sons take a third with them? The grandfather is the one who overshadows the half-siblings by the mother and keeps them from inheriting. He is more entitled to what they have because they are omitted for his sake. If the grandfather did not take that third, the half-siblings by the mother would take it and would take what does not return to the half-siblings by the father. The half-siblings by the mother are more entitled to that third than the half-siblings by the father while the grandfather is not less entitled to that than the half-siblings by the mother."

27.10 Paternal aunts

8 Yaḥyā related to me from Mālik from Muḥammad ibn Abī Bakr ibn Muḥammad ibn 'Amr ibn Ḥazm that 'Abd ar-Raḥmān ibn Ḥanẓala az-Zuraqī was informed by a *mawlā* of Quraysh, who used to be known as Ibn Mirsa, that he was sitting with 'Umar ibn al-Khaṭṭāb, and when they had prayed *Ẓuhr*, he said, "Yarfā! Bring that letter! (A letter which he had written about the paternal aunt). We asked about her and asked for information about her." Yarfā brought it to him. He called for a small vessel or drinking-bowl in which there was water. He erased the letter in it. Then he said, "Had Allah approved of you as an heir, we would have confirmed you. Had Allah approved of you, He would have confirmed you."

9 Yaḥyā related to me from Mālik that Muḥammad ibn Abī Bakr ibn Ḥazm heard his father say many times, "'Umar ibn al-Khaṭṭāb used to remark, 'It is a wonder that the paternal aunt is inherited from but does not inherit.'"

27.11 Inheritance of paternal relations (*'aṣaba*)

Mālik said, "The generally agreed-on way of doing things among us, in which there is no dispute, and which I saw the people of knowledge in our city doing, about paternal relations, is that full-brothers are more entitled to inherit than half-brothers by the father, and half-brothers by the father are more entitled to inherit than the children of the full-brothers. The sons of the full-brothers are more entitled to inherit than the sons of the half-brothers by the father. The sons of the half-brothers by the father are more entitled to inherit than the sons of the sons of the full-brothers. The sons of the sons of the half-brothers on the father's side are more entitled to inherit than the paternal uncle, the full brother of the father. The paternal uncle, the full brother of the father, is more entitled to inherit than the paternal uncle, the half-brother of the father on the father's side. The paternal uncle, the half-brother of the father on the father's side, is more entitled to inherit than the sons of the paternal uncle, the full-brother of the father. The son of the paternal uncle on the father's side is more entitled to inherit than the paternal great uncle, the full-brother of the paternal grandfather."

Mālik said, "Everything about which you are questioned concerning the inheritance of the paternal relations is like this. Trace the genealogy of the deceased and whoever among the paternal relations contends for inheritance. If you find that one of them reaches the deceased by a father, and none of them except him reaches him by a father, then grant the inheritance to the one who reaches him by the nearest father, rather than the one who reaches him by what is above that. If you find that they all reach him by the same father who joins them, then see who is the nearest of kin. If there is only one half-brother by the father, give him the inheritance rather than more distant paternal relations. If there is a full-brother and you find them equally related from a number of fathers or to one particular father, so that they all reach the genealogy of the deceased and they are all half-brothers by the father or full-brothers, then divide the inheritance equally among them. If the parent of one of them is an uncle (the full-brother of the father of the deceased) and whoever is with him is an uncle (the paternal half-brother of the father of the deceased), the inheritance goes to the sons of the full brother of the father rather than the sons of the paternal half-brother of the father. That is because Allah, the Blessed, the Exalted, says, *'But blood relations are closer to one another in Allah's Book. Allah has knowledge of all things.'* (8:75)"

Mālik said, "The paternal grandfather is more entitled to inherit than the sons of the full-brother, and more entitled than the uncle, the full brother of the father. The son of the father's brother is more entitled to inherit from *mawālī* retainers (freed slaves) than the grandfathers."

27.12 People who do not inherit

Mālik said, "The generally agreed-on way of doing things among us in which there is no dispute, and which I saw the people of knowledge in our city doing, is that the child of the half-sibling by the mother, the paternal grandfather, the paternal uncle who is the maternal half-brother of the father, the maternal uncle, the great grandmother who is the mother of the mother's father, the daughter of the full-brother, the paternal aunt, and the maternal aunt do not inherit anything by their kinship."

Mālik said, "Any woman who is more distantly related to the deceased than those who were named in this Book, does not inherit anything by her kinship, and women do not inherit anything apart from those that are named in the Qur'ān. Allah, the Blessed, the Exalted, mentions in His Book the inheritance of the mother from her children, the inheritance of the daughters from their father, the inheritance of the wife from her husband, the inheritance of the full-sisters, the inheritance of the half-sisters by the father and the inheritance of the half-sisters by the mother. The grandmother is made an heir by the example the Prophet ﷺ made about her. A woman inherits from a slave she frees herself because Allah, the Blessed, the Exalted, says in His Book, *'They are your brothers in the dīn and people under your patronage.'* (33:5)"

27.13 Inheritance from the people of other religions

10 Yaḥyā related to me from Mālik from Ibn Shihāb from 'Alī ibn Ḥusayn ibn 'Alī from 'Umar ibn Uthmān ibn 'Affān from Usāma ibn Zayd that the Messenger of Allah ﷺ said, "A Muslim does not inherit from a unbeliever."

11 Yaḥyā related to me from Mālik from Ibn Shihāb that 'Alī ibn Ḥusayn in 'Alī ibn Abī Tālib told him that 'Aqīl and Ṭālib inherited from Abū Ṭālib, and 'Alī did not inherit from him. 'Alī said, "Because of that, we have given up our portion of ash-Shi'b (a house belonging to the Banū Hāshim)."

12 Yaḥyā related to me from Mālik from Yaḥyā ibn Sa'īd from Sulaymān ibn Yasār that Muḥammad ibn al-Ash'ath told him that he had a Christian or Jewish paternal aunt who died. Muḥammad ibn al-Ash'ath mentioned that to 'Umar ibn al-Khaṭṭāb and asked him, "Who inherits from her?" 'Umar ibn al-Khaṭṭāb said to him, "The people of her *dīn* inherit from her." Then he went to 'Umar ibn 'Affān, and asked him about that. 'Uthmān said to him, "Do you think that I have forgotten what 'Umar ibn al-Khaṭṭāb told you? The people of her *dīn* inherit from her."

13 Yaḥyā related to me from Mālik from Yaḥyā ibn Sa'īd from Ismā'īl ibn Abī Ḥakīm that 'Umar ibn 'Abd al-'Azīz freed a Christian who then died. Ismā'īl said, "'Umar ibn 'Abd al-'Azīz ordered me to put his property in the Treasury."

14 Yaḥyā related to me from Mālik from a reliable source of his who had heard Sa'īd ibn al-Musayyab say, "'Umar ibn al-Khaṭṭāb refused to let anyone inherit from the non-Arabs except for one who was born among the Arabs."

Mālik said, "If a pregnant woman comes from the land of the enemy and gives birth in Arab land then he is considered to be her child. He inherits from her if she dies, and she inherits from him if he dies, by the Book of Allah."

Mālik said, "The generally agreed-on way of doing things among us and the *sunna* in which there is no dispute, and what I saw the people of knowledge in our city doing, is that a Muslim does not inherit from a unbeliever by kinship, clientage (*walā'*), or maternal relationship, nor does he (the Muslim) bar any (of the unbelievers) from his inheritance."

Mālik said, "Similarly, someone who forgoes his inheritance when he is the chief heir does not bar anyone from his inheritance."

27.14 People killed in battle or otherwise whose situation in inheritance is not known

15 Yaḥyā related to me from Mālik from Rabi'a ibn Abī 'Abd ar-Raḥmān from more than one of the people of knowledge of that time, that those who were killed on the Day of the Camel, the Day of Ṣiffīn, the Day of al-Ḥarra, and the Day of Qudayd did not inherit from each other. None of them inherited anything from his companion unless it was known that he had been killed before his companion.

Mālik said, "That is the way of doing things about which there is no dispute, and which none of the people of knowledge in our city doubt. The procedure with two mutual heirs who are drowned, or killed in another way, when it is not known which of them died first is the same – neither of them inherits anything from his companion. Their inheritance goes to whoever remains of their heirs. They are inherited from by the living."

Mālik said, "No one should inherit from anyone else when there is doubt, and one should only inherit from the other when there is certainty of knowledge and witnesses. That is because a man and his *mawlā* whom his father has freed might die at the same time. The sons of the free man could say, 'Our father inherited from the *mawlā*.' They should not inherit from the *mawlā* without knowledge or testimony that he died first. The living people most entitled to his *walā'* inherit from him."

Mālik said, "Another example is two full brothers who die. One of them has children and the other does not. They have a half-brother by their father. It is not known which of them died first, so the inheritance of the childless one goes to his half-brother by the father. The children of the full-brother get nothing."

Mālik said, "Another example is when a paternal aunt and the son of her brother die, or else the daughter of the brother and her paternal uncle. It is not known which of them died first. The paternal uncle does not inherit anything from the daughter of his brother, and the son of the brother does not inherit anything from his paternal aunt."

27.15 The inheritance of the child of *li'ān* and the child of fornication

16 Yaḥyā related to me from Mālik that he had heard that 'Urwa ibn az-Zubayr said about the child of *li'ān* and the child of fornication, that, if they died, the mother inherited her right from them according to the Book of Allah, the Mighty, the Majestic! The siblings by the mother had their rights. The rest was inherited by the former masters of the mother if she was a freed slave. If she was a free woman by origin, she inherited her due and the siblings by the mother inherited their due, and the rest went to the Muslims.

Mālik said, "I heard the same as that from Sulaymān ibn Yasār."

Mālik said, "That is what I have seen the people of knowledge in our city doing."

28. Marriage

28.1 Asking for someone's hand in marriage

1 Yaḥyā related to me from Mālik from Muḥammad ibn Yaḥyā ibn Ḥabbān from al-A'raj from Abū Hurayra that the Messenger of Allah ﷺ said, "Do not ask for a woman in marriage when another Muslim has already done so."

2 Yaḥyā related to me from Mālik from Nāfi' from 'Abdullāh ibn 'Umar that the Messenger of Allah ﷺ said, "Do not ask for a woman in marriage when another Muslim has already done so."

Mālik said, "The explanation of the statement of the Messenger of Allah ﷺ according to what we think – and Allah, the Blessed, the Exalted, knows best – is that, 'Do not ask for a woman in marriage when another Muslim has already done so,' means that when a man has asked for a woman in marriage, and she has inclined to him and they have agreed on a bride-price and are mutually satisfied (with the arrangement), and she has made any conditions for herself, it is forbidden for another man to ask for that woman in marriage. It does not mean that when a man has asked for a woman in marriage and his suit does not agree with her and she does not incline to him that no one else can ask for her in marriage. That is a door to misery for people."

3 Yaḥyā related to me from Mālik from 'Abd ar-Raḥmān ibn al-Qāsim that his father said about the words of Allah, the Blessed, the

Exalted, "*Nor is there anything wrong in any allusion to marriage you make to a woman, nor for any you keep to yourself. Allah knows that you will say things to them. But do not make secret arrangements with them, rather only speak with correctness and courtesy,*" (2:235) that it referred to a man saying to a woman while she was still in her *'idda* after the death of her husband, "You are dear to me, and I desire you, and Allah brings provision and blessing to you," and such words as these.

28.2 Asking the consent of virgins and women previously married

4 Mālik related to me from 'Abdullāh ibn al-Faḍl from Nāfi' ibn Jubayr ibn Muṭ'im from 'Abdullāh ibn 'Abbās that the Messenger of Allah ﷺ said, "A woman who has been previously married is more entitled to her person than her guardian, and a virgin must be asked for her consent and her silence is her consent."

5 Yaḥyā related to me from Mālik that he had heard that Sa'īd ibn al-Musayyab had said that 'Umar ibn al-Khaṭṭāb said, "A woman is only married with the consent of either her guardian or someone of her family with sound judgment or the ruler."

6 Yaḥyā related to me from Mālik that he had heard that al-Qāsim ibn Muḥammad and Sālim ibn 'Abdullāh would marry off their virgin daughters without consulting them.

Mālik said, "That is what is done among us about the marriage of virgins."

Mālik said, "A virgin has no right to her property until she enters her house and her state (competence, maturity, etc.) is known for sure."

7 Yaḥyā related to me from Mālik that he had heard that al-Qāsim ibn Muḥammad and Sālim ibn 'Abdullāh and Sulaymān ibn Yasār said about the virgin given by her father in marriage without her permission, "It is binding on her."

28.3 The bride-price and unreturnable gifts

8 Yaḥyā related to me from Mālik from Abū Ḥāzim ibn Dīnār from Sahl ibn Sa'd as-Sā'idī that a woman came to the Messenger of Allah ﷺ and said, "Messenger of Allah! I have given myself to you." She stood for a long time, and then a man got up and said, "Messenger of Allah, marry her to me if you have no need of her." The Messenger of Allah ﷺ said, "Do you have anything to give her as a bride-price?" He said, "I possess only this lower garment of mine." The Messenger of Allah ﷺ said, "If you give it to her you will not have a garment to wear, so look for something else." He said, "I have nothing else." He said, "Look for something else, even if it is only an iron ring." He looked, and found that he had nothing. The Messenger of Allah ﷺ said, "Do you know any of the Qur'ān?" He said, "Yes, I know such-and-such a *sūra* and such-and-such a *sūra*," which he named. The Messenger of Allah ﷺ said to him, "I have married her to you for what you know of the Qur'ān."

9 Yaḥyā related to me from Mālik from Yaḥyā ibn Sa'īd that Sa'īd ibn al-Musayyab had said that 'Umar ibn al-Khaṭṭāb said, "If a man marries a woman who is insane, or has leprosy or white leprosy, without being told of her condition by her guardian, and he has sexual relations with her, she keeps her bride-price in its entirety. Her husband is entitled to damages against her guardian."

Mālik said, "The husband is entitled to damages against her guardian when the guardian is her father, brother, or one who is deemed to have knowledge of her condition. If the guardian who gives her in marriage is a nephew, a *mawlā*, or a member of her tribe who is not deemed to have knowledge of her condition, there are no damages against him, and the woman returns what she has taken of her bride-price, and the husband leaves her whatever amount is thought to be fair."

10 Yaḥyā related to me from Mālik from Nāfi' that the daughter of 'Ubaydullāh ibn 'Umar, whose mother was the daughter of Zayd ibn al-Khaṭṭāb, married the son of 'Abdullāh ibn 'Umar. He died and had not yet consummated the marriage or specified her bride-price. Her mother wanted the bride-price and 'Abdullāh ibn 'Umar said, "She is not entitled to a bride-price. Had she been entitled to a bride-price, we would not

have kept it and we would not do her an injustice." The mother refused to accept that. Zayd ibn Thābit was brought to adjudicate between them and he decided that she had no bride-price, but that she did inherit.

11 Yaḥyā related to me from Mālik that he had heard that 'Umar ibn 'Abd al-'Azīz, during his khalifate, wrote to one of his governors, "Whatever a father or guardian, giving someone in marriage, makes a condition in the way of unreturnable gift or favour belongs to the woman if she wants it."

Mālik spoke about a woman whose father gave her in marriage and made an unreturnable gift a condition of the bride-price which was to be given. He said, "Whatever is given as a condition, by which marriage occurs, belongs to the woman if she wants it. If the husband parts from her before the marriage is consummated, the husband has half of the unreturnable gift, by which the marriage occurred."

Mālik said about a man who married off his young son and the son had no wealth at all, that the bride-price was obliged of the father if the young man had no property on the day of marriage. If the young man did have property, the bride-price was taken from his property, unless the father stipulated that he would pay the bride-price himself. The marriage was affirmed for the son if he was a minor and was under the guardianship of his father.

Mālik said that if a man divorced his wife before he had consummated the marriage, and she was a virgin, her father returned half of the bride-price to him. That half was permitted to the husband from the father to compensate him for his expenses.

Mālik said that was because Allah, the Blessed, the Exalted, says in His Book, "*unless they* (*women with whom he had not consummated marriage*) *forgo it or the one in charge of the marriage contract forgoes it.*" (2:237) (He being the father of a virgin daughter or the master of a female slave).

Mālik said, "That is what I have heard about the matter, and that is how things are done among us."

Mālik said that a Jewish or Christian woman who was married to a Jew or Christian and then became Muslim before the marriage had been consummated was not owed any bride-price.

Mālik said, "I do not think that women should be married for less than a quarter of a dinar. That is the lowest amount for which cutting off the hand is obliged."

28.4 Consummating a marriage

12 Yaḥyā related to me from Mālik from Yaḥyā ibn Sa'd from Sa'īd ibn al-Musayyab that 'Umar ibn al-Khaṭṭāb decided, in the case of a woman who was married by a man and the marriage had been consummated, that the bride-price was obligatory.

13 Yaḥyā related to me from Mālik from Ibn Shihāb that Zayd ibn Thābit said, "When a man takes his wife to his house and cohabits with her, then the bride-price is obliged."

Yaḥyā related to me from Mālik that he had heard that Sa'īd ibn al-Musayyab said, "When a man comes to his wife in her room, he is believed. When she comes to him in his room, she is believed."

Mālik commented, "I think that this refers to sexual intercourse. When he comes into her in her room and she says, 'He has had intercourse with me' and he says, 'I have not touched her,' he is believed. When she comes to him in his room and he says, 'I have not had intercourse with her' and she says, 'He had intercourse with me,' she is believed."

28.5 Wedding nights of virgins and of women previously married

14 Yaḥyā related to me from Mālik from 'Abdullāh ibn Abī Bakr ibn Muḥammad ibn 'Amr ibn Ḥāzim from 'Abd al-Malik ibn Abī Bakr ibn 'Abd ar-Raḥmān ibn al-Ḥārith ibn Hishām al-Makhzūmī from his father that when the Messenger of Allah ﷺ married Umm Salama and then spent the night with her, he said to her, "You are not being humbled in

your right. If you wish, I will stay with you for seven nights and stay seven nights (each) with the others. If you wish, I will stay with you for three nights, and then visit the others in turn." She said, "Stay three nights."

15 Yaḥyā related to me from Mālik from Humayd aṭ-Ṭawīl that Anas ibn Mālik said, "A virgin has seven nights, and a woman who has been previously married has three nights."

Mālik affirmed, "That is what is done among us."

Mālik said, "If a man takes another wife, he divides his time equally between them after the wedding nights. He does not count the wedding nights against the one he has just married."

28.6 Stipulations not permitted in marriage

16 Yaḥyā related to me from Mālik that he had heard that Sa'īd ibn al-Musayyab was asked about a woman who made a stipulation on her husband not to take her away from her town. Sa'īd ibn al-Musayyab said, "He takes her away if she wishes."

Mālik said, "The custom among us is that when a man marries a woman, and he makes a condition in the marriage contract that he will not marry after her or take a concubine, it means nothing unless there is an oath of divorce or setting-free attached to it. Then it is obliged and required of him."

28.7 Marriage of a *muḥallil* and its like

17 Yaḥyā related to me from Mālik from al-Miswar ibn Rifā'a al-Quraẓī from az-Zubayr ibn 'Abd ar-Raḥmān ibn az-Zubayr that Rifā'a ibn Simwāl divorced his wife, Tamīma bint Wahb, in the time of the Messenger of Allah ﷺ three times. She then married 'Abd ar-Rahmān ibn az-Zubayr and he turned from her and could not consummate the marriage and so he parted from her. Rifā'a wanted to marry her again and it was mentioned to the Messenger of Allah ﷺ and he forbade him to marry

her. He said, "She is not lawful for you until she has tasted the sweetness of intercourse."

18 Yaḥyā related to me from Mālik from Yaḥyā ibn Sa'īd from al-Qāsim ibn Muḥammad that 'Ā'isha, the wife of the Prophet ﷺ said when asked whether it was permissible for a man to marry again a wife he had divorced irrevocably, if she had married another man who divorced her before consummating the marriage, "Not until she has tasted the sweetness of intercourse."

19 Yaḥyā related to me from Mālik that he had heard that, when asked whether it was permissible for a man to return to his wife if he had divorced her irrevocably and then another man had married her after him and had died before consummating the marriage, al-Qāsim ibn Muḥammad said, "It is not lawful for the first husband to return to her."

Mālik said that the *muḥallil* could not remain in such a marriage so as to allow a new marriage. If he had intercourse with her in that marriage, she kept her dowry.

28.8 Combinations of women not to be married together

20 Yaḥyā related to me from Mālik from Abū az-Zinād from al-A'raj from Abū Hurayra that the Messenger of Allah ﷺ said, "One cannot be married to a woman and her paternal aunt, or a woman and her maternal aunt at the same time."

21 Yaḥyā related to me from Mālik from Yaḥyā ibn Sa'īd that Sa'īd ibn al-Musayyab said, "It is forbidden to be married to a woman and her paternal or maternal aunt at the same time, and for a man to have intercourse with a female slave who is carrying another man's child."

28.9 Prohibition against marrying mothers of wives

22 Yaḥyā related to me from Mālik from Yaḥyā ibn Sa'īd that Zayd ibn Thābit asked whether it was lawful for a man, who married a

woman and then separated from her before he had cohabited with her, to marry her mother. Zayd ibn Thābit said, "No. The mother is prohibited unconditionally. There are conditions, however, about foster-mothers."

23 Yaḥyā related to me from Mālik from more than one source that when 'Abdullāh ibn Mas'ūd was in Kufa, he was asked for an opinion about marrying the mother after marrying the daughter when the marriage with the daughter had not been consummated. He permitted it. When Ibn Mas'ūd came to Madīna, he asked about it and was told that it was not as he had said, and that this condition referred to foster-mothers. Ibn Mas'ūd returned to Kufa, and he had just reached his dwelling when the man who had asked him for the opinion came to visit and he ordered him to separate from his wife.

Mālik said that if a man married the mother of a woman who was his wife and he had sexual relations with the mother, then his wife was unlawful for him and he had to separate from both of them. They were both unlawful to him forever if he had had sexual relations with the mother. If he did not have relations with the mother, his wife was not unlawful for him, and he is separated from the mother.

Mālik explained further about the man who married a woman, and then married her mother and cohabited with her, "The mother will never be lawful for him, and she is not lawful for his father or his son, and any daughters of hers are not lawful for him, and so his wife is unlawful for him."

Mālik said, "Fornication, however, does not make any of that unlawful because Allah, the Blessed, the Exalted, mentions '*the mothers of your wives*,' as one whom marriage made unlawful, and He did not mention the making unlawful through fornication. Every marriage in a lawful manner in which a man cohabits with his wife is a lawful marriage.

"This is what I have heard, and this is how things are done among us."

28.10 Marriage to mothers of women with whom one has had sexual relations in a disapproved manner

Mālik said that a man who had committed fornication with a woman, for which the *ḥadd*-punishment had been applied to him, could marry that woman's daughter and his son could marry the woman herself if he wished. That was because he had unlawful relations with her, and the relations Allah had made unlawful were from the relations made in a lawful manner or in a manner resembling marriage. Allah, the Blessed, the Exalted, says, *"Do not marry any women your fathers married."* (4:21)

Mālik said, "If a man were to marry a woman in her *'idda* period in a lawful marriage and have relations with her, it would be unlawful for his son to marry the woman. That is because the father married her in a lawful manner, and the *ḥadd*-punishment would not have been applied to him. Any child who was born to him would be attached to the father. Just as it would be unlawful for the son to marry a woman whom his father had married in her *'idda* period and had relations with, so the woman's daughter would be unlawful for the father if he had had sexual relations with the mother."

28.11 What is not permitted in marriage in general

24 Yaḥyā related to me from Mālik from Nāfi' from 'Abdullāh ibn 'Umar that the Messenger of Allah ﷺ forbade *shighār*, which means one man giving his daughter in marriage to another man on the condition that the other gives his daughter to him in marriage without either of them paying the bride-price.

25 Yaḥyā related to me from Mālik from 'Abd ar-Raḥmān ibn al-Qāsim from his father from 'Abd ar-Raḥmān and Mujammi', the sons of Yazīd ibn Jāriya al-Anṣārī from Khansā' bint Khidām al-Anṣāriya, that her father gave her in marriage and she had been previously married. She disapproved of that and went to the Messenger of Allah ﷺ and he revoked the marriage.

26 Yaḥyā related to me from Mālik from Abū az-Zubayr al-Makkī that a case was brought to 'Umar about a marriage which had only been witnessed by one man and one woman. He said, "This is a secret marriage and I do not permit it. Had I been the first to come upon it, I would have ordered them to be stoned."

27 Yaḥyā related to me from Mālik from Ibn Shihāb from Sa'īd ibn al-Musayyab and from Sulaymān ibn Yasār that Ṭulayha al-Asadiya was the wife of Rushayd ath-Thaqafī. He divorced her and she got married in her *'idda* period. 'Umar ibn al-Khaṭṭāb beat her and her husband with a stick several times, and separated them. Then 'Umar ibn al-Khaṭṭāb said, "If a woman marries in her *'idda* period, and the new husband has not consummated the marriage, then separate them, and when she has completed the *'idda* of her first husband, the other becomes a suitor. If he has consummated the marriage, then separate them. Then she must complete her *'idda* from her first husband, and then the *'idda* from the other one, and they are never to be reunited."

Mālik added, "Sa'īd ibn al-Musayyab said that she had her dowry because he had consummated the marriage."

Mālik said, "The practice with us concerning a freewoman whose husband dies is that she does an *'idda* of four months and ten days and she does not marry if she doubts her period until she is free of any doubt or if she fears that she is pregnant."

28.12 Marrying slaves when already married to free women

28 Yaḥyā related to me from Mālik that he had heard that 'Abdullāh ibn 'Abbās and 'Abdullāh ibn 'Umar were asked about a man who had a freewoman as a wife and then wanted to marry a slave-girl. They disapproved that he should be married to both of them.

29 Yaḥyā related to me from Mālik from Yaḥyā ibn Sa'īd that Sa'īd ibn al-Musayyab said, "One does not marry slave-girl when married to a freewoman unless the freewoman wishes it. If the freewoman complies, she has two-thirds of the division of time."

Mālik said, "A freeman must not marry a slave-girl when he can afford to marry a freewoman, and he should not marry a slave-girl when he cannot afford a freewoman unless he fears fornication. That is in His Book, '*If any of you who do not have the means to marry believing free women (muḥṣanāt), you may marry believing slave-girls.*' (4:24). He says, '*This is for those of you who are afraid of committing al-'anat.*'"

Mālik said, "*Al-'anat* is fornication."

28.13 A man's owning a slave whom he has married and then divorced

30 Yaḥyā related to me from Mālik from Ibn Shihāb from Abū 'Abd ar-Raḥmān that Zayd ibn Thābit said that if a man divorced his slave-girl three times and then bought her, she was not lawful for him until she had married another husband.

31 Yaḥyā related to me from Mālik that he had heard that Sa'īd ibn al-Musayyab and Sulaymān ibn Yasār were asked whether, when a man married a slave of his to a slave-girl and the slave divorced her irrevocably, and then her master gave her to the slave, she was then lawful for the slave by virtue of ownership. They said, "No, she is not lawful until she has married another husband."

32 Yaḥyā related to me from Mālik that he had asked Ibn Shihāb about a man who had a slave-girl as a wife, and then he bought her and divorced her once. He said, "She is lawful for him by virtue of ownership as long as he does not make his divorce irrevocable. If he irrevocably divorces her, she is not lawful for him by virtue of ownership until she has married another husband."

Mālik said that if a man married a female slave and then she had a child by him and then he bought her, she was not an *umm walad* for him because of the child born to him while she belonged to another until she had had a child by him while she was in his possession after he had purchased her.

Mālik said, "If he buys her when she is pregnant by him and she then gives birth while she belongs to him, she is his *umm walad* by virtue of that pregnancy according to what we think, and Allah knows best."

28.14 Reprehensibility of intercourse with two sisters or a mother and daughter that one owns

33 Yaḥyā related to me from Mālik from Ibn Shihāb from 'Ubaydullāh ibn 'Abdullāh ibn 'Utba ibn Mas'ūd from his father that 'Umar ibn al-Khaṭṭāb was asked about a woman and her daughter who were both owned, and whether one could have intercourse with one of them after the other. 'Umar said, "I dislike both being permitted together." He then forbade that.

34 Yaḥyā related to me from Mālik from Ibn Shihāb from Qabīṣa ibn Dhū'ayb that a man asked 'Uthmān ibn 'Affān whether one could have intercourse with two sisters whom one owned. 'Uthmān said, "One *āyat* makes them lawful, and one *āyat* makes them unlawful. As for me, I would not like to do it." The man left him and met one of the Companions of the Messenger of Allah ﷺ and asked him about it, and he said, "Had I any authority and I found someone who had done it, I would punish him as an example."

Ibn Shihāb added, "I think that it was 'Alī ibn Abī Ṭālib."

35 Yaḥyā related to me from Mālik that he had heard that az-Zubayr ibn al-'Awwām said the like of that.

Mālik said that if a man had sexual relations with a female slave that he owned, and then he wanted to also have relations with her sister, the sister was not lawful for the man until intercourse with the slave-girl had been made unlawful for him by marriage, setting-free, *kitāba*, or the like of that – for instance, if he had married her to his slave or someone other than his slave.

28.15 Prohibition against intercourse with a slave-girl who belonged to one's father

36 Yaḥyā related to me from Mālik that he had heard that 'Umar ibn al-Khaṭṭāb gave his son a slave-girl and said, "Do not touch her, for I have uncovered her."

Yaḥyā related to me from Mālik that 'Abd ar-Raḥmān ibn al-Mujabbar said that Sālim ibn 'Abdullāh gave his son a slave-girl and said, "Do not go near her, for I wanted her, and did not act towards her."

37 Yaḥyā related to me from Mālik from Yaḥyā ibn Sa'īd that Abū Nahshal ibn al-Aswad said to al-Qāsim ibn Muḥammad, "I saw a slave-girl of mine uncovered in the moonlight, and so I sat on her as a man sits on a woman. She said that she was menstruating, so I stood up and have not gone near her after that. Can I give her to my son to have intercourse with?" Al-Qāsim forbade that.

38 Yaḥyā related to me from Mālik from Ibrāhīm ibn Abī 'Abla from 'Abd al-Malik ibn Marwān that he gave a slave-girl to a friend of his, and later asked him about her. He said, "I intended to give her to my son to do such-and-such with her." 'Abd al-Malik said, "Marwān was more scrupulous than you. He gave a slave-girl to his son, and then he said, 'Do not go near her, for I have seen her leg uncovered.'"

28.16 Prohibition against marrying slave-girls who are People of the Book

Mālik said, "It is not lawful to marry a Christian or Jewish slave-girl because Allah, the Blessed, the Exalted, says in His Book, '*So are chaste women* (*muḥṣanāt*) *from among the believers and women who are muḥṣanāt among those given the Book before you,*' (5:6), and they are freewomen from the Christians and Jews. Allah, the Blessed, the Exalted, says in His Book, '*If any of you who do not have the means to marry believing free women* (*muḥṣanāt*), *you may marry believing slave-girls.*' (4:24).'"

Mālik said, "In our opinion, Allah made marriage to believing slave-girls lawful, but He did not make lawful marriage to Christian and Jewish slave-girls from the People of the Book."

Mālik said, "Christian and Jewish slave-girls are lawful for their master by right of possession, but intercourse with a Magian slave-girl is not lawful by the right of possession."

28.17 *Muḥsanāt*

39 Yaḥyā related to me from Mālik from Ibn Shihāb that Sa'īd ibn al-Musayyab said, "The *muḥṣanāt* among women are those who have husbands." That referred to the fact that Allah has made fornication *ḥarām*.

40 Yaḥyā related to me from Mālik from Ibn Shihāb, and he had heard from al-Qāsim ibn Muḥammad that they said, "When a freeman marries a slave-girl and consummates the marriage, she makes him a *muḥṣan*."

Mālik said, "All (of the people of knowledge) I have seen have said that a slave-girl makes a freeman *muḥṣan* when he marries her and consummates the marriage."

Mālik said, "A slave makes a freewoman *muḥṣana* when he consummates a marriage with her, but a freewoman only makes a slave *muḥṣan* when he has been set free and he is her husband and has had sexual relations with her after he has been set free. If he parts from her before he is free, he is not a *muḥṣan* unless he marries her after having been set free and he consummates the marriage."

Mālik said, "When a slave-girl is married to a freeman and then he separates from her before she is set free, his marriage to her does not make her *muḥṣana*. She is not *muḥṣana* until she has married after she has been set free and she has had intercourse with her husband. This accords her the iḥṣān status. If she is the wife of a freeman and then she is set free while she is his wife before he separates from her, the man makes her *muḥṣana* if he has intercourse with her after she has been set free."

Mālik said, "Christian and Jewish freewomen and Muslim slave-girls all render a Muslim freeman muḥṣān when he marries one of them and has intercourse with her."

28.18 Temporary marriage

41 Yaḥyā related to me from Mālik from Ibn Shihāb from 'Abdullāh and Ḥasan, the sons of Muḥammad ibn 'Alī ibn Abī Ṭālib, from their father ﷺ that the Messenger of Allah ﷺ forbade temporary marriage with women, and the flesh of domestic donkeys, on the Day of Khaybar.

42 Yaḥyā related to me from Mālik from Ibn Shihāb from 'Urwa ibn az-Zubayr that Khawla ibn Ḥakīm came to 'Umar ibn al-Khattāb and said, "Rabi'a ibn Umayya contracted a temporary marriage with a woman and she is pregnant by him." 'Umar ibn al-Khattāb went out in dismay dragging his cloak, saying, "This temporary marriage, had I come across it, I would have ordered stoning and done away with it!"

28.19 Marriage of slaves

43 Yaḥyā related to me from Mālik that he heard Rabi'a ibn 'Abd ar-Raḥmān say that a slave could marry four women.

Mālik said, "This is the best of what I have heard about the matter."

Mālik said, "The slave differs with the *muḥallil* if the slave is given permission by his master for his ex-wife. If his master does not give him permission, he separates them. The *muḥallil* is separated in any case if he merely intends to make the woman lawful [for her prior husband] by virtue of marriage."

Mālik said, "When a slave is owned by his wife, or a husband owns his wife, the act of possession by either of them renders marriage void without divorce. If a man, for instance, is married to a slave-girl, and then he buys her, he must divorce her as a matter of course. They can then re-marry. If they re-marry afterwards, that separation was not divorce."

Mālik said, "When a slave is freed by his wife who owns him and she is in the *'idda*-period from him, they can only return to each other after she has contracted another marriage."

28.20 The marriage of idolators when their wives become Muslim before them

44 Mālik related to me from Ibn Shihāb that he had heard that in the time of the Messenger of Allah ﷺ women were becoming Muslim in their own lands, and they did not do *hijra* while their husbands were still unbelievers, although they themselves had become Muslim. Among them was the daughter of al-Walīd ibn al-Mughīra; she was the wife of Ṣafwān ibn Umayya. She became Muslim on the day that Makka was conquered, and her husband, Ṣafwān ibn Umayya, fled from Islam. The Messenger of Allah ﷺ sent Ṣafwān's paternal cousin, Wahb ibn 'Umayr with the cloak of the Messenger of Allah ﷺ as a safe-conduct for Ṣafwān ibn Umayya, and the Messenger of Allah ﷺ called him to Islam and asked for him to come to him and if he was pleased with the matter to accept it. If not, he would have a respite for two months.

When Ṣafwān came to the Messenger of Allah ﷺ with his cloak, he called out to him over the heads of the people, "Muḥammad! Wahb ibn 'Umayr brought me your cloak and claimed that you had summoned me to come to you and if I was pleased with the matter, I should accept it and if not, you would give me a respite for two months." The Messenger of Allah ﷺ said, "Come down, Abu Wahb." He said, "No, by Allah! I will not come down until you make it clear to me!" The Messenger of Allah ﷺ said, "You have a respite of four months." The Messenger of Allah ﷺ went to meet the Hawāzin at Ḥunayn. He sent to Ṣafwān ibn Umayya to borrow some equipment and arms that he had. Ṣafwān said, "Willingly or unwillingly?" He said, "Willingly." Therefore he lent him the equipment and arms which he had. Then Ṣafwān went out with the Messenger of Allah ﷺ while he was still an unbeliever. He was present at the Battles of Ḥunayn and at-Ṭā'if while he was still an unbeliever and his wife was a

Muslim. The Messenger of Allah ﷺ did not separate Ṣafwān and his wife until he had become Muslim, and his wife remained with him by that marriage.

45 Yaḥyā related to me from Mālik that Ibn Shihāb said, "There was about one month between the Islam of Ṣafwān and the Islam of his wife."

Ibn Shihāb said, "We have not heard about any woman doing *hijra* for Allah and His Messenger while her husband was an unbeliever abiding in the land of disbelief, but that her *hijra* separated her and her husband, unless her husband came in *hijra* before her period of *'idda* had been completed."

46 Yaḥyā related to me from Mālik from Ibn Shihāb that Umm Ḥakīm bint al-Ḥārith ibn Hishām, who was the wife of 'Ikrima ibn Abī Jahl, became Muslim on the day that Makka was conquered, and her husband 'Ikrima fled from Islam as far as the Yemen. Umm Ḥakīm set out after him until she came to him in the Yemen and she invited him to Islam, and he became Muslim. He went to the Messenger of Allah ﷺ in the year of the Conquest (of Makka). When the Messenger of Allah ﷺ, saw him, he rushed to him in joy and did not bother to put on his cloak until he had received his allegiance. The couple were confirmed in their marriage.

Mālik said, "If a man becomes Muslim before his wife, a separation occurs between them when he presents Islam to her and she does not become Muslim, because Allah, the Blessed, the Exalted, says in His Book, *'Do not hold to any marriage ties with women who reject.'* (60:10)"

28.21 The wedding feast

47 Yaḥyā related to me from Mālik from Ḥumayd aṭ-Ṭawīl from Anas ibn Mālik that 'Abd ar-Rahmān ibn 'Awf came to the Messenger of Allah ﷺ and he had a trace of yellow on him. The Messenger of Allah ﷺ asked about it. He told him that he had just been married. The Messenger of Allah ﷺ asked, "How much did you hand over to her?" He replied, "The weight of a date pit in gold." The Messenger of Allah ﷺ said, "Hold a feast, even if it is only with a sheep."

48 Yaḥyā related to me from Mālik that Yaḥyā ibn Sa'īd said, "I have heard that the Messenger of Allah ﷺ held a wedding-feast in which there was neither meat nor bread."

49 Yaḥyā related to me from Mālik from Nāfi' from 'Abdullāh ibn 'Umar that the Messenger of Allah ﷺ said, "When you are invited to a wedding-feast, you must go to it."

50 Yaḥyā related to me from Mālik from Ibn Shihāb from al-A'raj that Abū Hurayra said, "The worst food is the food of a wedding feast to which the rich are invited and the poor are left out. If anyone rejects an invitation, he has rebelled against Allah and His Messenger."

51 Yaḥyā related to me from Mālik that Ishāq ibn 'Abdullāh ibn Abī Ṭalḥa heard Anas ibn Mālik say that a certain tailor invited the Messenger of Allah ﷺ to eat some food which he had prepared.

Anas said, "I went with the Messenger of Allah ﷺ to eat the food. He served barley bread and a soup with pumpkin in it. I saw the Messenger of Allah ﷺ going after the pumpkin around the dish, so I have always liked pumpkin since that day."

28.22 Marriage in general

52 Yaḥyā related to me from Mālik from Zayd ibn Aslam that the Messenger of Allah ﷺ said, "When you marry a woman or buy a slave-girl, take her by the forelock and ask for blessing. When you buy a camel, take the top of its hump, and seek refuge with Allah from Shayṭān."

53 Yaḥyā related to me from Mālik from Abū az-Zubayr al-Makkī that somebody asked a man for his sister in marriage and the man mentioned that she had committed fornication. 'Umar ibn al-Khaṭṭāb heard about it, and he beat the man or almost beat him, and said, "What did you mean by giving him such information!"

54 Yaḥyā related to me from Mālik from Rabi'a ibn Abī 'Abd ar-Raḥmān that al-Qāsim ibn Muḥammad and 'Urwa ibn az-Zubayr said that a man,

who had four wives and then divorced one of them irrevocably, could marry straightaway if he wished, and he did not have to wait for the completion of her *'idda.*

55 Yaḥyā related to me from Mālik from Rabi'a ibn 'Abd ar-Raḥmān that al-Qāsim ibn Muḥammad and 'Urwa ibn az-Zubayr gave the same judgement to al-Walīd ibn 'Abd al-Malik in the year of his arrival in Madīna, except that al-Qāsim ibn Muḥammad said that he divorced his wife on separate occasions (i.e. not at one time).

56 Yaḥyā related to me from Mālik from Yaḥyā ibn Sa'īd that Sa'īd ibn al-Musayyab said, "There are three things in which there is no jest: marriage, divorce and setting-free."

57 Yaḥyā related to me from Mālik from Ibn Shihāb that Rāfi' ibn Khadīj married the daughter of Muḥammad ibn Maslama al-Anṣārī. She was with him until she grew older, and then he married a young girl and preferred the young girl to her. She begged him to divorce her, so he divorced her and then he gave her time until she had almost finished her *'idda* period and then he returned and still preferred the young girl. She therefore asked him to divorce her. He divorced her once, and then returned to her, and still preferred the young girl, and she asked him to divorce her. He said, "What do you want? There is only one divorce left. If you like, continue and put up with what you see of preference, and if you like, I will separate from you." She said, "I will continue in spite of the preference." He kept her in spite of that, Rāfi' did not see that he had done any wrong action when she remained with him in spite of preference.

29. Divorce

29.1 The 'irrevocable' divorce

1 Yaḥyā related to me from Mālik that he had heard that a man said to 'Abdullāh ibn 'Abbās, "I have divorced my wife by saying 'I divorce you a hundred times.' What do you think my situation is?" Ibn 'Abbās said to him, "She was divorced from you by three pronouncements, and by the ninety-seven you have mocked the *āyats* of Allah."

2 Yaḥyā related to me from Mālik that he had heard that a man came to 'Abdullāh ibn Mas'ūd and said, "I have divorced my wife by saying 'I divorce you' eight times." Ibn Mas'ūd said to him, "What have people told you?" He replied, "I have been told that I have to part absolutely from her." Ibn Mas'ūd said, "They have spoken the truth. If someone divorces in the way that Allah has said, Allah has made it clear for him. But if someone makes matters confused for himself, then we make him responsible for what he has made confused. So do not confuse yourselves and then expect us to bear the burden for you. It is as they have said."

3 Yaḥyā related to me from Mālik from Yaḥyā ibn Sa'īd from Abū Bakr ibn Ḥazm that 'Umar ibn 'Abd al-'Azīz had asked him what people said about the 'irrevocable' divorce, and Abū Bakr had replied that Abān ibn 'Uthmān had clarified that it was declared only once. 'Umar ibn 'Abd al-'Azīz said, "Even if divorce had to be declared a thousand times, the 'irrevocable' would use them all up. A person who says 'irrevocably' has cast the furthest limit."

4 Yaḥyā related to me from Mālik from Ibn Shihāb that Marwān ibn al-Ḥakam decided that if someone made three pronouncements of divorce, he had divorced his wife irrevocably.

Mālik said, "That is what I like best of what I have heard on the subject."

29.2 Divorce by euphemistic statements

5 Yaḥyā related to me from Mālik that he had heard that 'Umar ibn al-Khaṭṭāb had heard in a letter from Iraq that a man had said to his wife, "Your rein is on your withers" (i.e. you have free rein). 'Umar ibn al-Khaṭṭāb wrote to his governor to order the man to come to him at Makka at the time of the *ḥajj*. While 'Umar was doing *ṭawāf* around the House, a man met him and greeted him. 'Umar asked him who he was, and he replied that he was the man that he had ordered to be brought to him. 'Umar said to him, "I ask you by the Lord of this building, what did you mean by your statement, 'Your rein is on your withers'?" The man replied, "Had you made me swear by other than this place, I would not have told you the truth. I intended separation by that." 'Umar ibn al-Khaṭṭāb said, "It is what you intended."

6 Yaḥyā related to me from Mālik that he had heard that 'Alī ibn Abī Ṭālib used to say that if a man said to his wife, "You are unlawful for me," it counted as three pronouncements of divorce.

Mālik said, "That is the best of what I have heard on the subject."

7 Yaḥyā related to me from Mālik from Nāfi' that 'Abdullāh ibn 'Umar said that the statement like, "I cut myself off from you," or "You are abandoned" were considered as three pronouncements of divorce.

Mālik said that any strong statements such as these or others were considered as three pronouncements of divorce for a woman whose marriage had been consummated. In the case of a woman whose marriage had not been consummated the man was asked to make an oath on his *dīn*, as to whether he had intended one or three pronouncements of divorce. If he had intended one pronouncement, he was asked to make an oath by Allah to confirm it, and he became a suitor among her suitors, because a woman whose marriage had been consummated, required three pronouncements of divorce to make her inaccessible for the husband, whilst only one pronouncement was needed to make a woman whose marriage had not been consummated inaccessible.

Mālik added, "That is the best of what I have heard about the matter."

8 Yaḥyā related to me from Mālik from Yaḥyā ibn Sa'īd from al-Qāsim ibn Muḥammad that a certain man had taken a slave-girl belonging to somebody else as a wife. He said to her people, "She is your concern," and people considered that to be one pronouncement of divorce.

9 Yaḥyā related to me from Mālik that he heard Ibn Shihāb say that if a man said to his wife, "You are free of me, and I am free of you," it counted as three pronouncements of divorce as if it were an 'irrevocable' divorce.

Mālik said that if a man made any strong statement such as these to his wife, it counted as three pronouncements of divorce for a woman whose marriage had been consummated, or it was written as one of three for a woman whose marriage had not been consummated, whichever the man wished. If he said that he intended only one divorce he swore to it and he became one of the suitors because, whereas a woman whose marriage had been consummated was made inaccessible by three pronouncements of divorce, the woman whose marriage had not been consummated was made inaccessible by only one pronouncement.

Mālik said, "That is the best of what I have heard."

29.3 Giving wives the right of full divorce

10 Yaḥyā related to me from Mālik that he had heard that a man came to 'Abdullāh ibn 'Umar and said, "Abū 'Abd ar-Raḥmān! I placed the command of my wife in her hand, and she has divorced herself from me, what do you think?" 'Abdullāh ibn 'Umar said, "I think that it is as she said." The man said, "Do not do it, Abū 'Abd ar-Raḥmān!" Ibn 'Umar said, "You did it, it has nothing to do with me."

11 Yaḥyā related to me from Mālik from Nāfi' that 'Abdullāh ibn 'Umar said, "When a man gives a woman command over herself, then the result is as she decides unless he denies it and says that he only meant to give her one divorce and he swears to it – then he has access to her while she is in her *'idda.*"

29.4 When a wife's authority must be considered as only a single pronouncement of divorce

12 Yaḥyā related to me from Mālik from Sa'īd ibn Sulaymān ibn Zayd ibn Thābit that Khārija ibn Zayd ibn Thābit told him that he was sitting with Zayd ibn Thābit when Muḥammad ibn Abī 'Atīq came to him with his eyes brimming with tears. Zayd asked him what the matter was. He said, "I gave my wife command of herself, and she separated from me." Zayd said to him, "What made you do that?" He said, "The Decree." Zayd said, "Take her back if you wish for it is only one pronouncement, and you have the right to her."

13 Yaḥyā related to me from Mālik from 'Abd ar-Raḥmān ibn al-Qāsim from his father that a man of Thaqīf gave his wife command over herself, and she said, "You are divorced." He was silent. She said, "You are divorced." He said, "May a stone be in your mouth." She said, "You are divorced." He said, "May a stone be in your mouth." They argued and went to Marwān ibn al-Ḥakam. Marwān made him take an oath that he had only given her control over one pronouncement, and then he gave her back to him.

Mālik said that 'Abd ar-Raḥmān said that al-Qāsim was very pleased with Marwān's decision and thought it the best he had heard on the subject.

Mālik added, "That is also the best of what I have heard on this subject and I prefer it."

29.5 When allowing a wife her authority does not constitute a divorce

14 Yaḥyā related to me from Mālik from 'Abd ar-Raḥmān ibn al-Qāsim from his father that 'Ā'isha, *Umm al-Mu'minīn*, proposed to Qurayba bint Abī Umayya on behalf of 'Abd ar-Raḥmān ibn Abī Bakr. They married her to him and her people found fault with 'Abd ar-Raḥmān and said, "We only gave in marriage because of 'Ā'isha." 'Ā'isha therefore sent to 'Abd ar-Raḥmān and told him about it. He gave Qurayba authority over herself and she chose her husband and so there was no divorce.

15 Yaḥyā related to me from Mālik from 'Abd ar-Raḥmān ibn al-Qāsim from his father that 'Ā'isha, the wife of the Prophet ﷺ gave Ḥafṣa bint 'Abd ar-Rahmān in marriage to al-Mundhir ibn az-Zubayr while 'Abd ar-Raḥmān was away in Syria. When 'Abd ar-Raḥmān arrived, he said, "Shall someone like me have this done to him? Am I the kind of man to have something done to him without his consent?" 'Ā'isha spoke to al-Mundhir ibn az-Zubayr, and al-Mundhir said, "It is in the hands of 'Abd ar-Raḥmān." 'Abd ar-Raḥmān said, "I will not oppose something that you have already completed." Hafṣa was confirmed with al-Mundhir, and there was no divorce.

16 Yaḥyā related to me from Mālik that he had heard that 'Abdullāh ibn 'Umar and Abū Hurayra were asked about a man who gave his wife power over herself, and she returned it to him without doing anything with it. They said that there was no divorce. (i.e. the man's giving his wife power over herself was not interpreted as an actual expression of divorce on his part.)

Yaḥyā related to me from Mālik from Yaḥyā ibn Sa'īd that Sa'īd ibn al-Musayyab said, "If a man gives his wife authority over herself, and she does not separate from him and remains with him, there is no divorce."

Mālik said about a woman whose husband gave her power over herself and they then separated while she refused to do that, that she had no longer has power to invoke the divorce. She only had power over herself as long as they remained together in the same meeting.

29.6 Annulment of marriage by the husband's vow to refrain from intercourse (*īlā'*)

17 Yaḥyā related to me from Mālik from Ja'far ibn Muḥammad from his father that 'Alī ibn Abī Ṭālib said, "When a man takes a vow to abstain from intercourse, divorce does not occur immediately. If four months pass, he must declare his intent and either he is divorced or he revokes his vow."

Mālik said, "That is what is done among us."

18 Yaḥyā related to me from Mālik from Nāfi' that 'Abdullāh ibn 'Umar said, "When a man makes a vow to abstain from intercourse with his wife, and four months have passed, he must declare his intent and either he is divorced or he revokes his vow. Divorce does not occur until four months have passed and he is made to declare his intent."

Yaḥyā related to me from Mālik from Ibn Shihāb that Sa'īd ibn al-Musayyab and Abū Bakr ibn 'Abd ar-Raḥmān said about a man who made a vow to abstain from intercourse with his wife, "If four months pass it is a divorce. The husband can go back to his wife as long as she is still in her *'idda*."

19 Yaḥyā related to me from Mālik that he had heard that Marwān ibn al-Ḥakam decided about a man who had made a vow to abstain from intercourse with his wife that when four months had passed, it was a divorce but he could return to her as long as she was still in her *'idda*.

Mālik added, "That was also the opinion of Ibn Shihāb."

Mālik said that if a man made a vow to abstain from intercourse with his wife and at the end of four months he declared his intent to continue to abstain, he was divorced. He could go back to his wife, but if he did not have intercourse with her before the end of her *'idda*, he had no access to her and could not go back to her unless he had an excuse: illness, imprisonment, or a similar excuse. His return to her maintained her as his wife. If her *'idda* passed and then he married her after that and did not have intercourse with her until four months had passed and he declared his intent to continue to abstain, divorce was applied to him by the first vow. If four months passed, and he had not returned to her, he had no *'idda* against her nor access because he had married her and then divorced her before touching her.

Mālik said that a man who made a vow to abstain from intercourse from his wife and continued to abstain after four months and so divorced her, but then took her back but did not touch her and four months were completed before her *'idda* was completed, did not have to declare his intent and divorce did not befall him. If he had intercourse with her before the end of her *'idda*, he was entitled to her. If her *'idda* passed before he had intercourse with her, then he had no access to her.

Mālik said, "This is the best that I have heard about this matter."

Mālik said that if a man made a vow to abstain from intercourse with his wife and then divorced her, and the four months of the vow were completed before completion of the *'idda* of the divorce, it counted as two pronouncements of divorce. If he declared his intention to continue to abstain and the *'idda* of the divorce finished before the four months, the vow of abstention was not a divorce. That was because the four months had passed and she was not his on that day.

Mālik said, "If someone makes a vow not to have sexual intercourse with his wife for a day or a month, and then waits until more than four months have passed, it is not *īlā'*. *Īlā'* only applies to someone who vows more than four months. As for the one who vows not to have intercourse with his wife for four months or less than that, I do not think that it is *īlā'* because when the term enters into it at which it stops, he comes out of his oath and he does not have to declare his intention."

Mālik said, "If someone vows to his wife not to have intercourse with her until her child has been weaned, that is not *īlā'*. I have heard that 'Alī ibn Abī Ṭālib was asked about that and he did not think that it amounted to *īlā'*."

29.7 The *īlā'* (vow of abstention) of slaves

Yaḥyā related to me from Mālik that he had asked Ibn Shihāb about the *īlā'* of the slave. He said that it was like the *īlā'* of the freeman and it put an obligation on him. The *īlā'* of the slave was two months.

29.8 *Ẓihār* of freemen

20 Yaḥyā related to me from Mālik from Sa'īd ibn 'Amr ibn Sulaym az-Zuraqī that he asked al-Qāsim ibn Muḥammad about a man who made divorce conditional on his marrying a woman (i.e. if he married her he would automatically divorce her.) Al-Qāsim ibn Muḥammad said, "A man once made a woman like his mother's back, (i.e. has made unlawful for him by *ẓihār*) if he were to marry her, and 'Umar ibn al-Khaṭṭāb ordered him not to go near her if he married her until he had done *kaffāra* as one would for pronouncing *ẓihār*."

21 Yaḥyā related to me from Mālik that he had heard that a man asked al-Qāsim ibn Muḥammad and Sulaymān ibn Yasar about a man who pronounced *ẓihār* from his wife before he had married her. They said, "If he marries her, he must not touch her until he has done the *kaffāra* for pronouncing *ẓihār*."

22 Yaḥyā related to me from Mālik from Hishām ibn 'Urwa that his father said that a man who pronounced a *ẓihār* from his four wives in one statement had only to do one *kaffāra*.

Yaḥyā related the same as that to me from Mālik from Rabi'a ibn Abī 'Abd ar-Raḥmān.

Mālik said, "That is what is done among us. Allah, the Exalted, says about the *kaffāra* for pronouncing *ẓihār*, '*Anyone who cannot find the means must fast for two consecutive months before the two of them may touch one another again. And anyone who is unable to do that must feed sixty poor people.*'" (58:3-4)

Mālik said that a man who pronounced *ẓihār* from his wife on various occasions had only to do one *kaffāra*. If he pronounced *ẓihār*, and then did *kaffāra*, and then pronounced *ẓihār* after he had done the *kaffāra*, he had to do *kaffāra* again.

Mālik said, "Someone who pronounces *ẓihār* from his wife and then has intercourse with her before he has done *kaffāra*, only has to do one *kaffāra*. He must abstain from her until he has completed the *kaffāra* and ask forgiveness of Allah. That is the best of what I have heard."

Mālik said, "It is the same with *ẓihār* using any prohibited relations of either fosterage or ancestry."

Mālik said, "Women cannot pronounce *ẓihār*."

Mālik said that he had heard that the commentary on the word of Allah, the Blessed, the Exalted, *"Those who divorce their wives by equating them with their mothers, and then wish to go back on what they said"* (56:3), was that a man pronounced *ẓihār* on his wife and then decided to keep her and have intercourse with her. If he divorced her and, without having, after pronouncing *ẓihār* on her, decided to keep her and have intercourse with her, there would be no *kaffāra* incumbent on him.

Mālik said, "If he marries her after that, he does not touch her until he has completed the *kaffāra* of pronouncing *ẓihār*."

Mālik said that if a man who pronounced *ẓihār* from his slave-girl wanted to have intercourse with her, he had to do the *kaffāra* of the *ẓihār* before he could sleep with her.

Mālik said, "There is no *īlā'* in a man's *ẓihār* unless it is evident that he does not intend to retract his *ẓihār*."

23 Yaḥyā related to me from Mālik from Hishām ibn 'Urwa that he heard a man ask 'Urwa ibn az-Zubayr about a man who said to his wife, "Any woman I marry along with you as long as you live will be like my mother's back to me." 'Urwa ibn az-Zubayr said, "Freeing a slaves is enough to release him from that."

29.9 *Ẓihār* done by slaves

24 Yaḥyā related to me from Mālik that he asked Ibn Shihāb about the *ẓihār* of a slave. He said, "It is like the *ẓihār* of a freeman."

Mālik said, "He meant that the same conditions were applied in both cases."

Mālik said, "The *ẓihār* of the slave is incumbent on him, and the fasting of the slave in the *ẓihār* is two months."

Mālik said that there was no *īlā'* for a slave who pronounced a *ẓihār* from his wife. That was because if he were to fast the *kaffāra* for pronouncing a *ẓihār*, the divorce of the *īlā'* would come to him before he had finished the fast.

29.10 The option (of slave-girls married to slaves when freed)

25 Yaḥyā related to me from Mālik from Rabi'a ibn Abī 'Abd ar-Raḥmān from al-Qāsim ibn Muḥammad that 'Ā'isha, *Umm al-Mu'minīn*, said, "There were three sunnas established in connection with Barīra: firstly was that when she was set free she was given her choice about her husband; secondly, the Messenger of Allah ﷺ said about her, 'The right of inheritance belongs to the person who has set a person free'; and thirdly, the Messenger of Allah ﷺ came in and there was a pot with meat on the boil. Bread and condiments were brought to him from the stock of the house. The Messenger of Allah ﷺ said, 'Did I not see a pot with meat in it?' They said, 'Yes, Messenger of Allah. That is meat which was given as *ṣadaqa* for Barīra, and you do not eat *ṣadaqa*.' The Messenger of Allah ﷺ said, 'It is *ṣadaqa* for her, and it is a gift for us.'"

26 Yaḥyā related to me from Mālik from Nāfi' that 'Abdullāh ibn 'Umar said that a female slave who was the wife of a slave and then was set free had the right of choice as long as he did not have intercourse with her.

Mālik said, "If her husband has intercourse with her and she claims that she did not know, she still has the right of choice. If she is suspect and one does not believe her claim of ignorance, then she has no choice after he has had intercourse with her."

27 Yaḥyā related to me from Mālik from Ibn Shihāb from 'Urwa ibn az-Zubayr that a *mawlā* of the tribe of Banū 'Adī called Zabrā' told him that she had been the wife of a slave when she was a slave-girl. Then she was set free and she sent a message to Ḥafṣa, the wife of the Prophet ﷺ. Ḥafṣa called her and said, "I will tell you something, but I would prefer that you did not act upon it. You have authority over yourself as long as your husband does not have intercourse with you. If he has intercourse with you, you have no authority at all." Therefore she pronounced her divorce from him three times.

28 Yaḥyā related to me from Mālik that he had heard that Sa'īd ibn al-Musayyab said that if a man married a woman, and he was insane or had a physical defect, she had the right of choice. If she wished she could separate from him.

29 Mālik said that if a slave-girl, who was the wife of a slave, was set free before he had consummated the marriage, and she chose herself, then she had no bride-price and it was a pronouncement of divorce.

Mālik said, "That is what is done among us."

30 Yaḥyā related to me that Mālik heard Ibn Shihāb say, "When a man gives his wife the right of choice, and she chooses him, that is not divorce."

Mālik said, "That is the best of what I have heard."

Mālik said that if a woman who had been given the right of choice by her husband chose herself, she was divorced trebly. If her husband said, "But I only gave her the right of divorce in one," he was not allowed to do that.

Mālik said, "If the man gives his wife the right of choice and she says, 'I accept one', and he says, 'I did not mean that. I have given the right of choice in all three together,' then if she only accepts one, she remains with him in her marriage, and that is not separation if Allah, the Exalted, wills."

29.11 Separating from wives for compensation (*khul'*)

31 Yaḥyā related to me from Mālik from Yaḥyā ibn Sa'īd that 'Amra bint 'Abd ar-Raḥmān told him from Ḥabība bint Sahl al-Anṣārī that she had been married to Thābit ibn Qays ibn Shammās. The Messenger of Allah ﷺ went out for the Dawn Prayer, and found Ḥabība bint Sahl at his door in the darkness. The Messenger of Allah ﷺ asked her, "Who is this?" She said, "I am Ḥabība bint Sahl, Messenger of Allah." He asked, "What do you want?" She replied, "That Thābit ibn Qays and I separate." When her husband, Thābit ibn Qays, came, the Messenger of Allah ﷺ said to him, "This is Ḥabība bint Sahl. She has mentioned what Allah willed that she mention." Ḥabība said, "Messenger of Allah, I have all that he has given me!" The Messenger of Allah ﷺ said to Thābit ibn Qays, "Take it from her." He took it from her and she stayed in the house of her family.

32 Yaḥyā related to me from Mālik from Nāfi' from a *mawlā* of Ṣafiyya bint Abī 'Ubayd that she gave all that she possessed to her husband as compensation for her divorce from him, and 'Abdullāh ibn 'Umar did not disapprove of that.

Mālik said that the divorce was ratified for a woman who ransomed herself from her husband, when it was known that her husband was injurious to her and was oppressive to her and it was known that he wronged her, and he had to return her property to her.

Mālik added, "That is what I have heard, and it is what is done among us."

Mālik said, "There is no harm if a woman ransoms herself from her husband for more than he gave her."

29.12 The *khul'* divorce

33 Yaḥyā related to me from Mālik from Nāfi' that Rubayyi' bint Mu'awwidh ibn 'Afrā' came with her paternal uncle to 'Abdullāh ibn 'Umar and told him that she had been divorced from her husband by compensating him in the time of 'Uthmān ibn 'Affān, and 'Uthmān heard about it and did not disapprove.

'Abdullāh ibn 'Umar said, "Her *'idda* is the *'idda* of a divorced woman."

Yaḥyā related to me from Mālik that he had heard that Sa'īd ibn al-Musayyab and Sulaymān ibn Yasār and Ibn Shihāb all said that a woman who divorced her husband for compensation had the same *'idda* as a divorced woman: three menstrual periods.

Mālik said that a woman who ransomed herself could not return to her husband except by a new marriage. If he then married her (again) and then separated from her before he had had intercourse with her, there was no *'idda* for her to observe from her second divorce, and she continued on from when her first *'idda* stopped.

Mālik said, "That is the best that I have heard on the matter."

Mālik said, "If, when a woman offers to compensate her husband, he divorces her straightaway, then that compensation is confirmed for him. If he makes no response and then at a later date does divorce her, he is not entitled to that compensation."

29.13 *Li'ān* (invoking mutual curses)

34 Yaḥyā related to me from Mālik from Ibn Shihāb that Sahl ibn Sa'īd as-Sā'idī told him that 'Uwaymir al-'Ajlānī came to 'Āsim ibn 'Adī al-Ansārī and said to him, "'Āsim! What do you think a man who finds another man with his wife should do? Should he kill him and then be killed himself, or what should he do, 'Āsim? Ask the Messenger of Allah ﷺ about that for me." 'Asim asked the Messenger of Allah ﷺ about it. The Messenger of Allah ﷺ was revolted by the questions and reproved them until what 'Āsim heard from the Messenger of Allah ﷺ became too much for him to bear.

When 'Āsim returned to his people, 'Uwaymir came to him and said, "'Āsim! What did the Messenger of Allah ﷺ say to you?" 'Āsim said to 'Uwaymir, "You did not bring me any good. The Messenger of Allah ﷺ was revolted by the question which I asked him." 'Uwaymir said, "By Allah! I will not stop until I ask him about it myself!" 'Uwaymir stood up and went to the Messenger of Allah ﷺ in the middle of the people and said, "Messenger of Allah! What do you think a man who finds another man with his wife should do? Should he kill him and then be killed himself, or what should he do?" The Messenger of Allah ﷺ said. "Something has been sent down about you and your wife, so go and bring her."

Sahl continued, "They engaged in the process of *li'ān* in the presence of the Messenger of Allah ﷺ and I was present with the people. When they finished the process of *li'ān*, 'Uwaymir said, 'I shall have lied about her, Messenger of Allah, if I keep her,' and pronounced the divorce three times before the Messenger of Allah ﷺ ordered him to do it."

Mālik said that Ibn Shihāb said, "That then became the *sunna* for a couple engaging in the process of *li'ān*."

35 Yaḥyā related to me from Mālik from Nāfi' from 'Abdullāh ibn 'Umar that a man engaged in the process of *li'ān* with his wife in the time of the Messenger of Allah ﷺ and disowned her child. The Messenger of Allah ﷺ separated them and gave the child to the woman.

Mālik said, "Allah the Blessed, the Exalted, says, *'Those who make an accusation against their wives and have no witnesses except themselves, the legal proceeding of such a one is to testify four times by Allah that he is telling the truth and a fifth time that Allah's curse will be upon him if he is lying. And the punishment is removed from her if she testifies four times by Allah that he is lying and a fifth time that Allah's anger will be upon her if he speaks the truth.'"* (24:6-9)

Mālik said, "The *sunna* with us is that those who engage in the process of *li'ān* are never to be remarried. If the man calls himself a liar (i.e. takes back his accusation), he is flogged with the *ḥadd* punishment, and the child is attributed to him, and his wife can never return to him. There is no doubt or dispute about this *sunna* among us."

Mālik said, "If a man separates from his wife by an irrevocable divorce after which he cannot take her back, and then denies the paternity of the child she is carrying whilst she claims that he is the father, and it is possible by the timing that he is the father, then he must engage in the process of *li'ān* with her, so that there is no acknowledgement that the pregnancy is by him."

Mālik said, "That is what is done among us, and it is what I have heard from the people of knowledge."

Mālik said that a man who accused his wife after he had divorced her triply while she was pregnant, and he had at first accepted being the father but then claimed that he had seen her committing adultery before he separated from her, was flogged with the *ḥadd* punishment, and did not engage in the process of *li'ān* with her.

If he denied the paternity of her child after he had divorced her triply, and he had not previously accepted it, then he engaged in the process of *li'ān* with her.

Mālik said, "This is what I have heard."

Mālik said, "The slave is in the same position as the freeman as regards making accusations and engaging in the process of *li'ān*. He acts in the *li'ān* as the freeman acts although no *ḥadd* applies for slandering a female slave."

Mālik said, "The Muslim slave-girl and the Christian and Jewish freewoman also engage in the process of *li'ān* when a free Muslim marries one of them and has intercourse with her. That is because Allah – may He be blessed and exalted, says in His Book, '*Those who make an accusation against their wives,*' and they are their wives. This is what is done among us."

Mālik said, "If a slave marries a free Muslim woman, or a Muslim slave-girl, or a free Christian or Jewish woman, he can engage in the process of *li'ān* with her."

Mālik said that if a man engaged in the process of *li'ān* with his wife, and then stopped and called himself a liar after one or two oaths without having asked for curses on himself in the fifth one, he should be flogged with the *ḥadd* punishment [for slander], but they did not have to be separated.

Mālik said that if a man divorced his wife and then after three months the woman said, "I am pregnant," and he denied paternity, then he had to do *li'ān*.

Mālik said that the husband of a female slave who engaged in the process of *li'ān* with her and then bought her was not to have intercourse with her, even if he owned her, and the *sunna* which had been handed down about a couple who engaged in the process of *li'ān* was that they were never to return to each other.

Mālik said that when a man engaged in the process of *li'ān* with his wife before he had consummated the marriage, she only had half of the bride-price.

29.14 Inheritance of children of women against whom *li'ān* has been pronounced

36 Yaḥyā related to me from Mālik that he had heard that 'Urwa ibn az-Zubayr said that if the child of a woman against whom *li'ān* had been pronounced or the child of fornication died, his mother inherited from him her right as mentioned in the Book of Allah the Exalted, and his maternal half-brothers had their rights. The rest was inherited by the owners of his mother's *walā'* if she was a freed slave. If she was an ordinary freewoman, she inherited her right, his maternal brothers inherited their rights, and the rest went to the Muslims."

Mālik said, "I heard the same as that from Sulaymān ibn Yasār, and it is what I have seen the people of knowledge in our city doing."

29.15 Divorce of virgins

37 Yaḥyā related to me from Mālik from Ibn Shihāb from Muḥammad ibn 'Abd ar-Raḥmān ibn Thawbān that Muḥammad ibn Iyās ibn al-Bukayr said, "A man divorced his wife three times before he had consummated the marriage, and then it seemed good to him to marry her. He wanted, therefore, an opinion, and I went with him to ask 'Abdullāh ibn 'Abbās

and Abū Hurayra on his behalf about it, and they said, 'We do not think that you should marry her until she has married another husband.' He protested that his divorcing her had been only once. Ibn 'Abbās said, 'You threw away what you had of blessing.'"

38 Yaḥyā related to me from Mālik from Yaḥyā ibn Sa'īd from Bukayr ibn 'Abdullāh al-Ashajj from an-Nu'mān ibn Abī 'Ayyāsh al-Anṣārī from 'Aṭā' ibn Yasār that a man came and asked 'Abdullāh ibn 'Amr ibn al-'Āṣ about a man who divorced his wife three times before he had had intercourse with her. 'Aṭā' said, "The divorce of the virgin is one. 'Abdullāh ibn 'Amr ibn al-'Āṣ said to me, 'You say one pronouncement completely separates her from her husband and three makes her unlawful until she has married another husband.'"

39 Yaḥyā related to me from Mālik from Yaḥyā ibn Sa'īd that Bukayr ibn 'Abdullāh al-Ashajj informed him that Mu'āwiya ibn Abī 'Ayyāsh al-Anṣārī told him that he was sitting with 'Abdullāh ibn az-Zubayr and 'Āṣim ibn 'Umar ibn al-Khaṭṭāb when Muḥammad ibn Iyās ibn al-Bukayr came up to them and said, "A man from the desert has divorced his wife three times before consummating the marriage. What do you think?" 'Abdullāh ibn az-Zubayr said, "This is something about which we have no statement. Go to 'Abdullāh ibn 'Abbās and Abū Hurayra. I left them with 'Ā'isha. Ask them and then come and tell us." He went and asked them. Ibn 'Abbās said to Abū Hurayra, "Give an opinion, Abū Hurayra! A difficult one has come to you." Abū Hurayra said, "One pronouncement separates her and three makes her unlawful until she has married another husband." Ibn 'Abbās said something similar to that.

Mālik said, "That is what is done among us, and when a man marries a woman who has been married before, and he has not had intercourse with her, she is treated as a virgin – one pronouncement separates her and three make her unlawful until she has married another husband."

29.16 Divorce of sick men

40 Yaḥyā related to me from Mālik from Ibn Shihāb that Talha ibn 'Abdullāh ibn 'Awf said, and he knew better than them, from Abū Salama

ibn 'Abd ar-Raḥmān ibn 'Awf that 'Abd ar-Raḥmān ibn 'Awf divorced his wife irrevocably while he was terminally ill and 'Uthmān ibn 'Affān made her an heir after the end of her *'idda.*

41 Yaḥyā related to me from Mālik from 'Abdullāh ibn al-Faḍl from al-A'raj that 'Uthmān ibn 'Affān made the wives of Ibn Mukmil inherit from him, and he had divorced them while he was terminally ill.

42 Yaḥyā related to me from Mālik that he heard Rabi'a ibn Abī 'Abd ar-Raḥmān say, "I heard that the wife of 'Abd ar-Raḥmān ibn 'Awf asked him to divorce her. He said, 'When you have menstruated and are pure, then let me know.' She did not menstruate until 'Abd ar-Raḥmān ibn 'Awf was ill. When she was purified, she told him and he divorced her irrevocably or made a pronouncement of divorce which was all that he had left over her. 'Abd ar-Raḥmān ibn 'Awf was terminally ill at the time, so 'Uthmān ibn 'Affān made her one of the heirs after the end of her *'idda.*"

43 Yaḥyā related to me from Mālik from Yaḥyā ibn Sa'īd that Muḥammad ibn Yaḥyā ibn Ḥabbān said, "My grandfather Ḥabbān had two wives, one from the Banū Hāshim and one from the Ansār. He divorced the Anṣārī wife while she was nursing, and a year passed and he died and she had still not menstruated. She said, 'I inherit from him. I have not menstruated yet.' The wives quarrelled and went to 'Uthmān ibn 'Affān. He decided that she did inherit and the Hāshim wife rebuked 'Uthmān. He said, 'This is the practice of the son of your paternal uncle. He pointed this out to us.' He meant 'Alī ibn Abī Ṭālib."

44 Yaḥyā related to me from Mālik that he had heard Ibn Shihāb say, "When a man who is terminally ill divorces his wife three times, she still inherits from him."

Mālik said, "If he divorces her while he is terminally ill before he has consummated the marriage, she has half of the bride-price and inherits, and she does not have to do an *'idda.* If he has consummated the marriage, she has all the dowry and inherits. The virgin and the previously married woman are the same in this situation according to us."

29.17 Compensatory gift after divorce

45 Yaḥyā related to me from Mālik that he had heard that 'Abd ar-Raḥmān ibn 'Awf divorced his wife, and gave her a compensatory gift in the form of a slave-girl.

Yaḥyā related to me from Mālik from Nāfi' that 'Abdullāh ibn 'Umar said, "Every divorced woman has compensation except for the one who is divorced and is allocated a bride-price and has not been touched. She receives half of what was allocated to her."

46 Yaḥyā related to me from Mālik that Ibn Shihāb said, "Every divorced woman receives compensation."

Mālik said, "I have also heard the same as that from al-Qāsim ibn Muḥammad."

Mālik said, "There is no fixed limit among us as to how small or large the compensation is."

29.18 The divorce of a slave

47 Yaḥyā related to me from Mālik from Abū az-Zinād from Sulaymān ibn Yasār that Nufay', a *mukātab* of Umm Salama, the wife of the Prophet ﷺ, or a slave of hers, had a freewoman as a wife. He divorced her twice, and then he wanted to return to her. The wives of the Prophet ﷺ ordered him to go to 'Uthmān ibn 'Affān to ask him about it. He found him at ad-Daraj with Zayd ibn Thābit. He asked them, and they both replied to him immediately and said, "She is unlawful for you. She is unlawful for you."

48 Yaḥyā related to me from Mālik from Ibn Shihāb from Sa'īd ibn al-Musayyab that Nufay', a *mukātab* of Umm Salama, the wife of the Prophet ﷺ divorced his free wife twice, so he asked 'Uthmān ibn 'Affān for an opinion, and he said, "She is unlawful for you."

49 Yaḥyā related to me from Mālik from 'Abdu Rabbih ibn Sa'īd from Muḥammad ibn Ibrāhīm ibn al-Ḥārith at-Taymī that Nufay', a *mukātab*

of Umm Salama, the wife of the Prophet ﷺ asked Zayd ibn Thābit for an opinion. He said, "I have divorced my free wife twice." Zayd ibn Thābit said, "She is unlawful for you."

50 Yaḥyā related to me from Mālik from Nāfi' that 'Abdullāh ibn 'Umar said, "When a slave divorces his wife twice, she is unlawful for him until she has married another husband, whether she is free or a slave. The *'idda* of a free woman is three menstrual periods, and the *'idda* of a slave-girl is two periods."

51 Yaḥyā related to me from Mālik from Nāfi' that 'Abdullāh ibn 'Umar said, "If a man gives his slave permission to marry, the divorce is in the hand of the slave, and nobody else has any power over his divorce. Nothing is held against a man who takes the slave-girl of his male slave or the slave-girl of his female slave."

29.19 Maintenance of slave-girls divorced when pregnant

Mālik said, "Neither a freeman nor a slave who divorces a slave-girl nor a slave who divorces a freewoman, in an irrevocable divorce, is obliged to pay maintenance even if she is pregnant and he no longer has any right to return to her."

Mālik said, "A freeman is not obliged to pay for the suckling of his son when his son is a slave belonging to others, nor is a slave obliged to spend his money on what his master owns except with the permission of his master."

29.20 *'Idda* of women with missing husbands

52 Yaḥyā related to me from Mālik from Yaḥyā ibn Sa'īd from Sa'īd ibn al-Musayyab that 'Umar ibn al-Khaṭṭāb said, "The woman who loses her husband and does not know where he is waits for four years, then does *'idda* for four months, and then she is free to marry."

Mālik said, "If she marries after her *'idda* is over, regardless of whether the new husband has consummated the marriage or not, her first husband has no means of access to her."

Mālik said, "That is what is done among us. If her husband reaches her before she has re-married, he is more entitled to her."

Mālik said that he had seen people disapproving of what one person said that one of the people (i.e. one of the people of knowledge) had attributed to 'Umar ibn al-Khaṭṭāb that he had said, "Her first husband chooses when he comes: either her bride-price or his wife."

Mālik said, "I have heard that 'Umar ibn al-Khaṭṭāb, speaking about a woman whose husband divorced her while he was absent from her and then took her back, and the news of his taking her back had not reached her while the news of his divorcing her had, and so she had married again, said, 'Her first husband who divorced her has no means of access to her whether or not the new husband has consummated the marriage.'

Mālik said, "This is what I like best of what I have heard about the missing man."

29.21 *'Idda* of divorce and divorce of menstruating women

53 Yaḥyā related to me from Mālik from Nāfi' that 'Abdullāh ibn 'Umar divorced his wife while she was menstruating in the time of the Messenger of Allah ﷺ. 'Umar ibn al-Khaṭṭāb asked the Messenger of Allah ﷺ about it. The Messenger of Allah ﷺ said, "Go and tell him to take her back and keep her until she is purified and then has a period and then is purified. Then if he wishes, he can keep her, and if he wishes, he should divorce her before he has had intercourse with her. That is the *'idda* which Allah has commanded for women who are divorced."

54 Yaḥyā related to me from Mālik from Ibn Shihāb from 'Urwa ibn az-Zubayr from 'Ā'isha, *Umm al-Mu'minīn*, that she took Ḥafṣa ibn 'Abd ar-Raḥmān ibn Abī Bakr aṣ-Ṣiddiq into her house when she had entered the third period of her *'idda*. Ibn Shihāb said, "That was mentioned to 'Amra bint 'Abd ar ar-Raḥmān, and she said that 'Urwa had spoken the

truth and people had argued with 'Ā'isha about it, saying that Allah, the Blessed, the Exalted, says in His Book, '*Three qurū'*.' 'Ā'isha said, 'You spoken the truth. Do you know what *qurū'* are? *qurū'* are times of becoming pure after menstruation."

55 Yaḥyā related to me from Mālik that Ibn Shihāb said that he heard Abū Bakr ibn 'Abd ar-Raḥmān say, "I have never seen any of our *fuqahā'* who did not say that this was what the statement of 'Ā'isha meant."

56 Yaḥyā related to me from Mālik from Nāfi' and Zayd ibn Aslam from Sulaymān ibn Yasār that al-Aḥwaṣ died in Syria when his wife had begun her third menstrual period after he had divorced her. Mu'āwiya ibn Abī Sufyān wrote and asked Zayd ibn Thābit about that. Zayd wrote to him, "When she began her third period, she was free from him and he was free from her. He does not inherit from her nor she from him."

57 Yaḥyā related to me from Mālik that he had heard that Abū Bakr ibn 'Abd ar-Raḥmān, Sulaymān ibn Yasār and Ibn Shihāb used to say, "When a divorced woman enters the beginning of her third period, she is clearly separated from her husband and she cannot inherit from him and he cannot inherit from her and he has no access to her."

58 Yaḥyā related to me from Mālik from Nāfi' that 'Abdullāh ibn 'Umar said, "When a man divorces his wife and she begins her third period, she is free from him and he is free from her."

Mālik said, "This is how things are done among us."

59 Yaḥyā related to me from Mālik from al-Fuḍayl ibn Abī 'Abdullāh, the *mawlā* of al-Mahrī that al-Qāsim ibn Muḥammad and Sālim ibn 'Abdullāh said, "When a woman is divorced and begins her third period, she is clearly separated from him and is free to marry again."

60 Yaḥyā related to me from Mālik that he had heard that Sa'īd ibn al-Musayyab, Ibn Shihāb, and Sulaymān ibn Yasār all said, "The *'idda* of a woman in a *khul'* divorce is three periods."

61 Yaḥyā related to me from Mālik that he heard Ibn Shihāb say, "The

'idda of a divorced woman is reckoned by the menstrual cycles even if she is estranged." (The reason the *'idda* is normally reckoned by the menstrual cycle is to see whether the woman is pregnant or not.)

62 Yaḥyā related to me from Mālik from Yaḥyā ibn Sa'īd from a man of the Anṣār that his wife asked him for a divorce, and he said to her, "When you have had your period, then tell me." When she had her period, she told him. He said, "When you are purified then tell me." When she was purified, she told him and he divorced her.

Mālik said, "This is the best of what I have heard about it."

29.22 *'Idda* of women in their houses when divorced in them

63 Yaḥyā related to me from Mālik that Yaḥyā ibn Sa'īd heard al-Qāsim ibn Muḥammad and Sulaymān ibn Yasār both mention that Yaḥyā ibn Sa'īd ibn al-'Āṣ divorced the daughter of 'Abd ar-Raḥmān ibn al-Hakam irrevocably, so 'Abd ar-Raḥmān ibn al-Hakam took her away. 'Ā'isha, *Umm al-Mu'minīn*, sent to Marwān ibn al-Ḥakam who was the governor of Madīna at that time. She said, "Fear Allah and make him return the woman to her house."

Marwān said in what Sulaymān related, "'Abd ar-Raḥmān has the upper hand over me." Marwān said in what al-Qāsim related, "Have you not heard about the affair of Fāṭima bint Qays?" 'Ā'isha said, "It will not harm you to mention the story of Fāṭima." Marwān said, "If you see some evil, there is enough evil in what occurred between those two." (see *ḥadīth* 67)

64 Yaḥyā related to me from Mālik from Nāfi' that the daughter of Sa'īd ibn Zayd ibn 'Amr ibn Nufayl was the wife of 'Abdullāh ibn 'Amr ibn 'Uthmān ibn 'Affān, and he divorced her irrevocably and she moved out. 'Abdullāh ibn 'Umar rebuked her for that.

65 Yaḥyā related to me from Mālik from Nāfi' that 'Abdullāh ibn 'Umar divorced one of his wives in the house of Ḥafṣa, the wife of the Prophet ﷺ. It was on his way to the mosque so he went by a different route which

went behind the houses as he was averse to asking her permission to enter until he took her back.

66 Yaḥyā related to me from Mālik from Yaḥyā ibn Sa'īd that Sa'īd ibn al-Musayyab was asked who was obliged to pay the rent for a woman whose husband divorced her while she was in a leased house. Sa'īd ibn al-Musayyab said, "Her husband is obliged to pay it." Someone asked, "What if her husband does not have it?" He said, "Then she must pay it." Someone asked, "And if she does not have it?" He said, "Then the ruler must pay it."

29.23 Maintenance of divorced women

67 Yaḥyā related to me from Mālik from 'Abdullāh ibn Yazīd, the *mawlā* of al-Aswad ibn Sufyān from Abū Salama ibn 'Abd ar-Raḥmān ibn 'Awf from Fāṭima bint Qays that Abū 'Amr ibn Ḥafṣ divorced her absolutely while he was away in Syria. His agent sent her some barley and she was displeased with it, saying, "By Allah, I don't expect anything from you." She went to the Messenger of Allah ﷺ and mentioned it to him. He said, "You have no maintenance. He then ordered her to spend her *'idda* in the house of Umm Sharīk. Then he said, "This is a woman whom my Companions visit. Spend the *'idda* in the house of 'Abdullāh Ibn Umm Maktum. He is a blind man and you can undress in his home. When you are free to marry, tell me."

She continued, "When I was free to remarry, I mentioned to him that Mu'āwiya ibn Abī Sufyān and Abū Jahm ibn Hishām had asked for me in marriage. The Messenger of Allah ﷺ said, 'As for Abū Jahm, he never puts down his stick from his shoulder (i.e. he is always travelling), and as for Mu'āwiya, he is a poor man with no property. Marry Usāma ibn Zayd.' I objected to him and he repeated, 'Marry Usāma ibn Zayd.' So I married him, and Allah put good in it and I was content with him.'"

68 Yaḥyā related to me from Mālik that he heard Ibn Shihāb say, "A woman who is absolutely divorced does not leave her house until she is free to remarry. She is not entitled to maintenance unless she is pregnant. In that case the husband supports her until she gives birth."

Mālik said, "This is what is done among us."

29.24 *'Idda* of slave-girls divorced by their husbands

69 Mālik said, "What is done among us when a slave divorces a slave-girl when she is a slave and then she is set free, is that her *'idda* is the *'idda* of a slave-girl, and her being set free does not change her *'idda,* whether or not he can still take her back. Her *'idda* is not altered."

Mālik said, "The *ḥadd* punishment which a slave incurs is treated in the same way. When he is freed after he has incurred the penalty but before the punishment has been executed, his *ḥadd* is the *ḥadd* of a slave."

Mālik said, "A freeman can divorce a slave-girl three times, and her *'idda* is two periods. A slave divorces a freewoman twice, and her *'idda* is three periods."

Mālik said about a man who had a slave-girl as a wife, and he bought her and set her free, "Her *'idda* is the *'idda* of a slave-girl, i.e. two periods, as long as he has not had intercourse with her. If he has had intercourse with her after buying her and before he has set her free, she only has to wait until one period has passed."

29.25 General chapter on *'idda* of divorce

70 Yaḥyā related to me from Mālik from Yaḥyā ibn Sa'īd and from Yazīd ibn 'Abdullāh ibn Qusayṭ al-Laythī that Sa'īd ibn al-Musayyab said, "'Umar ibn al-Khaṭṭāb said, 'If a woman is divorced and has one or two periods and then stops menstruating, she must wait nine months. If it is clear that she is pregnant, then that is that. If not, she must do an *'idda* of three months after the nine, and then she is free to marry."

Yaḥyā related to me from Mālik from Yaḥyā ibn Sa'īd that Sa'īd ibn al-Musayyab said, "Divorce belongs to men, and women have the *'idda.*"

71 Yaḥyā related to me from Mālik from Ibn Shihāb that Sa'īd ibn al-

Musayyab said, "The *'idda* of the woman who bleeds constantly is a year."

Mālik said, "What is done among us about a divorced woman whose periods stop when her husband divorces her is that she waits nine months. If she has not had a period in that time, she has an *'idda* of three months. If she has a period before the end of the three months, she accepts the period. If another nine months pass without her having a period, she does an *'idda* of three months. If she has a second period before the end of those three months, she accepts the period. If nine months then pass without a period, she does an *'idda* of three months. If she has a third period, the *'idda* of the period is complete. If she does not have a period, she waits three months, and then she is free to marry. Her husband can return to her before she becomes free to marry unless he made her divorce irrevocable."

Mālik said, "The *sunna* with us is that when a man divorces his wife and has the option to return to her, and she does part of her *'idda* and then he returns to her and then parts from her before he has had intercourse with her, she does not add to what has passed of her *'idda*. Her husband has wronged himself and erred if he returns to her and has no need of her."

Mālik said, "What is done among us is that if a woman becomes a Muslim while her husband is an unbeliever and then he becomes a Muslim, he is entitled to her as long as she is still in her *'idda*. If her *'idda* is finished, he has no access to her. If he re-marries her after the end of her *'idda*, however, that is not counted as divorce. Islam removed her from him without divorce."

29.26 The two arbiters

72 Yaḥyā related to me from Mālik that he had heard that 'Alī ibn Abī Ṭālib said about the two arbiters about whom Allah, the Exalted, says, *"If you fear a breach between a couple, send an arbiter from his people and an arbiter from her people. If the couple desire to put things right, Allah will bring about a reconciliation between them. Allah is All-Knowing, All-Aware"* (4:35) that both separation and joining were overseen by the two of them.

Mālik said, "That is the best of what I have heard from the people of knowledge. Whatever the two arbiters say concerning separation or joining is taken into consideration."

29.27 Oath of men to divorce while not yet married

73 Yaḥyā related to me from Mālik that he had heard that 'Umar ibn al-Khattāb, 'Abdullāh ibn 'Umar, 'Abdullāh ibn Mas'ūd, Sālim ibn 'Abdullāh, al-Qāsim ibn Muḥammad, Ibn Shihāb, and Sulaymān ibn Yasār all said, "If a man has vowed to divorce his wife before marrying her and then he breaks his vow, divorce is obligatory for him when he marries her."

Yaḥyā related to me from Mālik that he had heard that 'Abdullāh ibn Mas'ūd said that there was nothing binding on someone who said, "Every woman I marry is divorced" if he did not name a specific tribe or woman.

Mālik said, "That is the best of what I have heard."

Mālik said about a man saying to his wife, "You are divorced, and every woman I marry is divorced," or that all his property would be *ṣadaqa* if he did not do such-and-such and then broke his oath, "As for his wives, it is divorce as he said. As for his statement, 'Every woman I marry is divorced', if he did not name a specific woman, tribe, or land, or so on, it is not binding on him and he can marry as he wishes. As for his property, he gives a third of it away as *ṣadaqa*."

29.28 Deadline of men who do not have intercourse with their wives

74 Yaḥyā related to me from Mālik from Ibn Shihāb that Sa'īd ibn al-Musayyab said, "If someone marries a woman and cannot have intercourse with her, there is a deadline of a year set for him to have intercourse with her. If he does not, they are separated."

75 Yaḥyā related to me from Mālik that he had asked Ibn Shihāb about whether the deadline was set from the day he had married her, or from

the day she presented the case before the ruler. He said, "It is from the day she presents her complaint before the ruler."

Mālik said, "As for someone who has intercourse with his wife and then is prevented from intercourse with her, I have not heard that there is a deadline set for him or that they have been separated."

29.29 General section on divorce

76 Yaḥyā related to me from Mālik that Ibn Shihāb said, "I have heard that the Messenger of Allah ﷺ said to a man from Thaqīf who had ten wives when he became Muslim, 'Take four and separate from the rest.'"

77 Yaḥyā related to me from Mālik that Ibn Shihāb said that he had heard Sa'īd ibn al-Musayyab, Ḥumayd ibn 'Abd ar-Raḥmān ibn 'Awf, 'Ubaydullāh ibn 'Abdullāh ibn 'Utba ibn Mas'ūd, and Sulaymān ibn Yasār all say that they had heard Abū Hurayra say that he had heard 'Umar ibn al-Khaṭṭāb say, "If a woman is divorced by her husband once or twice, and he leaves her until she is free to marry and she marries another husband and he dies or divorces her, and then she re-marries her first husband, she is with him according to what remains of her divorce (i.e. there is only one or two divorces left)."

Mālik said, "That is what is done among us and there is no dispute about it."

78 Yaḥyā related to me from Mālik from Thābit ibn al-Aḥnaf that he married an *umm walad* of 'Abd ar-Raḥmān ibn Zayd ibn al-Khaṭṭāb. He said, "'Abdullāh ibn 'Abd ar-Raḥmān ibn Zayd ibn al-Khaṭṭāb summoned me and I went to him. I came in upon him and there were whips and two iron fetters placed there, and two of his slaves whom he had made to sit there. He said, 'Divorce her, or, by Him by whom one swears, I will do such-and-such to you!' I said, 'It is divorce a thousand times.' Then I left him and saw 'Abdullāh ibn 'Umar on the road to Makka and I told him about my situation. 'Abdullāh ibn 'Umar was furious, and said, 'That is not a divorce and she is not unlawful for you, so return to your home.' I was still not at ease so I went to 'Abdullāh ibn az-Zubayr who was the

governor of Makka at that time. I told him about my situation and what 'Abdullāh ibn 'Umar had said to me. 'Abdullāh ibn az-Zubayr said to me, 'She is not unlawful for you, so return to your home,' and he wrote to Jābir ibn al-Aswad az-Zuhrī who was the governor of Madīna and ordered him to punish 'Abdullāh ibn 'Abd ar-Raḥmān and to make him leave me and my family alone. I went to Madīna and Ṣafiyya, the wife of 'Abdullāh ibn 'Umar, fitted out my wife so that she could bring her to my house with the knowledge of 'Abdullāh ibn 'Umar. Then I invited 'Abdullāh ibn 'Umar on the day of my wedding to the wedding feast and he came."

79 Yaḥyā related to me from Mālik that 'Abdullāh ibn Dīnār said, "I heard 'Abdullāh ibn 'Umar recite from the Qur'ān, *'O Prophet! When you divorce women, divorce them at the beginning of their 'idda.'*" (65:1)

Mālik said, "He meant by that to make one pronouncement of divorce at the beginning of each period of purity."

80 Yaḥyā related to me from Mālik from Hishām ibn 'Urwa that his father said, "It used to be that a man would divorce his wife and then return to her before her *'idda* was over, and that was all right, even if he divorced her a thousand times. The man went to his wife and then divorced her and when the end of her *'idda* was in sight, he took her back and then divorced and said, 'No! By Allah, I will not go back to you and you will never be able to marry again.' Allah, the Blessed, the Exalted, sent down, *'Divorce can be pronounced twice; then wives should be retained with correctness and courtesy or released with good will.'* (2:229) People then turned towards divorce in a new light from that day whether they were divorced or not."

81 Yaḥyā related to me from Mālik from Thawr ibn Zayd ad-Dīlī that Allah, the Blessed, the Exalted, revealed about a man who divorced his wife and then returned to her while he had no need of her and did not mean to keep her so as to make the *'idda* period long for her by that in order to do her harm: *"Do not retain them by force, thus overstepping the limits. Anyone who does that has wronged himself."* (2:231) Allah warns them by that *āyat.*

82 Yaḥyā related to me from Mālik that he had heard that Sa'īd ibn al-Musayyab and Sulaymān ibn Yasār were asked about a man who divorced when he was drunk. They said, "When a drunk man divorces, his divorce is allowed. If he kills, he is killed for it."

Mālik said, "That is what is done among us."

Yaḥyā related to me from Mālik that he had heard that Sa'īd ibn al-Musayyab said, "If a man does not find the means to spend on his wife, they are to be separated."

Mālik said, "That is what I have seen the people of knowledge in our city doing."

29.30 *'Idda* of widows when pregnant

83 Yaḥyā related to me from Mālik from 'Abdu Rabbih ibn Sa'īd ibn Qays that Abū Salama ibn 'Abd ar-Rahmān said that 'Abdullāh ibn 'Abbās and Abū Hurayra were asked when a pregnant woman whose husband had died could remarry. Ibn 'Abbās said, "Whichever of two periods is the longest." Abū Hurayra said, "When she gives birth, she is free to marry." Abū Salama ibn 'Abd ar-Rahmān visited Umm Salama, the wife of the Prophet ﷺ and asked her about it. Umm Salama said, "Subay'a al-Aslamiya gave birth half a month after the death of her husband and two men asked to marry her. One was young and the other was old. She preferred the young man and so the older man said, "You are not free to marry yet." Her family were away and he hoped that when her family returned, they would give her to him. She went to the Messenger of Allah ﷺ and he said, "You are free to marry, so marry whomever you wish."

84 Yaḥyā related to me from Mālik from Nāfi' that 'Abdullāh ibn 'Umar was asked about a woman whose husband died while she was pregnant, and he said, "When she gives birth, she is free to marry." A man of the Anṣār who was with him told him that 'Umar ibn al-Khaṭṭāb had said, "Had she given birth while her husband was still on his bed, unburied, she would still be free to marry."

85 Yaḥyā related to me from Mālik from Hishām ibn 'Urwa from his father that al-Miswar ibn Makhrama told him that Subay'a al-Aslamiya gave birth a few nights after the death of her husband. The Messenger of Allah ﷺ told her, "You are free to marry, so marry whomever you wish."

86 Yaḥyā related to me from Mālik from Yaḥyā ibn Sa'īd from Sulaymān ibn Yasār that 'Abdullāh ibn 'Abbās and Abū Salama ibn 'Abd ar-Raḥmān ibn 'Awf differed on the question of a woman who gave birth a few nights after the death of her husband. Abū Salama said, "When she gives birth to the child she is carrying, she is free to marry." Ibn 'Abbās said, "Whichever of the end of two periods is the longest." Abū Hurayra came and said, "I am with my nephew," meaning Abū Salama. They sent Kurayb, a *mawlā* of 'Abdullāh ibn 'Abbās, to Umm Salama, the wife of the Prophet ﷺ, to ask her about it. He came back and told them that she had said that Subay'a al-Aslamiya had given birth a few nights after the death of her husband, and she had brought the matter to the Messenger of Allah ﷺ and he had said, "You are free to marry, so marry whomever you wish."

Mālik said, "This is how the people of knowledge here continue to act."

29.31 Widows remaining in their houses until free to marry

87 Yaḥyā related to me from Mālik from Sa'īd ibn Isḥāq ibn Ka'b ibn 'Ujra from his paternal aunt, Zaynab bint Ka'b ibn 'Ujra, that al-Furay'a bint Mālik ibn Sinān, the sister of Abū Sa'īd al-Khudrī, informed her that she went to the Messenger of Allah ﷺ and asked to be able to return to her people among the Banū Khudra since her husband had gone out in search of some of his slaves who had run away and he had caught up with them near al-Qudūm (which is six miles from Madīna) and they had killed him.

She said, "I asked the Messenger of Allah ﷺ if I could return to my people in the Banū Khudra, as my husband had not left me a dwelling which belonged to him, and had left me with me no maintenance. The Messenger of Allah ﷺ said, 'Yes,' so I left. When I was in the courtyard, the Messenger of Allah ﷺ called me or summoned me, and I answered him. He said, 'What did you say?' I repeated the story about my husband. He said, 'Stay in your house until what is written reaches its term.' I did the *'idda* in the house for four months and ten days."

She said, "When 'Uthmān ibn 'Affān sent for me, I told him that, and he followed it and made judgements accordingly."

88 Yaḥyā related to me from Mālik from Ḥumayd ibn Qays al-Makkī from 'Amr ibn Shu'ayb from Sa'īd ibn al-Musayyab that 'Umar ibn al-Khaṭṭāb sent back widows from the desert and prevented them from performing the *ḥajj*.

Yaḥyā related to me from Mālik from Yaḥyā ibn Sa'īd that he had heard that as-Sa'ib ibn Khabbāb died and his wife went to 'Abdullāh ibn 'Umar. She mentioned to him that her husband had died and mentioned some land which they had at Qanāh (a district on the outskirts of Madīna), and asked him if it would be all right for her to stay overnight there. He forbade her to do so. So, she used to go out before dawn from Madīna and spent the whole day on their land, and then, when evening came, she would go back to Madīna and spend the night in her house.

89 Yaḥyā related to me from Mālik that Hishām ibn 'Urwa said about a Bedouin woman whose husband died, that she was to stay where her people stayed.

Mālik said, "This is what is done among us."

90 Yaḥyā related to me from Mālik from Nāfi' that 'Abdullāh ibn 'Umar said, "The only place a woman whose husband has died and a woman who is absolutely divorced can spend the night is in their houses."

29.32 *'Idda* of an *umm walad* on her master's death

91 Yaḥyā related to me from Mālik that Yaḥyā ibn Sa'īd said that he had heard al-Qāsim ibn Muḥammad say that Zayd ibn 'Abd al-Malik separated some men and their wives who were slave-girls who had borne children to men who had died, because they had married them

after one or two menstrual periods. He separated them until they had done an *'idda* of four months and ten days. Al-Qāsim ibn Muḥammad said, "Glory be to Allah! Allah says in His Book, *'Those of you who die, leaving wives.'* (2:234) They are not wives."

92 Mālik related that 'Abdullāh ibn 'Umar said, "The *'idda* of an *umm walad* when her master dies is one menstrual period."

Yaḥyā related to me from Mālik from Yaḥyā ibn Sa'īd that al-Qāsim ibn Muḥammad said, "The *'idda* of an *umm walad* when her master dies is one menstrual period."

Mālik said, "This is what is done among us."

Mālik added, "If she does not have periods, then her *'idda* is three months."

29.33 *'Idda* of slave-girls whose master or husband dies

93 Yaḥyā related to me from Mālik that he had heard that Sa'īd ibn al-Musayyab and Sulaymān ibn Yasār said, "The *'idda* of a slave-girl when her husband dies is two months and five days."

94 Yaḥyā related to me the like of that from Mālik from Ibn Shihāb.

Mālik said about a slave who divorced a slave-girl but did not make it absolute, "He can return to her. If he then dies while she is still in the *'idda* from her divorce, she does the *'idda* of a slave-girl whose husband dies, which is two months and five days. If she has been set free and he can return to her, and she does not choose to separate after she has been set free, and he dies while she is in the *'idda* from the divorce, she does the *'idda* of a freewoman whose husband has died, four months and ten days. That is because the *'idda* of widowhood befell her while she was free, so her *'idda* is the *'idda* of a freewoman."

Mālik said, "This is what is done among us."

29.34 *Coitus interruptus*

95 Yaḥyā related to me from Mālik from Rabi'a ibn Abī 'Abd ar-Raḥmān from Muḥammad ibn Yaḥyā ibn Ḥabbān that Muḥayriz said, "I went into the mosque and saw Abū Sa'īd al-Khudri and so I sat by him and asked him about *coitus interruptus*. Abū Sa'īd al-Khudrī said, "We went out with the Messenger of Allah ﷺ on the expedition against the Banū al-Muṣṭaliq. We took some Arabs prisoner, and we desired the women as celibacy was hard for us. We wanted the ransom, so we wanted to practise *coitus interruptus*. We asked, 'Shall we practise *coitus interruptus* while the Messenger of Allah ﷺ is among us before we have asked him?' We asked him about that and he said, 'You do not have to not do it. There is no self which is to come into existence up to the Day of Rising but that it will come into existence.'"

96 Yaḥyā related to me from Mālik from Abū an-Naḍr, the *mawlā* of 'Umar ibn 'Ubaydullāh, from 'Āmir ibn Sa'd ibn Abī Waqqāṣ from his father that he used to practise *coitus interruptus*.

97 Yaḥyā related to me from Mālik from Abū an-Naḍr, the *mawlā* of 'Umar ibn 'Ubaydullāh, from Ibn Aflaḥ, the *mawlā* of Abū Ayyūb al-Anṣārī, from an *umm walad* of Abū Ayyūb al-Anṣārī that he practised *coitus interruptus*.

98 Yaḥyā related to me from Mālik from Nāfi' that 'Abdullāh ibn 'Umar did not practise *coitus interruptus* and thought that it was disapproved.

99 Yaḥyā related to me from Mālik from Ḍamra ibn Sa'īd al-Māzinī from al-Ḥajjāj ibn 'Amr ibn Ghaziyya that he was sitting with Zayd ibn Thābit when Ibn Faḍl came to him. He was from the Yemen. He said, "Abū Sa'īd! I have slave-girls. None of the wives in my keep are more pleasing to me than them, and not all of them please me so much that I want a child by them. Shall I then practise *coitus interruptus*?" Zayd ibn Thābit said, "Give an opinion, Ḥajjāj!" I said, "May Allah forgive you! We sit with you in order to learn from you!" He said, "Give an opinion!" I said, "She is your field. If you wish, water it, and if you wish, leave it thirsty. I heard that from Zayd." Zayd said, "He has spoken the truth."

100 Yaḥyā related to me from Mālik from Ḥumayd ibn Qays al-Makkī that a man called Dhafif said that Ibn 'Abbās was asked about *coitus interruptus*, He called a slave-girl and said, "Tell them," She was embarrassed. He said, "It is all right, and I do it myself."

Mālik said, "A man does not practise *coitus interruptus* with a freewoman unless she gives her permission. There is no harm in practising *coitus interruptus* with a slave-girl without her permission. Someone who has someone else's slave-girl as a wife does not practise *coitus interruptus* with her unless her people give him permission."

29.35 Limit of abstaining from adornment in mourning

101 Yaḥyā related to me from Mālik from 'Abdullāh ibn Abī Bakr ibn Muḥammad ibn 'Amr ibn Ḥazm from Ḥumayd ibn Nāfi' that Zaynab bint Abī Salama related these three traditions to him. Zaynab said, "I visited Umm Ḥabība, the wife of the Prophet ﷺ, when her father Abū Sufyān ibn Ḥarb had died. Umm Ḥabība called for a yellowy perfume, perhaps *khalūq* or something else. She rubbed the perfume first on a slave-girl and she then wiped it on the sides of her face and said, 'By Allah! I have no need of perfume but I heard the Messenger of Allah ﷺ say, "It is not lawful for a woman who trusts in Allah and the Last Day to abstain from adornment in mourning for someone who has died for more than three nights, except for four months and ten days for a husband."'"

102 Zaynab said, "I went to the house of Zaynab bint Jaḥsh, the wife of the Prophet ﷺ, when her brother had died. She called for perfume and put some on and said, 'By Allah! I have no need of perfume, but I heard the Messenger of Allah ﷺ, say, "It is not lawful for a woman who trusts in Allah and the Last Day to abstain from adornment in mourning for someone who has died for more than three nights, except for four months and ten days for a husband."'"

103 Zaynab said, "I heard my mother, Umm Salama, the wife of the Prophet ﷺ, say that a woman came to the Messenger of Allah ﷺ and said, 'Messenger of Allah! My daughter's husband has died and her eyes are troubling her, can she put kohl on them?' The Messenger of Allah ﷺ said,

'No' two or three times. Then he said, 'It is only four months and ten days (i.e. the period of mourning). In the *Jāhiliyya* none of you threw away the piece of dung until a year had passed.'"

Ḥumayd ibn Nāfi' said, "I asked Zaynab to explain what 'throwing away the piece of dung at the end of a year' meant. Zaynab said, 'In the *Jāhiliyya* when a woman's husband died, she went into a small tent and dressed in the worst of clothes. She did not touch perfume or anything until a year had passed. Then she was brought an animal – a donkey, a sheep, or a bird – and she would break her *'idda* with it, by rubbing her body against it (*taftaḍḍu*). Rarely did she break her *'idda* with anything (by rubbing herself against it) but that it died. Then she would come out and would be given a piece of dung. She would throw it away and then return to whatever she wished of perfumes or whatever.'"

Mālik explained, "*Taftaḍḍu* means to wipe her skin with it in the same way as with a healing charm."

104 Yaḥyā related to me from Mālik from Nāfi' from Ṣafiyya bint Abī 'Ubayd from 'Ā'isha and Ḥafṣa, the wives of the Prophet ﷺ, that the Messenger of Allah ﷺ said, "It is not lawful for a woman in mourning for someone who has died, if she trusts in Allah and the Last Day, to abstain from adornment for more than three nights, except for a husband."

105 Yaḥyā related to me from Mālik that he had heard that Umm Salama, the wife of the Prophet ﷺ said to a woman in mourning for her husband whose eyes were troubling her and the pain had become severe, "Apply *jilā'* kohl at night and wipe it off in the day."

106 Yaḥyā related to me from Mālik that he had heard that Sālim ibn 'Abdullāh and Sulaymān ibn Yasār said that if a woman whose husband had died feared that an inflammation of her eyes might affect her sight or that some complaint might befall her, she should put kohl on and seek a remedy with kohl or some other cure even if it had perfume in it.

Mālik said, "If there is a necessity, the *dīn* of Allah is ease."

107 Yaḥyā related to me from Mālik from Nāfi' that Ṣafiyya bint Abī 'Ubayd suffered from an eye-complaint while she was in mourning for her husband, 'Abdullāh ibn 'Umar. She did not apply kohl until her eyes almost had *ramas* (a dry white secretion in the corners of the eye).

Mālik said, "A woman whose husband has died should anoint her eyes with olive oil and sesame oil and the like of that since there is no perfume in it."

Mālik said, "A woman in mourning for her husband should not put on any jewelry – rings, anklets or such-like, neither should she dress in any sort of colourful, striped garment unless it is coarse. She should not wear any cloth dyed with anything except black, and she should only dress her hair with things like lotus-tree leaves which do not dye the hair."

108 Yaḥyā related to me from Mālik that he had heard that the Messenger of Allah ﷺ visited Umm Salama while she was in mourning for Abū Salama and she had put aloes on her eyes. He asked, "What is this, Umm Salama?" She said, "It is only aloes, Messenger of Allah." He said, "Put it on at night and wipe it off in the daytime."

Mālik said, "The mourning of a young girl who has not yet had a menstrual period takes the same form as the mourning of one who has had a period. She avoids what a mature woman avoids if her husband dies."

Mālik said, "A slave-girl mourns her husband when he dies for two months and five nights like her *'idda*."

Mālik said, "An *umm walad* does not have to mourn when her master dies, and a slave-girl does not have to mourn when her master dies. Mourning is for those with husbands."

109 Yaḥyā related to me from Mālik that he had heard that Umm Salama, the wife of the Prophet ﷺ said, "A mourning woman can rub her head with lotus leaves and olive oil."

30. Suckling

30.1 Suckling of the young

1 Yaḥyā related to me from Mālik from ʻAbdullāh ibn Abī Bakr from ʻAmra bint ʻAbd ar-Raḥmān that ʻA'isha, *Umm al-Mu'minīn,* informed her that the Messenger of Allah ﷺ was with her when she heard the voice of a man asking permission to enter the room of Ḥafṣa. ʻĀ'isha said that she had said, "Messenger of Allah! There is a man asking permission to enter your house!" The Messenger of Allah ﷺ said, "I think it is so-and-so" (referring to a paternal uncle of Ḥafṣa by suckling). ʻĀ'isha asked, "Messenger of Allah, if so-and-so were alive (referring to her paternal uncle by suckling), could he enter where I am?" The Messenger of Allah ﷺ replied, "Yes, suckling makes unlawful what birth makes unlawful."

2 Yaḥyā related to me from Mālik from Hishām ibn ʻUrwa from his father that ʻĀ'isha, *Umm al-Mu'minīn,* said "My paternal uncle by suckling came to me and I refused to give him permission to enter until I had asked the Messenger of Allah ﷺ about it. He said, 'He is your paternal uncle, so give him permission.' I said, 'Messenger of Allah, the woman nursed me, not the man!' He said, 'He is your paternal uncle, so let him enter.'"

ʻĀ'isha said, "That was after we had been commanded to adopt the veil."

ʻĀ'isha added, "What is unlawful by birth is also made unlawful by suckling."

3 Yaḥyā related to me from Mālik from Ibn Shihāb from Urwa ibn az-Zubayr that ʻĀ'isha, *Umm al-Mu'minīn,* told him that Aflaḥ, the brother

of Abū al-Qu'ays, came and asked permission to visit her after the veil had been lowered, and he was her paternal uncle by suckling. She said, "I refused to give him permission to enter. When the Messenger of Allah ﷺ came, I told him about what I had done, and he told me to give him permission to enter."

4 Yaḥyā related to me from Mālik from Thawr ibn Zayd ad-Dīlī that 'Abdullāh ibn 'Abbās said, "The milk which a child under two years old sucks, even if it is only one suck, makes the foster-relatives unlawful."

5 Yaḥyā related to me from Mālik from Ibn Shihāb from 'Amr ibn ash-Sharīd that 'Abdullāh ibn 'Abbās was asked whether, if a man had two wives, and one of them had nursed a slave-boy, and the other had nursed a slave-girl, the slave-boy could marry the slave-girl. He said, "No, the husband is the same."

6 Yaḥyā related to me from Mālik from Nāfi' that 'Abdullāh ibn 'Umar said, "There is no kinship by suckling except for a person who is nursed when he is small. There is no kinship by suckling for an older person over the age of two years."

7 Yaḥyā related to me from Mālik from Nāfi' that Sālim ibn 'Abdullāh ibn 'Umar informed him that 'Ā'isha, *Umm al-Mu'minīn*, sent him away while he was being nursed to her sister, Umm Kulthūm bint Abī Bakr aṣ-Ṣiddīq, and said, "Suckle him ten times so that he can come in to see me."

Sālim said, "Umm Kulthūm nursed me three times and then fell ill, so that she only nursed me three times. I could not go in to see 'Ā'isha because Umm Kulthūm did not finish the ten times for me."

8 Yaḥyā related to me from Mālik from Nāfi' that Ṣafiyya bint Abī 'Ubayd told him that Ḥafṣa, *Umm al-Mu'minīn*, sent 'Āṣim ibn 'Abdullāh ibn Sa'd to her sister, Fāṭima bint 'Umar ibn al-Khaṭṭāb, for her to suckle him ten times so that he could come in to see her. She did it, so he used to come in to see her.

9 Yaḥyā related to me from Mālik from 'Abd ar-Raḥmān ibn al-Qāsim that his father told him that 'Ā'isha, the wife of the Prophet ﷺ admitted

those whom her sisters and the daughters of her brother had nursed, but she did not admit those who had been nursed by the wives of her brothers.

10 Yaḥyā related to me from Mālik that Ibrahīm ibn 'Uqba asked Sa'īd ibn al-Musayyab about suckling. Sa'īd said, "Anything that takes place in the first two years, even if it is only a drop, makes unlawful. Whatever is after two years, is only food that is eaten."

Ibrāhīm ibn 'Uqba said, "Then I asked 'Urwa ibn az-Zubayr and he told me the same as what Sa'īd ibn al-Musayyab said."

11 Yaḥyā related to me from Mālik that Yaḥyā ibn Sa'īd said that he heard Sa'īd ibn al-Musayyab say, "Suckling is only while the child is in the cradle. If not, it does not cause flesh and blood relations."

Yaḥyā related to me from Mālik that Ibn Shihāb said, "Suckling, however little or much, makes unlawful. Kinship by suckling makes men *maḥram*."

Yaḥyā said that he heard Mālik say, "Suckling, however little or much, when it is in the first two years makes unlawful. As for what is after the first two years, little or much, it does not make anything unlawful. It is like food."

30.2 Suckling of older people

12 Yaḥyā related to me from Mālik from Ibn Shihāb that he was asked about the suckling of an older person. He said, "'Urwa ibn az-Zubayr informed me that Abū Ḥudhayfa ibn 'Utba ibn Rabi'a, one of the Companions of the Messenger of Allah ﷺ who was present at Badr, adopted Sālim (who is called Sālim, the *mawlā* of Abū Ḥudhayfa) as the Messenger of Allah ﷺ adopted Zayd ibn Hāritha. He thought of him as his son, and Abū Hudhayfa married him to his brother's sister, Fāṭima bint al-Walīd ibn 'Utba ibn Rabi'a, who was at that time among the first emigrants. She was one of the best unmarried women of the Quraysh. When Allah the Exalted sent down in His Book what He sent down

about Zayd ibn Ḥāritha, '*Call them after their fathers. That is juster in Allah's sight. And if you do not know who their fathers were then they are your brothers in the dīn and people under your patronage*' (33:5), people in this position were traced back to their fathers. When the father was not known, they were traced to their *mawlā*.

"Sahla bint Suhayl, who was the wife of Abū Ḥudhayfa, and one of the tribe of 'Amr ibn Lu'ayy, came to the Messenger of Allah ﷺ and said, 'Messenger of Allah! We think of Sālim as a son and he comes in to see me when I am uncovered. We only have one room, so what do you think about the situation?' The Messenger of Allah ﷺ said, 'Give him five drinks of your milk and he will become a *maḥram* by that.' She then saw him as a foster-son. 'Ā'isha, *Umm al-Mu'minīn*, took that as a precedent for whatever men she wanted to be able to come to see her. She ordered her sister, Umm Kulthūm bint Abī Bakr aṣ-Ṣiddīq and the daughters of her brother to give milk to whichever men she wanted to be able to come in to see her. The rest of the wives of the Prophet ﷺ refused to let anyone come in to them by such nursing. They said, 'No, by Allah! We think that what the Messenger of Allah ﷺ ordered Sahla bint Suhayl to do was only by an indulgence concerning the nursing of Sālim alone. No, by Allah! No one will come in upon us by such nursing!'

"This is what the wives of the Prophet ﷺ thought about the suckling of an older person."

13 Yaḥyā related to me from Mālik that 'Abdullāh ibn Dīnār said, "A man came to 'Abdullāh ibn 'Umar when I was with him at the place where judgements were given and asked him about the suckling of an older person. 'Abdullāh ibn 'Umar replied, 'A man came to 'Umar ibn al-Khaṭṭāb and said, 'I have a slave-girl and I used to have intercourse with her. My wife went to her and suckled her. When I went to the girl, my wife told me to watch out because she had suckled her!' 'Umar told him to beat his wife and to go to his slave-girl because kinship by suckling was only by the suckling of the young."

14 Yaḥyā related to me from Mālik from Yaḥyā ibn Sa'īd that a man said to Abū Mūsā al-Ash'arī, "I drank some milk from my wife's breasts and it went into my stomach." Abū Mūsā said, "I can only but think that she is

unlawful for you." 'Abdullāh ibn Mas'ūd said, "Look at what opinion you are giving the man." Abū Mūsā said, "Then what do you say?" 'Abdullāh ibn Mas'ūd replied, "There is only kinship by suckling in the first two years."

Abū Mūsā said, "Do not ask me about anything while this learned man is among you."

30.3 Suckling in general

15 Yaḥyā related to me from Mālik from 'Abdullāh ibn Dīnar from Sulaymān ibn Yasār and from 'Urwa ibn az-Zubayr from 'Ā'isha, *Umm al-Mu'minīn*, that the Messenger of Allah ﷺ said, "What is unlawful by birth is unlawful by suckling."

16 Yaḥyā related to me from Mālik that Muḥammad ibn 'Abd ar-Raḥmān ibn Nawfal said, "'Urwa ibn az-Zubayr informed me from 'Ā'isha, *Umm al-Mu'minīn*, that Judāma bint Wahb al-Asadiya informed her that she heard the Messenger of Allah ﷺ say, 'I intended to prohibit *ghīla* but I remembered that the Greeks and Persians do that without it causing any injury to their children.'"

Mālik explained, "*Ghīla* is that a man has intercourse with his wife while she is suckling."

17 Yaḥyā related to me from Mālik from 'Abdullāh ibn Abī Bakr ibn Ḥazm from 'Amra bint 'Abd ar-Raḥmān that 'Ā'isha, the wife of the Prophet ﷺ said, "Amongst what was sent down of the Qur'ān was 'ten known sucklings make unlawful'. Then it was abrogated by 'five known sucklings'. When the Messenger of Allah ﷺ died, it was what is now recited of the Qur'ān."

Yaḥyā said that Mālik said, "One does not act on this."

31. Business Transactions

31.1 Non-returnable deposits (*'urbūn*)

1 Yaḥyā related to me from Mālik from a reliable source from 'Amr ibn Shu'ayb from his father from his father's father that the Messenger of Allah ﷺ forbade transactions in which non-refundable deposits were paid (*'urbūn*).

Mālik said, "That is, in our opinion, but Allah knows best, when a man buys a slave or slave-girl or rents an animal and then says to the person from whom he bought the slave or leased the animal, 'I will give you a dinar or a dirham or whatever on the condition that if I actually take the goods or ride what I have rented from you, then what I have given you already goes towards payment for the goods or hire of the animal. If I do not purchase the goods or hire the animal, then what I have given you is yours without any liability.'"

Mālik said, "According to the way of doing things with us there is nothing wrong in bartering an Arabic-speaking merchant-slave for Abyssinian slaves or any other type that are not his equal in eloquence, trading, shrewdness and know-how. There is nothing wrong in bartering one such slave for two or more other slaves with a stated delay in the terms if he is clearly different. If there is no appreciable difference between the slaves, two should not be bartered for one with a stated delay in the terms even if their racial type is different."

Mālik said, "There is nothing wrong in selling what has been bought in such a transaction before taking possession of all of it as long as you receive the price for it from someone other than the original owner."

Mālik said, "An addition to the price must not be made for a foetus in the womb of his mother when she is sold because that is *gharar* (an uncertain transaction). It is not known whether the child will be male or female, good-looking or ugly, normal or handicapped, alive or dead. All these things will affect the price."

Mālik said about a transaction where a slave or slave-girl was bought for one hundred dinars with a stated credit period that, if the seller regretted the sale, there was nothing wrong in him asking the buyer to revoke it for ten dinars by which he would forgo his right to the hundred dinars which he was owed.

Mālik said, "There is nothing wrong in that. If, however, the buyer regrets and asks the seller to revoke the sale of a slave or slave-girl in consideration of which he will pay an extra ten dinars immediately or on credit terms extended beyond the original term, that should not be done. It is disapproved of because it is as if, for instance, the seller is buying the one hundred dinars which is not yet due on a year's credit before the year expires for a slave-girl and ten dinars which is to be paid immediately or on credit term longer than the year. This falls into the category of selling gold with a delayed term."

Mālik said that it was not proper for a man to sell a slave-girl to another man for one hundred dinars on credit and then to buy her back for more than the original price or on a credit term longer than the original term for which he sold her. To understand why that was disapproved of, the example of a man who sold a slave-girl on credit and then bought her back on a credit term longer than the original term was looked at. He might have sold her for thirty dinars with a month to pay and then have bought her back for sixty dinars with a year or half a year to pay. The outcome would only be that his goods would have returned to him just like they were and the other party would have given him thirty dinars on a month's credit against sixty dinars on a year or half a year's credit. That should not be done.

31.2 Wealth of slaves

2 Yaḥyā related from Mālik from Nāfi' from 'Abdullāh ibn 'Umar that 'Umar ibn al-Khaṭṭāb said, "If a slave who has wealth is sold, that wealth belongs to the seller unless the buyer stipulates its inclusion."

Mālik said, "The generally agreed-upon way of doing things among us is that, if the buyer stipulates the inclusion of the slave's property whether it be cash, money owed to him, or goods of known or unknown value, then they belong to the buyer, even if the slave possesses more than what he was purchased for, whether he was bought for cash, as payment for a debt, or in exchange for goods. This is possible because a master is not asked to pay *zakāt* on his slave's property. If a slave owns a slave-girl, it is lawful for him to have intercourse with her by his right of possession. If a slave is freed or put under contract (*kitāba*) to purchase his freedom, then his property goes with him. If he becomes bankrupt, his creditors take his property and his master is not liable for any of his debts.

31.3 Built-in liability agreements

3 Yaḥyā related from Mālik from 'Abdullāh ibn Abī Bakr ibn Muḥammad ibn 'Amr ibn Ḥazm that Abān ibn 'Uthmān and Hishām ibn Ismā'īl used to mention in their *khuṭbas* built-in liability agreements in the sale of slaves, covering both a three day period and a similar clause covering a year.

Mālik explained, "The defects a slave or slave-girl is found to have from the time they are bought until the end of the three days are the responsibility of the seller. The year agreement is to cover insanity, leprosy, and loss of limbs due to disease. After a year, the seller is free from any liability."

Mālik said, "An inheritor or someone else who sells a slave or slave-girl without any such in-built guarantee is not responsible for any defect in a slave and there is no liability agreement held against him unless he was aware of a defect and concealed it. If he was aware of a defect, the lack of guarantee does not protect him: the purchase is returned. In our view, built-in liability agreements only apply to the purchase of slaves."

31.4 Defects in slaves

4 Yaḥyā related from Mālik from Yaḥyā ibn Sa'īd from Sālim ibn 'Abdullāh that 'Abdullāh ibn 'Umar sold one of his slaves for eight hundred dirhams with the stipulation that he was not responsible for defects. The person who bought the slave complained to 'Abdullāh ibn 'Umar that the slave had a disease which he had not told him about. They argued and went to 'Uthmān ibn 'Affān for a decision. The man said, "He sold me a slave with a disease which he did not tell me about." 'Abdullāh said, "I sold to him on the stipulation that I was not responsible." 'Uthmān ibn 'Affān decided that 'Abdullāh ibn 'Umar should take an oath that he had sold the slave without knowing that he had any disease. 'Abdullāh ibn 'Umar refused to take the oath, so the slave was returned to him and recovered his health in his possession. 'Abdullāh sold him afterwards for 1500 dirhams.

Mālik said, "The generally agreed-upon way of doing things among us about a man who buys a female slave and she becomes pregnant, or who buys a slave and then frees him, or if there is any other such matter which has already happened so that he cannot return his purchase, and a clear proof is established that there was a defect in that purchase when it was in the possession of the seller or the defect is acknowledged by the seller or someone else, is that the slave or slave-girl is assessed for their value with the fault they are found to have had on the day of purchase, and the buyer is refunded, from what he paid, the difference between the price of a slave when sound and their price with that defect."

Mālik said, "The generally agreed-upon way of doing things among us regarding a man who buys a slave and then finds that the slave has a defect for which he can be returned and meanwhile another defect has happened to the slave whilst in his possession, is that if the defect which occurred to the slave in his possession has harmed him, like the loss of a limb, loss of an eye, or something similar, then he has a choice. If he wants, he can have the price of the slave reduced commensurate with the defect (he bought him with) according to the prices on the day he bought him, or, if he likes, he can pay compensation for the defect which the slave has suffered in his possession and return him. The choice is up to him. If the slave dies in his possession, the slave is valued with the defect which he had on the day of his purchase. It is seen what his price would really have been. If the price of the slave on the day of his purchase without fault was one hundred dinars, and his price on the day of purchase with fault would been eighty dinars, then the price is reduced by the difference. These prices are assessed according to the market value on the day the slave was purchased."

Mālik said, "The generally agreed-upon way of doing things among us is that, if a man returns a slave-girl in whom he has found a defect and he has already had intercourse with her, he must pay what he has reduced of her price if she was a virgin. If she was not a virgin, there is nothing against his having had intercourse with her because he had charge of her."

Mālik said, "The generally agreed-upon way of doing things among us regarding a person, whether he is an inheritor or not, who sells a slave, slave-girl or animal, which is meant to be free of defects, is that he is not responsible for any defect in what he sold unless he knew about the fault and concealed it. If he knew that there was a fault and concealed it, his declaration that it was free of faults does not absolve him, and what he sold is returned to him."

Mālik spoke about a situation where a slave-girl was bartered for two other slave-girls and then one of the slave-girls was found to have a defect for which she could be returned. He said, "The slave-girl worth two other slave-girls is valued for her price. Then the other two slave-girls are valued, ignoring the defect which one of them has. Then the price of the slave-girl sold for two slave-girls is divided between them according to their prices so that the proportion of each of them in the price is arrived at – to the higher-priced one according to her higher price, and to the other according to her value. Then one looks at the one with the defect, and the buyer is refunded according to the amount her share is affected by the defect, be it little or great. The price of the two slave-girls is based on their market value on the day that they were bought."

Mālik spoke about a man who bought a slave and hired him out on a long-term or short-term basis and then found out that the slave had a defect which necessitated his return. He said that if the man returned the slave because of the defect, he kept the hire and the revenue. "This is the way in which things are done in our city. That is because, had the man bought a slave who then built a house for him and the value of the house was many times the price of the slave, and he then found that the slave had a defect for which he could be returned, he would not have to make payment for the work the slave had done for him. Similarly, he would keep any revenue from hiring him out because he had charge of him. This is the way of doing things among us."

Mālik said, "The way of doing things among us when someone buys several slaves in one lot and then finds that one of them has been stolen, or has a defect, is that he looks at the one he finds has been stolen or the one in which he finds a defect. If he is the pick of those slaves, or the most expensive, or it was for his sake that he bought them, or he is the one in whom people see the most excellence, then the whole sale is returned. If the one who is found to be stolen or to have a defect is not the pick of the slaves, and he did not buy them for his sake, and there is no special virtue which people see in him, the one who is found to have a defect or to have been stolen is returned as he is, and the buyer is refunded his portion of the total price."

31.5 The purchase of slave-girls with conditions attached

5 Yaḥyā related from Mālik from Ibn Shihāb that 'Ubaydullāh ibn 'Abdullāh ibn 'Utba ibn Mas'ūd told him that 'Abdullāh ibn Mas'ūd bought a slave-girl from his wife, Zaynab ath-Thaqafiyya. She made a condition to him that, if he bought her, she could always buy her back for the price that he paid. 'Abdullāh ibn Mas'ūd asked 'Umar ibn al-Khaṭṭāb about that and 'Umar ibn al-Khaṭṭāb said, "Do not go near her while anyone has a condition concerning her over you."

6 Yaḥyā related from Mālik from Nāfi' that 'Abdullāh ibn 'Umar would say, "A man should not have intercourse with a slave-girl except one whom, if he wished, he could sell, and if he wished, he could give away,

and if he wished, he could keep, and if he wished, he could do with her what he wanted."

Mālik said that a man who bought a slave-girl on condition that he did not sell her, give her away, or do something of that nature, was not to have intercourse with her. That was because he was not permitted to sell her or to give her away, so if he did not own that from her, he did not have complete ownership of her, because an exception had been made concerning her by the hand of someone else. If that sort of condition entered into it, it was an improper situation and such a sale was disliked.

31.6 Prohibition against intercourse with married slave-girls

7 Yaḥyā related from Mālik from Ibn Shihāb that 'Abdullāh ibn 'Āmir gave 'Uthmān ibn 'Affān a slave-girl, who had a husband, that he had purchased at Basra. 'Uthmān said, "I will not go near her until her husband has separated from her." Ibn 'Āmir compensated the husband and he separated from her.

8 Yaḥyā related from Mālik from Ibn Shihāb from Abū Salama ibn 'Abd ar-Rahmān ibn 'Awf that 'Abd ar-Raḥmān ibn 'Awf bought a slave-girl and then found that she had a husband, so he returned her.

31.7 Ownership of the fruit of trees sold

9 Yaḥyā related to me from Mālik from Nāfi' from 'Abdullāh ibn 'Umar that the Messenger of Allah ﷺ said, "If palm-trees are sold after they have been pollinated, the fruit belongs to the seller unless the buyer makes a stipulation about its inclusion."

31.8 Prohibition against selling fruit until starting to ripen

10 Yaḥyā related to me from Mālik from Nāfi' from Ibn 'Umar that the Messenger of Allah ﷺ forbade selling fruit until it had started to ripen. He forbade the transaction to both buyer and seller.

11 Yaḥyā related to me from Mālik from Ḥumayd aṭ-Ṭawīl from Anas ibn Mālik that the Messenger of Allah ﷺ forbade selling fruit until it had become mellow. He was asked, "Messenger of Allah, what do you mean by 'become mellow'?" He replied, "When it becomes rosy."

The Messenger of Allah ﷺ added, "Allah may prevent the fruit from maturing, so how can you take payment from your brother for it?"

12 Yaḥyā related to me from Mālik from Abū ar-Rijāl Muḥammad ibn 'Abd ar-Raḥman ibn Ḥāritha from his mother, 'Amra bint 'Abd ar-Raḥmān, that the Messenger of Allah ﷺ forbade selling fruit until it was clear of blight.

Mālik said, "Selling fruit before it has begun to ripen is an uncertain transaction (*gharar*)."

13 Yaḥyā related to me from Mālik from Abū az-Zinād from Kharīja ibn Zayd ibn Thābit that Zayd ibn Thābit did not sell fruit until the Pleaides were visible [at the beginning of the summer].

Mālik said, "The way of doing things among us about selling melons, cucumbers, water-melons, and carrots is that it is lawful to sell them when it is clear that they have begun to ripen. Then the buyer has what grows until the season is over. There is no specific timing laid down for that because the time is well-known to people, and it may happen that the crop will be affected by blight and put a premature end to the season. If blight strikes and a third or more of the crop is damaged, an allowance for that is deducted from the price of purchase."

31.9 The sale of *'ariyyas*

14 Yaḥyā related to me from Mālik from Nāfi' from 'Abdullāh ibn 'Umar from Zayd ibn Thābit that the Messenger of Allah ﷺ allowed the holder of an *'ariyya* to barter the dates on the palm for the amount of dried dates it was estimated that the palms would produce.

14.1 Yaḥyā related to me from Mālik from Dāwud ibn al-Ḥusayn from

Abū Sufyān, the *mawlā* of Ibn Abī Aḥmad, from Abū Hurayra that the Messenger of Allah ﷺ allowed the produce of an *'ariyya* to be bartered for an estimation of what the produce would be when the crop was less than five *awsāq* or equal to five *awsāq*. Dāwud was unsure whether he said five *awsāq* or less than five.

Mālik said, "*'Ariyyas* can be sold for an estimation of what amount of dried dates will be produced. The crop is examined and estimated while still on the palm trees. This is allowed because it comes into the category of delegation of responsibility, handing over rights, and involving a partner. Had it been like a form of sale, no one would have made someone else a partner in the produce until it was ripe nor would he have renounced his right to any of it or put someone in charge of it until the buyer had taken possession."

31.10 The effect of crop damage on the sale of agricultural produce

15 Yaḥyā related to me from Mālik that Abū ar-Rijāl Muḥammad ibn 'Abd ar-Raḥmān heard his mother, 'Amra bint 'Abd ar-Raḥmān say, "A man bought the fruit of an enclosed orchard in the time of the Messenger of Allah ﷺ and he tended it while staying on the land. It became clear to him that there was going to be some loss, he asked the owner of the orchard to reduce the price for him or to revoke the sale, but the owner made an oath not to do so. The mother of the buyer went to the Messenger of Allah ﷺ and told him about it. The Messenger of Allah ﷺ said, 'By this oath he has sworn not to do good.' The owner of the orchard heard about that and went to the Messenger of Allah ﷺ and said, 'Messenger of Allah, the choice is his.'"

16 Yaḥyā related to me from Mālik that he had heard that 'Umar ibn 'Abd al-'Azīz decided in a case to make a reduction for crop damage.

Mālik said, "This is what we do in this situation."

Mālik added, "Crop damage refers to whatever causes loss of a third or more for the purchaser. Anything less is not counted as crop damage."

31.11 Keeping back a portion of the fruit

17 Yaḥyā related to me from Mālik from Rabi'a ibn 'Abd ar-Raḥmān that al-Qāsim ibn Muḥammad would sell produce from his orchard and keep some of it aside.

18 Yaḥyā related to me from Mālik from 'Abdullāh ibn Abī Bakr that his grandfather, Muḥammad ibn 'Amr ibn Ḥazm sold the fruit of an orchard of his called al-Afraq for 4000 dirhams, and he kept aside 800 dirhams worth of dry dates.

19 Yaḥyā related to me from Mālik from Abū ar-Rijāl Muḥammad ibn 'Abd ar-Raḥmān ibn Ḥāritha that his mother, 'Amra bint 'Abd ar-Rahmān, used to sell her fruit and keep some of it aside.

Mālik said, "The generally agreed-upon way of doing things among us is that when a man sells the fruit of his orchard, he can keep aside up to a third of the fruit, but that is not to be exceeded. There is no harm in what is less than a third."

Mālik added that he thought there was no harm for a man to sell the fruit of his orchard and keep aside only the fruit of a certain palm-tree or palm-trees which he had chosen and whose number he had specified, because the owner was only keeping aside certain fruit of his own orchard and everything else he sold.

31.12 Disapproved practices in the sale of dates

20 Yaḥyā related to me from Mālik from Zayd ibn Aslam that 'Aṭā' ibn Yasār said, "The Messenger of Allah ﷺ said, 'Dried dates for dried dates should be exchanged like for like.' It was said to him, 'Your agent in Khaybar takes one *ṣā'* for two.' The Messenger of Allah ﷺ said, 'Call him to me.' So he was summoned. The Messenger of Allah ﷺ asked, 'Do you take one *ṣā'* for two?' He replied, 'Messenger of Allah! Why should they sell me good dates for assorted low quality dates, *ṣā'* for *ṣā'*!' The Messenger of Allah ﷺ said, 'Sell the assorted ones for dirhams, and then buy the good ones with those dirhams.'"

21 Yaḥyā related to me from Mālik from ʻAbd al-Ḥamīd ibn Suhayl ibn ʻAbd ar-Raḥmān ibn ʻAwf from Saʻīd ibn al-Musayyab from Abū Saʻīd al-Khudrī and from Abū Hurayra that the Messenger of Allah ﷺ appointed a man as an agent in Khaybar, and he brought him some excellent dates. The Messenger of Allah ﷺ said to him, "Are all the dates of Khaybar like this?" He said, "No, by Allah, Messenger of Allah! We take *ṣāʻ* of this kind for two *ṣāʻ* or two *ṣāʻ* for three." The Messenger of Allah ﷺ said, "Do not do that. Sell the assorted ones for dirhams and then buy the good ones with the dirhams."

22 Yaḥyā related to me from Mālik from ʻAbdullāh ibn Yazīd that Zayd ibn ʻAyyāsh told him that he had once asked Saʻd ibn Abī Waqqāṣ about selling white wheat for a type of good barley. Saʻd asked him which was the better and when he told him the white wheat, he forbade the transaction. Saʻd said, "I heard the Messenger of Allah ﷺ being asked about selling dried dates for fresh dates and the Messenger of Allah ﷺ said, 'Do the dates diminish in size when they become dry?' When he was told that they did, he forbade that."

31.13 *Muzābana* and *muḥāqala*

23 Yaḥyā related to me from Mālik from Nāfiʻ from ʻAbdullāh ibn ʻUmar that the Messenger of Allah ﷺ forbade *muzābana. Muzābana* was selling fresh dates for dried dates by measure, and selling grapes for raisins by measure.

24 Yaḥyā related to me from Mālik from Dā'ūd ibn al-Ḥusayn from Abū Sufyān, the *mawlā* of Ibn Abī Aḥmad, from Abū Saʻīd al-Khudrī that the Messenger of Allah ﷺ forbade *muzābana* and *muḥāqala. Muzābana* is selling fresh dates for dried dates while they were still on the trees. *Muḥāqala* is renting land in exchange for wheat.

25 Yaḥyā related to me from Mālik from Ibn Shihāb from Saʻīd ibn al-Musayyab that the Messenger of Allah ﷺ forbade *muzābana* and muhāqala. *Muzābana* was selling fresh dates for dried dates. *Muḥāqala* was buying unharvested wheat in exchange for threshed wheat and renting land in exchange for wheat.

Ibn Shihāb added that he had asked Sa'īd ibn al-Musayyab about renting land for gold and silver. He said, "There is no harm in it."

Mālik said, "The Messenger of Allah ﷺ forbade *muzābana*. The explanation of *muzābana* is that it is buying something whose number, weight and measure is not known with something whose number, weight or measure is known; for instance, if a man has a stack of food whose measure is not known, either of wheat, dates, or whatever food, or the man has goods of wheat, date kernels, herbs, safflower, cotton, flax, silk, and does not know its measure or weight or number, and then a buyer approaches him and proposes that he weigh or measure or count the goods, but before he does, he specifies a certain weight, or measure, or number and guarantees to pay the price for that amount, agreeing that whatever falls short of that amount is a loss against him and whatever is in excess of that amount is a gain for him. That is not a sale. It is taking risks and it is an uncertain transaction. It falls into the category of gambling because he is not buying something from him for something definite which he pays. Everything which resembles this is also forbidden."

Mālik said that another example of that was, for instance, a man proposing to another man, "You have cloth. I will guarantee you from this cloth of yours so many hooded cloaks, the measure of each cloak to be such-and-such (naming a measurement). Whatever loss there is, is against me and I will fulfil you the specified amount. Whatever excess there is, is mine." Or perhaps the man proposes, "I will guarantee you from this cloth of yours so many shirts, the measurement of each shirt to be such-and-such, and whatever loss there is, is against me and I will fulfill the specified amount. Whatever excess there is, is mine." Or perhaps a man proposes to a man who has cattle or camel hides, "I will cut up these hides of yours into sandals on a pattern I will show you. I will make up the loss of whatever falls short of a hundred pairs. Whatever is over is mine because I guaranteed you." Another example was that a man says to a man who has ben-nuts, "I will press these nuts of yours. I will make up whatever falls short of such-and-such a weight by the pound. Whatever is more than that is mine."

Mālik said that all this and whatever else was like it or resembled it was in the category of *muzābana*, and was neither good nor permitted. It was also the same case for a man to say to a man who had fodder-leaves, date kernels, cotton, flax, herbs or safflower, "I will buy these leaves from you in exchange for such-and-such a *ṣāʿ*, (indicating leaves which were pounded like his leaves) or these date kernels for such-and-such a *ṣāʿ* of kernels of them, and the like of that in the case of safflower, cotton, flax and herbs."

Mālik said, "All this is included in what we have described of *muzābana*."

31.14 General remarks about selling produce at its source

26 Mālik said, "There is no harm in buying dates from specified trees or a specified orchard or buying milk from specified sheep when the buyer starts to take them as soon as he has paid the price. That is like buying oil from a container. A man buys some of it for a dinar or two and gives his gold and stipulates that it be measured out for him. There is no harm in that. If the container breaks and the oil is wasted, the buyer takes his gold back and there is no transaction between them."

Mālik said, "There is no harm in anything which is taken right away as it is, like fresh milk and fresh picked dates, which the buyer can take on a day to day basis. If the supply runs out before the buyer has what he has paid for in full, the seller gives him back the portion of the gold that is owed to him, or else the buyer takes other goods from him to the value of what he is owed and about which they are in mutual agreement. The buyer should stay with the seller until he has taken it. It is disapproved of for the seller to leave because the transaction would then come into the forbidden category of a debt for a debt. If a stated time period for payment or delivery enters into the transaction, it is also disapproved. Delay and deferment are not permitted in it, and are only acceptable when it is standard practice on definite terms by which the seller guarantees it to the buyer, but this is not to be from one specific orchard or from any specific sheep."

Mālik was asked about a man who bought an orchard from another man in which there were various types of palm-trees – excellent *'ajwa* palms, good *kabīs* palms, *'adhq* palms and other types. The seller kept aside the produce of a certain palm of his choice from the sale. Mālik said, "That is not proper because if he does that and keeps aside, for instance, dates of the *'ajwa* variety whose yield would be fifteen *ṣā's* and he picks the *kabīs* dates in their place, and the yield of their dates is ten *ṣā's*, or he picks the *'ajwa* which yield fifteen *ṣā's* and leaves the *kabīs* which yield ten *ṣā's*, it is as if he bought the *'ajwa* for the *kabīs* making allowances for their difference of quality. This is the same as a man dealing *kabīs* another man who has heaps of dates before him – a heap of fifteen *ṣā's* of *'ajwa*, a heap of ten *ṣā's* of *kabīs*, and a heap of twelve *ṣā's* of *'adhq*. The first man gives the owner of the dates a dinar to let him choose and take whichever of the heaps he likes."

Mālik said, "That is not proper."

Mālik was asked what a man who bought fresh dates from the owner of an orchard and advanced him a dinar was entitled to if the crop ran out. Mālik said, "The buyer makes a reckoning with the owner of the orchard and takes takes the remainder of his dinar. If the buyer has taken two-thirds of a dinar's worth of dates, he gets back the third of a dinar which is owed him. If the buyer has taken three-quarters of a dinar's worth of dates, then he gets back the quarter which is owed to him, or they come to a mutual agreement and the buyer takes what is owed him from his dinar from the owner of the orchard in something else of his choosing. If, for instance, he prefers to take dry dates or some other goods, he takes them according to what is due. If he takes the dry dates or some other goods, he should stay with him until he has been paid in full."

Mālik said, "This is the same situation as hiring out a specified riding-camel or hiring out a slave tailor, carpenter or some other kind of worker, or letting a house and taking payment in advance for the hire of the slave or the rent of the house or camel. Then an accident happens to what has been hired resulting in death or something else. The owner of the camel, slave or house returns what remains of the rent of the camel, the hire of the slave or the rent of the house to the one who advanced him the money, and the owner reckons what will settle that up in full. If, for instance, he has provided half of what the man paid for, he returns the remaining half of what he advanced, or according to whatever amount is due."

Mālik said, "Paying in advance for something which is on hand is only good when the buyer takes possession of what he has paid for as soon as he hands over the gold, whether it be a slave, camel, or house, or in the case of dates, he starts to pick them as soon as he has paid the money. It is not good that there be any deferment or credit in such a transaction."

Mālik said, "An example illustrating what is disapproved of in this situation is that, for instance, a man may say that he will pay someone in advance for the use of his camel on the *ḥajj*, and the *ḥajj* is still some time off, or he may say something similar to that about a slave or a house. When he does that, he only pays the money in advance on the understanding that if he finds the camel to be sound at the time the hire is due to begin, he will take it by virtue of what he has already paid. If an accident, or death, or something happens to the camel, then he will get his money back and the money he paid in advance will be considered as a loan."

Mālik said, "This is not the same as someone who takes immediate possession of what he rents or hires, so that it does not fall into the category of 'uncertainty' or disapproved payment in advance. That is following a common practice. An example of it is that a man buys a slave, or slave-girl, and takes possession of them and pays their price. If something happens to them within the period of the year indemnification contract, he takes his gold back from the one from whom he made the purchase. There is no harm in that. This is the precedent of the *sunna* in the matter of selling slaves."

Mālik said, "Someone who hires a specific slave, or rents a specific camel, up until a certain time, taking possession of that camel or slave, has acted properly because he did not take possession of what he wanted to rent or hire, nor did he advance any money as a loan which will be the responsibility of the other until the first man gets it back."

31.15 Selling fruit

27 Mālik said, "The generally agreed-upon way of doing things among us is that someone who buys some fruit, whether fresh or dry, should not resell it until he gets full possession of it. He should not barter things of

the same type, except hand to hand. Whatever can be made into dried fruit to be stored and eaten should not be bartered for its own kind, except hand to hand, like for like, when it is the same kind of fruit. In the case of two different kinds of fruit, there is no harm in bartering two of one kind for one of another, hand to hand on the spot. It is not good to set delayed terms. As for produce which is not dried and stored but is eaten fresh like watermelons, cucumbers, melons, carrots, citrons, bananas, pomegranates and so on, which when dried no longer counts as fruit, and is not a thing which is stored up as fruit is, I think that it is quite proper to barter such things two for one of the same variety hand to hand. If no term enters into it, there is no harm in it."

31.16 Selling gold for silver, minted and unminted

28 Yaḥyā related to me from Mālik that Yaḥyā ibn Sa'īd said, "The Messenger of Allah ﷺ ordered the two Sa'ds to sell a vessel made of either gold or silver from the booty. They either sold each three units of weight for four units weight of coins or each four units of weight for three units of coins. The Messenger of Allah ﷺ said to them, 'You have taken usury, so return it.'"

29 Yaḥyā related to me from Mālik from Musā ibn Abī Tamīm from Abū al-Ḥubāb Sa'īd ibn Yasār from Abū Hurayra that the Messenger of Allah ﷺ said, "A dinar for a dinar, a dirham for a dirham, no excess between the two."

30 Yaḥyā related to me from Mālik from Nāfi' from Abū Sa'īd al-Khudrī that the Messenger of Allah ﷺ said, "Do not sell gold for gold except like for like and do not increase one part over another part. Do not sell silver for silver, except like for like and do not increase one part over another part. Do not sell some of it which is not there for some of it which is."

31 Yaḥyā related to me from Mālik from Ḥumayd ibn Qays al-Makkī that Mujāhid said, "I was with 'Abdullāh ibn 'Umar when an artisan came to him and said, 'Abū 'Abd ar-Raḥmān, I fashion gold and then sell what I have made for more than its weight. I take an amount equivalent to the work of my hand.' 'Abdullāh forbade him to do that, so the artisan repeated the question to him, and 'Abdullāh continued to forbid him

until he came to the door of the mosque or to an animal that he intended to mount. Then 'Abdullāh ibn 'Umar said, 'A dinar for a dinar, and a dirham for a dirham. There is no increase between them. This is the command of our Prophet to us and our advice to you.'"

32 Yaḥyā related to me from Mālik that he had heard from his grandfather, Mālik ibn Abī 'Āmir that 'Uthmān ibn 'Affān said, "The Messenger of Allah ﷺ said to me, 'Do not sell a dinar for two dinars nor a dirham for two dirhams.'"

33 Yaḥyā related to me from Mālik from Zayd ibn Aslam from 'Aṭā' ibn Yasār that Mu'āwiya ibn Abī Sufyān sold a gold or silver drinking-vessel for more than its weight. Abū ad-Dardā' said, "I heard the Messenger of Allah ﷺ forbidding such sales except like for like." Mu'āwiya said to him, "I do not see any harm in it." Abū ad-Dardā' said to him, "Who will excuse me from Mu'āwiya? I tell him something from the Messenger of Allah ﷺ and he gives me his own opinion! I will not live in the same land as you!" Then Abū ad-Dardā' went to 'Umar ibn al-Khaṭṭāb and mentioned that to him. 'Umar ibn al-Khaṭṭāb therefore wrote to Mu'āwiya, "Do not sell it except like for like, weight for weight."

34 Yaḥyā related to me from Mālik from Nāfi' from 'Abdullāh ibn 'Umar that 'Umar ibn al-Khaṭṭāb said, "Do not sell gold for gold except like for like, and do not increase one part over another part. Do not sell silver for silver except like for like, and do not increase one part over another part. Do not sell silver for gold, one of them at hand and the other to be given later. If someone asks you to wait for payment until he has been to his house, do not leave him. I fear *ramā'* for you." *Ramā'* is usury.

35 Yaḥyā related to me from Mālik from 'Abdullāh ibn Dīnār from 'Abdullāh ibn 'Umar that 'Umar ibn al-Khaṭṭāb said, "Do not sell gold for gold except like for like. Do not increase part of it over another part. Do not sell silver for silver except for like, and do not increase part of it over another part. Do not sell some of it which is there for some of it which is not. If someone asks you to wait for payment until he has been to his house, do not leave him. I fear *ramā'* for you." *Ramā'* is usury.

36 Yaḥyā related to me from Mālik that he had heard that al-Qāsim ibn

Muḥammad said, "'Umar ibn al-Khaṭṭāb said, 'A dinar for a dinar, and a dirham for a dirham, and a *ṣā'* for a *ṣā'*. Something to be collected later is not to be sold for something at hand.'"

37 Yaḥyā related to me from Mālik that Abū az-Zinād heard Sa'īd ibn al-Musayyab say, "There is usury only in gold or silver or what is weighed or measured of what is eaten or drunk."

37 Yaḥyā related to me from Mālik that Yaḥyā ibn Sa'īd heard Sa'īd ibn al-Musayyab say, "Clipping gold and silver is part of causing corruption in the land."

Mālik said, "There is no harm in buying gold with silver or silver with gold without measuring, if it is unminted, or a piece of jewellery which has been made. Counted dirhams and counted dinars should not be bought without reckoning until they are known and counted. To abandon number and buy them at random would only be to speculate. That is not part of the business transactions of Muslims. As for what is weighed of unminted objects and jewellery, there is no harm in buying such things without measuring. To buy them without measuring is like buying wheat, dried dates, and such food-stuffs, which are sold without measuring, even though things like them are measured."

Mālik spoke about buying a Qur'ān, a sword or a signet ring, which had some gold or silver work on it, with dinars and dirhams. He said, "The value of the object bought with dinars, which has gold in it is looked at. If the value of the gold is up to one-third of the price, it is permitted and there is no harm in it if the sale is hand to hand and there is no deferment in it. When something which has silver in it is bought with silver, the value is looked at. If the value of the silver is one-third, it is permitted and there is no harm in it if the sale is hand to hand. That is still the way that people act among us."

31.17 Money-changing

38 Yaḥyā related to me from Mālik from Ibn Shihāb from Mālik ibn Aws ibn al-Ḥadathān an-Naṣrī that one time he asked to exchange 100 dinars.

He said, "Ṭalha ibn 'Ubaydullāh called me over and we made a mutual agreement that he would make the exchange with me. He took the gold and turned it about in his hand and then said, 'I can't do it until my treasurer brings the money to me from al-Ghāba.' 'Umar ibn al-Khaṭṭāb was listening and 'Umar said, 'By Allah! Do not leave him until you have taken it from him!' Then he said, 'The Messenger of Allah ﷺ said, "Gold for silver is usury except hand to hand. Wheat for wheat is usury except hand to hand. Dates for dates is usury except hand to hand. Barley for barley is usury except hand to hand."'"

Mālik said, "When a man exchanges dirhams with dinars and then finds a bad dirham among them and wants to return it, the exchange of the dinars breaks down, and he returns the silver and takes back his dinars. The explanation of what is disapproved in that is that the Messenger of Allah ﷺ said, 'Gold for silver is usury except hand to hand,' and 'Umar ibn al-Khaṭṭāb said, 'If someone asks you to wait to be paid until he has gone back to his house, do not leave him.' When he returns a dirham to him from the exchange after he has left him, it is like a debt or something deferred. For that reason, it is disapproved of, and the exchange collapses. 'Umar ibn al-Khaṭṭāb wanted that all gold, silver and food should not be sold for goods to be paid later. He did not want there to be any delay or deferment in any such sale, whether it involved one commodity or different sorts of commodities."

31.18 Selling gold for gold and silver for silver by weight

39 Yaḥyā related to me from Mālik that Yazīd ibn 'Abdullāh ibn Qusayṭ saw Sa'īd ibn al-Musayyab sell gold, counterpoising it for gold. He poured his gold into one pan of the scales and the man with whom he was counterpoising put his gold in the other pan of the scale and, when the pivot of the scales was balanced, they took and gave.

Mālik said, "According to the way things are done among us, there is no harm in selling gold for gold and silver for silver by counterpoising the weight, even if eleven dinars are taken for ten dinars hand to hand, when the weight of gold is equal, coin for coin, even if the number is different. Dirhams in such a situation are treated the same way as dinars."

Mālik said, "If, when counterpoising gold for gold or silver for silver, there is a difference of weight, one party should not give the other the value of the difference in silver or something else. Such a transaction is ugly and a means to usury because if one of the parties were permitted to take the difference for a separate price, it could be as if he had bought it separately, and so it would be permitted. Then it would be possible for him to ask for many times the value of the difference in order to permit the completion of the transaction between the two parties."

Mālik said, "If he had really been sold the difference without anything else with it, he would not have taken it for a tenth of the price for which he took it in order to put a 'legal front' on the transaction. This leads to allowing what is forbidden. The matter is forbidden."

Mālik said that it was not good when counterpoising to give good old gold coins and put along with them unminted gold in exchange for worn Kufic gold, which was unpopular, and to then treat the exchange as like for like.

Mālik said, "The commentary on why that is disapproved is that the owner of the good gold uses the excellence of his old gold coins as an excuse to throw in the unminted gold with it. Had it not been for the superiority of his (good) gold over the gold of the other party, the other party would not have counterpoised the unminted gold for his Kufic gold and the deal would have been refused.

"It is like a man wanting to buy three *ṣā's* of *'ajwa* dried dates for two *ṣā's* and a *mudd* of *kabīs* dates and, on being told that it was not good, then offering two *ṣā's* of *kabīs* and a *ṣā's* of poor dates desiring to make the sale possible. That is not good because the owner of the *'ajwa* should not give him a *ṣā'* of *'ajwa* for a *ṣā'* of poor dates. He would only be giving him that because of the excellence of *kabīs* dates.

"Or it is like a man asking someone to sell him three *ṣā's* of white wheat for two and a half *ṣā's* of Syrian wheat, and being told that it was not good except like for like, and so offering two *ṣā's* of wheat and one *ṣā'* of barley, intending to make the sale possible between them. That is not good because no one would have given a *ṣā'* of barley for a *ṣā'* of white wheat had that *ṣāʿ* been by itself. It was only given because of the excellence of Syrian wheat over the white wheat. This is not good. It is the same as the case of the unminted gold."

Mālik said, "Where gold, silver and food – things which should only be sold like for like – are concerned, something disliked and of poor quality should not be put with something good and desirable in order to make the sale possible and to make a bad situation lawful. When something of desirable quality is put with something of poor quality and it is only included so that its excellence in quality is noticed, something is being sold which, if it had been sold on its own, would not have been accepted and to which the buyer would not have paid any attention. It is only accepted by the buyer because of the superiority of what comes with it over his own goods. Transactions involving gold, silver or food must not have anything of this description enter into them. If the owner of the poor quality items wants to sell them, he sells them on their own, and does not put anything with them. There is no harm if it is like that."

31.19 Buying on delayed terms and re-selling for less on more immediate terms

40 Yaḥyā related to me from Mālik from Nāfiʿ from ʿAbdullāh ibn ʿUmar that the Messenger of Allah ﷺ said, "Whoever buys foodstuffs should not then sell them until he has received the whole amount."

41 Yaḥyā related to me from Mālik from ʿAbdullāh ibn Dīnār from ʿAbdullāh ibn ʿUmar that the Messenger of Allah ﷺ said, "Someone who buys food must not sell it until he has taken possession of it."

42 Yaḥyā related to me from Mālik from Nāfiʿ that ʿAbdullāh ibn ʿUmar said, "In the time of the Messenger of Allah ﷺ we used to buy food. He sent orders for us to move our purchases from the place in which we purchased them to another place before we re-sold them."

43 Yaḥyā related to me from Mālik from Nāfiʿ that Ḥakīm ibn Ḥizām had bought some food that ʿUmar ibn al-Khattāb had ordered people to have, and then re-sold it to people. ʿUmar ibn al-Khattāb heard about

this and he revoked the sale and said, "Do not sell food which you have purchased until you take delivery of it."

44 Yaḥyā related to me from Mālik that he had heard that receipts were given to people in the time of Marwān ibn al-Ḥakam for the produce of the market at al-Jār. People bought and sold the receipts among themselves before they had taken actual delivery of the goods. Zayd ibn Thābit and one of the Companions of the Messenger of Allah ﷺ went to Marwān ibn al-Ḥakam and said, "Marwān! Do you make usury lawful?" He said, "I seek refuge with Allah! What is that?" He said, "These receipts which people buy and sell before they take delivery of the goods." Marwān therefore sent guards to follow them and to take them from people's hands and return them to their owners.

45 Yaḥyā related to me from Mālik that he had heard that a man wanted to buy food from a man in advance. The man who wanted to sell the food to him went with him to the market and he began to show him heaps, saying, "Which one would you like me to buy for you?" The buyer said to him, "Are you selling me what you do not have?" So they went to 'Abdullāh ibn 'Umar and mentioned that to him. 'Abdullāh ibn 'Umar said to the buyer, "Do not buy from him what he does not have." He said to the seller, "Do not sell what you do not have."

46 Yaḥyā related to me from Mālik that Yaḥyā ibn Sa'īd heard Jamīl ibn 'Abd ar-Raḥmān the Mu'adhdhin say to Sa'īd ibn al-Muysayyab, "I am a man who buys whatever Allah wills of the receipts for the provisions which people are offered at al-Jār. I want to take payment for goods that I guarantee to deliver at a future date." Sa'īd said to him, "Do you intend to settle these things with receipts for provisions you have bought?" He said, "Yes." So he forbade that.

Mālik said, "The generally agreed-on way of doing things among us in which there is no dispute about buying food – wheat, barley, durra-sorghum, pearl millet, or any pulse or anything resembling pulses on which *zakāt* is obliged, or condiments of any sort, oil, ghee, honey, vinegar, cheese, sesame oil, milk and so on – is that the buyer should not re-sell any of that until he has taken possession and complete delivery of it."

31.20 What is disapproved of in selling food with delayed payment or delivery

47 Yaḥyā related to me from Mālik that Abū az-Zinād heard Sa'īd ibn al-Musayyab and Sulaymān ibn Yasār forbid a man to sell wheat for gold on delayed terms and then to buy dried dates with the gold before he had taken delivery of the gold.

48 Yaḥyā related to me from Mālik that Kathīr ibn Farqad asked Abū Bakr ibn Muḥammad ibn 'Amr ibn Ḥazm about a man who sold food to be delivered at a future date to a man for gold and then with the gold he bought dates before he had taken delivery of the gold. He disapproved of that and forbade it.

Yaḥyā related the like of that to me from Mālik from Ibn Shihāb.

Mālik said, "Sa'īd ibn al-Musayyab, Sulaymān ibn Yasār, Abū Bakr ibn Muḥammad ibn 'Amr ibn Ḥazm, and Ibn Shihāb forbade a man to sell wheat for gold and then buy dates with that gold before he had received the gold from the transaction in which he sold the wheat. There is no harm in someone buying dates on delayed terms, on the strength of the gold for which he sold the wheat, from someone other than the person to whom he sold the wheat before taking possession of the gold, and to refer the one from whom he bought the dates to his debtor who bought the wheat, for the gold he is owed for the dates."

Mālik said, "I asked more than one of the people of knowledge about that and they did not see any harm in it."

31.21 Pre-payment on food

49 Yaḥyā related to me from Mālik from Nāfi' that 'Abdullāh ibn 'Umar said that there was no harm in a man making an advance to another man for food, with a set description and price until a set date, as long as it was not in crops or dates which had not begun to ripen.

Mālik said, "The Messenger of Allah ﷺ forbade selling food before getting delivery of it."

Mālik said that it was not good if the buyer regretted his purchase and asked the seller to revoke the sale for him and he would not press him immediately for what he had paid. The people of knowledge forbade that. That was because when the food was made ready for the buyer by the seller, the buyer deferred his due from the seller in order that he might revoke the sale for him. That was selling food with delayed terms before taking delivery of the food.

Mālik said, "The explanation of that is that when the date of delivery comes and the buyer dislikes the food, the seller takes goods for money to be paid later and so it is not revocation. Revocation is that in which neither the buyer nor the seller is increased. When increase occurs by deferment of payment for a time period, or by anything which increases one of them over the other or anything which gives one of them profit, it is not revocation. When either of them do that, revocation becomes a sale. There is an indulgence for revocation, partnership, and transfer, as long as increase, decrease, or deferment does not come into them. If increase, decrease, or deferment comes into it, it becomes a sale. Whatever makes a sale lawful makes it lawful and whatever makes a sale unlawful makes it unlawful."

Mālik said, "If someone pays in advance for Syrian wheat, there is no harm if he takes a load after the term falls due."

Mālik said, "It is the same with whoever advances for any kind of thing. There is no harm in him taking better than whatever he has made an advance for or worse than it after the agreed delivery date. The explanation of that is that if, for instance, a man makes an advance for a certain weight of wheat. There is no harm if he decides to take some barley or Syrian wheat. If he has made an advance for good dates, there is no harm if he decides to take poor quality dates. If he paid in advance for red raisins, there is no harm if he takes black ones when it happens after the agreed delivery date, and when he takes like measure of what he paid for in advance."

31.22 Bartering food for food with no increase between them

50 Yaḥyā related to me from Mālik that he had heard that Sulaymān ibn Yasār said, "The fodder of the donkeys of Sa'd ibn Abī Waqqāṣ ran out and so he told his slave to take some of the family's wheat and buy barley with it, and to only take a like quantity."

51 Yaḥyā related to me from Mālik from Nāfi' that Sulaymān ibn Yasār told him that one time the fodder of the animals of 'Abd ar-Raḥmān ibn al-Aswad ibn 'Abd Yaghūth was finished so he said to his slave, "Take some of your family's wheat as food and buy barley with it, and take only a like quantity."

52 Yaḥyā related to me from Mālik that he had heard the same as that from al-Qāsim ibn Muḥammad from Ibn Mu'ayqib ad-Dawsī.

Mālik said, "This is the way of doing things among us."

Mālik said, "The generally agreed-on way of doing things among us is that wheat is not sold for wheat, dates for dates, wheat for dates, dates for raisins, wheat for raisins, nor any kind of food sold for food at all, except from hand to hand. If there is any sort of delayed terms in the transaction, it is not good. It is unlawful. Condiments are not bartered except from hand to hand."

Mālik said, "Food and condiments are not bartered when they are the same type, two of one kind for one of the other. A *mudd* of wheat is not sold for two *mudds* of wheat, nor a *mudd* of dates for two *mudds* of dates, nor a *mudd* of raisins for two *mudds* of raisins, nor is anything of that sort done with grains and condiments when they are of one kind, even if it is hand to hand.

"This is the same position as with silver for silver and gold for gold. No increase is lawful in the transaction, and only like for like, from hand to hand, is lawful."

Mālik said, "If there is a clear difference in food-stuffs which are measured and weighed, there is no harm in taking two of one kind for one of another, hand to hand. There is no harm in taking a *ṣā'* of dates for two *ṣā's* of raisins, and a *ṣā'* of wheat for two *ṣā's* of ghee. If the two sorts in the transaction are different, there is no harm in two for one or more than that from hand to hand. If delayed terms enter into the sale, it is not lawful."

Mālik said, "It is not lawful to trade a heap of wheat for a heap of wheat. There is no harm in a heap of wheat for a heap of dates, from hand to hand. That is because there is no harm in buying wheat with dates without precise measurement."

Mālik said, "With kinds of foods and condiments that differ from each other, and the difference is clear, there is no harm in bartering one kind for another, without precise measurement from hand to hand. If delayed terms enter into the sale, there is no good in it. Bartering such things without precise measurement is like buying it with gold and silver without measuring precisely."

Mālik said, "That is because you buy wheat with silver without measuring precisely, and dates with gold without measuring precisely, and it is lawful. There is no harm in it."

Mālik said, "It is not good for someone to make a heap of food knowing its measure and then to sell it as if it had not been measured precisely, concealing its measure from the buyer. If the buyer wants to return such food to the seller, he can, because he concealed its measure and it is an uncertain transaction. This is done with any kind of food or other goods whose measure and number the seller knows, and which he then sells without measurement and the buyer does not know that. If the buyer wants to return that to the seller, he can return it. The people of knowledge still forbid such a transaction."

Mālik said, "There is no good in selling one round loaf of bread for two round loaves, nor large for small when some of them are bigger than others. When care is taken that they are like for like, there is no harm in the sale, even if they are not weighed."

Mālik said, "It is not good to sell a *mudd* of butter and a *mudd* of milk for two *mudds* of butter. This is like what we described of selling dates when two *ṣā'*s of *kabīs* and a *ṣā'* of poor quality dates were sold for three *ṣā'*s of *'ajwa* dates after the buyer had said to the seller, 'Two *ṣā'*s of *kabīs* dates for three *ṣā'*s of *'ajwa* dates is not good,' and then he did that to make the transaction possible. The owner of the milk puts the milk with his butter so that he can use the superiority of his butter over the butter of the other party to include his milk along with it."

Mālik said, "Flour for wheat is like for like, and there is no harm in that. That is if he does not mix up anything with the flour and sell it for wheat, like for like. Had he put half a *mudd* of flour and half of wheat, and then sold that for a *mudd* of wheat, it would be like what we have described previously, and it would not be good because he would want to use the superiority of his good wheat to put flour along with it. Such a transaction is not good."

31.23 General section on selling food

53 Yaḥyā related to me from Mālik that Muḥammad ibn 'Abdullāh ibn Abī Maryam asked Sa'īd ibn al-Musayyab's advice. "I am a man," he said, "who buys food with receipts from al-Jār. Perhaps I will buy something for a dinar and half a dirham, and will be given food for the half dirham." Sa'īd said, "No. You give a dirham and take the rest in food." (A half dirham did not exist as a coin.)

54 Yaḥyā related to me from Mālik that he had heard that Muḥammad ibn Sīrīn used to say, "Do not sell grain on the ear until it is white."

Mālik said, "If someone buys food for a known price to be delivered at a stated date, and when the date comes, the one who owes the food says, 'I do not have the food. Sell me the food which I owe you with delayed terms.' The owner of the food says, 'This is not good because the Messenger of Allah ﷺ forbade selling food until the transaction has been completed.' The one who owes the food says to his creditor, 'Sell me any kind of food on delayed terms until I discharge the debt to you.' This is not good because he gives him food and then he returns it to him. The gold which he gave him becomes the price of that which is his right against him and the food which he gave him becomes what clears what is between them. If they do that, it becomes the sale of food before the deal is complete."

Mālik spoke about a man who was owed food which he had purchased from a man and this other man was owed the like of that food by another man. The one who owed the food said to his creditor, "I will refer you to my debtor who owes me the same amount of food as I owe you, so that you may obtain the food which I owe you."

Mālik said, "If the man who has to deliver the food, goes and buys the food to pay off his creditor, that is not good. That is selling food before taking possession of it. If the food is an advance which falls due at that particular time, there is no harm in paying off his creditor with it because that is not a sale. It is not lawful to sell food before receiving it in full since the Messenger of Allah ﷺ forbade that. However, the people of knowledge agree that there is no harm in partnership, transfer of responsibility and revocation in sales of food and other goods."

Mālik said, "That is because the people of knowledge consider it as a favour rendered. They do not consider it as a sale. It is like a man lending light dirhams. He is then paid back in dirhams of full weight, and so gets back more than he lent. That is lawful for him and permitted. Had a man bought defective dirhams from him as being the full weight, that would not be lawful. Had it been stipulated to him that he lend full weight in dirhams, and then he gave faulty ones, that would not be lawful for him."

55 Mālik said, "Another example of that is that the Messenger of Allah ﷺ forbade the sale called *muzābana* but granted an indulgence in the *'ariyya* for computing the equivalent in dates. It was distinguished between them that while the *muzābana*-sale was based on shrewdness and trade, the *'ariyya* sale was based on a favour rendered and there was no shrewdness involved on it."

Mālik said, "A man must not buy food for a fourth, a third, or a fraction of a dirham on the basis that he be given that food on credit. There is no harm in a man buying food for a fraction of a dirham on credit and then giving a dirham and taking goods with what remains of his dirham because he gave the fraction he owed as silver, and took goods to make up the rest of his dirham. There is no harm in such a transaction."

Mālik said, "There is no harm in a man placing a dirham with another man and then taking from him agreed goods for a fourth, third or a known fraction. If there was not an agreed price on the goods and the man said, 'I will take them from you for the price of each day,' this is not lawful because there is uncertainty. It might be less one time and more another time, and they would not part with an agreed sale."

Mālik said, "If someone sells some food without measuring precisely and does not exclude any of it from the sale and then it occurs to him to buy some of it, it is not good for him to buy any of it, except what it would be permitted for him to exclude from it: that is a third or less. If it is more than a third, it becomes *muzābana* and is disapproved. He must only purchase from what he would be permitted to exclude, and he is only permitted to exclude a third or less than that. This is the way of doing things in which there is no dispute with us."

31.24 Hoarding and raising prices by stockpiling[4]

56 Yaḥyā related to me from Mālik that he had heard that 'Umar ibn al-Khaṭṭāb said, "There is no hoarding in our market and men who have excess gold in their hands should not buy up one of Allah's provisions, which He has sent to our courtyard, and then hoard it up against us. Someone who brings imported goods through great fatigue to himself in the summer and winter, such a person is the guest of 'Umar. Let him sell what Allah wills and keep what Allah wills."

57 Yaḥyā related to me from Mālik from Yūnus ibn Yūsuf from Sa'īd ibn al-Musayyab that 'Umar ibn al-Khaṭṭāb passed by Ḥatab ibn Abī Baltha'a who was underselling some of his raisins in the market. 'Umar ibn al-Khaṭṭāb said to him, "Either increase the price or leave our market."

4 Hoarding (*ḥukra*) applies to essential commodities like staple foods.

58 Yaḥyā related to me from Mālik that he had heard that 'Uthmān ibn 'Affān forbade hoarding.

31.25 What is permitted in bartering animals for other animals and advances on animals

59 Yaḥyā related to me from Mālik from Ṣāliḥ ibn Kaysān from Ḥasan ibn Muḥammad ibn 'Alī ibn Abī Ṭālib that 'Alī ibn Abī Ṭālib sold one of his camels called 'Usayfir for twenty camels to be delivered later.

60 Yaḥyā related to me from Mālik from Nāfi' that 'Abdullāh ibn 'Umar bought a female riding-camel for four camels and guaranteed to deliver them in full to the buyer at ar-Rabadha.

61 Yaḥyā related to me that Mālik asked Ibn Shihāb about selling animals, two for one with delayed terms. He said, "There is no harm in it."

Mālik said, "The generally agreed-on way of doing things among us is that there is no harm in bartering a camel for a camel like it and adding some dirhams to the exchange, from hand to hand. There is no harm in bartering a camel for a camel like it with some dirhams on top of the exchange, the camels to be exchanged from hand to hand, and the dirhams to be paid within a period."

He said, "There is no good in bartering a camel for a camel like it with some dirhams on top of it, with the dirhams paid immediately and the camel to be delivered later. If both the camel and the dirhams are deferred there is no good in that either."

Mālik said, "There is no harm in buying a riding-camel with two or more pack-camels, if they are from inferior stock. There is no harm in bartering two of them for one with delayed terms if they are different and their difference is clear. If they resemble each other whether their species are different or not, two are not to be taken for one with delayed terms."

Mālik said, "The explanation of what is disapproved of in that is that a camel should not be bought with two camels when there is no distinction between them in speed or hardiness. If this is according to what I have described to you, then one does not buy two of them for one with delayed terms. There is no harm in selling those of them you buy before you complete the deal to somebody other than the one from whom you brought them if you get the price in cash."

Mālik said, "It is permitted for someone to advance something on animals for a fixed term and describe the amount and pay its price in cash. Whatever the buyer and seller have described is obliged for them. That is still the permitted behaviour between people and what the people of knowledge in our land do."

31.26 What is not permitted in the sale of animals

62 Yaḥyā related to me from Mālik from Nāfi' from 'Abdullāh ibn 'Umar that the Messenger of Allah ﷺ forbade the transaction called *ḥabal al-ḥabala*. It was a transaction which the people of *Jāhiliyya* practised. A man would buy the unborn offspring of the unborn offspring of a she-camel.

63 Yaḥyā related to me from Mālik from Ibn Shihāb that Sa'īd ibn al-Musayyab said, "There is no usury in animals. There are three things forbidden in animals: *al-maḍamīn*, *al-malāqīh* and *ḥabal al-ḥabala*. *Al-maḍāmīn* is the sale of what is in the wombs of female camels. *Al-malāqīḥ* is the sale of the breeding qualities of camels" (i.e. for stud).

Mālik said, "No-one should buy a specified animal when it is concealed from him or in another place, even if he has already seen it very recently or not so recently and was pleased enough with it to pay its price in cash."

Mālik said, "That is disapproved of because the seller makes use of the price and it is not known whether or not those goods will be found to be as the buyer saw them or not. For that reason, it is disapproved of. There is no harm in it if it is described and guaranteed."

31.27 Selling animals in exchange for meat

64 Yaḥyā related to me from Mālik from Zayd ibn Aslam from Sa'īd ibn al-Musayyab that the Messenger of Allah ﷺ forbade bartering live animals for meat.

65 Yaḥyā related to me from Mālik from Dāwūd ibn al-Ḥusayn that he heard Sa'īd ibn al-Musayyab say, "Part of the gambling of the people of *Jāhiliyya* was bartering live animals for slaughtered meat, for instance, one live sheep for two slaughtered sheep."

66 Yaḥyā related to me from Mālik from Abū az-Zinād that Sa'īd ibn al-Musayyab said, "Bartering live animals for dead meat is forbidden." Abū az-Zinād said, "I said to Sa'īd ibn Musayyab, 'What do you think of a man buying an old camel for ten sheep?'" Sa'īd said, "If he buys it to slaughter it, there is no good in it."

Abū az-Zinād added, "All the people (i.e. Companions) that I have seen forbade bartering live animals for meat."

Abū az-Zinād said, "This used to be written in the appointment letters of governors in the time of Abān ibn 'Uthmān and Hishām ibn Ismā'īl."

31.28 Selling meat for meat

67 Mālik said, "It is the generally agreed-on way of doing things among us that the meat of camels, cattle, sheep and so on is not to be bartered one for one, except like for like, weight for weight, from hand to hand. There is no harm in that. If it is not weighed, then it is estimated to be like for like from hand to hand."

Mālik said, "There is no harm in bartering the meat of fish for the meat of camels, cattle and sheep and so on two or more for one, from hand to hand. If delayed terms enter into the transaction, however, there is no good in it."

Mālik said, "I think that poultry is different from the meat of cattle and fish. I see no harm in selling some of one kind for some of another kind, more of one than another, from hand to hand. None of that is to be sold on delayed terms."

31.29 Selling dogs

68 Yaḥyā related to me from Mālik from Ibn Shihāb from Abū Bakr ibn 'Abd ar-Raḥmān ibn al-Ḥārith ibn Hishām from Abū Mas'ūd al-Anṣārī that the Messenger of Allah ﷺ made unlawful the sale of a dog, the earnings of a prostitute and the earnings of a fortune-teller.

By the earnings of a prostitute he meant what a woman was given for fornication. The earnings of a fortune-teller were what he was given to tell a fortune.

Mālik said, "I disapprove of selling a dog, whether it is a hunting dog or otherwise, because the Messenger of Allah ﷺ forbade the sale of a dog."

31.30 Advance and sale of some goods for others

69 Yaḥyā related to me from Mālik that he had heard that the Messenger of Allah ﷺ forbade 'selling and lending'.

Mālik said, "The explanation of what that means is that one man says to another, 'I will take your goods for such-and-such if you lend me such-and-such,' If they agree to a transaction in this manner, it is not permitted. If the one who proposes the loan abandons his proposition, then the sale is permitted."

Mālik said, "There is no harm in exchanging linen from Shata for garments from Itribi or Qass or Ziq, or the cloth of Herat or Merv for Yemeni cloaks and shawls and such like, as one for two or three, from hand to hand or with delayed terms. If the goods are of the same kind, and deferment enters into the transaction, there is no good in it."

Mālik said, "It is not good unless they are different and the difference between them is clear. When they resemble each other, even if the names are different, do not take two for one with delayed terms, for instance, two garments of Herat for one from Merv or a Quhy with delayed terms, or two garments of Furqub for one from Shata. All these sorts conform to the same description, so do not buy two for one, on delayed terms."

Mālik said, "There is no harm in selling what you buy of such things, before you complete the deal, to someone other than the person from whom you purchased them, if the price was paid in cash."

31.31 An advance on goods

70 Yaḥyā related to me from Mālik from Yaḥyā ibn Sa'īd that al-Qāsim ibn Muḥammad said, "I heard 'Abdullāh ibn 'Abbās say to a man who asked him about someone making an advance on some garments and then wanting to sell them back before taking possession of them, 'That is silver for silver,' and he disapproved of it."

Mālik said, "Our opinion is – and Allah knows best – that was because he wanted to sell them to the person from whom he had bought them for more than the price for which he bought them. Had he sold them to someone other than the person from whom he had purchased them, there would not have been any harm in it."

Mālik said, "The generally agreed-on way of doing things among us, concerning making an advance for slaves, cattle or goods, is that when all of what is to be sold is described and an advance is made for them for a date, and the date falls due, the buyer does not sell any of that to the person from whom he purchased it for more than the price which he advanced for it before he has taken full possession of what he has advanced for it. It is usury if he does. If the buyer gives the seller dinars or dirhams and he profits with them, then, when the goods come to the buyer and he does not take them into his possession but sells them back to their owner for more than what he advanced for them, the outcome is that what he has advanced has returned to him and has been increased for him."

Mālik said, "If someone advances gold or silver for described animals or goods which are to be delivered before a named date, and the date arrives, or it is before or after the date, there is no harm in the buyer selling those goods to the seller for other goods to be taken immediately and not delayed, no matter how extensive the amount of those goods is, except in the case of food because it is not lawful to sell food before he has full possession of it. The buyer can sell those goods to someone other than the person from whom he purchased them for gold or silver or any goods. He takes possession of it and does not defer it because if he defers it, that is ugly and there enters into the transaction what is disapproved of – delay for delay. Delay for delay is to a sell debt against one man for a debt against another man."

Mālik said, "If someone advances for goods to be delivered after a time, and those goods are neither something to be eaten nor drunk, he can sell them to whomever he likes for cash or goods before he takes delivery of them to someone other than the person from whom he purchased them. He must not sell them to the person from whom he bought them except in exchange for goods which he takes possession of immediately and does not defer."

Mālik said, "If the delivery date for the goods has not arrived, there is no harm in selling them to the original owner for goods which are clearly different and which he takes immediate possession of and does not defer."

Mālik spoke about the case of a man who advanced dinars or dirhams for four specified pieces of cloth to be delivered before a specified time and, when the term fell due, he demanded delivery from the seller but the seller did not have them. He found that the seller had cloth of inferior quality, and the seller said that he would give him eight of those cloths. Mālik said, "There is no harm in that if he takes the cloths which are offered him before they separate. It is not good if delayed terms enter into the transaction. It is also not good if that is before the end of the term unless he sells him cloth which is not the type of cloth for which he made an advance."

31.32 Selling weighable items like copper and iron and similar things

71 Mālik said, "The generally agreed-on way of doing things among us about whatever is weighed but is not gold or silver, i.e. copper, brass, lead, black lead, iron, herbs, figs, cotton and any such things that are weighed, is that there is no harm in bartering all those sorts of things two for one, hand to hand. There is no harm in taking a *riṭl* of iron for two *riṭls* of iron, and a *riṭl* of brass for two *riṭls* of brass."

Mālik said, "There is no good in two for one of the same sort with delayed terms. There is no harm in taking two of one sort for one of another on delayed terms, if the two sorts are clearly different. If both sorts resemble each other but their names are different, like lead and black lead, brass and yellow brass, I disapprove of taking two of one sort for one of the other on delayed terms."

Mālik said, "When buying something of this nature, there is no harm in selling it before taking possession of it to someone other than the person from whom it was purchased, if the price is taken immediately and if it was bought originally by measure or weight. If it was bought without measuring, it should be sold to someone other than the person from whom it was bought, for cash or with delayed terms. That is because goods have to be guaranteed when they are bought by weight until they are weighed and the deal is completed. This is the best of what I have heard about all these things. It is what people continue to do among us."

Mālik said, "The way of doing things among us with what is measured or weighed of things which are not eaten or drunk, like safflower, date-stones, fodder-leaves, indigo dye and suchlike, is that there is no harm in bartering all such sorts of things two for one, hand to hand. Do not take two for one from the same variety with delayed terms. If the types are clearly different, there is no harm in taking two of one for one of the other with delayed terms. There is no harm in selling whatever is purchased of all these sorts, before taking delivery of them, if the price is taken from someone other than the person from whom they were purchased."

Mālik said, "In the case of anything of any variety that profits people, like gravel and gypsum, one quantity of them for two of its like with delayed terms is usury. One quantity of both of them for its equal plus any increase with delayed terms is usury."

31.33 Prohibition against two sales in one

72 Yaḥyā related to me from Mālik that he had heard that the Messenger of Allah ﷺ forbade two sales in one sale.

73 Yaḥyā related to me from Mālik that he had heard that a man said to another, "Buy this camel for me immediately so that I can buy it from you on credit." 'Abdullāh ibn 'Umar was asked about that and he disapproved of it and forbade it.

74 Yaḥyā related to me from Mālik that he had heard that al-Qāsim ibn Muḥammad was asked about a man who bought goods for ten dinars cash or fifteen dinars on credit. He disapproved of that and forbade it.

Mālik said that if a man bought goods from a man for either ten dinars cash or fifteen dinars on credit, then one of the two prices was obliged on the buyer. Such a thing was not to be done because if he postponed paying the ten, it would be fifteen on credit, and if he paid the ten, he would buy with it what was worth fifteen dinars on credit.

Mālik said that it was disapproved of for a man to buy goods from someone for either one dinar cash or for a described sheep on credit and that one of the two prices was obliged on him. It was not to be done because the Messenger of Allah ﷺ forbade two sales in one sale. This was a kind of two sales in the one.

Mālik spoke about a man saying to another, "I will either buy these fifteen *ṣā's* of *'ajwa* dates from you, or these ten *ṣā's* of *ṣayḥānī* dates, or I will buy these fifteen *ṣā's* of inferior wheat, or these ten *ṣā's* of Syrian wheat for a dinar, and one of them is obliged on me." Mālik said that it was disapproved of and was not lawful. That was because he obliged him ten *ṣā's* of *ṣayḥānī*, and left them and took fifteen *ṣā's* of *'ajwa*, or he was obliged fifteen *ṣā's* of inferior wheat and left them and took ten *ṣā's* of Syrian wheat. This was also disapproved of, and was not lawful. It resembled what was prohibited in the way of two sales in one sale. It was also included under the prohibition against buying two for one of the same sort of food.

31.34 Transactions with uncertainty in them

75 Yaḥyā related to me from Mālik from Abū Ḥāzim ibn Dīnār from Sa'īd ibn al-Musayyab that the Messenger of Allah ﷺ forbade the sale with uncertainty in it.

Mālik said, "An example of one type of uncertain transaction and risk is that a man postulates the price of a stray animal or escaped slave to be fifty dinars. A man says, 'I will take him from you for twenty dinars.' If the buyer finds him, the seller loses thirty dinars, and if he does not find him, the seller takes twenty dinars from the buyer."

Mālik said, "There is another fault in that. If that stray is found, it is not known whether it will have increased or decreased in value or what defects may have befallen it. This transaction is full of uncertainty and risk."

Mālik said, "According to our way of doing things, one kind of uncertain transaction and risk is selling what is in the wombs of females – both women and animals – because it is not known whether or not it will come out, and if it does comes out, it is not known whether it will be beautiful or ugly, normal or disabled, male or female. All that is disparate. If it is so, its price is such-and-such, and if it is so, its price is such-and-such."

Mālik said, "Females must not be sold with what is in their wombs excluded. That is, for instance, that a man says to another, 'The price of my sheep which has much milk is three dinars. She is yours for two dinars while I will have her future offspring.' This is disapproved of because it is an uncertain transaction and a risk."

Mālik said, "It is not lawful to sell olives for olive oil or sesame for sesame oil, or butter for ghee because *muzābana* comes into that on account of the fact that the person, who buys the raw product for something specified which comes from it, does not know whether more or less will come out of that, so it is an uncertain transaction and a risk."

Mālik said, "A similar case is the bartering of ben-nuts for ben-nut oil. This is an uncertain transaction because what comes from the ben-nut is ben-oil. There is no harm in selling ben-nuts for perfumed ben-oil because perfumed ben-oil has been perfumed, mixed and changed from the state of raw ben-nut oil."

Mālik, speaking about a man who sold goods to another on the provision that there was to be no loss for the buyer (i.e. sale or return), said, "This transaction is not permitted and it is part of risk. The explanation of why it is so is that it is as if the seller hired the buyer for the profit if the goods make a profit. If he sells the goods at a loss, he has nothing, and his efforts are not compensated. This is not good. In such a transaction, the buyer should have a wage according to the work that he has contributed. Whatever there is of loss or profit in such goods is for and against the seller. This is only when the goods are gone and sold. If they do not go, the transaction between them is null and void."

Mālik said, "As for a man who buys goods from a man and then the buyer regrets and asks to have the price reduced and the seller refuses and says, 'Sell it and I will compensate you for any loss,' there is no harm in this because there is no risk. It is something he proposes to him, and their transaction is not based on that. That is what is done among us."

31.35 *Al-mulāmasa* and *al-munābadha*

76 Yaḥyā related to me from Mālik from Muḥammad ibn Yaḥyā ibn Ḥabbān and from Abū az-Zinād from al-A'raj from Abū Hurayra that the Messenger of Allah ﷺ forbade *mulāmasa* and *munābadha*.

Mālik said, "*Mulāmasa* is when a man can feel a garment but does not know what is in it. *Munābadha* is that a man throws his garment to another, and the other throws his garment without either of them making any inspection. Each of them says, 'This is for this.' This is what is forbidden of *mulāmasa* and *munābadha*."

Mālik said that selling bundles with a list of their contents was different from the sale of the cloak concealed in a bag or the cloth folded up and such things. What made it different was that it was a common practice which people were familiar with, and which people had done in the past, and it was still among the permitted transactions and trading of people in which they saw no harm, because in the sale of bundles with a list of contents without undoing them, an uncertain transaction was not intended and it did not resemble *mulāmasa*.

31.36 *Murābaḥa* transactions (partnership between investors and borrowers in profit-sharing re-sales)

77 Yaḥyā related to me that Mālik said, "The generally agreed-on way of doing things among us, about a man buying cloth in one city and then taking it to another city to sell as a *murābaḥa,* is that he is not reckoned to have the wage of an agent or any allowance for ironing, folding, straightening, expenses, or the rent of a house. As for the cost of transporting the drapery, it is included in the basic price and no share of the profit is allocated to it unless the agent tells all of that to the investor. If they agree to share the profits accordingly after knowledge of it, there is no harm in that."

Mālik continued, "As for bleaching, tailoring, dyeing and such things, they are treated in the same way as drapery. The profit is reckoned in them as it is reckoned in drapery goods. So if he sells the drapery goods without clarifying the things we named as not getting profit, and the drapery has already gone, the transport is to be reckoned, but no profit is given. If the drapery goods have not gone, the transaction between them is null and void, unless they make a new mutual agreement on what is to be permitted between them."

Mālik spoke about an agent who bought goods for gold or silver and the exchange rate on the day of purchase was ten dirhams to the dinar. He took them to a city to sell as a *murābaḥa*, or sold them where he purchased them according to the exchange rate of the day on which he sold them. If he bought them for dirhams and sold them for dinars, or he bought them for dinars and sold them for dirhams, and the goods had not gone, then he had a choice. If he wished, he could accept to sell the goods, and if he wished, he could leave them. If the goods had been sold, he had the price for which the salesman bought them, and the salesman was reckoned to have the profit on what they were bought for, over what the investor gained as profit.

Mālik said, "If a man sells goods worth one hundred dinars for one hundred and ten, and he hears afterwards that they are worth ninety dinars, and the goods have gone, the seller has a choice. If he likes, he has the price of the goods on the day they were taken from him, unless the price is more than the price for which he was obliged to sell them in the first place, and he does not have more than that – and it is one hundred and ten dinars. If he likes, it is counted as profit against ninety unless the price his goods reached was less than the value. He is given the choice between what his goods fetch and the capital plus the profit, which is ninety-nine dinars."

Mālik said, "If someone sells goods on the basis of a *murābaḥa* [cost plus sale] and says, 'If was valued for me at one hundred dinars,' and then finds later on that its value was one hundred and twenty dinars, the buyer is given a choice: he can give the buyer the price of the goods if he so wishes, or, if he wishes, he can give him the price for which he bought them based on reckoning the amount of the profit achieved in them, whatever it is, provided that it is not less than the price for which he purchased the goods. He should not give the owner of the goods a loss in the price for which he bought them because he consented to that. The owner of the goods cam to seek more, so the buyer has no argument against the seller in this by which he can reduce the price for which he bought them according to the list of contents."

31.37 Sales according to a list of contents

78 Mālik spoke about what was done among them in the case of a group of people which buys goods, drapery or slaves, when a man, hearing about it, says to one of the group, "I have heard the description and

situation of the drapery goods you bought from so-and-so, shall I give you such-and-such profit to take over your portion?" This person agrees, and the man gives him the profit and becomes a partner in his place. Then, when he looks at the purchase, he sees that is was ugly and finds it too expensive.

Mālik said, "It is obliged on him and there is no choice in it for him if he buys it according to a list of contents and the description is well-known."

Mālik spoke about a man who has had drapery goods sent to him, and merchants come to him and he reads to them his list of contents and says, "In each bag is such-and-such a wrap from Basra and such-and-such a light wrap from Sabir. Their size is such-and-such," and he names to them types of drapery goods by their sort and says, "Buy them from me according to this description." They buy the bags according to how he has described them and then, having bought them, they find them too expensive and regret it. Mālik said, "The sale is binding on them if the goods agree with the list of contents against which he sold them."

Mālik said, "This is the way of doing things which people still use today. They permit the sale which names the items when the goods agree with the list of contents and are not different from it."

31.38 The right of withdrawal (*khiyār*)

79 Yaḥyā related to me from Mālik from Nāfi' from 'Abdullāh ibn 'Umar that the Messenger of Allah ﷺ said, "Both parties in a business transaction have the right of withdrawal as long as they have not separated, unless it is a sale subject to an option."

Mālik said, "There is no specified limit nor any matter which is applied in this case according to us."

80 Mālik related to me that he had heard that 'Abdullāh ibn Mas'ūd used to relate that the Messenger of Allah ﷺ said, "When two parties dispute about a business transaction, the seller's word is taken, or they agree to annul the sale."

Mālik spoke about someone who sells goods to a man and says when the sale is contracted, "I will sell to you provided I consult so-and-so. If he is satisfied, the sale is permitted. If he dislikes it, there is no sale between us." They make the transaction on this basis and then the buyer regrets the transaction before the seller has consulted the person.

Mālik said, "The sale is binding on them according to what they described. The buyer has no right of withdrawal and the sale is binding on him if the person whom the seller stipulates to him permits it."

Mālik said, "The way of doing things among us about a man who buys goods from another and they differ about the price, and the seller says, 'I sold them to you for ten dinars,' and the buyer says, 'I bought them from you for five dinars,' is that it is said to the seller, 'If you like, give them to the buyer for what he has mentioned. If you like, swear by Allah that you only sold your goods for what you have mentioned.' If he swears it is said to the buyer, 'Either you take the goods for what the seller has mentioned or you swear by Allah that you bought them only for what you have mentioned.' If he swears, he is free to return the goods. That is when each of them testifies against the other."

31.39 Usury in debts

81 Yaḥyā related to me from Mālik from Abū az-Zinād from Busr ibn Sa'īd from 'Ubayd Abū Ṣāliḥ, the *mawlā* of aṣ-Ṣaffāh, that he said, "I sold some drapery to the people of Dār Nakhla on credit. Then I wanted to go to Kufa, so they proposed that I reduced the price for them and they would pay me immediately. I asked Zayd ibn Thābit about it and he said, 'I order you not to accept increase or to allow it to anybody.'"

82 Yaḥyā related to me from Mālik from 'Uthmān ibn Ḥafṣ ibn Khalda from Ibn Shihāb from Sālim ibn 'Abdullāh that 'Abdullāh ibn 'Umar was asked about a man who took a loan from another man for a set term. The creditor reduced the debt and the man paid it immediately. 'Abdullāh ibn 'Umar disliked that and forbade it.

83 Mālik related to me that Zayd ibn Aslam said, "Usury in the *Jāhiliyya*

was that a man would give a loan to a man for a set term. When the term was due, he would say, 'Will you pay it off or increase me?' If the man paid he took it. If not, he increased him in his debt and lengthened the term for him."

Mālik said, "The disapproved way of doing things about which there is no dispute among us is that a man gives a loan to a man for a term and then the demander reduces it and the one from whom it is demanded pays it in advance. To us that is like someone who delays repaying his debt after it is due to his creditor and his creditor increases his debt." Mālik said, "This is nothing else but usury – no doubt about it."

Mālik spoke about a man who loaned one hundred dinars to a man for two terms. When it was due, the person who owed the debt said to him, "Sell me some goods whose price is one hundred dinars in cash for one hundred and fifty on credit." Mālik said, "This transaction is not good, and the people of knowledge still forbid it."

Mālik said, "This is disapproved of because the creditor gives the debtor the price of what the man sells him, and he defers payment of the hundred of the first transaction for the debtor for the term which is mentioned to him in the second transaction, and the debtor increases him with fifty dinars for deferring him. That is disapproved of and it is not good. It also resembles the *ḥadīth* of Zayd ibn Aslam about the transactions of the people of the *Jāhiliyya*. When their loans came, they said to the person with the debt, 'Either you pay in full or you increase it.' If they paid, they took it. If not they increased the debtors in their debts and extended the term for them."

31.40 Debts and transfer of debts in general

84 Yaḥyā related to me from Mālik from Abū az-Zinād from al-A'raj from Abū Hurayra that the Messenger of Allah ﷺ said, "Delay in payment by a rich man is injustice, but when one of you is referred to a solvent man for payment, let him accept the referral."

85 Mālik related to me from Mūsā ibn Maysara that he heard a man say

to Sa'īd ibn al-Musayyab, "I am a man who sells for a debt." Sa'īd said, "Do not sell except for what you take directly to your camel."

Mālik spoke about a person who buys goods from a man provided that he provides him with those goods by a specific date, either in time for a market in which he hopes that he can sell them, or to fulfill a need whose time he stipulates. Then the seller fails him about the date and the buyer wants to return the goods to the seller. Mālik said, "The buyer cannot do that, and the sale is binding on him. If the seller does bring the goods before the completion of the term, the buyer cannot be forced to take them."

Mālik spoke about a person who buys food and measures it. Then someone comes to him to buy it and he tells him that he has measured it for himself and taken it in full. The new buyer wants to trust him and accept his measure. Mālik said, "Whatever is sold in this way for cash has no harm in it, but whatever is sold in this way on delayed terms is disapproved of until the new buyer measures it out for himself. The sale with delayed terms is disapproved of because it leads to usury and it is feared that goods will be circulated in this way without weight or measure. If the terms are delayed it is disapproved of and there is no disagreement about that with us."

Mālik said, "One should not buy a debt owed by a man whether present or absent, without the confirmation of the one who owes the debt, nor should one buy a debt owed to a man by a dead person even if one knows what the deceased man has left. That is because to buy it is an uncertain transaction and one does not know whether the transaction will be completed or not."

He said, "The explanation of what is disapproved of in buying a debt owed by someone absent or dead is that it is not known what unknown debtors may have claims on the dead person. If the dead person is liable for another debt, the price which the buyer gives on strength of the debt may become worthless."

Mālik said, "There is another fault in that as well. He is buying something which is not guaranteed for him and so, if the deal is not completed, what he has paid becomes worthless. This is an uncertain transaction and it is not good."

Mālik said, "One distinguishes between a man who is only selling what he actually has and a man who is being paid in advance for something which is not yet in his possession. The man advancing the money brings his gold which he intends to buy with. The seller says, 'This is ten dinars. What do you want me to buy for you with it?' It is as if he sold ten dinars cash for fifteen dinars to be paid later. Because of this, it is disapproved of. It is something leading to usury and fraud."

31.41 Partnership, transferral of responsibility to an agent and revocation

86 Mālik said that there was no harm if a man who was selling some drapery, and had excluded some garments by their markings, stipulated that he would chose the marked ones from that. If he did not stipulate that he would choose from them when he made the exclusion, I think that he is partner in the number of drapery goods which were purchased from him. That is because two garments can be alike in marking and greatly different in price.

Mālik said, "The way of doing things among us is that there is no harm in partnership, transferring responsibility to an agent and revocation when dealing with food and other things, whether or not possession was taken, when the transaction is with cash, and there is no profit, loss or deferment of its price. If profit or loss or deferment of the price from one of the two enters any of these transactions, it becomes a sale which is made lawful by what makes sales lawful, and made unlawful by what makes sale unlawful, and it is not partnership, transferring responsibility to an agent, or revocation."

Mālik spoke about someone who bought drapery goods or slaves, and the sale was concluded, then a man asked him to be his partner and he agreed and the new partner paid the whole price to the seller and then something happened to the goods which removed them from their possession. Mālik said, "The new partner takes the price from the original partner and the original partner demands from the seller the whole price, unless the original partner stipulated on the new partner during the sale and before the transaction with the seller was completed that the seller was responsible to him. If the transaction has ended and the seller has gone, the precondition of the original partner is void and the responsibility is his."

Mālik spoke about a man who asked another man to buy certain goods to share between them, and he wanted the other man to pay for him and he would sell the goods for the other man. Mālik said, "That is not good. When he says, 'Pay for me and I will sell it for you,' it becomes a loan which he makes to him in order that he sell it for him and, if those goods are destroyed or perish, the man who paid the price will demand from his partner what he put in for him. This is part of the advance which brings in profit."

Mālik said, "If a man buys goods and the sale is completed, and then a man says to him, 'Share half of these goods with me and I will sell them all for you,' that is lawful and there is no harm in it. The explanation of that is that this is a new sale and he sells him half of the goods provided that he sells the entire lot."

31.42 Bankruptcy of debtors

87 Yaḥyā related to me from Mālik from Ibn Shihāb from Abū Bakr ibn 'Abd ar-Raḥmān ibn al-Ḥārith ibn Hishām that the Messenger of Allah ﷺ said, "Whenever a man sells wares and then the buyer becomes bankrupt and the seller has not taken any of the price and he finds some of his property intact with the buyer, he is more entitled to it than anyone else. If the buyer dies, then the seller is the same as other creditors with respect to it."

88 Yaḥyā related to me from Mālik from Yaḥyā ibn Sa'īd from Abū Bakr ibn Muḥammad ibn 'Amr ibn Ḥazm from 'Umar ibn 'Abd al-'Azīz from Abū Bakr ibn 'Abd ar-Raḥmān ibn al-Ḥārith ibn Hishām from Abū Hurayra that the Messenger of Allah ﷺ said, "If anyone goes bankrupt and a man finds his own property intact with him, he is more entitled to it than anyone else."

Mālik spoke about a man who sold a man wares and the buyer went bankrupt. He said, "The seller takes whatever he finds of his goods. If the buyer has sold some of them and distributed them, the seller of the wares is more entitled to them than the creditors. What the buyer has distributed does not prevent the seller from taking whatever of it he finds. It is the seller's right if he has received any of the price from the buyer and he wants to return it to take what he finds of his wares, and in what he does not find he is like the other creditors."

Mālik spoke about someone who bought spun wool or a plot of land, and then did some work on it, like building a house on the plot of land or weaving the spun wool into cloth. Then he went bankrupt after he had bought it and the original owner of the plot said, "I will take the plot and whatever structure is on it." Mālik said, "That structure is not his. However, the plot and what is on it that the buyer has improved is appraised. Then one sees what the price of the plot is, and how much of that value is the price of the structure. They are partners in that. The owner of the plot has as much as his portion, and the creditors have the amount of the portion of the structure."

Mālik said, "The explanation of that is that the value of it all is fifteen hundred dirhams, and the value of the building is one thousand dirhams. The owner of the plot has a third, and the creditors have two-thirds."

Mālik said, "It is like that with spinning and other things of a similar nature in such circumstances when the buyer has a debt which he cannot repay. This is the normative practice in such cases."

Mālik said, "As for goods which have been sold and which the buyer has not improved, but those goods sell well and have gone up in price, so their owner wants them and the creditors also want them, then the creditors can choose between giving the owner of the goods the price for which he sold them and not giving him any loss and surrendering his goods to him.

"If the price of the goods has gone down, the one who sold them has a choice. If he likes, he can take his goods and then he has no claim to any of his debtor's property, and that is his right. If he likes, he can be one of the creditors and take a portion of his due and not take his goods. That is up to him."

Mālik said about someone who bought a slave-girl or animal and she gave birth while in his possession and then the buyer went bankrupt: "The slave-girl or the animal and the offspring belong to the seller unless the creditors desire it. In that case they give him his complete due and then they take it."

31.43 What is permitted of free loans

89 Yaḥyā related to me from Mālik from Zayd ibn Aslam from 'Atā' ibn Yasār that Abū Rāfi', the *mawlā* of the Messenger of Allah ﷺ, said, "The Messenger of Allah ﷺ borrowed a young camel and then the camels from the *zakāt* came to him."

Abū Rāfi' said, "He ordered me to repay the man his young camel. I said, 'I can only find a good camel in its seventh year among the camels.' The Messenger of Allah ﷺ said, 'Give it to him. The best of people are those who discharge their debts in the best manner.'"

90 Mālik related to me from Ḥumayd ibn Qays al-Makkī that Mujāhid said, "'Abdullāh ibn 'Umar borrowed some dirhams from a man, then he discharged his debt with dirhams better than them. The man said, "Abū 'Abd ar-Rahmān, these are better than the dirhams which I lent you.' 'Abdullāh ibn 'Umar said, 'I know that. But I am happy to do that.'"

Mālik said, "There is no harm in a person who has lent gold, silver, food or animals taking something better than what was lent when that is not a stipulation between them nor a custom. If that is by a stipulation or promise or custom, then it is disapproved, and there is no good in it."

He explained, "That is because the Messenger of Allah ﷺ discharged his debt with a good camel in its seventh year in place of a young camel which he borrowed, and 'Abdullāh ibn 'Umar borrowed some dirhams and repaid them with better ones. If that is from the goodness of the borrower, and it is not by a stipulation, promise or custom, it is lawful and there is no harm in it."

31.44 What is not permitted of free loans

91 Yaḥyā related to me from Mālik that he had heard that 'Umar ibn al-Khaṭṭāb said that he disapproved of one man lending another food on the condition that he gave it back to him in another city. He said, "Where is the transport?"

92 Mālik related to me that he had heard that a man came to 'Abdullāh ibn 'Umar and said, "Abū 'Abd ar-Rahmān, I gave a man a loan and stipulated that he gave me better than what I lent him." 'Abdullāh ibn 'Umar said, "That is usury."

'Abdullāh said, "Loans are of three types. A free loan which you lend by which you desire the pleasure of Allah, and so you have the pleasure of Allah. A free loan which you lend by which you desire the pleasure of your companion, so you have the pleasure of your companion. And a free loan which you lend by which you take what is impure by what is pure, and that is usury." He said, "What do you order me to do, Abū 'Abd ar-Raḥman?" He said, "I think that you should tear up the agreement. If he gives you less than what you lent him, take it and you will be rewarded. If he gives you better than what you lent him of his own good will, that is his gratitude to you and you have the wage of the period you gave him the loan."

93 Yaḥyā related to me from Mālik from Nāfi' that he heard 'Abdullāh ibn 'Umar say, "If someone lends something, let the only condition be that it is repaid."

94 Mālik related to me that he had heard that 'Abdullāh ibn Mas'ūd used to say, "If someone makes a loan, they should not stipulate better than it. Even if it is a handful of grass, it is usury."

Mālik said, "The generally agreed-on way of doing things among us is that there is no harm in borrowing any animals with a set description and itemisation, and one must return the like of them. This is not done in the case of female slaves. It is clear that it would lead to making lawful what is not lawful, so it is not good. The explanation of what is disapproved of in that, is that a man borrow a slave-girl and have intercourse with her as seems proper to him. Then he returns her to her owner. That is not good and it is not lawful. The people of knowledge still forbid it and do not give an indulgence to anyone in it."

31.45 What is forbidden of haggling and such transactions

95 Yaḥyā related to me from Mālik from Nāfi' from 'Abdullāh ibn 'Umar that the Messenger of Allah ﷺ said, "None of you should make a sale overriding the sale of his brother."

96 Mālik related to me from Abū az-Zinād from al-A'raj from Abū Hurayra that the Messenger of Allah ﷺ said, "Do not go out to meet the caravans for trade, do not bid against each other, outbidding in order to raise the price, and a townsman must not buy on behalf of a man of the desert, and do not tie up the udders of camels and sheep so that they appear to have a lot of milk, for a person who buys them after that has two recourses open to him after he milks them. If he is pleased with them, he keeps them and if he is displeased with them, he can return them along with a *ṣā'* of dates."

Mālik said, "The explanation of the words of the Messenger of Allah ﷺ according to what we think – and Allah knows best – 'do not bid against each other' is that it is forbidden for a man to offer a price over the price of his brother when the seller has inclined to the bargainer and made conditions about the weight of the gold and he has declared himself not liable for faults and such things by which it is recognised that the seller wants to make a transaction with the bargainer. This is what he forbade, and Allah knows best."

Mālik said, "There is no harm, however, in more than one person bidding against each other over goods put up for sale."

He said, "Were people to abandon haggling when the first person starts to haggle an unreal price might be taken and the disapproved would enter into the sale of the goods. This is still the way of doing things among us."

97 Mālik said from Nāfi' from 'Abdullāh ibn 'Umar that the Messenger of Allah ﷺ forbade *najsh*.

Mālik said, "*Najsh* is to offer a man more than the worth of his goods when you do not mean to buy them and someone else follows you in the bidding."

31.46 Business transactions in general

98 Yaḥyā related to me from Mālik from 'Abdullāh ibn Dīnār from 'Abdullāh ibn 'Umar that a man mentioned to the Messenger of Allah ﷺ that he was always being cheated in business transactions. The Messenger of Allah ﷺ said, "When you enter a transaction say, 'No trickery.' So whenever that man entered a transaction, he would say, 'No trickery.'"

99 Mālik related to me that Yaḥyā ibn Sa'īd heard Sa'īd ibn al-Musayyab say, "When you come to a land where they give full measure and full weight, stay there. When you come to a land where they shorten the measure and weight, then do not stay there very long."

100 Mālik related to me from Yaḥyā ibn Sa'īd that he heard Muḥammad ibn al-Munkadir say, "Allah loves his slave who is generous when he sells and generous when he buys, generous when he repays and generous when he asks for repayment."

Mālik said about a man who bought camels or sheep or dry goods or slaves or any goods without measuring precisely, "There is no buying without measuring precisely in anything which can be counted."

Mālik spoke about a man who gave a man goods to sell for him and set their price saying, "If you sell them for this price as I have ordered you to do, you will have a dinar (or something which he has specified which they are both satisfied with), if you do not sell them, you will have nothing." He said, "There is no harm in that when he names a price to sell them at and names a known fee. If he sells the goods, he takes the fee, and if he does not sell them, he has nothing."

Mālik said, "This is like saying to another man, 'If you capture my runaway slave or bring my stray camel, you will have such-and-such.'

This falls into the category of reward and not the category of giving a wage. If it had been in the category of giving a wage, it would not be good."

Mālik said, "As for a man who is given goods and told that, if he sells them, he will have a named percentage for every dinar, that is not good because whenever there is a dinar less than the price of the goods, he decreases the due which was named for him. This is an uncertain transaction. He does not know how much he will be given."

101 Mālik related to me that he asked Ibn Shihāb about a man who hired an animal and then re-hired it out for more than what he hired it for. He said, "There is no harm in that."

32. *Qirāḍ*

32.1 *Qirāḍ*

1 Mālik related to me from Zayd ibn Aslam that his father said, "'Abdullāh and 'Ubaydullāh, the sons of 'Umar ibn al-Khaṭṭāb, left with the army for Iraq. On the way home, they passed by Abū Mūsā al-Ash'arī, the Amīr of Basra. He greeted them and made them welcome and told them that if there was anything he could do to help them, he would do it. Then he said, 'There is some of the property of Allah which I want to send to the *Amīr al-Mu'minīn*, so I will lend it to you and you can buy wares from Iraq and sell them in Madīna. Then give the principal to the *Amīr al-Mu'minīn*, and you keep the profit.' They said that they would like to do that, and so he gave them the money and wrote to 'Umar ibn al-Khaṭṭāb to take the money from them. When they came to sell they made a profit. When they paid the principal to 'Umar he asked, 'Did he lend everyone in the army the like of what he lent you?' They said, 'No.' 'Umar ibn al-Khaṭṭāb said, 'He made you the loan because you are the sons of the *Amīr al-Mu'minīn*, so pay the principal and the profit.' 'Abdullāh was silent. 'Ubaydullāh said, 'You do not need to do this, *Amīr al-Mu'minīn*. Had the principal decreased or been destroyed, we would have guaranteed it.' 'Umar said, 'Pay it.' 'Abdullāh was silent and 'Ubaydullāh repeated what he had said. A man who was sitting with 'Umar said, '*Amīr al-Mu'minīn*, better that you make it a *qirāḍ* loan.' 'Umar said, 'I have made it a *qirāḍ*.' 'Umar then took the principal and half of the profit, and 'Abdullāh and 'Ubaydullāh, the sons of 'Umar ibn al-Khaṭṭāb, took half of the profit."

2 Mālik related to me from al-'Alā' ibn 'Abd ar-Raḥmān from his father

from his father that 'Uthmān ibn 'Affān gave him some money as *qirāḍ* to use provided the profit was shared between them.

32.2 What is permitted in *qirāḍ*

3 Mālik said, "The recognised and permitted form of *qirāḍ* is that a man take capital from an associate to use. He does not guarantee it and in travelling pays out of the capital for food and clothes and what he makes good use of, according to the amount of capital. That is, when he travels to do the work and the capital can support of it. If he remains with his people, he does not have expenses for clothing from the capital."

Mālik said, "There is no harm in the two parties in a *qirāḍ* helping each other by way of a favour when it is acceptable to them both."

Mālik said, "There is no harm in the investor of the capital buying some of the goods from the agent in the *qirāḍ* if that is acceptable and without conditions."

Mālik spoke about an investor making a *qirāḍ* loan to a man and his slave, to be used by both. He said, "That is permitted, and there is no harm in it because the profit is property for his slave, and the profit is not for the master until he takes it from him. It is like the rest of his earnings."

32.3 What is not permitted in *qirāḍ*

4 Mālik said, "When a man owes money to another man and he asks him to let it stay with him as a *qirāḍ*, that is disapproved of until the creditor receives his property. Then he can make it a *qirāḍ* loan or keep it. That is because the debtor may be in a tight situation and want him to defer that for an increase it in it."

Mālik spoke about an investor who made a *qirāḍ* loan to a man in which some of the principal was lost before being used. Then he used it and realised a profit. The agent wanted to make the principal the remainder of the money after what was lost from it.

Mālik said, "His statement is not accepted, and the principal is made up to its original amount from his profit. Then they divide what remains after the principal has been repaid according to the conditions of the *qirāḍ*."

Mālik said, "A *qirāḍ* loan is only good in gold and silver coin and it is never permitted in any kind of wares or goods or articles."

Mālik said, "There are certain transactions whose revocation becomes unacceptable if a long span of time passes after the transaction takes place. As for usury, there is never anything except its rejection whether it is a little or a lot. What is permitted in other than it is not permitted in it because Allah, the Blessed and the Exalted, said in His Book, '*But if you turn in repentance you may have your capital, without wronging and without being wronged.*' (2:279)"

32.4 Conditions permitted in *qirāḍ*

5 Yaḥyā said that Mālik spoke about an investor who made a *qirāḍ* loan and stipulated to the agent that only certain goods should be bought with his money or he forbade that certain goods, which he named, be bought. He said, "There is no harm in an investor making a condition on an agent in *qirāḍ* not to buy a certain kind of animal or goods which he specifies. It is disapproved of for an investor to make a such condition on an agent in *qirāḍ* unless what he orders him to buy is in plentiful supply and does not fail in winter or summer. There is no harm in that case."

Mālik spoke about an investor who loaned *qirāḍ* money and stipulated that a set sum out of the profit should be his alone without the agent sharing in it. He said, "That is not good, even if it is only one dirham – unless he stipulates that half the profit is his and half the profit is the agent's or a third or a fourth or whatever. When he names a percentage, whether great or small, everything specified by that is lawful. This is the *qirāḍ* of the Muslims."

He said, "It is also not good if the investor stipulates that one dirham or more of the profit is purely his, without the agent sharing it and then what remains of the profit to be divided in half between them. That is not the *qirāḍ* of the Muslims."

32.5 Conditions not permitted in *qirāḍ*

6 Yaḥyā said that Mālik said, "The person who puts up the principal must not stipulate that he has a portion of the profit alone without the agent sharing in it, nor must the agent stipulate that he has a portion of the profit alone without the investor sharing. In *qirāḍ*, there is no sale, no rent, no work, no advance, and no convenience which one party specifies to himself without the other party sharing, unless one party allows it to the other unconditionally as a favour which is accepted by both. Neither of the parties should make a condition over the other which increases him in gold or silver or food over the other party."

He said, "If any of that enters into the *qirāḍ*, it becomes hire, and hire is only good when it has known and fixed terms. The agent should not stipulate when he takes the principal that he repay or commission specific persons with the goods, nor that he take any of them for himself. When there is a profit, and it is time to separate the capital, then they divide the profit according to the terms of the contract. If the principal does not increase or there is a loss, the agent does not have to make up for what he spent on himself or for the loss. That falls to the investor from the principal. *Qirāḍ* is permitted upon whatever terms the investor and the agent make a mutual agreement – half the profit, or a third, or a fourth, or whatever."

Mālik said, "It is not permitted for the agent to stipulate that he use the *qirāḍ* for a certain number of years and that it not be taken back from him during that time."

He said, "It is not good for the investor to stipulate that the *qirāḍ* money should not be returned for a certain number of years which are specified, because the *qirāḍ* is not for a term. The investor loans it to an agent to use for him. If it seems proper to either of them to abandon the project and the money is coin, and nothing has been bought with it, it can be abandoned and the investor takes back his money. If it seems proper to the investor to take the *qirāḍ* loan back after goods have been purchased with it, he cannot do so until the buyer has sold the goods and they have become money. If it seems proper to the agent to return the loan, and it has been turned to goods, he cannot do so until he has sold them. He returns the loan in cash as he took it."

Mālik said, "It is not good for the investor to stipulate that the agent pay any *zakāt* due from his portion of the profit in particular, because by stipulating that, the investor stipulates fixed increase for himself from the profit because the portion of *zakāt* he would be liable for by his portion of the profit is removed from him.

"Nor is it permitted for the investor to stipulate to the agent to only buy from so-and-so, referring to a specific man. That is not permitted because by doing so he would become his hireling for a wage."

Mālik said about an investor in *qirāḍ* who stipulated a guarantee for an amount of money from the agent, "The investor is not permitted to stipulate conditions about his principal other than the conditions on which *qirāḍ* is based or according to the precedent of the *sunna* of the Muslims. If the principal is increased by the condition of guarantee, the investor has increased his share of the profit because of the position of the guarantee. But the profit is only to be divided according to what it would have been had the loan been given without the guarantee. If the principal is destroyed, I do not think that the agent has a guarantee held against him, because the stipulation of guarantee in *qirāḍ* is null and void."

Mālik spoke about an investor who gave *qirāḍ* money to a man and the man stipulated that he would only buy palms or animals with it because he sought to eat the dates or the offspring of the animals and he kept them for some time to use for himself. He said, "That is not permitted. It is not the *sunna* of the Muslims in *qirāḍ* unless he buys it and then sells it as other goods are sold."

Mālik said, "There is no harm in the agent stipulating on the investor the inclusion of a slave to help him, provided that the slave stands to gain along with them out of the investment, and when the slave only helps him with the investment, not with anything else."

32.6 *Qirāḍ* in Wares

7 Yaḥyā said that Mālik said, "No one should make a *qirāḍ* loan except in coin because the loan must not be in wares since loaning wares can only be worked in one of two ways: either the owner of the wares says to the agent, 'Take these wares and sell them. Buy and sell with the capital realized according to *qirāḍ*.' The investor stipulates increase for himself from the sale of his goods and what relieves him of expense in selling it. Or else he says, 'Barter with these goods and sell. When you are through, buy for me the like of my goods which I gave you. If there is increase, it is between you and me.' It may happen that the investor gives the goods to the agent at a time in which they are in demand and expensive, and then the agent returns them while they are cheap and having perhaps bought them for only a third of the original price or even less than that. The agent then has a profit of half the amount, by which the price of the wares has decreased, as his portion of the profit. Or he might take the wares at a time when their price is low and make use of them until he has a lot of money. Then those wares become expensive and their price rises when he returns them, so he buys them for all that he has, so that all his work and concern have been in vain. This is an uncertain transaction and it is not good. If, however, that is not known until it has happened, then the wage an agent in *qirāḍ* would be paid for selling that is looked at and he is given it for his concern. Then the money is *qirāḍ* from the day the money became cash and collected as coin and it is returned as a *qirāḍ* like that."

32.7 Hire in *qirāḍ*

8 Yaḥyā said that Mālik spoke about a man who made a *qirāḍ* loan to a man and he bought wares with it and transported them to a commercial centre. It was not profitable to sell them and the agent feared a loss if he sold them, so he hired transport to take them to another city, and he sold them there and made a loss, and the cost of the hire was greater than the principal.

Mālik said, "If the agent can pay the cost of the hire from what the wares realize, his way is that. Whatever portion of the hire is not covered by the principal, the agent must pay. The investor is not answerable for any of it. That is because the investor only ordered him to trade with the principal. The investor is not answerable for other than the principal. Had the investor been liable, it would have been an additional loss to him on top of the principal which he invested. The agent cannot put that onto the investor."

32.8 Overstepping in *qirāḍ*

9 Yaḥyā said that Mālik spoke about an investor who made a *qirāḍ* loan to a man who used it and made a profit. Then the man bought a slave-girl with all the profit and he had intercourse with her and she became pregnant by him, and so the capital decreased. Mālik said, "If he has money, the price of the slave-girl is taken from his property, and the capital is restored by it. If there is something left over after the money is paid, it is divided between them according to the first *qirāḍ*. If he cannot pay it, the slave-girl is sold so that the capital is restored from her price."

Mālik spoke about an investor who made a *qirāḍ* loan to a man, and the agent spent more than the amount of the *qirāḍ* loan when buying goods with it and paid the increase from his own money. Mālik said, "The investor has a choice if the goods are sold for a profit or loss or if they are not sold. If he wishes to take the goods, he takes them and pays the agent back what he put in for them. If the agent refuses, the investor is a partner for his share of the price in either increase and decrease according to what the agent paid extra for them from himself."

Mālik spoke about an agent who took *qirāḍ* money from a man and then gave it to another man to use as a *qirāḍ* without the consent of the investor. He said, "The agent is responsible for the property. If it is decreased, he is responsible for the loss. If there is a profit, the investor has his stipulation of the profit and then the agent has his stipulation of what remains of the money."

Mālik spoke about an agent who exceeded and borrowed some of the *qirāḍ* money he had and bought goods for himself with it. Mālik said, "If he has a profit, the profit is divided according to the condition between them in the *qirāḍ*. If he has a loss, he is responsible for the loss."

Mālik said about an investor who paid money to a man and the agent borrowed some of the cash and bought goods for himself with it, "The investor of the capital has a choice. If he wishes, he shares with him in the goods according to the *qirāḍ* and, if he wishes, he frees himself of them, and takes all of the principal back from *qirāḍ* agent. That is what is done with someone who oversteps."

32.9 Expenses permitted in *qirāḍ*

10 Yaḥyā said that Mālik spoke about an investor who made a *qirāḍ* loan to man. Mālik said, "When the investment is large, the travelling expenses of the agent are taken from it. He can use it to eat and clothe himself in an acceptable fashion according to the size of the investment. If it saves him from trouble he can take a wage from some of the capital if it is large and he cannot support himself. There are certain jobs which an agent or his like are not responsible for. Amongst them are collecting debts, transporting the goods, loading up and so forth. He can use the capital to hire someone to do that for him. The agent should not spend from the capital nor clothe himself from it while he resides with his family. It is only permitted for him to have expenses when he travels for the investment. The expenses are taken from the capital. If he is only trading with the property in the city in which he resides, he has no expenses or clothing from the capital."

Mālik spoke about an investor who paid *qirāḍ* money to an agent who went out with it and with his own capital. He said, "The expenses come from the *qirāḍ* and from his own capital according to their proportions."

32.10 Expenses not permitted in *qirāḍ*

11 Yaḥyā said that Mālik spoke about an agent who had *qirāḍ* money with him and he spent from it and clothed himself. He said, "He cannot give away any of it, and neither a beggar nor anyone else is to be given

any of it and he does not pay anyone compensation from it. If he meets some people and they bring out food and he brings out food, I hope it will be permitted for him to do so if he does not intend to bestow something on them. If he intends to do that or something like that without the permission of the investor, he must first get the sanction of the investor for it. If he sanctions it, there is no harm. If he refuses to sanction it, then he must repay it with like as compensation if he has something which is suitable."

32.11 Debts in *qirāḍ*

12 Yaḥyā said that Mālik said, "The generally agreed-on way of doing things among us about an investor, who extends *qirāḍ* money to an agent to buy goods, and the agent then sells the goods for a price to be paid later and has a profit in the transaction, and then the agent dies before he has received payment, is that, if his heirs want to take that money, they have their father's stipulated portion from the profit. That is theirs if they are trustworthy enough to take the payment. If they dislike collecting it from the debtor and they refer him to the investor, they are not obliged to collect it and there is nothing against them and nothing for them by their surrendering it to the investor. If they do collect it, they have a share of it and expenses, just as their father had. They take the place of their father. If they are not trustworthy enough to do so, they can bring someone reliable and trustworthy to collect the money. If he collects all the capital and all the profit, they are in the same position as their father was."

Mālik spoke about an investor who extended *qirāḍ* money to a man provided that he used it and was responsible for any delayed payment for which he sold it. He said, "This is an obligation on the agent. If he sells it for delayed payment, he is responsible for it."

32.12 Goods in *qirāḍ*

13 Yaḥyā said that Mālik spoke about the case when a man gives qirad money to another man and then that man asked the investor for a loan, or the investor asked him for a loan, or the investor left

some goods with that man to sell for him, or gave him some dinars with which to purchase merchandise for him. Mālik said, "There is nothing wrong if the investor leaves his goods with him when he knows that if he had asked the agent to do that when that agent was not in possession of his money, he would have done it because of the brotherhood existing between them or because that would have not been a burden for him, and also that if the agent had refused to do that, he would not have removed his money from him, or if the agent borrows from the investor or carries goods for him when he knows that if he had not had his money, he would still have done the same for him, and if he were to refuse to do that, he would not have demanded the return of his money. If that is true of both of them and it is by way of a mark of friendship between them and not a stipulation in the terms of the qirad, it is permitted and there is no harm in it. If there is a stipulation involved in that, or it is feared that the agent is doing that for the investor to ensure that he retains possession of his capital, or the investor does that because the agent is withholding his capital and will not return it to him, that is not permitted in a *qirāḍ* and it is part of what the people of knowledge forbid."

32.13 Loans in *qirāḍ*

14 Yaḥyā said that Mālik spoke about a man who loaned another man money and then the debtor asked him to leave it with him as a *qirāḍ*. Mālik said, "I do not like that unless he takes his money back from him, and then pays it to him as a *qirāḍ*, if he wishes, or, if he wishes, keeps it."

Mālik spoke about an investor who extended a man *qirāḍ* money and the man told him that it had gathered up with him and asked him to write it for him as a loan. He said, "I do not like that unless he takes his money from him and then lends it to him or keeps it as he wishes. That is only out of fear that he has lost some of it and wants to defer it so that he can make up what has been lost of it. That is disapproved of and is not permitted and it is not good."

32.14 Accounting in *qirāḍ*

15 Yaḥyā said that Mālik spoke about an investor extending *qirāḍ* money to an agent who made a profit and then wanted to take his share of the profit and the investor was away. He said, "He should not take any of it unless the investor is present. If he takes something from it, he is responsible for it until it is accounted for in the division of the capital."

Mālik said, "It is not permitted for the parties involved in a *qirāḍ* to account and divide property which is away from them until the capital is present and the investor is repaid the principal in full. Then they divide the profit into their agreed portions."

Mālik spoke about a man taking *qirāḍ* money and buying goods with it while he had a debt. Then his creditors sought and found him while he was in a city away from the investor and was in possession of profitable merchandise whose good quality was clear. They wanted him to sell the merchandise for them so that they could take his share of the profit. Mālik said, "None of the profit of the *qirāḍ* is taken until the investor is present. He takes his principal and then the profit is divided mutually between them."

Mālik spoke about an investor who put *qirāḍ* money with an agent and he used it and had a profit. Then the principal was set aside and the profit divided. He took his share and added the share of the investor to his principal in the presence of witnesses he had called. Mālik said, "It is not permitted to divide the profit unless the investor is present. If he has taken something he returns it until the investor has received the principal in full. Then what remains is divided into their respective portions."

Mālik spoke about an investor who put *qirāḍ* money with an agent. The agent used it and then came to the investor and said, "This is your portion of the profit, and I have taken the like of it for myself and I have retained your principal in full." Mālik said, "I do not like that unless all the capital is present, the principal is there, and he knows that it is complete and he receives it. Then they divide the profit between them. He returns the principal to him if he wishes, or he keeps it. The presence of the principal is necessary, out of fear that the agent might have lost some of it and so may want it not to be removed from him and to keep it in his hand."

32.15 A general view of *qirāḍ*

16 Yaḥyā said that Mālik spoke about an investor who put *qirāḍ* money with an agent who bought goods with it and the investor told him to sell them. The agent said that he did not see any way of selling them at that time and they quarrelled about it. He said, "One does not pay any attention to what either of them say. The people of experience and insight concerning such goods are asked about these goods. If they can see any way of selling them, they are sold for them. If they think that it is time to wait, then they should wait."

Mālik spoke about a man who took *qirāḍ* money from an investor and used it and, when the investor asked him for his money, he said that he had it in full. When he held him to his settlement, he admitted, "I have lost such-and-such," and named a certain amount of money. He further said, "I only told you that so that you would leave it with me." Mālik said, "He does not benefit by denying it after he had affirmed that he had all of it. He is answerable by his admission against himself unless he can produce evidence about the loss of that property, which confirms what he has said. If he does not produce an acceptable reason, he is answerable by his admission and his denial does not help him."

Mālik said, "Similarly, had he said, 'I have had such-and-such a profit from the capital,' and then the owner of the capital asks him to pay him the principal and his profit, and then he says that he did not have any profit in it and had only said that so that it might be left in his possession, that does not help him. He is taken to account for what he affirmed, unless he brings acceptable proof of what he has said so that the first statement is not binding on him."

Mālik spoke about an investor who put *qirāḍ* money with an agent who made a profit with it. The agent said, "I took the *qirāḍ* from you provided that I would have two-thirds." The owner of the capital says, "I gave you a *qirāḍ* on the condition that you took a third." Mālik said, "The statement taken is that of the agent, and he must take an oath on that if what he says resembles the known practice of *qirāḍ* or is close to it. If he brings a matter which is unacceptable and people do not make *qirāḍ* like that, he is not believed, and it is judged according to how a similar *qirāḍ* would normally be."

Mālik spoke about a man who gave a man one hundred dinars as a *qirāḍ*. He bought goods with it and then went to pay the one hundred dinars to the owner of the goods and found that they had been stolen. The investor says, "Sell the goods. If there is anything over, it is mine. If there is a loss, it is against you because you lost it." The agent says, "Rather you must fulfil what the seller is owed. I bought them with your capital which you gave me." Mālik said, "The agent is obliged to pay the price to the seller and the investor is told, 'If you wish, pay the hundred dinars to the agent and the goods are between you. The *qirāḍ* is according to what the first hundred was based on. If you wish, you are free of the goods.' If the hundred dinars are paid to the agent, it is a *qirāḍ* according to the conditions of the *qirāḍ*. If he refuses, the goods belong to the agent and he must pay their price."

Mālik spoke about two people in a *qirāḍ* who settled up and the agent still had some of the goods which he used – threadbare cloth or a waterskin or something like that. Mālik said, "Any of that which is insignificant is of no importance and belongs to the agent. I have not heard anyone give a decision calling for the return of that. Anything which has a price is returned. If it is something which has value like an animal, camel, coarse cloth or suchlike which fetches a price, I think that he should return what he has remaining of such things unless the owner overlooks it."

33. Cropsharing

33.1 Cropsharing

1 Yaḥyā said that Mālik from Ibn Shihāb from Sa'īd ibn al-Musayyab that the Messenger of Allah ﷺ said to the Jews of Khaybar on the day that Khaybar was conquered, "I confirm you in it as long as Allah, the Mighty, the Majestic, establishes you in it provided that the fruits are divided between you and us."

Sa'īd continued, "The Messenger of Allah ﷺ used to send 'Abdullāh ibn Rawāḥa to assess the division of the fruit crop between him and them, and he would say, 'If you wish, you can buy it back, and if you wish, it is mine.' They would take it."

2 Mālik related to me from Ibn Shihāb from Sulaymān ibn Yasār that the Messenger of Allah ﷺ used to send 'Abdullāh ibn Rawāḥa to Khaybar to assess the division of the fruit crop between him and the Jews of Khaybar.

The Jews collected pieces of their jewellery for 'Abdullāh and told him, "This is yours. Treat us lightly and do not be too exacting in the division!"

'Abdullāh ibn Rawāḥa said, "O tribe of Jews! By Allah, you are the most hateful to me of Allah's creation, but it does not prompt me to deal unjustly with you. What you have offered me as a bribe is forbidden. We will not touch it." They said, "This is what supports the heavens and the earth."

Mālik said, "If a cropsharer waters the palms and between them there is some uncultivated land, whatever he cultivates in the uncultivated land is his."

Mālik said, "If the owner of the land makes a condition that he will cultivate the uncultivated land for himself, that is not good because the cropsharer does the watering for the owner of the land and so he increases the property of the landowner (without any return for himself)."

Mālik said, "If the owner stipulates that the fruit crop is to be shared between them, there is no harm in that if all the maintenance of the property – seeding, watering and care etc. – are the concern of the cropsharer.

If the cropsharer stipulates that the seeds are the responsibility of the owner of the property, that is not permitted, because he has stipulated an outlay against the owner of the property. Cropsharing is contracted on the basis that all the care and expense is outlayed by the cropsharer, and the owner of the property is not obliged to do anything. This is the accepted method of cropsharing."

Mālik spoke about a spring which was shared between two men, and then the water dried up and one of them wanted to work on the spring and the other said, "I do not have the means to work on it." He said, "Tell the one who wants to work on the spring, 'Work and expend. All the water will be yours. You will have its water until your companion brings you half of what you have spent. If he brings you half of what you have spent, he can take his share of the water.' The first one is given all the water because he has spent out on it and, if he does not achieve anything by his work, the other has not incurred any expense."

Mālik said, "It is not good for a cropsharer to only expend his labour and to be hired for a share of the fruit while all the expense and work is incurred by the owner of the garden, because the cropsharer does not know what the exact wage is going to be for his labour, whether it will be little or great."

Mālik said, "No one who lends a *qirāḍ,* or grants a cropsharing contract, should except some of the wealth or some of the trees from his agent, because by that the agent becomes his hired man. He says, 'I will grant you a cropshare provided that you work for me on such-and-such a palm – water and tend it. I will give you a *qirāḍ* for so-much money, provided that you work for me for ten dinars. They are not part of the *qirāḍ* which I have given you.' That must not be done. It is not good. This is how things are done in our community."

Mālik said, "The *sunna* of what is permitted to an owner of a garden in cropsharing is that he can stipulate to the cropsharer the maintenance of walls, cleaning the spring, sweeping the irrigation canals, pollinating the palms, pruning branches, harvesting the fruit and such things, provided that the cropsharer has a share of the fruit fixed by mutual agreement. However, the owner cannot stipulate the beginning of new work which the agent will start – digging a well, raising the source of a well, instigating new planting, or building a cistern whose cost is great. That is as if the owner of the garden were to say to a certain man, 'Build me a house here or dig me a well or make a spring full for me or do some work for me for half the fruit of this garden of mine', before the garden is sound and it is lawful to sell it. This is the sale of fruit before its good condition is clear. The Messenger of Allah ﷺ forbade fruit to be sold before it was clear that it was in good condition."

Mālik continued, "If the fruits are good and their good condition is clear and selling them is lawful, and then the owner asks a man to do such a job for him, specifying the job, for half the fruit of his garden, for example, there is no harm in that. He has hired the man for something recognised and known. The man has seen it and it satisfied with it.

"As for cropsharing, if the garden has no fruit or little or bad fruit, he has only that. The labourer is only hired for a set amount, and hire is only permitted on these terms. Hire is a type of sale. One man buys another man's work from him. It is not good if uncertainty enters into it, because the Messenger of Allah ﷺ forbade uncertain transactions."

Mālik said, "The *sunna* in cropsharing with us is that it can be practised with any kind of fruit tree, palm, vine, olive tree, pomegranate, peach, and so on. It is permitted, and there is no harm in it, provided that the owner of the property has a share of the fruit: a half or a third or a quarter or whatever."

Mālik said, "Cropsharing is also permitted in any crop which emerges from the earth if it is a crop which is picked and its owner cannot water, work on it and tend it.

"Cropsharing becomes reprehensible in the case of anything in which cropsharing is normally permitted if the fruit is already sound and its good condition is clear and it is lawful to sell it. He must cropshare in it the next year. If a man waters fruit whose condition is clear and it is lawful to sell it, and he picks it for the owner for a share of the crop – it is not cropsharing. It is similar to him being paid in dirhams and dinars. Cropsharing is what is between pruning the palms and when the fruit becomes sound and its sale is lawful."

Mālik said, "If someone makes a cropsharing contract with fruit trees before the condition becomes clear and its sale is lawful, it is cropsharing and is permitted."

Mālik said, "Uncultivated land must not be involved in a cropsharing contract. That is because it is lawful for the owner to rent it for dinars and dirhams or the equivalent for an accepted price."

Mālik said, "As for a man who gives his uncultivated earth for a third or a fourth of what comes out of it, that is an uncertain transaction because crops may be scant one time and plentiful another time. It may perish completely and the owner of the land will have abandoned a set rent which would have been good for him to rent the land for. He takes an uncertain situation and does not know whether or not it will be satisfactory. This is disapproved. It is like a man having someone travel for him for a set amount and then saying, 'Shall I give you a tenth of the profit of the journey as your wage?' This is not lawful and must not be done."

Mālik summed up, "A man must not hire out himself or his land or his ship unless it is for set amount."

Mālik said, "A distinction is made between cropsharing in palms and in cultivated land because the owner of the palms cannot sell the fruit until its good condition is clear. The owner of the land can rent it when it is uncultivated with nothing on it."

Mālik said, "What is done in our community about palms is that they can also be cropshared for three and four years, and less or more than that."

Mālik said, "That is what I have heard. Any fruit trees like that are in the position of palms. Contracts for several years are permissible for the cropsharer as they are permissible in the palms."

Mālik said about the owner, "He does not take anything additional from the cropsharer in the way of gold or silver or crops which increase. That is not good. The cropsharer also must not take from the owner of the garden anything additional which will increase him in gold, silver, crops or anything. Increase beyond what is stipulated in the contract is not good. It is also not good for the lender of a *qirāḍ* to be in this position. If such an increase does enter cropsharing or *qirāḍ*, it becomes by it hire. It is not good when hire is involved. Hire must never occur in a situation which has uncertainty in it."

Mālik spoke about a man who gave land to another man in a cropsharing contract on some of which there were palms, vines, or other such fruit trees growing, and some of which was uncultivated. He said, "If the uncultivated land is secondary to the fruit trees, either in importance or in size of land, there is no harm in cropsharing. That is if the palms take up two-thirds of the land or more and the uncultivated land is a third or less. This is because when the land given over to fruit trees is secondary to the uncultivated land and the cultivated land in which the palms, vines, or the like is a third or less, and the uncultivated land is two-thirds or more, it is permitted to rent out that land and cropsharing in it is unlawful.

"One of the common practices of people is to enter into cropsharing contracts on property with fruit trees which has uncultivated land attached to it, and to rent land which has fruit trees on it, just as a

Qur'ān or a sword which has some silver embellishment on it is sold for silver, or a necklace or ring which have stones and gold in them are sold for dinars. These sales continue to be permitted. People buy and sell by them. No specific has been described or instituted about such things which, if exceeded, makes them unlawful, and, if fallen below makes them lawful. What is done in our community about them is what people have always practised and permitted among themselves. That is, if the gold or silver is secondary to what it is incorporated in, it is permitted to sell it. For instance, if the value of the blade, the Qur'ān, or the stones is two-thirds or more, and the value of the decoration is one-third or less."

33.2 The condition about slaves in cropsharing

3 Yaḥyā said that Mālik said, "The best of what has been heard about a cropsharer stipulating on the owner of the property the inclusion of some slave workers is that there is no harm in it if they are workers that are attached to the property. They are like the property. There is no profit in them for the cropsharer except to lighten some of his burden. If they did not come with the property, his toil would be harder. It is like cropsharing land with a spring or a watering-trough. You will not find anyone who receives the same share for cropsharing two lands which are equal in property and yield, when one property has a constant plentiful spring and the other has a watering-trough, because of the ease of working land with a spring and the hardship of working land with a watering-trough."

Mālik added, "This is what is done in our community."

Mālik said, "A cropsharer cannot employ workers from the property in other work, and he cannot make a stipulation with the contract holder. Nor is it permitted for the cropsharer to stipulate on the owner of the property inclusion of slaves for use in the garden who are not attached to it when he makes the cropsharing contract.

"Nor must the owner of the property stipulate to the cropsharer that the owner can take any particular slave attached to the property and remove him from the property. The cropsharing of property is based on the state which it is currently in.

"If the owner of the property wants to remove one of the slaves of the property, he removes him before the cropsharing, or if he wants to put someone into the property he does it before the cropsharing. Then he grants the cropsharing contract after that if he wishes. If any of the slaves die or go off or become ill, the owner of the property must replace them."

34. Renting Land

34.1 Renting land

1 Yaḥyā related to me from Mālik from Rabi'a ibn 'Abd ar-Raḥmān from Ḥanẓala ibn Qays az-Zuraqī from Rāfi' ibn Khadīj that the Messenger of Allah ﷺ forbade renting out fields.

Ḥanẓala said, "I asked Rāfi' ibn Khadīj about paying rent in gold and silver and he said, 'There is no harm in it'."

2 Mālik related to me that Ibn Shihāb said, "I asked Sa'īd ibn al-Musayyab about renting land for gold or silver and he said, 'There is no harm in it.'"

3 Mālik related to me from Ibn Shihāb that he asked Sālim ibn 'Abdullāh ibn 'Umar about renting out fields. He said, "There is no harm if it is done with gold or silver." Ibn Shihāb said, "I said to him, 'What do you think of the *ḥadīth* which is mentioned from Rāfi' ibn Khadīj?' He replied, 'Rāfi' has exaggerated. If I had a field, I would rent it out.'"

4 Mālik related to me that he had heard that 'Abd ar-Raḥmān ibn 'Awf rented some land which he remained on until he died. His son said, "I thought that it belonged to us, because of the length of time which it had been in his hands, until he mentioned it to us at his death. He ordered us to pay some rent which he owed in gold or silver."

5 Mālik related to me from Hishām ibn 'Urwa that his father used to rent out his land for gold and silver.

Mālik was asked about a man who rented out his field for one hundred *ṣā'ṣ* of dates or part of its produce of wheat or from produce from another source. He disapproved of that.

35. Pre-emption in Property

35.1 Cases in which pre-emption is possible

1 Yaḥyā related to me from Mālik from Ibn Shihāb from Sa'īd ibn al-Musayyab and from Abū Salama ibn 'Abd ar-Raḥmān ibn 'Awf that the Messenger of Allah ﷺ allocated partners the right of pre-emption in property which had not been divided up. When boundaries had been fixed between them, then there was no right of pre-emption.

Mālik said, "That is the *sunna* about which there is no dispute among us."

2 Mālik said that he had heard that Sa'īd al-Musayyab, when asked about pre-emption and whether there was any *sunna* about it, said, "Yes. Pre-emption applies to houses and land, and it only applies between shareholders."

3 Mālik related to me that he heard the like of that from Sulaymān ibn Yasār.

Mālik spoke about a man bringing one of his partners in a shared property by paying the man with an animal, a slave, a slave-girl or some such equivalent in goods. Then later on another of the partners decides to exercise his right of pre-emption, and he finds that the slave or slave-girl has died and no one knows what her value had been. The buyer claims that the value of the slave-girl was a hundred dinars while the partner with the right of pre-emption claims that her value was only fifty dinars.

Mālik said, "The buyer takes an oath that the value of his payment was a hundred dinars. Then, if the one with the right of pre-emption wishes, he can compensate him or else he can leave it, unless he can bring clear proof that the slave or slave-girl's value was less than what the buyer has said. If someone gives away his portion of a shared house or land and the recipient repays him for it with cash or goods, the partners can take it by pre-emption if they wish and pay off the recipient the value of what he gave in dinars or dirhams. If someone makes a gift of his portion of a shared house or land and does not take any remuneration and does not seek to do so, and a partner wants to take it for its value, he cannot do so as long as the original partner has not been given recompense for it. If there is any recompense, the one with the right of pre-emption can have it for the price of the recompense."

Mālik spoke about a man who bought into a piece of shared land for a price on credit and one of the partners wanted to possess it by right of pre-emption. Mālik said, "If it seems likely that the partner can meet the terms, he has the right of pre-emption for the same credit terms. If it is feared that he will not be able to meet the terms, but he can bring a wealthy and reliable guarantor of equal standing to the person who bought the land, he can also take possession."

Mālik said, "A person's absence does not sever his right of pre-emption. Even if he is away for a long time, there is no time limit after which the right of pre-emption is cut off."

Mālik said that if a man left land to a number of his children, then one of them who had a child died, and the child of the deceased sold his right in that land, the brother of the seller was more entitled to pre-empt him than his paternal uncles, the father's partners."

Mālik said, "This is what is done in our community."

Mālik said, "Pre-emption is shared between partners according to their existing shares. Each of them takes according to his portion – if it is small, he has little, if it is great, it is according to that. That is if they are obstinate and contend with each other about it."

Mālik said, "In the situation where a man buys out the share of one of his partners, and then one of the other partners says, 'I will take a portion according to my share,' and the first partner says, 'If you wish to take all the pre-emption, I will give it up to you. If you wish to leave it, then leave it,' then if the first partner gives him the choice and hands it over to him, the second partner can only take all the pre-emption or give it back. If he takes it, he is entitled to it. If not, he has nothing."

Mālik spoke about a man who bought land and developed it by planting trees or digging a well etc. and then someone came and, seeing that he had a right in the land, wanted to take possession of it by pre-emption. Mālik said, "He has no right of pre-emption unless he compensates the other for his expenditure. If he gives him a price which covers what he has developed, he is entitled to pre-emption. If not, he has no right to it."

Mālik said that someone who sold off his portion of a shared house or land and then, on learning that someone with a right of pre-emption was to take possession by that right, asked the buyer to revoke the sale, and he did so, did not have the right to do that. The pre-emptor has more right to the property for the price for which he sold it.

Referring to the case of someone buying an animal and goods (that are not shared property) along with a section of a shared house or land so that when anyone demands his right of pre-emption in the house or the land, he says, "Take what I have bought altogether, for I bought it together," Mālik said, "The pre-emptor need only take possession of the house or land. Each thing the man bought is assessed according to its share of the lump sum the man paid. Then the pre-emptor takes possession of his right for a price which is appropriate on that basis. He does not take any animals or goods unless he wants to do so."

Mālik said, "If someone sells a section of shared land and one of those who have the right of pre-emption surrenders it to the buyer and another insists on taking his pre-emption, the one who refuses to surrender has to take up all the pre-emption and he cannot take according to his right and leave what remains."

Mālik said, "In the case where one of a number of partners in a single house sells his share, when all his partners are away except for one man, and the one present, when given the choice of either taking the pre-emption or leaving it, declares, 'I will take my portion and leave the portions of my partners until they are present. If they take it, that is that. If they leave it, I will take all the pre-emption.'" Mālik said, "He can only take it all or leave it. If his partners come, they can take their portion from him or leave it as they wish. If this is offered to him and he does not accept it, I think that he has no pre-emption."

35.2 Cases in which pre-emption is not possible

4 Yaḥyā said that Mālik related from Muḥammad ibn 'Umāra from Abū Bakr ibn Ḥazm than 'Uthmān ibn 'Affān said, "There is no pre-emption in land in which boundaries have been fixed. There is no pre-emption in a well or in male palm-trees."

Mālik said, "This is what is done in our community."

Mālik said, "There is no pre-emption in a road, whether or not it is practicable to divide it."

Mālik said, "What is done in our community is that there is no pre-emption in the courtyard of a house, whether or not it is practicable to divide it."

Mālik spoke about a man who bought into a shared property, provided that he had the option of withdrawal, and the partners of the seller wanted to take what their partner was selling by pre-emption before the buyer had exercised his option. Mālik said, "They cannot do that until the buyer has taken possession and the sale is confirmed for him. When the sale is confirmed, they have the right of pre-emption."

Mālik spoke about a man who bought some land which remained in his possession for some time. Then a man came and saw that he had a share of the land by inheritance. Mālik said, "If the man's right of inheritance is established, he also has a right of pre-emption. If the land has produced a crop, the crop belongs to the buyer until the day when the right of the other is established, because he has tended what was planted against being destroyed or being carried away by a flood."

Mālik continued, "If it has been a very long time, or the witnesses are dead, or the seller has died, or they are both alive but the basis of the sale and purchase has been forgotten because of the length of time, pre-emption is discontinued. A man only takes his right by inheritance which has been established for him.

"If his situation is not like this because the sale transaction is a recent one and he sees that the seller has concealed the price in order to sever his right of pre-emption, the value of the land is estimated, and then he buys the land for that price by his right of pre-emption. Then the buildings, plants or structures which are extra to the land are looked at so that he is in the position of the person who has bought the land for a known price and then after that has built on it and planted. The holder of the pre-emption takes possession after this is concluded."

Mālik said, "Pre-emption applies to the property of the deceased as it does to the property of the living. If the family of the deceased fear to break up the property of the deceased, then they share in it and sell it, and they have no right of pre-emption over it."

Mālik said, "There is no pre-emption among us in the case of a slave or slave-girl, or a camel, any animal, nor in clothes, nor a well which does not have any uncultivated land around it. Pre-emption pertains to what can be usefully divided and to land in which boundaries occur. As for what cannot be usefully divided, there is no pre-emption in it."

Mālik said, "Someone who buys land, in which people at hand have a right of pre-emption, refers them to the Sultan and either they claim their right or the ruler surrenders it to him. However, if he were to leave them and not refer their situation to the ruler, whilst they knew about his purchase but leave it a long time before coming to demand their pre-emption, I do not think that they should have it."

36. Judgements

36.1 Stimulation of desire to judge correctly

1 Yaḥyā related to me from Mālik from Hishām ibn 'Urwa from his father from Zaynab bint Abī Salama from Umm Salama, the wife of the Prophet ﷺ, that the Messenger of Allah ﷺ said, "I am but a man to whom you bring your disputes. Perhaps one of you is more eloquent in his proof than the other and so I give judgement according to what I have heard from him. He must not take take any of whatever I decide for him that is part of the right of his brother, for I am granting him a portion of the Fire."

2 Mālik related to me from Yaḥyā ibn Sa'īd from Sa'īd ibn al-Musayyab that 'Umar ibn al-Khaṭṭāb had a dispute brought to him between a Muslim and a Jew. 'Umar thought that the Jew was in the right and gave judgement in his favour. The Jew said to him, "By Allah! You have judged correctly!" So 'Umar ibn al-Khaṭṭāb struck him with his whip and said, "How can you be sure?" The Jew said to him, "We find that there is no judge who judges correctly but that there is an angel on his right side and an angel on his left side who guide him and give him success in the truth as long as he is with the truth. When he leaves the truth, they rise and leave him."

36.2 Giving testimony

3 Yaḥyā related to me from Mālik from 'Abdullāh ibn Abī Bakr ibn Muḥammad ibn 'Amr ibn Ḥazm from his father from 'Abdullāh ibn 'Amr

ibn 'Uthmān from Abū 'Amra al-Anṣārī from Zayd ibn Khālid al-Juhanī that the Messenger of Allah ﷺ said, "Shall I not tell you who is the best of witnesses? The one who brings his testimony before he is asked for it or tells his testimony before he is asked for it."

4 Mālik related to me that Rabi'a ibn Abī 'Abd ar-Raḥmān said, "An Iraqi man came before 'Umar ibn al-Khaṭṭāb and said, 'I have come to you because of a matter which has no beginning and no end.' 'Umar asked him, 'What is it?' The man said, 'False testimony has appeared in our land.' 'Umar inquired, 'Is that so?' He replied, 'Yes.' 'Umar said, 'By Allah! A man is not detained in Islam without just witnesses.'"

Mālik related to me that 'Umar ibn al-Khaṭṭāb said, "The testimony of a litigant or a man who is suspect is not accepted."

36.3 Judgement on testimony of those who have received *ḥadd*-punishments

Yaḥyā said from Mālik that he heard from Sulaymān ibn Yasar and others that when they were asked whether the testimony of a man who had been flogged for a *ḥadd* crime was allowed, they replied, "Yes, when he shows repentance."

Mālik related to me that he heard Ibn Shihāb being asked about that and he said something similar to what Sulaymān ibn Yasār said.

Mālik said, "That is what is done in our community. It is by the word of Allah, the Blessed, the Exalted, '*But those who make accusations against chaste women and then do not produce four witnesses: flog them with eighty lashes and never again accept them as witnesses. Such people are the degenerate – except for those who after that repent and put things right. Allah is Ever-Forgiving, Most Merciful.*'" (24:4).

36.4 Judgement based on oaths along with the testimony of a single witness

5 Yaḥyā said that Mālik said from Ja'far ibn Muḥammad from his father that the Messenger of Allah ﷺ pronounced judgement on the basis of an oath along with a single witness.

6 From Mālik from Abū az-Zinād that 'Umar ibn 'Abd al-'Azīz wrote to 'Abd al-Ḥamīd ibn 'Abd ar-Raḥmān ibn Zayd ibn al-Khaṭṭāb who was the governor of Kufa, "Pronounce judgement on the basis of an oath along with one witness."

7 Mālik related to me that he heard that Abū Salama ibn 'Abd ar-Raḥmān and Sulaymān ibn Yasār were both asked, "Does one pronounce judgement on the basis of an oath along with a single witness?" They both replied, "Yes."

Mālik said, "The precedent of the *sunna* in judging by an oath along with a single witness is that, if the plaintiff takes an oath along with presenting his witness, he is confirmed in his right. If he draws back and refuses to take an oath, the defendant is made to take an oath. If he takes an oath, the claim against him is dropped. If he refuses to take an oath, the claim is confirmed against him."

Mālik said, "This procedure pertains to property cases in particular. It does not occur in any of the *ḥadd* punishments, nor in marriage, divorce, freeing slaves, theft or slander. If someone says, 'Freeing slaves comes under property,' he has erred. It is not as he says. Had it been as he says a slave could take an oath along with one witness, if he could find one, that his master had freed him.

"However, when a slave lays claim to a piece of property, he can take an oath along with presenting one witness and demand his right as the freeman demands his right."

Mālik said, "The *sunna* with us is that when a slave brings somebody who witnesses that he has been set free, his master is made to take an oath that he has not freed him, and the slave's claim is cancelled."

Mālik said, "The *sunna* about divorce is also like that with us. When a woman brings somebody who testifies that her husband has divorced her, the husband is made to take an oath that he has not divorced her. If he takes the oath, the divorce does not proceed."

Mālik said, "The *sunna* in cases of divorce and freeing a slave is one witness. The right to make an oath only belongs to the husband of the woman and the master of the slave. Freeing is a *ḥadd* matter, and the testimony of women is not permitted in it because, when a slave is set free, his inviolability is affirmed and the *ḥadd* punishments are applied for and against him. If he commits fornication and is *muḥṣan*, he is stoned for it. If he kills a slave, he is killed for it. Inheritance is established for him, between him and whoever inherits from him. If somebody disputes this, arguing that if a man frees his slave and then a man comes to demand from the master of the slave payment of the debt, and a man and two women testify to his right, that establishes the right against the master of the slave, so that his freeing of the slave is cancelled if the slave is his only property – inferring by this case that the testimony of women is permitted in cases of setting-free – the case is not as he suggests (i.e. it is a case of property, not freeing). It is rather like a man who frees his slave, and then the claimant of a debt comes to the man and takes an oath along with one witness, demanding his right. By this, the emancipation of a slave would be cancelled. Or else a man is brought who has frequent dealings and transactions with the master of the slave and he is asked to take an oath that he doesn't owe what the claimant claims. If he draws back and refuses to take an oath, the claimant takes an oath and his right against the master of the slave is confirmed. This would cancel the freeing of the slave, if it is confirmed that property is owed by the master."

Mālik said, "It is the same with a man who marries a slave-girl and then the master of the slave-girl comes to the man who has married her and claims, 'You and so-and-so have bought my slave-girl from me for such an amount of dinars.' The slave-girl's husband denies that. The master of the slave-girl brings a man and two women and they testify to what he has said. The sale is confirmed and his claim is considered to be true. So the slave-girl is unlawful for her husband and they have to separate even though the testimony of women is not accepted in divorce."

Mālik said, "It is also the same when a man accuses a supposedly free man of a *ḥadd* crime and then a man and two women come and testify that the accused is in fact a slave. That would remove the *ḥadd* from the accused after it has been proved against him, even though the testimony of women is not accepted in accusations involving *ḥadd* punishments."

Mālik said, "Another similar case in which judgement appears to go against the precedent of the *sunna* is when two women testify that a child was born alive. This would effect inheritance if a situation arose where he was entitled to inherit, and the child's property would go to those who inherited from him if he dies, and it is not necessary that the two women witnesses should be accompanied by a man or an oath, even though it may involve vast possessions of gold, silver, livestock, gardens and slaves and other properties. However, had two women testified to one dirham or more or less than that in a property case, their testimony would not affect anything and would not be permitted unless they came with a witness or took an oath."

Mālik said, "There are people who say that an oath is not acceptable with only one witness and they argue by the word of Allah, the Blessed, the Exalted whose word is the Truth, '*Two men among you should act as witnesses. But if there are not two men, then a man and two women with whom you are satisfied as witnesses.*' (2:282) Such people argue that if he does not bring one man and two women, he has no claim and he is not allowed to swear an oath with one witness."

Mālik said, "Part of the proof against those who argue in this way is to reply to them, 'Do you think that if a man claims property from another man, the one from whom he claims it should not swear that the claim is false?' If he swears, the claim against him is dropped. If he refuses to swear an oath, the claimant is made to swear an oath that his claim is true and his right against his companion is established. There is no dispute about this with any of the people nor in any country. By what does the doubter take this? In what place in the Book of Allah does he find it? So if he confirms this, let him confirm the oath with one witness, even if it is not in the Book of Allah, the Mighty, the Majestic. It is enough that this is the precedent of the *sunna*. However, man wants to recognise the proper course of action and the location of the proof. In this there is a clarification for what is obscure about that, if Allah wills."

36.5 Judgement on a deceased with a debt against him and a debt for him and only one witness

Yaḥyā said that Mālik spoke about a man who died with a debt owed to him that there was only a single witness for, and some people had a debt against him and they also had only a single witness. The heirs refused to take an oath about their rights and to present their witness. He said, "The creditors take an oath and take their rights. If there is anything left over, the heirs do not take any of it, because the oaths were offered to them before and they abandoned them, unless they say, 'We did not know that our companion had extra,' and it is known that they only abandoned the oaths because of that. I think that they should take an oath and take what remains after the debt is paid off."

36.6 Judgement on claims

8 Yaḥyā said that Mālik said that Jamīl ibn 'Abd ar-Rahmān al-Mu'adhdhin was present when 'Umar ibn 'Abd al-'Azīz was judging between people. If a man came to him with a claim against someone, he examined whether or not there were frequent transactions and dealings between them. If there were, the defendant could make an oath. If there was nothing of that nature he did not accept an oath from him."

Mālik summed up, "What is done in our community is that if someone makes a claim against a man, it is examined. If there are frequent transactions and dealings between them, the defendant is made to swear on oath. If he swears on oath, the claim against him is dropped. If the defendant refuses to swear on oath, and foregoes the oath to the claimant, the one claiming his right swears an oath and takes his due."

36.7 Judgement on the testimony of children

9 Yaḥyā said that Mālik said from Hishām ibn 'Urwa that 'Abdullāh ibn az-Zubayr gave judgement based on the testimony of children concerning the injuries which occurred between them.

Mālik said, "The generally agreed on way of doing things in our community is that the testimony of children is permitted concerning injuries between themselves. It is not accepted in anything else. It is only permitted between them if they make their testimony before they leave the scene of the incident or have been deceived or instructed. If they leave the scene, they have no testimony unless they call reputable witnesses to support their testimony about what happened before they left."

36.8 Perjury on the minbar of the Prophet

10 Yaḥyā said that Mālik related to me from Hishām ibn Hishām ibn 'Utba ibn Abī Waqqāṣ from 'Abdullāh ibn Nistās from Jābir ibn 'Abdullāh al-Anṣārī that the Messenger of Allah ﷺ said, "If someone swears a false oath near this minbar of mine, he will take his seat in the Fire."

11 Mālik related to me from al-'Alā' ibn 'Abd ar-Raḥmān from Ma'bad ibn Ka'b as-Salamī from his brother, 'Abdullāh ibn Ka'b ibn Mālik al-Anṣārī, from Abū Umāma that the Messenger of Allah ﷺ said, "If someone takes the right of a Muslim man by his oath, Allah will forbid him the Garden and make the Fire mandatory for him." They said, "Even if is something insignificant, Messenger of Allah?" He replied, "Even if it is a toothpick, even if it is a tooth pick," repeating that three times.

36.9 Taking oaths on the minbar in general

12 Yaḥyā said that Mālik had said from Dā'ūd ibn al-Ḥusayn that he heard Abū Ghaṭafān ibn Ṭarīf al-Murrī say, "Zayd ibn Thābit al-Anṣārī and Ibn Mutī' had a dispute about a house which they shared. They went to Marwān ibn al-Ḥakam who was the governor of Madīna. Marwān

decided that Zayd ibn Thābit must take an oath on the minbar. Zayd ibn Thābit said, 'I will swear to it where I am.' Marwān said, 'No, by Allah! Only in the place of sorting out claims (i.e. the minbar).' Zayd ibn Thābit began to swear on oath that his right was true, and he refused to take an oath near the minbar. Marwān ibn al-Ḥakam was surprised at that."

Mālik said, "I do not think anyone should be made to take an oath near the minbar for less than a fourth of a dinar, and that is three dirhams."

36.10 Prohibition against forfeiting pledges given on security

13 Yaḥyā said that Mālik related to him from Ibn Shihāb from Sa'īd ibn al-Musayyab that the Messenger of Allah ﷺ said, "The pledge given as security is not forfeited."

Mālik said, "The explanation of that according to what we think – and Allah knows best – is that a man gives a pledge to somebody in security for something and the pledge is superior to what it is pawned for. The pledger says to the pawnbroker, 'I will bring you your due after such-and-such a time. If not, the pledge is yours for what it was pawned for.'"

Mālik said, "This transaction is not good and it is not lawful, and this is what was forbidden. If the owner brings what he pledged it for after the period has lapsed, the pledge is his. I think that the time condition is void."

36.11 Judgement on pledging fruit and animals as security

Yaḥyā said, "I heard Mālik say that if a man pledges his garden for a stated period and the fruits of that garden are ready before the end of the period, the fruits are not included in the pledge with the real estate, unless it is stipulated by the pledger when making the pledge. However, if a man receives a slave-girl as a pledge, and she is pregnant or she becomes pregnant after his taking her as a pledge, her child is included with her.

"A distinction is made between the fruit and the child of the slave-girl. The Messenger of Allah ﷺ said, 'If someone sells a palm which has been pollinated, the fruit belongs to the seller unless the buyer stipulates its inclusion.' The undisputed way of doing things in our community is that when a man sells a slave-girl or an animal with a foetus in its womb, the foetus belongs to the buyer, whether or not the buyer makes it a stipulation. The palm is not like the animal. Fruit is not like the foetus in the mother's womb. Another thing that also makes this clear is that it is the custom of people to let a man pawn the fruit of the palm apart from the palm. No one pawns the foetus in its mother's womb, however, whether of slaves or animals."

36.12 Judgement on pledging animals as security

Yaḥyā said that he heard Mālik say, "The undisputed way of doing things in our community, concerning pledges is that in cases where land or a house or an animal are known to have been destroyed whilst in the possession of the pledge-holder, and the circumstances of the loss are known, the loss is against the pledger. There is no deduction made from what is due to the pledge-owner at all. Any pledge which perishes in the possession of the pledge-owner, and the circumstances of its loss are only known by his word, the loss is against the pledge-owner and he is liable for its value. He is asked to describe whatever was destroyed and then he is made to take an oath about his description and what he loaned on security for it.

"Then people of discernment evaluate the description. If the pledge was worth more than what the pledge-holder loaned, the pledger takes the extra. If the assessed value of the pledge is less than what he was loaned, the pledger is made to take an oath as to what the pledge-holder loaned and he does not have to pay the extra which the pledge-holder loaned above the assessed value of the pledge. If the pledge-holder says that he does not know the value of the pledge, the pledger is made to take an oath on the description of the pledge and it is his if he brings a matter which is not disapproved of."

Mālik said, "All this applies when the pledge-holder takes possession of the pledge and does not put it in the hands of another."

36.13 Judgement on pledges shared between two men

Yaḥyā said that he heard Mālik speak about two men who shared in making a pledge. One of them undertakes to sell his share of the pledge and the other one asks him to wait a year for his due. He said, "If it is possible to divide the pledge, and the due of the one who asked him to wait will not be decreased, half the pledge which is between them is sold for him and he is given his due. If it is feared that his right will be decreased, all the pledge is sold, and the one who undertook to sell his pledge is given his due from that. If the one who asked him to wait for his due is pleased in himself, half of the price is paid to the pledger. If not, the pledgee is made to take an oath that he only asked him wait so that he could 'transfer my pledge to me in its form'. Then he is given his due immediately."

Yaḥyā said that he heard Mālik say about a slave, whose master had pledged him and the slave had property of his own, "The property of the slave is not part of the pledge unless the pledge-broker makes it a stipulation."

36.14 Judgement on pledges in general

Yaḥyā said that he heard Mālik speak about someone who pledges goods as security for a loan, and they perish with the broker. The one who took out the loan confirms its specification. They agree on the amount of the loan, but challenge each other about the value of the pledge, the pledger saying that it was worth twenty dinars whilst the broker says that it was only worth ten, and that the amount loaned on security was twenty dinars. Mālik said, "The pledger is asked to describe it. If he describes it he is made to take an oath on it and then people of experience evaluate what he describes. If its value is more than what was loaned on security for it, it is said to the broker, 'Return the rest of his due to the pledger.' If the value is less than what was loaned on security for it, the broker takes the rest of his due from the pledger. If the value is the exact amount of the loan, the pledge is compensated for by the loan."

Yaḥyā said that he heard Mālik say, "What is done in our community about two men who have a dispute about an amount of money loaned on the security of a pledge – the pledger claiming that he pledged it for ten dinars and the broker insisting that he took the pledge as security for twenty dinars, and the pledge is clearly in the possession of the broker – is that the broker is made to take an oath when the value of the pledge is fully known. If the value of the pledge is exactly what he swore that he had loaned on security for it, the broker takes the pledge as his right. He is more entitled to take precedence in swearing the oath since he has possession of the pledge. If the owner of the pledge wants to give him the amount which he swears that he is owed, he can take the pledge back. If the pledge is worth less than the twenty dinars he loaned, then it is said to the pledger, 'Either you give him what he has sworn to and take your pledge back, or you swear to what you say you pledged for.' If the pledger takes the oath, then what the broker has increased over the value of the pledge will become invalid. If the pledger does not swear on oath, he must pay what the broker has sworn to."

Mālik said, "If a pledge given on security for a loan perishes, and both parties deny each other's rights, with, for instance, the broker who is owed the loan saying that he gave twenty dinars, and the pledger who owes the loan saying that he was given only ten, and with the broḳer who is owed the loan saying that the pledge was worth ten dinars, and the pledger who owes the loan saying that it was worth twenty, then the broker who is owed the loan is asked to describe the pledge. If he describes it, he must take an oath on its description. Then people with experience of such matters evaluate the descripton. If the value of the pledge is estimated to be more than what the broker claims it was, he takes an oath as to what he claimed, and the pledger is given what is over from the value of the pledge. If its value is less than what the broker claims about it, he is made to take an oath as to what he claims is his. Then he demands settlement according to the actual value of the pledge. The one who owes the loan is then made to take an oath on the extra amount which remains owing against him to the claimant after the price of the pledge has been reached. This is because the broker becomes a claimant against the pledger. If he takes an oath, the rest of what the broker swore to of what he claimed above the value of the pledge is invalidated. If he draws back, he is bound to pay what remains due to the broker after the value of the pledge."

36.15 Judgement on renting animals and going beyond specified destinations

Yaḥyā said that he heard Mālik say, "What is done is our community about a man who rents an animal for a journey to a specified place and then he goes beyond that place and further, is that the owner of the animal has a choice. If he wants to take extra rent for his animal to cover the distance overstepped, he is given that on top of the first rent and the animal is returned. If the owner of the animal wants to sell the animal from the place where the man has overstepped, he has the price of the animal on top of the rent. If, however, the hirer rented the animal to go and return, and then he overstepped when he reached the city to which he had rented it to go, the owner of the animal only has half the first rent. That is because half of the rent is going, and half of it is returning. If he oversteps with the animal, only half of the first rent is obliged for him. Had the animal died when he reached the city to which it was rented, the hirer would not be liable and the renter would only have half the rent."

Mālik said, "That is what is done with people who overstep and dispute about what they took the animal for."

Mālik said, "It is also like that with someone who takes *qirāḍ* money from his companion. The owner of the property says to him, 'Do not buy such-and-such animals or such-and-such goods,' naming the ones which he excludes and disapproves of his money being invested in. The one who takes the money then buys what he was forbidden. By that, he intends to be liable for the money and take the profit of his companion. When he does that, the owner of the money has an option. If he wants to enter with him in the goods according to the original stipulations between them about the profit, he does so. If he likes, he has his capital guaranteed against the one who took the capital and overstepped the mark."

Mālik said, "It is also like that with a man with whom another man invests some goods. The owner of the property orders him to buy certain goods for him which he names. He differs and exchanges the goods for something other than what he was ordered to buy, exceeding his orders. The owner of the goods has an option. If he wants to take what has been bought with his property, he takes it. If he wants the partner to be liable for his capital he has that."

36.16 Judgement about raped women

14 Mālik related to me from Ibn Shihāb that 'Abd al-Malik ibn Marwān gave a judgement that the rapist had to pay the raped woman her bride-price.

Yaḥyā said that he heard Mālik say, "What is done in our community about the man who rapes a woman, virgin or non-virgin, if she is free, is that he must pay the bride-price of someone like her. If she is a slave, he must pay what he has diminished of her worth. The *ḥadd* punishment in such cases is applied to the rapist, and there is no punishment applied to the raped woman. If the rapist is a slave, that is against his master unless he wishes to surrender him."

36.17 Judgement on consuming other people's animals

Yaḥyā said that he heard Mālik say, "What is done in our community about someone who consumes an animal without the permission of its owner is that he must pay its price on the day he consumed it. He is not obliged to replace it with any kind of animal. He must pay its price on the day it was consumed, and giving the value is more equitable in compensation for animals and goods."

Yaḥyā said that he heard Mālik say about someone who consumes some food without the permission of its owner, "He returns to the owner a like weight of the same kind of food. Food is in the position of gold and silver. Gold and silver are returned with gold and silver. The animal is not in the position of gold in such cases. What distinguishes between them is the *sunna* and the normative practice which is in force."

Yaḥyā said that he heard Mālik say, "If a man is entrusted with some wealth and then trades with it for himself and makes a profit, the profit is his because he is responsible for the property until he returns it to its owner."

36.18 Judgement on the abandonment of Islam

15 Yaḥyā related to me from Mālik from Zayd ibn Aslam that the Messenger of Allah ﷺ said, "If someone changes his religion – then strike off his head!"

The meaning of the statement of the Prophet ﷺ in our opinion – and Allah knows best – is that the words, "If someone changes his religion – then strike off his head!" refers to those who leave Islam for something else – like heretics and suchlike, about whom that is known. They are killed without being called to repent because their repentance is not recognised. They were concealing their disbelief and making their Islam public, so I do not think that one should call such people to repent and one does not accept their word. As for the person who leaves Islam for something else and divulges it, he is called on to repent. If he does not turn in repentance, he is killed. If there are people in that situation, I think that one should call them to Islam and call on them to repent. If they repent, that is accepted from them. If they do not repent, they are killed. That does not refer as we see it, and Allah knows best, to those who convert from Judaism to Christianity or from Christianity to Judaism, nor to someone who changes his religion from any of the various forms of religion except for Islam. Whoever leaves Islam for something else and makes that known, that is the one who is referred to, and Allah knows best!"

16 Mālik related to me from 'Abd ar-Raḥmān ibn Muḥammad ibn 'Abdullāh ibn 'Abd al-Qārī that his father said, "A man came to 'Umar ibn al-Khaṭṭāb from Abū Mūsā al-Ash'arī. 'Umar asked after various people, and he informed him about them. Then 'Umar inquired, 'Do you have any recent news from those far away?' He said, 'Yes. A man has become an unbeliever after he was Muslim.' 'Umar said, 'What have you done with him?' He replied, 'We let him approach and then struck off his head.' 'Umar said, 'Did you not imprison him for three days and feed him

a loaf of bread every day and call on him to repent that he might turn in repentance and return to the command of Allah?' Then 'Umar said, 'O Allah! I was not present and I did not order it and I am not pleased since it has come to me!"

36.19 Judgement on men finding other men with their wives

17 Yaḥyā related to me from Mālik from Suhayl ibn Abī Ṣarḥ as-Sammān from his father from Abū Hurayra that Sa'īd ibn 'Ubāda said to the Messenger of Allah ﷺ, "What do you think if I find a man with my wife? Shall I grant him a respite until I bring four witnesses?" The Messenger of Allah ﷺ replied, "Yes."

18 Mālik related to me from Yaḥyā ibn Sa'īd from Sa'īd ibn al-Musayyab that a Syrian man called Ibn Khaybarī found a man with his wife and killed him or killed them both. Mu'āwiya ibn Abī Sufyān found it difficult to make a decision and he wrote to Abū Mūsā al-Ash'arī to ask 'Alī ibn Abī Ṭālib and 'Alī said to him, "Has this thing occurred in my land? I adjure you, you must tell me." Abū Mūsā explained to him how Mu'āwiya ibn Abī Sufyān had written him to ask 'Alī about it. 'Alī said, "I am Abū al-Ḥasan. If he does not bring four witnesses, then let him be completely handed over (to the relatives of the murdered man)."

36.20 Judgement on the abandoned child

19 Yaḥyā said that Mālik related from Ibn Shihāb that Sunayn Abī Jamīla, a man from the Banū Sulaym, found an abandoned child in the time of 'Umar ibn al-Khaṭṭāb. Sunayn took him to 'Umar ibn al-Khaṭṭāb. He asked, "What made you take this person?" He answered, "I found him lost, so I took him." 'Umar's advisor said to him, "*Amīr al-Mu'minīn*, he is a man who does good!" 'Umar inquired of him, "Is that so?" He replied, "Yes." 'Umar ibn al-Khaṭṭāb said, "Go, he is free and you have his *walā'* inheritance rights and we will provide for him."

Yaḥyā said that he heard Mālik say, "What is done in our community about an abandoned child is that he is free and his *walā'* inheritance rights belongs to the Muslims, and they inherit from him and pay his blood-money."

36.21 Judgement on attaching paternity to children

20 Yaḥyā said from Mālik from Ibn Shihāb from 'Urwa ibn az-Zubayr that 'Ā'isha, the wife of the Prophet ﷺ, said, "'Utba ibn Abī Waqqāṣ disclosed to his brother, Sa'd ibn Abī Waqqāṣ, that he had fathered of the son of the slave-girl of Zam'a and made him promise to look after him (after his death). In the Year of the Conquest, Sa'd took him and said, 'He is the son of my brother. He made a covenant with me about him.' 'Abd ibn Zam'a stood up and said, 'He is my brother and the son of my father's slave-girl. He was born on his bed.' They went to the Messenger of Allah ﷺ. Sa'd said, 'He is my brother's son. He made a covenant with me about him.' 'Abd ibn Zam'a said, 'He is my brother and the son of my father's slave-girl and was born on my father's bed.' The Messenger of Allah ﷺ said, 'He is yours, 'Abd ibn Zam'a.' Then the Messenger of Allah ﷺ said, 'A child belongs to the household (where he was born) and the adulterer has stones.' Then he told Sawda bint Zam'a, 'Veil yourself from him,' since he saw that he resembled 'Utba ibn Abī Waqqāṣ." 'Ā'isha added, "He did not see her from then on until he met Allah, the Mighty, the Majestic."

21 Mālik related to me from Yazīd ibn 'Abdullāh ibn al-Hādī from Muḥammad ibn Ibrāhīm ibn al-Ḥārith at-Taymī from Sulaymān ibn Yasār from 'Abdullāh ibn Abī Umayya that a woman's husband died and she observed the *'idda* of four months and ten days. Then she married when she was free to marry. She stayed with her husband for four and a half months and then gave birth to a fully-developed child. Her husband went to 'Umar ibn al-Khaṭṭāb and mentioned that to him, so 'Umar called some of the old women of the *Jāhiliyya* and asked them about that. One of the women said, "I will tell you what happened with this woman. When her husband died, she was pregnant by him but then the blood flowed from her because of his death and the child became dry in her womb. When her new husband had intercourse with her and the water reached the child, the child moved in the womb and grew." 'Umar ibn al-Khaṭṭāb believed her and separated them (until she had

completed her *'idda*). 'Umar said, "Only good has reached me about you two," and he connected the child to the first husband.

22 Mālik related to me from Yaḥyā ibn Sa'īd from Sulaymān ibn Yasār that 'Umar ibn al-Khaṭṭāb used to attach the children of the *Jāhiliyya* to whoever claimed them in Islam. Two men came and each of them claimed a woman's child. 'Umar ibn al-Khaṭṭāb summoned a person who scrutinised features to look at them. The scrutiniser said, "They both share in him." 'Umar ibn al-Khaṭṭāb hit him with a whip. Then he summmoned the woman and said, "Tell me your tale." She said, "It was this one (indicating one of the two men) who used to come to me while I was with my people's camels. He did not leave me until both he and I thought that I was pregnant. Then he left me and blood flowed from me and this other one took his place. I do not know which of them is the father of the child." The scrutinser said, "Allah is greater." 'Umar said to the child, "Go to whichever of them you wish."

23 Mālik related to me that he had heard that 'Umar ibn al-Khaṭṭāb or 'Uthmān ibn 'Affān gave a judgement about a slave woman who misled a man about herself and said that she was free. He married her and she bore children. It was decided that he should ransom his children with their like of slaves.

Yaḥyā said that he heard Mālik say, "To ransom them with their price is more equitable in this case, Allah willing."

36.22 Judgement on inheritance of attached children

Yaḥyā said that he heard Mālik say, "The way of doing things generally agreed upon in our community in the case of a man who dies and has sons and one of them claims, 'My father acknowledged that so-and-so was his son,' is that the relationship is not established by the testimony of one man, and the confirmation of the one who confirmed it is only permitted as regards his own share in the division of his father's property. The one testified for is only given his due from the share of the testifier."

Mālik said, "An example of this is that a man dies leaving two sons and

600 dinars. Each of them takes 300 dinars. Then one of them testifies that his deceased father acknowledged that so-and-so was his son. The one who testified is obliged to give 100 dinars to the one thus connected. This is half of the inheritance of the one thought to be related had he indeed been related. If the other son also acknowledges him, he takes the other 100 and so he has his full right and his relationship is established. His position is similar to that of a woman who acknowledges a debt against her father or her husband which the other heirs deny. She must pay to the person whose debt she acknowledges the amount according to her share of the full debt if it had been established against all the heirs. If the woman inherits an eighth, she pays the creditor an eighth of his debt. If a daughter inherits a half, she pays the creditor half of his debt. Whichever women acknowledge the debt pay it according to this."

Mālik said, "If a man's testimony is in agreement with what the woman testified to, that so-and-so was owed a debt by his father, the creditor is then made to take an oath with one witness and he is given all his due. This is not the position with women because a man's testimony is allowed and the creditor must take an oath with the testimony of one witness and take all his due. If he does not take an oath, he only takes from the inheritance of the one who acknowledged him according to his share of the debt, because he acknowledged his right while the other heirs denied it. It is permitted for him to acknowledge it."

36.23 Judgement on women who are *umm walad*

24 Yaḥyā said that Mālik related from Ibn Shihāb from Sālim ibn 'Abdullāh ibn 'Umar from his father that 'Umar ibn al-Khaṭṭāb said, "What is the matter with men who have intercourse with their slave-girls and then dismiss them? No slave-girl comes to me whose master admits that he has had intercourse with her but that I connect the child to him whether or not he has practised *coitus interruptus* or stopped having intercourse with her."

25 Mālik related to me from Nāfi' that Ṣafiyya bint Abī 'Ubayd informed him that 'Umar ibn al-Khaṭṭāb said, "What is the matter with men who have intercourse with their slave-girls and then let them go? No slave-

girl comes to me whose master admits that he has had intercourse with her but that I connect the child to him, whether or not he has practised *coitus interruptus* or stopped having intercourse with her."

Yaḥyā said that he heard Mālik say, "What is done in our community about an *umm walad* who commits a crime is that her master is liable for what she has done up to her value. He does not have to surrender her and he cannot be made to bear more than her value for her crime."

36.24 Judgement on bringing barren land into cultivation

26 Yaḥyā related to me from Mālik from Hishām ibn 'Urwa from his father that the Messenger of Allah ﷺ said, "If anyone revives barren land, it belongs to him, and the root unjustly planted has no right."

Mālik explained, "The unjust root is whatever is taken or planted without right."

27 Mālik related to me from Ibn Shihāb from Sālim ibn 'Abdullāh from his father that 'Umar ibn al-Khaṭṭāb said, "When someone revives barren land, it belongs to him."

Mālik said, "That is what is done in our community."

36.25 Judgement on watering land

28 Yaḥyā related to me from Mālik from 'Abdullāh ibn Abī Bakr ibn Muḥammad ibn 'Amr ibn Ḥazm that he heard that the Messenger of Allah ﷺ said about the flood-channels of Mahzūr and Mudhaynib (in Madīna), "Dam them systematically so that the water is diverted into each property in turn up to ankle level, starting upstream."

29 Mālik related to me from Abū az-Zinād from al-A'raj from Abū Hurayra that the Messenger of Allah ﷺ said, "Excess water is not withheld in order to prevent pasturage from growing."

30 Mālik related to me from Abū'r-Rijal Muḥammad ibn 'Abd ar-Raḥmān from his mother, 'Amra bint 'Abd ar-Raḥmān, that she informed him that the Messenger of Allah ﷺ said, "Do not withhold the surplus water of a well from people."

36.26 Judgement on benefiting neighbours

31 Yaḥyā related to me from Mālik from 'Amr ibn Yaḥyā al-Māzinī from his father that the Messenger of Allah ﷺ said, "There is no injury nor return of injury."

32 Mālik related to me from Ibn Shihāb from al-A'raj from Abū Hurayra that the Messenger of Allah ﷺ said, "No one should prevent his neighbour from fixing a wooden peg in his wall." Then Abū Hurayra said, "Why do I see you turning away from it? By Allah! I shall keep on at you about it."

33 Mālik related to me from 'Amr ibn Yaḥyā al-Māzinī from his father that aḍ-Ḍahhāk ibn Khalīfa watered his irrigation ditch from a large source of water. He wanted to have it pass through the land of Muḥammad ibn Maslama and Muḥammad refused. Aḍ-Ḍahhāk asked him, "Why do you prevent me? It will benefit you. You can drink from it first and last and it will not harm you?" Muḥammad refused, so aḍ-Ḍahhāk spoke to 'Umar ibn al-Khaṭṭāb about it. 'Umar ibn al-Khaṭṭāb summoned Muḥammad ibn Maslama and ordered him to clear the way. Muḥammad said, "No." 'Umar said, "Why do you prevent your brother from what will benefit him and is also useful for you? You will take water from it first and last and it will not harm you." Muḥammad said, "No, by Allah!" 'Umar said, "By Allah, he will pass it through, even if it is over your belly!" 'Umar ordered him to allow its passage and aḍ-Ḍahhāk did so.

34 Mālik related to me from 'Amr ibn Yaḥyā al-Māzinī that his father said, "There was a stream in my grandfather's garden belonging to 'Abd ar-Raḥmān ibn 'Awf. 'Abd ar-Raḥmān ibn 'Awf wanted to transfer it to a corner of the garden nearer his land but my grandfather prevented him. 'Abd ar-Raḥmān ibn 'Awf spoke to 'Umar ibn al-Khaṭṭāb about it and he gave a judgement that 'Abd ar-Raḥmān ibn 'Awf should transfer it."

36.27 Judgement on division of properties

35 Yaḥyā related to me from Mālik that Thawr ibn Zayd ad-Dīlī said, "I heard that the Messenger of Allah ﷺ said, 'A house or land that has been divided up in the *Jāhiliyya* is according to the division of the *Jāhiliyya*. A house or land which has not been divided up before the coming of Islam is divided according to Islam.'"

36 Yaḥyā said that he heard Mālik speak about a man who died leaving properties in 'Āliya and Sāfila (outlying districts of Madīna). He said, "Unirrigated, naturally watered land is not in the same category as irrigated land unless the family is satisfied with that. Unirrigated land is only in the same category as land with a spring when it resembles it. When the properties are in the same land and are close together, each individual property is evaluated and then divided between the heirs. Dwellings and houses are treated in the same way."

36.28 Judgement on animals grazing on other people's crops and animals stolen from the herd

37 Yaḥyā related to me from Mālik from Ibn Shihāb from Ḥarām ibn Sa'd ibn Muḥayyiṣa that a female camel of al-Barā' ibn 'Āzib entered a man's garden and caused some damage. The Messenger of Allah ﷺ gave a judgement that the garden's owners were responsible for guarding it during the day and the owner of the animals was only liable for what the animals destroyed at night.

38 Mālik related to me from Hishām ibn 'Urwa from his father from Yaḥyā ibn 'Abd ar-Raḥmān ibn Ḥātib that some of Ḥātib's slaves stole a she-camel belonging to a man from the Muzayna tribe and slaughtered it. The case was brought before 'Umar ibn al-Khaṭṭāb and 'Umar ordered Kathīr ibn aṣ-Ṣalṭ to cut off their hands. Then 'Umar said to Ḥātib, "I think you must be starving them!" He added, "By Allah, I will make you pay such a fine that it will be heavy for you!" He enquired of the man from the Muzayna tribe, "What was the price of your camel?" The Muzaynī said, "By Allah, I refused to sell her for 400 dirhams." 'Umar said, "Give him 800 dirhams."

Yaḥyā said that he heard Mālik say, "Doubling the price is not the behaviour of our community. What people have settled on among us is that the man is obliged to pay the value of the camel or animal on the day they were taken."

36.29 Judgement on injuries to domestic animals

Yaḥyā said that he heard Mālik say, "What is done in our community about injury done to a domestic animal is that the one who causes the injury must pay the amount by which he has diminished the animal's price."

Yaḥyā said that he heard Mālik speak about a camel which attacked a man and he feared for himself and killed it or hamstrung it. He said, "If he has clear evidence that it was heading for him and had attacked him, there are no damages against him. If there is no clear evidence other than his word, he is responsible for the camel."

36.30 Judgement regarding articles given to artisans to work on

Yaḥyā related that he heard Mālik say that if a man gives a washer a garment to dye and he dyed it and then the owner of the garment says, "I did not order you to use this dye," and the washer protests that he had done so, then the washer was to be believed. It was the same with tailors and goldsmiths. They are to take an oath about it unless they produced something which they would not normally have been employed to do. In that situation their statement is not allowed and the owner of the garment has to take an oath. If he rejects that and refuses to swear on oath, then the dyer is made to take an oath.

Yaḥyā said, "I heard Mālik speak about a dyer who was given a garment and made a mistake and gave it to the wrong person, and then the person to whom he gave it wore it. He said, "The person who wears it has no damages against him and the washer pays damages to the owner of the garment. This happens when the man wears the garment which he was given without recognising that it is not his. If he wears it knowing that it is not his garment, then he is held responsible for it."

36.31 Judgement on taking on debts and transfers of debts

Yaḥyā related that he heard Mālik say, "What is done in our community about a man who refers a creditor to another man for the debt he owes him is that, if the one referred to goes bankrupt or dies and does not leave enough to discharge the debt, then the creditor has nothing against the one who referred him and the debt does not revert to the first party."

Mālik said, "This is the way of doing things about which there is no dispute in our community."

Mālik said, "If a man has his debt to somebody taken on for him by another man and then the man who took it on dies or goes bankrupt, then whatever was taken on by him reverts to the first debtor."

36.32 Judgement on garments bought which have defects

Yaḥyā related that he heard Mālik say, "If a man buys a garment which has a defect, a burn or something else which the seller knows about and it is testified against him or he acknowledges it, and the man who has bought it causes a new tear which decreases the price of the garment, he can return it to the seller and he is not liable for his tearing it.

"If a man buys a garment which has a defect, a burn or a flaw, and the one who sold it to him claims that he did not know about it, and the buyer has cut the garment or dyed it, then the buyer has an option. If he wishes, he can have a reduction according to what the burn or flaw detracts from the price of the garment and he can keep the garment, or if he wishes to pay damages for what the cutting or dyeing has decreased of the price of the garment and return it, he can do so.

"If the buyer has dyed the garment with a dye which increases the value, the buyer has an option. If he wishes, he has a reduction from the price of the garment according to what the defect diminishes or, if he wishes to become a partner with the one who sold the garment, he does so. The price of the garment with the burn or flaw is looked at. If the price is ten dirhams, and the amount by which the dyeing increases the value is five dirhams, then they are partners in the garment, each according to his share. Taken into reckoning is the amount by which the dyeing increases the price of the garment."

36.33 What is not permitted in giving gifts (1)

39 Yaḥyā related to me from Mālik from Ibn Shihāb from Ḥumayd ibn 'Abd ar-Raḥmān ibn 'Awf and from Muḥammad ibn an-Nu'mān ibn Bashīr and they related to him that an-Nu'mān ibn Bashīr said that his father, Bashīr, brought him to the Messenger of Allah ﷺ and said, "I have given this son of mine one of my slaves." The Messenger of Allah ﷺ asked, "Have you given each of your children something similar?" He said, "No." The Messenger of Allah ﷺ said, "Then take the slave back."

40 Mālik related to me from Ibn Shihāb from 'Urwa ibn az-Zubayr that 'Ā'isha, the wife of the Prophet ﷺ, said, "Abū Bakr aṣ-Ṣiddīq gave me some palm-trees which produced twenty *awsāq* from his property in al-Ghāba. When he was dying, he said, 'By Allah, little daughter, there is no one I would prefer to be wealthy after I die than you. There is no one it is more difficult for me to see poor after I die than you. I gave you some palm-trees which produce twenty *awsāq*. If you had cut them and taken possession of them, they would have been yours, but today they are the property of the heirs who are your two brothers and two sisters, so divide it according to the Book of Allah.'"

'Ā'isha continued, "I said, 'My father! By Allah, even if it had been more, I would have left it! There is only Asmā'. Who is my other sister?' Abū Bakr replied, 'What is in the womb of Kharīja. I think that it is going to be a girl.'"

41 Mālik related to me from Ibn Shihāb from 'Urwa ibn az-Zubayr from 'Abd ar-Raḥmān ibn 'Abd al-Qārī that 'Umar ibn al-Khattāb said, "What

is wrong with men who give their sons gifts and then keep hold of them? If the son dies, they say, 'My property is in my possession and I did not give it to anyone.' But if they themselves are dying, they say, 'It belongs to my son. I gave it to him.' If someone gives a gift and does not hand it over to the one to whom it was given, the gift is invalid and, if he dies, it belongs to the heirs in general."

36.34 What is not permitted in giving gifts (2)

Yaḥyā said that he heard Mālik say, "What is done in our community about someone who gives a gift, without intention of reward, is that he calls witnesses to it. It is confirmed as belonging to the one to whom it has been given unless the giver dies before the one to whom it was given receives the gift."

He added, "If the giver wants to keep the gift after he has had it witnessed he cannot. If the recipient claims it from him, he takes it."

Mālik said, "If someone gives a gift and then withdraws it and the recipient brings a witness to testify for him that he was given the gift, be it goods, gold, silver or animals, the recipient is made to take an oath. If he refuses, the giver is made to take an oath. If he also refuses to take an oath, he gives to the recipient what he claims from him, if he has at least one witness. If he does not have any witness, then he has no claim."

Mālik said, "If someone gives a gift, not expecting anything in return, and then the recipient dies, the heirs take his place. If the giver dies before the recipient has received his gift, the recipient has nothing. That is because he was given a gift which he did not take possession of. If the giver wants to keep it, and he has already called witnesses to the gift, he cannot do so. When the recipient claims his right, he takes it."

36.35 Judgement on gifts

42 Mālik related to me from Dāwūd ibn al-Husayn from Abū Ghaṭafān ibn Ṭarīf al-Murrī that 'Umar ibn al-Khaṭṭāb said, " If someone gives

a gift to strengthen ties with a relative or as *ṣadaqa*, he cannot have it returned. If someone, however, gives a gift seeking by it favour or reward, he has the right to his gift and can reclaim it, if he does not have satisfaction from it."

Yaḥyā said that he heard Mālik say, "The generally agreed on way of doing things in our community is that if the gift is returned to the one who gave it for some recompense, and its value has been either increased or decreased, the one to whom it has been given only gives the owner its value on the day he received it."

36.36 Taking back *ṣadaqa*

Yaḥyā said that he heard Mālik say, "The way of doing things in our community about which there is no dispute is that if a man gives *ṣadaqa* to his son – *ṣadaqa* which the son takes possession of or which is in the father's keeping and the father has had his *ṣadaqa* witnessed – he cannot take it back any of it because he cannot reclaim any *ṣadaqa*."

Yaḥyā said that he heard Mālik say, "The generally agreed on way of doing things in our community in the case of someone who gives his son a gift, or grants him a gift which is not *ṣadaqa*, is that he can take it back as long as the child does not start a debt, which people claim from him and which they trust him for, on the strength of the gift which his father has given him. The father cannot take back anything from the gift after debts are started against it."

"If a man gives his son or daughter something and a woman marries the son only on account of the wealth and property which his father has given him and then the father wants to take it back, or if a man marries a woman whose father has given her a gift and he marries her with an increased bride-price because of the wealth and property that her father has given her, and then the father says, 'I take it back,' the father cannot then take back any such gift from the son or the daughter if the situation is as described."

36.37 Judgement on life grants

43 Mālik related to me from Ibn Shihāb from Abū Salama ibn 'Abd ar-Raḥmān ibn 'Awf from Jābir ibn 'Abdullāh al-Anṣārī that the Messenger of Allah ﷺ said, "If someone is given a life grant for himself and his posterity, it belongs to the person to whom it has been given. It never reverts to the one who gave it because he gave a gift and the rules of inheritance apply to it."

44 Mālik related to me from Yaḥyā ibn Sa'īd that 'Abd ar-Raḥmān ibn al-Qāsim ibn Muḥammad heard Makḥūl ad-Dimashqī ask al-Qāsim ibn Muḥammad about the life grant and what people said about it. Al-Qāsim ibn Muḥammad said, "I have only come upon people who keep to the conditions they make about their property and what they are given."

Yaḥyā said that he heard Mālik say, "What is done in our community is that the life grant reverts to the one who makes it a life grant unless he says, 'It belongs to you and your posterity.'"

45 Mālik related to me from Nāfi' that 'Abdullāh ibn 'Umar inherited the house of Ḥafṣa bint 'Umar. He said, "Ḥafṣa gave lodging to the daughter of Zayd ibn al-Khaṭṭāb for as long as she lived. When Zayd's daughter died, 'Abdullāh ibn 'Umar took possession of the dwelling and considered it to be his."

36.38 The ruling on lost property which is found

46 Mālik related to me from Rabi'a ibn Abī 'Abd ar-Raḥmān from Yazīd, the *mawlā* of al-Munba'ith that Zayd ibn Khālid al-Juhanī said, "A man came to the Messenger of Allah ﷺ and asked him about finds. He said, 'Note the details of the object found and then publicise it for a year. If the owner comes, give it to him. If not, then it is your business.' He said, 'What about lost sheep, Messenger of Allah?' He replied, 'They are yours, your brother's or the wolf's.' He asked, 'And the lost camel?' He said, 'It is none of your concern. It has its water and its feet. It will reach water and eat trees until its owner finds it.'"

47 Mālik related to me from Ayyūb ibn Mūsā from Mu'āwiya ibn 'Abdullāh ibn Badr al-Juhanī that his father informed him that he stopped with some people on the way to Syria and found a purse which contained eighty dinars. He mentioned that to 'Umar ibn al-Khattāb. 'Umar told him, "Announce it at the doors of the mosques and mention it to everyone who comes from Syria for a year. When a year passes, it is your business."

48 Mālik related to me from Nāfi' that a man found something and went to Ibn 'Umar and said to him, "I have found something. What do you think I should do about it?" 'Abdullāh ibn 'Umar said to him, "Make it known!" He said, "I have done so." He said, "Do it again." He said, "I have done so." 'Abdullāh said, "I do not order you to use it. If you wished you could have left it."

36.39 Judgement on slaves using finds

Yaḥyā said that he heard Mālik say, "What is done in our community about a slave who finds something and uses it before the term which is set for finds has been reached – which is a year – is that it is held against his person. Either his master gives the price of what his slave has used or he surrenders his slave to them as compensation. If he refrains from using it until the term is reached which is set for finds and then uses it, it is a debt against him which follows him and is not against his person and there is nothing against his master for it."

36.40 Judgement on strays

49 Mālik related to me from Yaḥyā ibn Sa'īd from Sulaymān ibn Yasār that Thābit ibn aḍ-Ḍahhāk al-Anṣārī told him that he had found a camel at Ḥarra, so he hobbled it and mentioned it to 'Umar ibn al-Khaṭṭāb and 'Umar ordered him to make it known three times. Thabit said to him, "That would distract me from the running of my estate." 'Umar said to him, "Then let it go where you found it."

50 Mālik related to me from Yaḥyā ibn Sa'īd from Sa'īd ibn al-Musayyab that 'Umar ibn al-Khaṭṭāb said while he was leaning his back against the Ka'ba, "Whoever takes a stray is astray."

51 Mālik related to me that he heard Ibn Shihāb said, "There were many stray camels in the time of 'Umar ibn al-Khaṭṭāb and they were left alone. No one touched them until the time of 'Uthmān ibn 'Affān. He ordered that they be publicised and then sold, and if the owner came forward afterwards, he was given their price."

36.41 *Ṣadaqa* of the living for the dead

52 Mālik related to me from Sa'īd ibn 'Amr ibn Shuraḥbīl ibn Sa'īd ibn Sa'd ibn 'Ubāda from his father that his father said, "Sa'd ibn 'Ubāda accompanied the Messenger of Allah ﷺ on one of his raids while his mother was dying in Madīna. Someone told her, 'Leave a will.' She said, 'About what shall I leave a will? The property is Sa'd's property.' Then she died before Sa'd returned. When Sa'd ibn 'Ubāda returned, that was mentioned to him. Sa'd said, 'Messenger of Allah! Will it help her if I give *ṣadaqa* for her?' The Messenger of Allah ﷺ said, 'Yes.' Sa'd said, 'Such-and-such a garden is *ṣadaqa* for her,' naming the garden."

53 Mālik related to me from Hishām ibn 'Urwa from his father from 'Ā'isha, the wife of the Prophet ﷺ, that a man said to the Messenger of Allah ﷺ, "My mother died suddenly and I think that if she had spoken, she would have given *ṣadaqa*. Shall I give *ṣadaqa* for her?" The Messenger of Allah ﷺ said, "Yes."

54 Mālik related to me that he heard that a man of the Anṣār from the tribe of Banū al-Ḥārith ibn al-Khazraj gave *ṣadaqa* to his parents and then they died. Their son inherited the property he had given them, which was palm-trees. He asked the Messenger of Allah ﷺ about it and he said, "You are rewarded for your *ṣadaqa* and take it as your inheritance."

37. Wills and Testaments

37.1 The command to write wills

1 Mālik related to me from Nāfi' from 'Abdullāh ibn 'Umar that the Messenger of Allah ﷺ said, "It is the duty of a Muslim man who has something to be given as a bequest not to spend two nights without having a written will in his possession."

Mālik said, "The generally agreed on way of doing things in our community is that when the testator writes something in health or illness as a bequest, and it involves emancipation of a slave or such things, he can alter it in any way he chooses until he is on his death-bed. If he prefers to abandon a bequest or change it, he can do so unless he has made a slave *mudabbar* – there is no way to change what he has made *mudabbar*. He is allowed to change his testament because the Messenger of Allah ﷺ said, "It is the duty of a Muslim man who has something to be given as a bequest not to spend two nights without having a written will in his possession."

Mālik explained, "Had the testator not been able to change his will nor what was mentioned in it about freeing slaves, testators might withhold from making bequests from their property, whether it be freeing slaves or other than that. A man makes a bequest while he is healthy or travelling (i.e. he does not wait until he is on his death-bed)."

Mālik summed up, "The way of doing things in our community, about which there is no dispute, is that he can change whatever he likes of such things except for the granting of *mudabbar* status."

37.2 Permissibility of bequests made by children, simpletons, lunatics and idiots

2 Mālik related to me from 'Abdullāh ibn Abī Bakr ibn Ḥazm that 'Amr ibn Sulaym az-Zuraqī informed his father that it had been said to 'Umar ibn al-Khaṭṭāb, "There is an adolescent boy here who has not yet reached puberty. He is from the Ghassān tribe and his heir is in Syria. He has property and the only relative he has here is the daughter of one of his paternal uncles." 'Umar ibn al-Khaṭṭāb instructed, "Let him make her a bequest." He willed her a property called the well of Jusham.

Mālik added, "That property was sold for 30,000 dirhams, and the daughter of the paternal uncle to whom he willed it was none other than the mother of 'Amr ibn Sulaym az-Zuraqī."

3 Mālik related to me from Yaḥyā ibn Sa'īd from Abū Bakr ibn Ḥazm that a boy from Ghassān was dying in Madīna while his heir was in Syria. This was mentioned to 'Umar ibn al-Khaṭṭāb. He was told, "So-and-so is dying, should he make a bequest?" He said, "Let him make a bequest."

Yaḥyā ibn Sa'īd said that Abū Bakr had said, "He was a boy of ten or twelve." Yaḥyā said, "He made the well of Jusham a bequest, and her family sold it for 30,000 dirhams."

Yaḥyā said that he heard Mālik say, "The generally agreed on way of doing things in our community is that a simpleton, an idiot, or a lunatic who recovers from time to time can make wills if they have enough of their wits about them to recognise what they will. Someone who has not enough wits to recognise what he wills and is totally lacking in comprehension cannot make a bequest."

37.3 Limiting bequests to one-third of the estate

4 Mālik related to me from Ibn Shihāb from 'Āmir ibn Sa'd ibn Abī Waqqās that his father said, "The Messenger of Allah ﷺ came to me to treat me for a pain which had became hard to bear in the year of the Farewell *Ḥajj*. I said, 'Messenger of Allah, you can see how far the pain has reached me. I

have property and only my daughter to inherit from me. Shall I give two-thirds of my property as *ṣadaqa*?' The Messenger of Allah ﷺ said, 'No.' I asked, 'Half?' He said, 'No.' Then the Messenger of Allah ﷺ, said, 'A third, and a third is a lot. Leaving your heirs rich is better than leaving them poor to beg from people. You never spend anything on maintenance desiring the Face of Allah by it but that you are rewarded for it, even what you appoint for your wife.' Sa'd said, 'Messenger of Allah, will I be left here in Makka after my companions have left for Madīna?' The Messenger of Allah ﷺ said, 'If you are left behind and do righteous deeds you will increase your degree and elevation by them. Perhaps you will be left behind so that some people may benefit by you and others may be harmed by you. O Allah! make the *hijra* of my Companions complete and do not turn them back on their heels. The unfortunate one is Sa'īd ibn Khawla.' The Messenger of Allah ﷺ was distressed on his account for he had died at Makka."

Yaḥyā said that he heard Mālik speak about a man who willed a third of his property to a man and said as well, "My slave will serve so-and-so (another man) for as long as he lives, then he is free," then that was investigated and the slave was found to constitute a third of the property of the deceased. Mālik said, "The service of the slave is evaluated. Then the two of them divide it between them. The one who was willed a third takes his third and the one who was willed the service of the slave takes what was evaluated for him of the slave's service. Each of them takes from the service of the slave or from his wage, if he has a wage, according to his share. If the one who was given the service of the slave for as he long as lived dies, then the slave is set free."

Yaḥyā said that he heard Mālik speak about someone who willed his third and said, "So-and-so has such-and-such and so-and-so has such-and-such," naming some of his property and his heirs protested that it was more than a third." Mālik said, "The heirs then have an option between giving the beneficiaries their full bequests or dividing among the beneficiaries the third of the property of the deceased and surrendering to them their third. If they wish, their rights in it reach as far as they reach."

37.4 Dealing with the property of a pregnant woman, a sick person and someone present in battle

Yaḥyā said that he heard Mālik say, "The best of what I have heard about the testament of the pregnant woman and about what settlements she is permitted to make from her property is that the pregnant woman is like a sick person. When the sickness is slight and one does not fear for the sick person, he does with his property what he likes. If the illness is such that his life is feared for, he can only dispose of a third of his estate."

He said, "It is the same with a woman who is pregnant. The beginning of the pregnancy is good news and joy. It is not illness and not to be feared because Allah the Blessed, the Exalted, says in His Book, '*So We gave her the good news of Isḥāq and Ya'qūb after Isḥāq*' (11:71). And He says, '*She bore a light load and carried it around. Then when it became heavy they called on Allah, their Lord, 'If You grant us a healthy child, we will be among the thankful!'*' (7:189)

"When a pregnant woman becomes heavy, she is only permitted to dispose of a third of her estate. The beginning of this restriction is after six months. Allah, the Blessed, the Exalted, says in His Book, '*Mothers should nurse their children for two full years.*' (2:233) And He says, '*His bearing and weaning take thirty months.*' (46:15)

"When six months have gone by since the woman conceived, she is only permitted to dispose of a third of her property."

Yaḥyā said that he heard Mālik say, "A man who is advancing in the ranks for battle can only dispose of a third of his property. He is in the same position as a pregnant woman or an ill person who is feared for as long as that situation pertains."

37.5 Bequests to heirs and right of possession

Yaḥyā said that he heard Mālik say, "This *āyat* is abrogated. It is the word of Allah, the Blessed, the Exalted, '*If he has some goods to leave, to make a will in favour of his parents and relatives.*' (2:180) What came down about the division of the fixed shares of inheritance in the Book of Allah, the Mighty, the Exalted, abrogates it."

Yaḥyā said that he heard Mālik speak about an invalid who made a bequest and asked his heirs to give him permission to make a bequest, when he was so ill that he only had command of a third of his property, and they gave him permission to leave some of his heirs more than his third. Mālik said, "They cannot revoke that. Had they been permitted to do so, every heir would have done that and then when the testator died, they would take that for themselves and prevent him from bequeathing his third and what was permitted to him with respect to his property."

Mālik said, "If he asks permission of his heirs to grant a bequest to an heir while he is well and they give him permission, that is not binding on them. The heirs can rescind that if they wish. That is because when a man is well, he is entitled to all his property and can do what he wishes with it. If he wishes, he can spend all of it. He can spend it and give *ṣadaqa* with it or give it to whomever he likes. His asking permission of his heirs is permitted for the heirs when they give him permission when authority over all his property is closed off from him and nothing outside of the third is permitted to him, and when they are more entitled to two-thirds of his property than he himself is. That is when their permission becomes relevant. If he asks one of the heirs to give his inheritance to him when he is dying and the heir agrees and then the dying man does not dispose of it at all, it is returned to the one who gave it unless the dying man says to him, 'So-and-so (one of his heirs) is weak, and I would like you to give him your inheritance.' So he gives it to him. That is permitted when the dying man specifies it for him."

Mālik said, "When a man gives the dying man free use of his share of the inheritance, and the dying man distributes some of it and some remains, the residue is returned to the giver after the man has died."

Yaḥyā said that he heard Mālik speak about someone who made a bequest and mentioned that he had given one of his heirs something which he had not yet taken possession of, so the heirs refused to permit that. Mālik said, "Such a gift returns to the heirs as inheritance according to the Book of Allah, because the deceased did not mean that to be taken out of the third and the heirs do not have a portion in the third (which the dying man is allowed to bequeath)."

37.6 Effeminate men and the custody of children

5 Mālik said from Hishām ibn 'Urwa from his father that an effeminate man was once in the company of Umm Salama, the wife of the Prophet ﷺ. He said to 'Abdullāh ibn Abī Umayya while the Messenger of Allah ﷺ was listening. "'Abdullāh! If Allah grants you victory over Ṭā'if tomorrow, I will lead you to the daughter of Ghaylān. She has four folds on her front and eight folds on her back." The Messenger of Allah ﷺ said, "This sort of man should not mix freely with you." (It was customary to allow men with no sexual inclination to enter freely where there were women.)

6 Mālik related to me that Yaḥyā ibn Sa'īd said that he heard al-Qāsim ibn Muḥammad say, "A woman of the Anṣār was married to 'Umar ibn al-Khaṭṭāb. She bore to him 'Āṣim ibn 'Umar and then he separated from her. 'Umar came to Qubā' and found his son 'Āṣim playing in the courtyard of the mosque. He took him by the arm and placed him before him on his mount. The child's grandmother argued with 'Umar about the child, so they went to Abū Bakr aṣ-Ṣiddīq. 'Umar said, 'My son!' The woman said, 'My son!' Abū Bakr said, 'Do not interfere between a child and its mother.' 'Umar did not repeat his words."

Yaḥyā said that he heard Mālik say, "This is what I would have done in that situation."

37.7 Liability for defective goods

Yaḥyā said that he heard Mālik speak about a man who bought goods – animals or clothes or wares – and the sale was found to be not permitted so it was revoked and the one who had taken the goods was ordered to return the owner his goods. Mālik said, "The owner of the goods only has their value on the day they were taken from him, and not on the day they are returned to him. That is because the buyer is liable for them from the day he took them and whatever loss is in them after that is against him.

For that reason, their increase and growth is also his. A man may take the goods at a time when they are selling well and are in demand, and then have to return them at a time when they have fallen in price and no one wants them. For instance, the buyer may take the goods from the other man and sell them for ten dinars or keep them while at that price. Then he may have to return them while their price is only a dinar. He should not go off with nine dinars from the seller's property. Or perhaps they are taken by the buyer and he sells them for a dinar or keeps them while their price is only a dinar, then he has to return them and their value on the day he returns them is ten dinars. The buyer should not have to pay ten dinars from his property to the owner. He is only obliged to pay the value of what he took possession of on the day it was taken."

He added, "Part of what clarifies this is that when a thief steals goods, only their price on the day he stole them is considered. If cutting off the hand is necessary, because the thief is imprisoned until his situation is examined or he flees and then is caught, the delay of the cutting off of the hand does not cancel the *ḥadd* punishment which was obliged for him on the day he stole, even if those goods become cheap after that. Nor does delay oblige cutting off the hand if it was not obliged on the day he took those goods, even if they become expensive after that."

37.8 General chapter on rendering judgement and aversion to it

7 Mālik related to me from Yaḥyā ibn Sa'īd that Abū ad-Dardā' wrote to Salmān al-Farsī, "Come immediately to the Holy Land." Salmān wrote back to him, "Land does not make anyone holy. A man's deeds make him holy. I have heard that you were put up as a doctor to treat and cure people. If you are innocent, then may you have delight! If you are a quack, then beware lest you kill a man and enter the Fire!" When Abū ad-Dardā' judged between two men, and they turned from him to go, he would look at them and say, "Come back to me, and tell me your story again. A quack, by Allah!"

Yaḥyā said that he heard Mālik say, "If someone makes use of a slave without the permission of his master in anything involving danger to his person, whose equivalent has a fee, he is liable for what befalls the slave if anything befalls him. If the slave is safe and his master asks for his wage for what he has done, that is the master's right. This is what is done in our community."

Yaḥyā said that he heard Mālik say about a slave who is part free and part enslaved, "His property is suspended in his hand and he cannot begin anything with it. He eats from it and clothes himself in an approved fashion. If he dies, his property belongs to the one to whom he is enslaved."

Yaḥyā said that he heard Mālik say, "The way of doing things in our community is that a parent can take his child to account for what he spends on him from the day the child has property, cash or goods if the parent so desires."

8 Mālik related to me from 'Umar ibn 'Abd ar-Raḥmān ibn Dalāf al-Muzanī from his father that a man from the Juhayna tribe used to buy camels before people set out for the *ḥajj* and sell them at a higher price. Then he travelled quickly and used to arrive in Makka before the others who set out for *ḥajj*. He went bankrupt and his situation was put before 'Umar ibn al-Khattāb, who said, "O People! Al-Usayfi', al-Usayfi' of the Juhayna, was satisfied with his *dīn* and his trustworthiness because it was said of him that he arrived before the others on *ḥajj*. He used to incur debts which he was not careful to repay, so all of his property has been eaten up by it. Whoever has a debt against him, let him come to us tomorrow and we will divide his property between his creditors. Beware of debts! Their beginning is a worry and their end is destitution!"

37.9 Damages and injuries caused by slaves

Yaḥyā said that he heard Mālik say, "The *sunna* with us about crimes committed by slaves is that the hand is not cut off for any harm that a slave causes a man, or something he pilfers, or something guarded which he steals, or hanging dates he cuts down or ruins or steals. Such things are counted against the slave's person and do not exceed the price of the slave whether it is little or much. If his master wishes to give the value of what the slave has taken or ruined, or pay the blood-price for the injury he has caused, he pays it and keeps his slave. If he wishes to surrender him, he surrenders him, and none of that is against him. The master has the option in that."

37.10 What is permitted in gifts

9 Mālik related to me from Ibn Shihāb from Sa'īd ibn al-Musayyab that 'Uthmān ibn 'Affān said, "If someone gives something to his small child who is not old enough to look after it himself, and in order that his gift might be permitted he makes the gift public and has it witnessed, the gift is permitted, even if the father keeps charge of it."

Mālik said, "What is done in our community is that if a man gives his small child some gold or silver and then dies whilst it is in his own keeping, the child has none of it unless the father has set it aside in coin or placed it with a man to keep for the son. If he has done that, it is permitted for the son."

38. Setting Free and *Walā'*

38.1 Freeing a share held in a slave

1 Mālik related to me from Nāfiʿ from ʿAbdullāh ibn ʿUmar that the Messenger of Allah ﷺ said, "If a man frees his share of a slave and has enough money to cover the full price of the slave justly evaluated, he must buy out his partners so that the slave is completely freed. If he does not have the money, then he is partially free."

Mālik said, "The generally agreed on way of doing things among us in the case of a slave whose master makes a bequest to free part of him after his death: a third, a fourth, a half, or any such share, is that only the portion of him is freed that his master has named. This is because the freeing of that portion is only obliged to take place after the death of the master because the master has the option to withdraw the bequest as long as he lives. When the slave is freed from his master, the master is a testator and the testator only has access to free what he can take from his property, being the third of the property he is allowed to bequeath, and the rest of the slave is not free because the man's property has gone out of his hands. How can the rest of the slave which belongs to other people be free when they did not initiate the setting-free and did not confirm it and they do not have the *walā'* established for them? Only the deceased could do that. He was the one who freed him and the one for whom the *walā'* is confirmed. That is not to be borne by another's property unless he bequeaths, within the third of his property, what remains of a slave to be freed. That is a request against his partners and inheritors and the partners must not refuse the slave that when it is within the third of the dead man's property because there is no harm in that to the inheritors."

Mālik said, "If a man frees a third of his slave while he is critically ill, he must complete the emancipation so he is completely free of him, if it is within the third of his property that he has access to, because he is not considered to be the same as a man who frees a third of a slave after his death because had the one who freed a third of his slave after his death lived, he could have cancelled it and the slave's being set free would be of no effect. The master who made the freeing of the third of the slave irrevocable in his illness would still have to free all of him if he lived. If he died, the slave would be set free within the third of the bequest. That is because the command of the deceased is permissible in his third as the command of the healthy is permissible in all his property."

38.2 Making conditions when freeing a slave

2 Mālik said, "A master who frees a slave of his and settles his emancipation so that his testimony is permitted, his inviolability is complete, and his right to inherit confirmed, cannot impose stipulations on him like those imposed on a slave about property or service, nor can he get him to do anything connected with slavery because the Messenger of Allah ﷺ said, "If a man frees his share of a slave and has enough money to cover the entire price of the slave justly evaluated for him, he must give his partners their shares so that the slave is completely free."

Mālik commented, "If he owns the slave completely, it is more proper to free him completely and not mingle any slavery with it."

38.3 People who free slaves and own no other property

3 Mālik related to me from Yaḥyā ibn Sa'īd and somebody else from al-Ḥasan ibn Abī al-Ḥasan al-Baṣrī and from Muḥammad ibn Sīrīn that a man in the time of the Messenger of Allah ﷺ freed six of his slaves while he was dying. The Messenger of Allah ﷺ drew lots between them and freed a third of those slaves.

Mālik added that he had heard that the man did not have any property besides them.

4 Mālik related to me from Rabi'a ibn Abī 'Abd ar-Raḥmān that a man in the time of Abān ibn 'Uthmān's governorship freed all of his slaves and they were his sole property. Abān ibn 'Uthmān took charge of the slaves and they were divided into three groups. Then he drew lots on the basis that whichever group drew the short straw would be free. The straw fell to one of the thirds, and that third was set free.

38.4 Judgement on the property of slaves when they are set free

5 Mālik related to me that he heard Ibn Shihāb say, "The precedent in the *sunna* is that when a slave is set free, his property follows him."

Mālik said, "One thing which makes clear that a slave's property follows him when he is freed is that when the contract (*kitāba*) is written for his freedom, his property follows him even if he does not stipulate that. That is because the bond of *kitāba* is the bond of *walā'* when it is complete. The property of a slave and a *mukātab* are not treated in the same way as any children they may have. Their children are only treated in the same way as their property. This is because the *sunna*, about which there is no dispute, is that when a slave is freed, his property follows him and his children do not follow him, and when a *mukātab* writes the contract for his freedom, his property follows him but his children do not follow him."

Mālik said, "One thing which makes this clear is that, when a slave or *mukātab* becomes bankrupt, their property is taken but the mothers of their children and their children are not taken, because they are not their property."

Mālik said, "Another thing which makes it clear is that, when a slave is sold and the person who buys him stipulates the inclusion of his property, his children are not included in that property."

Mālik said, "Another thing which makes it clear is that, when a slave does injury to someone, he and his property are taken, but his children are not taken."

38.5 Freeing slaves who are *umm walads* and a general section on freeing

6 Mālik related to me from Nāfi' from 'Abdullāh ibn 'Umar that 'Umar ibn al-Khaṭṭāb said, "If a slave-girl gives birth to a child by her master, he must not sell her, give her away, or bequeath her. He enjoys her and when he dies, she is free."

7 Mālik related to me that he had heard that a slave-girl, who had been beaten by her master with a red-hot iron, came to 'Umar ibn al-Khaṭṭāb and he set her free.

Mālik said, "The generally agreed on way of doing things among us is that a man is not permitted to be set free while he has a debt which exceeds the value of his property. A boy is not allowed to be set free until he has reached puberty. The young person, whose affairs are managed, cannot be set free with his property, even when he reaches puberty, until he manages his property."

38.6 Slaves permitted to be freed when a slave must be freed by obligation

8 Mālik related to me from Hilāl ibn Usama from 'Aṭā' ibn Yasār that 'Umar ibn al-Ḥakam said, "I went to the Messenger of Allah ﷺ and said, 'Messenger of Allah, a slave-girl of mine was tending my sheep. I came to her and one of the sheep was missing. I asked her about it and she said that a wolf had eaten it. I became angry at her, as I am one of the children of Adam, and struck her on the face. As it happens, I have to set a slave free, so shall I free her?' The Messenger of Allah ﷺ questioned her, 'Where is Allah?' She said, 'In heaven.' He asked, 'Who am I?' She replied, 'You are the Messenger of Allah.' The Messenger of Allah ﷺ said, 'Free her.'"

9 Mālik related to me from Ibn Shihāb from 'Ubaydullāh ibn 'Abdullāh ibn 'Utba ibn Mas'ūd that one of the Anṣār came to the Messenger of Allah ﷺ with a black slave-girl of his. He said, "Messenger of Allah, I must set free a slave who is a believer. If you think that she is a believer, I will

set her free." The Messenger of Allah ﷺ questioned her, "Do you testify that there is no god but Allah?" She said, "Yes." He asked, "Do you testify that Muḥammad is the Messenger of Allah?" She said, "Yes." He went on, "Are you certain about the Rising after death?" She replied, "Yes." The Messenger of Allah ﷺ said, "Free her."

10 Mālik related to me that he had heard that al-Maqburī said that Abū Hurayra was asked whether a man who had to free a slave could free an illegitimate child to fulfil that obligation. Abū Hurayra said, "Yes, that will give satisfaction for him."

11 Mālik related to me that he had heard that Faḍāla ibn 'Ubayd al-Anṣārī, one of the Companions of the Messenger of Allah ﷺ, was asked whether it was permissible for a man who had to free a slave to free an illegitimate child. He said, "Yes, that will satisfy his obligation."

38.7 Slaves not permitted to be freed when a slave must be freed by obligation

12 Mālik related to me that he had heard that 'Abdullāh ibn 'Umar was asked whether a slave could be bought for the specific purpose of fulfilling the obligation of freeing a slave and he said, "No."

Mālik said, "That is the best of what I have heard on the obligation of freeing slaves. Someone who has to set a slave free because of an obligation on him may not buy one on the condition that he sets him free, because by doing so, whatever he buys is not completely a slave, since he has reduced its price by the condition he has made of setting him free."

Mālik added, There is no harm, however, in someone buying a person expressly to set him free."

Mālik said, "The best of what I have heard on the obligation of freeing slaves is that it is not permitted to free a Christian or a Jew to fulfil it, and one does not free a *mukātab* or a *mudabbar* or an *umm walad* or a slave to be freed after a certain number of years or a blind person. There is no harm in freeing a Christian, Jew, or Magian voluntarily because Allah, the Blessed, the Exalted, says in His Book, '*...either as a favour then or by ransom.*' (47:4) The favour is setting-free."

Mālik said, "As for obligations of freeing slaves which Allah has mentioned in the Book, one only frees a believing slave for them."

Mālik said, "It is like that when feeding poor people for *kaffāra*. One must only feed Muslims and one does not feed anyone who is following other than the *dīn* of Islam."

38.8 Freeing the living for the dead

13 Mālik related to me from 'Abd ar-Raḥmān ibn Abī 'Amra al-Anṣārī that his mother had wanted to make a bequest, but she delayed until morning and died. She had intended to set someone free so 'Abd ar-Raḥmān said, "I asked al-Qāsim ibn Muḥammad, 'Will it help her if I free a slave for her?' Al-Qāsim replied, 'Sa'd ibn 'Ubāda said to the Messenger of Allah ﷺ, "My mother has died, will it help her if I set a slave free for her?" The Messenger of Allah ﷺ replied, "Yes."'"

14 Mālik related to me that Yaḥyā ibn Sa'īd said, "'Abd ar-Raḥmān ibn Abī Bakr died in his sleep and 'Ā'isha, the wife of the Prophet ﷺ, set free many slaves for him."

Mālik said, "This is what I like best of what I have heard on the subject."

38.9 The excellence of freeing slaves, freeing adulteresses and illegitimate children

15 Mālik related to me from Hishām ibn 'Urwa from his father from 'Ā'isha, the wife of the Prophet ﷺ, that the Messenger of Allah ﷺ was asked what was the most excellent kind of slave to free. The Messenger of Allah ﷺ answered, "The most expensive and the most valuable to his master."

16 Mālik related to me from Nāfi' that 'Abdullāh ibn 'Umar freed an illegitimate child and its mother.

38.10 The right of the one who sets free to the *walā'*

17 Mālik related to me from Hishām ibn 'Urwa from his father that 'Ā'isha, the wife of the Prophet ﷺ, said, "Barīra came to me and said, 'I have written myself as a *mukātab* for my people for nine *ūqiyas*, one *ūqiya* per year, so help me.' 'Ā'isha said, 'If your people agree that I pay it all to them for you and that, if I pay it, your *walā'* is mine, then I will do it.' Barīra went to her masters and told them that and they did not agree. She came back from her masters while the Messenger of Allah ﷺ was sitting [there]. She said to 'Ā'isha, 'I offered that to them and they refused me unless they had the *walā'*.' The Messenger of Allah ﷺ heard that and asked her about it. 'Ā'isha told him and the Messenger of Allah ﷺ said, 'Take her and stipulate that the *walā'* is theirs, for the *walā'* is for the one who sets free.' So 'Ā'isha did that and then the Messenger of Allah ﷺ stood up in front of the people and praised Allah and gave thanks to Him. Then he said, 'What is wrong with people who make conditions which are not in the Book of Allah? Any condition which is not in the Book of Allah is invalid even if it is a hundred conditions. The decree of Allah is truer and the conditions of Allah are firmer and the *walā'* only belongs to the one who sets free.'"

18 Mālik related to me from Nāfi' from 'Abdullāh ibn 'Umar that 'Ā'isha, *Umm al-Mu'minīn*, wanted to buy a slave-girl and set her free. Her people said, "We will sell her to you provided that her *walā'* is ours." She mentioned that to the Messenger of Allah ﷺ and he said, "Do not let that hinder you for the *walā'* only belongs to the one who sets free."

19 Mālik related to me from Yaḥyā ibn Sa'īd from 'Amra bint 'Abd ar-Raḥman that Barīra came asking the help of 'Ā'isha, *Umm al-Mu'minīn*. 'Ā'isha said, "If your masters agree that I pay them your price in one lump sum and set you free, I will do it." Barīra mentioned that to her masters and they said, "No, not unless your *walā'* is ours." Yaḥyā ibn Sa'īd added that 'Amra bint 'Abd ar-Raḥmān claimed that 'Ā'isha mentioned that to the Messenger of Allah ﷺ and the Messenger of

Allah ﷺ said, "Buy her and set her free. The *walā'* only belongs to the one who sets free."

20 Mālik related to me from 'Abdullāh ibn Dīnār from 'Abdullāh ibn 'Umar that the Messenger of Allah ﷺ forbade selling or giving away the *walā'*.

Mālik said that it was not permissible for a slave to buy himself from his master on the provision that he could give the *walā'* to whomever he wished, as the *walā'* was for the one who set him free, and that, had a man given permission to his *mawlā* to give the *walā'* to whomever he wished, it would not have been permitted because the Messenger of Allah ﷺ had said, "The *walā'* belongs to the one who sets free." The Messenger of Allah ﷺ forbade selling or giving away the *walā'*. And so if it was permitted to his master to stipulate that for him and to give him permission to give the *walā'* to whomever he liked, then it would be a gift.

38.11 Slaves attracting the *walā'* when set free

21 Mālik related to me from Rabi'a ibn 'Abd ar-Raḥmān that Az-Zubayr ibn al-'Awwām bought a slave and set him free. The slave had children by a free woman. When Az-Zubayr freed him, he said, "They are my *mawālī*." The man argued, "They are the *mawālī* of their mother. Rather, they are our *mawālī*." They brought the dispute to 'Uthmān ibn 'Affān and 'Uthmān gave a judgement that Az-Zubayr had their *walā'*.

Mālik related to me that he had heard that Sa'īd ibn al-Musayyab was asked who had the *walā'* of the children whom a slave had by a free woman. Sa'īd said, "If their father dies and he is a slave who was not set free, their *walā'* belongs to the *mawālī* of their mother."

Mālik said, "Similarly, in the case of a child of a woman who is a *mawlā* who has been divorced by *li'ān*, the child is attached to the *mawālī* of his mother and they are his *mawālī*. If he dies, they inherit from him. If he commits a crime, they pay the blood-money for him. If his father acknowledges him, he is given a kinship to him and his *walā'* goes to the *mawālī* of his father – they are his heirs and pay his blood-money – and his father is punished with the *ḥadd* punishment."

Mālik said, "It is the same for a free-born woman divorced by *li'ān*. If the husband who curses her by *li'ān* does not acknowledge her child, the child is dealt with in the same way except that the rest of his inheritance, after the inheritance of his mother and his brothers from his mother, goes to all the Muslims as long as he was not given kinship to his father. The child of the *li'ān* is attached to the patronage of the *mawālī* of his mother until his father acknowledges him, because he does not have a lineage or paternal relations. If his parentage is confirmed, it goes to his paternal relations."

Mālik said, "The generally agreed on way of doing things among us, about a child of a slave by a free woman while the slave's father is free, is that the grandfather (the father of the slave) attracts the *walā'* of his son's free children by a free woman. They leave their inheritance to him as long as their father is a slave. If the father becomes free, the *walā'* returns to his *mawālī*. If he dies and he is still a slave, the inheritance and the *walā'* go to the grandfather. If the slave has two free sons, and one of them dies while the father is still a slave, the grandfather, the father of the father, attracts the *walā'* and the inheritance.

Mālik spoke about a slave-girl, married to a slave, who was set free while she was pregnant and then her husband became free before she gave birth or after she gave birth. He said, "The *walā'* of what is in her womb goes to the person who set the mother free because slavery touched the child before the mother was set free. It is not treated in the same way as a child conceived by its mother after she has been set free because the *walā'* of such a child is attracted by the father when he is set free."

Mālik said that, if a slave asked his master's permission to free a slave of his and his master gave him permission, the *walā'* of the freed slave went to the master of his master, and his *walā'* did not return to the master who had set him free, even if he were to become free himself."

38.12 The inheritance of the *walā'*

22 Mālik related to me from 'Abdullāh ibn Abī Bakr ibn Muḥammad ibn 'Amr ibn Ḥazm from 'Abd al-Malik ibn Abī Bakr ibn 'Abd ar-Raḥmān ibn al-Ḥārith ibn Hishām that his father told him that al-'Aṣī ibn Hishām had died leaving three sons, two by one wife and one by another wife. One of the two with the same mother died and left property and *mawālī*. His full brother inherited his property and the *walā'* of his *mawālī*. Then he also died and left as heirs his son and his paternal half-brother. His son said, "I obtain what my father inherited of property and the *walā'* of the *mawālī*." His brother said, "It is not like that. You obtain the property. As for the *walā'* of the *mawālī*, that is not the case. Do you think that, had it been my first brother who died today, I would not have inherited from him?" They argued and went to 'Uthmān ibn 'Affān. He gave a judgement that the brother had the *walā'* of the *mawālī*.

23 Mālik related to me from 'Abdullāh ibn Abī Bakr ibn Ḥazm that his father told him that he was sitting with Abān ibn 'Uthmān when an argument was brought to him between some people from the Juhayna tribe and some people from the Banū al-Ḥārith ibn al-Khazraj. A woman of the Juhayna tribe was married to a man from the Banū al-Ḥarith ibn al-Khazraj called Ibrāhīm ibn Kulayb. She died and left property and *mawālī* and her son and husband inherited from her. Then her son died and his heirs said, "We have the *walā'* of the *mawālī*. Her son obtained that." Those of the Juhayna said, "That is not the case. They are the *mawālī* of our female associate. When her child dies, we have their *walā'* and we inherit it." Abān ibn 'Uthmān gave a judgement that the people of the Juhayna tribe did indeed have the *walā'* of the *mawālī*.

24 Mālik related to me that he had heard that Sa'īd ibn al-Musayyab spoke about a man who died and left three sons and left *mawālī* whom he had freed. Then two of his sons died leaving children. He said, "The third remaining son inherits the *mawālī*. When he dies, his children and his brothers' children share equally in the *walā'* of the *mawālī*."

38.13 The inheritance of slaves set free and the *walā'* of Jews and Christians who set slaves Free

25 Mālik related to me that he had asked Ibn Shihāb about a slave who was released. He said, "His gives his *walā'* to whomever he likes. If he dies and has not given his *walā'* to anyone, his inheritance goes to the Muslims and his blood-money is paid by them."

Mālik said, "The best of what has been heard about a slave who is released is that no one gets his *walā'*, his inheritance goes to the Muslims and they pay his blood-money."

Mālik said that when the slave of a Jew or Christian became Muslim and was set free before being sold, the *walā'* of the freed slave went to the Muslims. If the Jew or Christian became Muslim later, the *walā'* still did not revert to him."

He said, "However, if a Jew or Christian frees a slave of their own religion, and then the freed person becomes Muslim before the Jew or Christian who set him free becomes Muslim, and then the one who freed him becomes a Muslim, his *walā'* reverts to him because the *walā'* was confirmed for him on the day he set him free."

Mālik said that the Muslim child of a Jew or Christian inherited the *mawālī* of his Jewish or Christian father, when the freed *mawlā* became Muslim before the one who set him free became Muslim. If the freed person was already Muslim when he was set free, the Muslim children of the Christian or Jew had nothing of the *walā'* of a Muslim slave because the Jew and the Christian did not have the *walā'*. The *walā'* of a Muslim slaves goes to the Muslim community.

39. The *Mukātab*

39.1 Judgement on the *mukātab*

1 Mālik related to me from Nāfiʿ that ʿAbdullāh ibn ʿUmar said, "A *mukātab* remains a slave as long as any of his *kitāba* remains unpaid."

2 Mālik related to me that he had heard that ʿUrwa ibn az-Zubayr and Sulaymān ibn Yasār said, "The *mukātab* remains a slave as long as any of his *kitāba* still remains to be paid."

Mālik said, "This is my opinion as well."

Mālik said, "If a *mukātab* dies and leaves more property than what remains to be paid of his *kitāba,* and he has children who were born during the time of his *kitāba* or whose *kitāba* has been written as well, they inherit any property that remains after the *kitāba* has been paid off."

3 Mālik related to me from Ḥumayd ibn Qays al-Makkī that a son of al-Mutawakkil had a *mukātab* who died at Makka and left (enough to pay off) the rest of his *kitāba* and he also owed some debts to people. He also left a daughter. The governor of Makka was not certain about how to judge in the case so he wrote to ʿAbd al-Malik ibn Marwān to ask him about it. ʿAbd al-Malik wrote to him, "Begin with the debts owed to people and then pay off what remains of his *kitāba*. Then divide what remains of the property between the daughter and the master."

Mālik said, "What is done among us is that the master of a slave does not have to give his slave a *kitāba* if he asks for it. I have not heard of any of the imāms forcing a man to give a *kitāba* to his slave. I have heard that when someone asked about that and said that Allah the Blessed, the Exalted said, '*Write a kitāba for them if you know of good in them*' (24:33), one of the people of knowledge recited these two *āyats*, '*When you have come out of iḥrām, then hunt for game*' (5:3) and '*Then when the prayer is finished spread through the earth and seek Allah's bounty*' (62:10)."

Mālik commented, "It is a way of doing things for which Allah the Mighty, the Majestic, has given permission to people, and it is not obligatory for them."

Mālik said, "I heard one of the people of knowledge say about the words of Allah the Blessed, the Exalted, '*Give them some of the wealth Allah has given you*' (24:33), that it meant that a man give his slave a *kitāba* and then reduce the end of his *kitāba* for him by some specific amount."

Mālik said, "This is what I have heard from the people of knowledge and what I have seen people doing here."

Mālik said, "I have heard that 'Abdullāh ibn 'Umar gave one of his slaves his *kitāba* for 35,000 dirhams and then reduced the end of his *kitāba* by 5,000 dirhams."

Mālik said, "What is done among us is that when a master gives a *mukātab* his *kitāba*, the *mukātab*'s property goes with him but his children do not go with him unless he stipulates that in his *kitāba*."

Yaḥyā said, "I heard Mālik say that in the case of a *mukātab* who was the owner of a slave-girl who was pregnant, and neither he nor his master knew that on the day he was given his *kitāba*, the child did not follow him because he was not included in the *kitāba*. He belonged to the master. As for the slave-girl, she belonged to the *mukātab* because she was his property."

Mālik said that if a man and his wife's son (by another husband) inherited a *mukātab* from the wife, and the *mukātab* died before he had completed his *kitāba*, they divided his inheritance between them according to the Book of Allah. If the slave paid off his *kitāba* and then died, the inheritance went to the son of the woman and the husband had nothing of the inheritance.

Mālik said that if a *mukātab* gave his own slave a *kitāba*, the situation was examined. If he wanted to do his slave a favour, and it was obvious by his making it easy for him, it was not permitted. If, however, he was giving him a *kitāba* from desire to find money to pay off his own *kitāba*, then he was permitted to do so.

Mālik said that if a man had intercourse with a *mukātaba* of his and she became pregnant by him, she had an option. If she liked she could be an *umm walad*. If she wished she could confirm her *kitāba*. If she did not conceive she still had her *kitāba*.

Mālik said, "The generally agreed on way of doing things among us, about a slave who is owned by two men, is that one of them does not give a *kitāba* for his share, whether or not his companion gives him permission to do so, unless they both write the *kitāba* together, because that alone would effect setting him free. If the slave were to fulfil what he had agreed on to free half of himself and then the one who had given a *kitāba* for half of him was not obliged to complete his setting-free, that would be in opposition to the words of the Messenger of Allah ﷺ, 'If someone frees his share in a slave and has enough money to cover the full price of the slave, justly evaluated for him, he must pay his partners their shares so that the slave is completely free.'"

Mālik said, "If he is not aware of that until the *mukātab* has met the terms, or before he has met them, the owner who has written the *kitāba* for him returns what he has taken from the *mukātab* to him, and then he and his partner divide him according to their original shares and the *kitāba* is invalid. He is the slave of both of them in his original state."

Mālik spoke about a *mukātab* who was owned by two men and one of them granted him a delay in the payment of the right which he was owed. His partner refused to defer payment and exacted his part of the due. Mālik said that if the *mukātab* then died and left property which did not complete the *kitāba*, "They divide it according to what they are still owed by him. Each of them takes according to his share. If the *mukātab* leaves more than his *kitāba*, each of them takes what remains to them of the *kitāba* and what remains after that is divided equally between them. If the *mukātab* is unable to pay his *kitāba* fully, and the one who did not allow him to defer his payment has exacted more than his associate did, the slave is still equally between them, and he does not return to his associates the excess of what he has exacted, because he only exacted his right with the permission of his associate. If one of them remits what is owed to him and then the *mukātab* is unable to pay, he belongs to both of them, and the one who has exacted something does not return anything, because he only demanded what he was owed. That is like the debt of two men in one writing against the same man. One of them grants him time to pay and the other is greedy and exacts his due. Then the debtor goes bankrupt. The one who exacted his due does not have to return any of what he took."

39.2 Assuming responsibility in *kitāba*

4 Mālik said, "The generally agreed on way of doing things among us is that when a group of slaves write their *kitāba* together in the same *kitāba* agreement, and some are responsible for others, and they are not reduced anything by the death of one of the responsible ones, and then one of them says, 'I cannot do it,' and gives up, his companions can use him in whatever work he can do, and they help each other with that in their *kitāba* until they are freed if they are freed, or remain slaves if they remain slaves."

Mālik said, "The generally agreed on way of doing things among us is that when a master gives a slave his *kitāba*, it is not permitted for the master to let anyone assume the responsibility for the *kitāba* of his slave if the slave dies or is incapable. This is not part of the *sunna* of the Muslims. That is because, when a man assumes responsibility to the master of a *mukātab* for what is owed of the *kitāba* and then the master of the *mukātab* pursues that from the one who has assumed that responsibility, he takes his money falsely. It is not as if he is buying the *mukātab*, so that what he gives is part of the price of something that is his, and neither is the *mukātab* being freed so that the price established for him buys his inviolability as a free man. If the *mukātab* is unable to meet the payments he reverts to his master and is his slave. This is because *kitāba* is not a fixed debt which can be guaranteed by the master of the *mukātab*. It is something which, when it is paid by the *mukātab*, sets him free. If the *mukātab* dies and has a debt, his master is not one of the creditors for what remains unpaid of the *kitāba*. The creditors have precedence over the master. If the *mukātab* cannot meet the payments and he owes debts to people, he reverts to being a slave owned by his master and the debts to people are the liability of the *mukātab*. The creditors do not enter with the master into any share of the price of his person."

Mālik said, "When people are written together in the same *kitāba* agreement and there is no kinship between them by which they inherit from each other, and some of them are responsible for others, then none of them are set free before the others until all the *kitāba* has been paid. If one of them dies and leaves property and it is more than all of what is against them, it pays all that is against them. The excess of the property goes to the master, and none of those who have been written in the *kitāba* with the deceased have any of the excess. The master's claims are overshadowed by their claims for the portions which remain against them of the *kitāba* which can be fulfilled from the property of the deceased because the deceased had assumed their responsibility and so they must use his property to pay for their freedom. If the deceased *mukātab* has a free child not born in *kitāba*, and who was not written in the *kitāba*, it does not inherit from him because the *mukātab* was not set free until he died."

39.3 Severance in the *kitāba* for an agreed price

5 Mālik related to me that he heard that Umm Salama, the wife of the Prophet ﷺ made a settlement with her *mukātab* for an agreed amount of gold and silver.

Mālik said, "The generally agreed on way of doing things among us in the case of a *mukātab* who is shared between two partners is that one of them cannot make a settlement with him for an agreed price, according to his portion, without the consent of his partner. That is because the slave and his property are owned by both of them and so one of them is not permitted to take any of the property except with his partner's consent. If one of them settles with the *mukātab* and his partner does not, and he takes the agreed price, and then the *mukātab* dies while he has property or is unable to pay, the one who made the settlement would not have anything of the *mukātab*'s property and he could not return what he settled for, so that his right to the slave's person would return to him. However, when someone settles with a *mukātab* with the permission of his partner and then the *mukātab* is unable to pay, it is preferable that the one who broke with him returns what he has taken from the *mukātab* in severance and he can have back his portion of the *mukātab*. This he can do. If the *mukātab* dies and leaves property, the partner who has kept hold of the *kitāba* is paid in full the amount of the *kitāba* which remains to him against the *mukātab* from the *mukātab*'s property. Then what remains of the property of the *mukātab* is between the partner who made severance and his partner, according to their shares in the *mukātab*. If one of the partners breaks off with him and the other keeps the *kitāba*, and the *mukātab* is unable to pay, it is said to the partner who settled with him, 'If you wish to give your partner half of what you took, so the slave is divided between you, then do so. If you refuse, then all of the slave belongs to the one who held on to possession of the slave.'"

Mālik spoke about a *mukātab* who was shared between two men and one of them made a settlement with him with the permission of his partner. Then the one who retained possession of the slave demanded the like of that for which his partner had settled, or more than that, and the *mukātab* could not pay it. He said, "The *mukātab* is shared between them because the man has only demanded what is owed to him. If he demands less than what the one who settled with him took, and the *mukātab* cannot manage that, and the one who settled with him prefers to return to his partner half of what he took so the slave is divided in halves between them, he can do that. If he refuses then all of the slave belongs to the one who did not settle with him. If the *mukātab* dies and leaves property, and the one who settled with him prefers to return to his companion half of what he has taken so that the inheritance is divided between them, he can do so. If the one who has kept the *kitāba* takes the like of what the one who has settled with him took, or more, the inheritance is between them according to their shares in the slave because he is only taking his right."

Mālik spoke about a *mukātab* who was shared between two men and one of them made a settlement with him for half of what was due to him with the permission of his partner, and then the one who retained possession of the slave was willing to take less than what his partner settled with him for, but the *mukātab* was unable to pay. He said, "If the one who made a settlement with the slave prefers to return half of what he was assigned to his partner, the slave is divided between them. If he refuses to return it, the one who retained possession has the portion of the share for which his partner made a settlement with the *mukātab*."

Mālik said, "The explanation of that is that the slave is divided into two halves between them. They write him a *kitāba* together and then one of them makes a settlement with the *mukātab* for half his due with the permission of his partner. That is a fourth of the entire slave. Then the *mukātab* is unable to continue, so it is said to the one who settled with him, 'If you wish, return to your partner half of what you were awarded and the slave is divided equally between you.' If he refuses, the one who held to the *kitāba* takes in full the fourth of his partner, for which he made settlement with the *mukātab*. He had half the slave, so that now gives him three-fourths of the slave. The one who broke off has a fourth of the slave because he refused to return the equivalent of the fourth share for which he settled."

Mālik spoke about a *mukātab* whose master made a settlement with him and set him free and what remained of his severance was written against him as debt, then the *mukātab* died owing debts to people. He said, "His master does not share with the creditors because of what he is owed from the severance. The creditors are dealt with first."

Mālik said, "A *mukātab* cannot become free of his master whilst he owes debts to people. He would be set free and find himself with nothing because the people to whom he is in debt have more right to his property than his master. He is not permitted to do that."

Mālik said, "According to the way things are done among us, there is no harm if a man gives a *kitāba* to his slave and settles with him for gold and reduces what he is owed of the *kitāba,* provided only that the gold is paid immediately. Whoever disapproves of that does so because he puts it in the category of a debt which a man has against another man for a set term and then gives him a reduction and he pays immediately. This is not like such a debt. The *mukātab*'s becoming free from his master is dependent on his giving money to speed up the setting-free. Inheritance, testimony and the *ḥudūd* are obliged for him and the inviolability of being set free established for him. He is not buying dirhams for dirhams or gold for gold. Rather it is like a man who, having said to his slave, 'Bring me such-and-such an amount of dinars and you are free,' then reduces that for him, saying, 'If you bring me less than that, you are free.' That is not a fixed debt. If it had been a fixed debt, the master would have been counted amongst the creditors of the *mukātab* when he died or went bankrupt. His claim on the property of the *mukātab* would be treated in the same way as theirs."

39.4 Injuries caused by *mukātabs*

6 Mālik said, "The best of what I have heard about a *mukātab* who injures a man so that blood-money must be paid is that if the *mukātab* can pay the blood-money for the injury along with his *kitāba* he does so and it is against his *kitāba.* If he cannot do that, and he cannot pay his *kitāba* because he must pay the blood-money of the injury before the *kitāba,* and he cannot pay the blood-money of the injury, then his master has an option. If he prefers to pay the blood-money of the injury, he does so and keeps his slave and he becomes an owned slave. If he wishes to surrender the slave to the injured person, he surrenders him. The master does not have to do more than surrender his slave."

Mālik spoke about people who were in a general *kitāba* and one of them caused an injury which entailed blood-money. He said, "If any of them does an injury involving blood-money, he and those who are with him in the *kitāba* are asked to pay all the blood-money of that injury. If they pay, they are confirmed in their *kitāba.* If they do not pay, and they are incapable of doing so, then their master has an option. If he wishes, he can pay all the blood-money of that injury and all the slaves revert to him. If he wishes, he can surrender the one who alone did the injury and all the others revert to being his slaves since they could not pay the blood-money of the injury which their companion caused."

Mālik said, "The way of doing things about which there is no dispute among us is that when a *mukātab* is injured in some way which entails blood-money or one of the *mukātab*'s children who is written with him in the *kitāba* is injured, their blood-money is the blood-money of slaves of their value, and what is appointed to them as their blood-money is paid to the master who has the *kitāba* and he reckons that for the *mukātab* at the end of his *kitāba* and there is a reduction for the blood-money that the master has taken for the injury."

Mālik said, "The explanation of that is, for example, that he has written his *kitāba* for three thousand dirhams and the blood-money taken by the master for his injury is one thousand dirhams. When the *mukātab* has paid his master two thousand dirhams and the blood-money for his injury is one thousand dirham he is free straightaway. If the blood-money of the injury is more than what remains of the *kitāba*, the master of the *mukātab* takes what remains of his *kitāba* and frees him. What remains after the payment of the *kitāba* belongs to the *mukātab*. One must not pay the *mukātab* any of the blood-money of his injury in case he might consume it and use it up. If he could not pay his *kitāba* completely, he would then return to his master one-eyed, with a hand cut off, or crippled in body. His master only wrote his *kitāba* against his property and earnings, and he did not write his *kitāba* so that he would take the blood-money for what happened to his child or to himself and then use it up and consume it. One pays the blood-money of injuries done to a *mukātab* and any children of his who are born in his *kitāba*, or whose *kitāba* is written, to the master and he takes it into account for him at the end of his *kitāba*."

39.5 Selling *mukātabs*

7 Mālik said, "The best of what is said about a man who buys the *mukātab* of a man is that if the man wrote the slave's *kitāba* for dinars or

dirhams, he does not sell him unless it is for merchandise which is paid immediately and not deferred, because, if it is deferred, it would be a debt for a debt. A debt for a debt is forbidden."

He said, "If the master has given a *mukātab* his *kitāba* in exchange for certain merchandise in the form of camels, cattle, sheep or slaves, it is more correct that a buyer buy him for gold, silver, or different goods than the ones his master wrote the *kitāba* for, and such a payment must be paid immediately, not deferred."

Mālik said, "The best of what I have heard about a *mukātab* when he is sold is that he is more entitled to buy his *kitāba* than the one who buys him, if he can pay his master the price for which he was sold in cash. That is because his buying himself is his freedom, and freedom has priority over whatever bequests accompany it. If one of those who have written the *kitāba* for the *mukātab* sells his portion of him so that a half, a third, a fourth or whatever share of the *mukātab* is sold, the *mukātab* does not have the right of pre-emption in what is sold of him. That is because it is like the severance of a partner, and he can only cut off part of his *kitāba* with the permission of his partners, because what is sold of him does not give him complete rights as a free man and his property is barred from him, and, by buying part of himself, it is feared that he will become incapable of completing payment because of what he has had to spend. That is not like the *mukātab* buying himself completely unless whoever has some of the *kitāba* remaining due to him gives him permission. If they give him permission, he is more entitled to what is sold of him."

Mālik said, "Selling one of the instalments of a *mukātab* is not lawful. This is because it is an uncertain transaction. If the *mukātab* cannot pay it, what he owes is nullified. If he dies or goes bankrupt and he owes debts to people, then the person who bought his instalment does not take any of his portion with the creditors. The person who buys one of the instalments of the *mukātab* is in the position of the master of the *mukātab*. The master of the *mukātab* does not have a share with the creditors of the *mukātab* for what he is owed of his slave's *kitāba*. It is the same with the *kharāj* (a set amount deducted daily from the slave against his earnings) which accumulates for a master from the earnings of his slave. The creditors of the slave do not allow him a share for whatever deductions have accumulated for him."

Mālik said, "There is no harm in a *mukātab* paying towards his *kitāba* with coin or merchandise other than the merchandise for which he wrote the *kitāba,* if it is identical with it, on time (for the instalment) or delayed."

Mālik said that if a *mukātab* died and left an *umm walad* and small children by her or by someone else, and they would not work and it was feared that they would be unable to fulfil their *kitāba,* the *umm walad* of the father was sold if her price would pay all the *kitāba* for them, whether or not she was their mother. They were paid for and set free because their father would not have forbidden her sale if he had feared that they would be unable to complete their *kitāba.* If her price would not cover the price for them, and neither she nor they could work, they all reverted to being slaves of the master.

Mālik said, "What is done among us in the case of a person who buys the *kitāba* of a *mukātab,* and then the *mukātab* dies before he has paid his *kitāba,* is that the person who bought the *kitāba* inherits from him. If, rather than dying, the *mukātab* cannot pay, the buyer has his person. If the *mukātab* pays his *kitāba* to the person who bought him and he is free, his *walā'* goes to the person who wrote the *kitāba* and the person who bought his *kitāba* does not have any of it."

39.6 The labour of *mukātabs*

8 Mālik related to me that he heard that 'Urwa ibn az-Zubayr, when asked whether the sons of a man who had a *kitāba* written for himself and his children and then died worked for the *kitāba* of their father or were slaves, said, "They work for the *kitāba* of their father and they have no reduction at all for the death of their father."

Mālik said, "If they are young and unable to work, one does not wait for them to grow up and they are slaves of their father's master unless the *mukātab* has left what will pay their instalments for them until they can work. If there is enough to cover their payments from what he has left, that is paid off on their behalf and they are left in their condition until they can work, and then if they pay, they are free. If they cannot manage it, they are slaves."

Mālik, speaking about a *mukātab* who died and left property which was not enough to cover his *kitāba* and he also left a child with him in his *kitāba* and an *umm walad*, and the *umm walad* wanted to work for them, said, "The money is paid to her if she is trustworthy and strong enough to work. If she is not strong enough to work and not trustworthy with property, she is not given any of it and she and the children of the *mukātab* revert to being slaves of the master of the *mukātab*."

Mālik said, "If people are written together in a single *kitāba*, and there is no kinship between them, and some of them are incapable and others work until they are all set free, those who worked can claim from those who were unable to the portion of what they paid for them, because some of them assumed the responsibility for others."

39.7 Freeing a *mukātab* on payment of his due before its term

9 Mālik related to me that he heard Rabi'a ibn Abī 'Abd ar-Rahmān and others mention that al-Furāfiṣa ibn 'Umar al-Ḥanafī had a *mukātab* who offered to pay him all of his *kitāba* that he owed. Al-Furāfiṣa refused to accept it and the *mukātab* went to Marwān ibn al-Ḥakam, who was the governor of Madīna, and brought up the matter. Marwān summoned al-Furāfiṣa and told him to accept the payment, but he refused. Marwān then ordered that the payment be taken from the *mukātab* and placed in the treasury. He said to the *mukātab*, "Go, you are free." When al-Furāfiṣa saw that, he took the money.

Mālik said, "What is done among us when a *mukātab* pays all the instalments he owes before their term is that he is permitted to do so. The master cannot refuse him that. That is because payment removes every condition from the *mukātab* as well as service and travel. The setting-free of a man is not complete while he has any remaining slavery, and in such a situation neither would his inviolability as a free man be complete and his testimony permitted and inheritance obliged and so on. His master must not make any stipulation of service on him after he has been set free."

Mālik said that it was permitted for a *mukātab* who became extremely ill and wanted to pay his master all his instalments because his heirs who were free would then inherit from him and he had no children with him in his *kitāba* to do so because by that he completed his inviolability as a free man, his testimony was permitted, and his admission of what debts he owed to people was permitted. His bequest was permitted as well. His master could not refuse him that by claiming that he was escaping from him with his property.

39.8 The inheritance of a *mukātab* on emancipation

10 Mālik related to me that he had heard that Sa'īd ibn al-Musayyab was asked about a *mukātab* who was shared between two men. One of them freed his portion and then the *mukātab* died leaving a lot of money. Sa'īd replied, "The one who kept his *kitāba* is paid what remains due to him, and then they divide what is left between them both equally."

Mālik said, "When a *mukātab* who fulfils his *kitāba* and becomes free dies, he is inherited from by the people who wrote his *kitāba* and their children and paternal relations – whoever is most deserving."

He said, "This is also for whoever is set free before he dies – his inheritance is for the nearest people to him of children or paternal relations who inherit by means of the *walā'*."

Mālik said, "Brothers, written together in the same *kitāba*, are in the same position as each other's children, when none of them have children written in the *kitāba* or born in the *kitāba*. When one of them dies and leaves property, he pays for them whatever remains against them of their *kitāba* and sets them free. The money left over after that goes to any children he may have rather than to his brothers."

39.9 Conditions concerning *mukātabs*

11 Mālik spoke to me about a man who wrote a *kitāba* for his slave for gold or silver and stipulated against him in his *kitāba* a journey, service, sacrifice or similar, which he specified by name, and then the *mukātab* was able to pay all his instalments before the end of the term. He said, "If he pays all his instalments and is set free and his inviolability as a free man is complete, but he still has this condition to fulfil, the condition is examined, and whatever involves his person in it, like service or a journey, etc., is removed from him and his master has nothing against him for it. Whatever there is of sacrifice, clothing or anything that he must pay that can be treated as dinars and dirhams, is valued, and he pays it along with his instalments, and he is not free until he has paid that along with his instalments."

Mālik said, "The generally agreed on way of doing things among us, about which there is no dispute, is that a *mukātab* is in the same position as a slave whom his master will free after a service of ten years. If the master dies before ten years, what remains of his service goes to his heirs and his *walā'* goes to the one who contracted to free him and to his male children or paternal relations."

Mālik spoke about a man who stipulated against his *mukātab* that he could not travel, marry, or leave his land without his permission, and that, if he did so without his permission, it was in his power to cancel the *kitāba*. He said, "If a *mukātab* does any of these things, it is not in the man's power to cancel the *kitāba*. Let the master put that before the ruler. A *mukātab*, however, should not marry, travel, or leave the land of his master without his permission, whether or not he stipulates it. That is because the man may write a *kitāba* for his slave for one hundred dinars and the slave may have one thousand dinars or more. He goes off and marries a woman and pays her bride-price which wipes away his money and then he cannot pay. He reverts to his master as a slave without property. Or else he may travel and his instalments fall due while he is away. He cannot do so, and *kitāba* is not based on such behaviour. That is in the hand of his master. If he wishes, he gives him permission for it. If he wishes, he refuses it."

39.10 The *walā'* of the *mukātab* when he is set free

12 Mālik said, "When a *mukātab* sets his own slaves free, it is only permitted with the consent of his master. If his master gives him consent, and the *mukātab* sets his slave free, his *walā'* goes to the *mukātab*. If a *mukātab* then dies before he has been set free himself, the *walā'* of the freed slave goes to the master of the *mukātab*. If the freed one dies before the *mukātab* has been set free, the master of the *mukātab* inherits from him."

Mālik said, "It is the same when a *mukātab* gives his slave a *kitāba* and his *mukātab* is set free before he is himself. The *walā'* goes to the master of the *mukātab* as long as he is not free. If the person who wrote the *kitāba* is set free, then the *walā'* of his *mukātab*, who was freed before him, reverts to him. If the first *mukātab* dies before he pays, or he cannot pay his *kitāba* and has free children, they do not inherit the *walā'* of their father's *mukātab* because the *walā'* has not been established for their father and he does not have the *walā'* until he is free."

Mālik, speaking about a *mukātab* who was shared between two men and one of them forewent what the *mukātab* owed him and the other insisted on his due, then the *mukātab* died and left property, said, "The one who did not abandon any of what he was owed is paid in full. Then the property is divided between them both, just as if a slave had died, because what the first one did was not setting him free – he only abandoned a debt that was owed to him."

Mālik explained, "One thing that makes this clear is that when a man dies and leaves a *mukātab*, and he also leaves male and female children, and one of the children frees his portion of the *mukātab*, that does not establish any of the *walā'* for him. Had it been a true setting-free, the *walā'* would have been established for whichever men and women freed him."

Mālik continued, "Another thing that makes this clear is that if one of them freed his portion and then the *mukātab* could not pay, the value of what was left of the *mukātab* would be adjusted because of the one who freed his portion. Had it been a true setting-free, his estimated value would have been taken from the property of the one who set free until he had been set completely free, as the Messenger of Allah ﷺ said, 'Whoever frees his share in a slave, justly evaluated for him, gives his partners their shares. If not he frees of him what he frees.'"

He added, "Another thing that makes this clear is that part of the *sunna* of the Muslims about which there is no dispute, is that whoever frees his share of a *mukātab*, the *mukātab* is not set fully free using his property. Had he been truly set free, the *walā'* would have been his alone rather than his partners. Another clarification is that part of the *sunna* of the Muslims is that the *walā'* belongs to whoever writes the contract of *kitāba*. The women who inherit from the master of the *mukātab* do not have any of the *walā'* of the *mukātab*. If they free any of their shares, the *walā'* belongs to the male children of the master of the *mukātab* or his male paternal relations."

39.11 What is not permitted in freeing a *mukātab*

13 Mālik said, "If people are together in the same *kitāba*, their master cannot free one of them without consulting any companions he may have in the *kitāba* and obtaining their consent. If they are young, however, their consultation means nothing and it is not permitted to them. That is because a man might work for all the people and he might pay their *kitāba* for them to complete their freedom. The master approaches the one who will pay for them, and on whom their delivery from slavery depends, and frees him and so makes those who remain unable to pay. He does it intending benefit and increase for himself. It is not permitted for him to do that to those of them who remain. The Messenger of Allah ﷺ said, 'There must be no harm nor return of harm.' This is the most severe harm."

Mālik said about slaves who wrote a *kitāba* together that it was permitted for their master to free the old and exhausted of them and the young, when such a one could not pay anything and there was no help nor strength contributed by them in the *kitāba*.

39.12 Freeing a *mukātab* and an *umm walad*

14 Mālik, speaking about a man who had his slave in a *kitāba* and then the *mukātab* died and left his *umm walad*, and there remained for him some of his *kitāba* to pay off and he left what would cover it, said, "The *umm walad* is a slave since the *mukātab* was not freed until he died, and he did not leave children that were set free by his paying what remained, so that the *umm walad* of their father was freed by their being set free."

Mālik said about a *mukātab* who set free a slave of his or gave *ṣadaqa* with some of his property and his master did not know about it until he had set the *mukātab* free, "That is what has been done and the master does not rescind it. If the master of the *mukātab* learns about it before he sets the *mukātab* free, he can reject it and not permit it. If the *mukātab* is then freed and it becomes in his power to do so, he does not have to free the slave nor give the *ṣadaqa* unless he does it voluntarily on his own."

39.13 Bequests involving *mukātabs*

15 Mālik said, "The best of what I have heard about a *mukātab* whose dying master frees him is that the *mukātab* is valued according to what he would fetch if he were sold. If that value is less than what remains against him of his *kitāba*, his freedom is taken from the third that the deceased can bequeath. One does not consider the number of dirhams which remain against him in his *kitāba*. That is because, had he been killed, his killer would not be in debt for other than his value on the day he killed him. Had he been injured, the one who injured him would not be liable for other than the blood-money of the injury on the day of his injury. One does not look at how much he has paid of dinars and dirhams of the contract he has written because he is a slave as long as any of his *kitāba* remains. If what remains in his *kitāba* is less than his value, only whatever of his *kitāba* remains owing from him is taken into account in the third of the property of the deceased. That is because the deceased leaves him what remains of his *kitāba* and so it becomes a bequest which the deceased has made."

Mālik said, "An illustration of that is that if the price of the *mukātab* is one thousand dirhams, and only one hundred dirhams of his *kitāba* remain, his master leaves him the one hundred dirhams which complete it for him. It is taken into account in the third of his master and by it he becomes free."

Mālik said that if a dying man wrote his slave a *kitāba*, the value of the slave was estimated. If there was enough to cover the price of the slave in one third of his property, it was permitted for him to do so.

Mālik said, "An illustration of that is that there is a slave worth one thousand dinars. His master writes him a *kitāba* for two hundred dinars as he is dying. A third of the property of the master is one thousand dinars, so that is permitted for him. It is simply a bequest which he makes from one third of his property. If the master has left bequests to people, and there is no surplus in the third after the value of the *mukātab*, one begins with the *mukātab*, they follow it because the *kitāba* is setting-free, and setting-free takes priority over other bequests. When those bequests are paid from the *kitāba* of the *mukātab*, the heirs of the testator have a choice. If they want to give the people with bequests all their bequests and the *kitāba* of the *mukātab* is theirs, they have that. If they refuse and hand over the *mukātab* and what he owes to the people with bequests they can do so, because the third commences with the *mukātab* and because all the bequests which he makes are as one."

If the heirs then say, "What our fellow bequeathed was more than one third of his property and he has taken what was not his," Mālik said, "His heirs choose. They are told, 'Your companion has made the bequests you know about and if you would like to give them to those who are to receive them according to the deceased's bequests, then do so. If not, hand over to the people with bequests one third of the total property of the deceased.'"

Mālik continued, "If the heirs surrender the *mukātab* to the people with bequests, the people with bequests have what he owes of his *kitāba*. If the *mukātab* pays what he owes of his *kitāba*, they take that as their bequests according to their shares. If the *mukātab* cannot pay, he is a slave of the people with bequests and does not return to the heirs, because they gave him up when they made their choice, and because when he was surrendered to the people with bequests, they were liable. If he died, they would not have anything against the heirs. If the *mukātab* dies before he pays his *kitāba* and he leaves property worth more than what he owes, his property goes to the people with bequests. If the *mukātab* pays what he owes, he is free and his *walā'* returns to the paternal relations of the one who wrote the *kitāba* for him."

Mālik, speaking about a *mukātab* who owed his master ten thousand dirhams in his *kitāba* and, when the master died, he remitted one thousand dirhams from it, said, "The *mukātab* is valued and his value is looked at. If his value is one thousand dirhams and the reduction is a tenth of the *kitāba*, that portion of the slave's price is one hundred dirhams, being a tenth of the price. A tenth of the *kitāba* is therefore reduced for him – that is converted to a tenth of the price in cash. That is as if he had had all of what he owed reduced for him. Had he done that, only the value of the slave – one thousand dirhams – would have been taken into account in the third of the property of the deceased. If that which he had remitted is half of the *kitāba*, half the price is taken into account in the third of the property of the deceased. If it is more or less than that, it is according to this reckoning."

Mālik said, "When a man reduces the *kitāba* of his *mukātab* by one thousand dirhams at his death from a *kitāba* of ten thousand dirhams, and he does not stipulate whether it is from the beginning or the end of his *kitāba*, each instalment is reduced for him by one-tenth."

Mālik said, "If a man dies and remits one thousand dirhams from his *mukātab* from the beginning or the end of his *kitāba*, and the original basis of the *kitāba* is three thousand dirhams, then the *mukātab*'s cash value is estimated. Then that value is divided. That thousand which is from the beginning of the *kitāba* is converted into its portion of the price according to its proximity to the term and its precedence, and then the thousand which follows the first thousand is according to its precedence in the order until the end. Every thousand is paid according to its place in advancing and deferring the term because what is deferred of that is less in respect of its price. Then it is placed in the third of the deceased according to whatever of the price befalls that thousand according to the difference in preference of that, whether it is more or less, then it is according to this reckoning."

Mālik, speaking about a man bequeathing another man a fourth of a *mukātab*, or freeing a fourth, and then the first man died and the *mukātab* died and left a lot of property, more than he owed, said, "The heirs of the first master and the one who was willed a fourth has a third of what is left over, and the one willed a fourth has a third of what is left over after the *kitāba* is paid. The heirs of his master get two-thirds. That is because the *mukātab* is a slave as long as any of his *kitāba* remains to be paid. He is inherited from by the possession of his person."

Mālik said about a *mukātab* whose dying master frees him, "If the third of the deceased will not cover him, he is freed from it according to what the third will cover and his *kitāba* is decreased accordingly. If the *mukātab* owed five thousand dirhams and his value is two thousand dirhams cash, and the third of the deceased amounts to one thousand dirhams, half of him is freed and half of the *kitāba* has been reduced for him."

Mālik said about a man who said in his will, "My slave so-and-so is free and write a *kitāba* for so-and-so" that the setting-free had priority over the *kitāba*.

40. The *Mudabbar*

40.1 Judgement on the *mudabbar*

1 Yaḥyā related to me that Mālik said, "What is done in our community in the case of a man who makes his slave-girl a *mudabbara* and she gives birth to children after that, and then the slave-girl dies before the one who gave her a *tadbīr,* is that her children are in her position. The conditions which were confirmed for her are confirmed for them. The death of their mother does not harm them. If the one who made her *mudabbara* dies, they are free if their value is less than one-third of his total property."

Mālik said, "For every mother by birth, as opposed to mother by suckling, her children are in her position. If she is free and she gives birth after she is free, her children are free. If she is a *mudabbara* or *mukātaba,* or freed after a number of years in service, or part of her is free and pledged, or she is an *umm walad,* any children she has are in the same position as their mother. They are set free when she is set free and they are slaves when she is a slave."

Mālik said about the *mudabbara* given a *tadbīr* while she was pregnant, "Her children are in her position. That is also the position of a man who frees his slave-girl while she is pregnant and does not know that she is pregnant."

Mālik said, "The *sunna* about such women is that their children follow them and are set free by their being set free."

Mālik said, "It is the same as if a man had bought a slave-girl while she was pregnant. The slave-girl and what is in her womb belong to the one who has bought her whether or not the buyer stipulates that."

Mālik continued, "It is not lawful for the seller to make an exception about what is in her womb because that is an uncertain transaction. It reduces her price and he does not know if that will reach him or not. It is as if one were selling the foetus in the womb of the mother. That is not lawful because it is an uncertain transaction."

Mālik said about the *mukātab* or *mudabbar* who bought a slave-girl and had intercourse with her and she became pregnant by him and gave birth, "The children of either of them by a slave-girl are in the same position as himself. They are set free when he is set free and they are slaves while he is a slave."

Mālik said, "When he is set free, the *umm walad* is part of his property which is surrendered to him when he is set free."

40.2 General section on *tadbīr*

2 Mālik, speaking about a *mudabbar* who says to his master, "Free me immediately and I will give you fifty dinars which I will have to pay in instalments," and his master says, "Yes, you are free and you must pay me fifty dinars and you will pay me ten dinars every year," and the slave is satisfied with this, then the master dies one, two or three days later, said, "The freeing is confirmed and the fifty dinars become a debt against him. His testimony is permitted, his inviolability as a free man is confirmed, as are his inheritance and his liability to the full *ḥudūd* punishments. The death of his master, however, does not reduce the debt for him at all."

Mālik said that if a man who made his slave a *mudabbar* died and he had some property on hand and some absent property, and in the property on hand there was not enough (in the third he was allowed to bequeath) to cover the value of the *mudabbar*, the *mudabbar* was kept there together with the property, and his tax (*kharāj*) was gathered until the master's absent property was clear. Then if a third of what his master left would cover his value, he was freed with his property and what had gathered of his tax. If there was not enough to cover his value in what his master had left, as much of him was freed as the third would allow, and his property was left in his hands.

40.3 Bequests involving *tadbīr*

3 Mālik said, "The generally agreed on way of doing things in our community is that any setting-free, which a man makes in a bequest that he wills in health or illness, can be rescinded by him when he likes and changed when he likes, as long as it is not a *tadbīr*. There is no way to rescind a *tadbīr* once he has made it.

"As for every child born to him by a slave-girl whom he wills to be set free but does not make *mudabbara*, her children are not freed with her when she is freed. That is because her master can change his will when he likes and rescind it when he likes, and being set free is not confirmed for her. She is in the position of a slave-girl whose master says, 'If so-and-so remains with me until I die, she is free.'" (i.e. he does not make a definite contract.)

Mālik said, "If she fulfils such a condition, that right is hers. If he wishes to do so before the fulfilment of the condition, he can sell her and her child, because he has not included her child in any condition he has made for her.

"The bequest of setting-free is different from *tadbīr*. The precedent of the *sunna* makes a distinction between them. Had a bequest been in the position of a *tadbīr*, no testator would be able to change his will and whatever he mentioned in it of setting-free. His property would be tied up and he would not be able to use it."

Mālik said about a man who made all his slaves *mudabbar* while he was well and they were his only property, "If he made some of them *mudabbar* before the others, one begins with the first until the third of his property is reached (i.e. their value is matched against the third, and those whose value are covered are free.) If he makes them all *mudabbar* in his terminal illness and says in one statement, 'So-and-so is free. So-and-so is free. So-and-so is free if my death occurs in this illness,' or he makes them all *mudabbar* in the same statement, they are matched against the third and one does not begin with any of them before the others. It is a bequest and they have a third of his property divided between them in shares. Then the third of his property frees each of them according to the extent of his share. No single one of them is given preference when that all occurs in his illness."

Mālik spoke about a master who made his slave a *mudabbar* and then he died and the only property he possessed was the *mudabbar* slave and the slave had property. He said, "A third of the *mudabbar* is freed and his property remains in his possession."

Mālik said about a *mudabbar* whose master gave him a *kitāba* and then the master died and did not leave any property other than him, "A third of him is freed and a third of his *kitāba* is reduced, and he owes two-thirds."

Mālik spoke about a man who freed half of his slave while he was ill and made irrevocable his freeing half of him or all of him, and he had made another slave of his *mudabbar* before that. He said, "One begins with the slave he made *mudabbar* before the one he freed while he was ill. That is because the man cannot revoke what he has made *mudabbar* and cannot follow it with a matter which will rescind it. When this *mudabbar* is freed, then what remains of the third goes to the one who had half of him freed so as to complete his setting-free entirely in the third of the property of the deceased. If what is left of the third does not cover that, whatever is covered by what is left of the third is freed after the first *mudabbar* is freed."

40.4 A master's intercourse with his *mudabbara*

4 Mālik related to me from Nāfi' that 'Abdullāh ibn 'Umar made two of his slave-girls *mudabbara*, and he had intercourse with them while they were *mudabbara*.

5 Mālik related to me from Yaḥyā ibn Sa'īd that Sa'īd ibn al-Musayyab used to say, "When a man makes his slave-girl *mudabbara* he can have intercourse with her. He cannot, however, sell her or give her away and her children are in the same position as her."

40.5 Selling *mudabbars*

6 Mālik said, "The generally agreed on way of doing things in our community about a *mudabbar* is that the owner cannot sell him or change the position in which he has put him. If a debt overtakes the master, his creditors cannot sell the *mudabbar* as long as the master is still alive. If the master dies and has no debts, the *mudabbar* is included in the third (of the bequest) because the master expected his work from him as long as he lived. He cannot serve the master all of his life, and then have the master free him from his heirs out of the main portion of his property when he dies. If the master of the *mudabbar* dies and has no property other than him, one third of him is freed, and two-thirds of him belong to the heirs. If the master of the *mudabbar* dies and owes a debt which encompasses the *mudabbar*, he is sold to meet the debt because he can only be freed in the third (which is allowed for the bequests)."

He said, "If the debt only includes half of the slave, half of him is sold for the debt. Then a third of what remains after the debt is freed."

Mālik said, "It is not permitted to sell a *mudabbar* and it is not permitted for anyone to buy him unless the *mudabbar* buys himself from his master. He is permitted to do that. Or else someone gives the master of a *mudabbar* money to free him. That is also permitted for him."

Mālik said, "His *walā'* belongs to his master who made him a *mudabbar*."

Mālik said, "It is not permitted to sell the service of a *mudabbar* because it is an uncertain transaction since one does not know how long his master will live. That is uncertain and it is not good."

Mālik spoke about a slave who was shared between two men and one of them made his portion *mudabbar.* He said, "They estimate his value between them. If the one who made him *mudabbar* buys him, he is all *mudabbar.* If he does not buy him, his *tadbīr* is revoked unless the one who retains ownership of him wishes to give his partner who made him *mudabbar* his value. If he gives him to him for his value, that is binding, and he is all *mudabbar.*"

Mālik spoke about the Christian man who made a Christian slave of his *mudabbar* and then the slave became Muslim. He said, "One separates the master and the slave, and the slave is removed from his Christian master and is not sold until his situation becomes clear. If the Christian dies owing a debt, his debt is paid from the price of the slave unless he has in his estate enough to cover the debt. Then the *mudabbar* is set free."

40.6 Injuries caused by *mudabbars*

7 Mālik related to me that he heard that 'Umar ibn 'Abd al-'Azīz gave a judgement about the *mudabbar* who did an injury. He said, "The master must surrender what he owns of him to the injured person. He is made to serve the injured person and recompense (in the form of service) is taken from him as the blood-money of the injury. If he completes that before his master dies, he reverts to his master."

Mālik said, "The generally agreed on way of doing things in our community about a *mudabbar* who does an injury and then his master dies and the master has no property except him is that the third (allowed to be bequeathed) is freed, and then the blood-money for the injury is divided into thirds. A third of the blood-money is against the third of him which was set free, and two-thirds are against the two-thirds which the heirs have. If they wish, they surrender what they have of him to the party with the injury, and if they wish, they give the injured person two-thirds of the blood-money and keep their portion of their slave. That is because that injury is a criminal action by the slave and it is not a debt against the master by which whatever setting-free and *tadbīr* the master had done would be abrogated. If there were a debt to people against the master of the slave, as well as the criminal action of the slave, part of the *mudabbar* would be sold in proportion to the blood-money of the injury and according to the debt. Then one would begin with the blood-money which was for the criminal action of the slave and it would be paid from the price of the slave. Then the debt of his master would be paid, and then one would look at what remained of the slave after that. His third would be set free, and two-thirds of him would belong to the heirs. That is because the criminal action of the slave is more pressing than the debt of his master, and so, if the man dies and leaves a *mudabbar* slave whose value is one hundred and fifty dinars, and the slave strikes a free man on the head with a blow that lays the skull open, and the blood-money is fifty dinars, and the master of the slave has a debt of fifty dinars, one begins with the fifty dinars which are the blood-money of the head wound, and it is paid from the price of the slave. Then the debt of the master is paid. Then one looks at what remains of the slave, and a third of him is set free and two-thirds of him remain for the heirs. The blood-money is more pressing against his person than the debt of his master. The debt of his master is more pressing than the *tadbīr* which is a bequest from the third of the property of the deceased. None of the *tadbīr* is permitted while the master of the *mudabbar* has a debt which is unpaid, since it is a bequest. That is because Allah, the Blessed, the Exalted, says, *'After any bequest made or any debts.'* (4:11)."

Mālik continued, "If there is enough in the third of the property that the deceased can bequeath to free all the *mudabbar*, he is freed and the blood-money due from his criminal action is held as a debt against him, which follows him after he is set free, even if that blood-money is the full blood-money. It is not a debt on the master."

Mālik spoke about a *mudabbar* who injured a man and his master surrendered him to the injured party, and then the master died and had a debt and did not leave any property other than the *mudabbar*. The heirs said, "We offered to surrender the *mudabbar* to the injured party." whilst the creditor said, "My debt exceeds that." Mālik said that if the creditor's debt did not exceed that at all, he was more entitled to it and it was taken from the one who owed the debt, according to what the creditor was owed in excess of the blood-money of the injury. If his debt did not exceed it at all, he did not take the slave.

Mālik spoke about a *mudabbar* who did an injury and had property, and his master refused to stand security for him. He said, "The injured party takes the property of the *mudabbar* for the blood-money of his injury. If there is enough to pay it, the injured party is paid in full for the blood-money of his injury and the *mudabbar* is returned to his master. If there is not enough to pay it, he takes the blood-money from it and uses the *mudabbar* for what remains of the blood-money."

40.7 Injuries caused by an *umm walad*

Mālik said in the case of an *umm walad* who injured someone, "The blood-money of the injury is the responsibility of her master from his property, unless the blood-money of the injury is greater than the value of the *umm walad*. Her master does not have to pay more than her value. That is because when the master of a slave or slave-girl surrenders his slave or slave-girl for an injury which one of them has done, he does not owe any more than that, even if the blood-money is greater. As the master of the *umm walad* cannot surrender her because of the precedent of the *sunna*, it is as if he had surrendered her when he pays her price. He does not have to pay more than that. This is the best of what I have heard about the matter. The master is not obliged to assume responsibility for more than an *umm walad*'s value because of her criminal action."

41. *Ḥudūd*

41.1 Stoning

1 Mālik related to me from Nāfi' that 'Abdullāh ibn 'Umar said, "The Jews came to the Messenger of Allah ﷺ and mentioned to him that a man and woman from among them had committed adultery. The Messenger of Allah ﷺ asked them, 'What do you find in the Torah about stoning?' They said, 'We make their wrong action known and flog them.' 'Abdullāh ibn Salām said, 'You have lied! It is stoning for it, so bring the Torah!' They spread it out and one of them placed his hand over the verse of stoning. Then he read what was before and after it. 'Abdullāh ibn Salām told him to lift his hand. He lifted his hand and there was the verse of stoning. They said, 'He has spoken the truth, Muḥammad. The verse of stoning is in it.' So the Messenger of Allah ﷺ gave the order and they were stoned."

'Abdullāh ibn 'Umar added, "I saw the man leaning over the woman to protect her from the stones."

Mālik commented, "By 'leaning' he meant throwing himself over her so that the stones fell on him."

2 Mālik related to me from Yaḥyā ibn Sa'īd from Sa'īd ibn al-Musayyab that a man from the Aslam tribe came to Abū Bakr aṣ-Ṣiddīq and told him, "I have committed adultery." Abū Bakr said to him, "Have you mentioned this to anyone else?" He replied, "No." Abū Bakr told him, "Then cover it up with the veil of Allah. Allah accepts repentance from His slaves." He was still unsettled so he went to 'Umar ibn al-Khaṭṭāb and told him the same as he had said to Abū Bakr and 'Umar gave him

the same answer as Abū Bakr had done. He was still unsettled so he went to the Messenger of Allah ﷺ and said to him insistently, "I have committed adultery." The Messenger of Allah ﷺ turned away from him three times. Each time the Messenger of Allah ﷺ turned away from him until it became too much. The Messenger of Allah ﷺ questioned his family, "Does he have some illness which affects his mind or is he mad?" They said, "Messenger of Allah, he is well." The Messenger of Allah ﷺ said, "Unmarried or married?" They replied, "Married, Messenger of Allah." The Messenger of Allah ﷺ then gave the order for him to be stoned.

3 Mālik related to me from Yaḥyā ibn Sa'īd that Sa'īd in al-Musayyab said, "I have heard that the Messenger of Allah ﷺ said to a man called Hazzāl from the Aslam tribe, 'Hazzāl, if you had veiled him with your cloak, it would have been better for you.'"

Yaḥyā ibn Sa'īd said, "I related this *ḥadīth* in an assembly which included Yazīd ibn Nu'aym ibn Hazzāl al-Aslamī. Yazīd said, 'Hazzāl was my grandfather. This *ḥadīth* is true.'"

4 Mālik related to me that Ibn Shihāb informed him that a man had confessed that he had committed adultery in the time of the Messenger of Allah ﷺ and he testified against himself four times, so the Messenger of Allah ﷺ gave the order for him to be stoned.

Ibn Shihāb said, "Because of this a man is to be taken for his own confession against himself."

5 Mālik related to me from Ya'qūb ibn Zayd ibn Ṭalḥa from his father, Zayd ibn Talha, that 'Abdullāh ibn Abī Mulayka informed him that a woman came to the Messenger of Allah ﷺ and informed him that she had committed adultery and was pregnant. The Messenger of Allah ﷺ told her, "Go away until you give birth." When she had given birth she came to him. The Messenger of Allah ﷺ told her, "Go away until you have suckled and weaned the baby." When she had weaned the baby, she came to him. He said, "Go and entrust the baby to someone." She entrusted the baby to someone and then came to him. He gave the order and she was stoned.

6 Mālik related to me from Ibn Shihāb from 'Ubaydullāh ibn 'Abdullāh ibn 'Utba ibn Mas'ud that Abū Hurayra and Zayd ibn Khālid al-Juhanī informed him that two men brought a dispute to the Messenger of Allah ﷺ. One of them said, "Messenger of Allah, judge between us by the Book of Allah!" The other, who was the wiser of the two, said, "Yes, Messenger of Allah, judge between us by the Book of Allah and give me permission to speak." He said, "Speak." He said, "My son was hired by this person and he committed fornication with his wife. He told me that my son deserved stoning and I ransomed him for one hundred sheep and a slave-girl. Then I questioned the people of knowledge and they told me that my son deserved to be flogged with one hundred lashes and exiled for a year, and they informed me that the woman deserved to be stoned." The Messenger of Allah ﷺ said, "By Him in whose Hand my self is, I will judge between you by the Book of Allah. As for your sheep and slave-girl, they should be returned to you. Your son should have one hundred lashes and be exiled for a year." He ordered Unays al-Aslamī to go the wife of the other man and to stone her if she confessed. She confessed and he stoned her.

7 Mālik related to me from Suhayl ibn Abī Ṣāliḥ from his father from Abū Hurayra that Sa'd ibn 'Ubāda said to the Messenger of Allah ﷺ, "What do you think I should do if I were to find a man with my wife? Should I leave him there until I have brought four witnesses." The Messenger of Allah ﷺ answered, "Yes."

8 Mālik related to me from Ibn Shihāb from 'Ubaydullāh ibn 'Abdullāh ibn 'Utba ibn Mas'ūd that 'Abdullāh ibn 'Abbās said, "I heard 'Umar ibn al-Khaṭṭāb say, 'Stoning is in the Book of Allah for those who commit adultery, men or women, when they are *muḥṣan* and when there is clear proof of pregnancy or a confession.'"

9 Mālik related to me from Yaḥyā ibn Sa'īd from Sulaymān ibn Yasār from Abū Wāqid al-Laythī that a man came to 'Umar ibn al-Khaṭṭāb while he was in Syria. He mentioned to him that he had found a man with his wife. 'Umar sent Abū Wāqid al-Laythī to the wife to question her about that. He came to her while there were women around her and mentioned to her what her husband had mentioned to 'Umar ibn al-Khaṭṭāb, and informed her that she would not be punished on his word

and began to suggest to her by that she should retract her confession. She refused to retract and held firm to her confession. ʻUmar gave the order and she was stoned.

10 Mālik related to me that Yaḥyā ibn Saʻīd heard Saʻīd ibn al-Musayyab say, "When ʻUmar ibn al-Khaṭṭāb came from Minā, he made his camel kneel at al-Abṭaḥ and then he gathered a pile of small stones and cast his cloak over them and dropped to the ground. Then he raised his hands towards the sky and said, 'O Allah! I have become old and my strength has weakened. My flock is scattered. Take me to You with nothing missed out and without having neglected anything.' Then he went to Madīna and addressed the people, saying, 'People! Sunan have been laid down for you. Obligations have been placed upon you. You have been left with a clear way unless you lead people astray right and left.' He struck one of his hands on the other and then said, 'Take care lest you destroy the *āyat* of stoning so that someone will say, "We do not find two ḥadds in the Book of Allah." The Messenger of Allah ﷺ, stoned, so we have stoned. By Him in Whose hand my soul is, had it not been that people would say that ʻUmar ibn al-Khaṭṭāb has added to the Book of Allah, I would have written it: "*The full-grown man and the full-grown woman, stone them absolutely.*" We have certainly recited that.'"

Mālik said, " Yaḥyā ibn Saʻīd said Saʻīd ibn al-Musayyab said, 'Dhū al-Ḥijja had not passed before ʻUmar was murdered, may Allah have mercy on him.'"

Yaḥyā said that he heard Mālik say, "As for his words, 'The full-grown man and the full-grown woman' he meant, 'The man and the woman who have been married, stone them absolutely.'"

11 Mālik related to me that he had heard that ʻUthmān ibn ʻAffān was brought a woman to be stoned. ʻAlī ibn Abī Ṭālib said to him, "She does not deserve that. Allah, the Blessed, the Exalted, says in His Book, '*His bearing and weaning take thirty months.*' (46:15) and he said, '*Mothers should nurse their children for two full years for those who wish to complete the full term of nursing.*' (2:233) Pregnancy therefore can be six months, so she does not deserve to be stoned." ʻUthmān ibn ʻAffān sent for her and found that she had already been stoned.

Mālik related to me that he asked Ibn Shihāb about someone who committed sodomy. Ibn Shihāb said, "He is to be stoned, whether or not he is *muḥṣan.*"

41.2 Self-confession of fornication

12 Mālik related to me from Zayd ibn Aslam that a man confessed to fornication in the time of the Messenger of Allah ﷺ. The Messenger of Allah ﷺ called for a whip and he was brought a broken whip. He said, "Better than this," and he was brought a new whip whose knots had not been frayed yet. He said, "Not so good as this," and he was brought a whip which had been used and was flexible. The Messenger of Allah ﷺ gave the order and he was flogged. Then he said, "People! The time has come for you to observe the limits of Allah. Whoever has had any of these ugly things befall him should cover them up with the veil of Allah. Whoever reveals his wrong action to us, we will perform what is in the Book of Allah against him."

13 Mālik related to me from Nāfi' that Ṣafiyya bint Abī 'Ubayd informed him that a man who had had intercourse with a virgin slave-girl and made her pregnant was brought to Abū Bakr aṣ-Ṣiddīq. He confessed to fornication and he was not *muḥṣan.* Abū Bakr gave the order for him to be flogged with the *ḥadd* punishment. Then he was banished to Fadak (thirty miles from Madīna).

Mālik spoke about a person who confessed to fornication and then retracted his confession, saying, "I did not do it. I said that for such-and-such a reason," and he mentioned the reason. Mālik said, "That is accepted from him and the *ḥadd* is not imposed on him. That is because the *ḥadd* is what is for Allah and it is only applied by one of two means, either by clear evidence which establishes guilt or by a confession which is persisted in so that the *ḥadd* is imposed. If someone persists in his confession, the *ḥadd* is imposed on him."

Mālik said, "I have not seen the people of knowledge exiling slaves who have committed adultery."

41.3 The *ḥadd* for fornication

14 Mālik related to me from Ibn Shihāb from 'Ubaydullāh ibn 'Abdullāh ibn 'Utba ibn Mas'ūd from Abū Hurayra and Zayd ibn Khālid al-Juhanī that the Messenger of Allah ﷺ was asked about a slave-girl who committed fornication and was not *muḥṣana*. He said, "If she commits fornication, then flog her. If she commits fornication again, then flog her, and if she commits fornication yet again, then sell her, if only for a rope."

Ibn Shihāb added, "I do not know whether it was three or four times."

15 Mālik related to me from Nāfi' that a slave was in charge of the slaves in the *khumus* and he forced a slave-girl among those slaves against her will and had intercourse with her. 'Umar ibn al-Khaṭṭāb had him flogged and banished him, but he did not flog the slave-girl because the slave had forced her.

16 Mālik related to me from Yaḥyā ibn Sa'īd that Sulaymān ibn Yasār informed him that 'Abdullāh ibn 'Abbās ibn Abī Rabi'a al-Makhzūmī said, "'Umar ibn al-Khaṭṭāb gave me orders about the slaves of Quraysh and we flogged some of the slave-girls in the Muslim lands fifty times for each act of fornication."

41.4 Rape

Mālik said, "The position with us about a woman who is found to be pregnant and has no husband and she says, 'I was forced,' or she says, 'I was married,' is that it is not accepted from her and the *ḥadd* is inflicted on her unless she has clear evidence of what she claims about the marriage or being forced or if she comes bleeding if she was a virgin or she calls out for help so that someone comes to her and she is in that state or what resembles of it of the situation in which the violation occurred." He said, "If she does not produce any of those, the *ḥadd* is inflicted on her and whatever such claims she makes are not accepted from her."

Mālik said, "A raped woman cannot marry until she has proved to be free of pregnancy by three menstrual periods."

He said, "If she doubts her periods, she does not marry until she has freed herself of that doubt."

41.5 The *ḥadd* for slander, denial of paternity and insinuation

17 Mālik related to me that Abū az-Zinād said, "'Umar ibn 'Abd al-'Azīz flogged a slave with eighty lashes for slander."

Abū az-Zinād said, "I asked 'Abdullāh ibn 'Āmir ibn Rabi'a about that and he said, 'I saw 'Umar ibn al-Khaṭṭāb, 'Uthmān ibn 'Affān, the Khalīfas, and so on, and I did not see any of them flog a slave with more than forty lashes for slander."

18 Mālik related to me from Zurayq ibn Hakim al-Aylī that a man called Miṣbaḥ asked his son for help and he thought him unnecessarily slow. When the son came, his father said to him, "O fornicator." Zurayq said, "So the son asked me to help him against the father. When I wanted to flog him, his son said, 'By Allah, if you flog him, I will acknowledge that I have committed fornication.' When he said that, the situation was unclear for me, so I wrote to 'Umar ibn 'Abd al-'Azīz who was the governor at that time and I mentioned it to him. 'Umar wrote me to permit his pardon."

Zurayq said, "I also wrote to 'Umar ibn 'Abd al-'Azīz asking, 'What do you think about a man who is slandered, or his parents are slandered, and both or only one of them are dead?' 'Umar wrote to me, 'If he forgives, his pardon is permitted on his own behalf. If his parents are slandered and one or both of them are dead, take the judgement of the Book of Allah for it unless he wants to veil it.'"

Yaḥyā said, "I heard Mālik say, 'That is because the slandered man might fear that if it is unveiled about him, a clear proof might be established. If it is according to what we have described, his pardon is permitted."

19 Mālik related to me from Hishām ibn 'Urwa that his father said that there was only one *ḥadd* against a man who slandered a group of people.

Mālik said, "If they are on separate occasions there is still only one *ḥadd* against him."

Mālik related to me from Abū ar-Rijāl Muḥammad ibn 'Abd ar-Raḥmān ibn Ḥāritha ibn an-Nu'mān al-Anṣārī, of the Banū an-Najjar from his mother, 'Amra bint 'Abd ar-Raḥmān, that two men cursed each other in the time of 'Umar ibn al-Khaṭṭāb. One of them said to the other, "By Allah, my father is not an adulterer and my mother is not an adulteress." 'Umar ibn al-Khaṭṭāb asked advice about that. One person said, "He has praised his father and mother." Another said, "His father and mother have praise other than this. We think that he should be flogged with the *ḥadd*." So 'Umar flogged him with the *ḥadd* of eighty lashes.

Mālik said, "There is no *ḥadd* in our view except for slander, denial of paternity or insinuation in which one sees that what the speaker intends by that is denial of paternity or slander. Then the full *ḥadd* is imposed on the one who said that."

Mālik said, "What is done in our community, when a man denies that another man is his father's child, is that such a person should receive the *ḥadd*. If the mother who is the subject of the denial is a slave, then he should receive the *ḥadd* as well."

41.6 That for which there is no *ḥadd* punishment

Mālik said, "The best of what is heard about a slave-girl with whom a man has intercourse while he has a partner in her is that the *ḥadd* is not inflicted on him and the child is connected to him. When the slave-girl becomes pregnant, her value is estimated and he gives his partners their shares of the price and the slave-girl is his. That is what is done among us."

Mālik, speaking about a man who made his slave-girl lawful to a man, said that if the said that if the one for whom she was made lawful had intercourse with her, her value was estimated on the day he had intercourse with her and he owed that to her owner whether or not she conceived. The *ḥadd* punishment was averted from him by that. If she conceived the child was connected to him.

Mālik said about a man who had intercourse with his son's or daughter's slave-girl, "The *ḥadd* is averted from him and he owes the estimated value of the slave-girl whether or not she conceives."

20 Mālik related to me from Rabi'a ibn Abī 'Abd ar-Raḥmān that 'Umar ibn al-Khaṭṭāb spoke about a man who went out with his wife's slave-girl on a journey and had intercourse with her and then the wife became jealous and mentioned it to 'Umar ibn al-Khaṭṭāb. 'Umar questioned him about it. He said, "She gave her to me." 'Umar said, "Bring me clear evidence or I will stone you."

Rabi'a added, "The wife admitted that she had given her to him."

41.7 That which obliges cutting off the hand

21 Mālik related to me from Nāfi' from 'Abdullāh ibn 'Umar that the Messenger of Allah ﷺ cut off the hand of a man who stole a shield whose price was three dirhams..

22 Yaḥyā related to me from Mālik from 'Abdullāh ibn 'Abd ar-Raḥmān Abū Ḥusayn al-Makkī that the Messenger of Allah ﷺ said, "The hand is not cut off for fruit hanging on the tree and for sheep kept in the mountains. But when they are taken from the fold or the place where the fruit is dried, the hand is cut off for whatever reaches the price of a shield."

23 Yaḥyā related to me from Mālik from 'Abdullāh ibn Abī Bakr from his father from 'Amra bint 'Abd ar-Raḥmān that a thief stole a citron in the time of 'Uthmān. 'Uthmān ibn 'Affān ordered its value to be estimated and it was estimated at three dirhams at the rate of exchange of twelve dirhams for the dinar, so 'Uthmān cut off his hand.

24 Yaḥyā related to me from Mālik from Yaḥyā ibn Sa'īd from 'Amra bint 'Abd ar-Raḥmān that 'Ā'isha, the wife of the Prophet ﷺ, said, "It has not been a long time for me and I have not forgotten. A thief's hand is cut off for a quarter of a dinar and upwards."

25 Yaḥyā related to me from Mālik from 'Abdullāh ibn Abī Bakr ibn Ḥāzim that 'Amra bint 'Abd ar-Raḥmān said, "'Ā'isha, the wife of the Prophet ﷺ, went out to Makka with two girl *mawlās* of hers and a slave belonging to the sons of 'Abdullāh ibn Abī Bakr aṣ-Ṣiddīq. She sent a figured cloak with the two *mawlās* which was sewn up in a piece of green cloth."

'Amra continued, "The slave took it and unstitched it and took out the cloak. In its place he put some felt or skin and sewed it up again. When the *mawlā* girls came to Madīna, they gave it to his people. When they opened it, they found felt in it and did not find the cloak. They spoke to the two women and they spoke to 'Ā'isha, the wife of the Prophet ﷺ, or they wrote to her, suspecting the slave. The slave was questioned about it and confessed. Ā'isha, the wife of the Prophet ﷺ, gave the order for his hand to be cut off. Ā'isha said, "A thief's hand is cut off for a quarter of a dinar and upwards."

Mālik said, "The limit I prefer above which cutting off the hand is obliged is three dirhams, whether the exchange is high or low. That is because the Messenger of Allah ﷺ cut off the hand of a thief for a shield whose value was three dirhams, and 'Uthmān ibn 'Affān cut off the hand of a thief for a citron which was estimated at three dirhams. This is what I prefer of what I have heard on the matter."

41.8 Cutting off the hands of runaway slaves who steal

26 Yaḥyā related to me from Mālik from Nāfi' that a slave of 'Abdullāh ibn 'Umar stole while he was a runaway. 'Abdullāh ibn 'Umar sent him to Sa'īd ibn al-'Āṣ, who was the governor of Madīna, to cut off his hand. Sa'īd refused to cut off his hand. He said, "The hand of a runaway slave is not cut off when he steals." 'Abdullāh ibn 'Umar said to him, "In what Book of Allah did you find this?" Then 'Abdullāh ibn 'Umar gave the order and his hand was cut off.

27 Yaḥyā related to me from Mālik that Zurayq ibn Ḥakīm informed him that he had a runaway slave who had stolen. He said, "The situation was unclear to me, so I wrote to 'Umar ibn 'Abd al-'Azīz to ask him about

it. He was the governor at that time. I informed him that I had heard that if a runaway slave stole while he was a fugitive, his hand was not cut off. 'Umar ibn 'Abd az-'Azīz wrote to contradict what I had said in my letter, 'You wrote to me that you have heard that when the runaway slave steals, his hand is not cut off. Allah, the Blessed, the Exalted, says in His Book, *"As for both male thieves and female thieves, cut off their hands in reprisal for what they have done: an object lesson from Allah. Allah is Almighty, All-Wise."* (5:41). When his theft reaches a quarter of a dinar or more, his hand is cut off.'"

Yaḥyā related to me from Mālik that he had heard that al-Qāsim ibn Muḥammad and Sālim ibn 'Abdullāh and 'Urwa ibn az-Zubayr said, "When a runaway slave steals something for which cutting off the hand is obliged, his hand is cut off."

Mālik said, "The way of doing things amongst us about which there is no dispute is that when a runaway slave steals what obliges cutting off the hand, his hand is cut off."

41.9 Intercession is cut off for thieves when cases reach the ruler

28 Yaḥyā related to me from Mālik from Ibn Shihāb from Ṣafwān ibn 'Abdullāh ibn Ṣafwān that it was said to Ṣafwān ibn Umayya, "Whoever does not make *hijra* is ruined." So Ṣafwān ibn Umayya went to Madīna and slept in the mosque with his cloak as a pillow. A thief came and took his cloak and Safwān grabbed hold of the thief and brought him to the Messenger of Allah ﷺ. The Messenger of Allah ﷺ said to him, "Did you steal this cloak?" He said, "Yes." So the Messenger of Allah ﷺ ordered that his hand be cut off. Ṣafwān told him, "I did not intend this. It is his as *ṣadaqa*. The Messenger of Allah ﷺ said, "Why did you not do it before you brought him to me?"

29 Yaḥyā related to me from Mālik from Rabi'a ibn Abī 'Abd ar-Raḥmān that az-Zubayr ibn al-'Awwām came across a man who had taken hold of a thief and was intending to take him to the ruler. Az-Zubayr ibn al-'Awwām interceded with him to let him go. He said, "No, not until I take him to the ruler." Az-Zubayr said, "Once you reach the ruler with

him, Allah curses the one who intercedes and the one who accepts the intercession."

41.10 General section on cutting off the hand

30 Yaḥyā related to me from Mālik from 'Abd ar-Raḥmān ibn al-Qāsim from his father that a man from Yemen who had his hand and foot cut off presented himself to Abū Bakr aṣ-Ṣiddīq and complained to him that the governor of the Yemen had wronged him, and the man used to pray part of the night. Abū Bakr said, "By your father, your night is not the night of a thief!" Then they missed the necklace of Asmā' bint 'Umays, the wife of Abū Bakr aṣ-Ṣiddīq. The man came to go around with them looking for it. He said, "O Allah, You are responsible for the one who invaded the people of this good house by night!" They found the jewellery with a goldsmith who claimed that the maimed man had brought it to him. The maimed man confessed or there was testimony against him. Abū Bakr aṣ-Ṣiddīq ordered that his left hand be cut off. Abū Bakr said, "By Allah, his supplication against himself is far more serious than his theft as far as I am concerned."

Yaḥyā said that Mālik said, "What is done among us, about the person who steals several times and is then called to reckoning, is that only his hand is cut off for all he stole when the *ḥadd* has not been applied against him. If the *ḥadd* has been applied against him previously and he steals what obliges cutting off, then the next limb is cut off."

31 Yaḥyā related to me from Mālik that Abū az-Zinād informed him that a governor of 'Umar ibn 'Abd al-'Azīz took some people captive in battle and had not killed any of them. He wanted to cut off their hands or kill them, so he wrote to 'Umar ibn 'Abd al-'Azīz about that. 'Umar ibn 'Abd al-'Azīz wrote to him, "Better to take less than that."

Yaḥyā said that he heard Mālik say, "What is done among us about a person who steals goods, which people place under guard in the markets and their owners put them in their containers and store them together, is that if anyone steals any such thing from where it is kept, and its value reaches that for which cutting off the hand is obliged, his hand must be cut off, whether or not the owner of the goods is with his goods and whether it is night or day."

Mālik, speaking about someone who stole something for which cutting off the hand was obliged, and what he stole was found with him and he returned it to its owner, said, "His hand is cut off."

Mālik said, "If someone says, 'How can his hand be cut off when the goods have been taken from him and returned to their owner?' It is because he is in the same position as the wine drinker when the smell of wine is found on his breath and he is not drunk. He is flogged with the *ḥadd.*

He said, "The *ḥadd* punishment is imposed for drinking wine, even if it does not make the man intoxicated, because he drank it to become intoxicated. It is the same situation with cutting off the hand of the thief for theft when it is taken from him, even if he has not profited from it and it has been returned to its owner. When he stole it, he stole it to take it away."

Mālik said that if some people came to a house and robbed it together and then they left with a sack or box or board or basket or something similar which they carried together, and when they took it out of its guarded place, they carried it together and the price of what they took reached what obliged cutting off the hand, namely three dirhams or more, each of them had his hand cut off.

"If each of them takes something by himself, whoever of them takes out something whose value reaches three dirhams and upwards must have his hand cut off. If any of them takes out something whose value does not reach three dirhams, he does not have his hand cut off."

Yaḥyā said that Mālik said, "What is done among us is that when a man's house is locked and he is the only one living in it, cutting off the hand is not obliged against the one who steals something from it until he takes it completely out of the house. That is because the house is a place of custody. If someone other than him lives in the house and each of them locks his door, and it is a place of custody for each of them, whoever steals anything from the apartments of that house must have his hand cut off when he leaves the apartment and goes into the main house. He has removed it from its place of custody to another place and so he must have his hand cut off."

Mālik said, "What is done in our community, about a slave who steals from the property of his master, is that if he is not in service and among those trusted in the house and he enters secretly and steals from his master something for which cutting off the hand is obliged, his hand is not cut off. It is like that with a slave-girl when she steals from her master's property. Her hand is not cut off."

Mālik then spoke about a slave who was not in service and not one of those trusted in the house and he entered secretly and stole from the property of his master's wife something for which cutting off the hand was obliged. He said, "His hand is cut off."

"It is like that with the wife's slave-girl when she does not serve her or her husband nor is she trusted in the house and she enters secretly and steals from her mistress's property something for which cutting off the hand is obliged. Her hand is not cut off.

Mālik said, "Similarly, a woman's slave-girl who was not in service to her or her husband and not one of those trusted in the house and she entered secretly and stole from the property of her mistress's husband something for which cutting off the hand was obliged, her hand is cut off."

"It is like that with the man who steals from his wife's goods or the wife who steals from her husband's goods something for which cutting off the hand is obliged. If the thing which one of them steals from his spouse's property is in a room other than the room which they both lock for themselves, or it is in a place of custody in a room other than the room which they are in, whichever of them steals something for which cutting off the hand is obliged, their hand should be cut off."

Mālik spoke about small children and foreigners who do not speak clearly. He said, "If they are robbed of something from its place of custody or from under a lock, the one who stole it has his hand cut off. If the property is outside its place of custody or locked room (when it is stolen), the one who robbed them does not have his hand cut off. It is then in the same position as sheep stolen from the mountain and uncut fruit hanging on the trees."

Mālik said, "What is done among us about a person who robs graves is that if what he takes from the grave reached what obliges cutting off the hand, his hand is cut off. That is because the grave is a place of custody for what is in it just as houses are a place off custody for what is in them."

Mālik added, "Cutting off the hand is not obliged until he removes it from the grave."

41.11 Things for which the hand is not cut off

32 Yaḥyā related to me from Mālik from Yaḥyā ibn Sa'īd from Muḥammad ibn Yaḥyā ibn Ḥabbān that a slave stole a small palm from a man's garden and planted it in his master's garden. The owner of the palm went out looking for the palm and found it. He asked Marwān ibn al-Ḥakam for help against the slave. Marwān jailed the slave and wanted to cut off his hand. The master of the slave rushed off to Rafi' ibn Khadīj and asked him about it. Rāfi' informed him that he heard the Messenger of Allah ﷺ say, "The hand is not cut off for fruit or palm pith." The man said, "Marwān ibn al-Ḥakam has taken a slave of mine and wants to cut off his hand. I would like you to go with me to him so you can tell him what you heard from the Messenger of Allah ﷺ." So Rāfi' went with him to Marwān ibn al-Ḥakam and said, "Did you arrest a slave for this?" He replied, "Yes." He said, "What will you do with him?" He replied, "I intend to cut off his hand." Rāfi' said to him, "I heard the Messenger of Allah ﷺ say, 'The hand is not cut off for fruit or palm pith.' Marwān therefore ordered that the slave be released."

33 Yaḥyā related to me from Mālik from Ibn Shihāb from as-Sā'ib ibn Yazīd that 'Abdullāh ibn 'Amr ibn al-Ḥaḍramī brought a slave of his to 'Umar ibn al-Khaṭṭāb and told him, "Cut off the hand of this slave of

mine. He has stolen." 'Umar asked, "What did he steal?" He said, "He stole a mirror belonging to my wife. Its value was sixty dirhams." 'Umar said, "Let him go. His hand is not to be cut off. He is your servant who has stolen your belongings."

34 Yaḥyā related to me from Mālik from Ibn Shihāb that Marwān ibn al-Ḥakam was brought a man who had snatched some goods and he wanted to cut his hand off. He sent to Zayd ibn Thābit to ask him about it. Zayd ibn Thābit told him, "The hand is not cut off for what is stolen by chance, openly, in haste."

35 Yaḥyā related to me from Mālik that Yaḥyā ibn Sa'īd said that Abū Bakr ibn Muḥammad ibn 'Amr ibn Ḥazm informed him that he had taken a Nabatean who had stolen some iron rings and jailed him in order to cut off his hand. 'Amra bint 'Abd ar-Raḥmān sent a girl *mawlā* called Umayya to him. Abū Bakr said that she had come to him while he was among the people and said that his aunt, 'Amra, sent word to him saying, "Nephew! You have taken a Nabatean for something insignificant which was mentioned to me. Do you mean to cut off his hand?" He had replied, "Yes." She said, "'Amra tells you not to cut off the hand except for a quarter of a dinar or more."

Abū Bakr added, "So I let the Nabatean go."

Mālik said, "The generally agreed on way of doing things among us about the confession of slaves is that, if a slave confesses something against himself, the *ḥadd* and punishment for it is inflicted on his own person. His confession is accepted from him and one does not suspect that he would inflict something on himself."

Mālik said, "As for one of them who confesses to a matter which will incur damages against his master, his confession is not accepted against his master."

Mālik said, "One does not cut off the hand of a hireling, or a man who is with some people to serve them, if he robs them, because his state is not the state of a thief. His state is that of a treacherous one. The treacherous one does not have his hand cut off."

Mālik said about a person who borrows something and then denies it, "His hand is not cut off. He is like a man who owes a debt to another man and denies it. He does not have his hand cut off for what he has denied."

Mālik said, "The generally agreed on way of dealing among us with the thief who is found in a house and has gathered up goods and has not taken them out is that his hand is not cut off. That is like the man who places wine before him to drink and does not drink it. The *ḥadd* is not imposed on him. That is like a man who sits with a woman and desires to have unlawful intercourse with her and does not do it and he does not reach her. There is no *ḥadd* against that either."

Mālik said, "The generally agreed on way of doing things among us is that there is no cutting off the hand for what is taken by chance, openly and in haste, whether or not its price reaches that for which the hand is cut off."

42. Drinks

42.1 The *ḥadd* punishment for drinking wine

1 Yaḥyā related to me from Mālik from Ibn Shihāb that as-Sā'ib ibn Yazīd informed him that 'Umar ibn al-Khaṭṭāb came out to them. He said, "I have found the smell of wine on so-and-so and he claims that it was the drink of boiled fruit juice. I am inquiring about what he has drunk. If it intoxicates, I will flog him." 'Umar then flogged him with the full *ḥadd.*

2 Yaḥyā related to me from Mālik from Thawr ibn Zayd ad-Dīlī that 'Umar ibn al-Khaṭṭāb asked advice about a man drinking wine. 'Alī ibn Abī Ṭālib said to him, "We think that you should flog him for it with eighty lashes, because when he drinks, he becomes intoxicated, and when he becomes intoxicated, he talks confusedly, and when he talks confusedly he tells lies." (Eighty Lashes is the same amount as for slander). 'Umar imposed eighty lashes for drinking wine.

3 Yaḥyā related to me from Mālik from Ibn Shihāb that he was asked about the *ḥadd* imposed on a slave for drinking wine. He said, "I heard that he receives half the *ḥadd* of a free man for drinking wine. 'Umar ibn al-Khaṭṭāb, 'Uthmān ibn 'Affān and 'Abdullāh ibn 'Umar flogged their slaves with half of the *ḥadd* of a free man when they drank wine."

4 Yaḥyā related to me from Mālik from Yaḥyā ibn Sa'īd that he heard Sa'īd ibn al-Musayyab say, "There is nothing that Allah does not like to be pardoned as long as it is not a *ḥadd.*"

Yaḥyā said that Mālik said, "The *sunna* with us is that the *ḥadd* is imposed against anyone who drinks something intoxicating, whether or not he becomes drunk."

42.2 Containers forbidden for preparation of *nabīdh*

5 Yaḥyā related to me from Mālik from Nāfi' from 'Abdullāh ibn 'Umar that the Messenger of Allah ﷺ addressed the people on one of his raids. 'Abdullāh ibn 'Umar said, "I went towards him, but he finished before I reached him. I asked about what he had said. Someone said to me, 'He forbade preparing *nabīdh* in a gourd or in a jug smeared with pitch.'"

6 Yaḥyā related to me from Mālik from al-'Alā' ibn 'Abd ar-Raḥmān ibn Ya'qūb from his father from Abū Hurayra that the Messenger of Allah ﷺ forbade preparing *nabīdh* in a gourd or in a jug smeared with pitch.

42.3 Mixtures of fruit disapproved for making *nabīdh*

7 Yaḥyā related to me from Mālik from Zayd ibn Aslam from 'Aṭā' ibn Yasār that the Messenger of Allah ﷺ forbade preparing *nabīdh* from nearly ripe dates and fresh dates together, and from dates and raisins together.

8 Yaḥyā related to me from Mālik from a reliable source from Bukayr ibn 'Abdullāh ibn al-Ashajj from 'Abd ar-Raḥmān ibn al-Ḥubāb al-Anṣārī from Abū Qatāda al-Anṣārī that the Messenger of Allah ﷺ forbade making *nabīdh* from dates and raisins together, and nearly ripe dates and fresh dates together.

Mālik said, "That is the way of doing things among us which the people of knowledge in our city continue to observe. It is disapproved of because the Messenger of Allah ﷺ forbade it."

42.4 The prohibition of wine

9 Yaḥyā related to me from Mālik from Ibn Shihāb from Abū Salama ibn 'Abd ar-Rahmān that 'Ā'isha, the wife of the Prophet ﷺ said, "The

Messenger of Allah ﷺ was asked about mead and he replied, 'Every drink which intoxicates is unlawful.'"

10 Yaḥyā related to me from Mālik from Zayd ibn Aslam from 'Aṭā' ibn Yasār that the Messenger of Allah ﷺ was asked about *al-ghubayrā'*. He said, "There is no good in it," and forbade it.

Mālik said, "I asked Zayd ibn Aslam, 'What is *al-ghubayrā'*?' He replied, 'It is an intoxicant.'"

11 Yaḥyā related to me from Mālik from Nāfi' from 'Abdullāh ibn 'Umar that the Messenger of Allah ﷺ said, "If someone drinks wine in this world and does not turn from it in repentance, it will be unlawful for him in the Next World."

42.5 General section on the prohibition of wine

12 Yaḥyā related to me from Mālik from Zayd ibn Aslam that Ibn Wa'lā al-Miṣrī asked 'Abdullāh ibn 'Abbās about what is squeezed from grapes. Ibn 'Abbās replied, "A man gave the Messenger of Allah ﷺ a small water-skin of wine. The Messenger of Allah ﷺ said to him, 'Do you not know that Allah has made it unlawful?' He answered, 'No.' Then a man at his side whispered to him. The Messenger of Allah ﷺ asked what he had whispered and the man replied, 'I told him to sell it.' The Messenger of Allah ﷺ 'The One who made drinking it unlawful has made selling it unlawful.' The man then opened the water-skins and poured out what was in them."

13 Yaḥyā related to me from Mālik from Isḥāq ibn 'Abdullāh ibn Abī Ṭalḥa that Anas ibn Mālik said, "I was serving wine to Abū 'Ubayda ibn al-Jarraḥ, Abū Ṭalḥa al-Anṣārī and Ubayy ibn Ka'b. The wine had been prepared from crushed ripe dates and dried dates. Someone came to them and said, 'Wine has been made unlawful.' Abū Ṭalḥa ordered me to go and take the jugs and break them. I stood up and went over and got a mortar of ours and I struck them with the bottom of it until they broke."

14 Yaḥyā related to me from Mālik from Dāwud ibn al-Ḥusayn that Wāqid ibn 'Amr ibn Sa'd ibn Mu'ādh informed him from Maḥmūd ibn Labīd al-Anṣārī that when 'Umar ibn al-Khaṭṭāb went to Syria, some Syrians complained to him about the bad climate of their country and its heaviness. They said, "Only this drink helps." 'Umar said, "Drink this honey preparation." They said, "Honey does not help us." A man from the people of that land said, "Can we give you something of this drink which does not intoxicate?" He said, "Yes." They cooked it until two-thirds of it had evaporated and one-third of it remained. Then they brought it to 'Umar who put his finger in it and then raised his head and extended it. He said, "This is fruit juice concentrated by boiling. This is like the distillation which you smear on camel's scabs." 'Umar ordered them to drink it. 'Ubāda ibn aṣ-Ṣāmit said to him, "You have made it lawful, by Allah!" 'Umar said, "No, by Allah! O Allah, I will not make anything lawful for them which You have made lawful for them! I will not make anything unlawful for them which You have made lawful for them!"

15 Yaḥyā related to me from Mālik from Nāfi' from 'Abdullāh ibn 'Umar that some men from Iraq said to him, "Abū 'Abd ar-Raḥmān, we buy the fruit of the palm and grapes and we squeeze them into wine and sell it." 'Abdullāh ibn 'Umar said, "I call on Allah and His angels and whatever jinn and men hear to testify to you that I order you not to buy it nor sell it nor press it nor to drink it nor to give it to people to drink. It is something impure from the work of Shayṭān."

43. Blood Money

43.1 Concerning blood-money

1 Yaḥyā related to me from Mālik from 'Abdullāh ibn Abī Bakr ibn Muḥammad ibn 'Amr ibn Ḥazm from his father that in a letter which the Messenger of Allah ﷺ sent to 'Amr ibn Ḥazm about blood-money, he wrote that it was one hundred camels for a life, one hundred camels for a nose if completely removed, a third of the blood-money for a wound in the brain, the same as that for a belly wound, fifty for an eye, fifty for a hand, fifty for a foot, ten camels for each finger, and five for teeth, and five for a head wound which laid the bone bare.

43.2 Procedure in blood-money

2 Mālik related to me that he had heard that 'Umar ibn al-Khaṭṭāb estimated the full blood-money for the people of urban areas. For those who had gold, he made it one thousand dinars, and for those who had silver, he made it ten thousand dirhams.

Mālik said, "The people of gold are the people of Syria and the people of Egypt. The people of silver are the people of Iraq."

Yaḥyā related to me from Mālik that he heard that the blood-money was divided into instalments over three or four years.

Mālik said, "Three years is the most preferable to me of what I have heard on that."

Mālik said, "The generally agreed on way of doing things in our community is that camels are not accepted from the people of cities for blood-money nor is gold or silver accepted from desert people. Silver is not accepted from the people of gold and gold is not accepted from the people of silver."

43.3 The blood-money for murder when accepted, and the criminal act of the insane

Yaḥyā related to me from Mālik that Ibn Shihāb said, "The full blood-money for murder, when it is accepted, is twenty-five yearlings, twenty-five two year olds, twenty-five four year olds, and twenty-five five year olds."

3 Yaḥyā related to me from Mālik from Yaḥyā ibn Sa'īd that Marwān ibn al-Ḥakam wrote to Mu'āwiya ibn Abī Sufyān that a madman was brought to him who had killed a man. Mu'āwiya wrote to him, "Tie him up and do not inflict any retaliation on him. There is no retaliation against a madman."

Mālik said about an adult and a child when they murder a man together: "The adult is killed and the child pays half the full blood-money."

Mālik said, "It is like that with a free man and a slave when they murder a slave. The slave is killed and the free man pays half of his value."

43.4 The blood-money for manslaughter

4 Yaḥyā related to me from Mālik from Ibn Shihāb from 'Irāk ibn Mālik and Sulaymān ibn Yasār that a man of the Banū Sa'd ibn Layth was running a horse and it trod on the finger of a man from the Juhayna tribe. It bled profusely and he died. 'Umar ibn al-Khaṭṭāb said to those against whom the claim was made, "Do you swear by Allah with fifty oaths that he did not die of it?" They refused and refrained from doing it. He said to the others, "Will you take an oath?" They refused, so 'Umar ibn al-Khaṭṭāb gave a judgement that the Banū Sa'd had to pay half the full blood-money.

Mālik said, "One does not act on this."

Yaḥyā related to me from Mālik that Ibn Shihāb, Sulaymān ibn Yasār, and Rabi'a ibn Abī 'Abd ar-Raḥmān said, "The blood money for manslaughter is twenty yearlings, twenty two-year olds, twenty male two-year olds, twenty four-year olds and twenty-five-year olds."

Mālik said, "The generally agreed on way with us is that there is no retaliation carried out against children. Their intention is accidental. The *ḥudūd* penalties are not obliged for them if they have not yet reached puberty. If a child kills someone it is only accidentally. Had a child and an adult killed a free man accidentally, each of them would pay half the blood-money."

Mālik said, "A person who kills someone accidentally pays blood-money with his property and there is no retaliation carried out against him. That money is like anything else from the dead man's property and his debt is paid with it and he is allowed to make a bequest from it. If he has a total property of which the blood-money is a third and then the blood-money is relinquished, that is permitted to him. If all the property he has is his blood-money, he is permitted to relinquish a third of it and to make that a bequest."

43.5 The blood-money for accidental injury

Mālik related to me that the generally agreed on way of doing things amongst the community in the event of an accident is that there is no blood-money paid until the victim is better. If a man's bone, either a hand, or a foot, or another part of his body, is broken accidentally and it heals and becomes sound and returns to its proper form, there is no blood-money for it. If the limb is impaired or there is a scar on it, there is blood-money for it according to the extent that it is impaired.

Mālik said, "If that part of the body has a amount of specific blood-money mentioned by the Prophet ﷺ, it is according to what the Prophet ﷺ specified. If it is something that does not have a specific blood-money mentioned by the Prophet ﷺ and there is no previous *sunna* about it or specific blood-money, one uses *ijtihād* about it."

Mālik said, "There is no blood-money for an accidental bodily injury when the wound heals and it returns to its proper form. If there is any scar or mark, *ijtihād* is used about it except for the belly-wound. There is a third of the blood-money of a life for it."

Mālik said, "There is no blood-money for the wound which splinters bone in the body, which is like the wound to the body which lays bare the bone."

Mālik said, "The generally agreed on way of doing things in our community is that when the doctor performs a circumcision and cuts off the glans, he must pay the blood-money. That is because it is an accident which the tribe is responsible for, and the full blood-money is payable for everything in which a doctor errs or exceeds, when it is not intentional."

43.6 The blood-money for women

Yaḥyā related to me from Mālik from Yaḥyā ibn Sa'īd that Sa'īd ibn al-Musayyab said, "The blood-money for a woman is the same as for a man up to one-third of the blood-money. Her finger is like his finger, her tooth is like his tooth, her injury which lays the bone is like his, and her head wound which splinters the bone is like his."

Yaḥyā related to me from Mālik that Ibn Shihāb and also 'Urwa ibn az-Zubayr said the same as Sa'īd ibn al-Musayyab said about a woman. Her blood-money from a man is the same up to a third of the blood-money of a man. If what she is owed exceeds a third of the blood-money of the man, she is given up to half of the blood-money of a man.

Mālik said, "The explanation of that is that she receives blood-money for a head wound that lays bare the bone and for a wound that splinters the bone and for what is less than the brain wound and the belly and any such wounds which oblige a third of the blood-money or more. If the amount owed her exceeds that, her blood-money for that is half of the full blood-money of a man."

Yaḥyā related to me from Mālik that he heard Ibn Shihāb say, "The precedent of the *sunna* when a man injures a woman is that he must pay the blood-money for that injury and there is no retaliation carried out against him."

Mālik said, "That is accidental injury, as when a man strikes a woman and the blow lands where he did not intend: for instance, if he struck her with a whip and cut her eye open and things like that."

Mālik, speaking about a woman who has a husband and children who are not from her paternal relatives or her people, said that since he is from another tribe there is no blood-money against her husband for her criminal action, nor against any of her children if they are not from her people, nor against her maternal brothers when they are not from her paternal relations or her people. These are entitled to her inheritance but only the paternal relations have paid blood-money since the time of the Messenger of Allah ﷺ. Until today it is like that with the *mawlā* of a woman. The inheritance they leave goes to the children of the woman even if they are not from her tribe, but the blood-money of the criminal act of the *mawlā* is only against her tribe."

43.7 The blood-money for the foetus

5 Yaḥyā related to me from Mālik from Ibn Shihāb from Abū Salama ibn 'Abd ar-Raḥmān ibn 'Awf from Abū Hurayra that a woman of the Hudhayl tribe threw a stone at a woman from the same tribe who then had a miscarriage. The Messenger of Allah ﷺ gave a judgement that a slave or a slave-girl of fair complexion and excellence should be given to her.

6 Yaḥyā related to me from Mālik from Ibn Shihāb from Sa'īd ibn al-Musayyab that the Messenger of Allah ﷺ gave a judgement that the compensation for a foetus killed in its mother's womb was a slave or a slave-girl of fair complexion and excellence. The one against whom the judgement was given said, "Why should I pay damages for that which did not drink or eat or speak or make any cry? The like of that is nothing." The Messenger of Allah ﷺ said, "This is only one of the brothers of the diviners."

Yaḥyā related to me from Mālik that Rabi'a ibn Abī 'Abd ar-Raḥmān said, "The slave of fair complexion and excellence is estimated at fifty dinars or six hundred dirhams. The blood-money of a free Muslim woman is five hundred dinars or six thousand dirhams."

Mālik said, "The blood-money of the foetus of a free woman is a tenth of her blood-money. The tenth is fifty dinars or six hundred dirhams."

Mālik said, "I have not heard anyone dispute that there is no slave in compensation for the foetus until it leaves its mother's womb and falls stillborn from her womb."

Mālik said, "I heard that if the foetus comes out of its mother's womb alive and then dies, the full blood-money is due for it."

Mālik said, "The foetus is not alive unless it cries at birth. If it comes out of its mother's womb and cries out and then dies, the complete blood-money is due for it. We think that the slave-girl's foetus has a tenth of the price of the slave-girl."

Mālik said, "When a woman murders a man or woman, and the murderess is pregnant, retaliation is not taken against her until she has given birth. If a woman who is pregnant is killed intentionally or unintentionally, the one who killed her is not obliged to pay anything for her foetus. If she is murdered, then the one who killed her is killed and there is no blood-money for her foetus. If she is killed accidentally, the tribe obliged to pay on behalf of her killer pays her blood-money, and there is no blood-money for the foetus."

Yaḥyā related to me, "Mālik was asked about the foetus of a Christian or Jewish woman which was aborted. He said, "I think that there is a tenth of the blood-money of the mother for it."

43.8 Injuries for which there is full blood-money

Yaḥyā related to me from Mālik from Ibn Shihāb that Sa'īd ibn al-

Musayyab used to say, "The full blood-money is payable for cutting off both lips, but when the lower one only is cut off, two-thirds of the blood-money is due for it."

Yaḥyā related to me from Mālik that he asked Ibn Shihāb what happened if a one-eyed man gouged out the eye of a healthy person. Ibn Shihāb said, "If the healthy person wants to take retaliation from him, he can have his retaliation. If he prefers, he has blood-money of one thousand dinars, twelve thousand dirhams."

Yaḥyā related to me from Mālik that he heard that full blood-money is payable for both of a pair of any parts of a man that occur in pairs, and the tongue incurs full blood-money. The ears, when their hearing has departed, incur full blood-money, whether or not they have been cut off, and a man's penis incurs full blood-money as do testicles.

Yaḥyā related from Mālik that he heard that the breasts of a woman incurred full blood-money.

Mālik said, "The least of that are the eyebrows and a man's breasts."

Mālik said, "What is done in our community when a man is injured in his extremities to an extent that obliges payment of more than the amount of his full blood-money, is that he has a right to it. If his hands, feet and eyes are all injured, he has three full blood-moneys."

Mālik said about the sound eye of a one-eyed man when it is accidentally gouged out, "The full blood-money is payable for it."

43.9 The blood-money for an eye whose sight is lost

Yaḥyā related to me from Mālik from Yaḥyā ibn Sa'īd from Sulaymān ibn Yasār that Zayd ibn Thābit used to say, "When the eye remains but the sight is lost, one hundred dinars are payable for it."

Yaḥyā said, "Mālik was asked about cutting off the lower lid of the eye and the bone around the eye. He said, 'There is only *ijtihād* about that unless the vision of the eye is impaired. He is entitled to an amount that is compatible to the extent that the vision of the eye has been impaired."

Yaḥyā said that Mālik said, "What is done in our community about removing the bad eye of a one-eyed man when it has already been blinded and still remains there in its place and the paralyzed hand when it is cut off is that *ijtihād* in that must be used. There is no prescribed blood-money."

43.10 The blood-money for head wounds

Yaḥyā related to me from Mālik that Yaḥyā ibn Sa'īd heard Sulaymān ibn Yasār mention that a face wound in which the bone was bared was like a head wound in which the bone was bared unless the face was scarred by the wound. Then the blood-money was increased by one half of the blood-money of a head wound in which the skin was bared so that seventy-five dinars are payable for it.

Mālik said, "What is done in our community is that a head wound with splinters gets fifteen camels."

He explained, "The head wound with splinters is a wound from which pieces of bone fly off but which does not reach the brain. It can be in the head or the face."

Mālik said, "The generally agreed on way of doing things in our community is that there is no retaliation for a wound to the brain or a belly wound, and Ibn Shihāb has said, 'There is no retaliation for a wound to the brain.'"

Mālik explained, "The wound to the brain is a wound which pierces the skull through to the brain. This type of wound only occurs in the head. It is one that reaches the brain when the skull is pierced."

Mālik said, "What is done in our community is that there is no blood-money paid on any head wound less than one which lays bare the skull.

Blood-money is payable only for a head wound that bares the bone and anything more severe than that. That is because the Messenger of Allah ﷺ stopped at the head wound which bared the bone in his letter to 'Amr ibn Ḥazm. He made the blood-money for it five camels. The imāms, past and present, have not made any blood-money payable for injuries less than the head wound which bares the bone."

Yaḥyā related to me from Mālik from Yaḥyā ibn Sa'īd that Sa'īd ibn al-Musayyab said, "For every piercing wound in any of the organs or limbs of the body, one third of the blood-money of that limb is payable."

Mālik related to me, "Ibn Shihāb did not think, and nor do I, that there is a generally agreed on way of doing things regarding a piercing wound in any of the organs or limbs of the body, but I think that *ijtihād* should be used in each case. The imām uses *ijtihād* about it, and there is no generally agreed on way of doing things in our community in this case."

Mālik said, "What is done in our community about a brain wound and a wound which splinters the bone and a wound that bares the bone is that they apply to the head and face. If such a wound occurs in the body it is subject to *ijtihād*."

Mālik said, "I do not think the lower jaw or the nose are part of the head in regard to injury because they are separate bones, and apart from them the head is made up of a single bone."

Yaḥyā related to me from Mālik from Rabi'a ibn Abī 'Abd ar-Raḥmān that 'Abdullāh ibn az-Zubayr allowed retaliation for a head wound which splintered the bone.

43.11 The blood-money for fingers

Yaḥyā related to me from Mālik that Rabi'a ibn Abī 'Abd ar-Raḥmān said, "I asked Sa'īd ibn al-Musayyab, 'How much is it for the finger of a woman?' He replied, 'Ten camels.' I said, 'How much for two fingers?' He said, 'Twenty camels.' I asked, 'How much for three?' He said, 'Thirty camels.' I said, 'How much for four?' He said, 'Twenty camels.' I said,

'When her wound is greater and her affliction stronger is her blood-money then less?' He asked, 'Are you an Iraqi then?' I said, 'Rather I am a scholar who seeks to verify things, or an ignorant man who seeks to learn.' Sa'īd said, 'It is the *sunna*, my nephew.'"

Mālik said, "What is done in our community about all the fingers of the hand being cut off is that complete blood-money is given. That is because when five fingers are cut, their blood-money is the blood-money of the hand: fifty camels. Each finger has ten camels."

Mālik said, "The reckoning of the fingers is thirty-three dinars for each fingertip, and that is three and a third shares of camels."

43.12 General section on the blood-money for teeth

7 Yaḥyā related to me from Mālik from Zayd ibn Aslam from Muslim ibn Jundub from Aslam, the *mawlā* of 'Umar ibn al-Khaṭṭāb, that 'Umar ibn al-Khaṭṭāb decided that there was a camel for a molar, a camel for a collar-bone, and a camel for a rib.

Yaḥyā related to me from Mālik that Yaḥyā ibn Sa'īd heard Sa'īd ibn al-Musayyab say, "'Umar ibn al-Khaṭṭāb decided on a camel for each molar, and Mu'āwiya ibn Abī Sufyān decided on five camels for each molar."

Sa'īd ibn al-Musayyab said, "The blood-money is less in the judgement of 'Umar ibn al-Khaṭṭāb and more in the judgement of Mu'āwiya. If it had been me, I would have made it two camels for each molar. That is the fair blood-money, and everyone who strives with *ijtihād* is rewarded."

Yaḥyā related to me from Mālik from Yaḥyā ibn Sa'īd that Sa'īd ibn al-Musayyab used to say, "When a tooth is struck and becomes black, there is complete blood-money for it. If it falls out after it becomes black, there is also the complete blood-money for it."

43.13 Procedure in the blood-money for teeth

8 Yaḥyā related to me from Mālik from Dāwūd ibn al-Ḥusayn that Abū Ghaṭafān ibn Ṭarīf al-Murrī informed him that Marwān ibn al-Ḥakam sent him to 'Abdullāh ibn 'Abbās to ask him what there was for the molar. 'Abdullāh ibn 'Abbās said, "There are five camels for it." He said, "Marwān sent me back again to 'Abdullāh ibn 'Abbās." He said, "Do you consider all teeth as molars?" 'Abdullāh ibn 'Abbās said, "It is enough that you take the fingers as the example for that, their blood-money being all the same."

Yaḥyā related to me from Mālik from Hishām ibn 'Urwa that his father made all the teeth the same with respect to the blood-money and did not prefer any kind over others.

Mālik said, "What is done in our community is that the front teeth, molars, and eye-teeth have the same blood-money. That is because the Messenger of Allah ﷺ said, 'The tooth has five camels.' The molar is one of the teeth and he did not prefer any kind over the others."

43.14 The blood-money for injuries to slaves

Yaḥyā related to me from Mālik that he had heard that Sa'īd ibn al-Musayyab and Sulaymān ibn Yasār said, "The head wound of a slave in which the bone is bared is a twentieth of his price."

Mālik related to me that he had heard that Marwān ibn al-Ḥakam gave a decision that when a slave was injured, the person who injured him had to pay the amount that the value of the slave had diminished due to the injury.

Mālik said, "What is done in our community is that for the head wound of a slave that bares the bone there is a twentieth of his price. The head wound which splinters the bone incurs three-twentieths of his price. Both the wound to the brain and the belly-wound incur a third of his price. Besides these four, any other types of injury that decrease the value of the slave are considered after the slave is better and well, and one sees what the value of the slave is after his injury and what his value whole was before he received the injury. Then the one who injured him pays the difference between the two values."

43.15 The blood-money of the People of Protection (*dhimma*)

Yaḥyā related to me from Mālik that he heard that 'Umar ibn 'Abd al-'Azīz gave a decision that when a Jew or Christian was killed, his blood-money was half the blood-money of a free Muslim.

Mālik said, "What is done in our community is that a Muslim is not killed in retaliation for the death of an unbeliever unless the Muslim killed him by treachery. In such a case he is killed for it."

Yaḥyā related to me from Mālik from Yaḥyā ibn Sa'īd that Sulaymān ibn Yasār said, "The blood-money of a Magian is eight hundred dirhams."

Mālik said, "This is what is done in our community."

Mālik said, "The blood money for injuries suffered by Jews, Christians and Magians is the same as for injuries to the Muslims. The head wound incurs a twentieth of the full blood-money. The wound that opens the head incurs a third. The belly-wound also incurs a third of his blood-money. All their injuries are assessed in this way."

43.16 Blood-money that has to be paid on an individual basis

Yaḥyā related to me from Mālik from Hishām ibn 'Urwa that his father said, "The tribe is not obliged to pay blood-money for intentional murder. They only pay blood-money for accidental killing."

Yaḥyā related to me from Mālik that Ibn Shihāb said, "The precedent in the *sunna* is that the tribe is not liable for any blood-money of an intentional killing unless they wish it to be."

Yaḥyā related the same as that to me from Mālik from Yaḥyā ibn Sa'īd.

Mālik said that Ibn Shihāb said, "The precedent in the *sunna* in the case of intentional murder is that when the relatives of the murdered person relinquish their right of retaliation, the blood-money is owed by the murderer from his own property unless the tribe helps him with it willingly."

Mālik said, "What is done in our community is that the blood-money is not taken from the tribe until it has reached a third of the full amount and upwards. If it reaches a third is it is owed by the tribe, and if it is below a third it is taken from the property of the one who inflicted the injury."

Mālik said, "The way of doing things about which there is no dispute among us in the case of someone who has the blood-money accepted from him in intentional murder, or in any injury in which there is retaliation, is that the blood-money is not due from the tribe unless they wish it. The blood-money for it comes from the property of the murderer or the injurer if he has property. If he does not have any property it is a debt against him, and none of it is owed by the tribe unless they wish it to be."

Mālik said, "The tribe does not pay blood-money to anyone who injures himself, intentionally or accidentally. This is the opinion of the people of fiqh in our community. I have not heard that anyone has made the tribe liable for blood-money incurred by intentional actions. Well-known evidence for that is that Allah, the Blessed, the Exalted, said in His Book, *'But if someone is absolved by his brother, blood-money should be claimed with correctness and paid with good will.'* (2:178). The commentary on that, in our view, and Allah knows best, is that whoever gives his brother something of the blood-money should follow it with what is accepted and pay him with good will."

Mālik spoke about a child who had no property and a woman who had no property. He said, "When one of them causes an injury incurring below a third of the total blood-money, it is taken on behalf of the child and woman from their personal property, if they have property from which it may be taken. If not, the injury which each of them has caused is a debt against them. Their tribe does not have to pay any of it, and the father of a child is not liable for the blood-money for an injury caused by his child and he is not responsible for it."

Mālik said, "The way of doing things in our community about which there is no dispute is that when a slave is killed, his value is the same as it was on the day on which he was killed. The tribe of the murderer is not liable for any of the slave's value, great or small. It is the responsibility of the one who killed him and must be paid from his own personal property as far as it covers it. If the value of the slave is the same as the blood-money or even more, that must be paid from his property. That is because the slaves are a category of goods."

43.17 Inheritance of blood-money and making it more severe

9 Yaḥyā related to me from Mālik from Ibn Shihāb that 'Umar ibn al-Khaṭṭāb demanded of the people at Minā, "If anyone has knowledge of blood-money, let him tell me." Aḍ-Ḍaḥḥāk ibn Sufyān al-Kilābī stood up and said, "The Messenger of Allah ﷺ wrote to me that the wife of Ashyam aḍ-Ḍibābī inherited from the blood-money of her husband." 'Umar ibn al-Khaṭṭāb said to him, "Go into the tent until I come to you." When 'Umar ibn al-Khaṭṭāb came in, aḍ-Ḍaḥḥāk told him about it and 'Umar ibn al-Khaṭṭāb gave a decision based on that.

Ibn Shihāb added, "The killing of Ashyam was accidental."

10 Mālik related to me from Yaḥyā ibn Sa'īd from 'Amr ibn Shu'ayb that a man of the Banū Mudlij called Qatāda threw a sword at his son and it struck his thigh. The wound bled profusely and he died. Suraqa ibn Ju'shum came to 'Umar ibn al-Khaṭṭāb and mentioned that to him. 'Umar told him, "At the watering-place of Qudayd count one hundred and twenty camels and wait until I come to you." When 'Umar ibn al-Khaṭṭāb came to him, he took thirty four-year old camels, thirty five-year old camels and forty pregnant camels from them. Then he said, "Where is the brother of the slain man?" He said, "Here." He said, "Take them. The Messenger of Allah ﷺ said, 'The killer gets nothing.'"

Mālik said that he had heard that Sa'īd ibn al-Musayyab and Sulaymān ibn Yasār were asked, "Does one make the blood-money more severe in the sacred month?" They replied, "No. But it is increased because of violating the month." Sa'īd was asked, "Does one impose an increase for a wound just as one increases for a life?" He replied, "Yes."

Mālik added, "I think that they meant the same as 'Umar ibn al-Khaṭṭāb did with respect to the blood-money of the Mudlijī when he struck his son (i.e. giving one hundred and twenty camels instead of a hundred.)"

11 Mālik related to me from Yaḥyā ibn Sa'īd from 'Urwa ibn az-Zubayr that a man of the Anṣār called Uḥayḥa ibn al-Julāḥ had a young paternal uncle who was younger than him and who was living with his maternal uncles. Uḥayḥa seized him and killed him. His maternal uncles said, "We brought him up from a baby to a youth till he stood firm on his feet, and we have had the right of a man taken from us by his paternal uncle." 'Urwa said, "For that reason a killer does not inherit from the one he killed."

Mālik said, "The way of doing things about which there is no dispute is that the intentional murderer does not inherit any of the blood-money of the person he has murdered nor any of his property. He does not stop anyone who has a share of inheritance from inheriting. The one who kills accidentally does not inherit any of the blood-money and there is dispute as to whether or not he inherits from the dead person's property, because there is no suspicion that he killed him for his inheritance and in order to take his property. I prefer that he inherit from the dead person's property and not inherit from the blood-money."

43.18 General section on blood-money

12 Yaḥyā related to me from Mālik from Ibn Shihāb from Sa'īd ibn al-Musayyab and Abū Salama ibn 'Abd ar-Raḥmān from Abū Hurayra that the Messenger of Allah ﷺ said, "The wound of an animal is of no account and no compensation is due for it. The well is of no account and no compensation is due for it. The mine is of no account and no compensation is due for it and a fifth is due for buried treasure." Mālik said, "That which is of no account is that for which there is no blood-money."

Mālik said, "Everyone leading an animal by the halter, driving it or riding it is responsible if the animal kicks out without anything being done to make it kick out. 'Umar ibn al-Khaṭṭāb imposed the blood-money on a person who was exercising his horse."

Mālik commented, "It is yet more fitting that a person who is leading an animal by the halter, driving it or riding it incur a loss than a person who is exercising his horse."

Mālik said, "What is done in our community about a person who digs a well on a road or ties up an animal or does something similar on a road used by Muslims is that, since what he has done is included among the things which he is not permitted to do in such a place, he is liable for whatever injury or other thing arises from that action. The blood-money for anything less than a third of the full blood-money is owed from his personal property. Whatever reaches a third or more is owed by his tribe. Anything that he does which he is permitted to do on the Muslims' roads is something for which he has no liability or loss. Such things include a hole which a man digs to collect rain, and a beast from which the man alights for some need and leaves standing on the road. There is no penalty against anyone for such as this."

Mālik spoke about a man who went down a well with another man following behind him. The lower one pulled the higher one, and they both fell into the well and died. He said, "The tribe of the one who pulled the other in is responsible for the blood-money."

Mālik spoke about a child whom a man ordered to go down a well or to climb a palm tree and he died as a result. He said, "The one who ordered him is liable for whatever befalls him, be it death or anything else."

Mālik said, "The way of doing things in our community about which there is no dispute is that women and children are not obliged to pay blood-money together with the tribe with respect to any blood-money which the tribe must pay. The blood-money is only obligatory for men who have reached puberty."

Mālik said that the tribe could bind themselves to the blood-money of *mawālī* if they wished. If they refused, they were people of the *Dīwān* or were cut off from their people. In the time of the Messenger of Allah ﷺ people paid the blood-money to each other, as well as in the time of Abū Bakr aṣ-Ṣiddīq, before there was a *Dīwān*. The *Dīwān* came about in the time of 'Umar ibn al-Khaṭṭāb. No one other than one's people and the ones holding the *walā'* paid blood-money for someone, because the *walā'* was not transferable and because the Prophet ﷺ, said, "The *walā'* belongs to the one who sets free."

Mālik commented, "The *walā'* is an established relationship."

Mālik said, "What is done in our community about animals that are injured is that the person who causes the injury pays the amount that their value has been diminished."

Mālik said about a man condemned to death who becomes liable for one of the other *ḥudūd* as well, "He is not punished for it. That is because killing overrides everything, except for slander. Slander remains hanging over the one to whom it was said because it will be said to him, 'Why do you not flog the one who slandered you?' I think that a condemned man is flogged with the *ḥadd* before he is killed, and then he is killed. I do not think that any retaliation is inflicted on him for any injury except killing because killing overrides everything else."

Mālik said, "What is done in our community is that when a murdered person is found among the main body of a people in a village or other place, the people of the nearest house or place to him are not held responsible. That is because the murdered person can be slain and then cast at the door of some people to shame them by it. No one is responsible for something like that."

Mālik said about a group of people who fight with each other and when the fight is broken up, a man is found dead or wounded, and it is not known who did it, "The best of what is heard about that is that there is blood-money for him, and the blood-money is against the people who argued with him. If the injured or slain person is not from either of the two parties, his blood-money is against both of the two parties together."

43.19 Killing secretly by trickery and sorcery

13 Yaḥyā related to me from Mālik from Yaḥyā ibn Sa'īd from Sa'īd ibn al-Musayyab that 'Umar ibn al-Khaṭṭāb killed five or seven people for one man whom they had killed secretly by trickery. 'Umar said, "Had all the people of San'a joined forces against him, I would have killed all of them."

14 Yaḥyā related to me from Mālik from Muḥammad ibn 'Abd ar-Raḥmān ibn Sa'd ibn Zurara that he had heard that Ḥafṣa, the wife of the Prophet ﷺ killed one of her slave-girls who had used sorcery against her. The girl was a *mudabbara*. Ḥafṣa gave the order and she was killed.

Mālik commented, "The sorcerer is the one who uses sorcery on his own account, not someone who has it done for him. It is like the one about whom Allah, the Blessed, the Exalted, said in His Book, '*They know that any who deal in it will have no share in the Next World.*' (2:102) I think that if someone practises it, he should be killed."

43.20 What is obligatory for intentional injury

15 Yaḥyā related to me from Mālik from 'Umar ibn Ḥusayn, the *mawlā* of 'Ā'isha bint Qudāma, that 'Abd al-Malik ibn Marwān imposed retaliation against a man who killed a *mawlā* with a stick – and so the *mawlā*'s patron killed the man with a stick.

Mālik said, "The generally agreed on way of doing things in our community about which there is no dispute is that when a man strikes another man with a stick or hits him with a rock or intentionally strikes him causing his death, that is an intentional injury and there is retaliation for it."

Mālik said, "Intentional murder in our opinion is that a man intentionally goes to a man and strikes him until his life departs. Part of intentional injury also is that a man strikes a man in a quarrel between them. He leaves him while he is alive and then he bleeds to death and so dies. There is retaliation for that."

Mālik said, "What is done in our community is that a group of free men are killed for the intentional murder of one free man, and a group of women for one woman, and a group of slaves for one slave."

43.21 Retaliation in killing

Yaḥyā related to me from Mālik that he had heard that Marwān ibn al-Ḥakam wrote to Mu'āwiya ibn Abī Sufyān to mention to him that a drunkard had been brought to him who had killed a man. Mu'āwiya wrote to him to kill him in retaliation for the dead man.

Yaḥyā said that Mālik said, "The best of what I have heard about the interpretation of this *āyat*, the words of Allah, the Blessed, the Exalted, '*The free man for the free man and the slave for the slave*' – these are men – '*and the female for the female*' (2:178), is that retaliation is between women as it is between men. The free woman is killed for the free woman as the free man is killed for the free man. Slave-girls are slain for slave-girls as the slave is slain for the slave. Retaliation is between women as it is between men. That is because Allah, the Blessed, the Exalted, says in His Book, '*We prescribed for them in it: is a life for a life, an eye for an eye, a nose for a nose, and an ear for an ear, and a tooth for a tooth, and retaliation for wounds.*' (5:45). Allah, the Blessed, the Exalted, mentioned that it is a life for a life. It is the life of a free woman for the life of a free man, and her injury for his injury."

Mālik said about a man who held a man fast so that another man could hit him, and he died on the spot, "If he held him and he thought that he meant to kill him, the two of them are both killed for him. If he held him thinking that he meant to hit him as people sometimes do, and he did not think that he meant to kill him, the murderer is slain and the one who held the victim is punished severely and jailed for a year. There is no right to kill him."

Mālik said about a man who murdered a man intentionally or gouged out his eye intentionally, and then was slain or had his eye gouged out himself before retaliation was inflicted on him, "There is no blood-money nor retaliation against him. The right of the one who was killed or had his eye gouged out goes when the thing which he is claiming as retaliation goes. It is the same with a man who murders another man intentionally and then the murderer dies. When the murderer dies, the one seeking blood revenge has no blood-money or anything else. That is by the word of Allah, the Blessed, the Exalted, *'Retaliation is prescribed for you in the case of people killed: free man for free man and slave for slave.'* (2:178)

Mālik said, "He only has retaliation against the one who killed him. If the man who murdered him dies, he has no right to retaliation or blood-money."

Mālik said, "There is no retaliation against a free man by a slave for any injury. The slave is killed for the free man but the free man is not slain for the slave, even if he murders him intentionally. This is the best of what I have heard."

43.22 Pardoning murder

Yaḥyā related to me from Mālik that those he was satisfied with among the people of knowledge said about a man who willed that his murderer be pardoned when he had murdered him intentionally, "That is permitted for him. He is more entitled to the man's blood than any of his relatives after him."

Mālik said about a man who pardoned murder after having previously claimed his right and it was obliged for him to be paid, "There is no blood-money against the murderer unless the one who pardons him actually stipulates that when he pardons him."

Mālik said about a murderer when he was pardoned, "He is flogged one hundred lashes and jailed for a year."

Mālik said, "When a man murders intentionally and there is a clear proof of that, and the murdered man has sons and daughters and the sons pardon and the daughters refuse to pardon, the pardon of the sons is permitted in opposition to the daughters and the daughters have no authority over the sons in demanding blood and pardoning."

43.23 Retaliation in Injury

Yaḥyā said that Mālik said, "The generally agreed on way of doing things in our community is that retaliation is taken from someone who breaks someone's hand or foot intentionally, and not blood-money."

Mālik said, "Retaliation is not inflicted on anyone until the wound of the injured party has healed. Then retaliation is inflicted on him. If the wound of the person on whom the retaliation has been inflicted is like the first person's wound when it heals, it is retaliation. If the wound of the one on whom the retaliation has been inflicted becomes worse or he dies, there is nothing held against the one who has taken retaliation. If the wound of the person on whom the retaliation has been inflicted heals and the injured party is paralysed or his injury has healed but he has a scar, defect or blemish, the person on whom the retaliation has been inflicted does not have his hand broken again and further retaliation is not taken for his injury."

He also said, "But there is blood-money from him according to what he has impaired or maimed of the hand of the injured party. The bodily injury is also like that."

Mālik said, "When a man intentionally goes to his wife and gouges out her eye or breaks her hand or cuts off her finger or such like, and does it intentionally, retaliation is inflicted on him. As for a man who strikes his wife with a rope or a whip and hits what he did not mean to hit or does what he did not intend to do, he pays blood-money for what he has struck according to this principle, and retaliation is not inflicted on him."

Yaḥyā related to me from Mālik that he had heard that Abū Bakr ibn Muḥammad ibn 'Amr ibn Ḥazm took retaliation for the breaking of a leg.

43.24 The blood-money and crime of the slave set free and from whom his former master does not inherit

Yaḥyā related to me from Mālik from Abū az-Zinād from Sulaymān ibn

Yasār that a slave was set free by one of the people on *ḥajj* and his master abandoned the right to inherit from him. The ex-slave then killed a man from the Banū 'Ā'idh tribe. An 'Ā'idhī, the father of the slain man, came to 'Umar ibn al-Khaṭṭāb seeking the blood-money of his son. 'Umar said, "He has no blood-money." The 'Ā'idhī said, "What would you think if it had been my son who killed him?" 'Umar said, "Then you would pay his blood-money." He said, "He is then like the black and white Arqam snake. If it is left, it devours, and if it is killed, it takes revenge."

44. The Oath of *Qasāma*

44.1 Beginning with the people seeking blood revenge in the oath

1 Yaḥyā related to me from Mālik from Abū Layla ibn 'Abdullāh ibn 'Abd ar-Raḥmān ibn Sahl from Sahl ibn Abī Ḥathma that some of the notable men of his people informed him that 'Abdullāh ibn Sahl and Muḥayyisa went out to Khaybar because extreme poverty had overtaken them. Muḥayyisa returned and said that 'Abdullāh ibn Sahl had been killed and thrown in a shallow well or spring. The Jews came and he said, "By Allah! You have killed him!" They said, "By Allah! We have not killed him!" Then he made for his people and mentioned that to them. Then he, his brother Ḥuwayyisa, who was older than him, and 'Abd ar-Raḥmān, set out. Muḥayyisa began to speak, as he he had been at Khaybar. The Messenger of Allah ﷺ said to him, "The elder first, the elder first.' So Ḥuwayyisa spoke and then Muḥayyisa spoke. The Messenger of Allah ﷺ said, "Either they pay your companion's blood-money or we will declare war against them." The Messenger of Allah ﷺ wrote that to them and they wrote back, "By Allah, we did not kill him!" The Messenger of Allah ﷺ said to Ḥuwayyisa, Muḥayyisa and 'Abd ar-Raḥmān, "Do you swear and claim the blood of your companion?" They said, "No." He said, "Shall the Jews swear to you?" They said, "But they are not Muslims." The Messenger of Allah ﷺ gave blood-money from his own property, and sent them one hundred camels to their house.

Sahl added, "A red camel among them kicked me."

Mālik said, "'*Faqīr*' means 'a well.'"

2 Yaḥyā said from Mālik from Yaḥyā ibn Sa'īd that Buhayr ibn Yasār informed him that 'Abdullāh ibn Sahl al-Anṣārī and Muḥayyisa ibn Mas'ūd went out to Khaybar and they separated on their various businesses and 'Abdullāh ibn Sahl was killed. Muḥayyisa, his brother Ḥuwayyisa and 'Abd ar-Raḥmān ibn Sahl went to the Prophet ﷺ, and 'Abd ar-Raḥmān began to speak before his brother. The Messenger of Allah ﷺ said, "The elder first, the elder first." Therefore Huwayyisa and Muhayyisa spoke and mentioned the affair of 'Abdullāh ibn Sahl. The Messenger of Allah ﷺ said to them, "Do you swear with fifty oaths and claim the blood-money of your companion or the life of the murderer?" They said, "Messenger of Allah, we did not see it and we were not present." The Messenger of Allah ﷺ said, "Will you acquit the Jews for fifty oaths?" They said, "Messenger of Allah, how can we accept the oaths of a people who are unbelievers?"

Yaḥyā ibn Sa'īd said, "Bushayr ibn Yasār claimed that the Messenger of Allah ﷺ paid the blood-money from his own property."

Mālik said, "The generally agreed on way of doing things in our community, and that which I heard from those I am content with, concerning the oath of *qasāma*, and that upon which the past and present imāms agree, is that those who claim revenge begin with the oaths and swear. The oath for revenge is only obligatory in two situations: either when the slain person says, 'My blood is against so-and-so,' or the relatives entitled to the blood bring a partial proof of it that is not irrefutable against the one who is the object of the blood-claim. This obliges taking an oath on the part of those who claim the blood against those who are the object of the blood-claim. With us, swearing is only necessary in these two situations."

Mālik said, "That is the *sunna* about which there is no dispute with us and which is what the people still do. The people who claim blood begin the swearing, whether it is an intentional killing or an accident."

Mālik said, "The Messenger of Allah ﷺ began with the Banū Ḥārith in the case of the killing of their kinsman who was murdered at Khaybar."

Mālik said, "If those who make the claim swear, they deserve the blood of their kinsman and whoever they swear against is slain. Only one man can be killed in the *qasāma*. Two cannot be killed in it. Fifty men from the blood-relatives must swear fifty oaths. If their number is less or some of them draw back, they can repeat their oaths, unless one of the relatives of the murdered man who deserves blood and who is permitted to pardon it draws back. If one of them draws back, there is no way to revenge."

Yaḥyā said that Mālik said, "The oaths can be made by those of them who remain if one of them, who is not permitted to pardon, draws back. If one of the blood-relatives, who is permitted to pardon, draws back, even if he is only one, more oaths cannot be made after that by the blood-relatives. If that occurs, the oaths can be on behalf of the one against whom the claim is made. So fifty of the men of his people swear fifty oaths. If there are not fifty men, more oaths can be made by those of them who already swore. If there is only the defendant, he swears fifty oaths and is acquitted."

Yaḥyā said that Mālik said, "One distinguishes between oaths for blood and oaths for one's rights. When a man has a money claim against another man, he seeks to verify his due. When a man wants to kill another man, he does not kill him in the midst of people. He keeps to a place away from people. If there had been only swearing in cases where there was a clear proof, and if one acted in it as one acts about one's rights, (i.e. requiring witnesses), the right of retribution would have been lost and people would have been quick to take advantage of it when they learned of the decision about it. However, the relatives of the murdered man were allowed to initiate swearing so that people might restrain themselves from blood and the murderer might beware lest he was put into a situation like that (i.e. *qasāma*) by the statement of the murdered man."

Yaḥyā said, "Mālik talked about a people, of whom a certain number are suspected of murder, and the relatives of the murdered man ask them to take oaths and they are numerous, so they ask that each man swears fifty oaths on his own behalf. The oaths are not divided out between them according to their number and they are not acquitted unless each man among them swears fifty oaths on his own behalf."

Mālik said, "This is the best I have heard about the matter."

He said, "Swearing goes to the paternal relatives of the slain. They are the blood relatives who swear against the killer and by whose swearing he is killed."

44.2 Blood relatives who are permitted to swear in the case of an intentional act

Yaḥyā said that Mālik said, "The way of doing things in our community about which there is no dispute is that women do not swear in the swearing for the intentional act. If the murdered man only has female relatives, the women have no right to swear for blood and no pardon in the case of murder."

Yaḥyā said that Mālik said about a man who is murdered, "If the paternal relatives of the murdered man or his *mawālī* say, 'We swear and we demand our companion's blood,' that is their right."

Mālik said, "If the women want to pardon him, they cannot do so. The paternal relatives and *mawālī* are more entitled to do so than them because they are the ones who can demand blood and swear for it."

Mālik said, "If the paternal relatives of *mawālī* pardon after they have demanded blood and the women refuse and say, 'We will not abandon our right against the murderer of our companion,' the women are more entitled in that case because whoever takes retaliation is more entitled to it than someone among the women and paternal relatives who relinquishes it, when the murder is established and killing obliged."

Mālik said, "At least two claimants must swear at the case of murder. The oaths are repeated by them until they swear fifty oaths, then they have the right to blood. That is how things are done in our community."

Mālik said, "When people beat a man and he dies in their hands, they are all slain for him. If he dies after their beating, there is swearing. If there is swearing, it is only against one man and only he is slain. We have never known the swearing to be against more than one man."

Mālik spoke about a slave who had his hand or foot broken and then the break mended. He said, "The one who injured him is not obliged to pay anything. If that break causes him loss or scar, the one who injured him must pay according to the amount the value of the slave has been diminished."

Mālik said, "What is done in our community about retaliation between slaves is that it is the same as retaliation between freemen: the life of a slave-girl for the life of a slave, and her injury for his injury. When a slave intentionally kills a slave, the master of the murdered slave has a choice. If he wishes, he kills the murderer, and if he wishes, he takes the blood-money. If he accepts the blood-money, he takes the value of his slave. If the owner of the slave who killed wishes to give the value of the murdered slave, he does so. If he wishes, he surrenders his slave. If he surrenders him, he is not obliged to do anything other than that. When the owner of the murdered slave takes the slave who murdered and is satisfied with him, he must not kill him. All retaliation between slaves for cutting off the hand and foot and such things are dealt with in the same way as in the case of murder."

Mālik said about a Muslim slave who injures a Jew or Christian, "If the master of the slave wishes to pay blood-money for him according to the injury, he does so. Otherwise he surrenders him and he is sold, and the Jew or Christian is given the blood-money of the injury or all the price of the slave if the blood-money is greater than his price. The Jew or Christian is not given a Muslim slave."

44.3 Swearing in the case of manslaughter

Yaḥyā said that Mālik said, "The procedure in swearing in the case of manslaughter is that those who claim blood swear and it becomes due by their swearing. They swear fifty oaths and there is blood-money for them according to the division of their rights of inheritance. If it is not possible to divide up the oaths they swear between them evenly, one looks to the one who has the most of those oaths against him, and that oath against him is taken."

Mālik said, "If the slain man has only female heirs, they swear and take the blood-money. If he has only one male heir, he swears fifty oaths and takes the blood-money. That is only in the case of accidental killing, not intentional."

44.4 Inheritance in cases of *qasāma*

Yaḥyā said that Mālik said, "When the relatives of the deceased accept the blood-money, then it is inherited according to the Book of Allah. Daughters of a dead man inherit and so do sisters, and whichever women would inherit from him ordinarily. If the women do not take all his inheritance* then what remains goes to the agnatic relations who most deserve to inherit from him in conjunction with the women."

* i.e. when there are no male Qur'anic heirs.

Mālik said, "If one of the heirs of a man who was killed by mistake attempts to take his due from the blood-money while his fellow heirs are absent, he may not do so, and he then has no right to any of the blood-money, however large or small, unless the *qasāma* has been completed by him. If he swears fifty oaths then he has the right to his portion of the blood-money. That is because the blood-money is not established as due without there being fifty oaths, and the blood-money is not established as due unless the responsibility for the blood is established. If any one of the heirs comes after that, he swears a number of the oaths commensurate with his fraction of the inheritance and takes his right until all the heirs exact their complete rights. If a maternal uncle comes he has one-sixth and must swear one-sixth of the fifty oaths. So whoever swears may take his due from the blood-money and whoever abstains annuls his right. If one of the heirs is absent or is a child who has not reached puberty, those who are present swear fifty oaths and if the one who was absent comes after that or the child reaches puberty, they swear, and they swear according to their due of the blood-money and according to their share of inheritance from it."

Yaḥyā said that Mālik said, "This is the best I have heard on the matter."

44.5 Swearing for blood revenge in cases involving slaves

Yaḥyā said that Mālik said, "What is done in our community about slaves is that when a save is struck intentionally or accidentally and the master brings a witness, he swears with his witness one oath and then he has the value of the slave. There is no swearing for revenge in the case of slaves, whether they were killed accidentally or intentionally, and I have not heard any of the people of knowledge say that there was."

Mālik said, "If a slave is killed intentionally or accidentally, the master of the slave who is slain has no rights of swearing or oath. The master cannot demand his right except with a fair proof or a witness if he swears with one witness."

Yaḥyā said that Mālik said, "This is the best of what I have heard on the matter."

45. A Comprehensive Book

45.1 Supplication for Madīna and its people

1 Yaḥyā related to me from Mālik from Isḥāq ibn 'Abdullāh ibn Abī Ṭalḥa al-Anṣārī from Anas ibn Mālik that the Messenger of Allah ﷺ said, "O Allah! Bless them in their measure and bless them in their *ṣā'* and *mudd.*" He meant the people of Madīna.

2 Yaḥyā related to me from Mālik from Suhayl ibn Abī Ṣāliḥ from his father that Abū Hurayra said, "When people saw the first fruits of the season, they brought them to the Messenger of Allah ﷺ. The Messenger of Allah ﷺ took them and said, 'O Allah, bless us in our fruits! Bless us in our city. Bless us in our *ṣā'* and bless us in our *mudd.* O Allah, Ibrāhīm is Your slave, Your Khalīl and Your Prophet. I am Your slave and Your Prophet. He prayed to You for Makka. I pray to You for Madīna the same that He prayed to You for Makka, and the like of it with it.' Then he called the smallest child he saw and gave him the fruits."

45.2 What has been narrated about dwelling in Madīna and leaving it

3 Yaḥyā related to me from Mālik from Qaṭan ibn Wahb ibn 'Umayr in al-Ajda' that Yuḥannas, the *mawlā* of az-Zubayr ibn al-'Awwām, informed him that he was sitting with 'Abdullāh ibn 'Umar during the troubles (at the time of al-Ḥajjāj ibn Yūsuf). A female *mawlā* of his came and greeted him. She said, "I want to leave, Abū 'Abd ar-Raḥmān. The times are harsh for us." 'Abdullāh ibn 'Umar told her, "Stay put, O you with little knowledge, for I heard the Messenger of Allah ﷺ say, 'No one will be

patient in hunger and hardship in Madīna without my being a witness or intercessor for him on the Day of Rising'."

4 Yaḥyā related to me from Mālik from Muḥammad ibn al-Munkadir from Jābir ibn 'Abdullāh that a Bedouin took an oath of allegiance in Islam with the Messenger of Allah ﷺ. A fever befell the Bedouin at Madīna and he went to the Messenger of Allah and said, "Messenger of Allah, release me from my pledge!" The Messenger of Allah ﷺ refused. Then the Bedouin went to him again and said, "Release me from my pledge!" The Messenger of Allah ﷺ refused. Then he came yet again and said, "Release me from my pledge!" He refused. The Bedouin left and the Messenger of Allah ﷺ said, "Madīna is like the blacksmith's furnace. It removes impurities and purifies the good."

5 Mālik related to me from that Yaḥyā ibn Sa'īd said, "I heard Abū al-Ḥubāb Sa'īd ibn Yasār say that he heard Abū Hurayra say that he heard the Messenger of Allah ﷺ say, 'I was ordered to a town which will eat up towns. They used to say "Yathrib" but it is Madīna. It expels bad people like the blacksmith's furnace expels impurities from the iron."

6 Mālik related to me from Hishām ibn 'Urwa from his father that the Messenger of Allah ﷺ said, "No one leaves Madīna preferring to live elsewhere but that Allah will give it better than him in his place."

7 Yaḥyā related to me from Mālik from Hishām ibn 'Urwa from his father from 'Abdullāh ibn az-Zubayr that Sufyān ibn Abī Zuhayr said, "I heard the Messenger of Allah ﷺ say, 'Yemen will be conquered and people will be attracted to it, taking their families and whoever obeys them. Madīna would have been better for them had they but known. Syria will be conquered and people will be attracted to it, taking their families and whoever obeys them. Madīna would have been better for them had they but known. Iraq will be conquered and people will be attracted to it, taking their families and whoever obeys them. Madīna would have been better for them had they but known.'"

8 Yaḥyā related to me from Mālik from Ibn Ḥimās from his paternal uncle from Abū Hurayra that the Messenger of Allah ﷺ said, "Madīna will be left in the best way until a dog or wolf enters it and urinates

on one of the pillars of the mosque or on the minbar." They asked, "Messenger of Allah, who will have the fruit at that time?" He replied, "Animals seeking food – birds and wild beasts."

9 Mālik related to me that he had heard that when 'Umar ibn 'Abd al-'Azīz left Madīna, he turned back towards it and wept. Then he said, "O Muzāḥim! Aren't you afraid that we might be among those that Madīna casts off?"

45.3 Making Madīna a *ḥaram*

10 Yaḥyā related to me from Mālik from 'Amr, the *mawlā* of al-Muṭṭalib, from Anas ibn Mālik that the Messenger of Allah ﷺ saw Uḥud and said, "This is a mountain which loves us and we love it. O Allah, Ibrāhīm made Makka a *ḥaram* and I will make what is between the two tracts of black stones (in Madīna) a *ḥaram*."

11 Mālik related to me from Ibn Shihāb from Sa'īd ibn al-Musayyab that Abū Hurayra said, "If I had seen a gazelle at Madīna, I would have left it to graze and would not have frightened it. The Messenger of Allah ﷺ said, 'What is between the two tracts of black stones is a *ḥaram*.'"

12 Mālik related to me from Yūnus ibn Yūsuf from 'Aṭā' ibn Yasār that Abū Ayyūb al-Anṣārī found some boys who had driven a fox into a corner and he chased them away from it.

Mālik said, "I only know that he said, 'Have you done this in the *ḥarām* of the Messenger of Allah ﷺ?'"

13 Yaḥyā related to me from Mālik from a man who said, "Zayd ibn Thābit came across me while I was at al-Aswāf (on the outskirts of Madīna). I had captured a hawk. He took it from my hands and set it free."

45.4 The epidemic of Madīna

14 Yaḥyā related to me from Mālik from Hishām ibn 'Urwa from his

father that 'Ā'isha, *Umm al-Mu'minīn,* said, "When the Messenger of Allah ﷺ came to Madīna, Abū Bakr and Bilāl came down with a fever. I visited them and said, 'Father, how are you? Bilāl, how are you?'" She continued, "When Abū Bakr's fever worsened, he would say,

"Every man is struck down among his people in the morning -

Death is nearer than the strap of his sandal."

When the fever left Bilāl, he raised his voice and said,

"Would that I knew whether I would spend a night in the valley of Makka

with the sweet rushes and panic grass around me!

Will I one day return to the waters of Majinna?

Will the mountains of Shāma and Ṭafīl loom before me?"

'Ā'isha continued, I went to the Messenger of Allah ﷺ, and told him. He said, 'O Allah! Make us love Madīna as much as we love Makka or even more! Make it healthy and bless us in our *ṣā'* and our *mudd*. Remove its fever and put it in al-Juḥfa!'"

15 Mālik said that Yaḥyā ibn Sa'īd had related to him that 'Ā'isha said that 'Āmir ibn Fuhayra had recited at the time of the epidemic:

"I have seen death before tasting it,

the coward's death is above him."

16 Yaḥyā related to me from Mālik from Nu'aym ibn 'Abdullāh al-Mujmir that Abū Hurayra said, "The Messenger of Allah ﷺ said, 'There are angels at the entries of Madīna, and neither plague nor the Dajjāl will enter it.'"

45.5 The expulsion of the Jews from Madīna

17 Yaḥyā related to me from Mālik from Ismā'īl ibn Abī Ḥakīm that he heard 'Umar ibn 'Abd al-'Azīz say, "One of the last things that the Messenger of Allah ﷺ said was, 'May Allah fight the Jews and the Christians! They took the graves of their Prophets as places of prostration. Two *dīns* shall not co-exist in the land of the Arabs.'"

18 Yaḥyā related to me from Mālik from Ibn Shihāb that the Messenger of Allah ﷺ said, "Two *dīns* shall not co-exist in the Arabian Peninsula."

Mālik said that Ibn Shihāb said, "'Umar ibn al-Khaṭṭāb searched for information about that until he was absolutely convinced that the Messenger of Allah ﷺ had said, 'Two *dīns* shall not co-exist in the Arabian Peninsula,' and he therefore expelled the Jews from Khaybar."

19 Mālik said, "'Umar ibn al-Khaṭṭāb expelled the Jews from Najrān (a Jewish settlement in the Yemen) and Fadak (a Jewish settlement thirty miles from Madīna). When the Jews of Khaybar left they had none of the fruit nor the land. The Jews of Fadak had half the fruit and half the land because the Messenger of Allah ﷺ had made a settlement with them for that. So 'Umar paid them the value in gold, silver, camels, ropes, and saddlebags of half the fruit and half the land, and handed the value over to them and then expelled them."

45.6 Concerning Madīna

20 Yaḥyā related to me from Mālik from Hishām ibn 'Urwa from his father that the Messenger of Allah ﷺ came in view of Uḥud and said, "This is a mountain which loves us and we love it."

21 Yaḥyā related to me from Mālik from Yaḥyā ibn Sa'īd from 'Abd ar-Raḥmān ibn al-Qāsim that Aslam, the *mawlā* of 'Umar ibn al-Khaṭṭāb, informed him that he had visited 'Abdullāh ibn 'Ayyāsh al-Makhzūmī. He saw that he had some *nabīdh* with him which he was taking to Makka at that moment. Aslam said to him, "'Umar ibn al-Khaṭṭāb loves this drink." 'Abdullāh ibn 'Ayyāsh therefore carried a large drinking

bowl and brought it to 'Umar ibn al-Khaṭṭāb and placed it before him. 'Umar brought it near to him and then raised his head and said, "This drink is good." 'Umar drank some of it and passed it to a man on his left. 'Abdullāh turned to go. 'Umar ibn al-Khaṭṭāb called him and asked, "Are you the person who says that Makka is better than Madīna?" 'Abdullāh said, "I said that it was the *ḥarām* of Allah and His place of security and that His House was in it." 'Umar said, "I am not saying anything about the House of Allah or His *ḥarām*." Then 'Abdullāh left.

45.7 About the plague

22 Yaḥyā related to me from Mālik from Ibn Shihāb from 'Abd al-Ḥamīd ibn 'Abd ar-Raḥmān ibn Zayd ibn al-Khaṭṭāb from 'Abdullāh ibn 'Abdullāh ibn al-Ḥārith ibn Nawfal from 'Abdullāh ibn 'Abbās that 'Umar ibn al-Khaṭṭāb set out for Syria. When he was at Sargh, near Tabūk, the commanders of the army, Abū 'Ubayda ibn al-Jarrāḥ and his companions, met him and told him that the plague had broken out in Syria. Ibn 'Abbās said that 'Umar ibn al-Khaṭṭāb said, "Call the first Muhājirūn to me." He assembled them and asked them for advice, informing them that the plague had broken out in Syria. They disagreed about what to do. Some said, "You have set out for something and we do not think that you should abandon it." Others said, "You have the Companions of the Prophet ﷺ and the rest of the people with you and we do not think that you should send them towards this plague." 'Umar said, "Leave me."

Then he said, "Summon the Anṣār to me." They were summoned and he asked them for advice. They behaved as the Muhājirūn had and disagreed just as they had disagreed previously. He said, "Leave me." Then he said, "Summon to me whoever is here of the aged men of Quraysh of the Muhājirūn of the Conquest." They were summoned and not one of them differed. They said, "We think that you should withdraw the people and not send them towards the plague." 'Umar called out to the people, "I am leaving by camel in the morning, so you should do the same." Abū 'Ubayda said, "Is it flight from the decree of Allah?" 'Umar said, "Better that someone other than you had said it, Abū 'Ubayda. Yes, we flee from the decree of Allah to the decree of Allah. What would you think if these camels had gone down into a valley which had two slopes, one of them fertile and the other barren? If you pastured in the fertile part, wouldn't you pasture them by the decree of Allah? If you pastured them in the barren part, wouldn't you pasture them by the decree of Allah?"

'Abd ar-Raḥmān, who had been off doing something, arrived and he said, "I have some knowledge of this. I heard the Messenger of Allah ﷺ say, 'If you hear about it in a land, do not go forward to it. If it comes upon a land where you are, then do not depart in flight from it.'" 'Umar praised Allah and then set off.

23 Yaḥyā related to me from Mālik from Muḥammad ibn al-Munkadir and from Sālim ibn Abī an-Naḍr, the *mawlā* of 'Umar ibn 'Ubaydullāh, that 'Āmir ibn Sa'd ibn Abī Waqqāṣ heard his father ask Usāma ibn Zayd, "Have you heard anything from the Messenger of Allah ﷺ about the plague?" Usāma said, "The Messenger of Allah ﷺ said, 'The plague is a punishment which was sent down on a party of the tribe of Isrā'īl or whoever was before them. When you hear of it in a land, do not enter it. If it comes upon a land where you are, do not depart in flight from it.'"

Mālik said that Abū an-Naḍr said, "That is, do not depart with no intention other than flight."

24 Yaḥyā related to me from Mālik from Ibn Shihāb from 'Abdullāh ibn 'Āmir ibn Rabi'a that 'Umar ibn al-Khaṭṭāb set out for Syria. When he reached Sargh, near Tabūk, he heard that the plague had broken out in Syria. 'Abd ar-Raḥmān ibn 'Awf told him that the Messenger of Allah ﷺ said, 'If you hear that a land has plague in it, do not advance to it. If it comes upon a land where you are, do not depart in flight from it.'" 'Umar ibn al-Khaṭṭāb came back from Sargh.

25 Yaḥyā related to me from Mālik from Ibn Shihāb from Sālim ibn 'Abdullāh that 'Umar ibn al-Khaṭṭāb turned people back at Sargh according to the *ḥadīth* of 'Abd ar-Raḥmān ibn 'Awf.

26 Yaḥyā related to me that Mālik said, "I heard that 'Umar ibn al-Khaṭṭāb said, 'I prefer a night in Rukba (a valley near Ṭā'if) to ten nights in Syria.'"

Mālik said, "He meant to lengthen and preserve their lives because of the severity of the plague in Syria."

46. The Decree

46.1 The Prohibition against talking about the Decree

1 Yaḥyā related to me from Mālik from Abū az-Zinād from al-A'raj from Abū Hurayra that the Messenger of Allah ﷺ said, "Ādam and Mūsā argued and Ādam got the better of Mūsā. Mūsā rebuked Ādam, saying, 'You are Ādam who led people astray and brought them out of the Garden.' Ādam said to him, 'You are Mūsā to whom Allah gave knowledge of everything and whom he chose above other people with His message.' He said, 'Yes.' Ādam said, 'Do you then censure me for a matter which was decreed for me before I was even created?'"

2 Yaḥyā related to me from Mālik from Zayd ibn Abī Unaysa that 'Abd al-Ḥamīd ibn 'Abd ar-Raḥmān ibn Zayd ibn al-Khaṭṭāb informed him from Muslim ibn Yasār al-Juhanī that 'Umar ibn al-Khaṭṭāb was asked about this *āyat*, "*When your Lord took out all their descendants from the loins of the children of Adam and made them testify against themselves: 'Am I not your Lord?' They said, 'We testify that indeed You are!' Lest you say on the Day of Rising, 'We were heedless of this.'*" (7:172) 'Umar ibn al-Khaṭṭāb said, "I heard the Messenger of Allah ﷺ being asked about it. The Messenger of Allah ﷺ said, 'Allah, the Blessed, the Exalted, created Adam. Then He stroked his back with His right hand and some of his progeny issued from it. He said, "I created these for the Garden and they will act with the behaviour of the people of the Garden." Then He stroked his back again and brought forth the rest of his progeny from him. He said, "I created these for the Fire and they will act with the behaviour of the people of the Fire."' A man asked, 'Messenger of Allah, then of what value are actions?' The Messenger of Allah ﷺ replied, 'When Allah creates a slave for the

Garden, He gives him the behaviour of the people of the Garden so that he dies on one of the actions of the people of the Garden and by it He brings him into the Garden. When He creates a slave for the Fire, He gives him the behaviour of the people of the Fire so that he dies on one of the actions of the people of the Fire and by it He brings him into the Fire.'"

3 Yaḥyā related to me from Mālik that he heard that the Messenger of Allah ﷺ said, "I have left two things with you. As long as you hold fast to them, you will not go astray. They are the Book of Allah and the *Sunna* of His Prophet."

4 Yaḥyā related to me from Mālik from Ziyād ibn Sa'd from 'Amr ibn Muslim that Ṭāwus al-Yamānī said, "I found some of the Companions of the Messenger of Allah ﷺ saying, 'Everything is by a decree.'"

Ṭāwus added, "I heard 'Abdullāh ibn 'Umar say that the Messenger of Allah ﷺ said, 'Everything is by a decree – even incapacity and ability.'"

5 Mālik related to me from Ziyād ibn Sa'd that 'Amr ibn Dīnār said, "I heard 'Abdullāh ibn az-Zubayr say in a *khuṭba*, 'Allah – He is the Guider and the One Who Tempts Away.'"

6 Yaḥyā related to me from Mālik that his paternal uncle, Abū Suhayl ibn Mālik, said, "I was a prisoner with 'Umar ibn 'Abd al-'Azīz. He said, 'What do you think of these Qadariyya (proponents of free will)?' I said, 'My opinion is that one should ask them to turn away from wrong action if they will do so. If not, subject them to the sword. 'Umar ibn 'Abd al-'Azīz said, 'That is my opinion.'"

Mālik added, "That is my opinion as well."

46.2 General section on the People of the Decree

7 Yaḥyā related to me from Mālik from Abū az-Zinād from al-A'raj from Abū Hurayra that the Messenger of Allah ﷺ said, "A woman should not ask for the divorce of her sister so as to have everything for herself and in order to marry. She will get what is decreed for her."

8 Yaḥyā related to me from Mālik from Yazīd ibn Ziyād that Muḥammad ibn Ka'b al-Quraẓī said, "Mu'āwiya ibn Abī Sufyān said from the minbar, 'O people! Nothing can keep away what Allah gives and nothing can give what Allah keeps away. The wealth of a wealthy person does not profit him. When Allah desires good for him, He gives him understanding in the *dīn*.' Then Mu'āwiya said, 'I heard these words from the Messenger of Allah ﷺ on these very planks of wood.'"

9 Yaḥyā related to me from Mālik that he had heard that this was said, "Praise be to Allah who created everything as is necessary, who does not hasten anything He defers and determines. Allah is enough for me and sufficient. Allah hears whoever makes supplication to him. There is no goal beyond Allah."

10 Yaḥyā related to me from Mālik that he heard that this was said, "No one will die until his provision is completed for him, so behave correctly in seeking it."

47. Good Character

47.1 Good character

1 Yaḥyā related to me from Mālik that Mu'ādh ibn Jabal said, "The last advice the Messenger of Allah ﷺ gave me when I put my foot in the stirrup was that he said, 'Make your character good for the people, Mu'ādh ibn Jabal!'"

2 Yaḥyā related to me from Mālik from Ibn Shihāb from 'Urwa ibn az-Zubayr that 'Ā'isha, the wife of the Prophet ﷺ said, "The Messenger of Allah ﷺ did not have to choose between two matters but that he chose the easier of them as long as it was not a wrong action. If it was a wrong action, he was the furthest of people from it. The Messenger of Allah ﷺ did not take revenge for himself unless the limits of Allah were violated. Then he took revenge for it for Allah."

3 Yaḥyā related to me from Mālik from Ibn Shihāb from 'Alī ibn Ḥusayn ibn 'Alī ibn Abī Ṭālib that the Messenger of Allah ﷺ said, "Part of the excellence of a man's Islam is that he leaves what does not concern him."

4 Yaḥyā related to me from Mālik that he had heard that 'Ā'isha, the wife of the Prophet ﷺ said, "A man asked permission to come in to see the Messenger of Allah ﷺ. I was with him in the house and the Messenger of Allah ﷺ said, 'He is an evil member of his tribe.' Then the Messenger of Allah ﷺ gave him permission."

'Ā'isha continued, "It was not long before I heard the Messenger of

Allah ﷺ laughing with him. When the man left, I said, 'Messenger of Allah, you said what you said about him and then before long you were laughing with him!' The Messenger of Allah ﷺ said, 'Among the most evil of people is the one whom people are cautious with because of his evil.'"

5 Yaḥyā related to me from Mālik from his paternal uncle, Abū Suhayl ibn Mālik, from his father that Ka'b al-Aḥbar said, "If you want to know what a slave has stored up with his Lord, then look at whatever good praise follows him."

6 Yaḥyā related to me from Mālik that Yaḥyā ibn Sa'īd said, "I have heard that by his good character a man can reach the degree of someone who stands in prayer at night and who is thirsty from fasting in the heat of the day."

7 Yaḥyā related to me from Mālik that Yaḥyā ibn Sa'īd said that he heard Sa'īd ibn al-Musayyab say, "Shall I tell you what is better than much prayer and *ṣadaqa*?" They said, "Yes." He said, "Mending discord. And beware of hatred – it strips you (of your *dīn*)."

8 Yaḥyā related to me from Mālik that he had heard that the Messenger of Allah ﷺ said, "I was sent to perfect good character."

47.2 Modesty

9 Yaḥyā related to me from Mālik from Salama ibn Ṣafwān az-Zuraqī that Zayd ibn Ṭalḥa ibn Rukāna, who attributed it to the Prophet ﷺ said, "The Messenger of Allah ﷺ said, 'Every *dīn* has an innate character. The character of Islam is modesty'."

10 Yaḥyā related to me from Mālik from Ibn Shihāb from Sālim ibn 'Abdullāh from 'Abdullāh ibn 'Umar that the Messenger of Allah ﷺ passed by a man who was chiding his brother about modesty. The Messenger of Allah ﷺ said, "Leave him. Modesty is part of belief."

47.3 Anger

11 Mālik related to me from Ibn Shihāb from Ḥumayd ibn 'Abd ar-Raḥmān ibn 'Awf that a man came to the Messenger of Allah ﷺ and said, "Messenger of Allah, teach me some words which I can live by. Do not make them too much for me in case I forget." The Messenger of Allah ﷺ said, "Do not get angry."

12 Yaḥyā related to me from Mālik from Ibn Shihāb from Sa'īd ibn al-Musayyab from Abū Hurayra that the Messenger of Allah ﷺ said, "A strong person is not the person who throws his adversaries to the ground. A strong person is the person who contains himself when he is angry."

47.4 Shunning People

13 Yaḥyā related to me from Mālik from Ibn Shihāb from 'Aṭā' ibn Yazīd al-Laythī from Abū Ayyūb al-Anṣārī that the Messenger of Allah ﷺ said, "It is not lawful for a Muslim to shun his brother for more than three nights; that is they meet, and this one turns away and that one turns away. The better of the two is the one who gives the greeting first."

14 Yaḥyā related to me from Mālik from Ibn Shihāb from Anas ibn Mālik that the Messenger of Allah ﷺ said, "Do not be angry with each other and do not envy each other and do not turn away from each other, and be slaves of Allah, brothers. It is not lawful for a Muslim to shun his brother for more than three nights."

15 Yaḥyā related to me from Mālik from Abū az-Zinād from al-A'raj from Abū Hurayra that the Messenger of Allah ﷺ said, "Beware of suspicion. Suspicion is the most untrue speech. Do not spy and do not eavesdrop. Do not compete with each other and do not envy each other and do not hate each other and do not shun each other. Slaves of Allah be brothers."

16 Yaḥyā related to me from Mālik from 'Aṭā' ibn Abī Muslim that 'Abdullāh al-Khurasānī said, "The Messenger of Allah ﷺ said, 'Shake hands and rancour will disappear. Give presents to each other and you will love each other and enmity will disappear.'"

17 Yaḥyā related to me from Mālik from Suhayl ibn Abī Ṣāliḥ from his father from Abū Hurayra that the Messenger of Allah ﷺ said, "The doors of the Garden are opened on Monday and Thursday. Every Muslim slave who does not associate anything with Allah is forgiven except for those between whom there is enmity. It is said, 'Leave these two until they have made a reconciliation. Leave these two until they have made a reconciliation.'"

18 Yaḥyā related to me from Mālik from Muslim ibn Abī Maryam from Abū Ṣāliḥ as-Sammān that Abū Hurayra said, "The actions of people are presented twice a week, on Monday and Thursday. Every trusting slave is forgiven except for those between whom there is enmity. It is said, 'Leave these two until they turn in repentance. Leave these two until they turn in repentance.'"

48. Dress

48.1 Wearing clothes for beautification

1 Yaḥyā related to me from Mālik from Zayd ibn Aslam that Jābir ibn 'Abdullāh al-Anṣārī said, "We went out with the Messenger of Allah ﷺ in the raid on the Banū Anmār tribe." Jābir said, "I was resting under a tree when the Messenger of Allah ﷺ came up. I said, 'Messenger of Allah, come into the shade.' So the Messenger of Allah ﷺ came and sat down, and I stood up and went to a bag that we had. I looked in it for something and found a small cucumber and broke it. Then I brought it to the Messenger of Allah ﷺ. He asked, 'Where did you get this from?' I said, 'We brought it from Madīna, Messenger of Allah.'"

Jābir continued, "We had a friend with us whom we used to equip to go out to guard our mounts. I gave him what was necessary and then he turned to go to the mounts. He was wearing two threadbare cloaks he owned. The Messenger of Allah ﷺ looked at him and asked, 'Does he have two garments other than these?' I said, 'Yes, Messenger of Allah. He has two garments in the bag. I gave them to him,' and he said, 'Let him go and put them on.' I told him to go out to put them on. As he turned to go, the Messenger of Allah ﷺ exclaimed, 'May Allah strike his neck! Isn't that better for him?' He said (taking him literally), 'Messenger of Allah, in the way of Allah!' The Messenger of Allah ﷺ said, 'In the way of Allah.'"

Jābir added, "The man was killed in the way of Allah."

2 Yaḥyā related to me from Mālik that he heard that 'Umar ibn al-

Khaṭṭāb said, "I love to look at a Qur'ān reader who is wearing white garments."

3 Yaḥyā related to me from Mālik from Ayyūb ibn Abī Tamīm that Ibn Sīrīn said, "'Umar ibn al-Khaṭṭāb said, 'Allah has been generous to you, so be generous to yourselves. A man should wear a combination of his garments.'"

48.2 Wearing dyed garments and gold

4 Yaḥyā related to me from Mālik from Nāfi' that 'Abdullāh ibn 'Umar wore garments dyed with red earth and dyed with saffron.

Yaḥyā said that he heard Mālik say, "I disapprove of youths wearing any gold because I heard that the Messenger of Allah ﷺ forbade wearing gold rings and I disapprove of it for males, old or young."

Yaḥyā said, "I heard Mālik say about men wearing wraps dyed with safflower in their houses and courtyards, 'I do not know that it is unlawful but I prefer other garments to them.'"

48.3 Wearing rough silk

5 Mālik related to me from Hishām ibn 'Urwa from his father that 'Ā'isha, the wife of the Prophet ﷺ dressed 'Abdullāh ibn az-Zubayr in a shawl of silk which 'Ā'isha used to wear.

48.4 Clothes disapproved for women to wear

6 Yaḥyā related to me from Mālik from 'Alqama ibn Abī 'Alqama that his mother said, "Ḥafṣa bint 'Abd ar-Raḥmān visited 'Ā'isha, the wife of the Prophet ﷺ, and Ḥafṣa was wearing a long thin head scarf. 'Ā'isha tore it in two and made a wide one for her."

7 Yaḥyā related to me from Mālik from Muslim ibn Abī Maryam from

Abū Ṣāliḥ that Abū Hurayra said, "Women who are naked, even though they are wearing clothes, go astray and make others go astray, and they will not enter the Garden nor will they experience its fragrance, and its fragrance can be experienced from as far as the distance travelled in five hundred years."

8 Yaḥyā related to me from Mālik from Yaḥyā ibn Sa'īd from Ibn Shihāb that the Messenger of Allah ﷺ stood up in the night and looked at the horizon and said, "What treasures has the night opened? What trials have occurred? How many are dressed in this world and will be naked on the Day of Rising! Warn the women in their rooms."

48.5 A man trailing his garments

9 Yaḥyā related to me from Mālik from 'Abdullāh ibn Dīnār from 'Abdullāh ibn 'Umar that the Messenger of Allah ﷺ said, "A person who trails his garment out of arrogance will not be looked at by Allah on the Day of Rising."

10 Yaḥyā related to me from Mālik from Abū az-Zinād from al-A'raj from Abū Hurayra that the Messenger of Allah ﷺ said, "On the Day of Rising, Allah, the Blessed, the Exalted, will not look at a person who trails his lower garment out of arrogance."

11 Yaḥyā related to me from Mālik from Nāfi', 'Abdullāh ibn Dīnār and Zayd ibn Aslam that all of them informed him from 'Abdullāh ibn 'Umar that the Messenger of Allah ﷺ said, "On the Day of Rising, Allah will not look at a person who trailed his garment out of arrogance."

12 Yaḥyā related to me from Mālik from al-'Alā' ibn 'Abd ar-Rahmān that his father said, "I asked Abū Sa'īd al-Khudrī about the lower garment. He said that he would inform me with knowledge and that he had heard the Messenger of Allah ﷺ say, 'The lower garment of the believer should reach the middle of his calves. There is no harm in what is between that and the ankles. What is lower than that is in the Fire. What is lower than that is in the Fire. On the Day of Rising, Allah will not look at a person who trails his lower garment out of arrogance.'"

48.6 A woman trailing her garments

13 Yaḥyā related to me from Mālik from Abū Bakr ibn Nāfi' from his father, Nāfi', the *mawlā* of Ibn 'Umar, that Ṣafiyya bint Abī 'Ubayd informed him that Umm Salama, the wife of the Prophet ﷺ, said that when the lower garment of women was mentioned to the Messenger of Allah, he said, "She should let it down a hand-span."* Umm Salama said, "And if it leaves her uncovered?" He said, "Then the length of a forearm and let her not increase it."

48.7 Wearing sandals

14 Yaḥyā related to me from Mālik from Abū az-Zinād from al-A'raj from Abūu Hurayra that the Messenger of Allah ﷺ said, "Do not wear one sandal. Wear both of them or go with both feet bare."

15 Yaḥyā related to me from Mālik from Abū az-Zinād from al-A'raj from Abū Hurayra that the Messenger of Allah ﷺ said, "When you put on sandals, begin with the right foot. When you take them off, begin with the left foot. The right foot is the first to be put in the sandal and the last to be taken out."

16 Yaḥyā related to me from Mālik from his paternal uncle, Abū Suhayl ibn Mālik, from his father that Ka'b al-Aḥbar said to a man who took off his sandals, "Why have you taken off your sandals? Perhaps you have interpreted this *āyat*, '*Take off your sandals. You are in the holy valley of Ṭuwā*'? (20:12) Do you know what the sandals of Musā were?"

Mālik (Abū Suhayl's father) said, "I do not know what the man answered." Ka'b said, "They were made from the skin of a dead donkey."

48.8 Ways of dressing

17 Yaḥyā related to me from Mālik from Abū az-Zinād from al-A'raj that Abū Hurayra said, "The Messenger of Allah ﷺ forbade two kinds of sale: *mulāmasa*, in which a man is obliged to buy whatever he touches without

any choice in the matter, and *munābadha*, in which two men throw their garment to each other without either seeing the other's garment. He also forbade two ways of dressing: one in which a man sits with his legs drawn up to his chest wrapped in one garment that does not cover his genitals, and the other in which a man wraps a single garment over one arm and shoulder restricting them."

18 Yaḥyā related to me from Mālik from Nāfi' from 'Abdullāh ibn 'Umar that 'Abdullāh saw a silk robe at the door of the mosque. He said, "Messenger of Allah, would you buy this robe and wear it on *jumu'a* and when envoys come to you?" The Messenger of Allah ﷺ said, "No one wears this but a person who has no portion in the Next World." Then the Messenger of Allah ﷺ was brought some robes of the same material and gave one of them to 'Umar ibn al-Khaṭṭāb. 'Umar said, "Messenger of Allah, do you clothe me in it when you said what you said about the robe of 'Uṭārid?" The Messenger of Allah ﷺ said, "I did not give it to you to wear." 'Umar gave it to a brother of his in Makka who was still an idolator.

19 Yaḥyā related to me from Mālik that Isḥāq ibn 'Abdullāh ibn Abī Talḥa said, "Anas ibn Mālik said, 'I saw 'Umar ibn al-Khaṭṭāb when he was the governor of Madīna. Three patches were sewn between his shoulders, one patched over the other.'"

49. The Description of the Prophet ﷺ

49.1 Description of the Prophet ﷺ

1 Yaḥyā related to me from Mālik that Rabi'a ibn 'Abd ar-Raḥmān heard Anas ibn Mālik say, "The Messenger of Allah ﷺ was neither excessively tall nor excessively short. He was neither very pallid nor very dark. He did not have curly hair or straight hair. Allah commissioned him at the age of forty. He stayed in Makka ten years and at Madīna for ten years. When Allah, the Mighty, the Majestic, caused him to die, he was sixty, and there were not twenty white hairs in his hair or beard ﷺ."

49.2 Description of 'Īsā ibn Maryam عليه السلام and the Dajjāl

2 Yaḥyā related to me from Mālik from Nāfi' from 'Abdullāh ibn 'Umar that the Messenger of Allah ﷺ said, "I dreamt one night that I was at the Ka'ba, and I saw a dark man like the most handsome of dark men you have ever seen. He had hair which reached to between his ears and his shoulders like the most excellent of such hair that you have ever seen. He had combed his hair and water was dripping from it. He was leaning on two men or on the shoulders of two men doing *ṭawāf* around the Ka'ba. I asked, 'Who is this?' I was told, 'The Messiah, son of Maryam.' Then we were with a man with wiry hair who was blind in his right eye, which resembled a floating grape. I asked, 'Who is this?' I was told, 'This is the Dajjāl (lit. Dajjāl Messiah).'"

49.3 *Sunna* of the *fiṭra* (natural form)

3 Yaḥyā related to me from Mālik from Sa'īd ibn Abī Sa'īd al-Maqburī from his father that Abū Hurayra said, "There are five things which are part of the *fiṭra*: cutting the nails, trimming the moustache, removing the hair from the armpit, shaving the pubic region and circumcision."

4 Yaḥyā related to me from Mālik from Yaḥyā ibn Sa'īd that Sa'īd ibn al-Musayyab said, "Ibrāhīm ﷺ was the first to offer hospitality to the guest and the first person to be circumcised and the first person to trim the moustache and the first person to see grey hair. He said, 'O Lord! What is this?' Allah, the Blessed, the Exalted, said, 'It is dignity, Ibrāhīm.' He said, 'Lord, increase me in dignity.'"

Yaḥyā said that he had heard Mālik say, "One takes from the moustache until the edge of the lip appears: that is the rim. One does not cut it off completely so that one disfigures oneself."

49.4 Prohibition against eating with the left hand

5 Yaḥyā related to me from Mālik from Abū az-Zubayr from Jābir ibn 'Abdullāh as-Salamī that the Messenger of Allah ﷺ forbade a man to eat with his left hand or walk in one sandal or wrap a single garment around his drawn-up legs exposing his genitals.

6 Yaḥyā related to me from Mālik from Ibn Shihāb from Abū Bakr ibn 'Ubaydullāh ibn 'Abdullāh ibn 'Umar from 'Abdullāh ibn 'Umar that the Messenger of Allah ﷺ said, "When you eat, eat with your right hand and drink with your right. Shayṭān eats with his left hand and drinks with his left hand."

49.5 The very poor

7 Yaḥyā related to me from Mālik from Abū az-Zinād from al-A'raj from Abū Hurayra that the Messenger of Allah ﷺ said, "The very poor are not those people who constantly walk from person to person and are given

one or two morsels and one or two dates." They asked, "Then who are the very poor, Messenger of Allah?" He said, "People who do not find enough for themselves and other people are not aware of them to give *ṣadaqa* to them, and they do not start begging from other people."

8 Yaḥyā related to me from Mālik from Zayd ibn Aslam from Ibn Bujayd al-Ḥārithī (formerly al-Anṣārī) from his grandmother that the Messenger of Allah ﷺ said, "Give to the very poor, if only a roasted hoof."

49.6 The intestines of the unbeliever

9 Yaḥyā related to me from Mālik from Abū az-Zinād from al-A'raj that Abū Hurayra said, "The Messenger of Allah ﷺ said, 'The Muslim eats in one intestine and the unbeliever eats in seven!'"

10 Yaḥyā related to me from Mālik from Suhayl ibn Abī Ṣāliḥ from his father from Abū Hurayra that the Messenger of Allah ﷺ gave hospitality to a guest who was an unbeliever. The Messenger of Allah ﷺ ordered a sheep to be brought for him and it was milked. He drank its milk. Then another came and he drank it. Then another came and he drank it until he had drunk the milk of seven sheep. In the morning he became Muslim, and the Messenger of Allah ﷺ ordered a sheep for him. It was milked and he drank its milk. Then he ordered another for him but he could not finish it. The Messenger of Allah ﷺ said, "The believer drinks in one intestine and the unbeliever drinks in seven intestines."

49.7 Prohibition against drinking from silver vessels and blowing into drinks

11 Yaḥyā related to me from Mālik from Nāfi' from Zayd ibn 'Abdullāh ibn 'Umar ibn al-Khaṭṭāb from 'Abdullāh ibn 'Abd ar-Raḥmān ibn Abī Bakr aṣ-Ṣiddīq from Umm Salama, the wife of the Prophet ﷺ, that the Messenger of Allah ﷺ said, "A person who drinks from a silver vessel is gulping the fire of Hell into his belly."

12 Yaḥyā related to me from Mālik from Ayyūb ibn Ḥabīb, the *mawlā*

of Sa'd ibn Abī Waqqāṣ that Abū al-Muthannā al-Juhanī said that he was with Marwān ibn al-Ḥakam when Abū Sa'īd al-Khudrī came to him. Marwān ibn al-Ḥakam asked Abū Sa'īd, "Have you heard that the Messenger of Allah ﷺ forbade blowing into drinks?" Abū Sa'īd said to him, "Yes. A man said to him, 'Messenger of Allah, I am not quenched in a single breath.' The Messenger of Allah ﷺ said to him, 'Remove the cup from your mouth and then breathe.' The man said, 'Sometimes I see something floating in it?' He said, 'Then pour it out.'"|

49.8 Drinking while standing

13 Yaḥyā related to me from Mālik that he had heard that 'Umar ibn al-Khaṭṭāb, 'Alī ibn Abī Ṭālib and 'Uthmān ibn 'Affān drank while standing.

14 Yaḥyā related to me from Mālik from Ibn Shihāb that 'Ā'isha, *Umm al-Mu'minīn*, and Sa'd ibn Abī Waqqāṣ did not see any harm in a man drinking while standing.

15 Yaḥyā related to me from Mālik that Abū Ja'far al-Qārī said, "I saw 'Abdullāh ibn 'Umar drink while standing."

16 Yaḥyā related to me from Mālik from 'Āmir ibn 'Abdullāh ibn az-Zubayr that his father used to drink while standing.

49.9 The *sunna* about drinking and passing to the right

17 Yaḥyā related to me from Mālik from Ibn Shihāb from Anas ibn Mālik that the Messenger of Allah ﷺ was brought some milk which was mixed with well-water. There was a Bedouin on his right and Abū Bakr aṣ-Ṣiddīq was on his left. He drank and then gave it to the Bedouin, saying, "The right hand to the right hand."

18 Yaḥyā related to me from Mālik from Abū Ḥāzim ibn Dīnār from Sahl ibn Sa'd al-Anṣārī that the Messenger of Allah ﷺ was brought a drink and he drank some of it. There was a boy on his right and some old men on his left. He said to the boy, "Will you give me permission to give it to

these people?" The boy said, "No, Messenger of Allah. I will not prefer anyone to get my portion from you." Sahl said, "So the Messenger of Allah ﷺ placed it in his hand."

49.10 General section on food and drink

19 Yaḥyā related to me from Mālik that Isḥāq ibn 'Abdullāh ibn Abī Talḥa heard Anas ibn Mālik say that Abū Talḥa had said to Umm Sulaym, "I have just been listening to the Messenger of Allah ﷺ and his voice was very weak. I recognised hunger in it, so do you have anything?" She replied, "Yes," and brought out some barley loaves. She took her long head scarf and wrapped up the bread in part of it and put it into Anas' hand and gave him part of it to wear. Then she sent him to the Messenger of Allah ﷺ.

Anas continued, "I took it and found the Messenger of Allah ﷺ sitting in the mosque with some people. The Messenger of Allah ﷺ said, 'Did Abū Talḥa send you?' I replied, 'Yes.' He said, 'For food?' I said, 'Yes.' The Messenger of Allah ﷺ said to those with him, 'Let us go.' He set off and I went along with them until I came to Abū Talḥa and told him. Abū Talḥa said, 'Umm Sulaym! The Messenger of Allah ﷺ has brought people and we have no food. What shall we give them to eat?' She said, 'Allah and His Messenger know best.'

"Abū Talḥa went out and met the Messenger of Allah ﷺ approached with Abū Talḥa until they entered the house. The Messenger of Allah ﷺ said, 'Come now, Umm Sulaym, what have you got?' She brought out bread. The Messenger of Allah ﷺ ordered it to be broken into pieces, and Umm Sulaym squeezed out onto it a container of clarified butter which she had seasoned. Then the Messenger of Allah ﷺ said whatever Allah wished him to say and said, 'Will you give permission for ten of them to come in?' He gave them permission and they ate until they were full and then left. He said, 'Go and give permission to ten more.' He gave them permission, and they ate until they were full and left. Then he said, 'Give permission to ten more.' He gave them permission and they ate until they were full and left. He said, 'Give permission to ten more.' He gave permission and they ate until they were full and left. There were seventy or eighty men."

20 Yaḥyā related to me from Mālik from Abū az-Zinad from al-A'raj from Abū Hurayra that the Messenger of Allah ﷺ said, "The food of two is enough for three, and the food of three is enough for four."

21 Yaḥyā related to me from Mālik from Abū az-Zubayr al-Makkī from Jābir ibn 'Abdullāh that the Messenger of Allah ﷺ said, "Lock the door, tie up the waterskin, turn the vessel over or cover it and put out the lamp. Shayṭān does not open a locked door or untie a tied knot or uncover a vessel. A mouse may set fire to people's houses about them."

22 Yaḥyā related to me from Mālik from Sa'īd ibn Abī Sa'īd al-Maqburī from Abū Shurayḥ al-Ka'bī that the Messenger of Allah ﷺ said, "Whoever believes in Allah and the Last Day should speak good words or be silent. Whoever believes in Allah and the Last Day should be generous to his neighbour. Whoever believes in Allah and the Last Day should be generous to his guest. His welcome is for a day and a night, and his hospitality is for three days. Whatever is more than that is *ṣadaqa*. It is not lawful for a guest to stay with a man until he becomes a burden."

23 Yaḥyā related to me from Mālik from Sumayy, the *mawlā* of Abū Bakr, from Abū Ṣāliḥ as-Sammān from Abū Hurayra that the Messenger of Allah ﷺ said, "A man was walking on a road when he became very thirsty. He found a well and went into it and drank and then came out. There was a dog panting and eating earth out of thirst. The man said, 'This dog has become as thirsty as I was.' He went down into the well and filled his shoe and then held it in his mouth until he climbed out and gave the dog water to drink. Allah thanked him for it and forgave him." They said, "Messenger of Allah, do we have a reward for taking care of beasts?" He said, "There is a reward for every one with a moist liver."

24 Yaḥyā related to me from Mālik from Wahb ibn Kaysān that Jābir ibn 'Abdullāh said, "The Messenger of Allah ﷺ sent a delegation to the coast. Abū 'Ubayda ibn al-Jarrāḥ was in command of them. There were three people and I was one of them. We went out until head gone part of the way and our provisions were finished. Abū 'Ubayda ordered that the provisions of the army be gathered up and they amounted to two containers of dates. He used to give us a little provision from it each

day until it was finished, and we used to have only a single date each. I said, 'What is the use of one date?' He said, 'We will certainly feel its loss when they are finished.'"

Jābir continued, "Then we reached the sea and there was a fish like a small mountain (*ẓarib*). The army ate from it for eighteen nights. Then Abū 'Ubayda ordered two ribs from it to be set up. Then he commanded that a camel be ridden underneath them and it did not touch them."

"*Ẓarib*" is a small mountain.

25 Yaḥyā related to me from Mālik from Zayd ibn Aslam from 'Amr ibn Sa'd ibn Mu'ādh from his grandmother that the Messenger of Allah ﷺ said, "O believing women, none of you must consider even a roasted sheep's trotter too small to give to her neighbour."

26 Yaḥyā related to me from Mālik that 'Abdullāh ibn Abī Bakr said, "The Messenger of Allah ﷺ said, 'May Allah curse the Jews! They were forbidden to eat fat, so they sold it and ate its price'."

27 Yaḥyā related to me from Mālik that he heard that 'Īsā ibn Maryam used to say, "O tribe of Israel! You must drink pure water and the green things of the land, and barley bread. Beware of having wheat bread, for you will not be grateful enough for it."

28 Yaḥyā related to me from Mālik that he heard that the Messenger of Allah ﷺ entered the mosque and found Abū Bakr aṣ-Ṣiddīq and 'Umar ibn al-Khaṭṭāb there. He questioned them and they said, "Hunger has driven us out." The Messenger of Allah ﷺ said, "And hunger has brought me out." They went to Abū al-Haytham ibn at-Tayyihān al-Anṣārī who ordered some barley that was in the house be prepared and he got up to slaughter a sheep for them. The Messenger of Allah ﷺ said, "Leave the one with milk." He slaughtered a sheep for them and brought them pure sweet water which was hanging on a palm tree. Then they were brought the food and ate it and drank the water. The Messenger of Allah ﷺ recited, "*Then you will be asked that Day about the pleasures you enjoyed.*" (102:8)

29 Yaḥyā related to me from Mālik from Yaḥyā ibn Sa'īd that 'Umar ibn al-Khaṭṭāb was eating bread with ghee. He summoned one of the desert people and he began to eat and mop up the grease in the dish with a morsel of bread. 'Umar said, "It is as if you were lacking." He said, "By Allah, I have not eaten ghee nor have I seen food with it since such-and-such a time!" 'Umar declared, "I shall not eat clarified butter until people are give life again like they were first given life (i.e. on the Day of Rising)."

30 Yaḥyā related to me from Mālik from Isḥāq ibn 'Abdullāh ibn 'Abdullāh ibn Abī Ṭalḥa that Anās ibn Mālik said, "I saw 'Umar ibn al-Khaṭṭāb when he was *Amīr al-Mu'minīn* being given a *ṣā'* of dates and he ate all of them, even the inferior ones."

Yaḥyā related to me from Mālik from 'Abdullāh ibn Dīnar that 'Abdullāh ibn 'Umar said, "'Umar ibn al-Khaṭṭāb was asked about locusts. He said, 'I would like to have a basket of them from which we could eat.'"

31 Yaḥyā related to me from Mālik from Muḥammad ibn 'Amr ibn Ḥalḥala that Ḥumayd ibn Mālik ibn Khuthaym said, "I was sitting with Abū Hurayra on his land at al-'Aqīq. Some people rode out from Madīna to call upon Abū Hurayra. He told me to go to his mother, sending his greetings and asking her to prepare some food."

Ḥumayd continued, "She set down three loaves on a plate and some oil and salt. Then she put it on my head and I carried it to them. When I set it before them, Abū Hurayra said, 'Allah is greater,' and added, 'Praise be to Allah who has filled us with bread after our food had previously only been water and dates,' as the people did not touch any of the food.

"When they left, he said, 'O son of my brother, be good to your sheep and wipe the mucus from them and clean their pen. Pray in their quarter for they are among the animals of the Garden. By Him in Whose Hand my soul is, a time is about to come upon people when a small group of sheep will be more beloved to their owner than the house of Marwān.'"

32 Yaḥyā related to me from Mālik from Abū Nu'aym that Wahb ibn Kaysān said, "The Messenger of Allah ﷺ was brought food while his

stepson, 'Umar ibn Salama, was with him. The Messenger of Allah ﷺ told him, ' Say "Bismillāh" and eat what is in front of you.'"

33 Yaḥyā related to me from Mālik that Yaḥyā ibn Sa'īd said that he had heard al-Qāsim ibn Muḥammad say that a man came to 'Abdullāh ibn 'Abbās and said to him, "I have an orphan who has camels. Can I drink from the camels' milk?" Ibn 'Abbās said, "If you search for the lost camels of his and treat the camels' mange and fill in the cracks in their water basin and give them water on the day they drink, then drink the milk without doing any harm to the suckling camels by milking their mothers excessively."

34 Yaḥyā related to me from Mālik from Hishām ibn 'Urwa that his father never brought food nor drink, nor even a remedy which he consumed but that he said, "Praise be to Allah who has guided us and given us to drink and blessed us! Allah is greater! O Allah! We have found Your blessing accompanying every evil, give us every good in the morning and evening! We ask You for its completion and for gratitude. There is no good except Your good. There is god other than You, the God of the right-acting and the Lord of the Worlds. Praise be to Allah! There is no god but Allah. What Allah wills. There is no power except in Allah. O Allah, bless us in what You have provided us with and protect us from the punishment of the Fire!"

Al-ḥamdu lillāhi'lladhī hadānā wa aṭ'amanā wa saqānā wa na''amanā. Allāhu akbar. Allāhumma alfatnā ni'matuka bi kulli sharr. Fa aṣbaḥnā minhā wa amsaynā bi kulli khayr. Nas'aluka tamāmahā wa shukrahā. Lā khayra illā khayruk. Wa lā ilāha ghayruk. Ilāha'ṣ-ṣāliḥīn wa rabba'l-'ālamīn. Al-ḥamdu lillāh. Wa lā ilāha illa'llāh. Mā shā'a'llāh. Wa lā quwwata illā billāh. Allāhumma bārik lanā fīmā razaqtanā wa qinā 'adhāba'n-nār.

35 Yaḥyā said that Mālik was asked, "Can a woman eat with other than her relative or slave?" Mālik said, "There is no harm in that if it is in a manner which is accepted for a woman to eat with men."

Mālik said, "A woman sometimes eats with her husband and with others he dines with or with her brother in the same way. It is disapproved of for a woman to be alone with a man when there is no relationship between them by blood, marriage or suckling that would prevent him marrying her."

49.11 Eating meat

36 Yaḥyā related to me from Mālik from Yaḥyā ibn Sa'īd that 'Umar ibn al-Khaṭṭāb said, "Beware of meat. It has addictiveness like the addictiveness of wine."

Yaḥyā related to me from Mālik from Yaḥyā ibn Sa'īd that 'Umar ibn al-Khaṭṭāb saw Jābir ibn 'Abdullāh carrying some meat. He said, "What is this?" He replied, "*Amīr al-Mu'minīn*, we desired meat and I bought some meat for a dirham." 'Umar said, "Does one of you want to fill his belly to the exclusion of his neighbour or nephew? How can you overlook this *āyat*? '*You dissipated the good things you had in your worldly life and enjoyed yourself in it.*' (46:20)"

49.12 Wearing rings

37 Yaḥyā related to me from Mālik from 'Abdullāh ibn Dīnār from 'Abdullāh ibn 'Umar that the Messenger of Allah ﷺ used to wear a gold ring. Then the Messenger of Allah ﷺ stood up and threw it away and said, "I will never wear it." He said, "So the people threw away their rings."

38 Yaḥyā related to me from Mālik that Ṣadaqa ibn Yasār said, "I asked Sa'īd ibn al-Musayyab about wearing a ring. He said, "Wear it and tell people that I gave you that decision."

49.13 Pulling off necklaces and bells from the necks of camels

39 Yaḥyā related to me from Mālik from 'Abdullāh ibn Abī Bakr from 'Abbād ibn Tamīm that Abū Bashīr al-Ansārī told him that he was with the Messenger of Allah ﷺ on one of his journeys. He related, "The Messenger of Allah ﷺ sent a messenger." ('Abdullāh ibn Abī Bakr said, "I

think that he said it was while the people were in their resting place.") The messenger said, "Do not let a single-string necklace or any necklace remain unbroken on the neck of a camel."

Yaḥyā said, "I heard Mālik say, 'I think that was because of the evil eye.'"

50. The Evil Eye

50.1 *Wuḍū'* against the Evil Eye

1 Yaḥyā related to me from Mālik that Muḥammad ibn Abī Umāma ibn Sahl ibn Ḥunayf heard his father say, "My father, Sahl ibn Ḥunayf, had a *ghusl* at al-Kharrār. He removed the *jubbah* he had on while 'Āmir ibn Rabi'a was watching, and Sahl was a man with beautiful skin. 'Āmir said to him, 'I have never seen anything like I have seen today, not even the skin of a virgin.' Sahl fell ill on the spot and his condition worsened. Somebody went to the Messenger of Allah ﷺ and told him that Sahl was ill and could not go with him. The Messenger of Allah ﷺ came to him, and Sahl told him what had happened with 'Āmir. The Messenger of Allah ﷺ said, 'Why does one of you kill his brother? Why did you not say, "May Allah bless you (*tabāraka'llāh*)"? The evil eye is real. Do *wuḍū'* against its effects.' 'Āmir did *wuḍū'* against it and Sahl went with the Messenger of Allah ﷺ and there was nothing wrong with him."

2 Mālik related to me from Ibn Shihāb that Abū Umāma ibn Sahl ibn Ḥunayf said, "'Āmir ibn Rabi'a saw Sahl ibn Hunayf having a *ghusl* and said, 'I have not seen the like of what I see today, not even the skin of a maiden who has never been outdoors.' Sahl fell to the ground. The Messenger of Allah ﷺ arrived and it was said, 'Messenger of Allah! Can you do anything about Sahl ibn Hunayf? By Allah, he cannot even lift his head.' He said, 'Do you suspect anyone of it?' They said, 'We suspect 'Āmir ibn Rabi'a.'"

He continued, "The Messenger of Allah ﷺ summoned 'Āmir and was furious with him, saying, 'Why does one of you kill his brother? Why did you not say, "May Allah bless you"? Do *ghusl* for it!' 'Āmir washed his face, hands, elbows, knees, the end of his feet, and inside his lower garment in a vessel. Then he poured it over him and Sahl went off with the people, and there was nothing wrong with him."

50.2 Guarding against the Evil Eye

3 Yaḥyā related to me from Mālik that Ḥumayd ibn Qays al-Makkī said, "A man came to the Messenger of Allah ﷺ with the two sons of Ja'far ibn Abī Ṭālib. He asked their nursemaid, 'Why are they so thin?' Their nursemaid answered, 'Messenger of Allah, the evil eye goes quickly to them. Nothing stops us from asking someone to make talismans (using *āyats* of Qur'ān) for them, except that we do not know what you approve of in that.' The Messenger of Allah ﷺ said, 'Make talismans for them. Had anything been able to outstrip the decree, the evil eye would do so.'"

4 Yaḥyā related to me from Mālik from Yaḥyā ibn Sa'īd from Sulaymān ibn Yasār that 'Urwa ibn az-Zubayr told him that the Messenger of Allah ﷺ entered the house of Umm Salama, the wife of the Prophet ﷺ. There was a child weeping in the house and they said that it was from the evil eye. 'Urwa said, "The Messenger of Allah ﷺ said, 'Why do you not find someone to make a talisman to protect him from the evil eye?'"

50.3 The invalid's reward

5 Yaḥyā related to me from Mālik from Zayd ibn Aslam from 'Aṭā' ibn Yasār that the Messenger of Allah ﷺ said, "When the slave is ill, Allah sends two angels to him." He said, "They look at what he says to his visitors. If he praises Allah when they come to him, they take that up to Allah, the Mighty, the Majestic – and He knows best – and He says, 'If I make My slave die, I will make him enter the Garden. If I heal him, I will replace his flesh with better flesh and his blood with better blood and I will efface his wrong actions."

6 Yaḥyā related to me from Mālik from Yazīd ibn Khuṣayfa that 'Urwa ibn az-Zubayr said that he heard 'Ā'isha, the wife of the Prophet ﷺ, said,

'When a believer is afflicted by something, even a thorn, it removes (or effaces) his wrong actions.'"

Yazīd did not know which word 'Urwa said.

7 Yaḥyā related to me from Mālik that Muḥammad ibn 'Abdullāh Ibn Abī Ṣa'ṣa'a said that he heard Abū al-Hubāb Sa'īd ibn Yasār say that he had heard Abū Hurayra say, "The Messenger of Allah ﷺ said, 'Allah afflicts the one for whom He desires good.'"

8 Yaḥyā related to me from Mālik from Yaḥyā ibn Sa'īd that death came to a man in the time of the Messenger of Allah ﷺ. A man said, "He was fortunate," as he had died without being tried by illness. The Messenger of Allah ﷺ said, "Alas for you, what will let you know that if Allah had tried him with illness, He would have wiped out his wrong actions."

50.4 Seeking refuge and using talismans in illness

9 Yaḥyā related to me from Mālik from Yazīd ibn Khuṣayfa that 'Amr ibn 'Abdullāh ibn Ka'b as-Salamī told him that Nāfi' ibn Jubayr came to the Messenger of Allah ﷺ. 'Uthmān ibn Abī al-'Āṣ also came to the Messenger of Allah ﷺ. 'Uthmān said that he had a pain which was enough to kill him. The Messenger of Allah ﷺ said, "Rub it with your right hand seven times and say, 'I take refuge with the might of Allah and His power from the evil of what I feel.'"

'Uthmān added, "I said that and Allah removed what I had. I still command my family and others to say it."

10 Yaḥyā related to me from Mālik from Ibn Shihāb from 'Urwa ibn az-Zubayr from 'Ā'isha that when the Messenger of Allah ﷺ had a complaint, he would recite the last three *sūras* of the Qur'ān over himself and blow. She said, "When his pain was great, I would recite it over him and wipe him with his right hand hoping for its blessing."

11 Yaḥyā related to me from Mālik from Yaḥyā ibn Sa'īd from 'Amra bint 'Abd ar-Raḥmān that Abū Bakr aṣ-Ṣiddīq visited 'Ā'isha at a time when

she had a complaint and a Jewish woman was writing a talisman for her. Abū Bakr said, "Write it for her from the Book of Allah."

50.5 Treating the invalid

12 Yaḥyā related to me from Mālik from Zayd ibn Aslam that a man received a wound in the time of the Messenger of Allah ﷺ. The blood clotted in the wound and the man called two men from the Banū Anmār tribe. They looked at it and claimed that the Messenger of Allah ﷺ asked them, "Which of you is the better doctor?" They said, "Is there any good in medicine, Messenger of Allah?" Zayd claimed that the Messenger of Allah ﷺ said, "The One who sent down the disease also sent down the remedy."

13 Yaḥyā related to me from Mālik that Yaḥyā ibn Sa'īd said, "I heard that Sa'īd ibn Zurāra cauterized himself because of a pain in the throat accompanied by blood and he died."

14 Yaḥyā related to me from Mālik from Nāfi' that 'Abdullāh ibn 'Umar cauterized for palsy and he had a talisman made for the sting of scorpions.

50.6 Washing with water for a fever

15 Yaḥyā related to me from Mālik from Hishām ibn 'Urwa from Fāṭma bint al-Mundhir that whenever a woman who had a fever was brought to Asmā' bint Abī Bakr, she made supplication for her and took water and poured it inside her collar. She said, "The Messenger of Allah ﷺ ordered us to cool it with water."

16 Yaḥyā related to me from Mālik from Hishām ibn 'Urwa from his father that the Messenger of Allah ﷺ said, "Fever comes from the vehemence of the heat of Hell, so cool it with water."

Mālik related to me from Nāfi' from Ibn 'Umar that the Messenger of Allah ﷺ said, "Fever comes from the vehemence of the heat of Jahannam, so put it out with water."

50.7 Visiting invalids, and evil omens

17 Yaḥyā related to me from Mālik that he had heard from Jābir ibn 'Abdullāh that the Messenger of Allah ﷺ said, "When a man visits an invalid, he plunges into mercy to the extent that when he sits with him, it settles in him" or something like that.

18 Yaḥyā related to me from Mālik that he had heard from Bukayr ibn 'Abdullāh ibn al-Ashajj from Ibn 'Aṭiya that the Messenger of Allah ﷺ said, "There is no contagion, no *hāma*, and no serpent in a hungry belly. However, the possessor of sick livestock must not stop his animals at the same place as the possessor of healthy livestock, but the possessor of healthy livestock may stop wherever he wishes."

They said, "Messenger of Allah, why is that?" The Messenger of Allah ﷺ said, "It is harmful."

51. Hair

51.1 The *sunna* regarding hair

1 Yaḥyā related to me from Mālik from Abū Bakr ibn Nāfi' from his father Nāfi' from 'Abdullāh ibn 'Umar that the Messenger of Allah ﷺ ordered the moustache to be trimmed and the beard to be left.

2 Yaḥyā related to me from Mālik from Ibn Shihāb that Ḥumayd ibn 'Abd ar-Raḥmān ibn 'Awf heard Mu'āwiya ibn Abī Sufyān say from the minbar in the year that he performed the *ḥajj*, holding a lock of hair (i.e. a hairpiece) which he took from one of his guards, "People of Madīna! Where are your learned men? I heard the Messenger of Allah ﷺ forbid things like this, saying, 'The tribe of Israel were destroyed when their women started to use this.'"

3 Yaḥyā related to me from Mālik that Ziyād ibn Sa'd heard Ibn Shihāb say, "The Messenger of Allah ﷺ let his hair hang down his forehead as Allah willed, and afterwards he parted it."

Mālik said, "There is no harm in a man looking at the hair of his son's wife or the hair of his wife's mother."

4 Yaḥyā related to me from Mālik from Nāfi' that 'Abdullāh ibn 'Umar disapproved of castration and said, "The completeness of the created form is in the testicles."

5 Yaḥyā related to me from Mālik that Ṣafwān ibn Sulaym heard that the Messenger of Allah ﷺ said, "I and the one who guards the orphan,

whether for himself or someone else, will be like these two in the Garden, when he has *taqwā*," indicating his middle and index fingers.

51.2 Caring for hair

6 Yaḥyā related to me from Mālik from Yaḥyā ibn Sa'īd that Abū Qatāda al-Anṣārī said to the Messenger of Allah ﷺ, "I have a lot of hair which comes down to my shoulders, shall I let it down?" The Messenger of Allah ﷺ said, "Yes, and honour it." Sometimes Abū Qatāda oiled it twice in the same day because the Messenger of Allah ﷺ told him, "Honour it."

7 Yaḥyā related to me from Mālik from Zayd ibn Aslam that 'Aṭā' ibn Yasār told him that the Messenger of Allah ﷺ was in the mosque when a man came in with dishevelled hair and beard. The Messenger of Allah ﷺ motioned with his hand that he should be sent out to groom his hair and beard. The man did so and then returned. The Messenger of Allah ﷺ said, "Is this not better than that one of you should come with his head dishevelled as if he were a *shayṭān*?"

51.3 Dyeing the hair

8 Yaḥyā related to me from Mālik that Yaḥyā ibn Sa'īd said that Muḥammad ibn Ibrāhīm at-Taymī had informed him that Abū Salama ibn 'Abd ar-Raḥmān said, "'Abd ar-Raḥmān ibn al-Aswad ibn 'Abd al-Yaghūth used to sit with us and he had a white beard and hair. One day he came to us and he had dyed his beard and head red, and the people told him, 'This is better.' He said, "Ā'isha, the wife of the Prophet ﷺ, sent her slave-girl Nukhayla to me yesterday. She entreated me to dye my hair and she informed me that Abū Bakr aṣ-Ṣiddīq used to dye his hair.'"

Yaḥyā said that he heard Mālik say about dyeing the hair black, "I have not heard anything certain on that, but I prefer other colours."

Yaḥyā said, "Not to dye at all is permitted, Allah willing, and there is no constraint on people concerning it."

Yaḥyā said that he had heard Mālik say, "There is a clear indication in this *ḥadīth* that the Messenger of Allah ﷺ did not dye his hair. Had the Messenger of Allah ﷺ dyed his hair, 'Ā'isha would have sent a message to that effect to 'Abd ar-Raḥmān ibn al-Aswad."

Chapters on Seeking Refuge and Those who Love Each other for the Sake of Allah

51.4 What is commanded of seeking refuge in Allah

9 Yaḥyā related to me from Mālik that Yaḥyā ibn Sa'īd said that he had heard that Khālid ibn al-Walīd said to the Messenger of Allah ﷺ, "I have nightmares." The Messenger of Allah ﷺ said to him, "Say, 'I seek refuge with the complete words of Allah from His anger and His punishment and the evil of His slaves, and from the evil suggestions of the *shayṭāns* and from their being present (at death).'"

A'ūdhu bi kalimāti'llāhi't-tāmmati min ghaḍabihi wa 'iqābihi wa sharri 'ibādhihi wa min hamazāti'sh-shayāṭīni wa an yaḥḍurūn.

10 Yaḥyā related to me from Mālik that Yaḥyā ibn Sa'īd said, "When the Messenger of Allah ﷺ was taken on the Night Journey, he saw an evil jinn seeking him out with a fiery torch. Whenever the Messenger of Allah ﷺ turned, he saw him. Jibrīl said to him, 'Shall I teach you some words to say? When you say them, his torch will be extinguished and fall from him.' The Messenger of Allah ﷺ said, 'Yes, indeed.' Jibrīl said, 'Say, "I seek refuge with the Noble Face of Allah and with the complete words of Allah, which neither a good person nor a corrupt one can exceed, from the evil of what descends from the sky and the evil of what ascends in it, and from the evil of what is created in the earth and the evil of what comes out of it, and from the trials of the night and day, and from the visitations of the night and day, except for one that knocks with good, O Merciful!"'"

A'ūdhu bi wajhi'llāhi'l-karīm, wa bi kalimāti'llāhi't-tāmmāti'llatī lā yujāwizuhunna barrun wa lā fājir, min sharri mā yanzilu mina's-samā', wa sharri mā ya'ruju fīhā, wa sharri mā dhara'a fi'l-arḍ, wa sharri mā yakhruju minhā, wa min fitani'l-layli wa'n-nahār, wa min ṭawāriqi'l-layl, illā ṭāriqan yaṭruqu bikhayr, ya Raḥmān.

11 Yaḥyā related to me from Mālik from Suhayl ibn Abī Ṣāliḥ from his father from Abū Hurayra that a man of the Aslam tribe said, "I did not sleep last night." The Messenger of Allah ﷺ, said to him, "For what reason?" He replied, "A scorpion stung me." The Messenger of Allah ﷺ said, "Had you said in the evening, 'I seek refuge with the complete words of Allah from the evil of what He has created,' it would not have happened."

A'ūdhu bi kalimāti'llāhi't-tāmmāti min sharri mā khalaq.

12 Yaḥyā related to me from Mālik from Sumayy, the *mawlā* of Abū Bakr, from al-Qa'qā' ibn Ḥakīm that Ka'b al-Aḥbar said, "If it had not been for some words which I said, the Jews would have made me into a monkey." Someone asked him what they were. He said, "I seek refuge with the Immense Face of Allah – there is nothing greater than it – and with the complete words of Allah which neither the good person nor the corrupt can exceed and with all the most beautiful names of Allah, what I know of them and what I do not know, from the evil, of what He has created, originated and multiplied."

A'ūdhu bi wajhi'llāhi'l-'aẓīm, alladhī laysa shay'un a'ẓama minhu, wa bi kalimāti'llāhi't-tāmmāti'llatī lā yujāwizuhunna barrun wa lā fājir, wa bi asmā'i'llāhi'l-ḥusnā kullihā, mā 'alimtu minhā wa mā lam a'lam, min sharri mā khalaqa wa bara'a wa dhara'a.

51.5 Those who love each other in Allah

13 Yaḥyā related to me from Mālik from 'Abdullāh ibn 'Abd ar-Raḥmān ibn Ma'mar from Abū al-Ḥubāb Sa'īd ibn Yasār that Abū Hurayra said, "The Messenger of Allah ﷺ said, 'Allah, the Blessed, the Exalted, will say on the Day of Rising, "Where are those who loved each other for My majesty? Today I will shade them in My shade on the day when there is no shade except My shade."'"

14 Yaḥyā related to me from Mālik from Khubayb ibn ʿAbd ar-Raḥmān al-Anṣārī from Ḥafṣ ibn ʿĀsim that either Abū Saʿīd al-Khudrī or Abū Hurayra said, "The Messenger of Allah ﷺ said, 'There are seven whom Allah will shade in His shade on the day on which there is no shade except His shade: a just imām, a youth who grows up worshipping Allah, a man whose heart is attached to the mosque when he leaves it until he returns to it, two men who love each other in Allah and meet for that and part for that, a man who remembers Allah when he is alone and his eyes overflow with tears, a man who refuses the approaches of a noble, beautiful woman, saying, "I fear Allah", and a man who gives *ṣadaqa* and conceals it so that his left hand does not know what his right hand gives.'"

15 Yaḥyā related to me from Mālik from Suhayl ibn Abī Sālih from his father from Abū Hurayra that the Messenger of Allah ﷺ said, "If Allah loves a slave, he says to Jibrīl, 'I love so-and-so, so love him,' so Jibrīl loves him and then calls out to the people of heaven, 'Allah loves so-and-so, so love him,' and the people of heaven love him. Then acceptance is placed in the earth for him."

As for when Allah is angry with a slave, Mālik said, "I consider that He says the like of that about His anger."

16 Yaḥyā related to me from Mālik from Abū Ḥāzim ibn Dīnār that Abū Idrīs al-Khawlanī said, "I entered the Damascus mosque and there was a young man with a beautiful mouth and white teeth sitting with some people. When they disagreed about something, they referred it to him and acted according to his statement. I inquired about him, and was told, 'This is Muʿādh ibn Jabal.' The next day I went to the noon prayer and I found that he had got to the noon prayer before me and I found him praying."

Abū Idrīs continued, "I waited for him until he had finished the prayer. Then I came to him from in front of him and greeted him and said, 'By Allah! I love you for Allah!' He said, 'By Allah?' I said, 'By Allah.' He said, 'By Allah?' I said, 'By Allah.' He said, 'By Allah?' I said, 'By Allah!'"

He continued, "He took me by the upper part of my cloak and pulled me to him and said, 'Rejoice! I heard the Messenger of Allah ﷺ say, "Allah, the

Blessed and Exalted, said, 'My love is obliged for those who love each other in Me, and those who sit with each other in Me, and those who visit each other in Me and those who give to each other generously in Me.'"'"

17 Yaḥyā related to me from Mālik that he had heard that 'Abdullāh ibn 'Abbās said, "Equanimity, gentleness, and good behaviour are one twenty-fifth part of prophethood."

52. Visions

52.1 Visions

1 Yaḥyā related to me from Mālik from Isḥāq ibn 'Abdullāh ibn Abī Ṭalḥa al-Anṣārī from Anas ibn Mālik that the Messenger of Allah ﷺ said, "A good dream of a man who is right-acting is a forty-sixth part of prophethood."

Yaḥyā related the like of that to me from Mālik from Abū az-Zinād from al-A'raj from Abū Hurayra from the Messenger of Allah ﷺ.

2 Yaḥyā related to me from Mālik from Isḥāq ibn 'Abdullāh ibn Abī Ṭalḥa from Zufar ibn Ṣa'ṣa'a from his father from Abū Hurayra that when the Messenger of Allah ﷺ left the morning prayer, he would say, "Did any of you have a dream last night? All that will remain of prophethood after me will be the true dream."

3 Yaḥyā related to me from Mālik from Zayd ibn Aslam from 'Aṭā' ibn Yasār that the Messenger of Allah ﷺ said, "All that will be left of prophethood after me are the *mubashshirāt*." They asked, "What are the *mubashshirāt*, Messenger of Allah?" He said, "A true dream which a man who is right-acting sees – or which is shown to him – is a forty-sixth part of prophecy."

4 Yaḥyā related to me from Mālik from Yaḥyā ibn Sa'īd that Abū Salama ibn 'Abd ar-Raḥmān said that he heard Abū Qatāda ibn Rib'iyy say that he heard the Messenger of Allah ﷺ say, "Good dreams are from Allah and bad dreams are from Shayṭān. When you see what you dislike in

a dream, spit to your left side three times when you wake up and seek refuge with Allah from its evil. Then it will not harm you, Allah willing."

Abū Salama said, "I would see dreams which weighed on me more heavily than a mountain. When I heard this *ḥadīth*, I was no longer concerned about it."

5 Yaḥyā related to me from Mālik from Hishām ibn 'Urwa that his father said that the *āyat*, *"There is good news for them in the life of this world and in the Next World,"* (10:64), refers to a good dream which a man who is righteous has or which was shown to him.

52.2 Games of dice

6 Yaḥyā related to me from Mālik from Mūsā ibn Maysara from Sa'īd ibn Abī Hind from Abū Mūsā al-Ash'arī that the Messenger of Allah ﷺ said, "Whoever plays games of dice has disobeyed Allah and His Messenger."

Yaḥyā related to me from Mālik from 'Alqama from his mother that 'Ā'isha, the wife of the Prophet ﷺ, heard that the people who lived in a room in her house had some dice. She sent a message to them, "If you do not remove them, I will remove you from my house," and she reproached them for it.

7 Yaḥyā related to me from Mālik from Nāfi' from 'Abdullāh ibn 'Umar that when he found one of his family playing dice, he beat him and destroyed the dice.

Yaḥyā said that he heard Mālik say, "There is no good in chess," and he disapproved of it. Yaḥyā said, "I heard him disapprove of playing it and other worthless games. He recited this *āyat*: '*What is there after truth except misguidance*?' (10:32)"

53. Greetings

53.1 Behaviour in greeting

1 Yaḥyā related to me from Mālik from Zayd ibn Aslam that the Messenger of Allah ﷺ said, "Someone riding should greet someone walking, and when one of a group of people gives a greeting, it is enough for all of them."

2 Yaḥyā related to me from Mālik from Wahb ibn Kaysān that Muḥammad ibn 'Amr ibn 'Aṭā' said, "I was sitting with 'Abdullāh ibn 'Abbās when a Yemeni man came in. He said, 'Peace be upon you and the mercy of Allah and His blessing (*as-Salāmu 'alaykum wa raḥmatullāh wa barakātuhu*)' and then he added something more to that. Ibn 'Abbās asked (at that time his eyesight had gone), 'Who is this?' People said, 'This is a Yemeni who has come to see you,' and they introduced him, Ibn 'Abbās said, 'The greeting ends with the word blessing.'"

Yaḥyā said that Mālik was asked, "Does one greet a woman?" He said, "As for an old woman, I do not disapprove of it. As for a young woman, I do not like it."

53.2 Greeting Jews and Christians

3 Yaḥyā related to me from Mālik from 'Abdullāh ibn Dīnār that 'Abdullāh ibn 'Umar said that the Messenger of Allah ﷺ said, "When a Jew greets you and says, 'Poison to you (*as-sāmu 'alaykum*)', say, 'And to you.'"

Yaḥyā said that Mālik was asked whether a person who greeted a Jew or Christian should apologise for it. He said, "No."

53.3 General section on the greeting

4 Yaḥyā related to me from Mālik from Isḥāq ibn 'Abdullāh ibn Abī Ṭalḥa from Abū Murra, the *mawlā* of 'Aqīl ibn Abī Ṭālib, from Abū Wāqid al-Laythī that the Messenger of Allah ﷺ was sitting in the mosque with some people when three people came in. Two of them came towards the Messenger of Allah ﷺ and one went away. When the two stopped at the assembly of the Messenger of Allah ﷺ they gave the greeting. One of them saw a gap in the circle and sat in it. The other sat down behind the circle. The third turned away and left. When the Messenger of Allah ﷺ finished, he said, "Shall I tell you about three people? One of them sought shelter with Allah, so Allah gave him shelter. The other was shy, so Allah was shy to him. The other turned away, so Allah turned away from him."

5 Yaḥyā related to me from Mālik from Isḥāq ibn 'Abdullāh ibn Abī Ṭalḥa that Anas ibn Mālik heard 'Umar ibn al-Khaṭṭāb return the greeting of a man who greeted him. Then 'Umar asked the man, "How are you?" He answered, "I praise Allah to you (*aḥmadu ilayka'llāh*)." 'Umar said, "That is what I wanted from you."

6 Yaḥyā related to me from Mālik from Isḥāq ibn 'Abdullāh ibn Abī Ṭalḥa that at-Ṭufayl ibn Ubayy ibn Ka'b told him that he visited 'Abdullāh ibn 'Umar one morning and went out with him to the market. When they were out, 'Abdullāh ibn 'Umar did not pass by anyone selling poor merchandise or selling commodities or a needy person or anyone without greeting them.

At-Ṭufayl said, "I came to 'Abdullāh ibn 'Umar one day and he asked me to follow him to the market. I said to him, 'What will you do in the market if you will not stop to sell nor seek any goods or barter with them or sit in any of the assemblies of the market?' 'Abdullāh ibn 'Umar said that we should sit down and talk, and then he said, 'Abū Baṭn (lit. father of the belly, as at-Ṭufayl had a prominent stomach), we go out in the morning only for the sake of the greeting. We greet whomever we meet.'"

7 Yaḥyā related to me from Mālik from Yaḥyā ibn Sa'īd that a man greeted 'Abdullāh ibn 'Umar. He said, "Peace be upon you and the mercy of Allah and His blessings, on and on." 'Abdullāh ibn 'Umar said to him, "And on you, a thousand times" as if he disliked that.

8 Yaḥyā related to me from Mālik that he heard that when one entered an unoccupied house, one should say, "Peace be upon us and on the slaves of Allah who are right-acting (*as-salāmu 'alayna wa 'alā 'ibādillāhi'ṣ-ṣāliḥīn*)."

54. General

54.1 Asking permission to enter

1 Mālik related to me from Ṣafwān ibn Sulaym from 'Aṭā' ibn Yasār that the Messenger of Allah ﷺ was questioned by a man who said, "Messenger of Allah, should I ask permission of my mother to enter?" He said, "Yes." The man said, "I live with her in the house." The Messenger of Allah ﷺ said, "Ask her permission." The man said, "I am her servant." The Messenger of Allah ﷺ said, "Ask her permission. Do you want to see her naked?" He said, "No." He said, "Then ask her permission."

2 Mālik related to me from a reliable source of his from Bukayr ibn 'Abdullāh ibn al-Ashajj from Basr ibn Sa'īd from Abū Sa'īd al-Khudrī that Abū Mūsā al-Ash'arī said, "The Messenger of Allah ﷺ said, 'One asks permission three times. If you are given permission, then enter. If not, go away.'"

3 Mālik related to me from Rabi'a ibn 'Abd ar-Raḥmān from another of the scholars of that time that Abū Mūsā al-Ash'arī came and asked permission from 'Umar ibn al-Khaṭṭāb to enter. He asked permission three times and then went away. 'Umar ibn al-Khaṭṭāb sent after him and said, "What is wrong with you? Why did you not come in?" Abū Mūsā said, "I heard the Messenger of Allah ﷺ say, 'Ask permission to enter three times. If you are given permission, then enter. If not, go away.'"

'Umar said, "Who can confirm this? If you do not bring me someone to confirm, I will do such-and-such to you."

Abū Mūsā went out until he came to an assembly in the mosque which was called the Majlis al-Anṣār. He said, "I told 'Umar ibn al-Khaṭṭāb that I heard the Messenger of Allah ﷺ say, 'Ask permission three times. If you are given permission, then enter. If not, go away.' 'Umar said, 'If you do not bring me someone who can confirm it, I will do such-and-such to you.' If any of you have heard that, let him come with me." They said to Abū Sa'īd al-Khudrī, "Go with him." Abū Sa'īd was the youngest of them. He went with him and told 'Umar ibn al-Khaṭṭāb about that.

'Umar ibn al-Khaṭṭāb said to Abū Mūsā, "I did not suspect you, but I feared lest people forge sayings of the Messenger of Allah ﷺ."

54.2 Blessing someone who sneezes

4 Mālik related to me from 'Abdullāh ibn Abī Bakr from his father that the Messenger of Allah ﷺ said, "If a man sneezes, invoke a blessing on him. Then if he sneezes, invoke a blessing on him. Then if he sneezes, invoke a blessing on him. Then if he sneezes again, say, 'You have a cold.'" 'Abdullāh ibn Abī Bakr said, "I don't know whether it was after the third or the fourth."

5 Mālik related to me from Nāfi' that when 'Abdullāh ibn 'Umar sneezed and someone said to him, "May Allah have mercy on you (*yarḥamuka'llāh*)," he said, "May Allah have mercy on us and you and forgive us and you (*yarḥamuna'llāh wa yaghfir lanā wa lakum*)."

54.3 Pictures and images

6 Mālik related to me from Isḥāq ibn 'Abdullāh ibn Abī Ṭalḥa that Rāfi' ibn Ishāq, the *mawlā* of ash-Shifā', informed him that he and 'Abdullāh ibn Abī Ṭalḥa had gone to visit Abū Sa'īd al-Khudrī while he was ill. Abū Sa'īd said to them, "The Messenger of Allah ﷺ informed us, 'Angels do not enter a house which contains pictures or images.'"

Isḥāq was not sure which of them Abū Sa'īd said.

7 Mālik related to me from Abū an-Naṣr that 'Ubaydullāh ibn 'Abdullāh ibn 'Utba ibn Mas'ūd went to visit Abū Ṭalḥa al-Anṣārī when he was ill. He said, "I found Sahl ibn Ḥunayf with him. Abū Ṭalḥa summoned a man and removed a rug which was under him. Sahl ibn Ḥunayf asked him, 'Why did you remove it?' He replied, 'Because there were pictures on it and the Messenger of Allah ﷺ said you know what about them,' Sahl said, 'Did not the Messenger of Allah ﷺ say, "except for markings on a garment"?' He said, 'Yes, but it is more pleasing to me.'"

8 Mālik related to me from Nāfi' from al-Qāsim ibn Muḥammad from 'Ā'isha, the wife of the Prophet ﷺ, that she bought a cushion which had pictures on it. When the Messenger of Allah ﷺ saw it, he stopped at the door and did not enter. She recognised disapproval on his face and said, "Messenger of Allah, I turn in repentance to Allah and His Messenger. What have I done wrong?" The Messenger of Allah ﷺ said, "What is the meaning of this cushion?" She answered, "I bought it for you to sit and recline on." The Messenger of Allah ﷺ said, "Those who make such pictures will be punished on the Day of Rising. They will be told, 'Bring to life what you have created.'" Then he added, "The angels do not enter a house in which there are images."

54.4 Eating lizards

9 Mālik related to me from 'Abd ar-Raḥmān ibn 'Abdullāh ibn 'Abd ar-Raḥman ibn Abī Ṣa'ṣa'a that Sulaymān ibn Yasār said that the Messenger of Allah ﷺ entered the house of Maymūna bint al-Ḥārith and there was a lizard in which there were eggs to eat. 'Abdullāh ibn 'Abbās and Khālid ibn al-Walīd were with him. He asked, "From where did you get this?" She replied, "My sister, Huzayla bint al-Ḥārith, gave it to me." He then told 'Abdullāh ibn 'Abbās and Khālid ibn al-Walīd to eat. They said, "Will you not eat, Messenger of Allah?" He said, "There are those who visit me from Allah." Maymūna said, "Messenger of Allah, shall we give you some milk we have to drink?" He replied, "Yes." When he drank, he asked, "From where did you get this?" She said, "My sister, Huzayla, gave it to me." The Messenger of Allah ﷺ asked, "Do you see your slave-girl whom you asked me for permission to free? Give her to your sister and bring her to your maternal relatives to take care of her. That is better for you."

10 Mālik related to me from Ibn Shihāb from Abū Umāma ibn Sahl ibn Ḥunayf from 'Abdullāh ibn 'Abbās that Khālid ibn al-Walīd ibn al-Mughīra entered the house of Maymūna, the wife of the Prophet ﷺ, with the Messenger of Allah ﷺ and he was brought a roasted lizard. The Messenger of Allah ﷺ stretched out his hand toward it. One of the women who was in Maymūna's house said, "Tell the Messenger of Allah ﷺ what he is about to eat." Someone said, "It is a lizard, Muḥammad." He drew back his hand. Khālid asked, "Is it unlawful, Messenger of Allah?" He answered, "No, but there were none in my father's land and I find that I dislike them."

Khālid added, "I chewed and ate it while the Messenger of Allah ﷺ was looking."

11 Mālik related to me from 'Abdullāh ibn Dīnār from 'Abdullāh ibn 'Umar that a man called the Messenger of Allah ﷺ and said, "Messenger of Allah, what do you think about lizards?" The Messenger of Allah ﷺ said, "I do not eat them and I do not forbid them."

54.5 Concerning dogs

12 Mālik related to me from Yazīd ibn Khuṣayfa that as-Sā'ib ibn Yazīd informed him that he heard Sufyān ibn Abī Zuhayr, who was from the Azd Shanu'a tribe and among the Companions of the Messenger of Allah ﷺ, speaking with some people who were at the door of the mosque. He said, "I heard the Messenger of Allah ﷺ say, 'If anyone acquires a dog, which he does not use as a sheepdog or for hunting, a *qīrāṭ* will be deducted from the reward of his good deeds each day." He was asked, "Did you hear this from the Messenger of Allah ﷺ?" He said, "Yes, by the Lord of this mosque."

13 Mālik related to me from Nāfi' from 'Abdullāh ibn 'Umar that the Messenger of Allah ﷺ said, "Whoever acquires a dog, other than a sheepdog or hunting dog, will have two *qīrāṭs* deducted from the reward of his good actions every day."

14 Mālik related to me from Nāfi' from 'Abdullāh ibn 'Umar that the Messenger of Allah ﷺ ordered dogs to be killed.

54.6 Concerning sheep

15 Mālik related to me from Abū az-Zinād from al-A'raj from Abū Hurayra that the Messenger of Allah ﷺ said, "The main source of disbelief (*kufr*) lies towards the east. Boasting and pride are found in the people who have horses and camels. The loud-mouthed people are the people of the tents (the Bedouin). Tranquillity is found with the people who have sheep."

16 Mālik related to me from 'Abd ar-Raḥmān ibn 'Abd ar-Raḥmān ibn Ṣa'ṣa'a from his father from 'Abd ar-Raḥmān ibn Ṣa'ṣa'a from his father that the Messenger of Allah ﷺ said, "It will soon happen that the best property of a Muslim will be sheep which he takes to the peaks of the mountains and the valleys, fleeing with his *dīn* from trials."

17 Mālik related to me from Nāfi' from Ibn 'Umar that the Messenger of Allah ﷺ said, "No one should milk someone else's cow without permission. Would any of you like someone to come to his apartment, break into his larder and take his food? The udders of cows guard their food for their owners, so no one should milk someone else's cow without his permission."

18 Mālik related to me that he had heard that the Messenger of Allah ﷺ said, "There is no Prophet who has not herded sheep," and someone asked, "You included, Messenger of Allah?" He said, "Myself included."

54.7 Mice falling into clarified butter, and giving precedence to food over the prayer

19 Mālik related to me from Nāfi' that one time as Ibn 'Umar was served his evening meal, he heard the recitation of the imām while he was in his house and he did not hurry from his food until he had finished what he needed.

20 Mālik related to me from Ibn Shihāb from 'Ubaydullāh ibn 'Abdullāh ibn 'Utba ibn Mas'ūd from 'Abdullāh ibn 'Abbās from Maymūna, the wife of the Prophet ﷺ, that the Messenger of Allah ﷺ was asked about a mouse falling into clarified butter. He said, "Remove it and throw away what is around it."

54.8 Guarding against ill luck

21 Mālik related to me from Abū Ḥāzim ibn Dīnār from Sahl ibn Sa'd as-Sā'idī that the Messenger of Allah ﷺ said, "If it exists, it is in a horse, a woman, and a house" meaning ill luck.

22 Mālik related to me from Mālik from Ibn Shihāb from Ḥamza and Sālim, the sons of 'Abdullāh ibn 'Umar, from 'Abdullāh ibn 'Umar that the Messenger of Allah ﷺ said, "Ill luck is in a house, a woman and a horse."

23 Mālik related to me that Yaḥyā ibn Sa'īd said, "A woman came to the Messenger of Allah ﷺ and said, 'Messenger of Allah, we moved into a house when our number was great and our wealth was abundant. Now our number has dwindled and the wealth has gone.' The Messenger of Allah ﷺ said, 'Leave it as blameworthy.'"

54.9 Names that are disliked

24 Mālik related to me from Yaḥyā ibn Sa'īd that the Messenger of Allah ﷺ asked about a milk camel about to be milked, "Who is going to milk this camel?" A man stood up. The Messenger of Allah ﷺ asked, "What is your name?" The man said, "Murra (bitterness)." The Messenger of Allah ﷺ said to him, "Sit down." Then he said, "Who will milk this one?" A man stood up and the Messenger of Allah ﷺ asked, "What is your name?" He said, "Ḥarb (war)." The Messenger of Allah ﷺ said, "Sit down." Then he said, "Who will milk this camel?" A man stood up and the Messenger of Allah ﷺ said to him, "What is your name?" The man said, "Ya'īsh (he lives)." The Messenger of Allah ﷺ told him, "Milk!"

25 Mālik related to me from Yaḥyā ibn Sa'īd that 'Umar ibn al-Khaṭṭāb asked a man what his name was. He said, "Jamra (live coals)." "The son of whom?" he asked. He replied, "Ibn Shihāb (meteor, flame)." "From whom?" He asked. He said, "From al-Ḥuraqa (burning)." He asked, "Where do you live?" He replied, "At Ḥarra an-Nār (lava-field of the fire)." "At which one of them?" he asked?" He said, "At Dhāt Laẓā (one with flames)." 'Umar said, "Go and look to your family – they have been burned."

Yaḥyā added, "It was as 'Umar ibn al-Khaṭṭāb ﷺ said."

54.10 Cupping and the reward of the cupper

26 Mālik related to me from Ḥumayd aṭ-Ṭawīl that Anas ibn Mālik said, "The Messenger of Allah ﷺ was cupped. Abū Ṭayba cupped him, and the Messenger of Allah ﷺ ordered him to be given a *ṣā'* of dates and ordered his family to lessen what he paid them for his *kitāba* or *kharāj*."

27 Mālik related to me that he heard that the Messenger of Allah ﷺ said, "If there is a remedy that will reach the disease, then cupping will reach it."

28 Mālik related to me from Ibn Shihāb from Ibn Muḥayyisa al-Anṣārī, one of the Banū Ḥāritha, that he asked permission from the Messenger of Allah ﷺ to give payment for cupping and he forbade him to do so. He continued to ask and seek permission until he said, "Feed the ones who drive your water-carrying camels" meaning "your slaves."

54.11 Concerning the East

29 Mālik related to me from 'Abdullāh ibn Dīnār that 'Abdullāh ibn 'Umar said, "I saw the Messenger of Allah ﷺ pointing at the east and saying, 'The cause of dissension (*fitna*) is there. The cause of dissension is there, from where the helpers of Shayṭān arise."

30 Mālik related to me that he heard that 'Umar ibn al-Khaṭṭāb wanted to go to Iraq, and Ka'b al-Aḥbar said to him, "Do not go there, *Amīr al-*

Mu'minīn. Nine-tenths of sorcery is there and it is the place of rebellious jinn and the disease which the doctors are unable to cure."

54.12 Killing snakes and what is said about them

31 Mālik related to me from Nāfi' from Abū Lubāba that the Messenger of Allah ﷺ forbade killing snakes which were in houses.

32 Mālik related to me from Nāfi' from Sā'iba, the female *mawlā* of 'Ā'isha, that the Messenger of Allah ﷺ forbade killing the snakes which were in the houses except those with two white stripes on their back and two short ones. They make a person go blind and cause miscarriages in women.

33 Mālik related to me from Ṣayfī, the *mawlā* of Ibn Aflaḥ, that Abū as-Sā'ib, the *mawlā* of Hishām ibn Zuhra, said, "I went to Abū Sa'īd al-Khudrī and found him praying. I sat to wait for him until he finished the prayer. I heard a movement under a bed in his room, and it was a snake. I got up to kill it and Abu Sa'id gestured for me to sit down. When he had finished, he pointed to a room in the house and said, 'Do you see this room?' I replied, 'Yes.' He said, 'There was a youth in it who had just got married. He went with the Messenger of Allah ﷺ to al-Khandaq (the Ditch which the Muslims dug in the fifth year of the *Hijra* to defend Madīna against the Quraysh and their allies). While he was there, the youth came and asked his permission, saying, "Messenger of Allah, give me permission to return to my family." The Messenger of Allah ﷺ gave him permission and said, "Take your weapons with you, for I fear the Banū Qurayẓa tribe. They may harm you."

'The youth went to his family and found his wife standing between the two doors. He lifted his spear to stab her as jealousy had been aroused in him. She said, "Do not be hasty before you have gone in and seen what is in your house." He entered and found a snake coiled up on his bed. He transfixed it with his spear and then went out with it and set it upright in the house. The snake stirred on the end of the spear and the youth fell dead. No one knew which of them had died first, the snake or the youth. The Messenger of Allah ﷺ was told about that and he said, "There are jinn in Madīna who have become Muslim. When you see one of them, call out to it for three days. If it appears after that, then kill it, for it is a *shayṭān*.'"'

54.13 What to say on journeys

34 Mālik related to me that he heard that, when the Messenger of Allah ﷺ set foot in the stirrup intending to travel, he would say, "In the name of Allah. O Allah! You are my Companion in the journey and my replacement in my family. O Allah! Shorten the earth for us and make the journey easy for us. O Allah! I seek refuge with You from the hardship of the journey and from returning to sorrow and a distressing sight regarding property and family."

Bismi'llāh. Allāhumma anta'ṣ-ṣāḥibu fi's-safari wa'l-khalīfatu fi'l-ahl. Allāhumma'zwi lana'l-arḍa wa hawwin 'alayna's-safar. Allāhumma innī a'ūdhu bika min wa'thā'i's-safari wa min ka'ābati'l-munqalabi wa min sū'il-manẓari fi'l-māli wa'l-ahl.

Mālik related to me from a reliable source of his from Ya'qūb ibn 'Abdullāh al-Ashajj from Busr ibn Sa'īd from Sa'd ibn Abī Waqqāṣ from Khawla bint Ḥakīm that the Messenger of Allah ﷺ said, "Whoever dismounts to rest in a place should say, 'I seek refuge with the complete words of Allah from the evil of what He created', and nothing will harm him until he remounts."

A'ūdhu bi kalimāti'llāhi't-tāmmāti min sharri mā khalaq.

54.14 Travelling alone in the case of men and women

35 Mālik related to me from 'Abd ar-Raḥmān ibn Ḥarmala from 'Amr ibn Shu'ayb from his father from his grandfather that the Messenger of Allah ﷺ said, "One rider is a *shayṭān*. Two riders are two *shayṭāns*, and three are a riding party."

36 Mālik related to me from 'Abd ar-Raḥmān ibn Ḥarmala that Sa'īd

ibn al-Musayyab heard the Messenger of Allah ﷺ say, "Shayṭān concerns himself with one and two. When there are three, he does not concern himself with them."

37 Mālik related to me from Sa'īd ibn Abī Sa'īd al-Maqburī from Abū Hurayra that the Messenger of Allah ﷺ said, "It is not lawful for a woman who believes in Allah and the Last Day to travel the distance of a day and a night without a man who is her *maḥram*."

54.15 How to behave on journeys

38 Mālik related to me from Abū 'Ubayd, the *mawlā* of Sulaymān ibn 'Abd al-Malik from Khālid ibn Ma'dan who attributed it to the Prophet ﷺ, "Allah, the Blessed and Exalted, is kind and loves kindness. Kindness pleases Him and He helps you with kindness as long as it is not misplaced. When you ride dumb beasts, stop them in their stopping-places, and quicken their pace when the land is barren. Travel by night, because the land is travelled faster at night than it is during the day. Beware of pitching tents on the road for it is the path of animals and the abode of snakes."

39 Mālik related to me from Sumayy, the *mawlā* of Abū Bakr, from Abū Ṣaliḥ from Abū Hurayra that the Messenger of Allah ﷺ said, "Travelling is a portion of torment. It denies you your sleep, food and drink. When you have accomplished your purpose, you should hurry back to your family."

54.16 The command to be kind to slaves

40 Mālik related to me that he heard that Abū Hurayra said that the Messenger of Allah ﷺ said, "A slave should have normal food and clothing, and he is only obliged to do such work as he is capable of doing."

41 Mālik related to me that he heard that 'Umar ibn al-Khaṭṭāb went to the villages every Saturday. If he found a slave doing work which he was not capable of doing he lightened it for him.

42 Mālik related to me from his paternal uncle, Abū Suhayl ibn Mālik, that his father heard 'Uthmān ibn 'Affān say in a *khuṭba*, "Do not oblige a slave-girl to earn money unless she has a skill. If you oblige her to do that, she will earn money by prostitution. Do not oblige a child to earn money. If he does not find it, he will steal. Pardon, since Allah will pardon you, and you must feed them good food."

54.17 A slave and his reward

43 Mālik related to me from Nāfi' from 'Abdullāh ibn 'Umar that the Messenger of Allah ﷺ said, "When a slave gives good counsel to his master and worships Allah correctly, he has his reward twice over."

44 Mālik related to me that he heard that 'Umar ibn al-Khaṭṭāb saw a female slave belonging to 'Abdullāh ibn 'Umar ibn al-Khattāb. She was dressed in the way that a free woman dresses. He went to his daughter, Hafṣa, and said, "Did I not see your brother's slave-girl dressed in the way that a free woman dresses walking among the people and causing trouble?" 'Umar disapproved of that.

55. The Oath of Allegiance

55.1 About the oath of allegiance

1 Mālik related to me from 'Abdullāh ibn Dīnār that 'Abdullāh ibn 'Umar said, "When we took an oath of allegiance with him to hear and obey, the Messenger of Allah ﷺ said to us, 'In what you are able.'"

2 Mālik related to me from Muḥammad ibn al-Munkadir that Umayma bint Ruqayqa said, "I went to the Messenger of Allah ﷺ with the women who took an oath of allegiance with him in Islam. They said, 'Messenger of Allah! We take a pledge with you not to associate anything with Allah, not to steal, not to commit adultery, not to kill our children, nor to produce any lie that we have devised between our hands and feet, and not to disobey you in what is known.' The Messenger of Allah ﷺ said, 'In what you can do and are able.'"

Umayma continued, "They said, 'Allah and His Messenger are more merciful to us than ourselves. Come, let us give our hands to you, Messenger of Allah!' The Messenger of Allah ﷺ, said, 'I do not shake hands with women. My word to a hundred women is like my word to one woman.'"

3 Mālik related to me from 'Abdullāh ibn Dīnār that 'Abdullāh ibn 'Umar wrote to 'Abd al-Malik ibn Marwān, making an oath of allegiance. He wrote, "In the name of Allah, the All-Merciful, the Most Merciful. To the slave of Allah, 'Abd al-Malik, the *Amīr al-Mu'minīn*. Peace be upon you. I praise Allah to you. There is no god but Him. I acknowledge your right to my hearing and my obedience according to the *sunna* of Allah and the *sunna* of His Prophet in what I am able."

56. Speech

56.1 Disliked speech

1 Mālik related to me from 'Abdullāh ibn Dīnār from 'Abdullāh ibn 'Umar that the Messenger of Allah ﷺ said, "If a man says to his Muslim brother, 'O unbeliever!' it is true about one of them."

2 Mālik related to me from Suhayl ibn Abū Ṣāliḥ from his father from Abū Hurayra that the Messenger of Allah ﷺ said, "When you hear a man say, 'The people are ruined,' he himself is the most ruined of them all."

3 Mālik related to me from Abū az-Zinād from al-A'raj from Abū Hurayra that the Messenger of Allah ﷺ said, "Let none of you complain about time, for Allah is time.""

4 Mālik related to me from Yaḥyā ibn Sa'īd that 'Īsā ibn Maryam encountered a pig on the road. He said to it, "Go in peace." Somebody asked, "Do you say this to a pig?" 'Īsā replied, "I fear lest I accustom my tongue to evil speech."

56.2 The order to be mindful in speech

5 Mālik related to me from Muḥammad ibn 'Amr ibn 'Alqama from his father from Bilāl ibn al-Ḥārith al-Muzanī that the Messenger of Allah ﷺ said, "A man says what is pleasing to Allah and he does not suspect that it will have the result that it does, and Allah will write for him His good pleasure for it until the day when he meets Him. And a man says what

excites the wrath of Allah and he does not suspect that it will have the result that it does, and Allah will write His wrath for him for it until the day when he meets Him."

6 Mālik related to me from 'Abdullāh ibn Dīnār that Abū Ṣāliḥ as-Sammān informed him that Abū Hurayra said, "Truly a man utters words to which he attaches no importance, and by them he falls into the Fire of Hell, and truly a man utters words to which he attaches no importance, and by them Allah raises him into the Garden."

56.3 Disliked speech and speech without the mention of Allah

7 Mālik related to me from Zayd ibn Aslam that 'Abdullāh ibn 'Umar said, "Two men from the east stood up and spoke, and people were amazed at their eloquence. The Messenger of Allah ﷺ said, 'Some eloquence is sorcery,' and he said, 'Part of eloquence is sorcery.'"

8 Mālik related to me that 'Īsā ibn Maryam used to say, "Do not speak much without mentioning Allah because you will harden your hearts. A hard heart is far from Allah, but you do not know. Do not look at the wrong actions of people as if you were lords. Look to your wrong actions as if you were slaves. Some people are afflicted by wrong action and some people are protected from it. Be merciful to the people of affliction and praise Allah for His protection."

9 Mālik related to me that 'Ā'isha, the wife of the Prophet ﷺ, sent a message to one of her family after the evening prayer, saying, "Will you not allow the recording angel to rest?"

56.4 Backbiting

10 Mālik related to me from al-Walīd ibn 'Abdullāh ibn Sayyād that al-Muṭṭalib ibn 'Abdullāh ibn Ḥantab al-Makhzūmī informed him that a man asked the Messenger of Allah ﷺ, "What is backbiting?" The Messenger of Allah ﷺ said, "It is to mention about a man what he does not want to hear." He said, "Messenger of Allah, even if it is true?"

The Messenger of Allah ﷺ said, "If you utter something false, then it is slander."

56.5 What is feared from the tongue

11 Mālik related to me from Zayd ibn Aslam from 'Aṭā' ibn Yasār that the Messenger of Allah ﷺ said, "Whoever Allah protects from the evil of two things will enter the Garden?" A man said, "Messenger of Allah, do not tell us!" The Messenger of Allah ﷺ was silent. Then the Messenger of Allah ﷺ repeated what he had said the first time. The man said to him, "Do not tell us, Messenger of Allah!" The Messenger of Allah ﷺ was silent. Then the Messenger of Allah ﷺ said the same thing again. The man said, "Do not tell us, Messenger of Allah!" Then the Messenger of Allah ﷺ said the same thing again. Then the man began to say what he had said previously and a man at his side silenced him. The Messenger of Allah ﷺ said, "Whomever Allah protects from the evil of two things will enter the Garden. They are what is between his jaws and what is between his legs, what is between his jaws and what is between his legs, what is between his jaws and what is between his legs."

12 Mālik related to me from Zayd ibn Aslam from his father that 'Umar ibn al-Khaṭṭāb came upon Abū Bakr aṣ-Ṣiddīq pulling his tongue. 'Umar said to him, "Stop, may Allah forgive you!" Abū Bakr replied, "This has brought me to dangerous places."

56.6 Two people conversing to the exclusion of another

13 Mālik related to me from 'Abdullāh ibn Dīnār, saying, "'Abdullāh ibn 'Umar and I were at the house of Khālid ibn 'Uqba, who was away at the market. A man came who wanted to speak to 'Abdullāh ibn 'Umar and I was the only other person present. 'Abdullāh ibn 'Umar called another man so that we were four and said to me and the man whom he had called, 'Go a little way off together because I heard the Messenger of Allah ﷺ say, "Two should not converse to the exclusion of a third."'"

14 Mālik related to me from Nāfi' from 'Abdullāh ibn 'Umar that the

Messenger of Allah ﷺ said, "Two must not converse secretly to the exclusion of a third person."

56.7 Truthfulness and lying

15 Yaḥyā related to me from Mālik from Ṣafwān ibn Sulaym that a man asked the Messenger of Allah ﷺ, "Can I lie to my wife, Messenger of Allah?" The Messenger of Allah ﷺ answered, "There is no good in lying." The man said, "Messenger of Allah! Shall I make her a promise and tell her?" The Messenger of Allah ﷺ said, "It will not be held against you."

16 Mālik related to me that he heard that 'Abdullāh ibn Mas'ūd used to say, "You must tell the truth. Truthfulness leads to right action. Right action leads to the Garden. Beware of lying. Lying leads to corruption and corruption leads to the Fire. Do you not see that it is said, 'He speaks the truth and acts rightly,' and 'He lies and is corrupt.'"

17 Mālik related to me that he heard that someone said to Luqmān, "What has brought you to what we see?" meaning his high rank. Luqmān replied, "Truthful speech, fulfilling the trust and leaving what does not concern me."

18 Mālik related to me that he heard that 'Abdullāh ibn Mas'ūd used to say, "A slave of Allah continues to lie and a black spot grows in his heart until all his heart becomes black. Then he is written in the sight of Allah among the liars."

19 Mālik related to me that Ṣafwān ibn Sulaym said, "The Messenger of Allah ﷺ was asked, 'Can a believer be a coward?' He said, 'Yes.' He was asked, 'Can a believer be a miser?' He replied, 'Yes.' He was asked, 'Can a believer be a liar?' He said, 'No.'"

56.8 Squandering property and being two-faced

20 Mālik related to me from Suhayl ibn Abī Ṣāliḥ from his father from Abū Hurayra that the Messenger of Allah ﷺ said, "Allah is pleased with

three things from you, and He is angry with three things from you. He is pleased that you worship Him and do not associate anything with Him, and that you take hold of the rope of Allah altogether and that you give good counsel to the one to whom Allah gives command over you. He is angry with you for gossip, squandering property and asking too many questions."

21 Mālik related to me from Abū az-Zinād from al-A'raj from Abū Hurayra that the Messenger of Allah ﷺ said, "One of the most evil of people is the two-faced person who shows one face to some people and another face to other people."

56.9 Punishing the many for the actions of the few

22 Mālik related to me that he had heard that Umm Salama, the wife of the Prophet ﷺ, said, "Messenger of Allah! Shall we be destroyed while there are people who are right-acting among us?" The Messenger of Allah ﷺ said, "Yes, if there is much wickedness."

23 Mālik related to me that Ismā'īl ibn Abī Ḥakīm heard 'Umar ibn 'Abd al-'Azīz say, "Some say that Allah, the Blessed, the Exalted, will not punish the many for the wrong action of the few. However, when the objectionable action is committed openly, then they all deserve to be punished."

56.10 About people with *taqwā*

24 Mālik related to me from Isḥāq ibn 'Abdullāh ibn Abī Ṭalḥa that Anas ibn Mālik said, "When I was going out with 'Umar ibn al-Khaṭṭāb to visit an orchard, I heard him talking to himself. There was a wall between us and he was inside the garden. He said, "'Umar ibn al-Khaṭṭāb, *Amīr al-Mu'minīn*! Well done! Well done! By Allah, fear Allah or He will punish you!"

25 Mālik said that he heard that al-Qāsim ibn Muḥammad used to say, "I have seen the people (i.e. the Companions), and they were not impressed

by speech." Mālik said, "He meant that only action and deeds would be looked at, not words."

56.11 What to say when it thunders

26 Mālik related to me that 'Āmir ibn 'Abdullāh ibn az-Zubayr would stop speaking when he heard thunder and say, "Glory be to the One whom the thunder glorifies with His praise and the angels from fear of Him" (*Subḥāna'llādhi yusabbihu'r-ra'du bi-ḥamdihi wa'l-malā'ikatu min khīfatihi*).

56.12 The legacy of the Prophet ﷺ

27 Mālik related to me from Ibn Shihāb from 'Urwa ibn az-Zubayr from 'Ā'isha, *Umm al-Mu'minīn*, that when the Messenger of Allah ﷺ died, the wives of the Prophet ﷺ, wanted to send 'Uthmān ibn 'Affān to Abū Bakr aṣ-Ṣiddīq to ask him about their inheritance from the Messenger of Allah ﷺ. 'Ā'isha said to them, "Did the Messenger of Allah ﷺ not say, 'No one inherits from us. What we leave is *ṣadaqa*.'"

28 Mālik related to me from Abū az-Zinād from al-A'raj from Abū Hurayra that the Messenger of Allah ﷺ said, "My inheritance is not divided up by the dinar. What I leave, apart from the maintenance of my wives and provision for my servant, is *ṣadaqa*."

57. Jahannam

57.1 Description of Jahannam

1 Mālik related to me from Abū az-Zinād from al-A'raj from Abū Hurayra that the Messenger of Allah ﷺ said, "The fire of the descendants of Ādam which they kindle is a seventieth part of the fire of Jahannam." They said, "Messenger of Allah, this fire is certainly enough." he said, "That fire is sixty-nine times greater."

2 Mālik related to me from his paternal uncle, Abū Suhayl ibn Mālik, from his father that Abū Hurayra said, "Do you think that it is red like this fire of yours? It is blacker than tar."

58. *Ṣadaqa*

58.1 Stimulation of desire for *ṣadaqa*

1 Mālik related to me from Yaḥyā ibn Sa'īd from Abū al-Ḥubāb Sa'd ibn Yasār that the Messenger of Allah ﷺ said, "Whoever gives *ṣadaqa* from good earnings – and Allah only accepts the good – it is as if he placed it in the palm of the All-Merciful to raise it, as one of you might raise his foal or young camel until it is like the mountain."

2 Mālik related to me that Ishāq ibn 'Abdullāh ibn Abī Ṭalḥa heard Anas ibn Mālik say, "Abū Ṭalḥa had the greatest amount of property in palm-trees among the Ansar in Madīna. The dearest of his properties to him was Bayraḥā' which was in front of the mosque. The Messenger of Allah ﷺ used to go and drink from the pleasant water which was in it."

Anas continued, "When the *āyat* was revealed: '*You will not attain true goodness until you give of what you love*' (3:92) Abū Ṭalḥa went to the Messenger of Allah ﷺ and said, 'Messenger of Allah! Allah, the Blessed, the Exalted, has said, "*You will not obtain true goodness until you give of what you love.*" The property which I love the best is Bayraḥā'. It is *ṣadaqa* for Allah. I hope for its good and for it to be stored up with Allah. Place it wherever you wish, Messenger of Allah.'

"The Messenger of Allah ﷺ said, 'Well done! That is property which profits! That is property which profits! I have heard what you said about it and I think that you should give it to your relatives.' Abū Ṭalḥa said, 'I will do it, Messenger of Allah!' Abū Ṭalḥa therefore divided it among his relatives and the children of his paternal uncle."

3 Mālik related to me from Zayd ibn Aslam that the Messenger of Allah ﷺ said, "Give to a beggar even if he comes on a horse."

4 Mālik related to me from Zayd ibn Aslam from 'Amr ibn Mu'ādh al-Ashhalī al-Anṣārī that his grandmother said, "The Messenger of Allah ﷺ said, 'O believing women! Let none of you despise giving to her neighbour even if it is only a roasted sheep's trotter.'"

5 Yaḥyā related to me from Mālik that he heard that a beggar asked 'Ā'isha, the wife of the Prophet ﷺ, for something while she was fasting and there was only a loaf of bread in her house. She said to her female client, "Give it to him." The client protested, "You will not have anything to break your fast with." 'Ā'isha repeated, "Give it to him," so she did so. When evening came, the people of a house or a man who did not usually give to them, gave them a sheep and some food to go with it. 'Ā'isha, *Umm al-Mu'minīn*, called her client and said, "Eat from this. This is better than your loaf of bread."

6 Yaḥyā related to me that Mālik said, "I heard that a beggar asked for food from 'Ā'isha, *Umm al-Mu'minīn*, while she had some grapes. She told someone to take him one grape. He began to look in amazement. 'Ā'isha said, "Are you amazed? How many atoms' weights do you see in this grape?" (referring to Qur'ān 99:7)

58.2 Refraining from asking

7 Mālik related to me from Ibn Shihāb from 'Aṭā' ibn Yazīd al-Laythī from Abū Sa'īd al-Khudrī that some people of the Ansar asked the Messenger of Allah ﷺ and he gave to them. Then they asked him again and he gave to them until he used up what he had. Then he said, "What wealth I have I will not hoard from you. Whoever abstains, Allah will help him. Whoever tries to be independent, Allah will enrich him. Whoever tries to be patient, Allah will give him patience, and no one is given a better or vaster gift than patience."

8 Yaḥyā related to me from Mālik from Nāfi' from 'Abdullāh ibn 'Umar that the Messenger of Allah ﷺ said from the minbar when mentioning

ṣadaqa and refraining from asking, "The upper hand is better than the lower hand. The upper hand is the one which expends and the lower one is the one which asks."

9 Yaḥyā related to me from Mālik from Zayd ibn Aslam from 'Aṭā' ibn Yasār that the Messenger of Allah ﷺ sent a gift to 'Umar ibn al-Khaṭṭāb and 'Umar returned it. The Messenger of Allah ﷺ asked, "Why did you return it?" He replied, "Messenger of Allah, didn't you tell us that it is better for us not to take anything from anyone?" The Messenger of Allah ﷺ said, "That is by asking. Provision which Allah gives you is not the same as asking." 'Umar ibn al-Khaṭṭāb said, "By the One in whose hand my self is, I will not ask anything from anyone, and anything that comes to me without my asking for it, I will accept."

10 Yaḥyā related to me from Mālik from Abū az-Zinād from al-A'raj from Abū Hurayra that the Messenger of Allah ﷺ said, "By Him in whose hand my self is! To take your rope and gather firewood on your back is better for you than that you come to a man to whom Allah has give some of His favour and ask him and then he either gives something to you or refuses."

11 Yaḥyā related to me from Mālik from Zayd ibn Aslam from 'Aṭā' ibn Yasār that a man of the Banū Asad said, " My family and I dismounted to rest at Baqī'. My family said to me, 'Go to the Messenger of Allah ﷺ and ask him for something that we can eat,' and they began to mention what they needed. I went to the Messenger of Allah ﷺ and found that a man was asking for something, and the Messenger of Allah ﷺ was saying, 'I do not have anything to give you.' The man turned away from him in anger, saying, 'By my life! You give to whomever you wish!' The Messenger of Allah ﷺ remarked, 'He is angry with me because I do not have anything to give him. Whoever asks you for something while he has an *ūqiya* or its equivalent has asked with importunity.'"

The man continued, "I told myself that a camel we had was worth more than an *ūqiya*.' (Mālik explained that an *ūqiya* was forty dirhams) So I returned without having asked him for anything, and the Messenger of Allah ﷺ sent me barley and raisins later on. He gave us from his share until Allah, the Mighty, the Majestic, gave us relief."

12 Yaḥyā related to me that Mālik heard al-'Alā' ibn 'Abd ar-Raḥmān say, "*Ṣadaqa* does not decrease property, and Allah only increases a person in worth for his restraint, and no one is humble but that Allah raises him."

Mālik said, "I do not know whether this *ḥadīth* goes back to the Prophet ﷺ or not."

58.3 What is disliked in *ṣadaqa*

13 Yaḥyā related to me from Mālik that he heard that the Messenger of Allah ﷺ said, "*Ṣadaqa* to the family of Muḥammad is not lawful. It is only people's impurities."

14 Yaḥyā related to me from Mālik from 'Abdullāh ibn Abī Bakr from his father that the Messenger of Allah ﷺ gave a man from the Banū 'Abd al-Ashhal charge over some *ṣadaqa*. When he came to ask him for some camels from the *ṣadaqa*, the Messenger of Allah ﷺ was so angry that the anger showed in his face. One way in which anger could be recognised in his face was that his eyes became red. Then he said, "This man has asked me for what is not good for me or for him. If I refuse it, I hate to refuse. If I give it to him, I will give him what is not good for me or for him." The man said, "Messenger of Allah! I will never ask you for any of it."

15 Yaḥyā related to me from Mālik from Zayd ibn Aslam that his father said, "'Abdullāh ibn al-Arqam said, 'Show me a riding-camel which the *Amīr al-Mu'minīn* can give me to use.' I said, 'Yes, one of the *ṣadaqa* camels.' 'Abdullāh ibn al-Arqam said, 'Would you want a stout man on a hot day to wash for you what is under his lower garment and its folds and then give it to you to drink?' I was angry and said, 'May Allah forgive you! Why do you say such things to me?' 'Abdullāh ibn al-Arqam said, '*Ṣadaqa* is the impurities of people which they wash off themselves.'"

59. Knowledge

59.1 Seeking Knowledge

1 Yaḥyā related to me from Mālik that he heard that Luqmān the Sage made his will and counselled his son, saying, "My son! Sit with the learned men and keep close to them. Allah gives life to the hearts with the light of wisdom as Allah gives life to the dead earth with the abundant rain of the sky."

60 The Supplication of the Unjustly Wronged

60.1 Supplication of someone unjustly wronged

1 Yaḥyā related to me from Mālik from Zayd ibn Aslam from his father that 'Umar ibn al-Khaṭṭāb gave a *mawlā* of his called Ḥunayy charge over the *ḥimā*. He said, "Ḥunayy! Do not harm the people. Fear the supplication of the wronged for the wronged person is answered. Let the one with a small herd of camels and the one with a small herd of sheep enter, but be wary of the livestock of Ibn 'Awf and the livestock of Ibn 'Affān. If their livestock is destroyed, they will bring their children to me crying, '*Amīr al-Mu'minīn*! *Amīr al-Mu'minīn*!' Shall I neglect them? Water and pasturage are of less value to me than gold and silver. By Allah, they think that I have wronged them. This is their land and their water. They fought for it in the *Jāhiliyya* and became Muslims on it in Islam. By Him in whose hand my soul is! Were it not for the mounts, which I give to be ridden in the way of Allah, I would not have turned a span of their land into *ḥimā*."

61. The Names of the Prophet ﷺ

61.1 The names of the Prophet ﷺ

1 Mālik related to me from Ibn Shihāb from Muḥammad ibn Jubayr ibn Muṭ'im that the Prophet ﷺ said, "I have five names. I am Muḥammad. I am Aḥmad. I am al-Māḥī (the effacer) by whom Allah effaces disbelief. I am al-Ḥāshir (the gatherer) before whom people are gathered. I am al-'Āqib (the last)."

Glossary

'Abasa: He frowned, *Sūra* 80 of the Qur'ān.

Aḍḥā: *see 'Īd al-Aḍḥā.*

adhān: the call to prayer.

'adhq ibn ḥubayq: a kind of spoiled date.

'ajwā: an excellent variety of date.

amīr: literally 'one who commands', the source of authority in any situation.

Amīr al-Mu'minīn: the Commander of the Believers (*mu'minīn*), a title of respect given to the Caliph.

'anat: fornication.

Anṣār: the 'Helpers', the people of Madīna, who welcomed and aided the Messenger of Allah ﷺ. *See also Muhājirūn.*

al-'Aqaba: literally "the Steep Slope", a mountain pass to the north of Makka just off the caravan route to Madīna, where the Messenger of Allah ﷺ met in secret with the first Muslims from Madīna, in two successive years. On the first occasion, they pledged to follow the Messenger ﷺ, and on the second or Great Pledge of 'Aqaba to defend him and his companions as they would their own wives and children. This led to the *Hijra* (*see below*).

al-'Āqib: a name of the Messenger of Allah ﷺ meaning 'the last'.

al-'Aqīq: a valley four and a half miles west of Madīna.

'aqīqa: an animal killed in celebration of the birth of a child and *ṣadaqa* (see below) equal to the weight of the child's hair given in the way of Allah for the same reason. *See* Book 26.

'ariyya: loan for use – putting another temporarily and gratuitously in possession of the use of a thing, whilst the right of ownership is retained.

Used in particular reference to the allocation to poor families of the produce of certain date-palms by the owner of a date grove. *See* Book 31.

arkān: literally 'pillars', used in reference to the five indispensable 'pillars' of Islam.

'aṣaba: male relatives from the father's side. Paternal ties of kinship dominate over maternal. *See* Book 27.

'Arafa: a plain fifteen miles to the east of Makka on which stands the Jabal ar-Raḥma, the Mount of Mercy. One of the essential rites of the *hajj* is to stand on 'Arafa on the 9th of Dhū al-Ḥijja (Dhū al-Ḥijja, *see below*).

arwāḥ, pl. of **rūḥ**: (*See below*).

'Āshūrā': the 10th day of Muḥarram, the first month of the Muslim lunar calendar. It is considered a highly desirable day to fast.

'Aṣr: afternoon, and in particular the afternoon obligatory prayer.

awāq, pl. of **ūqiya** (*see below*).

awsāq, pl. of **wasq**: *see below.*

āyat: literally 'a sign', a verse of the Qur'ān.

Bāb ar-Rayyān: 'The Gate of the Well-Watered,' a special gate of the Garden by which the people of fasting enter.

Badr: a place near to the coast about ninety-five miles to the south of Madīna where, in 2 AH in the first battle fought by the newly established Muslim community, the three hundred outnumbered Muslims led by the Messenger of Allah ﷺ overwhelmingly defeated a thousand Makkan idolaters.

al-Balāṭ: a paved area of Madīna between the Mosque and the Market.

Banū: literally 'sons', a tribe or clan.

Banū Isrā'īl: the tribe of Israel.

al-Baqī': the cemetery of the people of Madīna where many of the family of the Messenger of Allah ﷺ and his Companions are buried.

baraka: a subtle beneficent spiritual energy which can flow through things and people or places.

barīd, pl. **burūd**: a mail stage, approximately twelve miles.

bay'a: an oath of allegiance, see Book 55.

al-Bayḍā': a place sixty kilometres south of Madīna on the route to

Makka, near Dhū al-Ḥulayfa.

bayt al-māl: literally 'the house of wealth'. The treasury of the Muslims where income from *zakāt* (*see below*) and other sources is gathered for re-distribution.

Bayt al-Maqdis: literally 'The Pure House', a name of Jerusalem.

ben-nut: the fruit of the Moringa Oleifera tree.

bid'a: innovation. For an example of use see Book 18.12. 16.

burdī: a variety of date noted for its good quality.

burnūs: a hooded cloak.

Day of Khaybar: *See Khaybar.*

Day of Ṣiffīn: *see Ṣiffīn.*

dīn: the life-transaction, literally 'the debt between two-parties', in this usage between the Creator and created.

Dhāt al-Jaysh: a place about twelve miles from Madīna.

dhikr: literally 'remembrance'. In a general sense all *'ibāda* (*see below*) is *dhikr*. In common usage it has come to mean invocation of Allah by repetition of His names or particular formulae.

dhimma: obligation or contract, in particular a treaty of protection for non-Muslims living in Muslim territory.

dhimmī: a non-Muslim living under the protection of Muslim rule.

Dhū al-Ḥijja: the twelfth month of the Muslim calendar, the month of the Hajj (Pilgrimage). One of the four Sacred Months in which fighting is prohibited.

Dhū al-Ḥulayfa: the *mīqāt* (*see below*) of the people of Madīna, now called Bayar 'Ali.

Dhū al-Qa'da: the eleventh month of the Muslim calendar. One of the four Sacred Months in which fighting is prohibited.

Dhū Ṭuwā: well-known well, now within Makka, but in earlier times outside of it.

dīnār: gold coinage. One dinar is 4.25 gs of gold.

dirham: silver coinage. One dirham is 2.975 gs of silver.

diya: financial compensation (blood-money) for injuries. See Book 43.

du'ā': supplication to Allah as opposed to ritual prayer (*salat*).

ḍuḥā: forenoon, and in particular the voluntary morning prayer of *Ḍuḥā*.

dulūk ash-shams: the sun's declining from the meridian.

fajr: dawn, first light, and in particular the post-dawn *sunna* prayer.

faqīh, pl. **fuqahā'**: a man learned in knowledge of *fiqh* (*see below*) who by virtue of his knowledge can give a legal judgement (*fatwā*).

farā'iḍ: the fixed shares of inheritance, instituted by the Qur'ān.

faraq: a kind of pot, containing about three *ṣā's* (*see below*) of water.

farḍ: obligatory, particularly applies to acts of worship.

farsakh: a measurement of length, about three miles.

al-Fātiḥa: "The Opening", the opening *sūra* of the Qur'ān.

fatwā: an authoritative legal opinion or judgement made by a *faqīh* (*see above*).

fidya: literally ransom. Compensation paid for rites missed or wrongly performed because of ignorance or ill-health.

fiqh: science of the application of *Sharī'a* (see below).

Fiṭr: *see 'Īd al-Fiṭr.*

fiṭra: the first nature, the natural, primal condition of mankind in harmony with nature.

al-Furqān: "The Discrimination", a name of the Qur'ān.

gharar: an uncertain transaction, particularly the sale of something which is not present.

ghasaq al-layl: the gathering of night, the dusk between *Maghrib* and *'Ishā'* (*see below*).

ghazwa, pl. **ghazawāt**: a military expedition.

ghusl: the full ritual washing of the body.

ḥabal al-ḥabala: a forbidden business transaction in which a man buys the unborn offspring of a female animal.

ḥadd, pl. **ḥudūd**: literally, 'the limits', Allah's boundary limits for lawful (*ḥalāl*) and unlawful (*haram*) (*see below*). The *ḥadd* punishments are the specific fixed penalties laid down by *Sharī'a* for the specified crimes.

ḥadīth, pl. **aḥādīth**: reported speech, particularly that of the Prophet

Muḥammad ﷺ.

ḥadīth qudsī: those words of Allah on the tongue of his Prophet ﷺ which are not part of the Revelation of the Qur'ān.

hady: an animal offered as a sacrifice during the *Hajj* (pilgrimage).

Ḥajj: the greater pilgrimage, see Book 20.

Ḥajj al-Ifrād: *ḥajj* 'by itself', the simplest way to perform *ḥajj*, see Book 20, section 11.

Ḥajj al-Qirān: the 'joined' *ḥajj*, see Book 20, section 12.

Ḥajj at-Tamattu': the 'interrupted' *ḥajj*, see Book 20, sections 19, 20, 83.

Ḥajj al-Wadā': the final *ḥajj* of the Prophet Muḥammad ﷺ.

ḥalāl: lawful, permitted by *Sharī'a*.

ḥama': a superstitious belief of the Arabs of the Period of Ignorance (*Jāhiliyya*). It was the unavenged spirit of a slain person that took the form of a night bird.

ḥarām: unlawful, forbidden by *Sharī'a*.

Ḥaram: a protected area in which certain behaviour is forbidden and other behaviour necessary. The area around the Ka'ba in Makka is a *ḥaram*, and the area around the Prophet's Mosque in Madīna is a *ḥaram*.

al-Ḥarra: a tract of volcanic black rock in Madīna.

ḥaṣan: an adjective describing a married person, from the noun *ḥiṣn*, a fortress. A person who has been made *ḥaṣan* by marriage (*muḥṣan*) has the full *ḥadd* punishment of death inflicted for illicit sexual relations.

al-ḥawḍ: the watering-place or basin of the Prophet ﷺ in the Next World, whose drink will refresh those who have crossed the Ṣirāṭ (before entering the Garden.

al-Ḥāshir: a name of the Prophet ﷺ meaning the Gatherer, before whom people are gathered on the Day of Gathering (*Yawm al-Ḥashr*).

al-Ḥashr: Gathering, *Sūra* 59 of the Qur'ān.

Ḥijāz: the region along the western seaboard of Arabia, in which Makka, Madīna, Jidda and Ṭā'if are situated.

Ḥijr: a semi-circular unroofed enclosure at one side of the Ka'ba, whose low wall outlines the shape of the original Ka'ba built by the Prophet Ibrāhīm عليه السلام.

hijra: emigration in the way of Allah. Islam takes its dating from the *Hijra* of the Prophet ﷺ to Madīna.

ḥill: the boundaries of a *ḥaram* (*see above*).

ḥimā: pasturage devoted to grazing livestock from the *zakāt* (*see below*) and other sources.

ḥudūd: plural of **ḥadd** (*see above*).

'ibāda: act of worship

'Īd: a festival. There are two main festivals of the Muslim year, on the first day of which *'id* prayers, are prayed.

'Īd al-Aḍḥā: a four day festival at the time of *hajj*. The *'Īd* of the Sacrifice, it starts on the 10th day of Dhū al-Ḥijja (the month of *Hajj*), the day that the pilgrims sacrifice their animals.

'Īd al-Fiṭr: the festival at the end of the month of fasting (Ramadan).

'idda: a period after divorce or the death of her husband for which a woman must wait before re-marrying to ensure that there is no confusion about the paternity of children.

Ifrād: (*see Ḥajj al-Ifrād above.*)

iḥrām: the condition adopted by the person on *hajj* or *'umra*: specially robed and under particular constrictions of behaviour.

iḥṣān: the state of being *ḥaṣan* (*see above*).

ijtihād: literally 'to struggle', to exercise personal judgement in legal matters.

īlā': a vow by a husband to abstain from sexual relations with his wife. If four months pass and the husband decides to continue to abstain, the *īlā'* pronouncement is considered a divorce.

Īlyā': a name for Jerusalem.

al-Inshiqāq: "The Bursting", *Sūra* 84 of the Qur'ān.

iqāma: the call which announces that the obligatory prayer is about to begin.

'Ishā': evening, and in particular *'Ishā'* prayer, the evening obligatory prayer.

istislām: literally 'submission', particularly greeting the Black Stone and the Yemeni corner of the Ka'ba during *ṭawāf* by kissing, touching or outstretched hand.

i'tikāf: seclusion, while fasting, in a mosque particularly during the last ten days of Ramadan, *see* Book 19.

izār: a piece of cloth used as a waist-wrapper both by men and women.

Jāhiliyya: the Time of Ignorance, before the coming of Islam.

jamra: literally 'a small walled place', but in this usage a stone-built pillar. There are three *jamras* at Mina. One of the rites of *hajj* is to stone them. Stoning the *jamras* is sometimes referred to as stoning the *shayṭāns*. (*Hajj, see above*, Minā, *shayṭān, see below*).

Jamrat al-'Aqaba: one of the three *jamras* at Minā. It is situated at the entrance of Mina from the direction of Makka. (Minā, *see below*).

janāba: the state of impurity in which a person requires *ghusl* (*see above*).

janib: a good variety of dates.

Ji'rāna: a place near Makka, where the Messenger of Allah ﷺ distributed the booty from the Battle of Ḥunayn and from where he went into *iḥrām* to perform *'umra*.

jizya: a protection tax imposed on non-Muslims under the protection of Muslim rule.

jubba: a cloak.

al-Juḥfa: the *mīqāt* (see below) of the people of Syria and Europe.

Jumādā al-Ākhir: the sixth month of the Muslim calendar.

Jumādā al-Awwal: the fifth month of the Muslim calendar.

Jumu'a: the Day of Gathering, Friday, and in particular the *Jumu'a* prayer.

junub: being in a state of *janāba* (*see above*).

ju'rūr: a kind of spoiled date.

kaffāra: prescribed way of making amends for wrong actions, particularly missed obligatory actions.

kāfir, pl. **kāfirūn**: a person who commits *kufr* (*see below*).

kanz: treaure; wealth concealed to avoid *zakāt* (*see below*).

khalīfa, pl. **khulafā'**: literally "someone who stands in for someone else", the leader of the Muslim community. *See also Imām, Amīr al-Mu'minīn.*

khalūq: a kind of yellowy perfume.

al-Khandaq: 'the Ditch'. In 5 AH, the Makkan idol-worshippers, assisted by the Jewish tribe of Banū Naḍīr and the Arab tribes of Banū Ghaṭafān and Banū Asad, marched on Madīna with an army of ten thousand soldiers. The Messenger of Allah ﷺ ordered a ditch to be dug on the unprotected side of Madīna and manned constantly. The enemy were halted and forced to lay a dispirited siege.

kharāj: taxes imposed on revenue from land or the work of slaves.

Khaybar: Jewish colony to the north of Madīna which was laid siege to and captured by the Muslims in the seventh year after the *Hijra* because of the Jews' continual treachery.

khiyār: right of withdrawal in a business transaction.

khuff: leather socks.

khul': a form of divorce in which a woman seeking divorce returns her bride-price, part of it, or even in excess of it, in return for her freedom. *See* Book 29.12-13.

Khulafā' ar-Rāshidūn: the Righly-guided Caliphs, the first four successors to the Prophet ﷺ as leaders of the Muslim umma (*see below*): Abū Bakr, 'Umar, 'Uthmān and 'Alī ﷽.

khums: the fifth of the booty distributed by the Amīr in the cause of Islam.

khuṭba: literally 'a speech', and in particular the addresses given by the Imām on the day of *Jumu'a* and the two *'Īd*s. On *Jumu'a* there are two *khuṭba*s separated by a short pause during which the Imām sits down.

kiswa: the huge embroidered black and gold cloth that drapes the Ka'ba.

kitāba: a contract by which a slave acquires his freedom against a future payment, or instalment payments, to his owner.

kohl: antimony powder used both as decoration and a medicine for the eyes.

Kufa: a place in Iraq, near Najaf, that was the chief military garrison and administrative centre of the Muslims when they conquered Iraq.

kufr: to cover up, to reject Allah, to refuse to believe that Muḥammad is the Messenger of Allah.

kunyā: a respectful way of calling people such as the 'Father of so-and-so' or the 'Mother of so-and-so'.

labbayk: 'At your service'. It is part of the *talbiya* (*see below*), the call that the pilgrims make to their Lord on *hajj*.

Laylat al-Qadr: the Night of Power, an odd night during the last tne nights of Ramadan.

li'ān: mutual self-cursing, an oath taken by both the wife and the husband when the husband accuses his wife of committing adultery. He makes three oaths that he is truthful and a fourth that the curse of Allah will be on him if he is lying. The wife can free herself of guilt and thus punishment by avowing herself to be innocent three times and making a vow that the wrath of Allah will be on her if she is lying. A couple who make *li'ān* are automatically and irrevocably divorced and can never be remarried.

maḍāmīn: a forbidden sale in which the foetus in the womb of a pregnant animal is sold.

madhhab: a school of *fiqh* (*see above*). There are four main Sunni madhhabs: Ḥanafī, Mālikī, Shāfi'ī and Ḥanbalī.

al-Madīna: literally the City, more properly *al-Madīna al-Munawarra*, the Enlightened City.

Magians: Zoroastrian fire-worshippers.

Maghrib: sunset, literally 'the west'. In particular, the *Maghrib* prayer which is just after sundown.

Maghrib: the Muslim territories in the West of North Africa.

al-Māḥī: a name of the Messenger of Allah, Muḥammad ﷺ, meaning the Effacer by whom Allah effaces *kufr* (*see above*).

mahr: dowry given by a husband to his wife on marriage.

maḥram: a person with whom marriage is forbidden.

makrūh: disapproved of without being forbidden.

malāqīḥ: a forbidden sale in which the stud properties of an animal are sold.

Maqām of Ibrāhīm: The place where Ibrāhīm stood which marks the place of prayer following *ṭawāf* of the Ka'ba.

Marwa: *see Ṣafā and Marwa.*

Mash'ar al-Ḥarām: a venerated place in the valley of Muzdalifa (*see below*).

al-Masīḥ ad-Dajjāl: the anti-Messiah.

al-Masīḥ ibn Maryam: the Messiah Jesus.

masjid: a mosque, literally 'a place of *sajda*' (*see below*).

Masjid al-Ḥarām: The Protected Mosque, the name of the mosque built around the Ka'ba in the Ḥaram at Makka.

mawālī: plural of **mawlā** (*see below*).

mawāqif: plural of **mawqif** (*see below*).

mawāqīt: plural of **mīqāt** (*see below*).

mawlā, pl. **mawālī**: a person with whom a tie of *walā'* (*see below*) has been established by manumission. It usually refers to the freed slave, but it can also mean the former master.

mawqif, pl. **mawāqif**: literally 'a standing or stopping place'. There are two places on Ḥajj where the pilgrims must 'stop': 'Arafa and Muzdalifa.

minbar: steps on which the Imām stands to deliver the *khuṭba* on the day of *Jumu'a*.

Minā: a valley five miles on the road to 'Arafa, where the three *jamra*s stand. It is part of *hajj* to spend three nights in Mina during the days of *tashrīq* (*see below*).

mīqāt, pl. **mawāqīt**: one of the designated places for entering into *iḥrām* for *'umra* or *hajj*.

mu'adhdhin: someone who calls the *adhan*, the call to prayer.

mubashshirat: literally 'good news', good dreams.

mudabbar: a slave who has been given a *tadbir*, a contract to be set free after his master's death.

mudd: a measure of volume, approximating to a double-handed scoop.

Mufaṣṣal: the *sura*s of the Qur'ān starting from *Sūra Qaf* (*Sūra* 50) to the end of the Qur'ān.

Muhājirūn: Companions of the Messenger of Allah ﷺ who accepted Islam in Makka and made *hijra* (*see above*) to Madīna.

muḥallil: a man who marries a woman who has been triply divorced on the condition that he divorce her in order that her first husband can remarry her.

muḥāqala: a forbidden sale in which, for instance, unharvested wheat was bartered for harvested wheat or land was rented for wheat.

Muḥarram: the first month of the Muslim year, which is based on the lunar calendar, and one of the four inviolable months during which fighting is prohibited (*haram*), from which its name is derived.

muḥrim: a person in *iḥrām*.

muḥṣan: a person who is *ḥaṣan* (*see above*).

muḥṣana: the feminine of *muḥṣan*. As well as meaning a person guarded by marriage, it also refers to a chaste unmarried free woman, who is sexually protected, as opposed to an unmarried slave woman over whom her master has sexual rights.

muḥṣar: a person prevented from completing *hajj* by an enemy or an illness.

mushrik, pl. **mushrikūn**: someone who commits *shirk*.

mukātab: a slave who has been given a *kitāba* (*see above*).

mulāmasa: a forbidden sale in which the deal is completed if the buyer touches a thing without seeing or checking it properly.

al-Multazam: the area between the Black Stone and the door of the Ka'ba, where it is recommended to make *du'ā'* (*see above*).

munābadha: a forbidden sale in which the deal is completed when the seller throws a things towards the buyer without giving him a chance to see, touch or check it.

murābaḥa: partnership between an investor and a borrower in a profit-sharing re-sale.

Murābiṭūn: the Almoravids, a Muslim dynasty in Spain and North Africa.

muṣrān al-fāra: a kind of spoiled date.

mut'a: temporary marriage under strict conditions, allowed in the early part of Islam, but later forbidden by the Prophet ﷺ at the Battle of Khaybar as narrated in the *Muwaṭṭa'*.

al-Muwaṭṭa': literally 'the well-trodden path,' or the 'many times agreed on', because it was agreed upon by seventy of the learned men of Madīna.

muzābana: a forbidden sale in which something, whose number, weight or measure is known is sold for something whose number, weight or measure is not known.

Muzdalifa: a place between 'Arafa and Mina where the pilgrims returning from 'Arafa spend a night in the open between the ninth and tenth day of *Dhū al-Ḥijja* after performing the *Maghrib* and *'Ishā'* prayers there.

nabīdh: a drink made by soaking grapes, raisins, dates, etc. in water without allowing them to ferment.

nāfila, pl. **nawāfil**: literally 'a gift', from the same root as *al-anfāl*, booty taken in war. It means a voluntary act of *'ibāda* (*see above*).

Najd: the region around Riyadh.

an-Najm: 'The Star', *Sūra* 53 of the Qur'ān.

najash: bidding falsely in order to increase the price.

nikāḥ: marriage, see Book 28.

niṣāb: the minimum amount of wealth of whatever kind that *zakāt* can be deducted from (*zakāt, see below*).

nawāfil: plural of **nāfila** (*see above*).

Qarn: the *mīqāt* (*see above*) of the people of Najd between *Ṭā'if* and Makka.

qārin: a person who performs *Ḥajj al-Qirān*.

qasāma: an oath taken by fifty members of a tribe or a locality to refute accusations of complicity in unclear cases of homicide. *See* Book 44.

qassī: garments, shot with silk, from Qass, a place in Egypt.

qibla: the direction faced in prayer, which is towards the Ka'ba in Makka.

qirāḍ: wealth put by an investor in the trust of an agent for use in commercial purposes, the agent receiving no wage, but taking a designated share of the profits.

qirān: see *Ḥajj al-Qirān*.

qīrāṭ: a measure of weight with contrary meanings, either a twelfth of a dirham or a very great weight like that of Mount Uḥud.

qiṣāṣ: retaliation in injuries, see Book 43.

Qubā': a village on the outskirts of Madīna.

qunūṭ: supplication (*du'ā'*) in the prayer, particularly in the standing position after *rukū'* (*see below*) in the *Ṣubḥ* prayer.

Quraysh: One of the great tribes in Arabia. The Messenger of Allah ﷺ belonged to this tribe.

qurū': a woman's becoming pure after menses, used particularly in reference to the *'idda* (*see above*) of divorce.

Rabī' al-Ākhir: the fourth month of the Muslim calendar.

Rabī' al-Awwal: the third month of the Muslim calendar.

Rajab: the seventh month. One of the four Sacred Months in which fighting is prohibited.

rak'a: a unit of prayer (*ṣalāt*), a complete series of standings, bowing, prostrations and sittings.

ramā': a form of usury.

Ramaḍān: the month of fasting, the ninth month of the Muslim calendar.

ramy: throwing pebbles at the *jamras* at Minā.

raml: 'hastening' in the first three circuits of *ṭawāf*, a way of walking briskly, moving the shoulders vigorously.

ribā: usury.

rikaz: treasure buried in the pre-Islamic period which is recovered without great cost or effort. *Zakāt* (*see below*) is exacted from such finds.

riṭl: a measure of weight comprising 480 dirhams, or 1.426 kg.

rūḥ, pl. **arwāḥ**: the spirit.

riwāyāt: a reading or transmission of the Qur'ān or another text.

rukū': bowing, particularly the bowing position of the prayer.

ruqya: recitation of *āyats* of the Qur'ān for treatment of and protection againstillness.

ṣā': a measure of volume equal to four *mudds* (*see above*).

ṣadaqa: giving in the way of Allah, charity.

Ṣafā and **Marwa**: two hills close to the Ka'ba. It is part of the rites of *'umra* and *hajj* to go seven times between each hill. *See sa'y below.*

Ṣafar: the second month of the Muslim lunar calendar.

ṣaḥūr: the early morning meal taken before first light when fasting.

sajda: the act of making prostration, particularly in the prayer.

ṣalāt: translated in the text as prayer. It consists of fixed sets of standings, bowings, prostrations and sittings in worship to Allah.

as-Salaf: the 'early generations' of the Muslims, particularly the *Ṣaḥāba*, the Companions of the Messenger of Allah ﷺ.

salafī: adjective from *as-Salaf.*

ṣāliḥ, pl. **ṣāliḥūn**: a spiritually developed man.

sa'y: the main rite of *'umra* and part of *hajj*. It is proceeding between the hills of Ṣafā and Marwa seven times.

ṣayḥānī: a variety of excellent date.

Sha'bān: the eighth month of the Muslim calendar and one of the four Sacred Months.

shafaq: the redness in the sky after sunset.

shahāda: witnessing – the affirmation that there is no divinity but Allah and that Muḥammad is the Messenger of Allah.

shahīd: literally 'a witness', a martyr in the way of Allah.

Sharī'a, pl. **sharā'i**: literally 'a road'. It is the legal modality of a people based on the revelation of their Prophet. The last *Sharī'a* in history is that of Islam. It abrogates all previous *sharā'i.*

Shawwāl: the tenth month of the Muslim calendar.

shayṭān, pl. **shayāṭīn**: a devil, particularly Iblīs (Satan).

shighār: a forbidden form of marriage whereby a man gave his daughter in marriage to another man who gave his daughter to him without there being any bride-price.

shirk: literally 'to associate anything as a partner with Allah'. It is the opposite of *tawḥīd*, affirmation of Divine Unity.

aṣ-Ṣiddīq: 'The Truthful', a name of respect given to Abū Bakr.

Ṣiffīn: a place in Syria where, in 36 AH, a battle between forces loyal to 'Alī ibn Abī Ṭālib and forces supporting Mu'āwiya ibn Abī Sufyān took place.

ṣiyām: fasting, *see* Book 18.

siwāk: toothstick from the 'Araq tree. It is *sunna* (*see below*) to use it.

Ṣubḥ: morning, particularly the *Ṣubḥ* obligatory prayer, prayed between the first light (*Fajr*) and the onset of sunrise.

sujūd: the position of prostration, particularly in the prayers.

sult: a grain between wheat and barley; it tastes like wheat, but is like barley in its nature and coldness.

sunna, pl. **sunan**: literally 'a form, the customary practice of a person or group of people'. It has come to refer almost exclusively to the practice of the Messenger of Allah, Muḥammad ﷺ.

sūra: a large unit of Qur'ān linked by thematic content, composed of *āyat*s (*see above*). There are 113 *sūra*s in the Qur'ān.

sutra: an object placed in front of a man praying so that people will pass beyond it and not 'break' his *qibla* (*see above*) and concentration.

Tabūk: a town in northern Arabia close to Syria. In the ninth year after the *Hijra*, the Messenger of Allah ﷺ, hearing that the Byzantines were gathering a large army to march against the Muslims, led a large expedition, in his last campaign, to Tabūk, only to find the rumours premature.

tadbīr: a contract given by a master to a slave that the slave will be freed after the master dies.

tahajjud: voluntary prayer in the night between the *'Ishā'* prayer and *Fajr*.

Ṭā'if: an important town in the mountains, fifty miles to the east of Makka.

takbīr: the saying of *'Allāhu Akbar,'* 'Allah is Great'. The prayer begins with a *takbīr*.

talbiya: the calling of *'labbayk'* (*see Book 20*).

Tamattu': see *Ḥajj at-Tamattu'*.

taqlīd: garlanding sacrificial animals, especially *hady*s (*see above*). In reference to *fiqh* (*see above*), it means the following of previous authorities and the avoidance of *ijtihād* (*see above*).

taqwā: awe of Allah, which inspires a person to be on guard against wrong action and eager for actions which please Him.

tarāwīḥ: extra night prayers, usually done in congregation, in the month of fasting (Ramadan) in order to recite the Qur'ān as fully as possible, or completely.

tashahhud: literally 'to make *shahāda'* (*see above*). In the context of the prayer it is a formula which includes the *shahāda*. It is said in the final sitting position of each two *rak'a* (*see above*) cycle.

tashrīq : the days of the 10th, 11th and 12th of Dhū al-Ḥijja (the month of the *hajj*) when the pilgrims sacrifice their animals and stone the *jamras* at Mina.

taslīm: giving the Islamic greeting of *'as-salāmu 'alaykum,'* 'Peace be upon you.' The prayer ends with a *taslīm*.

ṭawāf: circling the Ka'ba, *ṭawāf* is done in sets of seven circuits.

Ṭawāf al-Ifāda: the *ṭawāf* of the Ka'ba that the pilgrims must perform after coming from Minā to Makka on the tenth of Dhū al-Hijjah. It is one of the essential rites of the *hajj*.

tawba: repentance, returning to correct action after error.

tayammum: purification for prayer with clean dust, earth or stone, when water for *ghusl* (*see above*) or *wuḍū'* (*see below*) is either unavailable or would be detrimental to health.

aṭ-Ṭūr: 'The Mount', *Sūra* 52 of the Qur'ān, refers to Mount Sinai, where Allah revealed the Torah to Mūsā (Moses) عليه السلام.

Uḥud: a mountain just outside of Madīna, much beloved of the Messenger of Allah ﷺ where five years after the *Hijra*, the Muslims lost a battle against the Makkan idol worshippers. Many great Companions and in particular the uncle of the Prophet, Ḥamza, the 'lion of Allah', were killed in this battle.

'ulamā': plural of **'ālim** (*see above*).

Umma: the body of the Muslims as one distinct and integrated community.

Umm al-Mu'minīn: literally 'Mother of the Believers", an honorary title given to the wives of the Prophet ﷺ.

Umm al-Qur'ān: literally 'the Mother of the Qur'ān', the opening *sūra* of the Qur'ān, *al-Fātiḥa*. Also said to be its source in the Unseen.

umm walad: literally 'mother of a child', a slave-girl who has given birth to a child by her master.

'umra: the lesser pilgrimage. It can be performed at any time of the year. See Book 20.

ūqiya: pl. **awāq**: a measurement of silver equivalent to forty dirhams (*see above*) or 123 gs of silver.

'ushr: one tenth of the yield of land to be levied as a tax.

wājib: a necessary part of *Sharī'a* (*see above*).

walā': the tie of clientage, established between a freed slave and the person who freed him, whereby the freed slave becomes integrated into the family of that person.

walī: guardian, person who has responsibility for another person, used particularly for the person who 'gives' a woman in marriage.

wasq, pl. **awsāq**: a measure of volume equal to sixty *ṣā's* (*see above*).

wiṣāl: 'unbroken' fasting.

witr: literally 'odd', a single *rak'a* (*see above*) prayed during the night which makes uneven the number of *sunna rak'as*. It is considered *wājib* (*see above*).

wuḍū': ritual washing to be pure for the prayer.

wuqūf: Stopping at 'Arafa and Muzdalifa.

Yalamlam: the *mīqāt* (*see above*) of the people of Yemen.

Yemeni corner: the corner of the Ka'ba facing south towards the Yemen.

Yathrib: the ancient name for *al-Madīna al-Munawarra.*

zakāt: a wealth tax. It is one of the *arkan* (indispensable pillars) of Islam.

Zakāt al-Fiṭr: a small obligatory head-tax imposed on every responsible Muslim who has the means, for himself and his dependants. It is paid once yearly at the end of Ramadan before the *'Īd al-Fiṭr* (*see above*).

ẓālim: a person who is unjust and oppressive.

Zamzam: the well of the Ḥaram of Makka.

ẓihār: an oath by a husband that his wife is like his mother's back, meaning that sexual relations with her are *ḥarām* (*see above*) for him.

Ẓuhr: noon, in particular the noon prayer.

Index

INDEX REFERS TO BOOK AND SECTION NUMBERS AND ḤADĪTH NUMBERS (WHERE APPLICABLE)

A

B

C

D

E

G

H

I

J

K

N

O

P

Q

R

S

T

U

V

VISITING: See GENERAL
VISITING GRAVES: See DEATH
VOLUNTARY PRAYERS: See PRAYER

W

Y

Z

CPSIA information can be obtained
at www.ICGtesting.com
Printed in the USA
BVHW052246100719
553084BV00002B/10/P

9 781908 892355